Multiagent Systems

Edited by
Salman Ahmed
and
Mohd Noh Karsiti

Published by In-Teh

In-Teh is Croatian branch of I-Tech Education and Publishing KG, Vienna, Austria.

www.in-teh.org
Additional copies can be obtained from:
publication@ars-journal.com

First published February 2009
Printed in Croatia

p. cm.
ISBN 978-3-902613-51-6
1. Multiagent Systems, Salman Ahmed and Mohd Noh Karsiti

Preface

Multi agent systems involve a team of agents working together socially to accomplish a task. An agent can be social in many ways. One is when an agent helps others in solving complex problems. The field of multi agent systems investigates the process underlying distributed problem solving and designs some protocols and mechanisms involved in this process. This book presents an overview about some of the research issues in the field of multi agents.

This book can be divided into 4 parts. The first part (Chapters 1-3) deals with resources distribution and sharing among agents. Chapter 1 presents the allocation of resources in multi agent societies. The objective function and available resources are mathematically modelled and a discrete time representation of the system is also presented. The objective is to cope with resource allocations in dynamic environments. Chapter 2 presents an overview of the negotiation protocols in decision making. A fuzzy constraint based model is presented, analyzed and simulated for automated purchase negotiations. In order to have a better allocation of resources, multi agents can be equipped with negotiation attributes. Chapter 3 presents goal oriented approach to dynamically model a system, which can be used for process optimization and automation. The chapter presents industry-proven BPMS employing goal-oriented approach to modelling and executing business processes.

The second part (Chapter 4-5) deals with the modelling and analysis of multi agent systems. Petri nets are graphical modelling tools used to describe and analyse systems. In chapter 4, the multi agent framework is modelled using Petri nets. The Petri net model is obtained locally for each agent. Furthermore, a combined global model is also obtained. The global model is then analysed to study the properties of the system. The liveness and boundedness properties in the Petri net domain are analysed, which can give information about the communication and interaction mechanism of the multi-agent system. Chapter 5 presents a simulation framework, in which Bluetooth piconet profile is used for communication. A state space model of multi agent robots is also presented. The model is used to design and simulate feedback control strategies for trajectory tracking of the agents. A critical analysis of nonlinear feedback and feedback linearized control strategies is presented.

The third part (Chapter 6-13) deals with the coordination and communication issues in multi agent systems. Chapter 6 investigates the coordination techniques used in semi-conductor manufacturing system, while maintaining the desired throughput. The design of a process for enabling agent based computing is presented in Chapter 7. The service agents negotiate to select a final solution via a negotiation process using service quality and service payoff as the criteria. Chapter 8 focuses on coordination control and fault diagnosis of production system. The ways of agents' information exchange and the cooperation behaviour of agents are also presented. Chapter 9 deals with cooperation approaches using game theory. The rational and selfish behaviour in agent societies in terms of individual as well as collective activities is defined. Chapter 10 focuses on the indirect coordination mechanisms in multi agents.

Multi agent bluffing is considered as an unexpected behaviour and multi agents should be equipped to learn to predict its opponents' reactions based not only on its own cards, but on the actions of those around it. Chapter 11 presents a comprehensive overview about multi agent bluffing. One of the important issues in multi agent coordination is the use of a common language in multi agent societies. Chapter 12 presents a language for coordination which is capable of describing agent behaviour globally, locally and in a team. In certain environments and applications, it is necessary to ensure secure communication among agents. Of particular interest are wireless networks, which are more vulnerable to threats. Chapter 13 presents an agent-oriented key distribution protocol for wireless networks.

The fourth part (Chapter 14-20) deals with the design of frameworks for different applications of multi agents. This part also includes research papers which focus on the applications of multi agent systems. A framework for process simulation to support flexible activity scheduling is presented in Chapter 14. Social rationality is used to represent the utility function. The decision making strategies along with communication mechanism are also presented. Chapter 15 focuses on the application of multi agents in production, economical and social domains. The coalition formation for large scale multi agent system is also presented. One of the objectives for multi agent robotic systems is to track moving objects. Chapter 16 focuses on multi agents executing different tactics over the tracked target and collaborating with the tracked target. Chapter 17 presents scheduling system for multi agents, in which machine agents and task agents interact to achieve optimal or near-optimal global performances. The scheduling system assumes the combination of meta-heuristics. Chapter 18 presents a new dimension for the applications of multi agents. In this chapter, multi agents are employed as educational agents, which allow instructive communication and interaction between human characters. Chapter 19 focuses on the deployment of multi agent systems in auction and electronic markets using the Internet. Different types of transactions in electronic markets are classified and accordingly mechanisms are designed for the markets. Chapter 20 presents a multi agent architecture for the transport multimodal information systems. The objective is to optimize the composition of services in terms of cost and total response delay.

In summary, this book presents a combination of different research issues which are pursued by researchers in the domain of multi agent systems. Multi agent systems are one of the best ways to understand and model human societies and behaviours. In fact, such systems are the systems of future.

Editors

Salman Ahmed
Electrical and Electronic Engineering,
Universiti Teknologi Petronas,
Malaysia.

Mohd Noh Karsiti
Electrical and Electronic Engineering,
Universiti Teknologi Petronas,
Malaysia.

Contents

Preface V

1. Agent-Based Distributed Resource Allocation in Continuous Dynamic Systems 001
Holger Voos

2. Constraint Based Automated Multi-attribute Negotiations 021
Miguel A. López-Carmona, Iván Marsá-Maestre and Juan R. Velasco

3. Goal-Oriented Autonomic Business Process Modelling and Execution 055
Dominic Greenwood and Roberto Ghizzioli

4. Modeling and Analysis Methods for Multi-agent Systems 073
Jose R. Celaya and Alan A. Desrochers

5. Control Analysis and Feedback Techniques for Multi Agent Robots 103
Salman Ahmed and Mohd Noh Karsiti and Robert N. K. Loh

6. Scalable Coordination Mechanism to Maintain Throughput of Dynamic Multiagent Networks 129
Rajesh Gautam and Kazuo Miyashita

7. Requirements Driven Service Agent Collaboration 153
Liwei Zheng, Jian Tang and Zhi Jin

8. Coordination Control and Fault Diagnosis of Production System Using Multi-agent Technology 173
Li Tiejun, Peng Yuqing and Wu Jianguo

9. Evolutionary Game Theory based Cooperation Algorithm in Multi-agent System 203
Yuehai Wang

10. Indirect Coordination Mechanism of MAS 221
Satoshi Kurihara, Kensuke Fukuda, Shinya Sato and Toshiharu Sugawara

11. A Multi-Agent Approach to Bluffing 233
Tshilidzi Marwala and Evan Hurwitz

12. MASL: a Language for Multi-Agent System 247
Michel Dubois, Yann Le Guyadec and Dominique Duhaut

13. Agent-Oriented Novel Quantum Key Distribution Protocol for the Security in Wireless Network 261
Xu Huang, Shirantha Wijesekera and Dharmendra Sharma

14. A Framework for Business Process Simulation Based on Multi-Agent Cooperation 277
Wenan Tan, Wei Xu, Fujun Yang, Song Li and Yi Du

15. Agent Oriented Engineering and Methodologies with Application to Production, Economical and Social Systems 289
Baltazár Frankovič, Than Tung Dang, Tomáš Kasanický, Viktor Oravec and Ivana Budinská

16. Effective Multi-Model Motion Tracking Under Multiple Team Member Actuators 315
Yang Gu and Manuela Veloso

17. MASDScheGATS - Scheduling System for Dynamic Manufacturing Environmemts 333
Ana Madureira, Joaquim Santos and Ivo Pereira

18. Conversational Characters that Support Interactive Play and Learning for Children 349
Andrea Corradini, Manish Mehta and Klaus Robering

19. Auctions and Electronic Markets 375
Donna Griffin and Dirk Pesch

20. Distributed Optimisation using the Mobile Agent Paradigm through an Adaptable Ontology: Multi-operator Services Research and Composition 397
Hayfa Zgaya and Slim Hammadi

1

Agent-Based Distributed Resource Allocation in Continuous Dynamic Systems

Holger Voos
University of Applied Sciences Ravensburg-Weingarten
Germany

1. Introduction

The automation of complex large-scale systems is one of the most challenging tasks of modern control engineering. Such systems comprise a huge number of spatially distributed subsystems with both frequent and infrequent interactions, resulting in a complex overall behavior. In addition, numerous disturbances can occur leading to a high degree of uncertainty. The automation of such systems therefore calls for highly flexible automatic control systems that fulfill the following requirements:

- In accordance with the system under control, the overall control system should also consist of a number of spatially distributed local control systems, interconnected via suitable communication systems. In addition, also the control algorithms should be decentralized without any central control and the local control decisions are then coordinated to an overall consistent decision.
- The control functionality is implemented in the form of software which requires that state-of-the-art software engineering methods and techniques be employed, see [Bussmann, 2003].
- Because of the complex structure and the uncertainty of the system under control, the control algorithms must be robust against any model inaccuracies as well as disturbances during operation.
- It should be easy to maintain, to reconfigure or to extend the control system.
- The control system should also provide cognitive capabilities in order to realize the necessary complex decision making.

Taking these requirements into account, intelligent agents and multiagent systems reveal new strategies to design automation systems especially when considering large-scale distributed applications [Unland, 2003]. Agents can be defined as computer or software systems which are situated in some environment and able to perform flexible autonomous action in order to meet their design objectives [Unland, 2003], [Jennings, 1998]. Furthermore, agents can be pro-active and social, which enables them to interact with each other to form multiagent systems. In a multiagent system, the agents coordinate their behavior and solve problems in a distributed fashion without global control and only local and limited resources and information. There are first promising industrial applications of multiagent systems for the control of manufacturing, logistics, traffic or multi-robot systems, see e.g. [Weiss, 1999], [Colombo, 2004], [Kluegl, 2005], [AAMAS, 2008] for a survey.

One special subproblem during the control of large-scale technical systems is automatic resource allocation. In manufacturing systems for instance, the capacities of the machines are resources that have to be allocated to the production orders. In logistic systems, trucks and transportation lines as resources must be allocated to the transportation demands of the customers. However, automatic resource allocation is not limited to the control of manufacturing and logistic systems but also occurs in computer and communication networks, production plants, traffic and transportation systems, energy networks or in building automation. In a distributed control system, the task of automatic resource allocation is preferably also performed in a distributed manner, leading to distributed resource allocation. Therefore it is very interesting to note that the previously proposed multiagent systems are especially suited to solve the problem of distributed resource allocation, see [Weiss, 1999], [Unland, 2003].

However, most of the resource allocation problems solved so far with the help of multiagent systems are static problems where the allocations do not depend on time. Many resource allocation problems of practical interest can be solved using these static considerations, even in discrete-event systems like manufacturing or logistic systems. In these cases, the necessary allocation is computed based on the current state of the system and that allocation is maintained until some new events or changes of the states occur. Unfortunately, problems especially in highly dynamic environments cannot be addressed by this pure static approach since the allocations, i.e. the decision variables, depend on time and previous states of the considered system. Hence, continuous-time allocation trajectories must be computed and this processing must be performed in real-time. These problems are hardly considered in the relevant agent literature and if, most often only discrete-event systems are considered. Therefore, this work focuses on dynamic resource allocation problems especially in continuous systems.

The design of a multiagent system for distributed resource allocation mainly comprises the design of the local capabilities of the single agents and the interaction mechanisms that makes them find the best or at least a feasible allocation without any central control. Many possible interaction mechanisms can be found in the literature, see e.g. [Weiss, 1999], [Sandholm, 1999] for an overview. This work proposes a more formal approach, where the decision process of resource allocation is expressed as an optimization problem under certain constraints. This optimization problem can be solved in a distributed fashion using multiple agents that act as local optimizers and coordinate their local solutions to an overall consistent solution, see also [Voos, 2003], [Voos, 2006], [Voos, 2007]. One special formulation of this optimization problem leads to an analogy with economic markets [Clearwater, 1996] and to so called market-based interaction mechanisms, see e.g. [Clearwater, 1996], [Voos, 2003]. Herein, supplies and demands of the resources are defined which are exchanged by agents and balanced using a virtual price. While the general approach of such a market-based resource allocation has already been investigated in the literature, this work adds two important contributions.

First, the market-based interaction mechanism is adapted here to a much more general class of resource allocation problems, extending this approach to more applications of practical interest. In addition, the method is further extended to cover resource allocation in dynamic systems. The corresponding mathematical formulation leads to dynamic optimization problems that could not be addressed so far by market-based algorithms. In the proposed solution, the agents calculate and negotiate complete supply and demand trajectories using model-based predictions which also leads to the calculation of a price trajectory. This novel approach does not only consider the dynamic behavior of the distributed system but also combines control tasks and resource allocation in a very consistent way. The agents are designed as two-level entities: while the low-level functions are responsible for the real-time allocation of the resources in the form of closed-loop feedback control, the high-level functionalities realize the deliberative capabilities such as long-term planning and negotiation of the resource allocations. The solutions are finally applied to a number of technical applications for proof of concept.

2. Resource allocation problems

2.1 Resource allocation in technical systems

In a technical environment, resources are all means that enable the operation of a technical process. Therefore, resources could be energy, information, materials, capacities of plants, machines etc. Therefore, if we consider a large production plant for instance, many examples of resource allocation problems can be found, see e.g. Fig. 1.

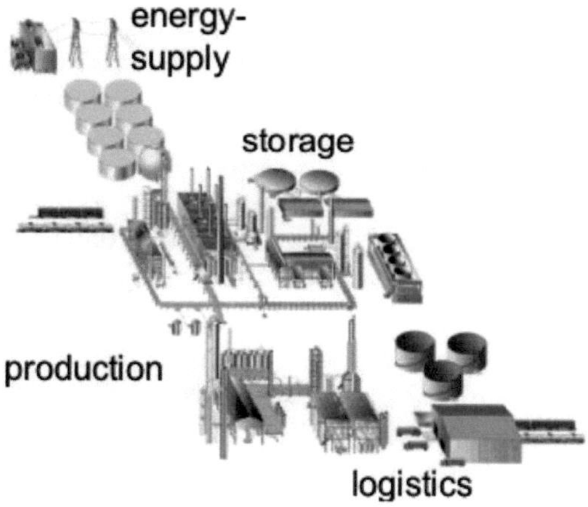

Fig. 1. Examples of resource allocation problems in a production plant.

It is characteristic that resources are always limited and quantities of a resource are always non-negative numbers. In a technical system, there are in general subsystems that offer resources and other subsystems (or entities) that need resources. Considering a communication network as an example, the channels offer the resource "bandwidth" which is used by the active communication connections. In a shop-job manufacturing system, the machines offer the production capacities as a resource which are then used by the production orders. In many technical systems however, the resources are not only used by one single entity but there are several of them that have to share limited quantities of the resources. Therefore, a sufficient quantity of each available resource must be allocated to each entity. Most often, several alternatives for that allocation exist which means that resource allocation is a decision process in general.

The resource allocation problem considered so far is static, i.e. the solution doesn't depend on time. In a technical realization, the allocation is calculated and maintained until a disturbance of that state occurs (e.g. if a new entity appears that also needs resources). In this case, the allocation is recalculated based on the new situation. Many problems of

practical interest could be solved like this, e.g. in computer or communication networks or production planning in manufacturing systems [Colombo, 2004], [Weiss, 1999].
One special resource allocation problem however appears in dynamic systems with continuous state variables, where the allocation of a certain amount of a resource also depends on the internal state of the system. An example is the allocation of heating energy as a resource to the single production processes e.g. in a chemical plant, where the allocation depends on the current temperatures in the different tanks. The temperature, however, can be described by a differential equation and also depends on previous allocations of heating energy. Thus allocation now depends on time and resource allocation is a dynamic continuous process. In addition, resource allocation then turns out to be a control problem in this case. The resource, i.e. the heating energy, is the controlled input variable of the considered process. The control goal is to maintain a certain temperature in the tank. Therefore the current temperature is measured, compared with the required setpoint temperature and the current allocation of the resource is adapted with regard to the deviation from this setpoint.
It is obvious that the dynamic behavior of the technical subsystems that need resources (e.g. the chemical reaction in the tank) now plays an important role during the solution of the allocation problem. One possible approach which will be derived in this contribution is a direct combination of the mathematical description of the resource allocation problem and the models of the dynamic behavior of the subsystems. Together with a market-based approach using a multiagent system, it leads to an interaction and control scheme that is similar to a model-predictive control algorithm. A second approach which will also be derived in this chapter is based upon a separation of the resource allocation process on the one side and the control problem on the other side. Here, while dealing with dynamic resource allocation, it is sufficient to work with a static mathematical formulation of the resource allocation problem and a static market-based interaction scheme.

2.2 Mathematical formulation of resource allocation

In many technical systems, the resources are not only used by one single entity but there is a number of entities that have to share limited quantities of the resources. Therefore, a sufficient quantity of each available resource must be allocated to each entity. Most often, several alternatives for that allocation exist which means that resource allocation is a decision process in general. Here we assume that we are interested in the best possible allocation based on the available information which leads to the formulation as an optimization problem, see also [Ibaraki, 1988].
In the following we assume that a number of L resources exists that have to be allocated to I entities. The allocation to entity $i \in \{1, \ldots, I\}$ can be expressed as an allocation vector $\boldsymbol{r}_i \in \mathbb{R}_+^L$ where r_{ij} denotes the allocated amount of resource j. If J is a suitable objective function that judges the overall allocation and if there is an overall maximum available amount of each resource given as the vector $\boldsymbol{r} \in \mathbb{R}_+^L$, the resource allocation problem can be expressed as follows:

$$
\begin{aligned}
&\min_{\{\boldsymbol{r}_i, \forall i\}} \quad J(\boldsymbol{r}_1, \ldots, \boldsymbol{r}_I) \\
\text{s.t.} \quad &\boldsymbol{C} \cdot \boldsymbol{r}_i = \boldsymbol{d}_i \quad \forall i \\
&\boldsymbol{r}_i \geq \boldsymbol{0} \quad \forall i \\
&\sum_{i=1}^{I} \boldsymbol{r}_i = \boldsymbol{r}
\end{aligned}
\tag{1}
$$

The best allocation is that set of non-negative allocation vectors $\{\mathbf{r}_i, \forall i\}$ that minimizes J while the overall sum of all allocations must be equal to the overall amount of the available resources. The equalities $\mathbf{C} \cdot \mathbf{r}_i = \mathbf{d}_i$ could be used to define some topological constraints where the topology of the system is described by a graph with incidence matrix $\mathbf{C}$ (see the example in the last section for further explanation).

Distributed resource allocation however means that there is no central control but a number of distributed agents assigned to the entities $i = 1, \ldots, I$ which communicate in order to coordinate the allocation in a distributed manner. Therefore, the description (1) of the resource allocation problem as one single optimization problem is not suitable. If we assume that an objective function $J_i(\mathbf{r}_i)$ for each entity i exists that measures the efficiency of the local resource allocation to that entity, the overall objective function J in (1) can be replaced by

$$J = \sum_{i=1}^{I} J_i(\mathbf{r}_i) \tag{2}$$

The resource allocation problem considered so far is a static description, i.e. the solution doesn't depend on time. In a technical realization, the allocation is calculated and maintained until a disturbance of that state occurs (e.g. if a new entity appears that also needs resources). In this case, the allocation is recalculated based on the new situation. Many problems of practical interest could be solved like this, e.g. in computer or communication networks or production planning in manufacturing systems [Weiss, 1999], [Colombo, 2004].

One special resource allocation problem however appears in dynamic systems with continuous state variables, where the allocation of a certain amount of a resource also depends on the internal state of the system. An example is the allocation of heating energy as a resource to the single rooms in a building where the allocation depends on the current temperatures in the rooms. The temperature, however, can be described by a differential equation and also depends on previous allocations of heating energy. Thus allocation now depends on time and resource allocation is a dynamic continuous process. A possible mathematical formulation of that problem will be derived in the following.

We assume that the I entities that need resources are dynamic systems, here described by a discrete-time state variable model with the vector $\mathbf{x}_i(k)$ as the vector of continuous state variables at instant k. In addition we assume that the states also depend on the allocated amount of the resources, where $\mathbf{r}_i(k)$ is the allocation to entity i at instant k. Hence the system i is described by the difference equation

$$\mathbf{x}_i(k+1) = \mathbf{F}_i(\mathbf{x}_i(k), \mathbf{r}_i(k)) \quad , \quad \mathbf{x}_i(0) = \mathbf{x}_{i0} \tag{3}$$

and we additionally assume that the full vector of state variables can be measured or at least estimated. Now we have to consider the problem to allocate resources over a certain period of time comprising K time steps. The allocation to system i is no longer a single allocation vector but a trajectory of allocations given by $\{\mathbf{r}_i(0), \mathbf{r}_i(1), \ldots, \mathbf{r}_i(K-1)\}$. The objective function is now a function of the trajectory of allocations and the trajectory of the states. The resource allocation problem is given by

$$
\begin{aligned}
&\min_{\{r_i(k),\forall i,k\}} \quad \sum_{i=1}^{I}\left(J_i(\boldsymbol{r}_i(0),\boldsymbol{x}_i(1),\ldots,\boldsymbol{r}_i(K-1),\boldsymbol{x}_i(K))\right)\\
\text{s.t.} \quad & \boldsymbol{x}_i(k+1)=\boldsymbol{F}_i(\boldsymbol{x}_i(k),\boldsymbol{r}_i(k)) \quad , \quad \boldsymbol{x}_i(0)=\boldsymbol{x}_{i0} \quad \forall i,k\\
& \boldsymbol{C}\cdot\boldsymbol{r}_i(k)=\boldsymbol{d}_i \quad \forall i,k\\
& \boldsymbol{r}_i(k)\geq\boldsymbol{0} \quad \forall i,k\\
& \sum_{i=1}^{I}\boldsymbol{r}_i(k)=\boldsymbol{r}(k) \quad \forall k
\end{aligned}
\tag{4}
$$

In order to apply agent-based resource allocation, we need some methodologies how to solve problems like (1) or (4) in a distributed fashion with communicating agents.

3. Agent-based resource allocation

3.1 Analogy between economies and resource allocation problems

The problem of distributed resource allocation has been addressed from the beginning of agent-based research and application. Here algorithms or methodologies have been developed that especially take into account the decentralized system structure of multiagent systems and their ability to communicate and coordinate. Well known methods of multiagent based resource allocation comprises blackboard structures or auction-like algorithms, see [Weiss, 1999], [Sandholm, 1999] for a summary. One method which will be investigated here is based on economic markets, since resource allocation is also a basic problem in human societies.

An abstract mathematical model of an idealized economic system[Debreu, 1959] consists of a certain number of commodities, agents and a price system. A commodity can either be a service or a good; any quantity of a commodity is a positive real number. Because of the limitation of the commodities, each is associated with a price while all prices together form the price system. The agents can either be consumers or producers and the task of an agent is to make the decision on a quantity of his input or output for each commodity. Each producer chooses his supply based on his production factors and has the objective of profit maximization. The consumers in the economy choose their demands, characterized by their choice criterions or preferences and certain constraints, mainly the limited wealth. In these models the consumer will always choose that demand he prefers the most and which is feasible by the wealth constraints.

On the market, overall supply and demand then has to be balanced by adjusting the price of the commodities: if the overall demand exceeds the overall supply, the prices are increased and vice versa. Under some strict conditions concerning the preferences and the production factors, such an economy can reach a competitive equilibrium where overall supply equals overall demand and where each consumer maximizes its preferences. Because of the principal and mathematical analogy between the distributed resource allocation problem and this model of an economic market, the idea of a market-based solution led to a number of solutions in agent-based distributed resource allocation, see [Clearwater, 1996], [Voos, 2003] for a first summary of applications.

One main drawback of this economic model are the constraints regarding the preferences of the consumers, most often expressed by so-called utility functions. To guarantee the existence of the competitive equilibrium, the utility of the consumer must be described by monotone, quasi-concave and strictly increasing functions. That means that the utility is increasing with increasing amounts of allocated commodities ("more is preferred"). The simple price adjustment algorithm called tâtonnement which is performed by the agents is only guaranteed to converge if these conditions hold. However, this may not be the case in technical systems, which causes problems for the direct adaption of the economic model to real technical applications. In addition, problems like (4) where additional variables such as the state variables appear in the objective function are not at all addressed in economic models. Therefore, from a mathematical point of view we have to consider two problems: 1.) how can problems of the form (1) be solved in a distributed market-based fashion even if the objective functions do not fulfill the mentioned strict conditions and 2.) how can we address dynamic problems like (4) by these market-based algorithms.

3.2 Market-based resource allocation with general objective functions

Now we consider (1) under the relaxed assumption that the objective functions $J_i(\boldsymbol{r}_i)$ are not strictly increasing, but strictly convex functions. The Lagrangian of optimization problem (1) is

$$\mathscr{L} = \sum_{i=1}^{I} J_i(\boldsymbol{r}_i) + \sum_{i=1}^{I} \boldsymbol{\lambda}_i^T (\boldsymbol{C}\boldsymbol{r}_i - \boldsymbol{d}_i) + \boldsymbol{p}^T \cdot (\sum_{i=1}^{I} \boldsymbol{r}_i - \boldsymbol{r}) - \sum_{i=1}^{I} \boldsymbol{\mu}_i^T \cdot \boldsymbol{r}_i \tag{5}$$

The conditions for optimality (which are necessary and sufficient for the existence of an optimum in the case of strictly convex functions J_i) are:

$$\begin{aligned}
&\frac{dJ_i(\boldsymbol{r}_i)}{d\boldsymbol{r}_i}\Big|_{(\boldsymbol{r}_i^*)} + \boldsymbol{C}^T \cdot \boldsymbol{\lambda}_i^* + \boldsymbol{p}^* - \boldsymbol{\mu}_i^* = \boldsymbol{0} \quad \forall i \\
&\boldsymbol{C}\boldsymbol{r}_i^* - \boldsymbol{d}_i = \boldsymbol{0} \quad \forall i \\
&-\boldsymbol{r}_i^* \le \boldsymbol{0} \quad \forall i \\
&\boldsymbol{r}_i^{*T} \cdot \boldsymbol{\mu}_i^* = 0 \quad \forall i \\
&\boldsymbol{\mu}_i^* \ge \boldsymbol{0} \quad \forall i \\
&\sum_{i=1}^{I} \boldsymbol{r}_i^* - \boldsymbol{r} = \boldsymbol{0}
\end{aligned} \tag{6}$$

It is obvious from (6) that this optimization problem could also be solved as follows: for a given Lagrange multiplier $\boldsymbol{p}$ that is associated with the balancing equality condition, (6) can be decomposed into I independent optimization problems of the form

$$\begin{aligned}
&\min_{\{\boldsymbol{r}_i\}} \quad J_i(\boldsymbol{r}_i) + \boldsymbol{p}^T \cdot \boldsymbol{r}_i \\
\text{s.t.} \quad &\boldsymbol{C} \cdot \boldsymbol{r}_i = \boldsymbol{d}_i \\
&\boldsymbol{r}_i \ge \boldsymbol{0}
\end{aligned} \tag{7}$$

That means that each agent i tries to solve its own optimization problem for a given parameter $\boldsymbol{p}$ that leads to the allocation $\boldsymbol{r}_i^*(\boldsymbol{p})$. All of these single solutions together form the function

$$z(\boldsymbol{p}) = \sum_{i=1}^{I} \boldsymbol{r}_i^*(\boldsymbol{p}) - \boldsymbol{r} \tag{8}$$

This equation then can be used to find the optimal parameter $\boldsymbol{p}^*$ by the evaluation of

$$z(\boldsymbol{p}^*) = \boldsymbol{0} \tag{9}$$

and therefore also leads to the fulfillment of the last equality condition in (6). Hence $\boldsymbol{p}$ can be interpreted as a price vector that is used to balance overall supply and demand. Each agent i tries to optimize its allocation while minimizing the costs $\boldsymbol{p}^T \cdot \boldsymbol{r}_i$ of its allocation for a given current price. This is done by the single agents independent from each other which results in I demands that all depend on the current price (most often, however, not in the form of an explicit function). On the common market, the overall demand and the overall supply (here only the fixed supply $\boldsymbol{r}$) must be balanced by adjusting the price vector in the right way (market clearing).

This solution process can be executed in an iterative way: starting with a first price vector, all customers calculate their allocation by solving their own independent allocation problems. These allocations depend on the current price which in general cannot be given as an explicit function. Nevertheless, all current demand values are taken together and compared with the overall supply. If overall supply and demand are not equal, i.e. $z(\boldsymbol{p}) \neq 0$, the price vector has to be adjusted in a suitable way. The price is distributed back to all agents that adapt their demands to that new price and so on. The basic problem is to adapt the price vector in a way that the overall process converges towards $z(\boldsymbol{p}) = 0$. In economic theory this iterative process is called tâtonnement and adjusts the price in the way

$$\boldsymbol{p}(\kappa+1) = \boldsymbol{p}(\kappa) + \boldsymbol{K} \cdot z(\boldsymbol{p}(\kappa)) \tag{10}$$

where κ is the index of the iteration steps and $\boldsymbol{K}$ is a suitable but constant matrix. If the conditions concerning the utility functions (e.g. strictly increasing) are fulfilled, it can be shown that a pure diagonal matrix $\boldsymbol{K}$ with elements $K_{ii} > 0$ on the main diagonal leads to convergence.

Since these conditions are no longer fulfilled here, a new algorithm for the iterative solution of (9) must be found. One algorithm that does not require the calculation of the Jacobian matrix is the algorithm of Broyden [Stoer, 1993]. This algorithm approximates the Jacobian matrix and works as follows:

$$\begin{aligned}
\boldsymbol{p}(\kappa+1) &= \boldsymbol{p}(\kappa) - \varphi(\kappa) \cdot \boldsymbol{d}(\kappa) \\
\boldsymbol{d}(\kappa) &= \boldsymbol{\Pi}^{-1}(\kappa) \cdot z(\boldsymbol{p}(\kappa)) \\
\boldsymbol{\delta}_1(\kappa) &= -\varphi(\kappa) \cdot \boldsymbol{d}(\kappa) \\
\boldsymbol{\delta}_2(\kappa) &= z(\boldsymbol{p}(\kappa+1)) - z(\boldsymbol{p}(\kappa)) \\
\boldsymbol{\Pi}(\kappa+1) &= \boldsymbol{\Pi}(\kappa) + \\
&\quad \frac{1}{\boldsymbol{\delta}_1^T(\kappa) \cdot \boldsymbol{\delta}_1(\kappa)} \cdot \left(\boldsymbol{\delta}_2(\kappa) - \boldsymbol{\Pi}(\kappa)\boldsymbol{\delta}_1(\kappa)\right) \boldsymbol{\delta}_1^T(\kappa)
\end{aligned} \tag{11}$$

The parameter $\varphi(\kappa)$ must be adjusted by optimization but can also be set to a constant value. It can be proven that this algorithm converges, see [Stoer, 1993]. This provides the mathematical basis for a first implementation of a multiagent market-based resource allocation.

3.3 Agent-based resource allocation

The first step during the engineering of a multiagent system is the derivation of a model with the help of a suitable modelling approach. One possibility to obtain such models is the application of the UML (Unified Modeling Language). However, the original version of the UML doesn't offer suitable constructs for the modelling of agent-based systems. Therefore, the UML was extended with some agent-specific constructs and diagrams leading to the so called AML (Agent Modelling Language), see [Cervenka, 2007]. Fig. 2 depicts a first AML model of the distributed resource allocation problem if we intend to solve it with the market-based approach.

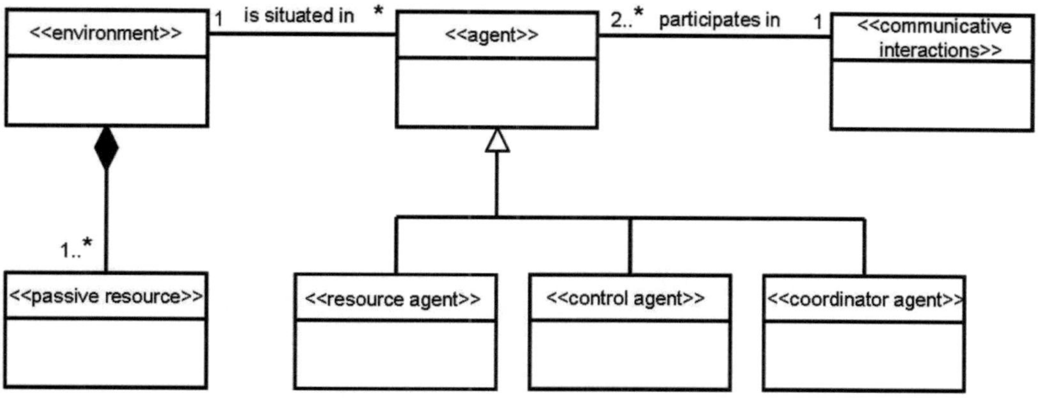

Fig. 2. AML model of the market-based resource allocation.

Both the resources that have to be allocated and the agents are situated in the environment. Here we distinguish between passive resources or resources with assigned resource agents. Resource agents however are only necessary if the (overall) amount of the resources can be influenced and therefore a further decision would be necessary. In the general case, the amount of the resources are fixed and no resource agents have to be assigned to them. The group of the agents itself can be further categorized into control agents and coordinator agents. The agents are interacting with the help of a suitable communicative interaction protocol which will be derived in the following.

The overall market-based resource allocation requires the assignment of one single control agent i to each of the I entities or subsystems that need resources and the definition of one coordinator agent. Then

1. The iteration index is set to $\kappa=0$. The coordinator agent chooses a start price $\boldsymbol{p}(\kappa=0)$ and a start matrix $\Pi(\kappa = 0)$. This price is transmitted to all other control agents via a communication network.
2. All control agents $i = 1, \ldots, I$ solve their local resource allocation problem (7). The result is a demand $\boldsymbol{r}_i^*(\kappa)$ which is locally optimal under the current price vector. All demands are transmitted to the coordinator agent.
3. The coordinator agent computes the current value of $z(\boldsymbol{p}(\kappa))$. If $z(\boldsymbol{p}(\kappa))=0$, the market is cleared and the allocation can be realized as calculated. Otherwise, the iteration index

κ is incremented by one and the coordinator agent calculates the new price vector $\boldsymbol{p}(\kappa+1)$ according to (11). The new price vector is distributed to the control agents and the algorithm proceeds with step two.

This interaction is shown in Fig. 3 in the form of an AML sequence diagram[Cervenka, 2007], using the multi-lifeline element for the control agents.

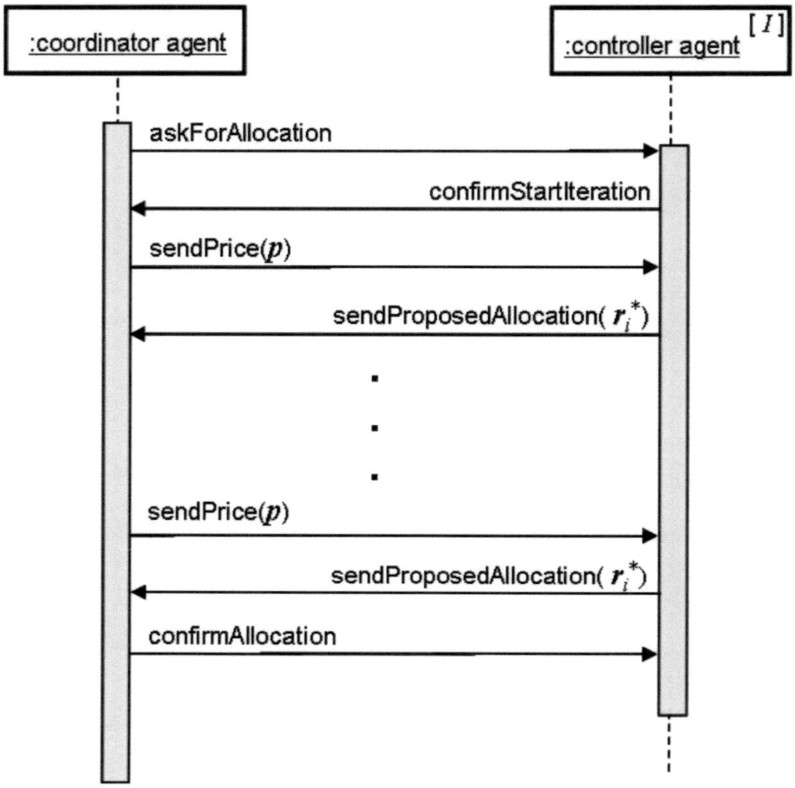

Fig. 3. AML sequence diagram of the interaction.

The only limitation we have so far is the condition of strict convexity of all objective functions $J_i(r_i)$ of the single agents. It is no problem to generalizes this approach further by also adding some suppliers in the system and work with a varying and not fixed overall amount of the available resources. In this case, each of such resources are accompanied with a resource agent that is then also included in the interaction. The next problem that we have to address is the problem of resource allocation to dynamic systems.

3.4 Market-based resource allocation to dynamic systems

Now we assume that resources have to be allocated to a number of I dynamic subsystems, where each subsystem i is described by the discrete-time state variable model (3). Herein, the allocated resources are the inputs of the system. In many cases however, the subsystems can be described by a linear state variable model (which can be obtained by linearization):

$$\boldsymbol{x}_i(k+1) = \boldsymbol{A}_i\boldsymbol{x}_i(k) + \boldsymbol{B}_i\boldsymbol{r}_i(k) \quad , \quad \boldsymbol{x}_i(0) = \boldsymbol{x}_{i0} \tag{12}$$

A first approach for market-based dynamic resource allocation directly uses these dynamic models of the subsystems to form the objective functions as given in (4). Since we are now interested in trajectories of the state variables and the resource allocations, we express trajectories over K time steps in the form of vectors as

$$\boldsymbol{x}_i^T = (\boldsymbol{x}_i(1),\ldots,\boldsymbol{x}_i(K)) \quad , \quad \boldsymbol{r}_i^T = (\boldsymbol{r}_i(0),\ldots,\boldsymbol{r}_i(K-1)) \tag{13}$$

With the help of the state variable model (12), the connection between the state variable trajectory and the resource trajectory is given by

$$\boldsymbol{x}_i = \tilde{\boldsymbol{A}}_i\boldsymbol{x}_i + \tilde{\boldsymbol{B}}_i\boldsymbol{r}_i + \tilde{\boldsymbol{a}}_i \tag{14}$$

with

$$\tilde{\boldsymbol{A}}_i = \begin{pmatrix} \boldsymbol{0} & \boldsymbol{0} & \cdots & \boldsymbol{0} \\ \boldsymbol{A}_i & \boldsymbol{0} & \cdots & \boldsymbol{0} \\ & \ddots & & \boldsymbol{0} \\ \boldsymbol{0} & \cdots & \boldsymbol{A}_i & \boldsymbol{0} \end{pmatrix}, \tilde{\boldsymbol{B}}_i = \begin{pmatrix} \boldsymbol{B}_i & \boldsymbol{0} & \cdots & \boldsymbol{0} \\ \boldsymbol{0} & \boldsymbol{B}_i & & \boldsymbol{0} \\ & & \ddots & \\ \boldsymbol{0} & \cdots & & \boldsymbol{B}_i \end{pmatrix} \tag{15}$$

and $\tilde{\boldsymbol{a}}_i^T = (\boldsymbol{A}_i\boldsymbol{x}_{i0}\,\boldsymbol{0}\cdots\boldsymbol{0})$. With the identity matrix $\boldsymbol{I}$ of a suitable size, (14) can then be reformulated to express the trajectory of the state variables as a linear transformation of the trajectory of the resources:

$$\boldsymbol{x}_i = (\boldsymbol{I}-\tilde{\boldsymbol{A}}_i)^{-1}\cdot\tilde{\boldsymbol{B}}_i\cdot\boldsymbol{r}_i + (\boldsymbol{I}-\tilde{\boldsymbol{A}}_i)^{-1}\cdot\tilde{\boldsymbol{a}}_i = \boldsymbol{\Psi}_i\boldsymbol{r}_i + \boldsymbol{c}_i \tag{16}$$

As in optimal control, the goal of a single agent i should be the minimization of the difference between the current states and required states $\boldsymbol{x}_{id}$ and the minimization of the resource consumption over a certain time interval. Since $\boldsymbol{x}_i$ and $\boldsymbol{r}_i$ are the trajectories of the states and allocations, the definition of the vector $\boldsymbol{x}_{id}$ as a vector of the trajectory of the required states and the diagonal weighting matrices $\boldsymbol{Q}_{i1}$ and $\boldsymbol{Q}_{i2}$ of suitable size yields the objective function of agent i

$$\begin{aligned} J_i(\boldsymbol{x}_i,\boldsymbol{r}_i) &= (\boldsymbol{x}_i-\boldsymbol{x}_{id})^T\boldsymbol{Q}_{i1}(\boldsymbol{x}_i-\boldsymbol{x}_{id}) + \boldsymbol{r}_i^T\boldsymbol{Q}_{i2}\boldsymbol{r}_i \\ &= \boldsymbol{x}_i^T\boldsymbol{Q}_{i1}\boldsymbol{x}_i - 2\boldsymbol{x}_{id}^T\boldsymbol{Q}_{i1}\boldsymbol{x}_i + \boldsymbol{x}_{id}^T\boldsymbol{Q}_{i1}\boldsymbol{x}_{id} + \boldsymbol{r}_i^T\boldsymbol{Q}_{i2}\boldsymbol{r}_i \end{aligned} \tag{17}$$

Now (16) can be inserted in (17) which results in

$$J_i(\boldsymbol{r}_i) = \boldsymbol{r}_i^T\boldsymbol{\Gamma}_i\boldsymbol{r}_i + \boldsymbol{h}_i^T\boldsymbol{r}_i + \alpha_i \tag{18}$$

with

$$\begin{aligned} \boldsymbol{\Gamma}_i &= \boldsymbol{\Psi}_i^T\boldsymbol{Q}_{i1}\boldsymbol{\Psi}_i + \boldsymbol{Q}_{i2} \\ \boldsymbol{h}_i^T &= 2\boldsymbol{c}_i^T\boldsymbol{Q}_{i1}\boldsymbol{\Psi}_i - 2\boldsymbol{x}_{id}^T\boldsymbol{Q}_{i1}\boldsymbol{\Psi}_1 \\ \alpha_i &= \boldsymbol{c}_i^T\boldsymbol{Q}_{i1}\boldsymbol{c}_i - 2\boldsymbol{x}_{id}^T\boldsymbol{Q}_{i1}\boldsymbol{c}_i + \boldsymbol{x}_{id}^T\boldsymbol{Q}_{i1}\boldsymbol{x}_{id} \end{aligned} \tag{19}$$

Since the two matrices $\boldsymbol{Q}_{i1}$ and $\boldsymbol{Q}_{i2}$ are both symmetric and positive defined, also the matrix Γ_i is positive defined and the objective function $J_i(r_i)$ as given in (18) is a strictly convex quadratic form. Therefore, the optimization problem for each single agent i again has the form(7) where the allocation now is a trajectory of allocations over K time instants taking into account the discrete-time dynamics of each subsystem. The previously derived distributed solution algorithm can be applied again with the only difference that the vector $\boldsymbol{p}$ represents a price trajectory.

The overall market-based dynamic resource allocation now again requires the assignment of one single control agent i to each of the I entities or subsystems that need resources and the definition of one coordinator agent. Each of the control agents has a model of the dynamic behavior of its assigned local subsystem, i.e. the control agent i knows the matrices $\boldsymbol{A}_i$ and $\boldsymbol{B}_i$ and it is able to measure the current vector of state variables, i.e. $\boldsymbol{x}_i(0)$. The coordinator agent then starts in iteration step $\kappa = 0$ with the definition of a first price trajectory $\boldsymbol{p}(\kappa = 0)$ which now has the dimension of K-times the dimension of one single price vector in one single instant. The price trajectory is distributed to all control agents which calculate their demand trajectories $\boldsymbol{r}_i(\boldsymbol{p}(\kappa))$ with the knowledge of the goal trajectories $\boldsymbol{x}_{id}$ over the next K time steps. This is done by solving the respective minimization problems (7) with the objective function (18).

All demand trajectories are transmitted to the coordinator agent which compares overall supply and demand and then adjusts the price trajectory as explained in the previous section. Again this iteration procedure stops until the overall (and also future market) is cleared and overall supply trajectory equals the overall demand trajectory. Then the allocation for that current time step is realized and the overall procedure starts again in the next time step. That means that the current allocation is calculated on the basis of model-based predictions of the future states, but the calculated future resource trajectory is not completely allocated. The reason for that approach is the possibility to consider disturbances of the state variables that can occur in the next time step. Thus the overall allocation scheme is similar to a model-predictive control algorithm but realized by distributed communicating control agents.

A second possible approach takes into account that the main goal of the local control agents is the control of the single subsystems via a suitable allocation of the resources. In a heating system for instance, each control agent has to allocate that amount of heating energy to the assigned room that a required temperature setpoint is maintained. This is done by a feedback of the room temperature and a conventional controller like a PID controller. There are many possibilities to develop suitable control algorithms and this is a well-known standard procedure in control engineering, see the corresponding literature. Without any loss of generality we can assume here that discrete-time state variable feedback controllers with a controller matrix $\boldsymbol{K}_i$ exist for all single subsystems $i = 1, \ldots, I$:

$$\tilde{\boldsymbol{r}}_i(k) = -\boldsymbol{K}_i \cdot \boldsymbol{x}_i(k) \tag{20}$$

Herein, $\tilde{\boldsymbol{r}}_i(k)$ is the allocation vector that is proposed from the pure control algorithm in each instant k. However, this computation only takes the fulfillment of the given control goals into account and not the fact that the overall allocated amount of the resources is limited to $\boldsymbol{r}$. For that purpose, each control agent also acts as a local optimizer in addition to the pure control task for the overall coordination of the resource allocation process. However, a suitable objective function $J_i(\boldsymbol{r}_i(k)$ has to be derived that again makes the market-based allocation scheme applicable.

Here, the following idea has been developed. If $\tilde{\boldsymbol{r}}_i(k)$ is the amount of the resources proposed for an allocation by the pure control algorithm in order to fulfill the local control goal and $\boldsymbol{r}_i(k)$ is the finally allocated amount negotiated by the control agent, the difference between these two vectors should be minimized, i.e.

$$\begin{aligned} J_i(\boldsymbol{r}_i(k)) &= (\boldsymbol{r}_i(k) - \tilde{\boldsymbol{r}}_i(k))^T \cdot (\boldsymbol{r}_i(k) - \tilde{\boldsymbol{r}}_i(k)) \\ &= \boldsymbol{r}_i^T(k)\boldsymbol{r}_i(k) - 2 \cdot \boldsymbol{r}_i^T(k)\tilde{\boldsymbol{r}}_i(k) + \tilde{\boldsymbol{r}}_i^T(k)\tilde{\boldsymbol{r}}_i(k) \end{aligned} \tag{21}$$

This objective function $J_i(\boldsymbol{r}_i(k))$ again is a strictly convex quadratic form and therefore the proposed market-based allocation algorithm can be applied in each instant k. However, this objective function also takes the control goal into account, because it also contains the corresponding vector $\tilde{\boldsymbol{r}}_i(k)$.

The overall market-based dynamic resource allocation then works as follows. In each discrete time step k, each local control agent i measures the full vector $\boldsymbol{x}_i(k)$ of state variables of the associated subsystem. With the help of a local control algorithm, each control agent proposes a local allocation $\tilde{\boldsymbol{r}}_i(k)$ which is then given to an included local optimizer i. Each optimizer i then calculates the current objective function $J_i(\boldsymbol{r}_i(k))$. From the viewpoint of the optimization, this objective function is a pure static function at each instant k and the dynamic behavior of the subsystem i has been taken into account during the development of the state variable feedback controller. With the help of that separation between control task and resource allocation, a realization of the proposed system is not very difficult since the control algorithms itself remain unchanged. With the help of a coordinator agent and the previously described iterative algorithm, the actual allocations $\boldsymbol{r}_i(k)$ are then calculated. The optimizers within the control agents then command these values to their local controllers to realize this allocation with the suitable actuators. The overall physical structure of the system is shown in figure 4.

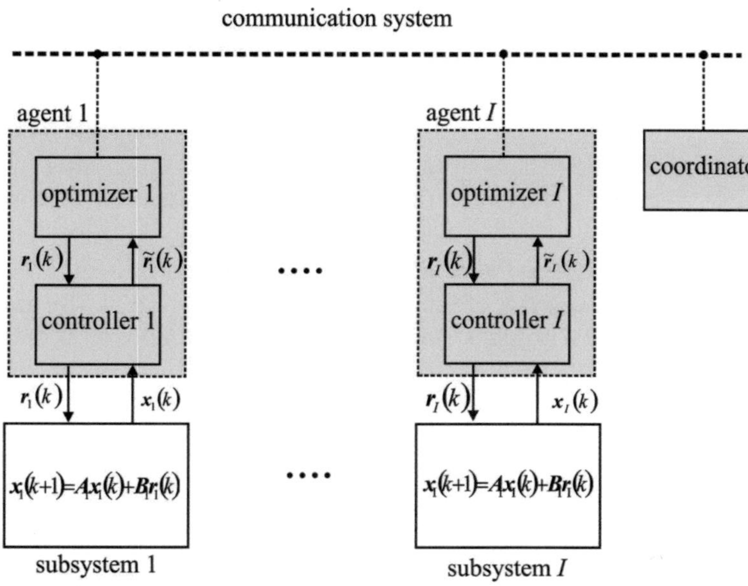

Fig. 4. Structure of the dynamic resource allocation which combines control and allocation task.

4. Application examples

In a first application example, we consider flow control in a network as a static distributed resource allocation problem given by (1) for a number of agents. The network is described by a directed graph with M nodes and N links between the nodes as given in Fig. 5. The nodes have no storage capability and act as routing elements. Each link L_j, $j = 1, \dots, N$ has a certain maximum transport capacity c_j and associated costs w_j for the transport over L_j. We assume several simultaneous transport requests where each comprises the injection of an input flow at a start node, the distributed transport over the inner links of the network and the extraction of the flow at one or several end nodes. Several of these requests with the related flows now have to be routed simultaneously through the network where the transport capacity of the single links are the resources that have to be shared and allocated to the requests. The goal of a single request is to minimize the costs of the overall transport. Such flow control problems without fixed single paths occur in packet-switched communication networks, in traffic systems and in energy and water supply networks.

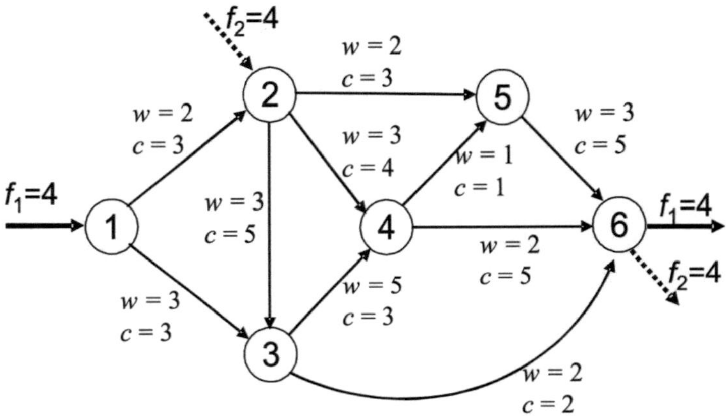

Fig. 5. Directed graph of the transport network.

Now each request is associated with a control agent i which is responsible for the allocation of the flows over each of the N links from the start to the end nodes. After the distributed allocation process between the agents is finished, this information is transmitted to the nodes for local routing. Each control agent has to determine the vector $\boldsymbol{r}_i \in \mathbb{R}_+^L$ of its corresponding allocations, where the single vector elements are ordered according to the link numbering, i.e r_{ij} is the amount of flow of request i through link j. The topology of the network given by the directed graph is described by its incidence matrix $\boldsymbol{C}$ that has M rows and N columns and the single matrix elements C_{kj} are

$$C_{kj} = \begin{cases} -1 & \text{if node } k \text{ is start node of link } j \\ 1 & \text{if node } k \text{ is end node of link } j \\ 0 & \text{else} \end{cases} \qquad (22)$$

The matrix-vector product $\boldsymbol{C} \cdot \boldsymbol{r}_i$ now defines the divergence of the nodes which allows the formulation of a condition of the injection and extraction of the flows of request i at the respective nodes in the form

$$\boldsymbol{C} \cdot \boldsymbol{r}_i = \boldsymbol{d}_i \tag{23}$$

where the elements of the vector $\boldsymbol{d}_i \in \mathbb{R}^M$ are

$$d_{ik} = \begin{cases} <0 & \text{injection of flow at node } k \\ >0 & \text{extraction of flow at node } k \\ 0 & \text{else} \end{cases} \tag{24}$$

The vector $\boldsymbol{d}_1$ for the first transport request in the example given in Fig. 5 is

$$\boldsymbol{d}_1^T = (-4, 0, 0, 0, 0, 4)$$

which means an injection flow of magnitude 4 at node one and and extraction of that flow at node six. Now the single optimization problems for the control agents i can be formulated in the form (7) where the objective function $J_i(\boldsymbol{r}_i)$ considers the transportation costs, e.g. in a linear form $J_i = \boldsymbol{w}^T \cdot \boldsymbol{r}_i$ where $\boldsymbol{w}$ is the vector of all costs of the links. However, these objective functions could be any suitable strictly convex functions which only influences the local optimization algorithm for the single control agent i. With the help of the proposed interaction scheme the price vector $\boldsymbol{p}$ is adjusted in a way that the overall condition for the allocation holds

$$\sum_{i=1}^{I} \boldsymbol{r}_i \leq \boldsymbol{c} \tag{25}$$

where the vector $\boldsymbol{c}$ is the vector of all link transport capacities. This inequality condition then can be transformed into the equality condition of form (1) by the introduction of slack variables. The allocation performed by the market-based multiagent system results in

$$\begin{aligned} \boldsymbol{r}_1^T &= (2, 2, 0, 1.02, 0.98, 0, 2, 0, 1.02, 0.98) \\ \boldsymbol{r}_2^T &= (0, 0, 0, 2.4, 1.6, 0, 0, 0, 2.4, 1.6) \end{aligned}$$

An example considering resource allocation in a dynamic system is the distribution of heating energy in an office building. Here we consider the building as a number of room modules connected according to the topology of the building. Each room module i comprises four connected elements for thermal storage: the air, the floor, the outer wall (to environment) and the inner wall with the temperatures T_i, T_{Fi}, T_{WOi} and T_{WIi}. The connections and heat flows between the elements are shown in Fig. 6. In the whole model, we neglect radiation heat and only consider convection of heat. To each office, i.e. to the air of the office, a certain heat flow r_i can be allocated as a part of the overall heating energy resource. The offices have windows that allow some direct loss heat flow j_{Li} from the room to the environment. From the air, there is a heat flow j_{Fi} to the floor and heat flows j_{WOi} to the outer wall and j_{WIi} to the inner wall. Since the inner walls connect two neighboring offices, there is an additional heat flow j_{ik} from that wall to the other office k with air temperature T_k (or several other offices). The outdoor temperature T_{Ei} is modelled as a virtual variable which is a superposition of two parts. One part is the general outdoor temperature that is independent from the orientation to the sun and only depends on the time of the day. The second part describes the influence of the radiation of the sun and therefore depends on the orientation to the sun. Therefore there are different virtual outdoor temperatures for different offices in the simulation model.

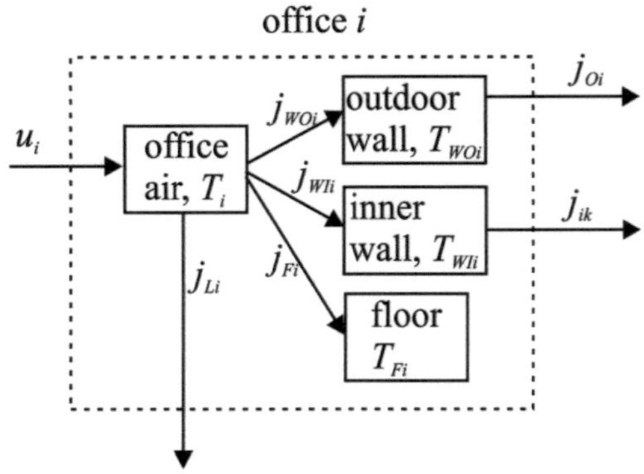

Fig. 6. Dynamic model of a single office.

The differential equation describing the air temperature T_i in office i under the assumption that the mass m_i of the air is constant is

$$c_i \cdot m_i \cdot \dot{T}_i = r_i - j_{Li} - j_{Fi} - j_{WIi} - j_{WOi} \tag{26}$$

with $j_{Li} = k_{Li} \cdot (T_i - T_{Ei})$, $j_{Fi} = k_{Fi} \cdot (T_i - T_{Fi})$, $j_{WIi} = k_{WIi} \cdot (T_i - T_{WIi})$ and $j_{WOi} = k_{WOi} \cdot (T_i - T_{WOi})$. Herein, c_i is the specific heat capacity of the air while the constants k_{Li}, k_{Fi}, k_{WIi} and k_{WOi} are the coefficients of heat transfer normalized to the effective surfaces, respectively. The other three elements for thermal storage floor, inner and outer wall are modelled in a similar way where the details are omitted here. One single room module i hence can be described by a state variable model of order four of the form

$$\begin{pmatrix} \dot{T}_i \\ \dot{T}_{Fi} \\ \dot{T}_{WIi} \\ \dot{T}_{WOi} \end{pmatrix} = \boldsymbol{A}_i \cdot \begin{pmatrix} T_i \\ T_{Fi} \\ T_{WIi} \\ T_{WOi} \end{pmatrix} + \boldsymbol{b}_i \cdot r_i + \boldsymbol{D}_i \cdot \begin{pmatrix} T_{Ei} \\ T_k \end{pmatrix} \tag{27}$$

where $\boldsymbol{A}_i$, $\boldsymbol{b}_i$ and $\boldsymbol{D}_i$ are all constant matrices or vectors that depend on the masses, heat capacities and coefficients of heat transfer. The matrix $\boldsymbol{D}_i$ describes the influence of the disturbances, i.e. the outdoor temperature and the temperatures of the neighboring office(s). In general, the trajectory of the outdoor temperature can be estimated and predicted while the trajectory of the temperature of the neighboring offices are unknown since they are a result of the allocation algorithm. However, if the heat transfer through the wall is not too big, these interconnections can be neglected with respect to the disturbance caused by the outdoor temperature. From a mathematical point of view however, the consideration of the predicted trajectory of the outdoor temperature only leads to an additional part in the vector $\tilde{\boldsymbol{a}}_i$ in (14).

Each office is associated with a control agent i that is responsible for the resource allocation, i.e. the allocation of heating energy r_i. The state variable model (27) can be transformed into a discrete-time state variable model of form (12) for each single office i. The goal of the resource allocation to office i is to minimize the difference between the trajectory of the air temperature (which can only be controlled by the input r_i) and a desired temperature trajectory while the energy consumption should be minimized simultaneously over an interval of K time steps. This leads to a definition of the objective function J_i as described in (17). Herein the matrix Q_{i1} has only the first element on the main diagonal as a non-zero element since there are no desired trajectories for the other temperatures of the walls and floor.

The dynamic allocation then can be processed by the agents as described in the previous section. Each control agent has the knowledge of the local model (27) while neglecting the interconnections between the offices and using an estimation of the future outdoor temperature. The control agent calculates the allocation trajectory for the next K time steps and all trajectories are balanced by the distributed coordination with the price trajectory. Then all control agents realize their local allocation for the next time step only and the overall procedure starts again. Especially the prediction of the future outdoor temperatures as the main disturbances leads to an early adaptation of the single allocations taking into account the inert behavior of a heating process. Thus the overall efficiency of the heating system and the comfort is considerably increased. One result for a building configuration with twelve offices is shown for four rooms in Fig. 7. Here it becomes obvious that the set-point temperatures are maintained except in intervals where the radiation of the sun is too strong (see offices four and eleven). These deviations are caused by the fact that in spite of zero allocation of heating energy the incoming heat still leads to an increase of the temperature. However, this problem could only be solved by a cooling system. Nevertheless, the algorithm works well in the simulation and the overall heating energy is always kept below a desired maximum.

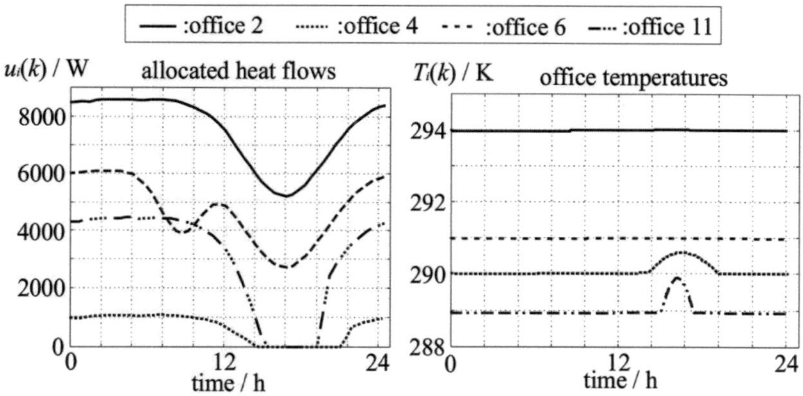

Fig. 7. Results of heat allocation for a simulated building.

The second proposed agent-based dynamic resource allocation scheme is finally applied to a real industrial production process in sugar industry. In Europe, sugar is mainly produced by extracting it from sugar beets. This extraction is performed by cutting the beets into small parts and giving them into hot water. Within that heating process, the sugar is dissolved in the water and steam is generated. In a following production step, the sugar cristallization, the sugar-water solution is given into several cooking stations where this solution is further heated until the solution is oversaturated and the sugar starts to cristallize. Hereby, the steam that is generated in the sugar extraction is then used in this second process of cristallization as heating energy, see Fig. 8. The overall amount of steam should be kept constant in order to avoid disturbances during the extraction. Therefore, the limited and constant amount of the resource "steam" has to be allocated in a suitable way to the different cooking stations and that resource allocation is accomplished here with the proposed distributed market-based algorithm using agents.

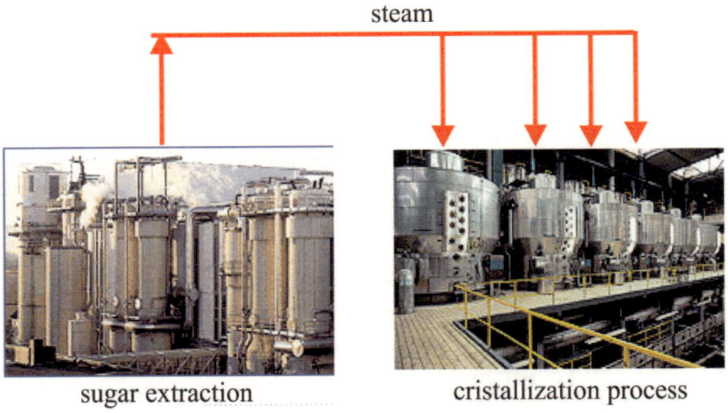

Fig. 8. Steam allocation in the sugar production process.

The resource allocation problem can be expressed as follows. Given the overall constant amount j_H of steam generated during the extraction, this steam must be allocated to a number of I cooking stations, each indexed by i. At each discrete time step k, the amount of steam allocated to a single cooking station i is $j_{H,i}(k)$ and the allocation problem expressed in the form (1) yields

$$\begin{aligned} &\min_{\{j_{H,i}(k),\forall i\}} \sum_{i=1}^{I} J_i(j_{H,i}(k)) \\ \text{s.t.} \quad & j_{H,i}(k) \geq 0 \quad \forall i \\ & \sum_{i=1}^{I} j_{H,i}(k) = j_H \end{aligned} \tag{28}$$

However, the allocation of the limited overall amount of steam at instant k to the different cooking stations must be done in a suitable way and the allocated amounts of steam depend on the current state of the stations and the control goal. A single cooking station is shown in Fig. 9.

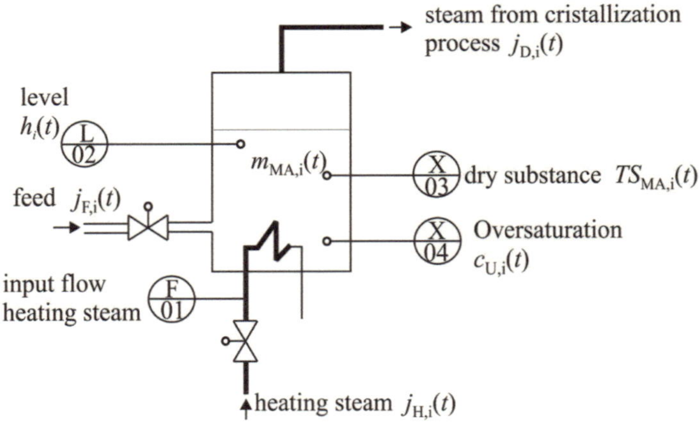

Fig. 9. A simplified scheme of a cooking station.

Herein, $m_{MA,i}$ is the overall mass, $j_{F,i}$ is the amount of sugar-water solution that flows into the tank, $j_{H,i}$ is the heating steam, $C_{U,i}$ is the oversaturation, $TS_{MA,i}$ is the dry substance and h_i is the level in the tank. Concerning that process, a discrete-time state space model was developed [Voos, 2003] in order to design a local state variable feedback controller as given in (20). Here, the main control goal is to keep the oversaturation constant while filling the tank with the solution and to reach a dry substance content in the solution of 90% at the end of the batch process. The input variable for that control task is the amount of the actually allocated amount of heating steam $j_{H,i}(k)$. The allocation proposed by this local controller then can be expressed here as

$$\tilde{j}_{H,i}(k) = -\boldsymbol{K}_i \cdot \boldsymbol{x}_i(k) \tag{29}$$

That leads to the formulation of the local objective function corresponding to (21) and the proposed distributed allocation algorithm can be applied.
The approach is currently tested in a simulation where some results are given in figure 10. Here a number of 3 cooking station is supplied with an overall amount of j_H = 8 kg/sec of heating steam. The different cooking stations are started at different start times and therefore the batches also end at different stop times. In figure 10, the three different allocated amounts $j_{H,i}(k)$ as well as the sum of all of them are depicted. It is obvious that the algorithm succeeds in keeping the sum constant and equal to the required overall amount j_H = 8 kg/sec of generated steam. In addition, in each single batch the control goals are fulfilled

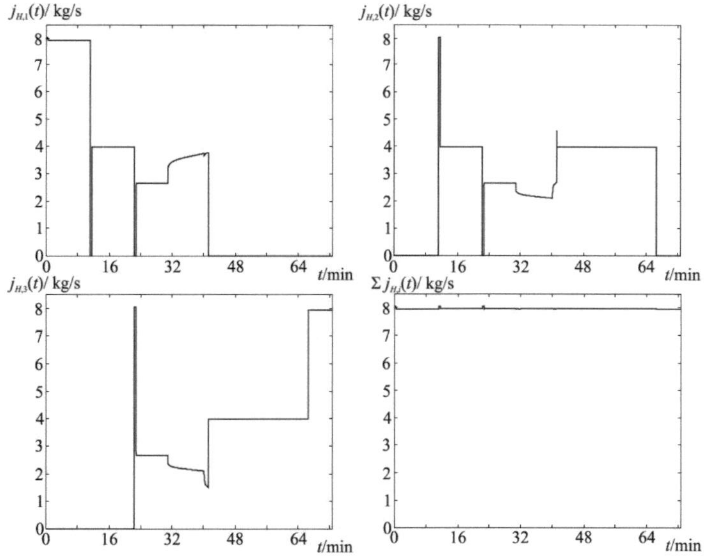

Fig. 10. Allocated amounts of steam in the simulation.

(not shown here). This example also illustrates the flexibility of the market-based approach since it can handle a flexible and varying number of agents (i.e. batches here) that take part in the allocation. At the beginning, only one agent takes part in the allocation process since only the first batch has been started. Then with the start of the second batch process, a second agent starts to take part in the allocation and so on.

5. Conclusions and future works

In this chapter a new approach for agent-based distributed resource allocation has been derived which is especially suited to cope with allocations in dynamic environments. The interaction scheme is inspired by economic markets and therefore called market-based allocation. Herein, the resource allocation problem is formulated as an optimization problem that can be decomposed into single optimization problems that only depend on a global price vector. That price vector is used to balance the overall allocations, i.e. the solutions of the single optimization problems. A general market-based approach has been extended here in two directions. First, more general objective functions now can be used which leads to a wider range of applications. Second, the idea of allocation to dynamic systems has been included. The approach is demonstrated using three technical examples for proof of concept. One interesting question that has to be solved in the future is the consideration of allocation to dynamic systems where a dynamic interconnection between the subsystems occurs.

6. References

[Unland, 2003] R. Unland, M. Klusch, M. Calisti, (Ed.) *Software Agent-Based Applications, Platforms and Developments Kits*, Birkh¨auser, Basel 2005.

[Maturana, 2006] F. Maturana et. al., *Agent Infrastructure for Distributed Control and Interoperability.* In proc. of the IEEE Workshop on Distributed Intelligent Systems DIS 2006, Prague, Czech Republic, 2006.

[Jennings, 1998] N.R. Jennings, K. Sycara, M.Wooldridge, "A Roadmap of Agent Research and Development", *Autonomous Agents and Multi-Agent Systems*, vol. 1 (1), pp. 7-38, 1998.

[Clearwater, 1996] S.H. Clearwater (ed.), *Market-Based Control: A Paradigm For Distributed Resource Allocation.* Singapore: World Scientific, 1996.

[Debreu, 1959] G. Debreu, *Theory of value.* New Haven and London: Yale University Press, 1959.

[Ibaraki, 1988] T. Ibaraki and N. Katoh, *Resource Allocation Problems - Algorithmic Approaches.* Cambridge (MA): MIT Press, 1988.

[Voos, 2003] H. Voos, *Market-based Control: Eine neue Methode zur automatisierten Ressourcenzuteilung.* (in German.) Ph.D. Thesis, Aachen: Shaker, 2003.

[Voos, 2006] H. Voos, *Agent-Based Distributed Resource Allocation in Technical Dynamic Systems.* in Proc. of the IEEE Workshop on Distributed Intelligent Systems DIS 2006, Prague, Czech Republic, 2006.

[Voos, 2007] H. Voos, *Resource allocation in Continuous Production using Market-Based Multiagent Systems.* in Proc. of the IEEE 5th International Conference on Industrial Informatics INDIN 2007, Wien, Austria, 2007.

[Colombo, 2004] A.W. Colombo, R. Schoop, R. Neubert, *Collaborative (Agent-based) Factory Automation.* Chapter 109 in "The Industrial Information Technology Handbook.", Richard Zurawski (Ed.), Boca Raton, USA,: CRC Press LLC, 2004.

[Sandholm, 1999] T. W. Sandholm, "Distributed Rational Decision Making", in Multiagent Systems, G. Weiss, ed., pp. 201-258, Cambridge: MIT Press, 1999.

[Stoer, 1993] Stoer, J.: *Numerische Mathematik 1.* 6. Aufl. Berlin, Heidelberg: Springer Verlag 1993

[Weiss, 1999] G. Weiss, ed.; *Multiagent Systems.* Cambridge, MA: MIT Press, 1999.

[Bussmann, 2003] N. Jennings, S. Bussmann, *Agent-Based Control Systems.* In IEEE Control Systems Magazine, Vol. 23, June 2003.

[Kluegl, 2005] F. Klügl, A. Bazzan, S. Ossowski (Eds.), *Applications of Agent Technology in Traffic and Transportation.* Basel: Birkhäuser 2005.

[AAMAS, 2008] Proceedings of the Seventh International Conference on Autonomous Agents and Multiagent Systems AAMAS 2008, Lissabon, Portugal, 2008.

[Cervenka, 2007] R. Cervenka, I. Trescansky, *The Agent Modeling Language - AML.* Berlin, Heidelberg: Springer 2007.

2

Constraint Based Automated Multi-attribute Negotiations

Miguel A. López-Carmona, Iván Marsá-Maestre and Juan R. Velasco
Universidad de Alcalá
Spain

1. Introduction

Multi-attribute (Multi-issue) negotiation protocols have been studied widely, and represent an important challenge in the multiagent systems community (Lai et al., 2004). Therefore, a lot of automated negotiation models and protocols have been developed, and manifold negotiation challenges have been already addressed. Most research in automated negotiation to date has focused on the competitive aspect (Vo et al., 2007). On the other hand, work by Dispute Resolution theorists in the social sciences has also focussed substantially on how to achieve negotiated agreements that are of a high value to all parties (Fischer & Ury, 1981). This approach is known as *Integrative* or *Interest-based negotiation*, and it has been recognised as the more successful approach to the negotiation problem. Example scenarios where such cases may arise are: business process management involving agents within the same organization, e-commerce negotiations where the seller is interested in having a satisfied buyer (e.g. long-term commercial relationships), or e-commerce scenarios where risk averse agents avoid the conflict in the negotiation processes. In the context of purchase negotiation scenarios, it is clear that every negotiation partner tries to maximize his preferences. However, when an agent aims at optimizing his own benefit with no regard for the others', it has been shown that negotiators more often than not reach inefficient compromises. Conflict theorists Lax and Sebenius (Lax & Sebenius, 1992) argue that negotiation necessarily includes both cooperative and competitive elements, and that these elements exist in tension. Therefore, he refers to the problem of deciding whether to pursue a cooperative or a competitive strategy at a particular time during a negotiation as the Negotiator's Dilemma. However, it is not always possible to separate the integrative bargaining process, i.e. when agents use cooperative strategies to search for joint gains, from the distributive bargaining process, i.e. when agents use competitive strategies in order to 'claim value'. The main problem is that distributive and integrative processes interplay with each other making information manipulation becomes part of the integrative bargaining process.□□*Integrative negotiation* contrasts with *distributive bargaining* in which the parties are trying to distribute a fixed resource, and where if an agent wins another agent looses. Distributive negotiation predicts that one party can only gain at the other party's expense. The key characteristics that distinguish integrative negotiations from distributive ones are: creation of value; focus on interests and not positions; openness and exchange of relevant information, and even learning; and problem restructuring. In order to achieve integrative approaches, literature of automated negotiation proposes a number of techniques such as *multi-attribute utility theory, distributed constraint satisfaction*, and *cojoint analysis*. A common aspect in all these techniques and in integrative negotiation approaches in general is that a multi-attribute negotiation scenario is required. Attributes are the characteristics of the negotiation item that are taken into account during the evaluation. The idea is that it may be beneficial for people to introduce multiple issues in a negotiation when they have different preferences over these issues because it may be possible to trade off one issue for another in order to reach agreements where both the negotiators are better off. So, in multi-attribute negotiations the parties involved need to settle more than one issue. For example, agents may need to come to agreements that are characterized by attributes such as price, quality, delivery time, and so on. If the impact of the issues under negotiation over the satisfaction function is different for each agent (that is, some issues are more important for a participant than for the others and vice versa), the issues may be traded-off against one another, increasing the social welfare of the deal.

Both in single and multi-issue negotiations the outcome depends on four key factors (Fatima et al., 2006): the *negotiation protocol*, the *participant's strategies*, the *players' preferences* over the possible outcomes, and the *information that the participants have about the others*. However, in multi-issue negotiations appears an additional factor: the *negotiation procedure*, which specifies how the issues will be settled. There are three ways of negotiating multiple issues: *Package deal* which links all the issues and discusses them together as bundle, *Simultaneous negotiation* which settles the issues simultaneously, but independently, and *Sequential negotiation* which negotiates the issues sequentially one after another. This chapter will focus on a package deal based procedure.

As we pointed out before, many automated negotiation models have been developed. They may be classified regarding many different criteria (Buttner, 2006). Regarding their theoretical approach, *game theoretic, heuristic* and *argumentation-based* approaches exist. The game-theoretic approach tries to find optimal strategies by the analysis of the equilibrium conditions (Nash, 1950). Game-theoretic models are deemed mathematically elegant, but are very restricted in use because of their assumptions of unlimited resources, perfect rationality and a perfect information situation. In heuristic approaches the mentioned assumptions are relaxed, and players try to find an approximate solution strategy according to principles of bounded rationality by utilizing heuristic search and evaluation techniques (Faratin et al., 1998; Ehtamo et al., 1999; Faratin et al., 2002; Klein et al., 2003; Gatti & Amigoni, 2005; Lai et al., 2006; Ito et al., 2008;). Both in game-theoretic and heuristic approaches, negotiation protocols are usually based on the communication of offers in the form of potential agreements. In contrast, in argumentation-based negotiations, the agents are able to reason their positions including a meta-level component that may use promises, rewards, threats, as well as issue various forms of appeal (Rahwan et al., 2003). In addition to the theoretical approach criterion, negotiation can be classified regarding its structure, regarding the negotiation process, and regarding the restrictions over time and information situations.

In addition to the problem of selecting the optimal strategies in the negotiation processes, the agent's decision making mechanisms in multi-attribute negotiations have to face the problem of characterize the preference on all attributes. The characterization of preferences has a critical influence on the negotiation protocols and decision-making mechanisms. To end up with this introduction we briefly review some of the most relevant approaches in negotiation to model preferences, and pick up one of them to propose a multi-attribute negotiation protocol that will be presented in the following sections.

A typical way to model preferences is to use *utility functions*. In the case of multiple attributes, we talk about *multi-attribute utility theory (MAUT)*. Another approach to model preferences is to employ *multi-criteria decision making (MCDM)* (also called *multi-objective* or *multi-criteria optimization*) theory. In MCDM an agent has several objectives that are statements that delineate the desires of a decision maker. Thus, an agent wishes to maximise his objectives, which in some cases will conflict which each other in that the improved achievement with one objective can only be accomplished at the expense of another. Given an assignment of values to the corresponding attributes an agent measures how much the different objectives are fulfilled. Finally, a utility function is applied over the set of different levels of satisfaction of the agent's objectives. Research on those topics is conducted mostly in the field of decision theory. In the negotiation models described in the literature which use the utility based approaches to the modelling of preferences, the negotiation protocols are based on the communication of offers and counteroffers expressed as an assignment of values to the corresponding attributes. This approach to negotiation is known as *positional bargaining*, and is the predominant form of negotiation in the game-theoretic and heuristic approaches to negotiation. On the other hand, in argumentation-based negotiation the exchange of offers and counteroffers includes meta-information with the aim of reason the agents' positions. In the area of interest-based negotiation, another way to modelling preferences is to use *constraints* to restrict the attribute values that are preferred. *Constraints* in different formats, from *fuzzy* to *probabilistic* or *weighted constraints*, have been used in several models and approaches to multi-attribute negotiation (Luo et al., 2003; Lai & Lin, 2003; Ito et al., 2008). There are three main reasons that make very convenient the use of constraints as the core of a negotiation model. First, it is an efficient way of capturing requirements; second, constraints are capable of representing trade-offs between the different possible values for attributes; and third, using constraints to express offers in turns means that the solution space can be explored in a given exchange and so means that the search for an agreement is more efficient than in positional bargaining. The negotiation framework presented in this chapter falls within the heuristic approaches to non-mediated multi-attribute bilateral negotiations under incomplete information settings, and uses fuzzy constraints to model agent's preferences. With incomplete information we mean that agents lack information about other's discounting factors, reservation prices, utility functions or deadlines, and with non-mediated we mean that agents negotiate without the intervention of a mediating agent. The negotiation model is based on the hypothesis that by means of an expressive approach to constraint based negotiation the negotiation processes may be more efficient than with other approaches where mainly positional bargaining is used. Behind this is the idea that with the cost of a bounded increase in the revelation of private information, the decision mechanisms are more accurate when searching the negotiation space.

The remainder of this chapter is organized as follows. The next Section recalls the most relevant concepts on modelling agent's preferences and presents some preliminaries. Section 3 presents an example negotiation scenario where two different negotiation techniques are applied in order to show the possible advantages of expressive negotiation. Then the negotiation framework followed by an empirical evaluation is described. Finally, Section 6 presents the conclusions.

2. Modelling agent's preferences

A multi-attribute negotiation can be seen as a distributed *multi-objective optimization problem*. The participants in a negotiation have their own preferences over the negotiated attributes, and these preferences can be formulated in its most extensive form as a multi-objective or multi-criteria decision making problem. By definition, objectives are statements that delineate the desires of a decision maker. Thus, an agent wishes to maximise his objectives. However, it is quite likely that a decision maker's objectives will conflict with each other in that the improved achievement with one objective can only be accomplished at the expense of another. Therefore, a negotiator agent has to settle at a compromise solution. This is the topic of the *multi-criteria decision making theory*. Part of the solution to this problem is that the agent has to identify or approximate the *Pareto frontier* in the *consequence space* (i.e. in the space of the satisfaction levels of the different objectives). This task can be accomplished using different methods based on standard optimization techniques. Regarding the negotiation process it can be seen as a special case of multi-objective optimization problem. In this case, we have a set of distributed agent's objectives that should be satisfied. Each agent's objective depends on his individual objectives. The question now is if we can compute the Pareto frontier in a similar way. Assuming a set of agents which formalize their preferences as a multi-objective decision making problem, and that each agent computes his Pareto frontier, the only way to solve this problem in a similar way would be to share this information to formulate the global multi-objective optimization problem. In practice, this could be done by means of a trusted mediator, but it has a fundamental problem, agents and humans try to minimise the revelation of private information in negotiation to avoid strategic manipulation. Moreover, though Pareto optimality is a key concept in multi-objective optimization, we cannot forget that the aim of the negotiation is to reach an agreement, and so, it is necessary to pick up a fair solution from the Pareto frontier. However, fairness is not an easy concept to manage in negotiations.

2.1 Multi-attribute decision problems

As we stated before, negotiator agents are decision makers, and their decisions are based on preferences over the values of the different attributes. Formally, a *Multi-Attribute Decision Problem (MADP)* is defined as a set of attributes $X = \{x_1, ..., x_n\}$; a set of domain values $D = \{D_1, ..., D_n\}$ where each D_i is a set of possible values for attribute x_i; a set of constraints $C = \{C_1, ..., C_m\}$ where each C_j is a constraint function on a subset of attributes to restrict the values they can take; a set of available outcomes $O = \{o_1, ..., o_l\}$ where each o_j is an element of the possible outcome space *D*, and *O* is a subset of *D*; and a set of decision maker's preference statements $P = \{P_1, ..., P_m\}$. Agents negotiate over the same set of attributes and domain values, but each agent has a different set of constraints, available outcomes and preference statements. In a negotiation process, agents try to maximize their preferences, and in order to compute those values they have to solve the MADP. Among the different approaches to model agents' preferences from the MADPs perspective we survey two different categories of methods: the *constraint satisfaction problem (CSP) framework*, and the *multi-attribute utility theory (MAUT)*. For a detailed survey including more methods on MADPs see (Zhang & Pu, 2005).

A **CSP** is defined by a 3-tuple <*X*,*D*,*C*>, where *X* is a set of variables, *D* is a set of domains and *C* is a set of constraints. A solution to a CSP is a set of value assignment

$v = \{x_1 = v_1, ..., x_n = v_n\}$ where all constraints in *C* are satisfied. Therefore, the constraints are crisp (hard) since they are either respected or violated. A number of different approaches have been developed for solving this problem. One simple approach is to simply *generate-and-test*. However, when the CSP is complex the algorithm is not practical due to the computational complexity. A more efficient method is the *backtracking algorithm* that essentially performs a depth-first search of the space of potential CSP solutions. However, the complexity of backtracking for most nontrivial problems is still exponential. Other search algorithms for classical CSPs include: *forward checking, partial lookahead, full lookahead,* and *really full lookahead.*

We can see how a solution of a classical CSP needs to satisfy all the crisp constraints. Comparing the definition of classical CSP and MADP we can see that the main difference between them is that the MADP has a set of preferences, some of which can be violated when finding the optimal solution. Classical CSPs have been extended to *soft CSPs* in which not all the given constraints need to be satisfied. In the following, we recall several kinds of soft CSPs and a general framework which describes both classical and soft CSPs.

Fuzzy CSPs (FCSPs) extend the hard constraints by *fuzzy constraints*. A fuzzy constraint is a mapping from the direct product of the finite domain of the variables referred by the constraint to the [0,1] interval. The solution of a fuzzy CSP is the set of n-tuples of values that have the maximal value. The value associated with each n-tuple is obtained by minimizing the values of all its sub-tuples. An FCSP can be solved in a similar way as classical-CSP turning all fuzzy constraints into hard constraints.

Probabilistic CSPs (PCSPs) model those situations where each constraint *c* has a certain independent probability *p(c)* to be part of the given real problem. Let v be an n-tuple value set, considering all the constraints that the n-tuple violates, we can see that the probability of n-tuple being a solution is $\prod_{\text{all c that v violates}} (1 - p(c))$. The aim of solving PCSPs is to get the n-tuple with the maximal probability. The main difference between FCSPs lies in the fact that PCSPs contain crisp constraints with probability levels, while FCSPs contain non-crisp constraints. Moreover, the criteria for choosing the optimal solutions are different.

Weighted CSPs (WCSPs) allow to model optimization problems where the goal is to minimize the total cost of a solution. There is cost function for each constraint, and the total cost is defined by summing up the costs of each constraint. Usually WCSPs can be solved by the *Branch and Bound algorithm.*

A semiring-based CSP framework describes both classical and soft CSPs. In this framework, a semiring is a tuple *(A,+,x,0,1)* such that: *A* is a set and $0,1 \in A$; + is a close, commutative, and associative operation on A and 0 is its unit element; x is a closed, associative, multiplicative operation on A; and 1 is its unit element and 0 is its absorbing element. Moreover, x distributes over +. A c-semiring is a semiring such that + is idempotent, x is commutative, and 1 is the absorbing element of +.

Both the classical CSPs and the different type of soft CSPs can be seen as instances of the semiring CSP framework. The classical CSPs are Semiring-CSPs over the semiring $S_{CSP} = (\{false, true\}, \vee, \wedge, false, true)$ which means that there are just two preferences (*false* or *true*), that the preference of a solution is the logic *and* of the preferences of their subtuples in the constraints, and that *true* is better than *false*. FCSPs can be represented by $S_{FCSP} = ([0,1], \max, \min, 0, 1)$ which means that the preferences are over [0,1], and that we want to maximize the minimum preference over all the constraints. Similarly, the semiring corresponding to a PCSP is $S_{PCSP} = ([0,1], \max, \times, 0, 1)$, and the WCSPs can be represented by the semiring $S_{WCSP} = (R^+, \min, +, +\infty, 0)$.

Utility theory and MAUT has been used in solving decision problems in economics especially for those involving uncertainty and risk. Given the utility function, the decision maker's preferences will be totally determined, and the optimal solution will be the outcome with the maximal utility. When using MAUT to solve a multi-attribute decision problem that only involves certainty, the main task is to assess the value function according to the decision maker's preferences.

Let $O = \{O_1, ..., O_n\}$ be a set of outcomes of the MADP, $\mathfrak{A}$ be the set of all lotteries on the set O where $\sum p_i o_i \in \mathfrak{A}$, $p_i \in [0,1]$, and $\sum p_i = 1$; and $\succsim$ be a binary relation on $\mathfrak{A}$. First we define 4 axioms: 1) $\succsim$ is complete, i.e. either $x \succsim y$ or $y \succsim x$; 2) $\succsim$ is transitive, i.e. if $x \succsim y$ and $y \succsim z$, then $x \succsim z$; 3) Continuity: given $x \succ y \succ z$, then there is an $\alpha, \beta \in (0,1)$ such that $\alpha x + (1-\alpha)z \succ y$ and $y \succ \beta x + (1-\beta)z$; 4) Independence: for all $x, y, z \in \mathfrak{A}$ and any $\alpha \in [0,1]$, $x \succsim y$ if and only if $\alpha x + (1-\alpha)z \succsim \alpha y + (1-\alpha)z$. Then the *von Neumann Morgenstern Theorem* proved the existence of utility function theoretically provided that the relation $\succsim$ satisfies the four axioms: Let $\mathfrak{A}$ be a convex subset of a linear space, and let $\succsim$ be a binary relation on $\mathfrak{A}$, then $\succsim$ satisfies the four axioms if and only if there is a real-valued function $u : \mathfrak{A} \to \mathfrak{R}$ such that:

a. $\forall x, y \in \mathfrak{A}, x \succsim y \Leftrightarrow u(x) \geq u(y)$;

b. $\forall x, y \in \mathfrak{A}$ and $\forall \alpha \in (0,1), u(\alpha x + (1-\alpha)y) = \alpha u(x) + (1-\alpha)u(y)$.

The function u is called the *utility function*.

Keeney and Raiffa (Keeney & Raiffa, 1976) extended the utility theory to the case of multi-attributes. Multi-attribute utility theory is concerned with the valuation of the consequences or outcomes of a decision maker's actions. For a decision problem where each action has a deterministic outcome, the decision maker needs only to express preferences among outcomes. The preference relation can be captured by an order-preserving, real-valued value function. Then, the optimal problem of the multi-attribute decision problem can be converted into the format of the standard optimization problem to maximize *u(x)*. When there is uncertainty involved in the decision problem, the outcomes are characterized by probabilities. It must be noted that a utility function is a value function, but a value function is not necessarily a utility function. In the case that only certainty is involved, the utility and value function are interchangeable.

3. A non-mediated bilateral negotiation model based on fuzzy constraints

Here we propose a non-mediated fuzzy constraint based negotiation framework for competitive e-marketplaces in which multiple buyer agents negotiate bilaterally with multiple seller agents to acquire products. In competitive markets, there is an inherent need to restrict the amount of private information the agent reveals. However, this restriction can have a detrimental effect on the search for a solution. As we stated above, especially in the case of multi-attribute negotiations, it is possible to reach a more satisfactory agreement by means of an adequate combination of attributes or constraints. However, most solutions put forward to tackle this problem are mediated, iterative and approach mechanisms, which are applicable to preference models based on linear-additive or quasi-concave utility functions (Ehtamo et al., 1999; Faratin et al., 2002; Lai et al., 2006). Other approaches based on non-linear utility spaces include a mediator in the negotiation processes (Klein et al., 2003; Gatti & Amigoni, 2005; Ito et al., 2008). As an alternative to these solutions, we propose one based on the concept of communicative rationality rather than one which is merely strategic and retains as the fundamental criteria the minimization of private information revealed. Our solution is therefore based on a dialogue of offers in which preferences or satisfaction degrees are partially disclosed. The hypotheses on which the work is based is that of an interactive model which is sufficiently expressive to allow a discussion of proposals by means of a partial declaration of preferences which permits the agents to reach a more satisfactory agreement, being confined to the need to minimize the loss of privacy. The negotiation framework is defined by: a fuzzy constraint based model of preferences; the expressive behaviors and strategies of the agents; an interaction model that permits the automatic generation of expressive or non-expressive dialogues with different degrees of symmetry; and finally a set of decision mechanisms adapted to the interaction model and the preferences of the agents.

There are several works using fuzzy constraints to model preferences, however, most of them use single point offers (i.e. positional bargaining). The FeNAs (Fuzzy e-Negotiation Agent system) platform (Kowalczyk & Bui, 2000) uses fuzzy constraints and permits correlated multiple bilateral negotiations. It is one of the first works in which the problem of multi-attribute negotiation is clearly presented using a preference model based on FCSP. The main problem with FeNAs resides in its being a positional approach. Lai (Lai & Lin, 2004) presents a general framework for multi-attribute and multilateral negotiation based on fuzzy constraints. The negotiation model is based on FCSP, which when applied to a distributed domain of agents is organized as a network of distributed fuzzy constraints (DFCN). This work makes some very important contributions to the regularization of the mechanisms for calculating the satisfaction degree and to the available concession and compensation strategies. It introduces fuzzy logic techniques to the relaxation decision making area that allow concession strategies to be defined that are a function of the beliefs and desires of the agents. The model is also based on single-point offers and there is no argumentation, but decision-making is based on the behavior of the opponent and the type of offers received. In accordance with the mentioned above procedures, if there is no convergence in the first relaxation steps, the number of offers increases exponentially. If there are a large number of attributes, the number of possible proposals for a particular cut level becomes intractable. Although the similarity function can help with convergence, a certain amount of knowledge of the utility functions of the opponent is assumed. Finally, Luo (Luo et al., 2003) develops a fuzzy constraint based model for bilateral multi-issue negotiations in semi-competitive environments. It uses crisp constraints to express offers and includes the idea of rewards and restrictions. The most noticeable aspects are related to the acceptability function and with the operators used to apply the prioritization of the fuzzy constraints. Assuming the seller agents' dominant strategy is to offer the first product that satisfies the constraints, the model isn't efficient enough because it exhibits a large lack of symmetry. In this model a buyer agent has a great communication power (expressing offers by means of constraints) while the seller agent can only offer specific products or request a relaxation of the constraints. In this way, the opportunity to apply some form of solution compensation technique so that a win-win solution is obtained is lost.

3.1 Expressive vs inexpressive negotiation dialogues

In this subsection a bilateral negotiation scenario is presented, comparing two approaches, one expressive and the other non-expressive, in which all the advantages that our approach contributes to the problem will be discussed.

A buyer agent and a seller agent begin a negotiation dialogue about the sale of a vehicle. The buyer agent expresses a desire to buy in the following way: "*I want to acquire a car at a low price, of high quality and as new as possible*". From this statement, it can be taken there are three issues that are of interest to the buyer agent, the *price*, the *quality* and the *age* of the car. The requirements of the buyer agent are therefore defined by these three fuzzy constraints, so that a priori, no specific range is defined for each issue to determine whether a constraint has been satisfied. In the seller agent's case we could propose a formulation of preferences or sale needs in a similar way, however, in trading scenarios the seller agent may be more inclined towards the use of catalogues of products. In Figures 1 and 2, the buyer agent's preferences and a summary of the seller agent's catalogue are shown respectively. The labels above each step represent the range of the attributes value domain, in such a way that the states can appear as intervals, numeric groups or as linguistic terms. The higher steps represent greater satisfaction degrees. If we analyse the diagram we can see that, for

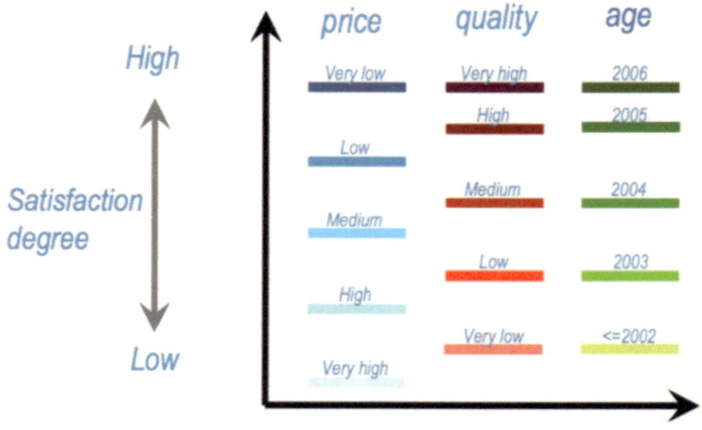

Fig. 1. Buyer agent's preferences

Fig. 2. Seller's catalogue of products

example, the fuzzy constraint expressed as low price is divided in intervals in accordance with the different satisfaction degrees of the buyer agent.□The catalogue of products is defined by a series of rows each one of which characterizes a product. For each product, the satisfied range of values of the buyer agent's attributes is shown. The last column represents the utility the seller agent obtains if the product is sold. This utility value does not have to have any direct correlation with the negotiable attributes, there may exist other private issues (non negotiated) that have a greater influence on the utility value.□
To give an example of our working hypothesis we first present a possible negotiation dialogue between a buyer and seller agent (see Figure 3) that we will call *non-expressive*. In this type of dialogue the argumentation capability with respect to the offers is minimal. The buyer agent makes offers in the form of crisp constraints taken strategically from the fuzzy constraints that represent its overall requirements. On the other hand, the seller agent is only able to accept or reject an offer. So, we see in the example that the buyer agent successively relaxes its demands, as after each offer the seller agent responds with a refusal (as it does not have products that satisfy the constraints). Finally, in the last stage, the seller agent finds a product p4 that satisfies the buyer agent's requirements. However, this solution provides a very low profit for the seller agent. It is clear that the negotiating position of the buyer agent is much stronger, their requirements are described in detail in each offer, and at no time does the seller agent give any clue as to its preferences. The limitations of the language used mean that the only possible criteria that can be used to find solutions are local preferences. The question we must ask ourselves is whether there exists a solution that would have been more satisfying for the seller agent without worsening the

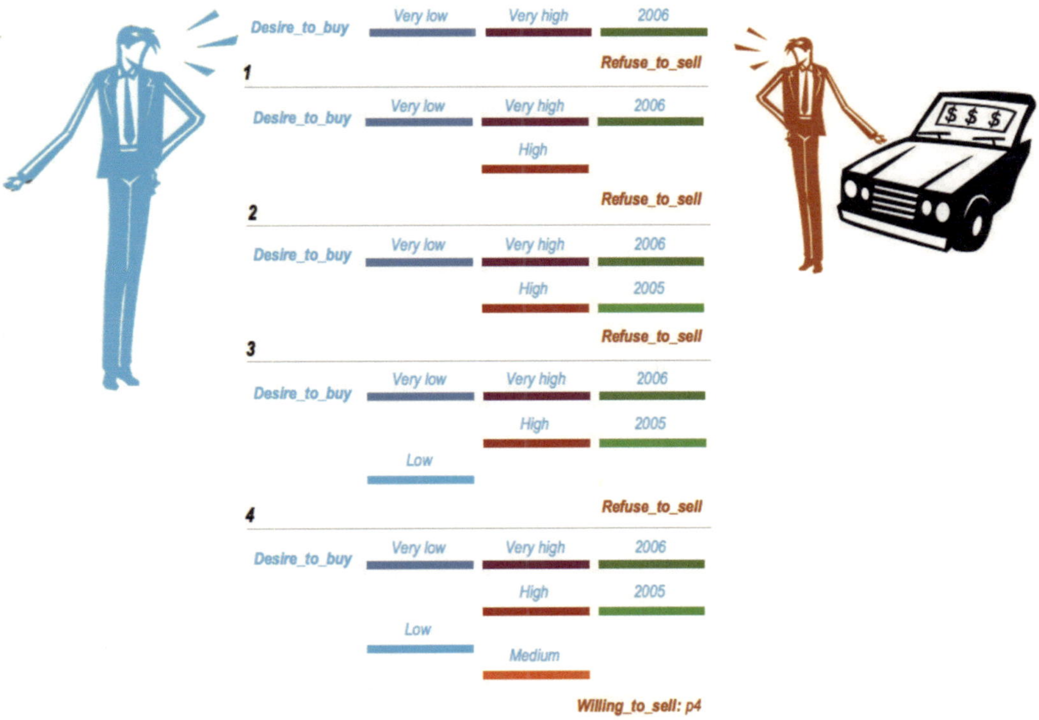

Fig. 3. Example of non-expressive dialogue

buyer agent satisfaction degree, and the answer rests in the solution p3, which would indeed have been more satisfactory for the seller agent without being less so for the buyer agent.□□As an alternative, we now present a new dialogue, which we term *expressive*, in which the concepts that form the basis of our hypothesis are applied.□□In Figure 4, the buyer agent and the seller agent negotiate the purchase of an automobile under the same preference conditions used in the previous dialogue. In this dialogue two important innovations appear: Firstly, the buyer agent is able to subjectively value its offers; and secondly, the seller agent is able to clarify its refusal to offer a product, by using expressions that allow it to state which constraints it wants the buyer agent to relax.

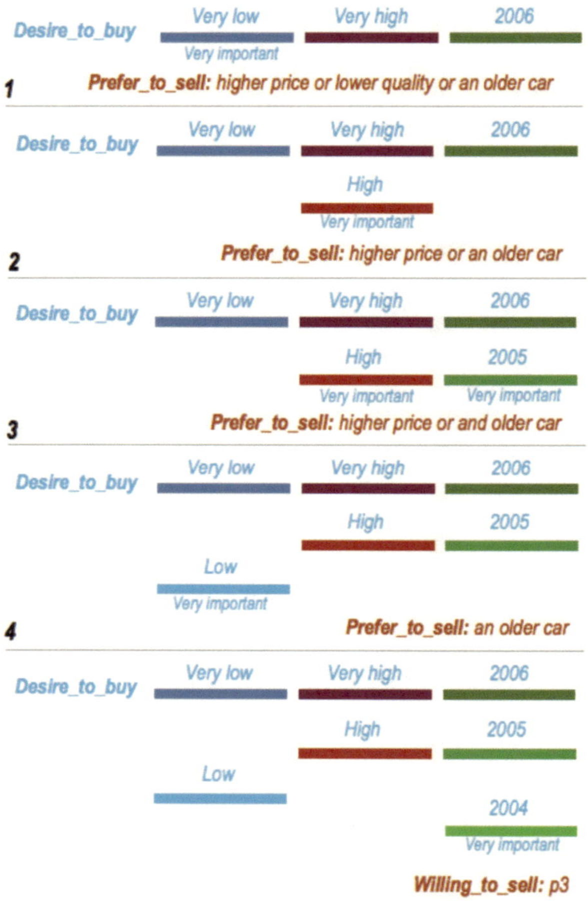

Fig. 4. Example of expressive dialogue

We will now analyse the course of the dialogue. □□

1. The first offer made by the buyer agent is the one that subjectively offers it the greatest satisfaction. Apart from the offer, defined as a set of crisp constraints, these constraints contain meta-information that grades them depending on the degree of importance each of them has. Thus, the constraint Very Low is considered as very important and it is expressed like this in the dialogue. The seller agent does not have a product that satisfies all the constraints, so it has no choice but to refuse the offer. However, it argues

its refusal with an attack based on preferences, suggesting that the buyer agent relax constraints with differing degrees of preference. From the seller agent point of view, any of the constraints in the initial dialogue can be relaxed.□

2. The buyer agent's second offer involves relaxing the quality constraint. As the seller agent had no preference for which constraint should be relaxed, the buyer agent relaxes at random one of the constraints (quality or age) that least affects its satisfaction degree. The quality constraint now becomes the buyer agent's choice, because to do so later would involve a greater loss of satisfaction than the relaxation of any other constraint. When the seller agent receives the offer, it is unable to find a product that satisfies all the constraints. However, it concludes that products p2 and p3 come close to the buyer agent's requirements. To be precise, the seller agent reasons in the following way: p2 will provide me with more profit, but on the other hand, although p3 will provide me with slightly less profit, it is closer to the buyer agent's requirements. After the seller agent has made the previous reasoning, it tries to persuade the seller agent by first asking it to relax the price and age constraints.□□
3. The third stage of the negotiation follows similar parameters to the previous one.
4. In the buyer agent's fourth offer, the price constraint is the most important. The seller agent analyses its catalogue and rejects p1 because of its low utility and estimated distance. With regards to p2, it decides that it satisfies the age and quality constraints, and that p3 satisfies the price and quality constraints, and finally, that p4 satisfies the price and age constraints. A priori, the three products are relatively close to the buyer agent requirements, but the description of the price constraint as very important affects the estimation of the closeness or distance of p2. The distance of products p3 and p4 is estimated to be similar, so the buyer agent discriminates depending on the utility of the solutions. The conclusion is that the seller agent decides that p3 is the best possible offer. He then puts all its effort into ensuring the sale of p3, although it does not satisfy the age constraint, which is why the request to relax concentrates on this constraint. □□
5. After receiving the request to relax, the buyer agent finds that a priori, it has no problem with relaxing either the quality or the age constraint. Under the assumption of negotiation based on interests or principles, the buyer agent accepts the request to relax the age constraint. The seller agent has a product, p3 that satisfies the present requirements. The overall satisfaction of the solution is greater than in the case with non-expressive negotiation. □□

The challenge of developing all the concepts in the example involves several aspects. Firstly, an agents' preference model formalization. Secondly, a definition of the negotiation profile for modelling the agent's behaviour towards their opponents. Creation of a communication model that, amongst other things, details the locutions needed to be able to deal with all the expressive nuances. Development of decision making mechanisms. Finally, a working language specification allowing the decision mechanisms to be linked to the expressions available to the agents.

4. Negotiation framework

The negotiation framework consists of a description of the *agent's domain knowledge*; a *dialogue model*; the *decision mechanisms*; and the *transition rules* that connect the locutions to the mechanisms.

4.1 Agent's domain knowledge

Buyer agent's requirements over the attributes of a product are described by means of a *fuzzy constraint satisfaction problem (FCSP)*, which is a 3-tuple (X,D,C^f) where $X=\{x_i \mid = 1,...,n\}$ is a finite set of variables, $D=\{d_i \mid = 1,...,n\}$ is the set of finite domains of the variables, and $C^f=\{R_j^f \mid j=1,...,m\}$ is a set of fuzzy constraints over the variables. It is worth noting that a fuzzy constraint may restrict more that one variable or attribute. A fuzzy constraint corresponds to the membership function of a fuzzy set. The function that numerically indicates how well a given constraint is satisfied is the satisfaction degree function $\mu_{R_j^f}: X \rightarrow [0,1]$, where 1 indicates completely satisfied and 0 indicates not satisfied at all. Given the *cut level* $\sigma \in [0,1]$, the induced crisp constraint of a fuzzy constraint R^f is defined as R^c. It simply means that if R^c is satisfied, the satisfaction degree for the corresponding fuzzy constraint will be at least σ. Therefore, the *overall (global) satisfaction degree (osd)* of a given solution $x^{'}=(x_1^{'},...,x_n^{'})$ is:

$$\alpha(x')=\min\{\mu_{R^f}(x') \mid R^f \in C^f\} \tag{1}$$

On the other hand, a seller agent owns a private catalogue of products $S=\{s_k \mid s_k=(p_k,u_k)\}$, where p_k is the vector of attributes and u_k is the profit the seller agent obtains if the product is sold. We assume that the profit u_k may depend not only on the negotiated attributes but also on non-negotiated ones (stock period for instance).

Let A_b and A_s represent a buyer and a seller agent, a negotiation process is a finite sequence of alternate proposals from one agent to the other. During the negotiation stage, A_b utters *purchase requirements,*

$$\pi=\bigcap\left\{R_j^{c(\sigma_j)} \mid j\in[1,m]\right\} \tag{2}$$

where $R_j^{c(\sigma_j)}$ is a crisp constraint induced from R_j^f at a cut level σ. Therefore, a purchase requirement is a purchase proposal that is formed by a set of crisp constraints extracted from the set of fuzzy constraints that describes the buyer's preferences regarding the attributes of the products. Each crisp constraint in the purchase requirement can be induced at a different cut level. Complementing the *osd* definition, the *potential or expected overall satisfaction degree (posd)* is the osd that a buyer agent may get if the corresponding purchase requirement is satisfied. It is defined as:

$$\alpha^{\pi}=\min\{\sigma_i \mid i=1,...,m\} \tag{3}$$

A seller agent may respond to a buyer agent in three different ways: *rejecting the proposal, offering a product* that satisfies the purchase requirement, or *suggesting the relaxation* of the purchase requirement. A *relaxation requirement* is defined as a set:

$$\rho=\{r_j \mid r_j \in[0,1]\} \tag{4}$$

where ρ_j is the preference for constraint j to be relaxed. The negotiation process and the agreements achieved will mainly vary depending on the strategies followed by the agents when generating purchase requirements and when requesting its relaxation. We cover all these aspects modeling the *agents' attitudes*. Agents' attitudes are related to the agents' strategic behavior in the negotiation process, where strategic behaviors are described in terms or expressiveness and receptiveness. A negotiation profile $Profile_{seller} = \{\psi, \beta\}$ describes the seller agent's attitude, where $\psi \in \{0,1\}$ controls whether it uses or not relaxation requests in order to express its preferences for a specific relaxation of the previous buyer's demands, and $\beta \in [0,1]$ modulates its attitude regarding a purchase requirement received from a buyer agent. Finally, a negotiation profile $Profile_{buyer} = \{\xi, \eta\}$ describes the buyer agent's attitude, where $\xi \in \{0,1\}$ controls whether it uses or not *purchase requirement valuations* defined as:

$$v = \{v_j \mid v_j \in [0,1]\} \tag{5}$$

where v_j is the degree of importance that the constraint j has for the buyer agent, and $\eta \in [0,1]$ modulates its attitude regarding a relaxation requirement received from a seller agent.

4.2 Negotiation dialogue

The framework of *formal dialogue games* is increasingly used as a base for structuring the interactions of agents communication protocols (McBurney et al., 2003), adopted from the theory of argumentation field. Formal dialogue games are those in which two or more players pronounce or transmit locutions in accordance with certain predetermined rules. In our negotiation model all dialogues are confined to two agents, one the buyer and the other the seller, so that the dialogues are exclusively bilateral. A dialogue is structured in accordance with the following stages:

1. *Opening* the dialogue.
2. *Negotiation*: this stage is defined by a sequence of iterations that are based on the domain knowledge mentioned earlier. These iterations are now itemised:
   - Buyer agent:
   - Transmit purchase requirements.
   - Transmit valuation of purchase requirements.
   - Reject sale offers.
   - Seller agent:
   - Transmit sale offers.
   - Rejects purchase requirements.
   - Propose the relaxation of purchase requirements.
   - Reject purchase obligations.
3. *Confirmation*: the participants come to a compromise and reach an agreement.
4. *Close* of dialogue: the dialogue ends.

Our dialogue proposal is subject to the following rules:

a. The first stage in the dialogue is Opening of the dialogue.
b. The Opening and Closing stages of the dialogue can only occur once in the whole dialogue.
c. The only stages that must appear in all dialogues that end normally are Opening and Closing of the dialogue.
d. The Confirmation stage requires the negotiation stage to have occurred previously.
e. The last stage of all dialogues that end normally is Close of dialogue.

The participants can commute between the negotiation and confirmation stages, subject only to the rules and the constraints defined by the combination of locutions rules, which we describe later.

Our purchase negotiation dialogue is defined as sequence of four stages: **open dialogue** (L1-2), **negotiate** (L3-8), **confirm** (L9-10) and **close dialogue** (L11).

L1: open_dialogue (P_b, P_s, θ) P_b suggests the opening of a purchase dialogue to a seller participant P_s on product category θ. P_s wishing to participate must respond with *enter_dialogue*(.).

L2: enter_dialogue (P_s, P_b, θ) P_s indicates a willingness to join a purchase dialogue with participant P_b. Within the dialogue, a participant P_b must have uttered the locution *open_dialogue*(.).

L3: willing_to_sell (P_s, P_b, p_j) P_s indicates to the buyer P_b a willingness to sell a product. A buyer P_b must have uttered a *desire_to_buy*(.) or a *prefer_to_buy*(.) locution.

L4: desire_to_buy $(P_b, P_s, \pi_{B_{req}})$ P_b, speaking to the seller P_s, requests to purchase a product that satisfies the purchase requirement $\pi_{B_{req}}$.

L5: prefer_to_sell $(P_s, P_b, \pi_{B_{req}}, \rho_{B_{req}})$ P_s, speaking to the buyer, requests to relax the purchase requirement $\pi_{B_{req}}$, and expresses which constraints are preferred to be relaxed, by means of the relax requirement $\rho_{B_{req}}$.

L6: prefer_to_buy $(P_b, P_s, \pi^k_{B_{req}}, \upsilon_{B_{req}})$ P_b, speaking to the seller, requests to purchase a product which satisfies the purchase requirement $\pi^k_{B_{req}}$, and expresses its preferences for the different constraints by means of the purchase requirement valuation $\upsilon_{B_{req}}$.

L7: refuse_to_buy (P_b, P_s, p_j) Buyer agent expresses a refusal to purchase a product. This locution cannot be uttered following a valid utterance of *agree_to_buy*(.).

L8: refuse_to_sell $(P_s, P_b, p_j \mid \pi_{B_{req}})$ Seller agent expresses a refusal to sell a product, or it expresses a refusal to sell products that satisfy the purchase requirement $\pi_{B_{req}}$. This locution cannot be uttered following a valid utterance of *agree_to_sell*(.).

L9: agree_to_buy (P_b, P_s, p_j) Buyer agent P_b speaking to P_s commits to buy a product. A locution of the form *willing_to_sell*(.) must have been uttered.

L10: agree_to_sell (P_s, P_b, p_j) Seller agent speaking to buyer agent commits to sell a product. A locution of the form *agree_to_buy*(.) must have been uttered.

L11: withdraw_dialogue (P_x, P_y, θ) For P_x and P_y participants with different roles (i.e. sellers and buyers). P_x announces agent P_y the withdrawal from the dialogue.

Next step is to specify the mechanisms that will invoke particular locutions in the course of a dialogue.

4.3 Decision mechanisms

Syntactic rules are not enough to ensure that the dialogues are generated automatically. It is essential to equip each participant with mechanisms that allow it to invoke the correct locution at the right time, as a response to previous locutions or in anticipation of future ones. This type of mechanism we term *semantic decision mechanism*. The mechanisms are grouped together depending on the role of the participant: Buyer (B) or Seller (S). We will now describe each mechanism's general directive and then detail their specific features. In addition, we specify the output generated by the mechanisms, a key point for describing, in the following Section, the working features or working semantics that connect the decision mechanisms and the locutions. We begin with the buyer agent's decision mechanisms.

B1: Recognize Need Allows a buyer agent to recognize the need to acquire a product. This recognition may be as a consequence of the explicit initiative of the user (e.g. through an interface the user gives an order to their personal agent of their intention to acquire a product), or it could be an automatic response based on thresholds that are triggered automatically (e.g. when a personal agent detects that it is within range of an electronic market that offers a particular type of product that falls within the preferences of the owner of the personal agent). When it detects the need and furthermore interprets that it is possible to begin a dialogue the mechanism's output is *have_need* (θ). Outputs: *wait, have_need* (θ), *have_no_need* (θ), where (θ) defines a *product category*.

B2: Generate Purchase Requirement This mechanism responds to a buyer agent's need to generate purchase requirements. Any purchase requirement must be compatible with the locution *desire_to_buy*(.) or *prefer_to_buy*(.). Two possible outputs are recognized, one that states that it is impossible to generate a requirement and another that specifies the requirement generated. Outputs: *empty_set* $\varnothing$, $\pi_{B_{req}}$

The method for extracting crisp constraints directly affects the way a purchase requirement is accepted, and indirectly affects the potential overall satisfaction degree the buyer agent hopes to obtain. There are two possible strategies when extracting crisp constraints to satisfy a purchase requirement and generate a specific potential overall satisfaction degree:

(Concession strategy) Given a purchase requirement $\pi^t_{B_{req}}$ sent at an instant $t \in \mathbb{N}$, a general concession strategy is defined as mechanism that generates a new purchase requirement $\pi^{t+1}_{B_{req}}$ so that $\alpha^{\pi^{t+1}_{B_{req}}} < \alpha^{\pi^{t}_{B_{req}}}$ and $\alpha^{\pi^{t+1}_{B_{req}}} \geq \alpha^{\pi^{t}_{B_{req}}} - \varepsilon$, where $\varepsilon \in (0,1]$.

According to this definition, ε is an arbitrary value that fixes the maximum loss of potential overall satisfaction that the buyer agent is willing to accept when generating a new purchase requirement. It determines the agent's behaviour with respect to how rapidly it is willing to make concessions over its purchase requirements.

(Compensation strategy) Given a purchase requirement $\pi^t_{B_{req}}$ sent in an instant $t \in \mathbb{N}$, a compensation strategy is a mechanism that generates a new purchase requirement $\pi^{t+1}_{B_{req}}$ so that $\alpha^{\pi^{t+1}_{B_{req}}} \geq \alpha^{\pi^{t}_{B_{req}}}$.

We now move on to the specific mechanisms that put these strategies into practice. There are two ways to generate a new purchase requirement:

Adding a new fuzzy constraint. This way of generating purchase requirements is intended for two specific situations: the start of the negotiation, when the first purchase requirement should be prepared, and during the negotiation, after a sale offer that does not satisfy the constraints not included in the purchase requirement. In the first case, the agent selects a fuzzy constraint and applies the highest cut level to extract the corresponding crisp constraint and create the purchase requirement $\pi^t_{B_{req}}$. By using this method, the agent is following the minimum revelation of information principle and the requirement obtained generates the greatest potential overall satisfaction degree. In the second case, a new constraint is selected from amongst those not satisfied by the sale offer received.

Modification of a previous purchase requirement. This way of creating a purchase requirement is intended for a specific situation: the locutions *prefer_to_sell*(.) or *refuse_to_sell*(.) sent by the seller agent during the negotiation with the intention of expressing its refusal to satisfy the buyer agent's requirements. Given a purchase requirement $\pi^{t}_{B_{req}}$, and after receiving one of these locutions as a reply, the cut levels associated with the fuzzy constraints included must be changed and this change affects the potential overall satisfaction degree. Therefore, the generation of a new requirement $\pi^{t+1}_{B_{req}}$ will be the aim of the application of one of the concession or compensation strategies and the problem is reduced to determining the plan for relaxing the previous purchase requirement $\pi^{t}_{B_{req}}$. We propose the meta-strategy, which consists, when possible, of applying the compensation method and in its absence the concession method. The following algorithm implements the required function.

Algorithm 1. (*Modification of purchase requirements*)

1. Given a purchase requirement $\pi^{t}_{B_{req}}$, a vector is obtained with the potential overall satisfaction degrees for all the possible purchase requirements resulting from the relaxation each time of only one of the constraints contained in $\pi^{t}_{B_{req}}$:

$$[\alpha^{\pi^{(t+1)k_1}_{B_{req}}} \ldots \alpha^{\pi^{(t+1)k_i}_{B_{req}}}]$$

where $\alpha^{\pi^{(t+1)k_x}_{B_{req}}}$ represents the potential overall satisfaction degree obtained if the constraint $R^{f}_{k_x}$ is relaxed the minimum possible. The constraints that cannot be relaxed must be eliminated from the vector. If none of the constraints can be relaxed the function returns $\varnothing$.

2. The maximum of the previous vector is calculated:

$$\alpha^{t+1}_{max} = max([\alpha^{\pi^{(t+1)k_1}_{B_{req}}} \ldots \alpha^{\pi^{(t+1)k_i}_{B_{req}}}])$$

3. A new vector $\overrightarrow{\alpha^{t+1}_{max}}$ is generated in which only the elements that satisfy the following equality are included:

$$\alpha^{t+1}_{max} = \alpha^{\pi^{(t+1)k_x}_{B_{req}}}$$

4. Finally, the following function is applied:

$$\arg\max_{\overrightarrow{\alpha^{t+1}_{max}},\rho^{t}_{max}} \alpha^{\pi^{(t+1)k_x}_{B_{req}}} + r_{k_x} * \eta$$

where ρ^{t}_{max} is a relax requirement from the seller agent, in which only those constraints included in the vector created in stage 3 are taken into account. If there are no relax requirements, r_{k_x} always takes the value 0. This function selects the constraint or constraints that maximize the total potential overall satisfaction that is induced if they are relaxed and of the relax requirement correspondingly weighted by the value η of the buyer agents receptive profile.

5. Once the constraint or constraints with the option of being relaxed are selected, one is chosen and a new purchase requirement is created $\pi_{B_{req}}^{t+1}$, in which only the chosen constraint is modified.

The first three stages of the algorithm focus on the search for those constraints in $\pi_{B_{req}}^{t}$ which if relaxed involve the smallest possible loss of potential overall satisfaction. Once these constraints have been detected, stage 4) takes into account only these constraints and, if there is a relax requirement, what the seller agent's preferences are in this respect. At one extreme if $\eta = 0$, the only criteria for relaxing is local, whereas if $\eta = 1$, the maximum importance possible is being given to the seller agent's recommendations. It is important to clarify that as we have defined in stage 2) the maximum value for filtering the potential satisfaction values, the function defined in 4) would only vary if r_{k_x} varies, being $\alpha^{\pi_{B_{req}}^{(t+1)k_x}}$ a constant the same as α_{max}^{t+1}. However, we have decided to show the function in a more general form so we can easily extend the criteria of the maximum to other criteria.

B3: Generate Purchase Requirement Valuation This mechanism allows a valuation argument to be generated for a purchase requirement that has not yet been sent, i.e. a purchase requirement valuation $\upsilon_{B_{req}}$. This can be communicated by the locution *prefer_to_buy*(.). The impossibility of obtaining a valuation generates the output an *empty_set*. Taking into account that the argumentation of a requirement is a reflection of the expressive character of the buyer agent, the mechanism will be controlled by its *expressive profile* ξ. If this has the value 1 the mechanism activates and tries to generate the valuation, if it has the value 0, the mechanism does not activate a valuation and returns an *empty_set*. When there are no valuations the buyer agent uses the locution *desire_to_buy*(.), whereas if there are valuations it uses the locution *prefer_to_buy*(.). Outputs: *empty_set* $\varnothing$, $\upsilon_{B_{req}}$

A valuation of a purchase requirement is an expression of how important for the buyer agent the satisfaction of each of the purchase requirements constraints is. We propose the following algorithm.

Algorithm 2. (*Valuation of a purchase requirement*)

1. Given a purchase requirement, by sending $\pi_{B_{req}}^{t+1}$, a vector is obtained with the potential overall satisfaction degrees for all the possible purchase requirements that result from relaxing only one of the constraints in $\pi_{B_{req}}^{t+1}$ each time. The potential overall satisfaction degrees of those constraints that cannot be relaxed have the value 0:

$$[\alpha^{\pi_{B_{req}}^{(t+2)k_1}} \ldots \alpha^{\pi_{B_{req}}^{(t+2)k_i}}]$$

2. The elements of the previous vector are taken and a new standardized vector is defined that represents the valuation of the purchase requirement:

$$\upsilon_{B_{req}} = [1-\alpha^{\pi_{B_{req}}^{(t+2)k_1}} \ldots 1-\alpha^{\pi_{B_{req}}^{(t+2)k_i}}] / sum([1-\alpha^{\pi_{B_{req}}^{(t+2)k_1}} \ldots 1-\alpha^{\pi_{B_{req}}^{(t+2)k_i}}])$$

The mechanism defines the valuation strategy of the purchase requirement as a strategy based on potential satisfaction degrees. To clarify which potential satisfaction degrees we are talking about we will describe a normal valuation process. When mechanism *B2:*

Generate Purchase Requirement is executed, a purchase requirement called $\pi_{B_{req}}^{t+1}$ is generated from a requirement sent earlier, termed $\pi_{B_{req}}^{t}$. To generate $\pi_{B_{req}}^{t+1}$ the fictitious potential satisfaction degrees $\pi_{B_{req}}^{t}$ have been used. However, in carrying out the valuation, the fictitious potential satisfaction degrees of the proposal $\pi_{B_{req}}^{t+1}$, which has not yet been sent, are being generated. To sum up, what is being estimated is the potential satisfaction degree that could be obtained if the buyer agent requests another new requirement.
As we also take into account in the definition of the mechanism, the valuation of a constraint is contrary to the potential satisfaction degree that is obtained if it is relaxed. For this reason, we have chosen to carry out the operation $1-\alpha^{\pi_{B_{req}}^{(t+2)k_x}}$ on each constraint. Finally, it is necessary to make clear that in the case of constraints that cannot be relaxed, by assigning a value of 0 to the potential overall satisfaction degrees in stage 1) a maximum valuation is obtained.
B4: Consider Offers This mechanism responds to the buyer agents need to decide at any given moment whether to: *accept or reject a sale offer* proposed by the seller agent, or *generate a new purchase requirement*. Sending a purchase requirement $\pi_{B_{req}}^{t}$, a buyer agent accepts a sale offer p_j when the overall satisfaction degree $\alpha(p_j)$ is greater than or equal to the potential overall satisfaction degree of the purchase requirement $\pi_{B_{req}}^{t+1}$. In this case the mechanism returns *accept_offer*(p_j). The acceptance of an offer opens the offer confirmation stage of the dialogue. If a sale offer cannot be accepted and the offer does not satisfy the constraints sent in $\pi_{B_{req}}^{t}$, the mechanism returns *reject_offer*(p_j) indicating that a rejection expression must be generated. Finally, if the sale offer cannot be accepted, but satisfies the constraints sent in $\pi_{B_{req}}^{t}$, the mechanism returns *generate_purchase_requirement*(p_j), indicating that a new purchase requirement must be generated.
Outputs: *accept_offer*(p_j), *reject_offer*(p_j), *generate_purchase_requirement*(p_j)
When a sale offer cannot be accepted, in one case the mechanism indicates that a new purchase requirement must be generated whilst in the other it indicates that a rejection expression must be generated. In both cases, the non-acceptance of the offer has its origin in the desired overall satisfaction degree not being reached. However, when the offer does not satisfy the constraints that have been sent we should interpret it as an anomaly. The seller agent may for example be sending offers indiscriminately. If however, a sale offer is not accepted, but satisfies the constraints that have been sent, this means that the sale offer does not adequately satisfy fuzzy constraints that have not been sent. In this case, we cannot assume that there is any anomaly in the seller agent's behaviour.
B5: Consider Withdrawal This mechanism responds to the buyer agent's need to decide at any given moment if it should terminate a dialogue with the seller agent. The mechanism can remain in wait mode and so returns *wait* or indicate whether the dialogue should be terminated in which case it returns *withdraw* (θ). Outputs: *wait*, *withdraw* (θ).
We now present the seller agent's decision mechanisms.
S1: Recognize Category Allows a seller agent to recognize the need to sell a product. The mechanism merely assures that the seller agent has available products of the *category* (θ) in

its catalogue. If the products are available the mechanism returns *wish_to_enter* (θ), and if not *wish_not_to_enter* (θ). The mechanism can remain in wait mode, and so returns wait. Outputs: *wait, wish_to_enter* (θ), *wish_not_to_enter* (θ)

S2: Assess Purchase_Requirement This mechanism responds to the seller agent's need to valuate purchase requirements. The main objective of a valuation is to detect the existence of products in the catalogue that satisfy the purchase requirements. If the products are not found, the mechanism decides whether to argue the rejection of the requirement received or not. This decision is function of the agent's expressive profile ψ, so that if it has value 1, the decision is to argue, and if it has value 0 not to argue. When there is a sale offer the mechanism returns *sale_offer*(p_j), if it decides to argue the purchase requirement it returns *purchase_requirement* ($\pi^t_{B_{req}}$), and if it decides not to argue it returns an *empty_set*. Outputs: *empty_set* $\varnothing$, *purchase_requirement* ($\pi^t_{B_{req}}$), *sale_offer*(p_j)

Next, we propose an algorithm for implementing the mechanism.

Algorithm 3. (*Selection of sale offers*)

1. The products of maximum utility are selected.
2. Of the products selected in 1) those that have been sent the least number of times are chosen.
3. Of the products selected in 2) one is chosen at random. The function returns this product.
4. The seller agent's working memory is updated, increasing the number of times the product chosen in 3) is sent.

Choosing the product with the greatest utility is consistent with the agent's rationality with respect to utility maximization. Selecting the product that has been offered the least number of times is a consequence of logical reasoning, by estimating that if a product has not been accepted previously, it is unlikely to be accepted now, so better to try with a product with the same utility, but which has not been offered yet.

S3: Generate Potential Sale-Offers This mechanism for generating potential sale offers responds to the seller agent's need to use introspection to analyse which products in its catalogue would be considered as good offers at any given moment. We denominate these offers *potential sale offers* because their purpose is to serve as a reference in the rejection argumentation process of a purchase requirement. This mechanism returns a set of products from the catalogue S that it considers would be a good choice for a future offer to the buyer agent. Outputs: S_p, that details the set of products the seller agent considers would be a good choice for a future offer.

This mechanism constitutes the nucleus of the seller agent argumentation system. When a seller agent cannot satisfy a purchase requirement, it can motivate the buyer agent to change its preferences and consequently its proposals or purchase requirements. In a non-argumentative approach, the seller agent's only tool is rejection, but a mechanism based solely on rejection does not allow the negotiation to be taken to a more favourable position for the seller agent and even less arrive at a win-to-win solution. One way of promoting convergence in the negotiation from the seller agent's point of view is to express how a received purchase requirement should be relaxed. This expression is finally specified by the relax requirement $\rho_{B_{req}}$. We understand a relax requirement as a two stage mechanism: the *generation of potential sale offers* (which are implemented in the mechanism we are describing), and *the generation of the relax requirement* $\rho_{B_{req}}$ (which is implemented in the mechanism S4 described below).

The relax requirement is an expression of the seller agents preferences for the relaxation of specific constraints. The problem therefore is to discover which criteria the seller agent should apply to lean towards one constraint or another. We should recall that the final objective of the seller agent is to sell a product, and in particular decide which products it prefers to sell. The selection of preferred products is developed during the generation of potential sale offers stage. Once the products it prefers to sell have been selected, the relax requirement will try to lead the buyer agent towards those products, which is basically the same as trying to get it to relax those constraints that are not satisfied by the products that have been chosen as sale offers. However, choosing the candidate products is by no means an easy task. If we focus the search on strictly local criteria, we can lose the idea of what the buyer agent really wants, and on the other hand, if we concentrate solely on the needs of the buyer agent, the utility obtained by the sale can be diminished. Anyway, it seems obvious that there are two abstract ideas that should govern the selection of candidates, local and external criteria. We have identified two fundamental aspects in particular for carrying out the selection process:

Utility

Dependents on the u_j parameter defined for each product in the catalogue, would be a strictly local criterion focused on the utility of the sale.

Viability

Dependents on the degree of similarity between each product p_j and the purchase requirement $\pi_{B_{req}}$, and the valuation the buyer agent is expected to make of the product on potential offer. This would be an external criteria connected to the buyer agents needs.

These two aspects are expressed by the function *prefer*(s_j)that assigns a preference value for each of the products in the catalogue. To modulate the importance and viability it turns to the agent's receptive profile β. So, we propose the following definition for the function *prefer*:

$$prefer(s_j) = \beta * u_j + (1-\beta) * \widehat{viability}(p_j, \pi^t_{B_{req}}, \upsilon_{B_{req}}) \tag{6}$$

At one extreme, if $\beta = 1$, the function remains as prefer $(s_j) = \beta * u_j$, whereas if $\beta = 0$ the function remains as $prefer(s_j) = \widehat{viability}(p_j, \pi^t_{B_{req}}, \upsilon_{B_{req}})$. Either the first case does not take into account the received purchase requirement or its possible valuation, which means the selection criteria, depends solely on the local utility. The second case does not take into account the utility, so the product selection criteria are based solely on the estimated viability of the sale. Intermediate β values consider both criteria at a specific rate.

Once the preference values for all the products in the catalogue have been calculated, by using a threshold filter for them, it is possible to generate a list of potential sale offers. The pre-set value threshold has a fundamental effect on the process of generating relax requirements. In general, a value below the threshold implies a high number of products in S_p, whereas a more selective or high threshold means that the number of products in S_p is smaller. If the seller agent tends to generate few products as candidates for potential sale offers, its behaviour can be interpreted as leaning towards leading the buyer agent towards a specific product. If, on the other hand, the seller agent is not very selective and the number of candidate products is always large, it can be assumed that it is not trying to lead the negotiation towards a specific area. Therefore, this threshold is an indication of the impatience of the seller agent for sending constraint arguments.

Estimate of viability $\widehat{viability}$

The estimate of the viability of the sale of a product must be based, in accordance with the characteristics of the mechanism, on: the degree of similarity between the product and the purchase requirement $\pi_{B_{req}}$; and an estimation of the valuation the buyer agent will make of the product in question if it is offered for sale. These aspects are condensed in the following definition of the estimation of viability:

$$\widehat{viability} = \widehat{sim}(p_j, \pi_{B_{req}}) \Diamond \widehat{E_{bv}}(\upsilon_{B_{req}}) \tag{7}$$

The first term represents an estimation of the similarity between the product and the purchase requirement $\pi_{B_{req}}$. The second defines the estimation of the buyer agent valuation as an estimation function that depends on the product, and the valuation of the purchase requirement sent by the buyer agent (if the buyer agent's profile is expressive). The operator $\Diamond$ has the function of considering both terms (this operator is described later). We approach each term separately.

Similarity

We can define *similarity* as a function of distance in the following way:

$$\widehat{sim}(p_j, \pi_{B_{req}}) = 1 - \widehat{dist}(p_j, \pi_{B_{req}}) \tag{8}$$

where $\widehat{dist}(p_j, \pi_{B_{req}})$ represents the estimation of the standardized distance between a product and a purchase requirement $\pi_{B_{req}}$. To estimate the distance we propose using a measure based on Euclidean distance, making it clear that the selection is arbitrary and that it is possible to use other distance estimates. Our proposal is the following:

$$\widehat{dist}(p_j, \pi^t_{B_{req}}) = sqrt(\sum_{i=1}^{n} \widehat{dist}(a_{ji}, \pi^{t,i}_{B_{req}})^2 / n) \tag{9}$$

where $\widehat{dist}(a_{ji}, \pi^{t,i}_{B_{req}})$ represents the distance of the attribute a_{ji} of the product to the set of constraints included in $\pi^t_{B_{req}}$ which refer to said attribute. This means that in the first place the distances between the attribute and each one of these constraints must be calculated. This calculation is a measure of the distance of the closest estimated limit, which limits the corresponding crisp constraint. However, this measure of distance between an attribute and the limit of a crisp constraint is an absolute measure that has to be normalized. The following values need to be defined: the *estimated reservation value* a_i^{res} for each attribute; the *farthest limit of each attribute* a_{ji}, which is obtained by use of the boundary function $boundary(\pi^{t,i}_{B_{req}})$; the *estimated relaxation speed* for each attribute a_{ji}, which we term $\tau_i^t \in (0,\infty)$; and finally, the *degree of certainty of the estimated distance* of an attribute a_{ji} which we term $\gamma_i^t \in [0,1]$. The reservation values, the relaxation velocity values and the degree of certainty make up part of the seller agent's requirement model, in particular the set of beliefs $\Delta^t = \{(\delta_i^t, \gamma_i^t), i = 1,...,m\}$, where $\delta_i^t = (a_i^{res}, \tau_i^t)$. We now comment on each of these values.

The reservation value a_i^{res} expresses the seller agent's belief as to what value of relaxation limit the buyer agent would be willing to assume for a particular attribute. From this partial belief, it should not be induced that the buyer agent would be willing to relax all the constraints to these reserve values simultaneously. If this were the case, the seller agent could simply reject all the proposals until the buyer agent relaxed all its constraints. However, in a multiple seller agent system, using this type of strategy is conditioned by the seller agent's aversion to the risk of losing a sale. In our proposal, we do not specify how the seller agent establishes its belief about these reservation values. Beliefs could come from local factors, or it could be determined by external factors, for example, a record of negotiations with the same or other buyer agents.

The farthest limit requires in the first place the calculation of the limits that define the crisp constraints that limit an attribute a_{ji}. It is assumed that these limits are the closest to the attribute. Once these limits are obtained, the absolute distances to the attribute can be calculated. The farthest limit will be the limit generated by the largest of these distances. In other words, the absolute distance of the attribute a_{ji} to a purchase requirement will be the greatest distance from said attribute to the crisp constraints that limit it.

The estimated relaxation trend is an estimate of the buyer agent's predisposition to relax the constraints of a particular attribute. In this case, it is not the reserve value that is estimated, but the speed at which the reserve value will be reached. The idea is that the distance calculated for an attribute for which a rapid relaxation is estimated should be interpreted as shorter than for an equal distance calculated for an attribute for which a slow relaxation is estimated.

The degree of certainty γ_i^t is a measure of how sure the buyer agent is of the distance measure made for the attribute a_{ji}.

Finally, we now present the function $\widehat{dist}(a_{ji}, \pi_{B_{req}}^{t,i})$ that binds all these concepts.

$$\widehat{dist}(a_{ji}, \pi_{B_{req}}^{t,i}) = \begin{cases} (abs(\frac{a_{ji} - boundary(\pi_{B_{req}}^{t,i})}{a_i^{res} - boundary(\pi_{B_{req}}^{t,i})})^{1/\tau_i^t} - 1) * \gamma_i^t + 1 & a_{ji} \in [a_i^{res}, boundary(\pi_{B_{req}}^{t,i})) \\ 0 & a_{ji} \in \pi_{B_{req}}^{t,i} \\ 1 & rest \end{cases} \quad (10)$$

The distance estimate has the following properties:

1. The distance is standardized at one in all the cases.
2. The attribute values that exceed the estimated reservation values are fixed at distance 1.
3. If the attribute satisfies the constraint the distance is 0.
4. If the attribute is within the reservation value and the limit of the constraints, the distance is function of the remoteness of the constraints, and it is standardized by the distance between the reservation value and the limit of the constraints.

5. For an equal attribute value a_{ji}, a high value for τ_i^t implies a higher distance estimate than of a low value. Therefore, a high value for τ_i^t should be used when the seller agent does not believe that the constraints for the attribute will be relaxed largely.
6. For $\gamma_i = 0$ the degree of certainty about the estimation of the distance of the attribute a_{ji} is nil, so the distance has value 1.
7. For a predetermined value of $abs(.)^{1/\tau_i^t}$, a low value for γ_i^t penalizes the distance estimate in comparison with a high value.

Lastly, it is important to point out the dynamic character the parameters a_i^{res}, τ_i^t and γ_i^t can have. By this, we mean that these values can be updated even during the course of the negotiation because of the seller agent's beliefs, which may vary over time. For example, it is clear that if it is seen that the estimated reservation value is exceeded by the buyer agent's relaxation, the seller agent's belief with respect to the reservation value must be modified.

Estimate of the buyer agent's valuation

The estimate of the valuation the buyer agent will make of a sale offer is directly related to the explicit valuation the buyer agent may make of a purchase requirement, that's to say, of $\upsilon_{B_{req}}$. This valuation follows a similar reasoning to that which causes us to define the relaxation velocity τ_i^t and the degree of certainty γ_i^t. It affects the distance estimate in the following way: if the constraints on an attribute are of high priority, the buyer agent will be much less predisposed to relax them, which means the distance measure should be increased, so, when the buyer agent sends purchase valuations we propose the operator implement the following viability function:

$$\widehat{viability} = 1 - sqrt(\sum_{i=1}^{n} (\widehat{dist}(a_{ji}, \pi_{B_{req}}^{t,i}) * v_{boundary(\pi_{B_{req}}^{t,i})})^2 / n) \tag{11}$$

where $v_{boundary(\pi_{B_{req}}^{t,i})}$ represents the preference the buyer agent has that the constraint furthest from the attribute a_{ji} be satisfied.

To extend the use of this viability function to those cases in which the buyer agent is non-expressive, the seller agent considers $v_{boundary(\pi_{B_{req}}^{t,i})} = 1$. The prefer function finally becomes:

$$prefer(s_j) = \beta * u_j + (1-\beta) * (1 - sqrt(\sum_{i=1}^{n} (\widehat{dist}(a_{ji}, \pi_{B_{req}}^{t,i}) * v_{boundary(\pi_{B_{req}}^{t,i})})^2 / n)) \tag{12}$$

S4: Generate Relax Requirement This mechanism responds to the seller agent's need to generate a relax requirement $\rho_{B_{req}}$. It conforms to the second stage of the generation of the relax requirement process that we described in mechanism S3. Given a set of potential sale offers S_p, the mechanism generates a relax requirement with the aim of leading the buyer agent towards the products contained in S_p. The mechanism returns a relax requirement $\rho_{B_{req}}$. Outputs: $\rho_{B_{req}}$

The basic principle of the generation of the relax requirement is to get the buyer agent to relax those constraints of the purchase requirement that are not satisfied by the products contained in S_p. We apply the following algorithm:

Algorithm 4. (*Generate relax requirement*)

1. The relax requirement is generated as a vector $r_{k_1},...,r_{k_i}$, where $r_{k_x}=0$ indicates that constraint R_{k_x} is not satisfied by any product, and $r_{k_x}=1$ indicates that constraint R_{k_x} is satisfied by at least one product.

S5: Accept or Reject Offer This mechanism responds to the seller agent's need to decide at any given moment whether or not to accept an offer to purchase a product sent by the buyer agent using the locution *agree_to_buy*(.). There are only two possible return values, *accept* (p_j) if it accepts the offer, and *reject*(p_j) if it rejects the offer. This mechanism is easy to itemise if we assume a non-strategic behaviour, that is to say, if, as we have mentioned earlier, the agent does not keep back sale offers that satisfy the seller agents purchase requirements, while waiting for the buyer agent to relax its requirements further. If this supposition is valid, the mechanism returns *accept*(p_j) when p_j exists, and *reject*(p_j) in the opposite case. Outputs: *accept*(p_j), *reject*(p_j)

S6: Consider Withdrawal This mechanism responds to a seller agents need at any given moment to decide whether or not to terminate the dialogue with a buyer agent. The mechanism can remain in wait mode, and so returns wait, or indicate that it must withdraw from the dialogue, in which case it returns $withdraw(\theta)$. Outputs: *wait*, $withdraw(\theta)$

Equipped with the expressive mechanisms described through locutions, and the corresponding internal decision mechanisms, the next stage is to link these elements to finally shape the complete negotiation framework.

4.4 Operational semantics

Operational semantics in a dialogue game indicate how the state of the dialogue changes after locutions have been sent. It is assumed that the agents participating in the dialogue have the previously described decision mechanisms implemented and that the dialogue states are defined by the mechanisms inputs and outputs. The locutions sent throughout the course of the dialogue generate transitions between the different states, so that the locutions sent are inputs of one or more decision mechanisms, which in turn generate new outputs in the form of locutions. Therefore, the operational semantics is a formalization of the connection between the locutions available in the dialogue model and the defined decision mechanisms. To express the operational semantics we define the tuple $\langle P_x, \mathbf{K}, s\rangle$ that the decision mechanism K of agent P_x describes when it generates an output s. Operational semantics is defined by a series of transition rules between states. When the transitions are between the mechanisms of different agents, they are defined by the locutions that are sent and when they are between the mechanisms of the same agent, they are defined without locutions. In the first case, an arrow and the denomination of the pertinent locution indicate the transition. In the second case only an arrow appears. We now present the transition rules:

TR1 $\langle P_b, \mathbf{B1}, have\_need(\theta)\rangle \underrightarrow{\mathbf{L1}} \langle P_s, \mathbf{S1}, .\rangle$ This transition rule indicates that a buyer agent that wishes to acquire a product from category θ, is trying to start a purchase negotiation dialogue using the locution *L1: open_dialogue*(.). Said locution activates the mechanism *S1: Recognize Category* of the seller agent with which it wants to establish the dialogue.

TR2 $\langle P_b, \mathbf{B1}, have\_no\_need(\theta)\rangle \rightarrow \langle P_b, \mathbf{B1}, wait\rangle$ This transition rule indicates that a buyer agent that does not wish to acquire a product from category θ, will not start a purchase negotiation dialogue and will review the situation later on.

TR3 $\langle P_s, \mathbf{S1}, wish\_not\_to\_enter(\theta)\rangle \rightarrow \langle P_s, \mathbf{S1}, wait\rangle$ A seller agent that does not wish to start a trading dialogue with a buyer agent will review the situation later.

TR4 $\langle P_s, \mathbf{S1}, wish\_to\_enter(\theta)\rangle \underline{\mathbf{L2}} \langle P_b, \mathbf{B2}, .\rangle$ A seller agent that wishes to participate in a purchase negotiation dialogue will do so by sending the locution *L2: enter_dialogue*(.). This transmission induces the buyer agent to execute mechanism *B2: Generate Purchase Requirement* with the objective of generating the first purchase requirement.

TR5 $\langle P_b, \mathbf{B2}, \varnothing\rangle \rightarrow \langle P_b, \mathbf{B5}, .\rangle$ This transition rule affirms that when mechanism *B2: Generate Purchase Requirement* returns an *empty_set* in by a buyer agent it also activates mechanism *B5: Consider Withdrawal* in a buyer agent. This result is produced when a buyer agent cannot produce any more purchase requirements. Then it should consider withdrawing from the dialogue.

TR6 $\langle P_b, \mathbf{B5}, withdraw(\theta)\rangle \underline{\mathbf{L11}} \langle P_s, \mathbf{S6}, .\rangle$ When a buyer agent positively consider withdrawing from a dialogue, it sends the locution *L11: withdraw_dialogue*(). This activates in the seller agent mechanism *S6: Consider Withdrawal* so that it in turn considers withdrawing.

TR7 $\langle P_s, \mathbf{S6}, withdraw(\theta)\rangle \underline{\mathbf{L11}} \langle P_b, \mathbf{B5}, .\rangle$ When a seller considers withdrawing from the dialogue it sends locution *L11: withdraw_dialogue*(.), which in turn activates mechanism *B5: Consider Withdrawal* in the buyer agent.

TR8 $\left\langle P_b, \mathbf{B2}, \pi_{B_{req}} \right\rangle \rightarrow \langle P_b, \mathbf{B3}, .\rangle$ This rule indicates that when a buyer agent generates a purchase requirement $\pi^t_{B_{req}}$, it subsequently activates internally mechanism *B3: Generate Purchase Requirement Valuation* of generate purchase requirement valuation.

TR9 $\langle P_b, \mathbf{B3}, \varnothing\rangle \underline{\mathbf{L4}} \langle P_s, \mathbf{S2}, .\rangle$ Rule TR9 affirms that if mechanism *B3: Generate Purchase Requirement Valuation* induces an *empty_set* output, the buyer agent sends the locution *L4: desire_to_buy*(.). The locution in turn activates the seller agent's mechanism *S2: Assess Purchase Requirement* for the valuation of the purchase requirement.

TR10 $\left\langle P_b, \mathbf{B3}, \upsilon_{B_{req}} \right\rangle \underline{\mathbf{L6}} \langle P_s, \mathbf{S2}, .\rangle$ This rule is identical to *TR9*, but the buyer agent sends the locution *L6: prefer_to_buy*(.) instead.

TR11 $\langle P_s, \mathbf{S2}, \varnothing\rangle \underline{\mathbf{L8}} \langle P_b, \mathbf{B2}, .\rangle$ This transition rule describes that when mechanism *S2: Assess Purchase Requirement* returns an *empty_set*, the seller agent sends the locution *L8: refuse_to_sell*(.). This locution activates mechanism *B2: Generate Purchase Requirement* in the buyer agent. This rule is the definitive one that generates a rejection locution without arguments to a previous purchase requirement.

TR12 $\left\langle P_s, \mathbf{S2}, sale\_offer(p_j)\right\rangle \underline{\mathbf{L3}} \langle P_b, \mathbf{B4}, .\rangle$ When the *S2:Assess Purchase Requirement* mechanism generates a sale offer that satisfies a purchase requirement, it is sent to the buyer agent by using the *L3: willing_to_sell*(.) locution, which in turn activates the buyer agents *B4:Consider Offers* mechanism for it to consider the offer.

TR13 $\left\langle P_s, \mathbf{S2}, purchase\_requirement(\pi^t_{B_{req}})\right\rangle \rightarrow \langle P_s, \mathbf{S3}, .\rangle$ When the *S2: Assess Purchase Requirement* mechanism returns a purchase requirement, then the buyer agent itself activates the *S3: Generate Potential Sale-Offer* mechanism to explore the potential offers. In some way the *S2* mechanism is indicating that the purchase requirement be used as an input procedure to generate arguments.

TR14 $\langle P_s, \mathbf{S3}, S_P\rangle \rightarrow \langle P_s, \mathbf{S4}, .\rangle$ This transition rule states that the set S_p of potential sale offers generated by the *S3: Generate Potential Sale-Offer* mechanism, automatically activates the *S4:*

Generate Relax Requirement mechanism of the seller agent itself to generate a relax requirement.

TR15 $\langle P_s, \mathbf{S4}, \rho_{B_{req}} \rangle \underrightarrow{\mathbf{L5}} \langle P_b, \mathbf{B2}, . \rangle$ This transition rule affirms that the relax requirement $\rho_{B_{req}}$ which is obtained when the seller agents *S4: Generate Relax Requirement* is executed, is incorporated in the *L5: prefer_to_sell*(.) locution sent to the buyer agent. The locution activates the *B2: Generate Purchase Requirement* in the buyer agent with the aim of getting it to generate a new purchase requirement using the relax requirement that it has received as a basis.

TR16 $\langle P_b, \mathbf{B4}, generate\_purchase\_requirement(p_j) \rangle \rightarrow \langle P_b, \mathbf{B2}, . \rangle$

The $generate\_purchase\_requirement(p_j)$ output in the buyer agent's *B4: Consider Offers* mechanism activates *B2: Generate Purchase Requirement*. This transition appears when the buyer agent cannot accept a sale offer, so it needs to generate a new purchase requirement.

TR17 $\langle P_b, \mathbf{B4}, accept\_offer(p_j) \rangle \underrightarrow{\mathbf{L9}} \langle P_s, \mathbf{S5}, . \rangle$ This transition rule specifies that when a sale offer from the *B4: Consider Offers* mechanism is considered, if the offer is accepted, the mechanism sends the *L9: agree_to_buy*(.) locution, which in turn activates the *S5: Accept or Reject Offer* mechanism in the seller agent. This transition describes the beginning of the confirmation stage of the negotiation.

TR18 $\langle P_b, \mathbf{B4}, reject\_offer(p_j) \rangle \underrightarrow{\mathbf{L7}} \langle P_s, \mathbf{S2}, . \rangle$ If, after considering a sale offer from the *B4: Consider Offers* mechanism, the output of the mechanism is *reject_offer*(p_j), the buyer agent sends the *L7: refuse_to_buy*(.) locution, which activates the *S2: Assess Purchase Requirement* mechanism in the seller agent. This transition reflects the buyer agents rejection of a badly structured sale offer.

TR19 $\langle P_s, \mathbf{S5}, accept(p_j) \rangle \underrightarrow{\mathbf{L10}} \langle P_b, \mathbf{B5}, . \rangle$ When a seller agent considers, through the execution of the *S5: Accept or Reject Offer* mechanism, that an offer to purchase p_j is valid, it sends the *L10: agree_to_sell*(.) locution, which in turn activates the *B5: Consider Withdrawal* mechanism in the buyer agent. This transition describes the definitive confirmation of a purchase.

TR20 $\langle P_s, \mathbf{S5}, reject(p_j) \rangle \underrightarrow{\mathbf{L8}} \langle P_b, \mathbf{B2}, . \rangle$ If a seller agent considers that p_j is an invalid offer to purchase, when it executes the *S5: Accept or Reject Offer* mechanism, it sends the *L8: refuse_to_sell*(.) locution, that automatically activates the *B2: Generate Purchase Requirement* mechanism in the buyer agent. This result is produced when the confirmation stage cannot be completed due to the disappearance of the product p_j from the seller agent's catalogue.

TR21 $\langle P_x, \mathbf{K}, wait \rangle \rightarrow \langle P_x, \mathbf{K}, . \rangle$ When any mechanism *K* returns wait as an output, it indicates that the agent intention is to execute the same mechanism later.

One of the fundamental aims of our work is to develop an automated negotiation system. Therefore, the first thing we must demonstrate is that the dialogue model, the decision mechanism, and the operational semantics, that is to say our dialogue game framework for automated purchase negotiation is able to generate dialogue automatically. To demonstrate that the negotiation is automated we need to demonstrate: (a) that all the locutions can be activated by one or more of the decision mechanisms, and (b) that every time one of these mechanisms is executed it ultimately activates a locution. To support these propositions we first present for (a), a list of the locutions, together with the mechanisms that activate them, and the transition rule in which the activation is featured.

L1: Mechanism B1 (Rule TR1).
L2: Mechanism S1 (Rule TR4).
L3: Mechanism S2 (Rule TR12).
L4: Mechanism B3 (Rule TR9).
L5: Mechanism S4 (Rule TR15).
L6: Mechanism B3 (Rule TR10).
L7: Mechanism B4 (Rule TR18).
L8: Mechanism S2 (Rule TR11); Mechanism S5 (Rule TR20).
L9: Mechanism B4 (Rule TR17).
L10: Mechanism S5 (Rule TR19).
L11: Mechanism B5 (Rule TR6); Mechanism S6 (Rule TR7).

For (b), we show for each mechanism and their possible states: whether they activate a locution, or whether they indirectly activate a mechanism that in turn activates a locution. We also present the transition rules where these connections are established.

B1: Output *have_need* activates L1 (Rule TR1).
B1: Output *have_no_need* activates the mechanism B1 (Rule TR2).
B2: Output *empty_set* activates the mechanism B5 (Rule TR5).
B2: Output $\pi_{B_{req}}$ activates the mechanism B3 (Rule TR8).
B3: Output *empty_set* activates the locution L4 (Rule TR9)
B3: Output $\upsilon_{B_{req}}$ activates the locution L6 (Rule TR10).
B4: Output *generate_purchase_requirement* invokes the mechanism B2 (Rule TR16).
B4: Output *accept_offer* invokes the locution L9 (Rule TR17).
B4: Output *reject_offer* invokes L7 (Rule TR18).
B5: Output *withdraw_dialogue* invokes L11 (Rule TR6).
S1: Output *wish_not_to_enter* activates the mechanism S1 (Rule TR3).
S1: Output *wish_to_enter* activates the locution L2 (Rule TR4).
S2: Output *emtpy_set* invokes L8 (Rule TR11).
S2: Output *sale_offer* invokes L3 (Rule TR12).
S2: Output *purchase_requirement* invokes the mechanism S3 (Rule TR13).
S3: Output S_p activates the mechanism S4 (Rule TR14).
S4: Output $\rho_{B_{req}}$ invokes the locution L5 (Rule TR15).
S5: Output *accept* invokes L10 (Rule TR19).
S5: Output *reject* invokes L8 (Rule TR20).
S6: Output *withdraw* invokes the locution L11 (Rule TR7).

We can easily prove that all the mechanisms generate a locution or activate a mechanism that then generates a locution, or activate a mechanism that then generates another mechanism that finally generates a locution.

5. Experimental analysis

Our negotiation framework allows us to test with different expressive and receptive strategies. An *expressive buyer* agent ($\xi = 1$) makes use of purchase valuations, whilst a *non-expressive* one ($\xi = 0$) does not. The *receptiveness* is determined by η, which has a continuous domain that we limit to *non-receptive* ($\eta = 0$) and *receptive* ($\eta = 1$). On the other hand, an *expressive seller* agent ($\psi = 1$) makes use of relax requirements, whilst a *non-expressive* one ($\psi = 0$) does not. The *receptive profile* determined by β has a continuous domain that we limit to *0, 0.5* and *1* (value 0 indicates no receptivity, 0.5 intermediate, and 1 maximum). However, not all the combinations of strategies are valid.

5.1 Analysis of validity of Individual strategies

We look first at agent level and we begin with the *buyer agent*:
(BAer) expressive and receptive, (BAner) non-expressive and receptive, and (BAnenr) non-expressive and non-receptive are valid strategies. However, **(BAenr) expressive and non-receptive** strategies make no sense as the purpose of the valuation is to redirect the negotiation in such a way that the seller agent sends useful relax requirements. If the agent does not analyse relax requirements, the valuation is of no use whatsoever. To sum up, the buyer agent can behave in three different ways: **BAer, BAner y BAnenr**.
We now analyse the *seller agent*:
(SAer1) expressive and receptive ($\beta = 0$), (SAer0.5) expressive and receptive ($\beta = 0.5$), (SAenr) expressive and non-receptive ($\beta = 1$), and **(SAnenr) non-expressive and non-receptive** are valid strategies. However, **(SAner1 or SAner0.5) non-expressive and any receptive** strategy makes no sense as a non-expressive seller agent does not send relax requirements, and the main purpose of a receptive strategy is to direct the relax requirements. To sum up, the seller agent can behave in accordance with four different strategies: **SAer1, SAer0.5, SAenr** and **SAnenr.**

5.2 Analysis of validity of combination of strategies

There are 12 possible combinations of strategies. However, some of these combinations are not coherent. In **BAer vs SAnenr** the buyer agent's valuations are not taken into account by the seller agent, which furthermore is not expressive. This aspect is detectable by the buyer agent, given that it does not receive relaxation requirements. A rational agent will not send valuations if it knows they are of no use. This combination is not stable and therefore equilibrium is not possible. The best strategy for a buyer agent under these circumstances is to change to a **non-expressive and non-receptive** strategy **BAnenr**. In **BAner vs SAnenr** neither of the agents is expressive, so for the buyer agent to be receptive makes no sense, and furthermore this fact it detectable by the buyer agent. A rational buyer agent would change to a **BAnenr** strategy. After this analysis, there are 10 pairs of balanced strategies : **BAer vs SAer1, BAer vs SAer0.5, BAer vs SAenr, BAner vs SAer1, BAner vs SAer0.5, BAner vs SAenr, BAnenr vs SAer1, BAnenr vs SAer0.5, BAnenr vs SAenr**, y **BAnenr vs SAnenr**. To simplify this repertoire we have made the following groupings:
BAer vs SAexrx This group has in common the fact that the buyer agent is simultaneously expressive and receptive, and the seller agent is expressive. Furthermore it seems obvious that the seller agents' different receptive profiles will affect the results of the negotiation, because the generation of relax requirements varies depending on this profile. Therefore, a priori we need to test with the three combinations that make up the group.
BAner vs SAexrx This group of strategies has in common the fact that the buyer agent is not expressive, but it is receptive and the seller agent is expressive. When the seller agent is receptive, intuitively we can affirm that the results of the negotiations are different to those

of the previous group. This is so because the buyer agent's valuations are not available to the seller agent. However, when the seller agent is not receptive the scenario is identical to the previous group. In other words, if the seller agent is not receptive it makes no difference whether the buyer agent sends valuations or not. In conclusion, the BAner vs SAenr pair is identical to BAer vs SAenr, as far as the results of the negotiation are concerned. To speed up the tests of this type, we have opted to define the test as BAner vs SAenr.

BAnenr vs SAxexrx This group of strategies is characterised by the non-expressivity and non-receptivity of the buyer agent. Therefore, it makes no difference whether the seller agent is expressive or receptive or not as the buyer agent will be unable to consider it. To speed up the execution of the tests in this group, we have opted to define as representative the BAnenr vs SAnenr pair.

Summarizing, there exist six pairs of representative strategies.

5.3 Buyer's preferences and seller's catalogue of products

The buyer agent's preferences are described as a 5 fuzzy constraint problem $R^f_{1...5}$ over 5 attributes $a_{1...5}$. Given a catalogue of products S, the set of products that may be a solution to a negotiation is the solution set $S_{sol} \subseteq S$. This set is comprised of the products that maximize the buyer agent's utility. This occurs when the seller agent is non-strategic with regards to the occultation of products and the buyer agent relaxes constraints minimizing the lost of *posd*. Finally, the noise set $S_{noise} \subseteq S$, is the set of complementary products to S_{sol}, so that $S_{sol} \cup S_{noise} = S$. In the experiments, the set S_{sol} is defined as a set of products where $\alpha(p_i) = 0.7$ for the buyer agent, while the utilities for the set S_{noise} are 0.1, 0.2 or 0.3. Once the products from the solution and noise sets have been generated, the next step is to assign utility values u_j to each of them. In the case of S_{noise} these are generated randomly using a uniform allocation between 0.9 and 1, while for S_{sol} a uniform allocation between 0 and 0.69 is used. To test the pareto-efficiency of the negotiations, also randomly, the utility of one of the products from the set S_{sol} is assigned 0.7. The aim is to see if this solution is reached after a negotiation. With this allocation of utilities, the seller agent's preferred sale offers are the noise set products. However, an intelligent seller agent would conclude that these products are not a valid sale offer and it would try to obtain the best solution from amongst those products that can really be a solution, in other words, from the solution set.

5.4 Test results

For each of the six pairs of strategies that we analyze and the different sizes of catalogues, 300 negotiations are carried out. We take as a reference the number of products from the solution set, so that the noise set is the same size as the solution set in every case. Taking into account that the buyer agent's overall satisfaction degree is known, the result we need to analyse is the utility the seller agent obtains from each negotiation. The results show the median and the success rate, where the success rate estimates the number of times that the pareto-optimal solution is obtained, that is to say, the solution in which $u_j = 0.7$. In every case, the calculated confidence interval is 95%. The summary of results is shown in Table 1.

It can be seen that with the *BAnenr vs SAnenr* strategies the success rate stabilizes around 10%, although for 4 and 8 products the rate is higher, which is logical, as the number of relax combinations is greater than the number of products. There is a dip in the median value with 16 products. However, the median grows again as the number of products increases. This effect was foreseeable, as when the number of products is augmented, the probability that the seller agent has products with a high utility for the purchase requirement is greater. The results for the *BAer/BAner vs SAer1* strategies are similar to the *BAnenr vs SAnenr* strategies. This result was foreseeable, taking into account that the seller agent is not a utility maximizer. In the *BAer vs SAer0.5* strategies the valuation of the purchase requirements distracts the seller agent, so it unfavourably modifies the preferences of the different sale offers and ends up concentrating the search in the noise set, and the results are similar to the *BAnenr vs SAnenr* strategies. The *BAner vs SAenr* strategies are also similar to those obtained with the *BAnenr vs SAnenr* strategies. These results are very important, because they allow us to appreciate how, when a seller agent limits to looking out for its best interest and only thinks about the utility, the results are not good. Finally, with the *BAner vs SAer0.5* strategies we can check how the results are significantly better in every case. This test shows that the expressivity of the seller agent is key to obtaining satisfactory solutions.

BAnenr vs SAnenr, BAer/BAner vs SAer1,□BAner vs SAenr, BAer vs SAer0.5□			
Number of products	*Success rate*	*Confidence interv.*	*Median*
4	0.4400	0.3830 0.4982	0.6432
8	0.32	0.2676 0.3760	0.5502□
16	0.15	0.1116 0.1955	0.4867□
32	0.12	0.0855 0.1622	0.5362□
64	0.15	0.1116 0.1955	0.6326□
128	0.11	0.0769 0.1510	0.6419□
256	0.07	0.0439 0.1050	0.6686□
	BAner vs SAer05□		
4	0.9500	0.9189 0.9717	0.7□
8	0.7600	0.7076 0.8072	0.7□
16	0.6900	0.6343 0.7419	0.7□
32	0.5200	0.4618 0.5778	0.7□
64	0.4500	0.3928 0.5082	0.6859□
128	0.3600	0.3056 0.4172	0.6647□
256	0.3300	0.2770 0.3864	0.6807□

Table 1. Summary of results

In Figure 5 the results obtained from the tests of the *BAnenr vs SAnenr*, and *BAner vs SAer05* strategies are summarised. In the top graphic the medians are shown, and in the bottom one the success rates. The success rates follow the same trend for all the catalogues, with a noticeable improvement in the case of the *BAner vs SAer05* strategies. As regards the medians, for catalogues with up to 64 products, the results are optimum. For catalogues with more than 256 products the strategies tend to converge, so expressivity is not a determinant factor. It should be recalled that a heavily populated catalogue means the seller agent will have high utility sale offers with a higher probability.

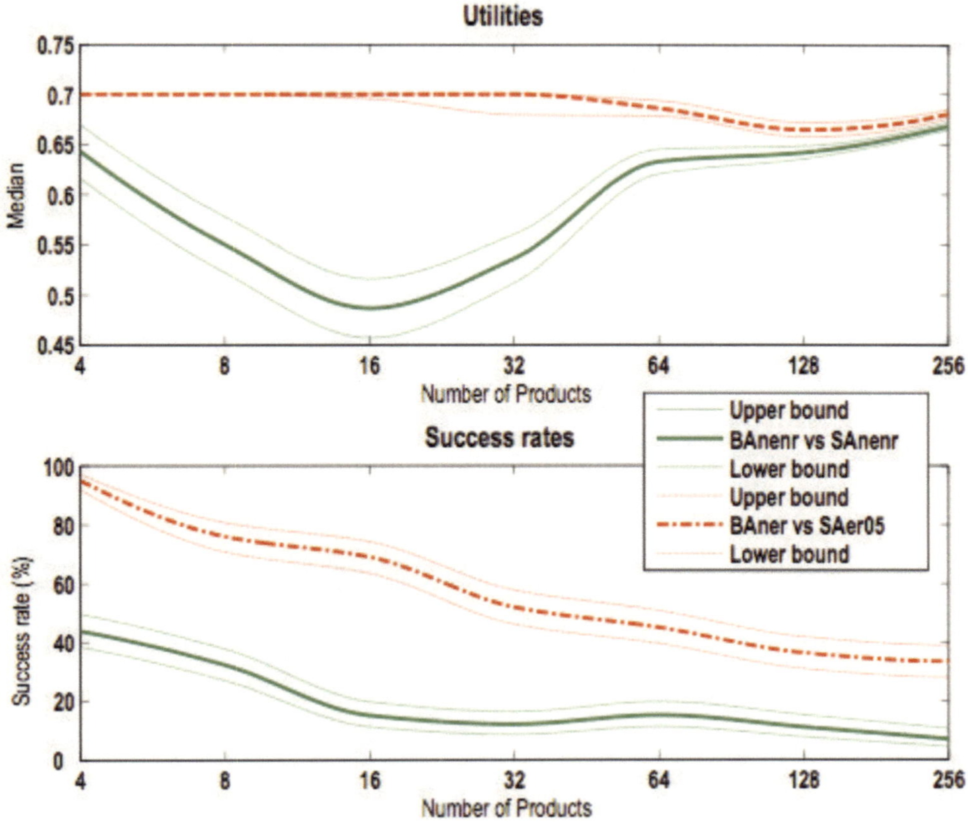

Fig. 5. Comparative of the *Banenr vs Sanenr* and the *Baner vs Saer05* strategies

Finally, in Figure 6 two graphs are presented that depict the percentage improvement in the success rates and the comparative percentage improvement in utility. The improvement in the success rates portrays the comparative between the percentage of success rates obtained with the *BAner vs SAer05* strategies and those obtained with the *BAnenr vs Sanenr* strategies. This graph presents a very important property, which is the exponential trend of comparative improvements in the success rates. For catalogues with a small solution set the improvement is of approximately 200%, with an increase of around 325% for medium sized catalogues of 16 and 32 products being observed. It should be taken into account that when there are very few products, the possibility of a good solution being found at random, is greater than when the catalogue is large, which is why the improvement is smaller for 4 and 8 products. Although for 64 products the success rate decreases to 250%, in general, as the size of the catalogues increases there is an exponential tendency for the rates to improve. As the catalogues become very large, the probability of obtaining an optimal solution without expressivity decreases exponentially down to zero, whereas with expressivity the optimal solution is explicitly searched.

The relative improvement in utility is a comparative measure that compares the improvements obtained with the *BAner vs SAer05* strategies with respect the maximum improvement obtained. It can be observed that the reference catalogue is the one with 16 products, which is the scenario with which the maximum utility is obtained. Therefore, the graph shows a percentage of relative improvement of 100% for this catalogue. For large catalogues, the percentage of relative improvement decreases to below 10%. The minimum percentage improvement for smaller catalogues is 10% with an average value of around 60%.

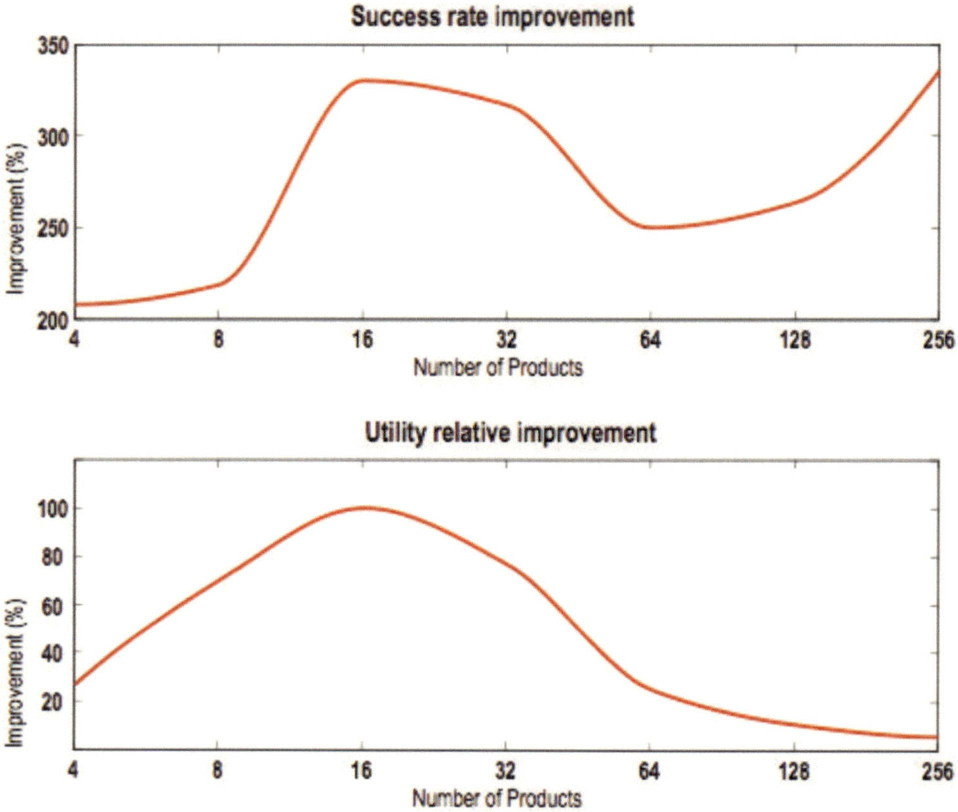

Fig. 6. Improvement in the success rate and relative improvement of utility

6. Conclusions and future work

This chapter presents a fuzzy constraint based model for automated purchase negotiations in competitive trading environments. The analysis of the model shows that the expressivity of the seller agent is essential to obtain an improvement in the negotiations. However, the expressivity of the buyer agent makes the results come close to those achieved with the reference non-expressive and non-receptive strategies. The viability of the potential sale offers is decisive in the improvement of the negotiations, and so, the *BAner vs SAenr* strategies, which focus on the seller agents' utility, are invalid. To sum up, we can affirm that the expressivity factor brings significant benefit to the negotiation process and the key element resides in the expressivity of the seller agent and the receptivity of the buyer agent. However, it must be pointed out that under our negotiation model, an 'inexpressive' buyer agent is more expressive than an 'inexpressive' seller agent because a buyer agent expresses offers as a set of constraints, while a seller agent expresses offers as concrete products or rejections to purchase requirements.

As future work, we propose the refinement of the mechanisms related to the purchase requirement valuation. As we have seen, the results using valuations of purchase requirements are not good because valuations distract the seller agent. We suggest to test different estimates for the viability parameter in the prefer function of the *generate potential sale offers seller's mechanism*. We believe that including valuations in the purchase requirements the negotiation processes may be improved.

7. Acknowledgements

This work has been supported by the Spanish Ministry of Education and Science grant TSI2005-07384-C03-03, and by the Comunidad de Madrid grant CCG07-UAH/TIC-1648.

8. References

Buttner, R. (2006). A Classification Structure for Automated Negotiations, *Proceedings of the 2006 IEEE/WIC/ACM Int. Conference on Web Intelligence and Intelligent Agent Technology*, pp. 1-8, ISBN 0-7695-2749-3, IEEE Computer Society

Faratin, P.; Sierra, C. & Jennings, N.R. (1998). Negotiation decision functions for autonomous agents. *Robotics and Autonomous Systems,* 24, 3-4, 159-182, ISSN 0921-8890

Faratin, P.; Sierra, C. & Jennings, N.R. (2002). Using similarity criteria to make issue trade-offs in automated negotiations. *Artificial Intelligence,* 142, 2, 205-237, ISSN 0004-3702

Ehtamo, H.; Hamalainen, P.; Heiskanen, P.; Teich, J.; Verkama, M. & Zionts, S. (2001). Generating Pareto Solutions in a Two-Party Setting: Constraint Proposal Methods. *Management Science,* 45, 12, 1697-1709, ISSN 1526-5501

Fatima, S. (2006). Multi-issue Negotiation with Deadlines. *Journal of Artificial Intelligence Research,* 27, 381-417, ISSN 11076 - 9757

Fisher, R. & Ury, W. (1981). *Getting to Yes: Negotiating an Agreement Without Giving In,* Houghton Mifflin Company, ISBN 0-395-63124-6, New York

Gatti, N. & Amigoni, F. (2005). An Approximate Pareto Optimal Cooperative Negotiation Model for Multiple Continuous Dependent Issues, *Proceedings of the 2005 IEEE/WIC/ACM Int. Conference on Web Intelligence and Intelligent Agent Technology,* pp. 1-8, ISBN 0-7695-2749-3, IEEE Computer Society

Ito, T.; Klein, M. & Hattori, H. (2008). A multi-issue negotiation protocol among agents with nonlinear utility functions. *Multiagent and Grid Systems,* 4, 67-83, ISSN 1574-1702

Keeney, R.L. & Raiffa, H. (1976). *Decisions with Multiples Objectives: Preferences and value Tradeoffs,* John Wiley and Sons, ISBN 0 521 43883 7, New York

Klein, M.; Faratin, P.; Sayama, H. & Bar-Yam, Y. (2003). Protocols for Negotiating Complex Contracts. *IEEE Intelligent Systems,* November-December 2003, 32-38, ISSN 1094-7167

Kowalczyk, R. & Bui, V. (2000). On fuzzy e-negotiation agents: Autonomous negotiation with incomplete and imprecise information, *Proceedings of the 11th Int. Workshop on Database and Expert Systems Applications*, pp. 1034-1038, London, ISBN 3-540-67978-2

Lai, G. ; Li, C. ; Sycara, K. & Giampapa, J. (2004). Literature Review on Multi-attribute Negotiations, *Technical Report CMU-RI-TR-04-66,* Carnegie Mellon University

Lai, G.; Li, C. & Sycara, K. (2006). Efficient Multi-Attribute Negotiation with Incomplete Information. *Group Decision and Negotiation,* 15, 511-528, ISSN 1572-9907

Lai, R. & Lin, M.W. (2004). Modelling agent negotiation via fuzzy constraints in e-business. *Computational Ingelligence,* 20, 4, 624-642, ISSN 1467-8640

Lax, D. & Sebenius, J. (1992). The manager as negotiator: The negotiators dilemma: Creating and claiming value, In: *Dispute Resolution,* F.S. Stephen Goldberg and N. Rogers, (2nd ed.), 49-62, Little Brown and Co., ISBN 978-0735528802, Boston

Luo, X.; Jennings, N.R.; Shadbolt, N.; Leung, H.F. & Lee, J.H. (2003). A fuzzy constraint based model for bilateral, multi-issue negotiations in semi-competitive environments. *Artificial Intelligence,* 148, 1-2, 53-102, ISSN 0004-3702

McBurney, P.; Van Eijk, R.M.; Parsons, S. & Amgoud, L. (2003). A Dialogue Game Protocol for Agent Purchase Negotiations. *Autonomous Agents and Multi-agents Systems,* 7, 235-273, ISSN 1573-7454

Nash, J. (2005). The Bargaining Problem. *Econometrica,* 18, 2, 155-162

Rahwan, I.; Ramchurn, S.; Jennings, N.; McBurney, P.; Parsons, S. & Sonenberg, L. (2003). Argumentation-based negotiation. *The Knowledge Engineering Review,*18, 4, 343-375, ISSN 1469-8005

Vo, Q.B.; Padgham, L. & Cavedon, L. (2007). Negotiating flexible agreements by combining distributive and integrative negotiation. *Intelligent Decision Technologies,* 1, 1-2, 33-47, ISSN 1872-4981

Zhang, J. & Pu, P. (2004). Survey on Solving Multi-Attribute Decision Problems, *Technical Report IC/2004/54,* EPFL

3

Goal-Oriented Autonomic Business Process Modelling and Execution

Dominic Greenwood and Roberto Ghizzioli
Whitestein Technologies AG
Switzerland

1. Introduction

Business processes are essential components of all enterprises and the use of models, languages and execution engines as components of a Business Process Management (BPM) deployment are now commonplace. By definition, these processes describe an enterprise in terms of its organizational knowledge, structure and activities, and are often essential to realizing an organization's competitive advantage. It thus follows that the design, execution and, critically, responsiveness to change in the system or environment they are affecting, is of prime significance toward establishing and maintaining efficient business operation.

Deploying a high quality and effective Business Process Management System (BPMS) is thus utterly essential to many modern enterprises. Yet current trends toward flexible methods of working, just-in-time organizational reaction times, distributed intra-organization and inter-organization collaboration and constantly changing markets are creating new and complex business landscapes. This brings about increased complexity, further motivating the need for real-time dynamic change throughout an enterprise's business processes; ever more dynamic environments require key business processes to be more flexible and automated in both their design and behaviour.

Yet many companies are now discovering that investments in conventional BPMS often suffers from poor return on investment due to a common inability to create business process models that are both meaningful to business people and capable of offering the real-time process flexibility and rapid process adaptation required to cope effectively with the fluid business conditions typifying many modern enterprises. As evidenced by our work with customers in the manufacturing domain, there is very often a need to alter executing process structures, sometimes in real-time, without perturbing the integrity of running process instances. If a BPMS is not built to innately support change in this manner the result can be reductions in both dependability and visibility, especially from a management perspective. Our observation is that many of the current procedural approaches to BPM are too inflexible and unresponsive to change, especially in any automated fashion.

In fact many BPMS solutions provide only design-time modelling, with neither support for run-time determination of process structure, nor direct execution of industry standard Business Process Modeling Notation (BPMN) process models without the need for first translating BPMN into intermediary formats, such as the Business Process Execution Language (BPEL), in preparation for execution. In practice, these issues imply that process models can tend to become overly complex and brittle through the necessity of coding-in all possible options at design-time due to the inability to change dynamically once in execution (Cordoso, 2006).

The alternative approach outlined in this chapter is to employ the notion of goals, which as recognised by other BPM vendors (Tibco, 2006) and practitioners (Benfield, 2006), are an intrinsically powerful and intuitive means to model business processes. We therefore propose an extension to standard BPMN to support the concepts of Goals and Plans, and moreover introduce an industry-validated process execution engine based on autonomic technologies, capable of directly executing Goal-Oriented BPMN (GO-BPMN) models and most importantly allowing safe, real-time alteration of both models and executing process instances. The GO-BPMN language is detailed in section 2.

The starting point for the goal-oriented approach was an observation of business management at the executive level which is typified by the assignment of achievement goals and decision points. This is also true at operational levels, but the degree of abstraction diminishes as the concrete knowledge of how to achieve goals and decision points is introduced through pre-established, or ad-hoc, processes. For humans it is natural to set goals, decompose goals into sub-goals, and to define or reuse plans to achieve those goals. This also extends to routine tracking of plan execution to detect problems as they occur, or even better before they do, in order to take timely and appropriate actions. On the other hand, computers are more easily instructed by providing them with fixed procedures. This is why many BPM solutions tend toward procedural automation where explicitly directed process specifications describe precisely which actions to take in all envisaged situations (such as with BPEL). This results in processes that are efficient in execution yet with limited expressivity and responsiveness to change.

To maintain effectiveness without sacrificing agility, we posit that the concepts of plan and goal be brought to center stage in BPM solutions. Our approach therefore uses a goal-oriented business process specification that offers a clean separation between the goals to be achieved (or maintained) and the set of task plans used to achieve or maintain them. This results in the creation of BPM deployments that are intrinsically capable of handling higher levels of complexity and change using directly executable goal-oriented process models whose structure can encode multiple degrees of freedom supporting real-time decision-making.

Goal-orientation offers a powerful, visually intuitive method of modelling and executing processes accessible to business managers and process analysts alike. Processes are described as goal hierarchies, with every leaf goal linked to one or more plans describing that part of the overall process to be executed in order to achieve the goal. Because plans can be selected at run-time, flexibility is built-in to the process structures allowing workflows to be altered safely in real-time without any need for halting or re-starting the overall process.

Autonomic Process Execution offers process responsiveness to change by creating feedback loops not only between the process engineer and the process model, but also between the underlying systems (human or computational) affected by the process tasks.

The purpose of this chapter is thus to present details of our approach and the Living Systems Autonomic Business Process Management (LS/ABPM) suite (Greenwood & Rimassa, 2007). To illustrate deployment, a current large-scale business case is described wherein Daimler AG is using the technology to manage their entire Engineering Change Management (ECM) and Procurement process catalogues. The ECM (Habhouba et al., 2006) aspect spans the documentation and execution of processes for the description, analysis, decision and implementation of changes to all products - from individual parts to assembled vehicles. ECM is a mission-critical business operation for Daimler that can reap substantial cost reduction and time-to-market benefits if handled effectively, but it is also subject to dynamic and unpredictable environmental effects, many of which do not fall under the direct and complete control of the enterprise.

Subsequent to this Introduction, section 2 of the chapter outlines our innovative approach to business process modelling, known as Goal-Oriented Process Modeling. Section 3 then describes how these models are directly executed using the Autonomic Process Navigation Engine with section 4 introducing some of the support tooling. Section 5 describes the current business case with Daimler AG. The final section offers a discussion and conclusions.

2. Goal-oriented process modeling with GO-BPMN

The visual modelling language Whitestein Technologies has created for specifying goal-oriented process models is called the Goal-Oriented Business Process Modelling Notation (GO-BPMN). This language represents an enhancement of standard BPMN with support for the explicit modelling of goals, plans and their relationships inspired by mental modelling as defined in the Agent Modeling Language, AML (Cervenka & Trencansky, 2007). This unique combination of declarative modelling of business goals with procedural specification of business processes offers a flexible way of modelling processes that is directly applicable to the design of agile business processes with support for dynamic variation in their path of execution.

In GO-BPMN a process model consists of goals and plans structured into one or more hierarchies as illustrated in Figure 1. Goals represent objectives to be achieved, and plans represent the activities to be performed in order to satisfy a goal. For example, in Figure 1 the three plans represent three different ways to achieve goal A. Plans contain BPMN workflows of activities performed by the process engine. For human-executable activities, a mapping with an organizational model is provided. The determination of which goals will be activated and which plans will be selected and executed at runtime for a specific instance of a process model depends on the values of context conditions associated with process goals and plans.

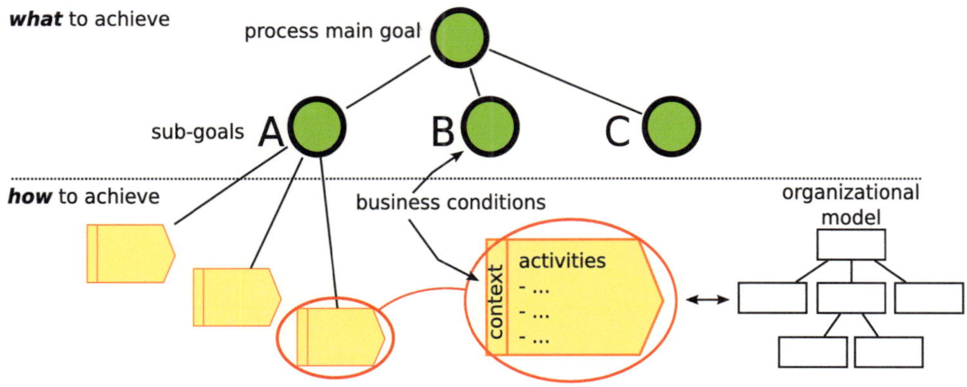

Fig. 1. The Goal-Oriented Modelling Elements

In GO-BPMN a whole process model can be divided into several independent *modules*, which represent re-usable, encapsulated, parameterizable and independently executable parts of the business process.

2.1 Goal concept

The common understanding of the term 'goal' is the result or achievement toward which effort is directed. The goal concept in GO-BPMN is essentially identical, in that goals define the states that must be reached or maintained by the process during its execution. GO-BPMN defines two types of goals, *achieve* and *maintain* goals. An *achieve goal* represents an explicit milestone, objective, desire, etc. that must be reached by the process during its execution, whereas a *maintain goal* represents the need to keep a particular condition in a persistent state, i.e., true. Goals can be composed into hierarchies with any goal considered complete only when all the associated sub-goals succeed.

A business process modelled in GO-BPMN can be seen as a set of goal hierarchies that have to be achieved or maintained. Only leaf goals in a goal-hierarchy have connected one or more *plans* which contains the activities to be performed toward achieving or maintaining the goal objective. Goals have business conditions, or rules, that control their execution, and thus the execution of the process. For example, achieve goals are defined in terms of pre-conditions, expressions that must be evaluated to true before the achieve goal can become active. For more details about business conditions please refer to Section 2.4.

When a GO-BPMN model is executed the modelled goals become stateful and the LS/ABPM Process Navigation Engine strives to achieve them. The possible states for achieve goals are: *inactive, ready, deactivated, running* or *failed.* The possible states for maintain goals are: *inactive, ready, running* or *deactivated.*

2.2 Plan concept

A GO-BPMN *plan* contains the BPMN-encoded specification of the functional activities to be taken toward achieving or maintaining a goal. A functional activity, called *task* in GO-BPMN, can be either human- or machine-executable. The LS/ABPM Process Navigation Engine automatically performs machine-executable tasks and issues ToDo actions to process participants for human-executable tasks. End-users, through a front-end, can browse their ToDo list and perform the required tasks.

The BPMN encoding used for plan bodies employs all standard elements of the language including flows, control gateways, sub-processes, tasks, BPMN start events, end events, intermediate events, transactions etc. Figure 2 shows a very simple example of GO-BPMN plan.

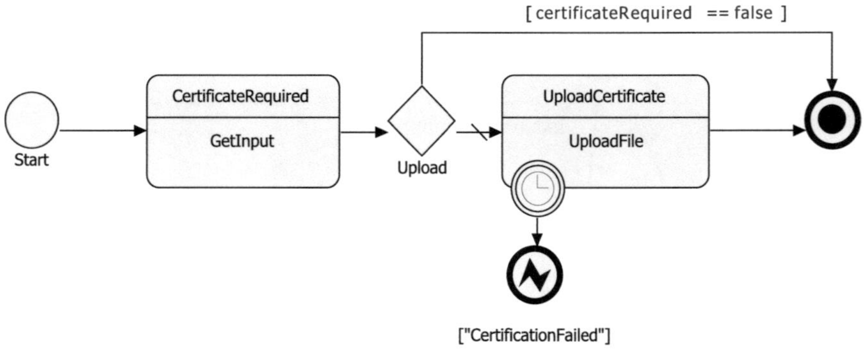

Fig. 2. Example of GO-BPMN Plan

GO-BPMN elements can be aggregated into *libraries*, with a *Standard Library* shipped with the LS/ABPM Suite providing GO-BPMN tasks, functions and data types elements for general-purpose activities. According to their domain and requirements, application-specific libraries can be created using the LS/ABPM Standard Development Kit.

During process execution, if a leaf goal has more than one plan, a selection of the most suitable plan based on the business conditions attached to the plans is performed by the LS/ABPM engine. The possible states for plans are *not triggered, running* or *finished.*

2.3 The GO-BPMN expression language

LS/ABPM employs an expression language to write business conditions, triggers, task parameters, conditional flows, etc., that control the execution flow of a GO-BPMN process.

The GO-BPMN expression language is a strongly typed language. It offers two kinds of data types: **built-in types** and **user-defined types**. The built in types are *Object, Null, Boolean, Decimal, Integer, Date, String, List, Set, Map, Reference* and *Closure*. The user-defined types are *record* types, that is, types combined through a Cartesian product operation, resulting in new types. For examples, the business objects, which hold the application data, are represented as record types. Record types also support sub-typing as a partial order on types used to express if a type (subtype) is substitutable for another (supertype).

The language also supports the definition of **variables**, that is, typed storage slots declared at compile-time. In GO-BPMN variables can have different scopes, that is, different visibility. The possible scopes are *GO-BPMN modules, plans* or *BPMN sub-processes.*

Application-specific **functions** can also be defined. Functions are composed by a declaration and an implementation. Function bodies can be written in Java, Groovy or using the expression language itself.

Within LS/ABPM process models other **named elements** can be referred to using *identifiers.* For example, process model names, goals, plans, organizational structure elements (see later), are automatically reflected into identifiers of appropriate names. Other named elements are modules names, module imports, module parameters, localization entities, etc.

Typed variables, functions and named elements can be used in conjunction with language operators (e.g., mathematical, relational, logical, etc.) to construct expressions. In GO-BPMN, all expressions have an expected type. For example, the expressions used to define goal and plan conditions expect a *Boolean* type, *Catch Signal Intermediate Event* filters expect a *Closure* type *{Object: Boolean}*, etc.

2.4 Business conditions

The conditions associated with goals and plans are used to control the execution flow of process models. They are evaluated at runtime ensuring that executing process instances remain flexible and responsive to changes in their operating environment. The conditions supported in GO-BPMN are:

- *Pre-conditions* for achieve goals: if *true,* it runs the associated goal. Sub-goals or plans are then triggered.
- *Deactivation conditions* for achieve goals: if *true,* it deactivates the goal. Such goals can be re-activated using appropriate Standard Library tasks.
- *Maintain conditions* for maintain goals: if *false,* it runs the associated goal.
- *Context conditions* for plans: if *true,* the plan is considered as selectable by the Plan Selection Algorithm.

For example, a pre-condition for an achieve goal could be something like *MyGoal.state == achieved (),* i.e., the engine tries to achieve the goal only when the referenced goal is finished.

MyGoal.state retrieves the status of the goal whereas *finished()* is a Standard Library function that represents the achieved, failed or deactivated goal states. The obtained result is that two objectives are achieved in sequence.

2.5 Organizational structures

An essential feature of LS/ABPM is the ability to route work to the correct process performers (e.g., workers, business roles, organizational units, business experts, etc.). This is achieved by:

- *Modelling organizational structures*: a feature of GO-BPMN for visually modelling selected organizational structures - organization units, roles, and their relationships (see Figure 3).
- *Managing Users*: managing process participants (i.e., the human workers who perform human tasks), the specification of their properties, and the connection of users to the defined organizational structure model(s).
- *Mapping of organizational models to process models*: specifying the task performers responsible for the execution of human tasks.

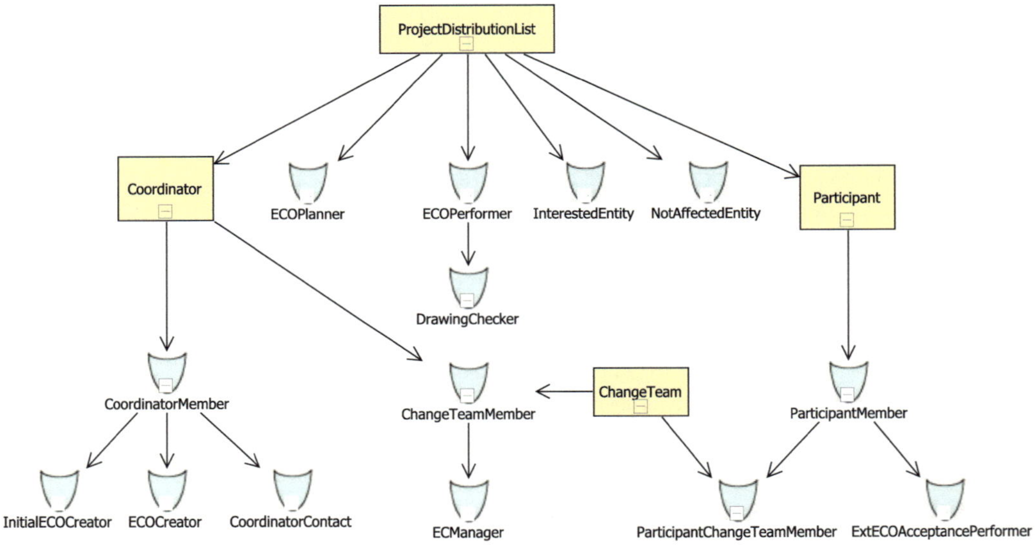

Fig. 3. Example of a GO-BPMN Organizational Model

LS/ABPM also supports escalation. It represents the set of activities that should be performed when a human-activity cannot be accomplished for several unpredictable reasons

3. Autonomic process execution

Once a process model has been created it is loaded into the autonomic process navigation engine for execution. Note that in this respect the model itself is directly executable with no requirement to translate it via an intermediary representation such as BPEL. The engine is composed of two primary computational layers, as illustrated in Figure 4: the LS/ABPM process navigation engine and the Living Systems technology Suite (LS/TS) (Rimassa et al.,

2006) autonomic middleware platform. The middleware layer executes directly over any J2EE compliant application server and can be seamlessly scaled across multiple machine clusters as demanded by deployment criteria.

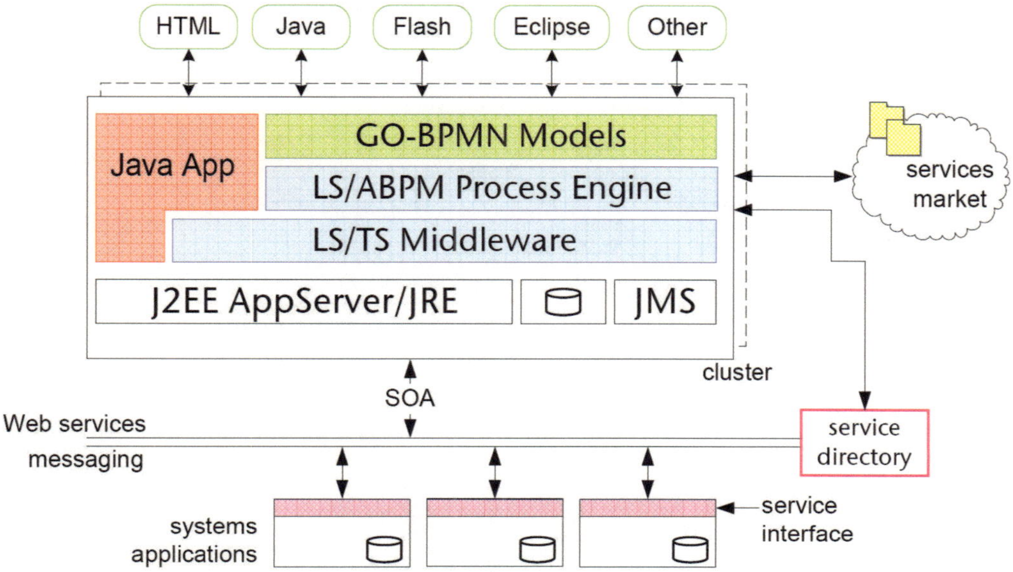

Fig. 4. Autonomic Business Process Navigation Engine system architecture

3.1 LS/ABPM process navigation engine

The LS/ABPM process navigation engine is an application developed for the LS/TS middleware runtime, consisting of a collection of goal-oriented agents acting as process instance controllers. An agent controller is assigned to each process instance, responsible for coordinating the process algebra and task structuring within goal-plan combinations, taking into account goal and plan preconditions.

When a process model is created using the Process Modeler it is directly loaded into a new process controller agent, wherein process goals are mapped onto logical goals within the goal-oriented execution engine (see section 3.2). The controller then executes the process instance by initiating the entire goal hierarchy and waiting for appropriate triggers to be sensed within the system environment to activate goals and move forward with process execution.

Each process controller is at the heart of its own autonomic feedback control loop (Pautasso et al., 2007; Tesauro et al., 2004) which uses observations made of the *system*[1] being affected by the process instance to effect decisions within the corresponding process instance relating to, for example, which goals should be activated and which plans selected to meet goal requirements. Such autonomic control allows process instances to be self-configured and self-optimized bringing about both process flexibility and resilience.

---

[1] The system may generally include software, hardware, human and physical resources including the constraints and policies defining their use.

Run-time execution agility is achieved as illustrated in Figure 5 wherein one of several alternative paths of execution may be taken by navigating through the goal-plan hierarchy in real time. For instance, in this example sub-goal B is satisfiable by any one of three available plans, the third plan being selected in this case according the state of a particular context parameter. In this manner the execution path of the process is determined as each goal becomes active, with context variables asserting decision criteria when multiple plans are available to satisfy any given goal.

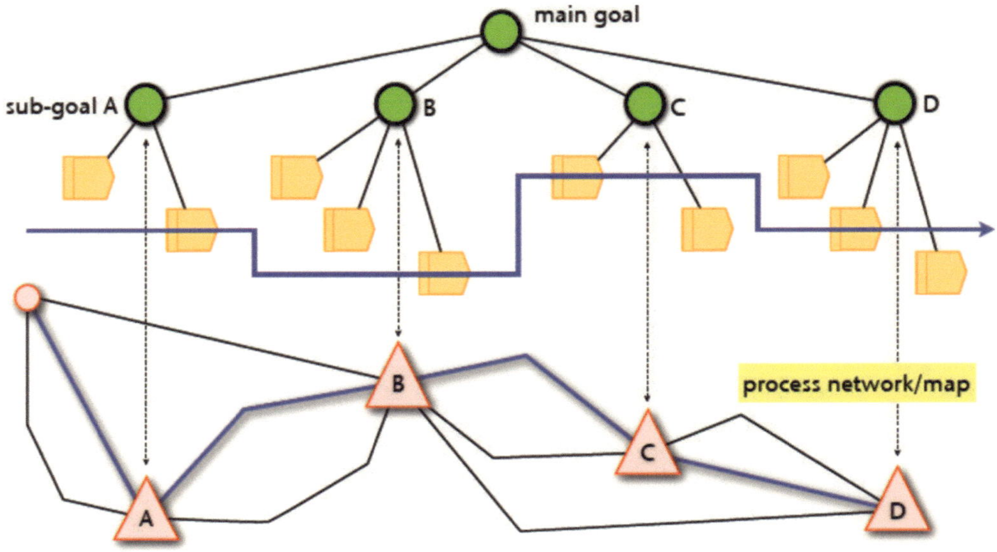

Fig. 5. Run-time agile navigation of an executing process instance

Interactions between executing process instances are managed via signal-based communication between the process controllers responsible for those instances. This is local if the instance is managed by the same controller and remote if not. Interactions can be simple bindings between the goals and plans of different processes or more complex (potentially semantic) relationships coordinating the activities of more that one controller. When multiple process instances are interacting, the influence from autonomic feedback loops is carefully monitored and controlled to ensure all effects are traceably causal and without unexpected side-effects.

3.2 LS/TS middleware

The LS/TS middleware (Rimassa, et al., 2006) is a J2EE/SE compliant runtime and associated tool suite for the development and deployment of autonomic applications driven by multi-agent technology. The runtime hosts the agents and services that define an application, providing them with life cycle support, messaging, persistence, resource management, monitoring, and more.

The tasks an agent can perform are represented as first-class objects that can be assembled into structured compounds and can be reasoned about prior to executing them. A process-algebraic model is employed to drive this task reification and assembly: tasks become Java objects and their composition follows the grammar and semantics of the operators of suitable process algebra. Building on this basic model one of the key execution engines available to application designers is the goal-oriented execution engine, inspired by the Belief-Desire-Intention (BDI) concept (Rao & Georgeff, 1995). Using this engine, software agents maintain their own belief base of logical formulae describing their observations of the world[2], and a set of desired goals, also expressed as logical formulae, which identify the states that the agent should attempt to reach. A goal is committed to according to belief revision from world observation, at which point it becomes an intention of the agent to satisfy the goal by dynamically selecting suitable plans from plan libraries located either internal or external to the agent. It is this observe-decide-act loop intrinsic to the execution engine that allows applications to be developed that exhibit autonomic features such as self-management.

Some of the benefits of goal-oriented programming are (i) implicit programming whereby application logic is resolved only a run-time when goals are activated and plans selected according to world observation (e.g., detection of available resources), (ii) encapsulation of multiple potential strategies denoted as plan, and (iii) intuitive means of comprehending what an application should do, especially when a logical link exists to the expression of goals at the user level as is the case with the goal-oriented process modeler of LS/ABPM.

4. The LS/ABPM suite

The LS/ABPM Suite is currently composed of five main components: the *Process Modeler* for goal-oriented process modelling, the *Process Navigation Engine* for autonomic process execution, the *Management Console* for process deployment and administration, the *GO-BPMN Standard Library* to model quickly and efficiently and the *Standard Development Kit* to easily build solutions for specific needs. All components are based on standard technologies such as J2EE application servers, JMS, DBMS, and the Eclipse environment.

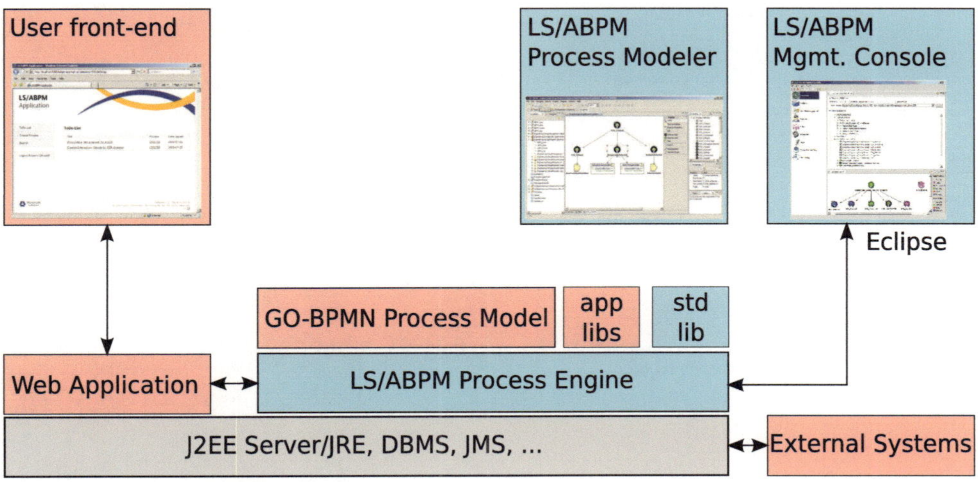

Fig. 6. The LS/ABPM Suite's Components

2 The 'world' in this respect implies the system environment, e.g., process execution environment

For LS/ABPM-based solutions, further components can be implemented using the provided SDK. These components include: interfaces with external systems to be integrated with the process, the interface with the process participants (e.g., a Web application), a set of domain-specific GO-BPMN libraries, and the GO-BPMN process models to be executed (see Figure 6).

4.1 The process modeler

The *LS/ABPM Process Modeler*, built using the Eclipse framework, offers facilities for model creation, validation, and deployment. Using this component, process designer are allowed to model in GO-BPMN their business processes, applying all the concepts presented in section 2.

Figure 7 shows a screenshot of the GO-BPMN Process Modeler. This offers several panels including a process explorer, visual editors with tool palette, outline list of all created GO-BPMN elements, model problems list, model element properties, and more. As models can often be large, the model editor panel supports model folding whereby hierarchies can be collapsed or expanded across multiple views to ease navigation.

The process modeler is equipped with several tools to simplify model design, including model refactoring. In particular it allows the renaming and the moving of GO-BPMN elements across multiple GO-BPMN modules. Furthermore, the Modeler enables team working, that is, it is possible to share the resources of GO-BPMN process models via CVS or SVN. To facilitate task development the LS/ABPM Process Modeler allows the auto generation of Java source code from task declarations.

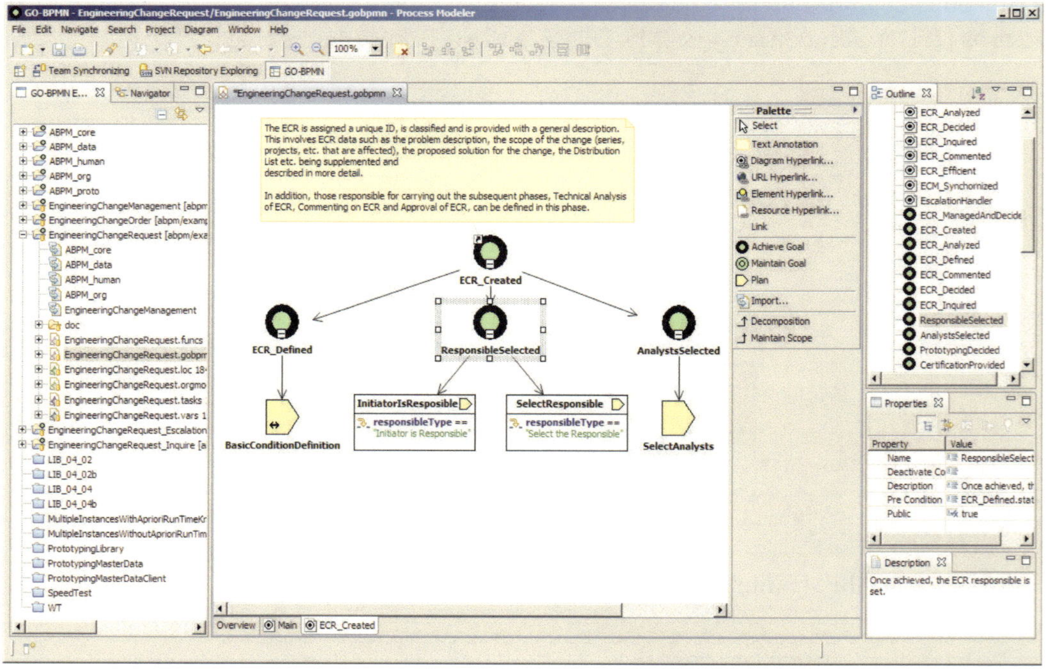

Fig. 7. The LS/ABPM Process Modeler

Every model created with the Process Modeler is automatically validated whenever the model is saved to disk with any detected problems reported in the Problems panel.

4.2 The management console

This component of the LS/ABPM suite provides powerful tools for the deployment, management and control of processes and other system administration tasks (see Figure 8). One of the main features of the Management Console is to enable process instance monitoring, controlling and debugging. At any point, a process administrator can explore the values of context variables, the states of goals and plans and evaluate GO-BPMN expressions. It can also alter the execution of a running process by changing the values of context data, activate or deactivate goals or updating the process model a running process instance is using. Additionally, process instances can be debugged, that is, the administrator can insert breakpoints related to goal states, changing of context variables and flow selections.

The Management Console contains other tools for browsing archived processes, deploy process models into the execution engine, manage the process participants and their roles, managing security rights, managing the ToDo actions assigned to the end-users and handling logs and exceptions.

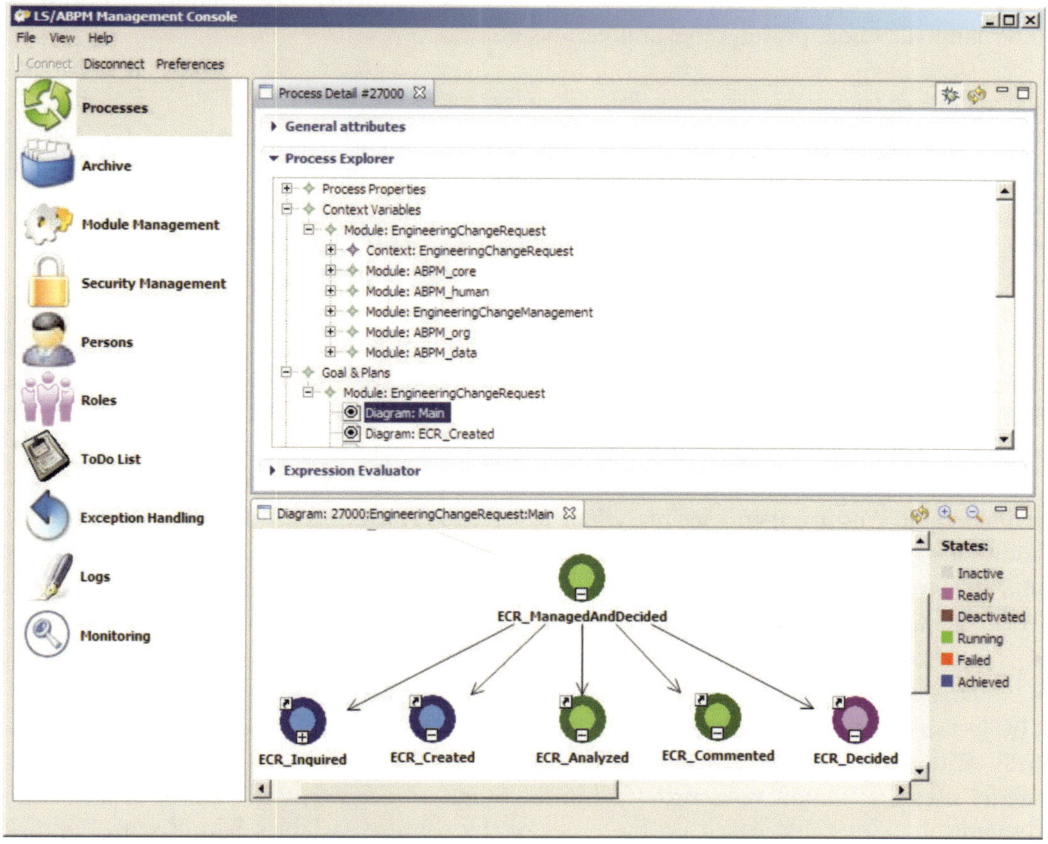

Fig. 8. The LS/ABPM Management Console

4.3 Process navigation engine

The *LS/ABPM Process Navigation Engine* is an application developed for the LS/TS middleware runtime, consisting of a collection of goal-oriented agents acting as process instance controllers. An agent controller is assigned to each process instance, responsible for coordinating the process algebra and task structuring within goal-plan combinations.

LS/ABPM runs within a J2EE environment and it is available in two distributions: a self-contained modeling suite and an enterprise suite deployable in 3rd-party J2EE servers (e.g., IBM WebSphere). The engine is capable to interact with Web applications that are used as front-ends with the process participants. Additionally, the engine can also be interfaced with external systems that have to be integrated into the modelled business processes.

4.4 Standard library

The *LS/ABPM Standard Library* contains a set of modules provided by the LS/ABPM Suite. The standard library defines the data types, functions, operation overloading and task types applicable in the following areas: reflection of the process and organization structure models, process status changing and control, process management, signal processing, data manipulation, support for large binary data, support for human processes, internationalization, prototyping, and various utilities.

4.5 SDK

The *LS/ABPM Standard Development Kit (SDK)* allows the implementation of LS/ABPM-based business process applications. In particular, the SDK enables the creation of:

- Application-specific GO-BPMN tasks and functions.
- Application-specific front-ends (either using a Web or other GUI technologies).
- Interface 3rd-party software components with the LS/ABPM engine.

Once the development environment is set up (see Figure 9), using the LS/ABPM Java API a developer is enabled to implement application-specific components. The created artifacts can be directly tested and executed within the development environment. The LS/ABPM SDK also provides Maven and ANT scripts able to build and deploy the LS/ABPM-based application into industry-grade J2EE runtime environments.

The LS/ABPM SDK includes a *Default Web Application,* that is, a simplified and domain-independent Web front-end usable when prototyping an LS/ABPM-based application. It allows a process participant to authenticate into the system, to create new process instances and to perform human-executable tasks. All the requested tasks are visible in the user's ToDo list. In general, two types of activities can be requested:

- *Input request*: the user is requested to provide input to a process instance.
- *Output notification*: the user is notified that some event occurred.

The Default Web Application, built using the Java Server Faces technology, supports a fully automatic, type-driven layout for input requests. This means that if the process model uses the human tasks provided in the Standard Library, the Web input forms are dynamically generated based on the types of the context variables bound with the task parameters.

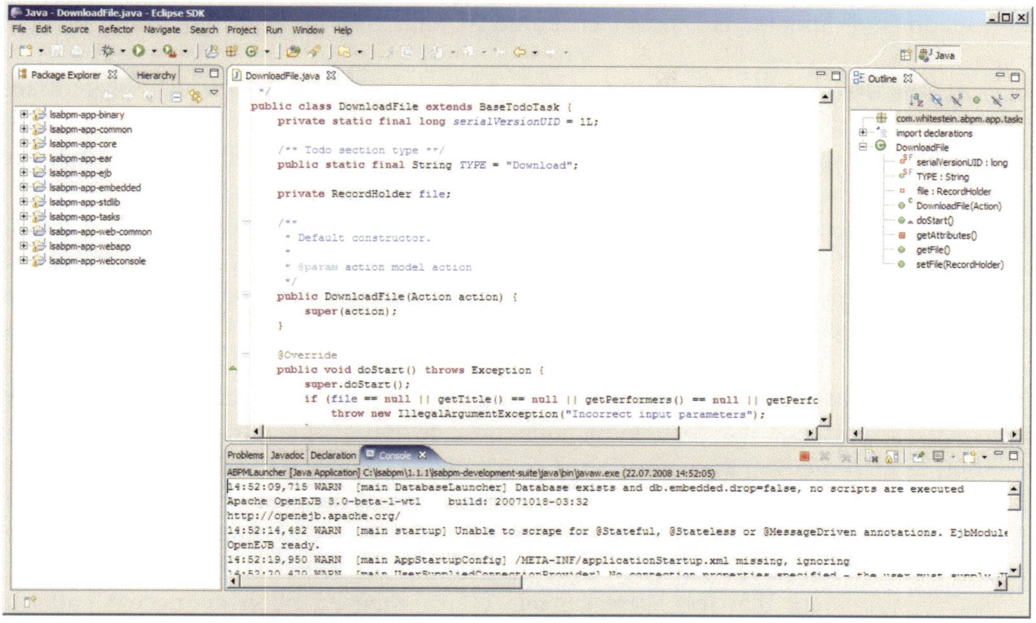

Fig. 9. The LS/ABPM SDK within the Eclipse environment

5. Engineering change management for daimler AG

In 2006 DaimlerChrysler, and now solely Daimler, took the strategic decision to radically update its approach to Engineering Change Management (ECM); the collection of integrated processes for handling the lifecycles of its entire products and parts range. The Strategic Automotive Product Data Standards Industry Group (SASIG) publishes a recommended ECM reference process (SASIG, 2008) with which many manufacturing enterprises comply, including Daimler AG. The reference process for ECM published by SASIG is illustrated in Figure 10.

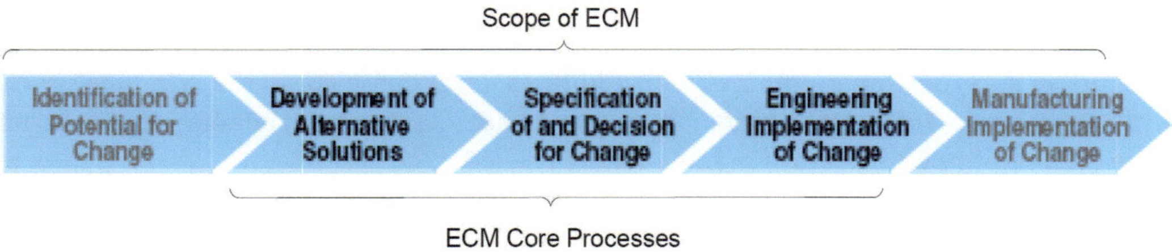

Fig. 10. SASIG ECM Reference Process

Within the context of ECM, Daimler had found that their existing BPM solution could not cope with their increasingly pressing demands for flexibility and robustness in the processes governing the lifecycles of their engineering assets. Product change and evolution is a dynamic activity by definition. Changes can be provoked by a host of reasons, most of which be neither easily be predicted nor controlled, e.g., market trends, partner integration, competition pressure, and normative regulations. Every change must be assessed and applied in consideration of critical factors such as quality, time-to-market and cost. Two of the fundamental limitations Daimler encountered with conventional approaches to BPM were:

Rigid system design processes - the ECM process has become increasingly significant to the management of change events calling for more flexible process development. The existing approach offers only rigid and costly system design processes, not allowing managers to rapidly and optimally adapt the processes to changing priorities.

Rigid process execution - the current system's process control is not capable of governing change requests in a situation-specific and purposeful manner, that is, adapted to process content and the project's context. For example, both minor and drastic changes follow the same process steps. This places excessive strain on the organisation and slows down the overall process.

A thorough examination of options to re-engineer aspects of Daimler's current BPM approach demonstrated that these limitations could be only partially mitigated, and only in the short term. Moreover, an evaluation of conventional BPM systems available from major industry vendors demonstrated that they uniformly lacked the goal-orientation dimension in their process models, a key requirement from the perspective of capturing business-level goals at model level.

It was also apparent that few were capable of real-time adaption of process paths in response to changing influences and goals. It was this assessment that led to Daimler's commitment to seek a novel approach to BPM that met their requirements for process agility and goal-orientation. The nascent LS/ABPM suite from Whitestein Technologies was selected as the result of two global evaluation phases due to its intrinsic support for the key requirements of Daimler. In March 2008 version 1.0 of the suite was released to Daimler, who are now employing it to manage ECM processes, beginning with the critical Specification and Decision for Change (see Figure 10) otherwise known as the Engineering Change Request (ECR). A highly simplified process model typical of that governing the ECR is illustrated in Figure 11, modelled using GO-BPMN and the Process Modeler.

The top-goal relates to the overall management of an ECR with the next level of child goals dealing with the various business objectives comprising the ECR. Each of these sub-goals can be active concurrently and must all be completed (unless deactivated) in order for top-goal to be achieved. The 'plus' symbol indicted on some of these achieve goal icons indicates that further sub-goals are present, with an additional level unfolded for the `ECR_Analyzed` and `ECR_Decided` goals. The hierarchy can be as deep as required, although typically no more than three or four layers of granularity are needed.

Attached to each leaf-goal in the model are the plans containing the particular BPMN-scripted tasks to be performed when the plan is selected for execution. In the case of the `CostsAssessed` goal, two plans are available for execution yet only one will be selected at runtime according to context conditions present in the process' execution environment (set by humans or software components perhaps activated within an earlier plan). Cost evaluation is a highly relevant assessment criterion in ECM and requires experts to calculate the production cost variation resulting from the change. This calculation can either be exact or estimated, with both procedures offering benefits and tradeoffs according to the situation. Sometimes either will do, sometimes exact costs are mandated, and sometimes estimates are preferred to relieve the complexity in calculating exact figures. The structure of the process lends itself to flexibility and thus plans can be added, replaced, or removed at runtime. For

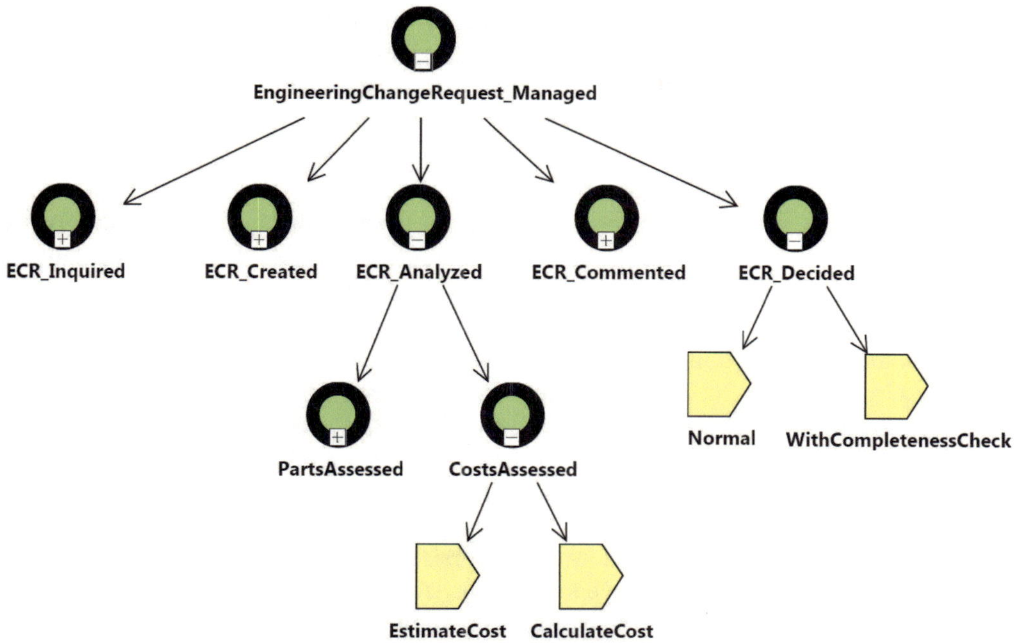

Fig. 11. A simplified model of the ECM Change Request process

example, the `CalculateCost` plan could be replaced with an alternative plan perhaps containing a new cost calculation function. Otherwise a new `CalculateCost_HighPrecision` plan could be added to accompany the two existing plans, offering a high precision calculation which may be preferred if time is available and/or extremely accurate cost assessment is required.

The goal-oriented approach thus allows the expression of a wide and diverse set of solutions while minimising the combinatorial complexity of process definition and execution.

The interface between the process structure and the environment it is affecting are actual plan tasks, typically grouped into general purpose and domain-specific task libraries. A general purpose task may be to generate a Web form, ask a human for input, or activate some domain agnostic software service. Domain-specific tasks are uniquely intended for use in processes used within a particular domain, such as ECM. Of particular interest are tasks that directly invoke SOA services, or service compositions, as is commonly the case with Service Delivery Platforms (SDPs) in the telecommunications domain. At this time we are preparing an adjunct product to LS/ABPM capable of performing goal-oriented dynamic service composition and invocation[3].

6. Discussion and conclusions

This chapter has introduced a novel, industry-proven BPMS employing a goal-oriented approach to modelling and executing agile business processes. We have demonstrated that this is an inherently flexible approach, allowing processes to be designed and executed

[3] LS/ASCO - Living Systems® Autonomic Service Composition and Orchestration.

following the logical ways in which humans naturally comprehend processes. Moreover, the approach uses autonomic self-management allowing processes to self-configure and self-optimize according to strategic requirements and changing operational constraints.

Three of the primary facets of the approach are illustrated in Figure 12: process governance, process optimization and process automation, all three with particular aspects of autonomic behaviour.

Process governance uses goal expressions to capture the purpose of a process in terms of business-level objectives and strategies. In this respect business-level knowledge and intention is expressed directly in the model providing a coherent relationship between the 'why, what, and how' of a process and a clean delineation of domain knowledge and execution logic. We have found through customer reports that goal modelling is an intuitive technique accessible to both Business Managers and Process Analysts alike.

Process optimization allows the structural and parametrical adaption of processes. Manual optimization of a model structure can induce automatic update of the corresponding process instances. Equivalently autonomic optimization of process instances can induce automatic update of process model structures in response to events/conditions arising in operational environments/controlled systems. Persistent monitoring of active models and process instances to ensure that change to in either respect is properly and safely reflected to the other. All optimizations are verifiable and reversible.

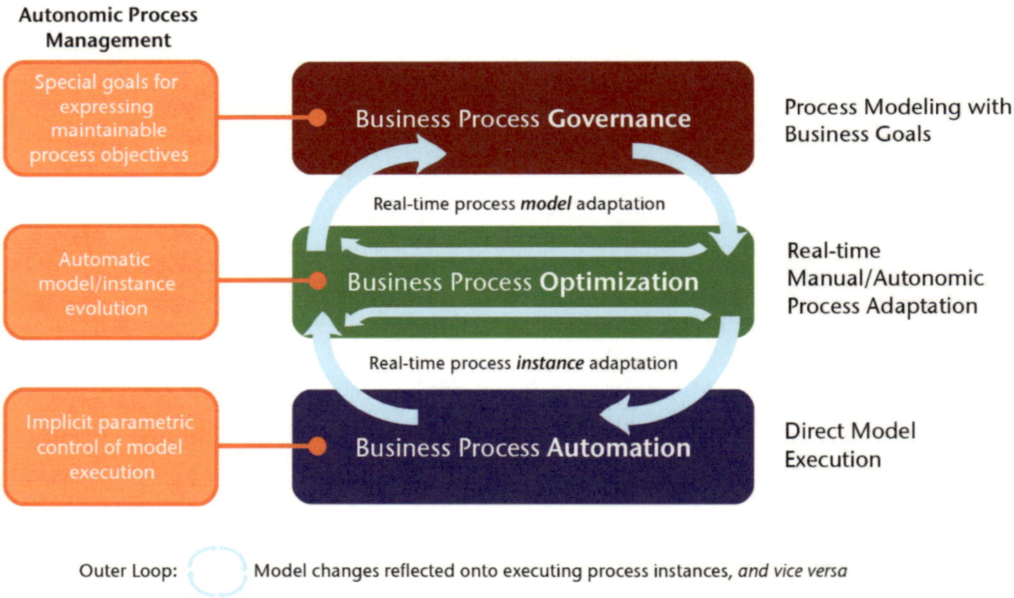

Fig. 12. Business Process Governance, Optimization and Automation

Process automation takes designed models and directly executes them using the process navigation engine. Visual process models are directly rendered into the goal-oriented execution logic of software agent process controllers; one process instance to one software agent. The activities, tasks, and resources required to attain goal objectives are selected or assembled dynamically at run-time. Executing process instances interact through inter-agent communication. Messages are as simple as required by the process context with advanced semantic communication available for complex interactions.

Autonomic behaviour is manifested at the governance level through the use of maintain goals in process models to express iteratively sustainable process objectives. At the optimization level it is manifested as automatic model/instance evolution through feedback loops propagating change and thereby keeping the entire system in balance. At the automation level, it is manifested as implicit parametric control of model execution.

As a product suite the combination of LS/ABPM and LS/TS offer a unique and compelling approach to BPMS developed with the needs of today's evolving, globally connected enterprise in mind. The suite is domain agnostic by design with the automotive, and in particular the ECM, domain being our first large scale deployment. The case described in the latter part of the chapter is currently in the early stages of full deployment and integration, with the customer, Daimler AG, working in close collaboration to assist with ongoing product refinement and next-stage development.

We are currently in the process of approaching several other domains of application including telecommunications, data center management and financial systems. In particular, the transformation to all-IP network architecture and SOA-driven software architecture is creating a pressing need for innovative approaches to BPM in the telecommunications domain. At the time of publication we have several showcases demonstrating the application of our goal-oriented LS/ABPM technology to telecommunications-specific processes (Whitestein Technologies, 2008), especially those associated with conventional and Next-Generation Networking (NGN) Product Lifecycle Management (PLM) and Order Management.

7. References

Benfield, S. (2006). Beyond BPM: Using goal-seeking agents to tackle highly-complex SOA applications, *SOA World Conference*, New York, U.S.A.

Cardoso, J. (2006). Complexity analysis of BPEL web processes, *Software Process: Improvement and Practice Journal - Special Issue on Design for Flexibility*, 12(1):35-49

Cervenka, R. & Trencansky, I. (2007). *A Comprehensive Approach to Modelling Multi-Agent Systems*, Birkhauser, ISBN 978-3764383954, Basel, Switzerland

Greenwood, D. & Rimassa, G. (2007). Autonomic goal-oriented business process management, *Proceedings of the Third International Conference on Autonomic and Autonomous Systems (ICAS)*, 43, Athens, Greece

Habhouba, D., Desrochers, A. & Cherkaoui, S. (2006). Engineering change management and decision-making assistance using software agent. *Proceedings of the Canadian Conference on Electrical and Computer Engineering*, 1694-97, Ottawa, Canada

Pautasso, C., Heinis, T. & Alonso, G. (2007). Autonomic resource provisioning for software business processes. *Information Software Technology*, 49(1):65-80

Rao, S. & Georgeff, M.P. (1995). BDI-agents: from theory to practice. *Proceedings of the First Intl. Conference on Multiagent Systems*, 312-319, San Francisco, USA

Rimassa, G., Greenwood, D. & Kernland, M. (2005). The Living Systems Technology Suite: An autonomous middleware for autonomic computing. *Proceedings of the Second*

International Conference on Autonomic and Autonomous Systems (ICAS), 33, Santa Clara, USA
SASIG: Strategic Automotive Product Data Standards Industry Group. (2008). Engineering Change Management (ECM) reference process.
Tesauro, G., Chess, D.M., Walsh, W.E., Das, R., Segal, A., Whalley, I., Kephart, J.O., & White, S.R. (2004). A multi-agent systems approach to autonomic computing. *Proceedings of the 3rd Intl. Conference on Autonomous Agents and Multi-Agent Systems (AAMAS)*, 464-471, New York, USA
Tibco. (2006). Goal-driven business process management: Creating agile business processes for an unpredictable environment. *Tibco Whitepaper*
Whitestein Technologies. (2008). Solution Profile Telecoms: Autonomic Business Process Management for Next Generation Networks. *Whitestein Technologies Whitepaper*

4

Modeling and Analysis Methods for Multi-agent Systems

Jose R. Celaya[1] and Alan A. Desrochers[2]
[1]*Decision Sciences and Engineering Systems Department*
[2]*Electrical, Computer, and Systems Engineering Department*
Rensselaer Polytechnic InstituteTroy, NY 12180
USA

1. Introduction

Multi-agent systems have been studied for the past few decades. At this point in time, several multi-agent systems frameworks have been defined in order to apply the multi-agent system concept to different applications. In a multi-agent system, several agents communicate and interact in order to solve a complex problem. A multi-agent system can be studied as a computer system that is concurrent, asynchronous, stochastic and distributed. These characteristics of multi-agent systems make them also a discrete-event dynamic system, and these have been studied under several analytical methodologies, particularly Petri nets. Petri nets have a well-defined mathematical structure that can be leveraged to provide formal analysis of discrete-event dynamic systems. From the discrete-event dynamic system point of view, multi-agent systems lack analysis and design methodologies. This chapter is concerned with the development of analytical methods for modeling and analysis of multi-agent systems, as well as the definition and assessment of system properties. The study of system properties is becoming more important due to the fact that we are faced more and more with handling large complex dynamic systems. Computer simulation is generally used to assess system properties and to verify that the system is achieving its design objectives. An important challenge in this field is the development of analytical methods to assess key properties of such systems. Such methods could be used to provide a preliminary analysis of the multi-agent system, providing design and operation feedback before the development of expensive simulation models. Furthermore, they will provide insight into design methodologies for multi-agent systems that will ensure that the system design under such methodologies complies with the required properties, hence being a dependable multi-agent system.

The communication and interaction among agents is critical for the overall multi-agent system design and for the proper functioning of the system. Several interaction frameworks have been defined and they range from collaboration among agents, through competition for resources requiring some level of negotiation in the multi-agent system. This work focuses particularly at the interaction level, and studies the interactions between different agents in the system.

The mission of the chapter is to present a methodology for modeling and analysis of multi-agent systems at the agent interaction level. This will be carried out by studying the discrete-

event characteristics of the interactions and using the Petri net methodologies as the modeling and analysis tool. Properties known to be important in the discrete event systems and Petri net domains will be used to study multi-agent systems. Here, properties like boundedness and liveness will be analyzed and demonstrated for multiagent systems, as they relate to deadlock avoidance in the Petri net domain. Furthermore, these properties will be related to characteristics of the interaction mechanism. If modeled properly, a deadlock found in a Petri net domain will mean that the interaction mechanism in use in the multi-agent system is prone to deadlocks in the interaction among agents.
In particular, this chapter will include methodologies for mapping multi-agent systems into Petri net models. These methodologies will present the right level of detail/abstraction in order to map all the important behaviors of the interaction framework into the resulting Petri net models. Petri net analysis methods such as the reachability graph and the analysis of the network invariants will be used for the assessment of properties. Furthermore, Petri net synthesis techniques will allow the ability to provide more or less detail to the models, giving the ability to add detail/abstraction to the behavior of the multi-agent system to be modeled.

1.1 Methodology

The problem addressed in this chapter can be considered in two parts: properties, and methodologies for modeling and analysis. The following is the methodology followed for this work.

Properties: If a multi-agent system is regarded as a discrete-event system and modeled using Petri nets, then properties known to be important in the discrete-event systems and Petri net domains could be used to study multi-agent systems. If we consider models of multi-agent systems as discrete-event systems, an important question to consider is which properties in the Petri net domain are important? As a starting point there are properties we would like to analyze and demonstrate for multi-agent systems. Examples of these are boundedness and liveness as related to deadlock avoidance in the Petri net domain. Other properties exist that are related to performance evaluation. These properties from the Petri net domain could be related to characteristics of the communication and interaction of the multi-agent system. If modeled properly, a deadlock found in a Petri net domain will mean that the interaction mechanism in use in the multi-agent system is prone to deadlocks in the interaction among individual agents.

Methodologies for modeling and analysis: Considering that a multi-agent system can be regarded as a discrete-event system, Petri nets can be used as a modeling tool. This will require methodologies for mapping multi-agent systems into Petri net models. These methodologies will require the right level of detail/abstraction in order to map all the important behaviors of the communication and interaction framework into the resulting Petri net models. Having Petri net models of multi-agent systems will allow us to use the existing analysis methodologies for Petri nets. Important properties of discrete-event systems could be obtained with Petri net analysis methods such as the reachability graph and the analysis of the network invariants. New analysis techniques related directly to the multi-agent system domain can be designed or tailored from existing Petri net techniques. Furthermore, Petri net synthesis techniques allow us to provide more or less detail to our models giving the ability to add detail/abstraction to the behavior of the multi-agent system that we would like to model.

1.2 Related work

Petri nets and Petri net extension methodologies have been used to model systems with more than one agent. Murata et al. [1] presented an algorithm to construct predicate/ transition models of robotic operations. Basically, robot actions were considered as firing transitions and the model was used for the planning of concurrent activities of multiple robots (agents). Even though the robotic system considered does not have direct interaction between the agents, the model used shows the ability of the Petri net-like models to capture interactions between the agents that are not evident in the design process. In a similar way, Xu et al. [2] proposed a methodology based on predicate/transition nets for multiple agents under static planning of activities. In addition, they proposed a validation algorithm for plans with parallel activities. The verification is done based on reachability graphs due to the fact that agents actions are modeled as transitions. Petri nets also have been used to model specific multi-agent system frameworks but the resulting models have not been used to provide a study of the properties of the multi-agent system. Ahn et al. [3] proposed a multi-agent system architecture for distributed and collaborative supply-chain management. The suggested architecture is aimed at discovering the structure of the supply-chain and predicting future demands based on local information sharing among the agents. A Petri net model is presented but no structural analysis of the model and no verification of the coordination activities were performed. The advantages of having a Petri net model were not exploited. The work of Leitao et al. [4], proposed a Petri net model approach to formal specification of holonic control systems for manufacturing. They developed a Petri net submodel for each of the four types of holons (agents) suggested in the ADACOR (Adaptive Holonic Control Architecture for Distributed Manufacturing Systems) architecture. There was no attempt to study the structural properties of the Petri net model in order to assess some sort of dependability in the proposed architecture. Formal modeling and specification of the multi-agent systems interaction framework has only been attempted in the holonic manufacturing system considering the contract net protocol as the interaction framework. The work presented by Hsieh in [5] proposed a new model called a *collaborative Petri* net and addressed the question of deadlock and undesirable state avoidance under the contract net protocol. Finally, multi-agent system survivability[1] and fault tolerance using Petri net models have been used in the mobile-agent area. Lyu et al. [6] used a *Stochastic Petri net* model to assess survivability and fault tolerance of mobile agents systems. They use the model for design and verification of their proposed agent architecture.

2. Introduction to Petri nets

Petri nets are a graphical and mathematical modeling tool used to describe and analyze different kinds of real systems. Petri nets were first introduced by Carl Adam Petri in 1962 in Germany [8], and evolved as a suitable tool for the study of systems that are concurrent, asynchronous, distributed, parallel and/or stochastic. Performance evaluation has been a very successful application area of Petri nets. In addition, Petri nets have been successfully used in several areas for the modeling and analysis of distributed-software systems, distributed-database systems, flexible manufacturing systems, concurrent and parallel programs and discrete-event dynamic systems (DEDS) to mention just a few [9][8][10][11]. A

[1] Survivability is the agent's ability to recognize, resist and recover from attacks [7].

multi-agent system is a kind of DEDS that is concurrent, asynchronous, stochastic and distributed. From the DEDS point of view, multi-agent systems lack analysis and design methodologies. Petri net methods are used in this work to develop analytical methodologies for multi-agent systems.

Petri nets are often used in the modeling and analysis of DEDS. They include explicit conditions under which an event can occur; capturing also the relations between concurrent and asynchronous events. As a result, Petri nets are suitable for studying complex and general DEDS [10][11].

This section presents an introduction to Petri nets. Petri nets are defined followed by important properties and analysis methodologies. Finally, an example of a manufacturing application is presented.

2.1 Petri nets definition

Definition 1 *The following is the formal definition of a Petri net [9][8][12][13]. A Petri net is a five-tuple*

$$(P, T, A, W, M_0) \tag{1}$$

where:
P is a finite set of places
T is a finite set of transitions
$A \subseteq (P \times T) \cup (T \times P)$ *is a set of arcs*
$W : A \rightarrow \{1, 2, 3, \ldots\}$ *is a weight function*
$M_0 : P \rightarrow Z_+$ *is the initial marking*

The meanings of *places* and *transitions* in Petri nets depend directly on the modeling approach. When modeling, several interpretations can be assigned to places and transitions. For a DEDS a transition is regarded as an event and the places are interpreted as a condition for an event to occur.

Table 1 presents several typical interpretations for transitions and places. A simple Petri net example is presented in figure 1. This example is used later to define additional Petri net characteristics.

Input Place	Transitions	Output Places
Preconditions	Event	Postconditions
Input data	Computation Step	Output data
Input signal	Signal processor	Output signal
Resources needed	Task or job	Resource released
Conditions	Clause in logic	Conclusion
Buffers	Processor	Buffer

Table 1. Modeling interpretations of transitions and places [8].

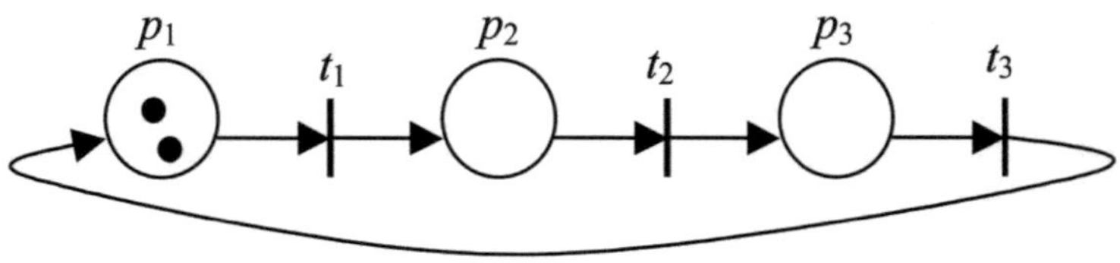

Fig. 1. Petri net example.

Places, transitions and arcs: Places are represented with circles and transitions are represented with bars. The arcs are directed from places to transitions or from transitions to places. The places contain *tokens* that travel through the net depending on the firing of a transition. A place p is said to be an input place to a transition t if an arc is directed from p to t. Similarly, an output place of t is any place in the net with an incoming arc from transition t. In the example (figure 1) p_1 is an input place of t_1, and p_2 is an output place of t_1.
Transition firing: A transition can fire only if it is *enabled*. For a transition t to be enabled, all the input places of t must contain at least one *token*[2]. When a transition is fired, a *token* is removed from each input place, and one *token* is added to each output place. In this way the *tokens* travel through the net depending on the transitions fired.
Definition 2 (Marking) *The marking m_i of a place $p_i \in P$ is a non-negative quantity representing the number of tokens in the place at a given state of the Petri net. The marking of the Petri net is defined as the function $M : P \rightarrow Z_+$ that maps the set of places to the set of non-negative integers. It is also defined as a vector $M_j = (m_1, m_2, \ldots, m_{|P|})$ were $m_i = M(p_i)$, which represents the j_{th}* state *of the net. M_j contains the marking of all the places and the initial marking is denoted by M_0.*
In the example of figure 1 only transition t_1 is enabled. When t_1 fires, one token is removed from place p_1 and one token is added to place p_2. Figure 2 shows the evolution of the Petri net in the previous example. Figure 2 a) presents the initial marking of the net M_0 = $[M(p_1),M(p_2),M(p_3)]$ = [2, 0, 0], only transition t_1 is enabled. Figure 2 b) presents the net with marking M_1 = [1, 1, 0] after t_1 is fired. Here, transitions t_1 and t_2 are enabled and they can be fired. Finally, figure 2 c) represents the net after t_2 is fired. In this case transitions t_1 and t_3 are enabled with marking M_2 = [1, 0, 1].

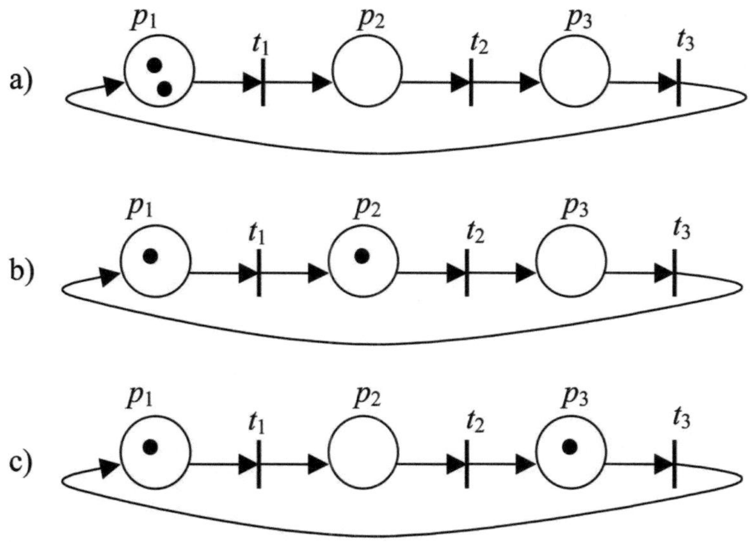

Fig. 2. Petri net evolution after firing transitions t_1 and t_2.

---

2 Assuming the weights W of the Petri net are equal to one. When the weights are not indicated they are assumed to be one. The weight on an arc coming to a transition from one of the incoming places indicates the minimum number of tokens needed in the incoming place in order for that transition to be enabled. When the transition fires, it will remove from the incoming place the amount of tokens indicated by the weight of the arc.

The marking of the Petri net represents the state of the net. As described above, the transitions change the state of the Petri net in the same way an event changes the state of a DEDS.

Definition 3 (Reachability graph) *The reachability graph has the marking of the Petri net (or state of the Petri net) as a node. An arc of the graph joining* M_i *with* M_j *represents the transition when firing takes the Petri net from the marking (state)* M_i *to the marking* M_j.

The *reachability graph* of the Petri net in figure 1 is presented in figure 3.

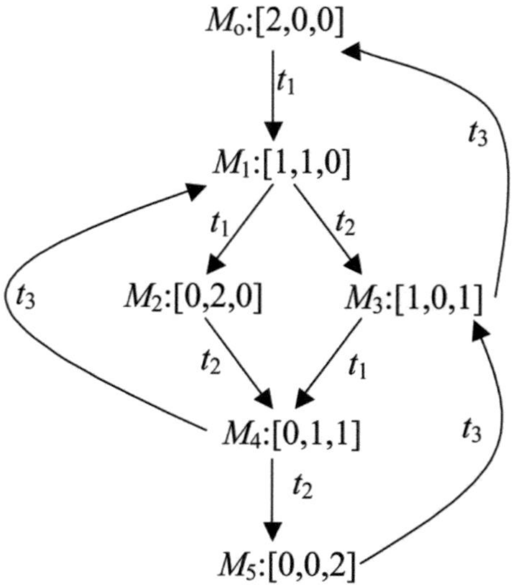

Fig. 3. Reachability graph.

2.2 Properties

This section covers some of the most important *properties* of Petri nets such as *Reachability, Liveness, Boundedness* and *Reversibility*. These properties are essential for the analysis of Petri net models. Furthermore, they are required characteristics for the use of Petri nets in performance evaluation [8][10][11].

These are properties that could be applied to multi-agent systems models. Examples of these properties are boundedness and liveness since they are related to deadlock avoidance in DEDS. Other properties are going to be relevant to multi-agent systems particularly to the communication, interaction, and single agent architectures. It is unknown how the available properties of Petri nets relate to models of multi-agent systems. This is a research question addressed in this study. In addition, the definition of new properties might be required to capture behaviors particular to multi-agent systems. A complete description of the available Petri net properties can be found in [8]. The analysis methods developed in this research will focus on the following properties.

Definition 4 (Reachability) *A marking* M_j *is said to be reachable from marking* M_i *if there exists a sequence of transitions that takes the Petri net from state* M_i *to* M_j. *The set of all possible markings that are reachable from* M_0 *is called the reachability set and is defined by* $R(M_0)$.

The concept of *reachability* is essential for the study of the dynamic properties of a Petri net. The reachability set can be obtained from the reachability graph presented previously, e.g., figure 3 [8][11].

Definition 5 (Liveness) *A Petri net is said to be live for a marking M_0 if for any marking in $R(M_0)$ it is possible to fire a transition.*
The *liveness* property guaranties the absence of deadlock in a Petri net. This property can also be observed from the reachability graph. If the reachability graph contains an absorbent state[3], then the Petri net is not live at that state and it is said to have a deadlock [8][11].
Definition 6 (Boundedness) *A Petri net is said to be* bounded *or* k-bounded *if the number of tokens in each place does not exceed a finite number k for any marking in $R(M_0)$. Furthermore, a Petri net is* structurally bounded *if it is bounded for any finite initial marking M_0. A Petri net is said to be safe if it is* 1-bounded *[8].*
Definition 7 (Reversibility) *A Petri net is* reversible, *if for any marking in $R(M_0)$, M_0 is reachable. This means that the Petri net can always return to the initial marking M_0 [8][11].*
For the example in figure 1 we have a reachability set $R(M_0) = \{M_1 = [1, 1, 0], M_2 = [0, 2, 0], M_3 = [1, 0, 1], M_4 = [0, 1, 1], M_5 = [0, 0, 2]\}$. The Petri net is live, reversible and *2-bounded* for the marking $M_0 = [2, 0, 0]$.

2.3 Structural analysis

This section considers the structural analysis of Petri nets by using invariant analysis as described in [8][13]. Basically, the liveness and boundedness of the net will be assessed by using *P-invariants* and *T-invariants*. These invariants are obtained from the incidence matrix of the net and they give information regarding token conservation and transition firing sequences that leave the marking of the net unchanged. These concepts are used to assess the overall liveness and boundedness of the net.
Definition 8 (Incidence matrix) *Let $a^+_{ij} = w(i, j)$ be the weight of the arc that goes from transition t_i to place p_j and $a^-_{ij} = w(j, i)$ be the weight of the arc from place p_j to transition t_i. The incidence matrix A of a Petri net has $|T|$ number of rows and $|P|$ number of columns. It is defined as $A = [a_{ij}]$ where $a_{ij} = a^+_{ij} - a^-_{ij}$.*
The example presented in figure 1 shows an ordinary Petri net (all the weights are equal to 1) and the following is its corresponding incidence matrix.

$$A_1 = \begin{bmatrix} -1 & 1 & 0 \\ 0 & -1 & 1 \\ 1 & 0 & -1 \end{bmatrix}$$

Definition 9 (Net-invariants) *Let A be the incidence matrix. A P-invariant is a vector that satisfies the equation*

$$Ax = 0 \tag{2}$$

and a T-invariant is a vector that satisfies the equation

$$A^T y = 0. \tag{3}$$

[3] If the net is not live for marking M_0 then at least one marking from $R(M_0)$ will not have any enabled outgoing transitions. If the reachability graph is considered as the state graph of the net, then an absorbent state is that from which the marking it is representing does not have any outgoing transitions enabled. As a result, when the net reaches an absorbent state, it will remain in it indefinitely.

2.3.1 Boundedness assessment

The P-invariants of the incidence matrix are used in Theorem 1 to make an assessment of the boundedness of the Petri net. A Petri net model is covered by P-invariants if and only if, for each place s in the net, there exists a positive P-invariant x such that $x(s) > 0$.

Theorem 1 *A Petri net is structurally bounded if it is covered by P-invariants and the initial marking M_0 is finite [13].*

2.3.2 Liveness assessment

The liveness of the Petri net model is assessed on Theorem 2 by means of the T-invariants of the incidence matrix. A Petri net model is covered by T-invariants if and only if, for each transition t in the net, there exists a positive T-invariant y such that $y(t) > 0$. This is a necessary condition but not sufficient. The liveness assessment by the use of T-invariants is still an open problem [8].

Theorem 2 *A Petri net that is finite is live and bounded if it is covered by T-invariants [13].*

3. Modeling of multi-agent systems with indirect interaction

The methodology presented here consists of defining a simple multi-agent system based on the abstract architecture for intelligent agents (M). The abstract architecture is modeled as a discrete-event system using Petri nets (N) and structural and reachability analysis provides an assessment of the interaction properties. Deadlock avoidance in the multiagent system is considered as a key property, and it is evaluated using the liveness and boundedness properties of the Petri net model.

The purpose of this work consists of the definition of an abstract architecture for multiagent systems with indirect interaction, analogous to the abstract architecture for intelligent agents. The proposed architecture allows the description of agent-to-agent interactions via changes in the environment and serves as an initial description of the discrete-event dynamics of the multi-agent system. In addition, this work presents an algorithm (algorithms 1 and 2) to obtain a Petri net model of a multi-agent system by making use of the multi-agent system's abstract architecture. Finally, a methodology to ensure that the multi-agent system is deadlock free is presented; it is based on the analysis of the properties of the Petri net model.

Here, the abstract architecture of intelligent agents is used as a starting point; particularly the abstract architecture for purely reactive agents. The level of abstraction of agents modeled by the abstract architecture makes it a good candidate for the study of multiagent systems as discrete-event dynamic systems. The study of interaction frameworks is first approached by studying the simplest means of interaction among agents (indirect interaction); assuming the agents have the perception/action capabilities and agents can interact by changing each others environment.

Modeling approach based on interaction among agents: The interactions between agents can be either a direct agent-to-agent interaction or an indirect interaction. The typical structure of a multi-agent system was presented in [14] and is reproduced in figure 4. It shows how the agents interact among each other and how they operate over a metalevel (multi-agent level) environment. Arrows define direct agent interactions from agent to agent; the indirect interactions are based on the environment. In the indirect interaction, an agent modifies another agent's environment triggering a reaction. The indirect interaction occurs in the cases when two or more agents share a subset of the environment. It should be noted that the overall multi-agent system acts over a meta-level environment. An agent that is part of the multi-agent system has its own environment that is somehow related to the meta-level environment of the multi-agent system. This meta-level environment of the multi-agent system is referred to in the literature as being an open environment [15]. A complex problem will provide an open environment, which is dynamic, has components that are unknown in advance, its structure changes over time and might be heterogeneous in its implementation [15]. By focusing on the interactions among agents as described above, it is natural to regard a multi-agent system as a discrete-event system.

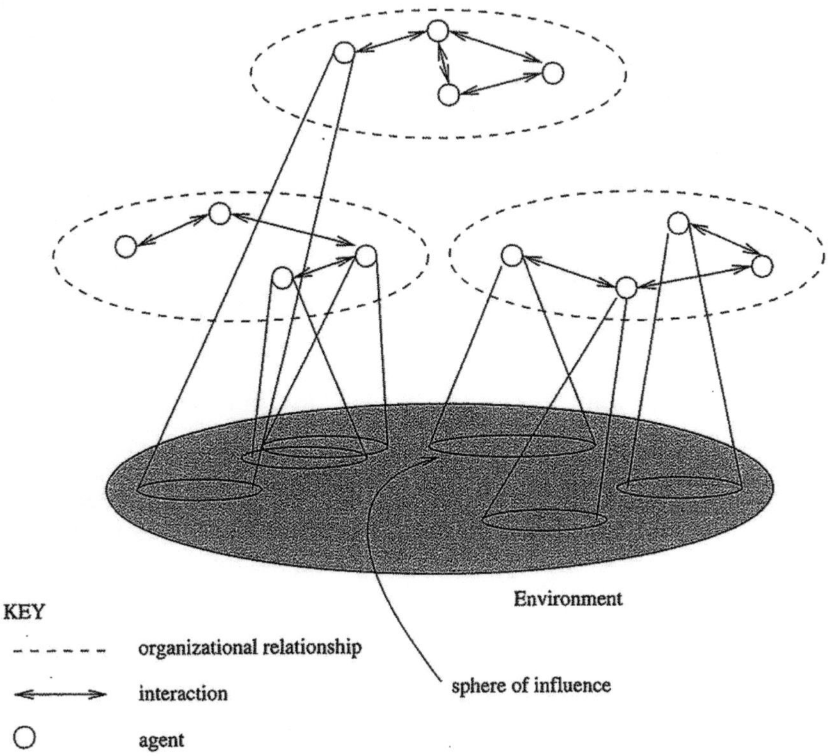

Fig. 4. Structure of a multi-agent system [14].

Following the goal of defining a methodology for modeling multi-agent systems, there is a need to define a modeling methodology that makes no use of the context of the system or at least abstracts itself from it. Basically, looking at an abstract architecture as a means of modeling single agents and multi-agent systems. The proposed modeling approach, uses the abstract architecture to obtain the Petri net models.

3.1 Petri net models from the abstract architecture

The artificial intelligence research considers three difierent paradigms for intelligent agents: a) reactive and b) deliberative; and c) hybrids between them. The abstract architecture models how an agent behaves with respect to changes in its environment. Here, an agent has its own environment and this environment is defined by the nature of the agent. The goals, objectives and the general purpose of the agent define its environment. This abstract architecture is based on the reactive paradigm of perception and action. A purely reactive agent has a perception of the environment and it is used in the decision mechanism that provides an action in the agent. A reactive agent can also have an internal state as a decision mechanism for the actions to be undertaken. An agent with perception and internal state capabilities has more computational power than an agent without them and its computational power is now comparable with that of the Belief-Desired-Intention architecture as described in [14].

Abstract model for purely reactive agents: In a purely reactive agent, the perception part records the changes in the state of the environment. The action part computes the actions to be taken in order to react to changes in the environment. The agent environment changes based on the actions applied by the agent, as well as actions by other agents, and it may be dynamic in that it may change by itself.

The environment consists of a set of states $S = \{s_1, s_2, \ldots\}$. The agent can undertake a set of actions $A = \{a_1, a_2, \ldots\}$ and perceive a set of percepts $P = \{p_1, p_2, \ldots\}$. For a purely reactive agent, the behavior of the agent can be represented as the function *action*: $P \rightarrow A$ and *perception* : $S \rightarrow P$. The deterministic behavior of an environment can be represented by the function *environment* : $S \times A \rightarrow S$.

Petri net modeling of multi-agent systems: A Petri net is defined as a five-tuple (P, T, A, W, M_0) where: P is a finite set of *places*, T is a finite set of *transitions*, $A \subseteq (P \times T)$ [$(T \times P)$ is a set of *arcs*, $W : A \rightarrow \{1, 2, 3, \ldots]$ is a *weight* function, and $M_0 : P \rightarrow Z_+^{|P|}$ is the initial *marking*. When modeling, several interpretations can be assigned to places and transitions. For a discrete-event dynamic system a transition is regarded as an event, and the places are interpreted as a condition for an event to occur.

There are properties we would like to show for multi-agent systems. Examples of these properties are boundedness and liveness since they are related to deadlock avoidance in discrete-event systems. Other properties are going to be relevant to multi-agent systems particularly to the communication, interaction and individual agent architectures. The reachability, liveness and boundedness properties of Petri nets are going to be used in the analysis presented in this chapter.

3.1.1 Obtaining Petri net models from the abstract architecture

Places model the environmental state of the agent. Having a token in a place representing state s_i means that the agent is currently in such a state.

Transitions model the actions of an agent. The environmental state is changed by actions so, for the Petri net model having tokens move from one place to another by firing transitions, this agrees with the execution process of the abstract architecture.

Algorithm 1 (Petri net submodel for agent *i*) *Let S_i be the set of environmental states of agent i, and $s_{ij} \in S_i$ be the jth environmental state of agent i. Similarly, let A_i be the set of actions of agent i, and $a_{ik} \in A_i$ be the kth action of agent i.*

1. *Add a place for each element of the environment S_i and label each place using notation P_{ij} for s_{ij}.*
2. *Add a transition for each action in A_i and label each transition using notation T_{ik} for a_{ik}.*
3. *For each instance of the function environment : $S_i \times A_i \rightarrow S_i$ say $s_{ij} \times a_{ik} \rightarrow s_{il}$: a) add an arc leaving from place P_{ij} and ending in transition T_{ik}; b) add an arc leaving from transition T_{ik} and ending in place P_{il}; c) add a weight of 1 to each arc.*
   If an arc from transition T_{ik} to place P_{il} already exists, add a new transition and label it T'_{ik}; perform this step using T'_{ik} instead of T_{ik}.
4. *Add a token in the place representing the initial state of the environment.*

Algorithm 2 (Petri net model of the multi-agent system) *The Petri net sub-models of each of the individual agents in the system should be joined based on their indirect interactions. In general, this indirect interaction will be in such a way that an agent i action will change an environment state of agent j. This communication act can be regarded as a regular action in the construction of the complete model. There will be arcs added from the places modeling the environmental states of agent j to the transition modeling the communication in agent i.*

3.1.2 Analysis of the Petri net model

The Petri net model of the multi-agent system can be analyzed to assess system properties like deadlock. Inspection of the reachability graph of the Petri net model can indicate if the model is live and bounded. On the other hand, liveness and boundedness properties can also be assessed using invariant analysis [13]. Basically, the liveness and boundedness of the net can be assessed by using the P-invariants and T-invariants obtained from the incidence matrix which give information regarding token conservation and transition firing sequences that leave the marking of the net unchanged.

Let $a_{ij}^{+} = w(i, j)$ be the weight of the arc that goes from transition t_i to place p_j and $a_{ij}^{-} = w(j, i)$ be the weight of the arc from place p_j to transition t_i. The incidence matrix A of a Petri net has $|T|$ number of rows and $|P|$ number of columns. It is defined as $A = [a_{ij}]$ where $a_{ij} = a_{ij}^{+} - a_{ij}^{-}$. Furthermore, a P-invariant is a vector that satisfies $Ax = 0$ and a T-invariant is a vector that satisfies $A^T y = 0$.

A Petri Net model is covered by P-invariants if and only if for each place s in the net, there exists a positive P-invariant x such that $x(s) > 0$. Furthermore, a Petri net is structurally bounded if it is covered by P-invariants and the initial marking M_0 is finite. In addition, a Petri net model is covered by T-invariants if and only if for each transition t in the net, there exists a positive T-invariant y such that $y(t) > 0$. Furthermore, a Petri Net is live and bounded if it is covered by T-invariants. This is a necessary condition but not sufficient.

3.2 Multi-agent system modeling and analysis example

This section presents a description of a simple multi-agent system consisting of two physical agents that work together at a task. This system will be used throughout this chapter to illustrate how the Petri net and abstract architecture models can be applied to multi-agent systems.

This system consists of two agents referred to as *agent A* and *agent B*. They move objects from one end of a path to the other. Figure 5 shows 4 scenarios in the operation of the system. Both agents are capable of moving objects and agent A moves faster than agent B. The objective of agent A is to go to the end of the path, pick an object, and return to the start of the path (figure 5a). Since it is faster than agent B it reaches the objects first (figure 5b). At the time they intersect in the path, agent A gives its object to agent B and returns to the end of the path to pick another object (figures 5c and 5d). On the other hand, the objective of agent B is to go in the direction of the end of the path, intersect with agent A and get its object. Once the agent has an object, it returns to the start of the path, places the object down and starts all over again.

The *meta-level environment* of the system consists of a single path with a set of objects on one side and no objects on the other side.

There is *indirect interaction* between the agents via changes in their environments. The exchange of the object between the agents should be regarded as a result of a change in the environment of both agents. The two agents are regarded as *purely reactive*, which implies they do not have a record of history and they do not have an internal state. The decisions they make are about which actions to undertake and those decisions are directly influenced by the location of the agent in the path and whether the agent has an object or not. It should be noted also, that the goal of the overall multi-agent system is a little different from the goal of each specific agent.

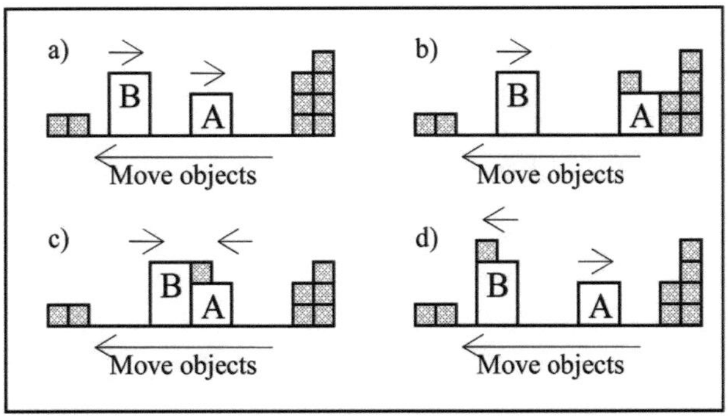

Fig. 5. Multi-agent system example for modeling and analysis.

3.2.1 Abstract architecture description

Under normal conditions, agent A will be walking to the end of the path to pick the object to be moved. The object is going to be taken away by the other agent at the intersection. Let M be the multi-agent system with agent A and B modeled with the abstract architecture. Agent A has environmental states S_A, a set of actions A_A, an action function $action_A$, and an environment evolution function $environment_A$. On the other hand, Agent B has environmental states S_B, a set of actions A_B, an action function $action_B$, and an environment evolution function $environment_B$. Tables 2 and 3 describe the possible environmental states (S_A) and the actions (A_A) that agent A can undertake.

State (S_A)	Description
s_1	Agent has object
s_2	Agent has no object and it is not at the end
s_3	Agent has no object and it is at the end

Table 2. Environmental states of agent A of M.

Actions (A_A)	Description
a_1	Walk to the end
a_2	Pick an object
a_3	Walk to start

Table 3. Actions for agent A of M.

Table 4 presents the mapping of the environment ($environment_A$) describing how it will be changing as the agent undertakes actions. It should be noted that the notion of exchanging the part with agent B at the intersection has not been considered explicitly in the description of the $environment_A : S \times A \rightarrow S$ for agent A. The agents decision mechanism is described by the $action_A$ function as presented in (4).

$$action_A(s) = \left\{ \begin{array}{ll} a_1 & \text{if } s = s_2 \\ a_2 & \text{if } s = s_3 \\ a_3 & \text{if } s = s_1 \end{array} \right\} \tag{4}$$

Agent B will be walking toward the end of the path until it intersects with agent A which is on its way back to the beginning of the path carrying an object. At the intersection point, agent B takes over the object of agent A and proceeds to return to the beginning of the path to drop the object and start the cycle again. The abstract architecture of agent B is presented in Tables 4 and 5, and the $action_B(s)$ function is described in (5).

A_A	S_A	S_A	Description
a_1	s_2	s_3	Walking towards the end of the path. Eventually will reach the end with no object.
a_2	s_3	s_1	Now the agent has an object.
a_3	s_1	s_1	Walking to the start of the path. Eventually will lose object to agent B.

Table 4. Environment function for agent A of *M*.

State (S_B)	Description
s_1	Agent has no object
s_2	Agent has object and it is not at the start
s_3	Agent has object and it is at the start
s_4	Agent is at the intersection with agent A

Table 5. Environmental states for agent B of *M*.

Actions (A_B)	Description
a_1	Walk to the end
a_2	Take over object from agent A
a_3	Walk to start
a_4	Put object down at start

Table 6. Actions for agent B of *M*.

$$action_B(s) = \left\{ \begin{array}{ll} a_1 & \text{if } s = s_1 \\ a_2 & \text{if } s = s_4 \\ a_3 & \text{if } s = s_2 \\ a_3 & \text{if } s = s_3 \end{array} \right\} \tag{5}$$

The mapping of the environment of agent B ($environment_B$) is presented in Table 7. The interaction with agent A (in the exchange of the part) is implicitly modeled by action a_2 although there is no indication in its abstract architecture that it will change the environment of agent A.

3.2.2 Petri net model

The Petri net model of the multi-agent system was obtained following the procedure described in algorithm 1 (*Petri net submodel for an agent*) and algorithm 2 (*Petri net model of the multi-agent system*). Basically, algorithm 1 is executed once for each agent in the system.

A_B	S_B	S_B	**Description**
a_1	s_1	s_4	Will walk toward the end until intersection with agent A
a_2	s_4	s_2	Object exchange, now it has an object
a_3	s_2	s_3	Will walk towards start until it reaches it
a_4	s_3	s_1	Will drop the object at start

Table 7. Environment function for agent B of *M*.

Furthermore, once all the individual agents' submodels are obtained, algorithm 2 is used to join the submodels of those agents that engage in indirect interaction.

Petri net submodel for agent A: The Petri net submodel for agent A presented in figure 6 is obtained as follows. Step 1 of the algorithm is concerned with the places of the Petri net. For each of the environmental states of agent A as described in table 2, a place is added to the new submodel following the described notation. In this step, three places are added in total, e.g., place p_{A2} which models the environmental state s_2. In this state, agent A does not have an object and it is not at the end of the path. The transitions of the model are added in the second step of the algorithm. For this agent, a total of three transitions are added which model the three actions agent A can undertake, e.g., transition t_{A2} models action a_2 which in turn is the *pick an object* action of agent A as described in table 3. The arcs of the Petri net are added in Step 3 of the algorithm. These arcs are related directly to the function that describes the evolution of the environment of the agent. This function maps the Cartesian product of *environmental states* and *actions* into the environmental states resulting from the agent undertaking a particular action. From the Petri net model point of view, this means a Cartesian product of places and transitions that is mapped into a set of places. The addition of arcs revolves around the transitions/actions of each instance of this mapping as described in table 4, e.g., $f(s_2, a_1) = s_3$ indicates that two arcs should be added to transition t_{A1}, an incoming arc from place p_{A2} and an outgoing arc to place p_{A3}. The last step of the algorithm consists of assigning the initial condition or current state to the model. A token is added to the place representing the current environmental state of the agent. A complete list with description of places and transitions is presented in table 8.

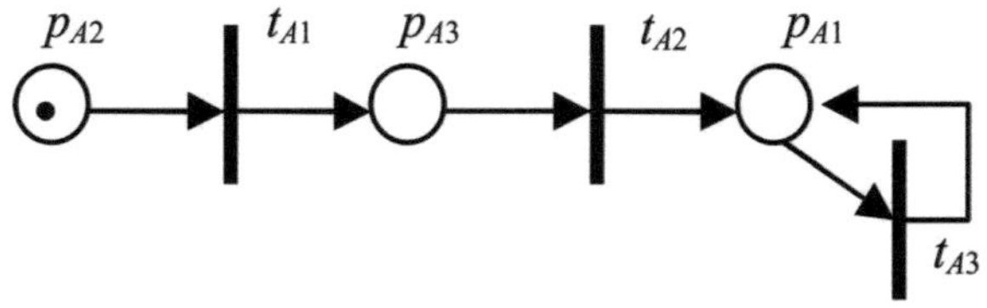

Fig. 6. Petri net model of agent A.

The Petri net submodel for agent A is not pure since place p_{A1} and transition t_{A3} form a self-loop. A Petri net is said to be *pure* if there is no place *p* that is both the input and output place to a transition *t* [8]. This self-loop is an artifact of the abstract architecture model of the agent. A token in place p_{A1} indicates that the agent is currently at environmental state S_1, which in turn means that *agent A has an object*. Furthermore, transition t_{A3} models action a_3 which indicates that *agent A walks to the start of the path*. This self-loop models agent A walking towards the start of the path while carrying an object. It does not model what will happen once the agent reaches the start of the path. It must be noted that this is not a deficiency in the Petri net construction model, but a choice made in generating the abstract

architecture description for this agent. This description assumes that when agent A is holding an object and walking towards the start of the path, the other agent will intersect with it and take over the object.
From the Petri net analysis point of view it can be seen that a token will eventually reach place p_{A1} and remain there indefinitely. This is consistent with the abstract architecture description since it does not model the capabilities of the agent once it reaches the start of the path having an object to drop there. As a result, the dynamics of this agent by itself reach a stationary state. A stationary state in this context means that the agent will keep doing the same activity and that the Petri net model indicates that the dynamics eventually get trapped at one state. It can be seeen from the reachability graph in figure 7 that the agent reaches state M_2 and remains there. The only transition enabled at state M_2 is transition t_{A3} and once it fires, the system remains in state M_2.
The states of the reachability graph are described in figure 7 as well. The initial marking M_0 describes the initial condition where agent A has no object and it is not at the end of the path. From the reachability graph it can be concluded that the net is bounded and live for $M_0 = [0, 1, 0]$. Even though the subnet is live, it will remain in state M_2 once such a state is reached, as a result, the subnet is not reversible.

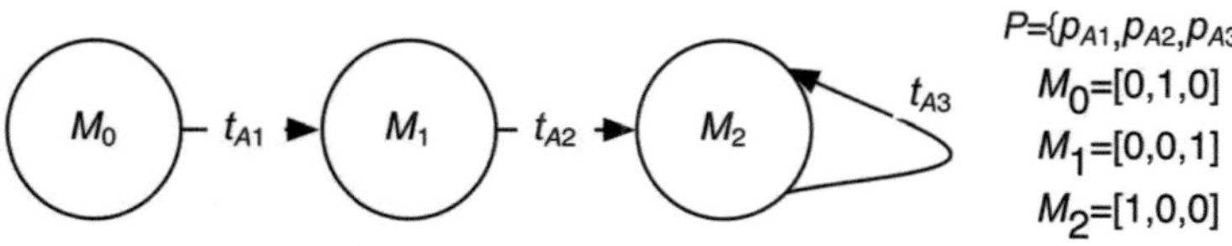

Fig. 7. Reachability graph of agent A.

The incidence matrix A_A of the Petri net submodel of agent A is presented in equation 6. The order of the places in the matrix is $P = \{p_{A1}, p_{A2}, p_{A3}\}$ and the order for transitions is $T = \{t_{A1}, t_{A2}, t_{A3}\}$. The incidence matrix A_A is a $m \times n$ matrix, where $m = |T|$ and $n = |P|$. Let x be a P-invariant of the subnet which satisfies equation $Ax = 0$, $x_1 = [1, 1, 1]^T$ is the only P-invariant of A_A with integer elements. Furthermore, let y be a T-invariant of the subnet which satisfies equation $A^T y = 0$, $y_1 = [0, 0, 1]^T$ is the only T-invariant of A_A with integer elements.

$$A_A = \begin{bmatrix} 0 & 1 & 0 \\ -1 & 0 & 0 \\ 1 & -1 & 0 \end{bmatrix} \quad (6)$$

The Petri net submodel of agent A is not covered by positive T-invariants. As a result, the necessary condition for liveness is not met and it can be concluded that the subnet is not structurally live. On the other hand, the subnet is covered by positive P-invariants, as a result, the subnet is bounded for finite initial markings.
Petri net submodel of agent B: The Petri net submodel of agent B is presented in figure 8. This submodel is obtained in a similar way as that of agent A, following the steps presented in algorithm 1 and the abstract architecture description of the agent presented in the previous section. The first step of the algorithm results in the addition of four places to the model based on the set of environmental states described in table 5. The four transitions are added in step 2, representing the set of actions in table 6. The four instances of the environment evolution function presented in table 7 result in the eight arcs of the model. The token was added to place p_{B1} to indicate that the agent does not have an object.

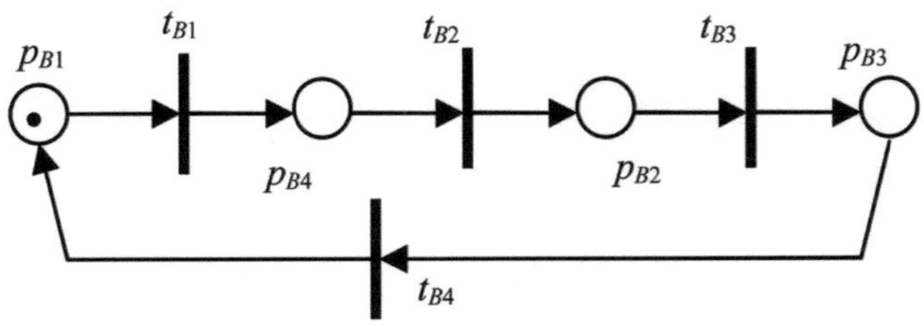

Fig. 8. Petri net model of agent B.

The reachability graph is presented in figure 9. The initial marking M_0 describes the initial condition where agent B has no object. From the reachability graph it can be concluded that the net is bounded and live for $M_0 = [1, 0, 0, 0]$.

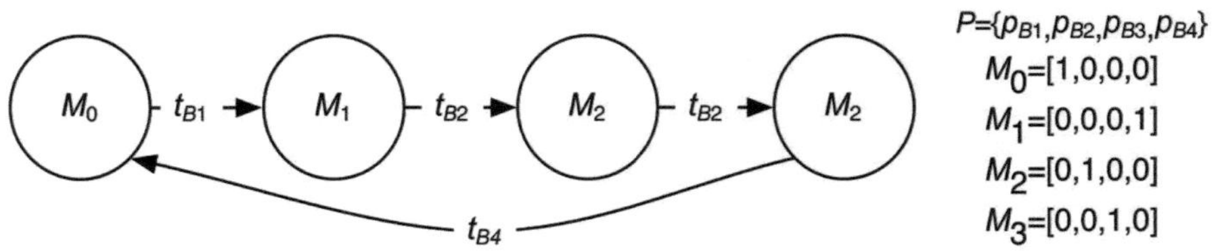

Fig. 9. Reachability graph of agent B.

The incidence matrix A_B of the Petri net submodel of agent B is presented in equation 7. The order of the places in the matrix is $P = \{p_{B1}, p_{B2}, p_{B3}, p_{B4}\}$ and the order for transitions is $T = \{t_{B1}, t_{B2}, t_{B3}, t_{B4}\}$. The incidence matrix A_B is a $m \times n$ matrix, where $m = |T|$ and $n = |P|$. Let x be a P-invariant of the subnet which satisfies equation $Ax = 0$, $x_1 = [1, 1, 1, 1]^T$ is the only P-invariant of A_B with integer elements. Furthermore, let y be a T-invariant of the subnet which satisfies equation $A^T y = 0$, $y_1 = [1, 1, 1, 1]^T$ is the only T-invariant of A_B with integer elements.

The Petri net submodel of agent B is covered by positive T-invariants. As a result, the necessary condition for liveness is met so it can be structurally live. On the other hand, the subnet is also covered by positive P-invariants, as a result, the subnet is bounded for finite initial markings.

$$A_B = \begin{bmatrix} -1 & 0 & 0 & 1 \\ 0 & 1 & 0 & -1 \\ 0 & -1 & 1 & 0 \\ 1 & 0 & -1 & 0 \end{bmatrix} \tag{7}$$

Petri net model of the complete multi-agent system: Let $N = (P, T, A, W, M_0)$ be the Petri net model of the complete system with places $P = \{p_{A1}, p_{A2}, p_{A3}, p_{B1}, p_{B2}, p_{B3}, p_{B4}\}$, transitions $T = \{t_{A1}, t_{A2}, t_{A3}, t_{B1}, t_{B2}, t_{B3}, t_{B4}\}$, and $M_0 = [0, 1, 0, 1, 0, 0, 0]$. Figure 10 shows N and the interpretation of places and transitions is presented in Table 8.

This model was obtained by joining the Petri net submodels of the two agents, by following the methodology presented in algorithm 2. The premise of the algorithm is to identify agents engaging in indirect interaction in order to join their models. Furthermore, a transition firing from one of the agents will modify the other agent's environmental state. For this example, transition t_{B2} which models an action of agent B, modifies the environmental state of agent A. The interpretation in terms of the system's description is that when agent B *takes over the object from agent A,* the environmental state of agent A changes from *having an object* to *not having an object and not being at the end of the path.* As a result, two additional arcs are added to the submodels in order to construct the overall multi-agent system model; an incoming arc to transition t_{B2} from place P_{A1}, and an outgoing arc from transition t_{B2} to place p_{A2}.

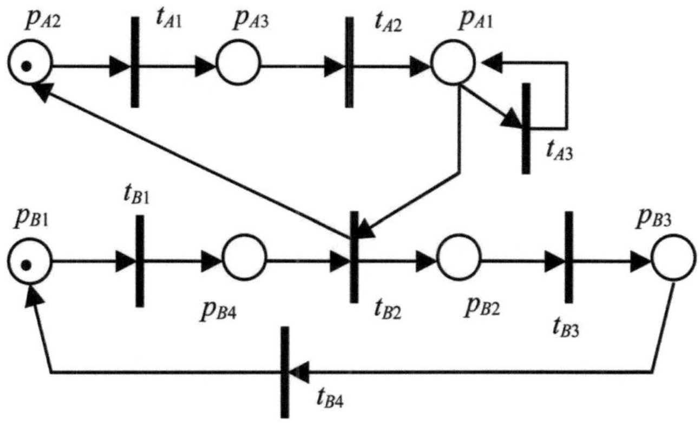

Fig. 10. Petri net model *N*.

Element	Name	Description
Places (P)	p_{A1}	A token in this place indicates the environment is at state s_1 for agent A
	p_{A2}	A token in this place indicates the environment is at state s_2 for agent A
	p_{A3}	A token in this place indicates the environment is at state s_3 for agent A
	p_{B1}	A token in this place indicates the environment is at state s_1 for agent B
	p_{B2}	A token in this place indicates the environment is at state s_2 for agent B
	p_{B3}	A token in this place indicates the environment is at state s_3 for agent B
	p_{B4}	A token in this place indicates the environment is at state s_4 for agent B
Transitions (T)	t_{A1}	Execution of action a_1 for agent A
	t_{A2}	Execution of action a_2 for agent A
	t_{A3}	Execution of action a_3 for agent A
	t_{B1}	Execution of action a_1 for agent B
	t_{B2}	Execution of action a_2 for agent B
	t_{B3}	Execution of action a_3 for agent B
	t_{B4}	Execution of action a_4 for agent B

Table 8. Description of Petri net model *N*.

The tokens in places p_{A2} and p_{B1} represent the initial conditions of agent A and B respectively. The tokens travel through the net representing different environment states for the agents as the system executes. The systems execution scenarios presented in figure 5 can be identified in the Petri net model, e.g., scenario d) of figure 5 will be represented in the Petri net model as having a token in p_{A2} and p_{B2}. The Petri net model can now be analyzed to assess the deadlock property in a systematic way.

3.2.3 Analysis of the Petri net model *N*

The Petri net model presented in figure 10 (*N*) can now be analyzed to assess the deadlock property of the underlying multi-agent system. The reachability graph of the model is presented in figure 11 and it shows that the net is live and bounded. Therefore, the multi-agent system is deadlock free.

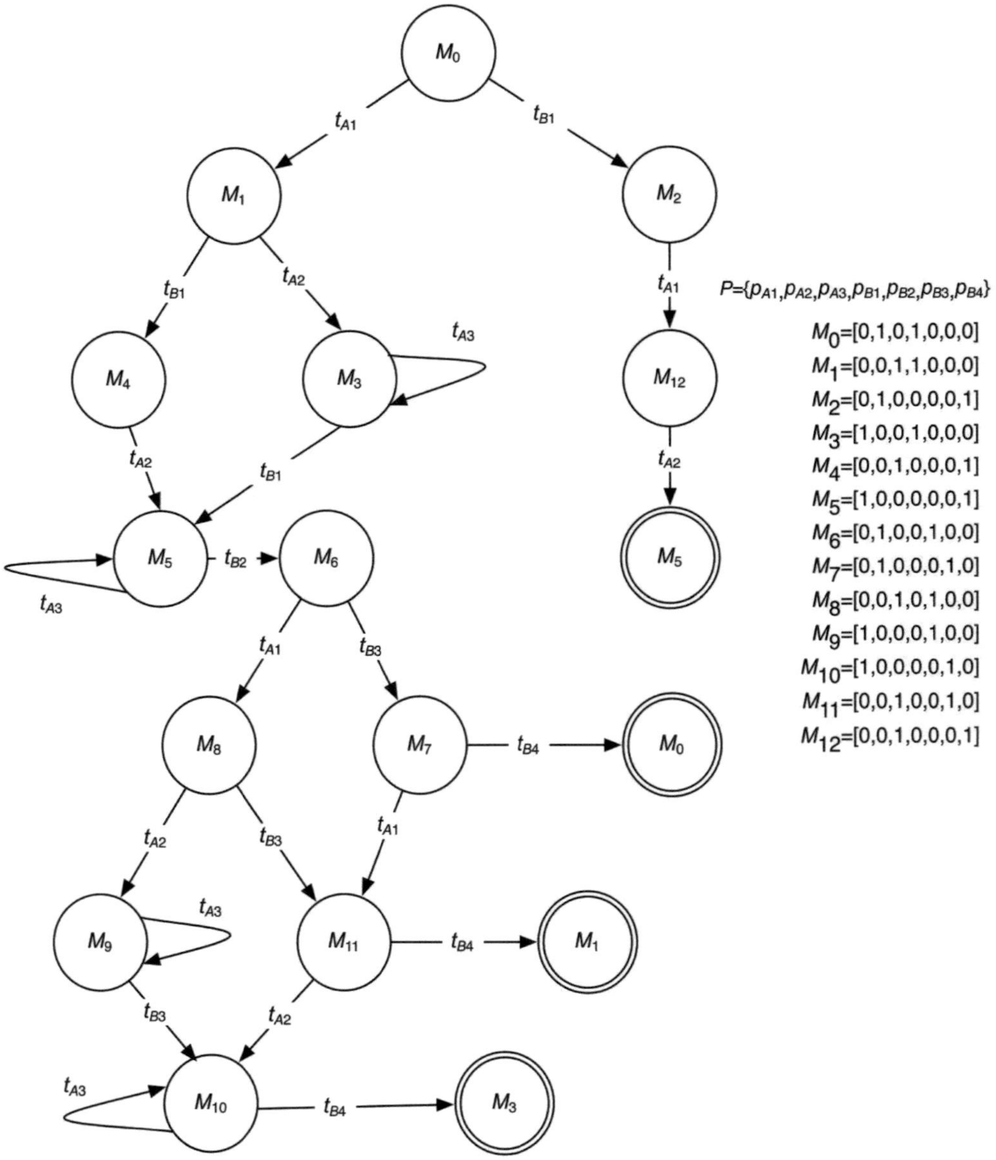

Fig. 11. Reachability graph of Petri net model *N*.

The reachability graph shows the different markings that can be reached by firing different enabled transitions in the model. Every node in the graph represents a marking from the reachability set $R(M_0)$ of the initial marking. The arcs leaving each node indicate the transitions that are enabled, e.g., at marking M_6 transitions t_{A1} and t_{B3} are enabled. The initial marking M_0 = [0, 1, 0, 1, 0, 0, 0] represents the initial state of the system where a token is present in place p_{A2} and p_{B1}, which in turn represents the initial state of both agents. It should be noted that the reachability graph is generated taking M_0 as a starting state, therefore, the assessment of properties using this graph will result in such properties being valid only when M_0 = [0, 1, 0, 1, 0, 0, 0].

It can be seen from this graph that at every marking of $R(M_0)$, there is always an enabled transition (every node in the graph has an outgoing arc). As a result the net is live when the initial marking (initial condition) is M_0 = [0, 1, 0, 1, 0, 0, 0].

The boundedness of the net when M_0 = [0, 1, 0, 1, 0, 0, 0] can also be observed from the reachability graph. The number of tokens present at a particular place is indicated for all the markings reachable from M_0, hence it is possible to observe the maximum number of tokens a place can have. The reachability graph of M_0 = [0, 1, 0, 1, 0, 0, 0] shows that the bound in the number of tokens for all the places in the net is one, therefore, the net is safe (*1-bounded*).

Structural analysis is done using the incidence matrix (9) of the net and its invariants (10). It shows that the net is bounded and that the necessary condition for liveness is satisfied; this is a slightly weaker conclusion on "liveness" than when both necessary and sufficient conditions are met. The incidence matrix A_4 for net N is a $m \times n$ matrix, where $m = |T|$ and $n = |P|$. The row order of transitions is given by $T = \{t_{A1}, t_{A2}, t_{A3}, t_{B1}, t_{B2}, t_{B3}, t_{B4}\}$ and the column order of places is $P = \{p_{A1}, p_{A2}, p_{A3}, p_{B1}, p_{B2}, p_{B3}, p_{B4}\}$.

The incidence matrix gives an indication on the number of tokens gained for every place in the net as a result of a transition firing. The *state equation* (8) presented below, models the marking evolution as a function of firing transitions. It is defined as

$$M_f = M_0 + uA, \tag{8}$$

were u is a row vector of m elements of nonnegative integers. The i_{th} element of u represents the number of times transition t_i is fired in order to reach M_f from M_0. M_0 is the current marking of the net, and M_f is the marking reached by firing the transitions indicated by u.

$$A_4 = \begin{bmatrix} 0 & -1 & 1 & 0 & 0 & 0 & 0 \\ 1 & 0 & -1 & 0 & 0 & 0 & 0 \\ 0 & 0 & 0 & 0 & 0 & 0 & 0 \\ 0 & 0 & 0 & -1 & 0 & 0 & 1 \\ -1 & 1 & 0 & 0 & 1 & 0 & -1 \\ 0 & 0 & 0 & 0 & -1 & 1 & 0 \\ 0 & 0 & 0 & 1 & 0 & -1 & 0 \end{bmatrix} \tag{9}$$

$$\text{T -invariants} = \begin{bmatrix} 0 & 1 \\ 0 & 1 \\ 1 & 0 \\ 0 & 1 \\ 0 & 1 \\ 0 & 1 \\ 0 & 1 \end{bmatrix} \text{ and P-invariants} = \begin{bmatrix} 1 & 0 \\ 1 & 0 \\ 1 & 0 \\ 0 & 1 \\ 0 & 1 \\ 0 & 1 \\ 0 & 1 \end{bmatrix} \tag{10}$$

The state equation for N is $M_f = M_0 + uA_4$. This equation can be used to find reachable markings as described by the reachability graph. Lets assume that a series of transition firings are executed in N starting from $M_0 = [0, 1, 0, 1, 0, 0, 0]$. These transitions are t_{A1}, t_{B1}, t_{A2}, t_{B2}, t_{A1} in this specific order, which renders $u = [2, 1, 0, 1, 1, 0, 0]$. Use the state equation to compute the current marking $M_f = [0, 0, 1, 0, 1, 0, 0]$. This is equivalent to marking M_8 from the reachability graph in figure 11 which was reached from M_0 after firing the same transitions in the same order.

The state equation is the basis for the structural analysis based on the P-invariants for boundedness and T-invariants for liveness (reachability). Let x be a P-invariant of the net which by definition satisfies $Ax = 0$, e.g., $x_1 = [1, 1, 1, 0, 0, 0, 0]^T$ is a P-invariant of A_4 from (10). Multiplying the state equation (8) by x we get $M_f x = M_0 x + uAx$. The last term of the right hand side of the equality is zero given that x is a P-invariant. As a result $M_f x = M_0 x$, which in turn indicates that the total number of tokens in the places for which the P-invariant is one (places p_{A1}, p_{A2} and p_{A3}, for P-invariant x_1) does not change; disregarding which transition or set of transitions was fired. This token conservation property is also independent from M_0, hence, it can be used to assess structural boundedness of such places.

For P-invariant x_1, $M_f x_1 = M_0 x_1$ implies that $M_f(p_{A1}) + M_f(p_{A2}) + M_f(p_{A3}) = M_0(p_{A1}) + M_0(p_{A2}) + M_0(p_{A3})$. This means that places $\{p_{A1}, p_{A2}, p_{A3}\}$ are bounded by $k = M_0(p_{A1}) + M_0(p_{A2}) + M_0(p_{A3})$. This result applies for every initial marking M_0. Furthermore, if the markings of these places are assumed to be finite, then it can be concluded that such places are *k bounded*. Further analysis can be done if more knowledge of M_0 is assumed. For $M_0 = [0, 1, 0, 1, 0, 0, 0]$, $k = M_0(p_{A1}) + M_0(p_{A2}) + M_0(p_{A3}) = 1$, therefore these places are *1-bounded* (safe).

The same methodology is used to make an assessment about the structural boundedness of the rest of the places of N. The second P-invariant vector in (10) is $x_2 = [0, 0, 0, 1, 1, 1, 1]^T$. It can be concluded that places $\{p_{B1}, p_{B2}, p_{B3}, p_{B4}\}$ are bounded by $k = M_0(p_{B1})+M_0(p_{B2})+M_0(p_{B3})+M_0(p_{B4})$ for every possible initial marking. Furthermore, since $M_0 = [0, 1, 0, 1, 0, 0, 0]$, then $k = M_0(p_{B1})+M_0(p_{B2})+M_0(p_{B3})+M_0(p_{B4}) = 1$, therefore these places are *1-bounded* (safe).

The structural boundedness by net invariants can also be assessed as described in theorem 1. The basis for the theorem is the same as presented above, even though it is more restrictive since it is focused on assessing boundedness of the whole net. From theorem 1 it can only be concluded that the net is bounded, but doing a more detailed analysis of the situation allowed the conclusion that the net is *safe*. For cases where the model complexity is large, it could be difficult to find instances in which the whole net is bounded. In such cases, knowledge of the details of token conservation should be leveraged to provide boundedness assessment of submodels of the net.

Another use of the state equation (8) is in the solution of the reachability problem. The reachability problem consists of knowing whether marking M_f can be reached by firing a sequence of transitions given that the net is currently on marking M_0. Basically, if $M_f \in R(M_0)$, then u is a nonnegative integer solution to $M_f = M_0 + uA$. Solution to the state equation is just a necessary condition for reachability. This is due to the fact that u tells only which transitions are firing and how many firings per transition will result in marking M_f. It does not tell the order in which such transitions should be fired (sequence of transition firings), furthermore, it does not warranty that firing sequences consistent with u will be feasible, given that there could exist transitions in the sequence that are not enabled in markings where they are expected to fire.

The reachability problem is closely related to the liveness assessment. Structural liveness is difficult to prove based on the network invariants. As a matter of fact, only a necessary condition for structural liveness is available; which was described earlier in theorem 2. For net N, which is bounded and covered by T-invariants (8), the necessary condition for liveness is satisfied.

Further interpretation of the T-invariants, in addition to the fact that the state equation solution provides only a necessary condition for reachability, gives further insight on why a T-invariant coverage provides only a necessary condition for liveness. The T-invariant of a net is defined as $A^T y = 0$, where A is the incidence matrix. This equation is equivalent to $y^T A = 0$. Let $u = y^T$, then the state equation $M_f = M_0 + y^T A$ becomes $M_f = M_0$. This means that firing the transitions described by the T-invariant does not change the marking of the network. Furthermore, by firing such transitions, the net returns to marking M_0. This property is key in the construction of theorem 2. In addition, the fact that only the set of transition firings is known, but not a feasible transition firing sequence, results in this theorem being a necessary condition only.

4. Analysis of Petri net models from multi-agent systems

This section presents the application of Petri net synthesis and reduction methods for the modeling and analysis of multi-agent systems using Petri nets. In particular, the use of synthesis and reduction methodologies for Petri net models of multi-agent systems with indirect interaction, and presents a simple example where the principles are demonstrated.

This work builds on the methodology presented in section 3 which presents a systematic approach to building Petri net models of multi-agent systems with indirect interaction. In the examples presented in section 3 only a mutli-agent system consisting of two agents was studied and liveness and boundedness properties were assessed. The question now is how could these properties be proved for larger systems or for any multi-agent system in general that has indirect interaction. One way to do it will be to build the Petri net model for the entire multi-agent system and apply the structural or behavioral analysis approaches to the entire model in order to make an assessment. The drawback of this approach is the complexity involved in a) generating a detailed Petri net model for the complete system, b) generating reachability graphs for large Petri nets, and c) finding the invariants of a large incidence matrix since the null space of the matrix must be computed. Structural analysis is also restrictive since results must apply to every initial marking. An additional drawback could be the interpretation of such an assessment and its usefulness. Another approach is the divide and conquer approach where we can leverage Petri net synthesis and reduction methodologies for analysis to prove liveness and boundedness of the whole system. This is done either by proving the properties at a subsystem level and then building them up, or by reducing the complete model while preserving its properties until a model of manageable size is obtained to assess properties [16].

The synthesis and reduction approaches have been successfully applied to the analysis of Petri net models of manufacturing systems [17][18][16]. There is no evidence that these methodologies have been applied in the analysis of Petri net models of multi-agent systems. In general, the focus has been on obtaining Petri net models of specific multi-agent systems, but not in the analysis of such models.

4.1 Introduction to synthesis and reduction methods for Petri nets

Petri net synthesis for analysis is the process of adding refinement to Petri net models in a manner in which certain properties like liveness and boundedness are preserved. The synthesis methodologies consist of starting with a simple model where certain properties hold, and then adding detail in the form of more places and transitions following rules that ensure that such properties will hold in the new more detailed model [17]. The synthesis and reduction methodologies can be described as: i) top-down, ii) bottom-up and iii) hybrid. The top-down approach starts with a high level model of the system under consideration and then adds stepwise refinements until the desired level of detail is achieved in the model [17][19][20]. The bottom-up approach also referred to as a *reduction* approach consists of joining Petri net sub-models that share places or transitions. This approach can also be described as transforming the detailed Petri net models using macroplaces and macrotransitions so as to obtain a smaller model where the desired properties can be proved [17][21][22].

Petri net transformations for analysis: Petri net transformations play a crucial role in the analysis and assessment of properties. Reduction and synthesis methodologies for analysis make use of transformations in order to facilitate the analysis. Such transformations are required to preserve system properties; which might vary depending on the focus of the analysis, e.g., liveness should be preserved if deadlock is to be assessed for the whole model. Transformations might involve places, transitions, or even sections of a Petri net. They range from removal of redundant transitions and places, to the exchange of a place or a transition by a submodel with higher level of detail. Property preserving transformations are usually bi-directional. If a type of transformation removes a redundant place preserving liveness, then the same transformation in reverse order can also be used the other way around to provide more detail preserving the liveness property.

Petri net model construction and analysis: In general, the differences between model assessment and model construction processes are well understood, since they are present for every type of modeling activity in engineering and science. The model analysis process starts when a model of a natural or man-made system is readily available, then analysis of key properties and behavior of such a model is performed. It is easy to visualize how reduction or even synthesis methodologies can be applied for this situation. On the other hand, model construction has subtle details that must be clarified in order to understand how the synthesis and reduction techniques can be applied to it.

For a model construction process for existing systems, either man-made or natural, the purpose is to build a model, often times a mathematical model which mimics the behavior of the existing system. There could be a multiple number of models ranging from different levels of detail to different methodologies. An example where different levels of detail are present is in dynamic systems, which could either be a lumped-parameter model (ordinary differential equations), a distributed parameter model (partial differential equation) or even a stochastic model (removing the assumption that some variables are deterministic). An example of different methodologies for modeling could be that of a manufacturing system; which can either be modeled as a queuing system, with discrete-event simulation, or even Petri nets. The selection of the level of detail and methodologies is often guided by the requirements of the problem at hand.

For the Petri net case, synthesis methodologies can be used in the model construction process. One can start with a high level of abstraction model which presents certain key properties, additional levels of detail are then added by following property preserving transformations. A similar approach is to construct models of different sections of the system, then use synthesis procedures to join the different submodels in such a way that the properties of interest are preserved.

For a model construction of a system that does not already exist, like the control logic for an automated manufacturing facility, the purpose is to build a model that satisfies a series of conditions and properties. In such cases, models can be constructed taking desired properties into account during the construction process.

The concepts described above apply to the multi-agent system domain directly. There are cases where a multi-agent system is used to model an existing system, as in the case studies presented in previous sections. In other situations, like the control of the national airspace system, multi-agent system controllers have been proposed to carry out space management operations in a safe and efficient manner. In both cases, analysis methodologies should be employed to assess properties of the system. Such multi-agent systems models can be translated into the Petri net domain to assess deadlock or other properties. For a multi-agent system construction process, the development can start with a high-level model and then add more detail to the individual agents. Furthermore, Petri net synthesis concepts could be used to aid the design of interaction mechanisms among the agents in such a way that properties of the individual agents are preserved through the interaction.

On synthesis and reduction methodologies: The reduction approach presented in figure 4.1a shows how starting from a high fidelity model with high-level of detail, the model is reduced to a size manageable to perform behavioral or structural analysis. The model N_{a1} is a high-level of detail model used as a starting point, transformation T_{a1} reduces the model in complexity resulting in a new model N_{a2}. Transformation T_{a1} should be a property preserving transformation so that N_{a2} preserves the properties of interest from N_{a1}. For example, if liveness and boundedness properties are to be assessed for N_{a1}, then transformations T_{a1} and T_{a2} must preserve these properties. The final model N_{a3} will have lower complexity than the high fidelity model. Analysis of N_{a3} is now easier or even possible if the complexity of N_{a1} is such that analysis is intractable. The following are situations when the reduction approach is helpful.

- When a high fidelity model is too large to assess behavioral properties of the complete model. For this situation, the number of markings in $R(M_0)$ is too large and the construction of the reachability graph is cumbersome even with the aid of computational tools.
- When there is more interest in the behavior of a section of the model and how it interacts with the rest of the model. In this situation, the rest of the net could be reduced as much as possible to facilitate the analysis of the section of interest.

The synthesis approach is also depicted in figure 4.1b. Synthesis methods focus on the composition of models from submodels. Two submodels can be joined to form a larger one or a place or transition can be exchanged for a submodel with higher level of detail. Similar to the reduction approach, these transformations should also be property preserving. Assuming that transformations T_{b1} and T_{b2} preserve properties like liveness and boundedness, then model N_{b3} will be live and bounded if model N_{b1} is live and bounded. This allows one to perform the analysis in the model of smaller complexity and then extrapolate those results for the larger model.

4.2 Literature review

The work by Suzuki in [23] and Suzuki and Murata in [20] presents a methodology for expanding and reducing Petri nets to a desired level of detail. This methodology consists of stepwise refinements of transitions and places, as well as abstraction of subnets into a single

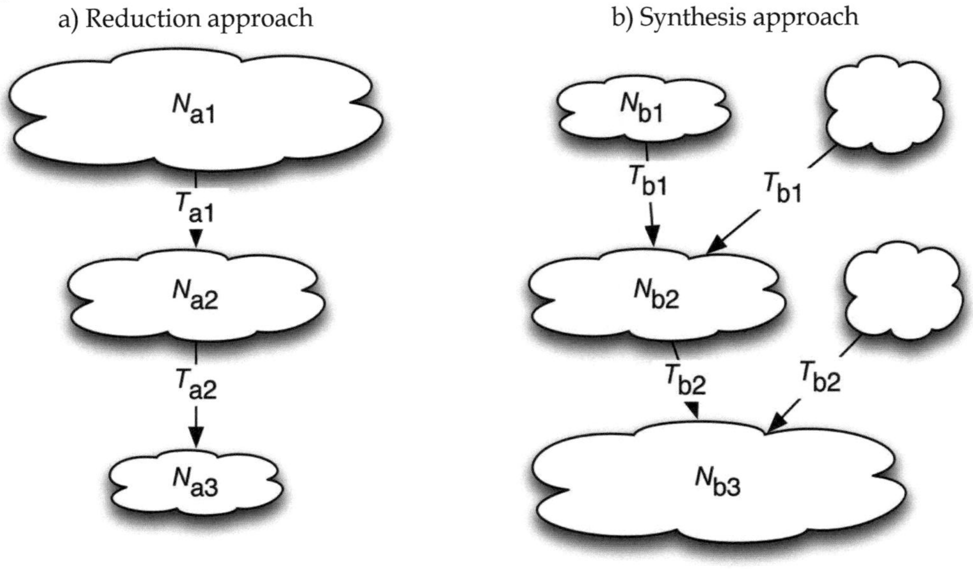

Fig. 12. Synthesis and reduction of Petri net models.

transition. The transformations presented preserve liveness and boundedness. Reduction is presented as a substitution of a subnet by a single transition, hence generating a new model with higher level of abstraction.

Synthesis is approached by way of stepwise refinements. Datta and Ghosh in [24] present a top-down approach to analysis of regular Petri nets. Regular Petri nets are live and bounded by construction. The properties considered to be preserved by the transformations are liveness and boundedness. The work by Lee and Favrel in [22] presents a hierarchical (bottom-up) approach to analysis. This consists of a hierarchical reduction and decomposition by transforming subnets into macroplaces or macrotransitions. Liveness and boundedness are preserved by these transformations. The work by Berthelot in [25] presents a series of transformations to provide reduction and synthesis. The properties considered include liveness, boundedness, safety, covering of P-invariants, return to home state and others. Place transformations and fusion of transitions are presented to provide reduction. Synthesis is considered by addition of submodels. Lee et al. in [21] present a reduction methodology for generalized Petri nets. In generalized Petri nets, multiple arcs are allowed between transitions and places, as a result, the weights of the arcs can be larger than one. The purpose of the methodology is to reduce the state-space of the net to a manageable size based on the structure of the net. Liveness, boundedness and proper termination properties are preserved by reducing subnets into macroplaces or macrotransitions. The work by Jeng and DiCesare in [26] presents a review of synthesis and reduction methods. Examples of applications in the manufacturing domain are presented as well. Zhou et al. in [18] present a hybrid methodology for synthesis of Petri net models of automated manufacturing systems. In this work, modeling details are included as increments by refining places. Reversibility, boundedness and liveness are preserved by this methodology. The work by Jeng and DiCesare [27] presents a review of reduction and synthesis technologies and their applications to manufacturing. Methodologies for synthesis are presented by considering merging of places from different subnets, and refinement of transitions. The properties preserved depend on the transformations applied. Synthesis and analysis of flexible manufacturing systems is presented in Zhou et al. [16]. In this work, the synthesis process is used for the model construction process. Petri net design approaches and the modeling process are considered, as well as the analysis of the system. Refinement is used to design a system that conforms to certain desired properties like liveness, boundedness and reversibility. The work by Jeng in [28] presents a methodology for synthesis of flexible manufacturing systems. A bottom-up approach is used to construct models and interactions among submodels is investigated. This is an application of reduction and refinement for the construction of Petri net models of flexible manufacturing systems.

4.3 Analysis of Petri net model *N* using reduction techniques

The Petri net model *N* from the example (figure 13) in the previous section is presented here to illustrate how reduction techniques are used for the assessment of liveness and boundedness. From the results presented in the previous section we learned that this Petri net model is live and bounded for the initial marking M_0 (which is indicated in figure 13). The Petri net is also structurally bounded given that the number of places in the model must be finite in the initial condition. For structural liveness, only the necessary condition is satisfied. From the individual agent submodels (figure 6 and figure 8) it can be concluded that only the model for agent B is live and bounded.

The objective here is to prove that the model is live and bounded. In order to do so, it is assumed that it is not known in advance that the model is live and bounded. By applying the reduction techniques, the model will be reduced in size until the liveness and boundedness properties are evident from the reduced model.

Transformations: The transformations considered for this example are presented in [17]. Basically, two transition transformations *fusion* and *pre-fusion* will be used to reduce the model. These transformations preserve liveness and boundedness, and they are intended to reduce the number of reachable markings of the net; making easier the analysis of the reduced model.

The *fusion* transformation combines two transitions t_i and t_j that are separated by a single place p_k. Place p_k must be the only output place of transition t_i and it is also an input place of transition t_j. The transformation removes place p_k and combines the transitions into a single transition t_{ij}, which will have the same input places as t_i and the same output places as t_j. This transformation preserves liveness and boundedness [17].

The *pre-fusion* is a liveness and boundedness preserving transformation that combines two transitions t_i and t_j that are separated by a single place p_k. Place p_k must be the only output place of transition t_i and it is also an input place of transition t_j . In addition, transition t_j can have additional input places besides p_k. The transformation removes place p_k and combines the transitions into a single transition t_{ij} , which will have the same input places as t_i and the same input and output places as t_j [17].

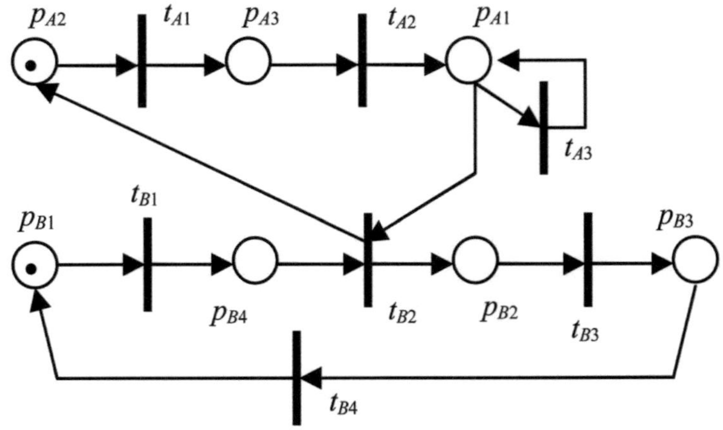

Fig. 13. Petri net model *N*.

Reduction procedure: The Petri net model *N* is presented in figure 14. In this figure, a series of fusion transformations are indicated. Transitions t_{A1} and t_{A2} will be fused, as a result, place p_{A3} will be removed resulting in the model in figure 15a. Fusion of transitions is applied twice in the bottom part of the model. First transitions t_{B1} and t_{B4} are fused. The resulting transition is then fused with transition t_{B3} to form transition t_{B134} in figure 15a. In addition, transition t_{A3} was removed since it does not change the marking when it fires.

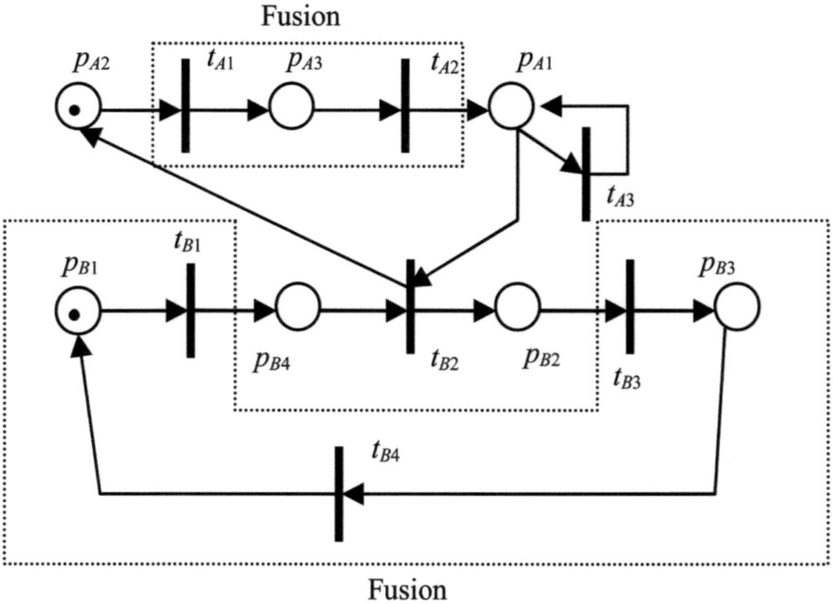

Fig. 14. Fusion transformations in Petri net model *N*.

The final model is presented in figure 15b. It is obtained after applying the pre-fusion transformation to the model in figure 15a.
The pre-fusion transformation will remove place p_{B4} and combine transition t_{B2} with transition t_{B134}. The resulting model is sufficiently simple to perform the assessment of liveness and boundedness by inspection. The size of the reachability set is two since there are only two possible markings in the model. The maximum number of tokens in all the places is one, as a result the net is 1-bounded (safe). It is also evident that there is always an enabled transition, as a result the model is live.

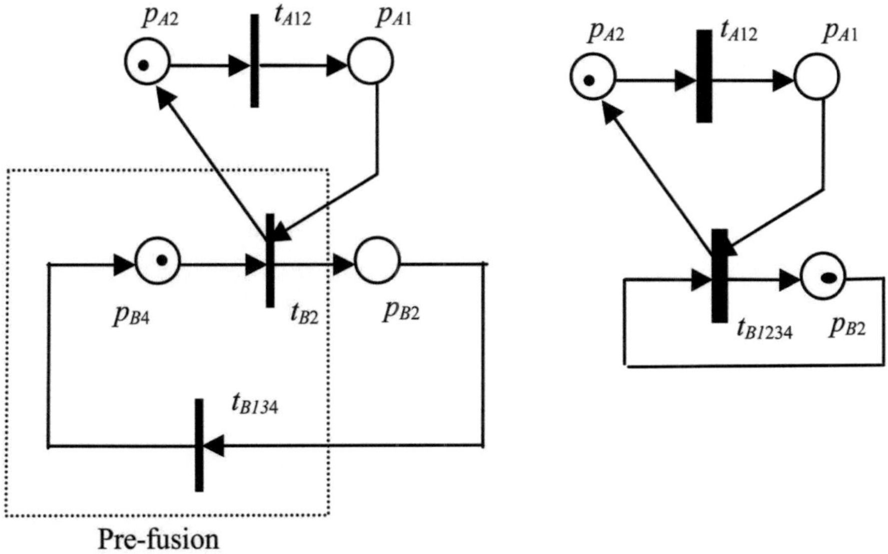

Fig. 15. Reduced Petri net model *N*.

Since all the transformations applied preserve liveness and boundedness, the fact that the reduced model is live and bounded implies that the original Petri net model (figure 13) is also live and bounded.

5. Discussion

This chapter presented a methodology for the modeling and analysis of multi-agent systems using Petri nets. Multi-agent systems with indirect interaction were considered as a starting point for the development of Petri net based tools for multi-agent systems.
The interaction framework considered was the simplest means of interaction among agents and referred to in this work as indirect interaction. In the indirect interaction framework agents can interact with each other by changing each other's environment. At the interaction level, it is natural to regard a multi-agent system as a discrete-event system, and by focusing at this level, this work presents a methodology to assess how indirect interactions will work with respect to the discrete-event system properties of the multiagent system. Petri nets have been used in several applications of discrete-event dynamic systems. In this work, multi-agent systems were regarded as a discrete event-system and modeled using the Petri net methodology. Thus, properties of Petri nets were analyzed and related to multi-agent

systems. The liveness and boundedness properties in the Petri net domain are important for multi-agent systems as they relate to deadlock avoidance. Furthermore, properties from the Petri net domain could be related to characteristics of the communication and interaction mechanism of the multi-agent system. The abstract architecture of intelligent agents is considered as a preliminary step of the Petri net model construction process. The methodology proposed in this work consists of describing a multi-agent system with the abstract architecture for intelligent agents, and then constructing a Petri net model systematically from the abstract architecture description of the system. Different scenarios were considered in order to indicate how the Petri net analysis methodologies can be used to assess key system properties, showing that there is a relationship between multi-agent systems with indirect interaction and Petri nets. The mapping of multi-agent systems models with the abstract architecture into Petri net models captured the discrete-event dynamics of the systems under consideration. This allowed the assessment of properties like deadlock avoidance in a multi-agent system, which can be assessed systematically from the Petri net model.

In general, the results presented in this work show the potential for using Petri nets to assess key properties of multi-agent systems. In addition, they provide the foundation to further investigate the application of Petri net methodologies for the modeling, analysis and design of multi-agent systems.

6. References

[1] T. Murata, P. C. Nelson, and J. Yim, "A predicate-transition net model for multiple agent planning," *Inf. Sci.*, vol. 57-58, pp. 361-384, 1991.

[2] D. Xu, R. Volz, T. Ioerger, and J. Yen, "Modeling and verifying multi-agent behaviors using predicate/transition nets," in *SEKE '02: Proceedings of the 14th international conference on Software engineering and knowledge engineering*, (New York, NY, USA), pp. 193-200, ACM Press, 2002.

[3] H. J. Ahn and S. J. Park, "Modeling of a multi-agent system for coordination of supply chains with complexity and uncertainty," in *Intelligent Agents and Multi-Agent Systems* (J. Lee and M. Barley, eds.), vol. 2891 of *Lecture Notes in Computer Science*, pp. 13-24, 6th Pacific Rim International Workshop on Multi-Agents, PRIMA 2003 Seoul, Korea, Springer-Verlag Berlin Heidelberg, November 2003.

[4] P. Leitão, A. W. Colombo, and F. Restivo, "An approach to the formal specification of holonic control systems," in *Holonic and Multi-Agent Systems for Manufacturing* (V. Marík, D. McFarlane, and P. Valckenaers, eds.), vol. 2744 of *Lecture Notes in Computer Science*, pp. 59-70, First International Conference on Industrial Applications of Holonic and Multi-Agent Systems, HoloMAS 2003 Prague, Czech Republic, September 1-3, 2003, Springer Berlin / Heidelberg, 2004.

[5] F.-S. Hsieh, "Model and control holonic manufacturing systems based on fusion of contract nets and Petri nets," *Automatica*, vol. 40, no. 1, pp. 51-57, 2004.

[6] M. R. Lyu, X. Chen, and T. Y. Wong, "Design and evaluation of a fault-tolerant mobile-agent system," *Intelligent Systems*, vol. 19, no. 5, pp. 32-38, 2004.

[7] A. W. Krings, "Agent survivability: An application for strong and weak chain constrained scheduling," in HICSS '04: Proceedings of the Proceedings of the 37th

Annual Hawaii International Conference on System Sciences (HICSS'04) - Track 9, (Washington, DC, USA), p. 90297.1, IEEE Computer Society, 2004.
[8] T. Murata, "Petri nets: Properties, analysis and applications," *Proceedings of the IEEE*, vol. 77, pp. 541-580, April 1989.
[9] T. Agerwala, "Putting Petri nets to work," *Computer*, vol. 12, pp. 85- 94, December 1979.
[10]C. G. Cassandras, *Discrete Event Systems, Modeling and Performance Analysis*. Aksen Associates Incorporated, 1993.
[11] A. A. Desrochers, "Performance analysis using Petri nets, "*Journal of Intelligent and Robotic Systems*, vol. 6, pp. 65-79, August 1992.
[12] J. L. Peterson, Petri net theory and the modeling of systems. Prentice Hall, 1981.
[13] W. Reisig, Petri nets, An Introduction, vol. 4 of EATCS: Monographs on Theoretical Computer Science. Springer-Verlag, 1985.
[14] M. J. Wooldridge, *Introduction to Multiagent Systems*. John Wiley & Sons, Inc., 2001.
[15] K. P. Sycara, "Multiagent systems," *AI Magazine*, pp. 79-92, 1998.
[16] M. Zhou, K. McDermott, and P. A. Patel, "Petri net synthesis and analysis of a flexible manufacturing system cell," *IEEE Transactions on Systems, Man, and Cybernetics*, vol. 23, pp. 523-531, March 1993.
[17] A. A. Desrochers and R. Y. Al-Jaar, Applications of Petri Nets in Manufacturing Systems: Modeling, Control, and Performance Analysis. IEEE Press, 1995.
[18] M. Zhou, F. DiCesare, and A. A. Desrochers, "A hybrid methodology for synthesis of Petri net models for manufacturing systems," *IEEE Transactions on Robotics and Automation*, vol. 8, no. 3, pp. 350-361, 1992.
[19] R. Valette, "Analysis of Petri nets by stepwise refinements," *Journal of Computer and System Sciences*, vol. 18, no. 1, pp. 35-46, 1979.
[20] I. Suzuki and T. Murata, "A method for stepwise refinement and abstraction of Petri nets,"*Journal of Computer and System Sciences*, vol. 27, no. 1, pp. 51-76, 1983.
[21] K. H. Lee, J. Favrel, and P. Baptiste, "Generalized Petri net reduction method.," *IEEE Transactions on Systems Man and Cybernetics*, vol. 17, no. 2, pp. 297-303, 1987.
[22] K. H. Lee and J. Favrel, "Hierarchical reduction method for analysis and decomposition of Petri nets," *IEEE Transactions on Systems, Man, and Cybernetics*, vol. 15, no. 2, pp. 272-280, 1985.
[23] I. Suzuki and T. Murata, "Stepwise refinements of transitions and places," in *Selected Papers from the First and the Second European Workshop on Application and Theory of Petri Nets*, (London, UK), pp. 136-141, Springer-Verlag, 1982.
[24] A. Datta and S. Gosh, "Synthesis of a class of deadlock-free Petri nets," *Journal of the Association for Computing Machinery*, vol. 31, pp. 486-506, July 1984.
[25] G. Berthelot, "Checking properties of nets using transformations," in Advances in Petri Nets 1985, covers the 6th European Workshop on Applications and Theory in Petri Nets-selected papers, pp. 19-40, Springer-Verlag, 1986.
[26] M. D. Jeng and F. DiCesare, "A review of synthesis techniques for Petri nets," in *Rensselaer's Second International Conference on Computer Integrated Manufacturing*, pp. 348-355, 1990.

[27] M. D. Jeng and F. DiCesare, "A review of synthesis techniques for Petri nets with applications to automated manufacturing systems," *IEEE Transactions on Systems, Man and Cybernetics*, vol. 23, no. 1, pp. 301-312, 1993.
[28] M. D. Jeng, "A Petri net synthesis theory for modeling flexible manufacturing systems," *IEEE Transactions on Systems, Man, and Cybernetics, Part B: Cybernetics*, vol. 27, pp. 169-183, April 1997.

5

Control Analysis and Feedback Techniques for Multi Agent Robots

Salman Ahmed[1] and Mohd Noh Karsiti[2] and Robert N. K. Loh[3]
[1,2]Electrical & Electronic Engineering, Universiti Teknologi PETRONAS
[3]Electrical and Computer Engineering, Oakland University,
[1,2]Malaysia
[3]United States

1. Introduction

Multi agent robots involve a team of robots working together socially to achieve a task. Collaboration among agents is motivated by a need to complete complex tasks that require more capabilities than a single robot can provide. Applications of multi agent robots can be found in the fields of underwater robotics, air traffic control, intelligent highways, security patrols, tele-surgery and mines and ores detection (Bichhi & Pallottino, 2000; Ferber, 1999; Parker, 1994). The accuracy of task completion by multi agent robots depends on the control strategies implemented in the robots to minimize the effect of external disturbances and errors. Multi agent unicycle robots can be represented as an underactuated system in which the number of control inputs is less than the number of states. In such a system, the controllable degrees of freedom are less than the total degrees of freedom. Hence, the motion control problems for underactuated systems are of particular interest for research (Kolmanovsky & McClamroch, 1995).

1.1 Motion planning

Motion planning for multi agent robots involves the following basic motion tasks (Luca et. al. 2000).
Point to point motion: In point to point motion, the multi agent robots must reach a final goal starting from a given initial configuration. The trajectory or path for the multi agent robots is not specified in advance.
Trajectory tracking: In trajectory tracking, the multi agent robots must reach a final configuration following a certain desired trajectory in the cartesian space. The desired trajectory is a function of time.
In terms of control systems, point to point motion can be compared with a regulation control for an equilibrium point in the state space. Trajectory tracking can be compared with a tracking problem such as to minimize the error between the reference and desired trajectory to zero.

1.2 Feedback control techniques

In automatic control systems, feedback improves the system performance by completing the task even if external disturbances and initial errors are present. Hence, the effect of unmodeled events at running time, such as slipping of wheels or wrong initial localization, is minimized. Furthermore, feedback control techniques can be used to stabilize the system. There are various feedback control design techniques available for feedback control, some of which are listed as follows (Nise, 2004; Khalil, 2002; Slotine & Li, 1991).

- Root locus method
- PID method
- Poles placement
- Cascaded systems theory
- Linearization of corresponding error model
- Approximate linearization
- Feedback linearization

The design of nonlinear feedback control strategies is a challenging task. A common practice is to linearize the system. After linearizing the model of multi agent robotic system, feedback control strategies can be designed for trajectory tracking and point to point motion.

1.3 Formation control strategies

The control of multi agent robotic system requires coordination at different levels. At the lowest level, it is necessary for each robot to control its motion and to avoid collisions with its neighbors. Furthermore, the robotic agent should move along a desired trajectory. At an immediate supervisory level, it is necessary to maintain a certain formation strategy.

The various approaches to formation control can be divided roughly into three categories: behavior-based, virtual structure formation and leader-follower formation (Tabuada, et al., 2005). The behavior-based formation is a distributed approach (Balch & Arkin, 1998), while the virtual structure formation is a centralized approach (Tan & Lewis, 1997). Majority of the current algorithms that focus on behavior-based or virtual structure formation are implemented on robots having visual capabilities (Langer et al., 1994; Clark, 2004). Similarly, behavior-based formation focuses on peer to peer communication, whereas in this paper Bluetooth is considered, which acts in a master-slave fashion (Morrow, 2002). Therefore, leader-follower formation is the best available formation control and it is used as a formation control strategy for the multi agent nonholonomic robots (Desai, 1998).

In the leader-follower formation, one of the agent robots is designated as the leader and the others as followers. The leader agent plans and follows a desired trajectory. The follower agents follow the leader agent with a desired distance and separation bearing angle. The leader agent is responsible for guiding the formation.

There has been considerable research in designing feedback linearized strategies for trajectory tracking of multi agent robots. However, most of the feedback linearized strategies are designed either for a single robot (Oriolo, 2002) or for the follower robots using the leader-follower formation (Desai, 1998). Similarly, there have been feedback linearized strategies for vision-based multi agent robots (Das, 2002). In this chapter, the multi agent robots have communication abilities only. The principal investigation of this chapter is to present a comparative analysis of different feedback control strategies for multi agent robots having communication abilities. The comparative analysis is presented for trajectory tracking as well as posture stabilization of the multi agent robots. In this chapter, a development framework for simulation and implementation based on communication abilities is also presented for multi agent robots.

2. Kinematic model of leader-follower formation

A multi agent robot system can be described by its state, X, which is a composition of the individual robots states as

$$X = [x_1, x_2, \ldots, x_n]^T \,, \quad \dot{X} = F(X,t) \tag{1}$$

The state of each robot varies as a function of its continuous state, x, and the input vector, u. Also each robot receives information about the rest of the system, z. The input vector, u, depends on the discrete state of the robot, h, which can be either the leader, l, or follower, f, state. The state equations of each robot, $i = l, f$, can be expressed as

$$\dot{x}_i = f_{i,h}(x_i, u_i, \hat{z}_i) \tag{2}$$

To model the kinematics of the leader robot, l, in the 2D plane, the configuration $p_l = [x_l, y_l, \theta_l]^T$ (with respect to the global frame (X_G, Y_G) in Fig. 1) is used. This configuration of the robot stands for three degrees of freedom. Let the control inputs for the leader robot be denoted by v_l and ω_l. The equations for the leader robot can be written as

$$\begin{pmatrix} \dot{x}_l \\ \dot{y}_l \\ \dot{\theta}_l \end{pmatrix} = \begin{pmatrix} \cos\theta_l \\ \sin\theta_l \\ 0 \end{pmatrix} v_l + \begin{pmatrix} 0 \\ 0 \\ 1 \end{pmatrix} \omega_l \tag{3}$$

The wheels in the model of Eq. 3 are assumed not to slip and exhibit purely rolling motion. The same constraint is observed for the follower robots, f. The nonholonomic constraint is expressed as

$$-\dot{x}_i \sin\theta_i + \dot{y}_i \cos\theta_i = 0 \tag{4}$$

The follower robots are modeled relatively to the leader robot. The modeling of the follower robots depend on the formation controllers, which are discussed as follows.

2.1 Separation-bearing controller (SBC)

The separation bearing controller is used for two robots. The follower robot follows the leader while maintaining a desired relative distance and separation bearing angle with respect to the leader robot. Such type of leader-follower formation control strategy is also denoted by l–φ control strategy. A schematic for this control strategy is shown in Fig. 1.

Let φ_{lf} denote the separation bearing angle between the leader and follower robot. The separation distance between the center of axis between the rear wheels of the leader, and the front castor of the follower robot is denoted by l_{lf}. The position coordinates for the front castor of the follower robot is represented by (x, y). The distance between the front castor and the center of axis between the rear wheels for each robot is denoted by d. Let (x_l, y_l) represent the mid point on the axis between the rear wheels. The leader robot position is expressed by $p_l = [x_l, y_l, \theta_l]^T$ and the control inputs by $u_l = [v_l, \omega_l]^T$.. The follower robot position is represented by $p_f = [x_f, y_f, \theta_f]^T$ and the control inputs by $u_f = [v_f, \omega_f]^T$.

Knowing the leader robot position and the separation distance, the follower robot position can be calculated as follows.

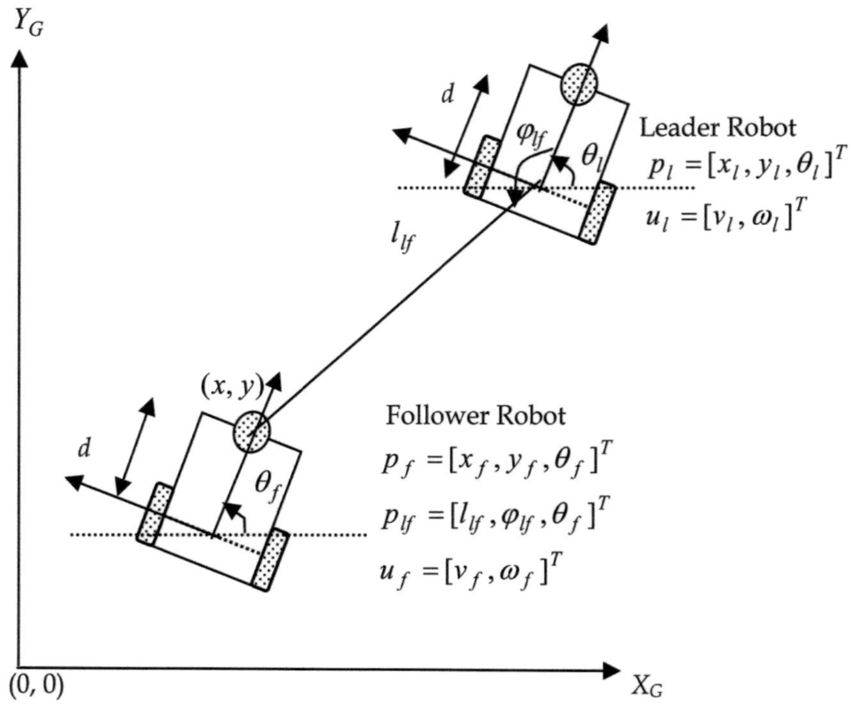

Fig. 1. Leader-follower formation using separation-bearing controller.

$$\begin{aligned} x_f &= x + d\cos\theta_f \\ y_f &= y + d\sin\theta_f \end{aligned} \tag{5}$$

where d is the distance between the mid point of the axis between rear wheel and the front castor wheel. The follower robot is modeled relatively to the leader robot as $p_{lf} = [l_{lf}, \varphi_{lf}, \theta_f]^T$. The new state vector, p_{lf}, can be expressed as given by Eq. (6).

$$\begin{aligned} l_{lf} &= \sqrt{(x_l - x_f - d\cos\theta_f)^2 + (y_l - y_f - d\sin\theta_f)^2} \\ \varphi_{lf} &= \pi - \arctan 2(y_f + d\sin\theta_f - y_l, x_l - x_f - d\cos\theta_f) - \theta_l \end{aligned} \tag{6}$$

Differentiating Eq. (6) and combining with Eq. (4), the kinematic model for the follower robot is obtained as

$$\begin{aligned} \dot{l}_{lf} &= v_f\cos\gamma - v_l\cos\varphi_{lf} + d\omega_f\sin\gamma \\ \dot{\varphi}_{lf} &= \frac{v_l\sin\varphi_{lf} - v_f\sin\gamma - \omega_l l_{lf} + d\omega_f\cos\gamma}{l_{lf}} \\ \dot{\theta}_f &= \omega_f \end{aligned} \tag{7}$$

where $\gamma = \theta_l - \theta_f + \varphi_{lf}$. In order to avoid collision between the leader and the follower robots, a requirement that $l_{lf} > 2d$ must be ensured.

2.2 Separation-separation controller (SSC)

This controller is used when multiple robots are present in the formation. Such type of control strategy is also denoted by l–l. A schematic for this control strategy is shown in Fig. 2. In the l – l formation strategy, the leader robot 2 is actually a follower relative to leader robot 1. The leader robot 2 can be modeled using l–φ controller. The follower robot can be expressed relative to the leader robot 1 and 2 as $p_f = [l_{1f}, l_{2f}, \theta_f]^T$. In the l – l control strategy, the aim is to maintain the desired lengths l_{1f}^d and l_{2f}^d with respect to both leader robots. Again, to avoid collision $l_{1f} > 2d$ and $l_{2f} > 2d$ must be ensured. The separation distances for the leader robots can be expressed as

$$\begin{aligned} l_{1f} &= \sqrt{(x_1 - x_f - d\cos\theta_f)^2 + (y_1 - y_f - d\sin\theta_f)^2} \\ l_{2f} &= \sqrt{(x_2 - x_f - d\cos\theta_f)^2 + (y_2 - y_f - d\sin\theta_f)^2} \end{aligned} \tag{8}$$

Differentiating Eq. (8), the kinematic model for the follower robot is obtained as

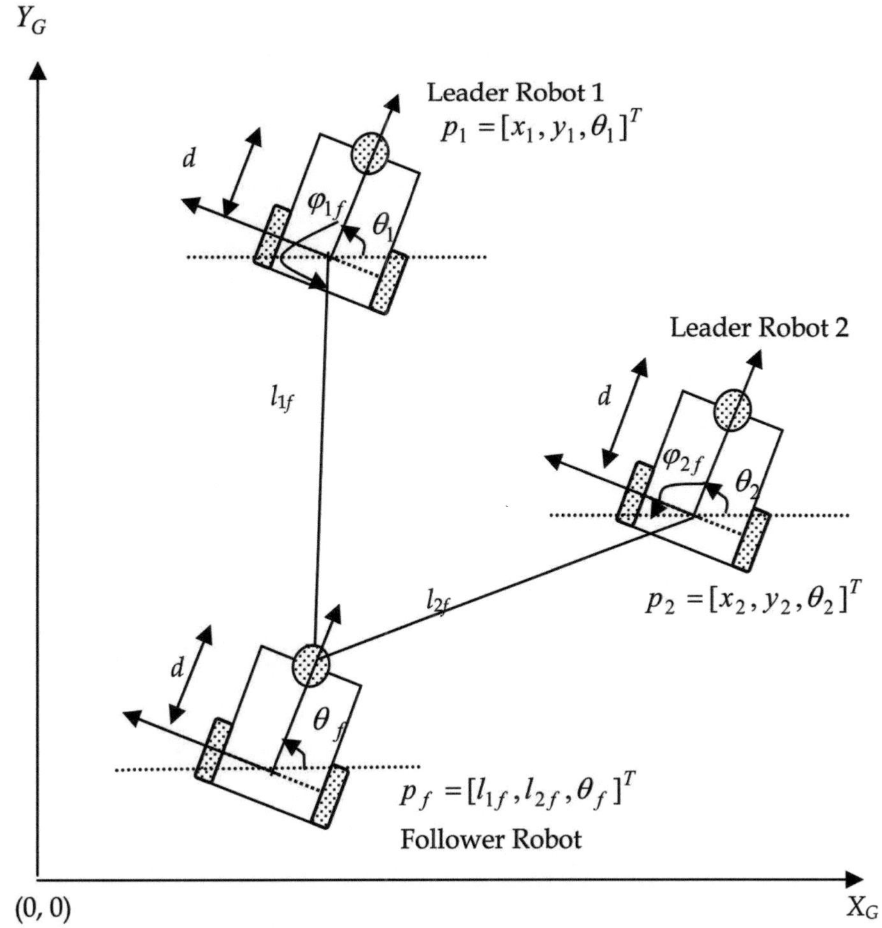

Fig. 2. Leader-follower formation using separation-separation controller.

$$\begin{aligned}
\dot{l}_{1f} &= v_f \cos\gamma_1 - v_1 \cos\varphi_{1f} + d\omega_f \sin\gamma_1 \\
\dot{l}_{2f} &= v_f \cos\gamma_2 - v_2 \cos\varphi_{2f} + d\omega_f \sin\gamma_2 \\
\dot{\theta}_f &= \omega_f
\end{aligned} \tag{9}$$

where $\gamma_1 = \theta_1 - \theta_f + \varphi_{1f}$ and $\gamma_2 = \theta_2 - \theta_f + \varphi_{2f}$.

3. Development framework for multi agent robots

3.1 Simulation platform

The simulation platform is implemented using MATLAB/Simulink. For simulation, Bluetooth USB dongles are used. Each dongle is connected to a computer. These dongles are configured to form a Bluetooth piconet. A MATLAB/Simulink session runs on each computer, which communicates with other sessions in the piconet. Each session models the leader-follower formation for the leader and follower robots. The master device in the piconet acts as the leader robot and the slaves act as follower robots. This simulation platform for the leader and follower robots is shown in Figs. 3 and 4, respectively.
For a desired and feasible goal trajectory, $[x_d(t), y_d(t)]^T$, the feedforward controller generates the feedforward control inputs, $[v_d, \omega_d]^T$, for the leader robot. Using the leader-follower strategy, the leader robot transmits its own control inputs to the follower robots. The control inputs are transmitted using the Bluetooth piconet. The follower robots receive the leader robot inputs and derive their own control inputs, $[v_f, \omega_f]^T$, using the leader-follower formation control and the information sent by the leader robot. The control inputs for both the leader and follower robots are fed into the feedback strategies. The feedback control strategies generate the actual inputs based on the feedforward inputs and feedback states of the robots.

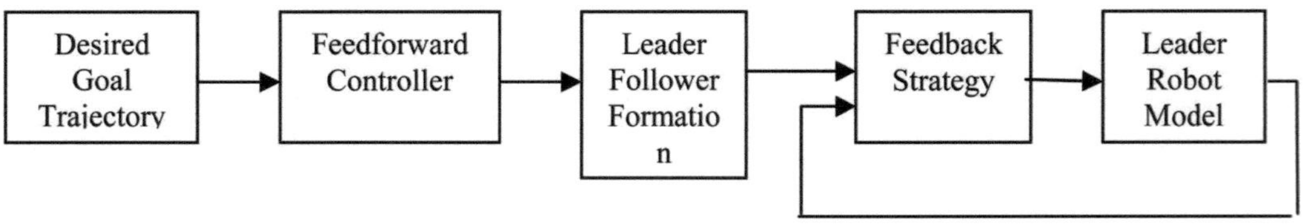

Fig. 3. Framework for the leader robot

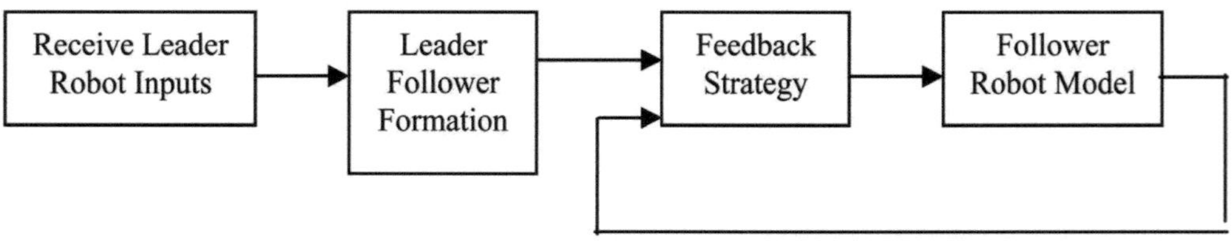

Fig. 4. Framework for the follower robot

3.2 Bluetooth library development

The Bluetooth protocol suite is implemented in software as well as in hardware device. The software protocol suite for Bluetooth piconet supports three modes of operation which includes Personal Area Network User, PANU, Group Adhoc Network, GN, and Network

Access Point, NAP. In this paper, the multi agent robots communicate using the GN mode. The message format used for communication conforms to the standard Agent Control Language, ACL, provided by Foundation for Intelligent Physical Agents (FIPA, 2002).
Currently, the TCPIP toolbox available in MATLAB does not provide support for TCP connections between two computers. Rather the TCPIP toolbox provides functions that can be used to acquire data from a network device such as an oscilloscope. So to overcome this limitation, a shared library was developed using Windows Socket programming (Rydesater, 2007). This shared library was then accessed in MATLAB to communicate with other MATLAB sessions in the Bluetooth piconet.

3.3 Feedforward controller

Assuming that the leader robot follows a desired cartesian trajectory $[x_d(t), y_d(t)]^T$ with $t \in [0, T]$. The flat outputs for the leader robot system are $[x_l(t), y_l(t)]^T$ (Luca et al., 2001). The flat outputs for a system are helpful in a way that all the system inputs, states and outputs can be determined algebraically from the flat outputs without integration. The desired orientation angle for the leader robot, θ_d, can be calculated as

$$\theta_d = \text{atan2}(\dot{y}_d, \dot{x}_d) \tag{10}$$

where atan2 is the fourth-quadrant inverse tangent and is undefined only if both arguments are zero. Assuming v_d and ω_d are the desired velocities for the leader robot, whereas the actual velocities are denoted by v and ω. Differentiating Eq. (3) with respect to time, the feedforward control inputs for the leader robot are computed as

$$v_d(t) = \pm\sqrt{\dot{x}_d^2(t) + \dot{y}_d^2(t)} \tag{11}$$

$$w_d(t) = \frac{\ddot{y}_d(t)\dot{x}_d(t) - \ddot{x}_d(t)\dot{y}_d(t)}{\dot{x}_d^2(t) + \dot{y}_d^2(t)} \tag{12}$$

The sign for $v_d(t)$ will determine the forward or backward motion of the robots. Eq. (12) is not defined when $v_d(t)$ is equal to zero.

4. Posture stabilization control strategies

The objective of posture stabilization controller is to reach a final desired configuration starting from an initial point, without the need to plan a trajectory. The available techniques are to use smooth time-varying feedback, non smooth time-varying feedback and design based on polar coordinates. All of these control strategies are discussed as follows.

4.1 Smooth time-varying feedback controller

The smooth time-varying feedback controller for posture stabilization was first presented in (Wit et al., 1994). Let the desired position for the leader robot be $p_d = [x_d, y_d, \theta_d]^T$, whereas the actual position is denoted by $p_l = [x_l, y_l, \theta_l]^T$. The error between the desired and actual position is expressed as

$$e = \begin{bmatrix} e_1 \\ e_2 \\ e_3 \end{bmatrix} = \begin{bmatrix} \cos\theta_l & \sin\theta_l & 0 \\ -\sin\theta_l & \cos\theta_l & 0 \\ 0 & 0 & 1 \end{bmatrix} \begin{bmatrix} x_d - x_l \\ y_d - y_l \\ \theta_d - \theta_l \end{bmatrix} \tag{13}$$

The feedback strategy using the smooth time-varying feedback controller is given as

$$\begin{aligned} u_1 &= -k_1(v_d(t), \omega_d(t))e_1, \\ u_2 &= -k_2 v_d(t)\frac{\sin e_3}{e_3}e_2 - k_3(v_d(t), \omega_d(t))e_3 \end{aligned} \tag{14}$$

where k_1, k_2 and k_3 are feedback gains, and. The feedback gains are expressed as

$$\begin{aligned} &k_1(v_d(t), \omega_d(t)) = k_3(v_d(t), \omega_d(t)) = 2\zeta a = 2\zeta\sqrt{w_d^2(t) + bv_d^2(t)} \\ &k_2 = b|v_d(t)| \end{aligned} \tag{15}$$

where b is a positive constant. For generating the actual control inputs, Eq. (16) is used.

$$\begin{aligned} v &= v_d \cos(\theta_d - \theta_l) + k_1(v_d(t), \omega_d(t))\,[\cos\theta(x_d - x_l) + \sin\theta(y_d - y_l)] \\ \omega &= \omega_d + k_4 v_d \frac{\sin(\theta_d - \theta_l)}{\theta_d - \theta_l}[\cos\theta(y_d - y_l) - \sin\theta(x_d - x_l)] + k_3(v_d, \omega_d)(\theta_d - \theta_l). \end{aligned} \tag{16}$$

The feedback control law expressed by Eq. (16) globally asymptotically stabilizes the origin at $e = 0$, which is demonstrated using Lyapunov stability theory.

4.2 Design based on polar coordinates

The control law for posture stabilization based on the polar coordinates was presented in (Aicardi et al., 1995; Luca et al., 2001). This control design is based on the change of original coordinates to polar coordinates. Let ψ be the distance of the reference point (x_l, y_l) of the leader robot from the goal, μ be the angle of the pointing vector to the goal with respect to the robot main axis and ϕ be the angle of the same pointing vector with respect to the x-axis of the robot. The state transformation is given as

$$\begin{aligned} \psi &= \sqrt{x^2 + y^2} \\ \mu &= \tan^{-1}(y/x) - \theta + \pi \\ \phi &= \mu + \theta \end{aligned} \tag{17}$$

Differentiating Eq. (17), the transformed kinematic equations can be written as

$$\begin{aligned} \dot{\psi} &= -v\cos\mu \\ \dot{\mu} &= \frac{\sin\mu}{\psi}v - \omega \\ \dot{\phi} &= v\frac{\sin\mu}{\psi} \end{aligned} \tag{18}$$

The feedback control law based on polar coordinates is given as follows

$$v = k_1 \psi \cos \mu$$
$$\omega = k_2 \mu + k_1 \frac{\sin \mu \cos \mu}{\mu}(\mu + k_3 \phi) \qquad (19)$$

The feedback law of Eq. (19) globally asymptotically stabilizes the system.

4.3 Dynamic feedback linearized controller

The dynamic feedback linearized controller was presented in (Luca et al., 2000) The feedback control law is given as

$$r_1 = -k_{p1}(x) - k_{d1}(\dot{x})$$
$$r_2 = -k_{p2}(y) - k_{d2}(\dot{y}) \qquad (20)$$

where k_{p1}, k_{p2}, k_{d1}, k_{d2} are the feedback gains. The feedback law of Eq. (20) yields exponential convergence from any initial configuration to the origin

5. Trajectory tracking control strategies for the leader robot

In order to track the correct goal trajectory, the feedforward controller generates the velocity inputs. The inputs commands are generated for the leader robot and transmitted to the follower robots using Bluetooth. The kinematics of the leader and the follower robots is modeled using Simulink. Different feedback control strategies are chosen from the literature based on their properties which are briefly discussed below.

Feedback control strategies are designed for the leader as well as follower robots. For the leader robot, the feedback control strategies involve designing strategies for point stabilization and trajectory tracking. For the follower robots, it involves designing strategies for trajectory tracking only. The feedback control strategies are presented as follows.

5.1 Feedback strategy based on approximate linearization

The control objective of feedback controller is to drive the errors $[x_d - x, y_d - y, \theta_d - \theta]^T$ to zero. Linearizing the error dynamics about the equilibrium point, $e = 0$ and $u = 0$, the feedback strategy is expressed as follows (Oriolo et al.,2002).

$$v = v_d \cos(\theta_d - \theta_l) + k_1[\cos\theta(x_d - x_l) + \sin\theta(y_d - y_l)]$$
$$\omega = \omega_d + k_2 \operatorname{sign}(v_d)[\cos\theta(y_d - y_l) - \sin\theta(x_d - x_l)] + \quad k_3(\theta_d - \theta_l) \qquad (21)$$

The feedback control strategy of Eq. (21) results in a time-varying system. This means that if the eigenvalues are constant and with negative real part, asymptotic stability is not guaranteed because the system is still time-varying.

5.2 Feedback strategy using cascaded systems theory

This controller was proposed in (Lefeber et al., 2001). The control law is given by Eq. (22)

$$v = v_d + c_2 e_1 - c_3 \omega_d e_2, \qquad c_2 > 0, c_3 > -1$$
$$\omega = \omega_d + c_1 e_3, \qquad c_1 > 0 \qquad (22)$$

The control law of Eq. (22) is K-exponentially stable if v_d is bounded and ω_d is persistently exciting. A small modification to this law was also proposed, which is

$$\begin{aligned} v &= v_d + c_2 e_1 - c_3 \omega_d e_2, \qquad && c_2 > 0, c_3 > -1 \\ \omega &= \omega_d + c_1 \sin e_3, && c_1 > 0 \end{aligned} \tag{23}$$

The feedback control strategy of Eq. (23) results in local uniform exponential stable system if v_d is bounded and ω_d is persistently exciting.

5.3 Feedback strategy based on linearization of error model

This control strategy was presented in (Kanayama et al., 1991). The control law is given as

$$\begin{aligned} v &= v_d \cos e_3 + K_x e_1, \qquad && K_x > 0 \\ \omega &= \omega_d + v_d (K_y e_2 + K_\theta \sin e_3), && K_y > 0, K_\theta > 0 \end{aligned} \tag{24}$$

The stability analysis of the control law expressed in Eq. (24) states that if $v_d > 0$, then the system is locally asymptotically stable. Furthermore, if v_d and ω_d are both continuous, v_d, ω_d, K_x, K_θ are all bounded and if $\dot{v}_d$ and $\dot{\omega}_d$ are both sufficiently small, then the system is locally uniformly asymptotically stable.

5.4 Feedback strategy based on full state linearized via dynamic feedback

This feedback strategy was proposed in (Oriolo et al., 2002). The dynamic state feedback compensator is given as

$$\begin{aligned} v &= a(q,\xi) + b(q,\xi) r \\ \xi &= c(q,\xi) + d(q,\xi) r \end{aligned} \tag{25}$$

where $\xi(t) \in \Re^v$ is the compensator state vector of dimensions v, and $r(t) \in \Re^v$ is the auxiliary input. For the system modeled by Eq. (3), the output is defined as

$$z = \begin{bmatrix} x \\ y \end{bmatrix}, \quad \dot{z} = \begin{bmatrix} \cos\theta & 0 \\ \sin\theta & 0 \end{bmatrix} \begin{bmatrix} v \\ \omega \end{bmatrix} \tag{26}$$

From Eq. (26), it can be observed that only v affects $\dot{z}$, while ω cannot be recovered. In order to proceed, an integrator, ξ, is added on the linear velocity input v, as

$$\xi = v, \quad \dot{\xi} = a \tag{27}$$

where a is the new input representing the linear acceleration of the leader robot. In terms of ξ, Eq. (26) can be expressed as

$$\dot{z} = \begin{bmatrix} \cos\theta & 0 \\ \sin\theta & 0 \end{bmatrix} \begin{bmatrix} \xi \\ \omega \end{bmatrix} \Rightarrow \dot{z} = \xi \begin{bmatrix} \cos\theta \\ \sin\theta \end{bmatrix} \tag{28}$$

Differentiating Eq. (27), the following is obtained

$$\ddot{z} = \dot{\xi}\begin{bmatrix} \cos\theta \\ \sin\theta \end{bmatrix} + \xi\begin{bmatrix} -\sin\theta \\ \cos\theta \end{bmatrix}\dot{\theta} \tag{29}$$

Substituting the value of $\dot{\xi}$ from Eq. (27) and $\dot{\theta} = \omega$, the following is obtained

$$\ddot{z} = a\begin{bmatrix} \cos\theta \\ \sin\theta \end{bmatrix} + \xi\begin{bmatrix} -\sin\theta \\ \cos\theta \end{bmatrix}\omega = \begin{bmatrix} \cos\theta & -\xi\sin\theta \\ \sin\theta & \xi\cos\theta \end{bmatrix}\begin{bmatrix} a \\ \omega \end{bmatrix} \tag{30}$$

From Eq. (30), it can be observed that the decoupling matrix multiplied with the modified input (a, ω) is nonsingular provided that $\xi \neq 0$. Let $\ddot{z} = r$, so the inputs can be obtained as

$$\begin{bmatrix} a \\ \omega \end{bmatrix} = \begin{bmatrix} \cos\theta & -\xi\sin\theta \\ \sin\theta & \xi\cos\theta \end{bmatrix}^{-1}\begin{bmatrix} r_1 \\ r_2 \end{bmatrix} = \begin{bmatrix} \cos\theta & \sin\theta \\ -\sin\theta/\xi & \cos\theta/\xi \end{bmatrix}\begin{bmatrix} r_1 \\ r_2 \end{bmatrix} \tag{31}$$

Substituting the values for original inputs, the resulting dynamic compensator and the inputs are

$$\begin{aligned} v &= \xi \\ \omega &= \frac{r_2\cos\theta - r_1\sin\theta}{\xi} \\ \dot{\xi} &= r_1\cos\theta + r_2\sin\theta \end{aligned} \tag{32}$$

As one integrator, ξ, was added, hence the order of the dynamic compensator is one. The new coordinates can be written as

$$\begin{aligned} z_1 &= x \\ z_2 &= y \\ z_3 &= \dot{x} = \xi\cos\theta \\ z_4 &= \dot{y} = \xi\sin\theta \end{aligned} \tag{33}$$

The extended system of Eq. (33) is fully linearized in a controllable form. The decoupled chain of input output integrators can be written as

$$\begin{aligned} \ddot{z}_1 &= r_1 \\ \ddot{z}_2 &= r_2 \end{aligned} \tag{34}$$

Assuming that the robot must follow a smooth output trajectory $[x_d(t), y_d(t)]^T$. The globally exponentially stabilizing feedback law for the trajectory is given as

$$\begin{aligned} r_1 &= \ddot{x}_d(t) + k_{p1}(x_d(t) - x) + k_{d1}(\dot{x}_d(t) - \dot{x}) \\ r_2 &= \ddot{y}_d(t) + k_{p2}(y_d(t) - y) + k_{d2}(\dot{y}_d(t) - \dot{y}) \end{aligned} \tag{35}$$

with PD gains chosen as $k_{pi} > 0$, $k_{di} > 0$, for $i = 1,2$. The values of $\dot{x}$ and $\dot{y}$ can be computed from Eq. (33) as a function of the robot state and the compensator state, ξ. The values of the feedback gains are chosen such that the polynomial expressed by Eq. (36) is Hurwitz.

$$\lambda^2 + k_{di}\lambda + k_{pi}, \quad i = 1,2 \tag{36}$$

6. Feedback strategies for the follower robots

In this section, the feedback strategies for the follower robots are presented. The follower robots follow the leader robot with a desired distance and angle. The feedback laws as presented for both of the formation control strategies.

6.1 Feedback strategy for separation bearing controller

The kinematic model for the follower robot using the separation bearing controller was expressed in Eq. (7). The kinematic model can be written in compact form as given as

$$\begin{aligned} \dot{z}_{lf} &= G_{\mathrm{SB}}(z_{lf}, \gamma)u_f + F_{\mathrm{SB}}(z_{lf})u_l \\ \dot{\theta}_f &= \omega_f \end{aligned} \tag{37}$$

where $z_{lf} = (l_{lf}, \varphi_{lf})$, $u_f = (v_f, \omega_f)$, $u_l = (v_l, \omega_l)$ and

$$\begin{aligned} G_{\mathrm{SB}} &= \begin{bmatrix} \cos\gamma & d\sin\gamma \\ \dfrac{-\sin\gamma}{l_{lf}} & \dfrac{d\cos\gamma}{l_{lf}} \end{bmatrix} \\ F_{\mathrm{SB}} &= \begin{bmatrix} -\cos\varphi_{lf} & 0 \\ \sin\varphi_{lf} / l_{lf} & -1 \end{bmatrix} \end{aligned} \tag{38}$$

The input-output linearization technique begins by defining the output as $z_{lf} = (l_{lf}, \varphi_{lf})$ (Desai, 1998). Differentiating the output, Eq. (39) is obtained.

$$\dot{z}_{lf} = G_{\mathrm{SB}}(z_{lf}, \gamma)u_f + F_{\mathrm{SB}}(z_{lf})u_l = A(z_{lf})u_f + B \tag{39}$$

The determinant of the decoupling matrix, $A(z_{lf})$, is $d/l \neq 0$. Since $A(z_{lf})$ is nonsingular, the control velocities for the follower robot can be expressed as

$$u_f = G_{\mathrm{SB}}^{-1}(p_{\mathrm{SB}} - F_{\mathrm{SB}}u_l) \tag{40}$$

where p_{SB} is an auxiliary control input given as

$$p_{\mathrm{SB}} = K\tilde{z}_{lf} = \begin{bmatrix} k_1 & 0 \\ 0 & k_2 \end{bmatrix} \begin{bmatrix} l_{lf}^d - l_{lf} \\ \varphi_{lf}^d - \varphi_{lf} \end{bmatrix} \tag{41}$$

with $k_1, k_2 > 0$ as the controller gains. The control inputs for the follower robot are expressed as

$$v_f = \rho - d\omega_f \tan\gamma$$

$$\omega_f = \frac{\cos\gamma}{d}\{k_a l_{lf}(\varphi_{lf}^d - \varphi_{lf}) - v_l \sin\varphi_{lf} + l_{lf}\omega_l + \rho\sin\gamma\}$$

where (42)

$$\rho = \frac{k_b(l_{lf}^d - l_{lf}) + v_l \cos\varphi_{lf}}{\cos\gamma}$$

$$\gamma = \varphi_{lf} + \theta_l - \theta_f$$

The stability of the controller expressed by Eq. (42) was presented in (Desai, 1998; Desai et. al., 1998). If the linear velocity of the leader robot is lower bounded *i.e.* $v_l > 0$, angular velocity is bounded *i.e.* $\omega_l < \omega_{max}$, and the initial orientation is such that $| \theta_l(0) - \theta_f(0) | < \pi$, then the system of Eq. (42) is stable and the output error converges to zero exponentially.

6.2 Feedback strategy for separation-separation controller

Using input-output linearization techniques the control law for the follower robot is given as

$$v_f = \frac{k_1(l_{1f}^d - l_{lf}) + v_1\cos\varphi_{1f} - d\omega_f \sin\gamma_1}{\cos\gamma_1}$$

$$\omega_f = \frac{k_1(l_{1f}^d - l_{lf})\cos\gamma_2 + v_1\cos\varphi_{1f}\cos\gamma_2}{d\sin(\gamma_1 - \gamma_2)} + \frac{v_2\cos\varphi_{2f}\cos\gamma_1 - k_2(l_{2f}^d - l_{2f})\cos\gamma_1}{d\sin(\gamma_1 - \gamma_2)} \qquad (43)$$

where

$$\gamma_i = \varphi_{if} + \theta_i - \theta_f, \qquad i = 1,2$$

The stability analysis of the feedback control strategy expressed in Eq. (43) was presented in (Desai, 1998; Desai et al., 1998). Assuming the linear velocity of the leader robot 1 is lower bounded *i.e.* $v_1 > 0$, angular velocity is bounded *i.e.* $\omega_1 < \omega_{max}$, and the relative orientation between the robots is such that $| \theta_l(0) - \theta_i(0) | < \pi$ with $i = 2, f$. If the control input u_{2f} is obtained using feedback linearization, then the system of Eq. (43) is stable and the output converges exponentially to the desired value z_d.

7. Simulation results

The above stated feedback laws for posture stabilization and trajectory tracking were simulated using MATLAB/Simulink. The multi agent robot system using leader-follower formation was modeled in MATLAB/Simulink. The results of simulation are summarized as follows.

7.1 Trajectory tracking controllers for the leader robot

In the first test, the desired trajectory was defined as follows.

$$x_d(t) = 10\sin(t/20),\; y_d(t) = 10\sin(t/40) \qquad (44)$$

The desired trajectory of Eq. (44) begins at the origin (0, 0). The trajectory completes a full cycle when $T = 2\pi\ (40) \approx 251.3$ sec. The actual trajectory and the error norm using full state dynamic feedback linearized controller are shown in Fig. 5. The values for different parameters in the feedback controllers are listed in Table 1. The error statistics for the given trajectory are summarized in Table 2.

Controllers	Parameters values
Feedforward	$v_d(0)$= 0.0125 m/sec
Approximate linearized feedback	$\zeta = 0.5$, $b = 2$
Cascaded systems feedback	$c_1 = 216.9$, $c_2 = 1.355$ and $c_3 = -0.414$
Linearization of corresponding error model	$K_x = 10$, $K_y = 0.0064$ and $K_\theta = 0.16$
Dynamic linearized feedback	$k_{d1} = k_{d2} = 0.7$, $k_{p1} = k_{p2} = 1$, $\zeta(0) = v(0)$

Table 1. Parameters values for different feedback controllers

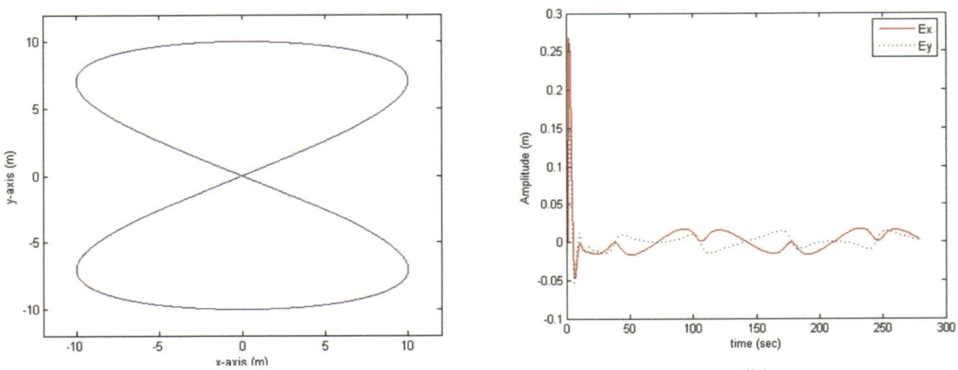

(a) (b)

Fig. 5. (a) Actual trajectory by the leader robot (Eq. 44) using full state dynamic feedback linearized controller (b) Norm of error for trajectory of Eq. (44) using full state dynamic feedback linearized controller

Statistical parameter	Mean (m)	Standard Deviation (m)	Variance (m)
Approximate linearized	0.1622	0.7746	0.6001
Cascaded systems controller	0.5154	0.6758	0.4568
Linearization of corresponding error model	3.3460	2.9895	8.9369
Full state linearized via dynamic feedback	0.0192	0.0410	0.00017

Table 2. Error statistics using different feedback controllers for trajectory of Eq. (44)

In the second series of simulation, the desired trajectory was defined as follows.

$$x_d(t) = t\,,\ y_d(t) = 10\sin(t) \tag{45}$$

The desired trajectory of Eq. (45) begins at the origin (0, 0) and is a sinusoidal signal. This trajectory is shown in for $T = 1000$ sec. The same values of Table 1 for the parameters of the feedback controllers were used. Table 3 summarizes the error statistics for the given trajectory using different feedback controllers. The actual trajectory using full state linearized via dynamic feedback controller is shown in Fig. 6. In the third series of simulation, the desired trajectory was defined as follows.

$$x_d(t) = 10\cos(t/20)\,, y_d(t) = 10\sin(t/20) \tag{46}$$

The desired trajectory of Eq. (46) begins at the origin (10, 0) and completes a full cycle when $T = 2\pi\,(20) \approx 125.67$ sec. The leader robot is assumed to be at the origin (0, 0). The actual trajectory for the leader robot using approximate linearized and cascaded systems controller is shown in Fig. 7. The actual trajectory using linearization of corresponding error model and full state linearized via dynamic feedback controller is shown in Fig. 8. Table 4 summarizes the error statistics for the given trajectory using different feedback controllers.

Statistical parameter	Mean (m)	Standard Deviation (m)	Variance (m)
Approximate linearized	0.2808	0.2619	0.0686
Cascaded systems controller	0.6908	0.6538	0.4274
Linearization of corresponding error model	1.0406	0.8041	0.6465
Full state linearized via dynamic feedback	0.2265	0.6846	0.4687

Table 3. Error statistics using different feedback controllers for trajectory of Eq. (45)

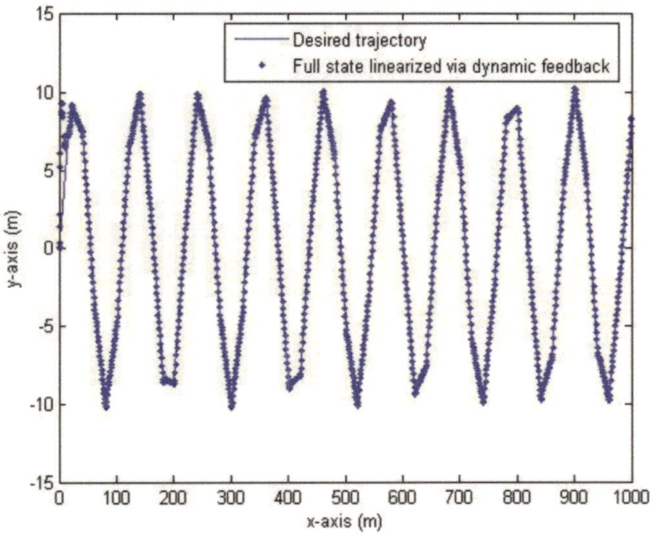

Fig. 6. Actual trajectory for Eq. (45) using full state dynamic feedback linearized controller

Statistical parameter	Mean (m)	Standard Deviation (m)	Variance (m)
Approximate linearized	0.9627	2.4787	6.1438
Cascaded systems controller	9.7688	0.7949	0.6319
Linearization of corresponding error model	11.3544	1.3286	1.7651
Full state linearized via dynamic feedback	1.0957	2.8231	7.9700

Table 4. Error statistics using different feedback controllers for trajectory of Eq. (46)

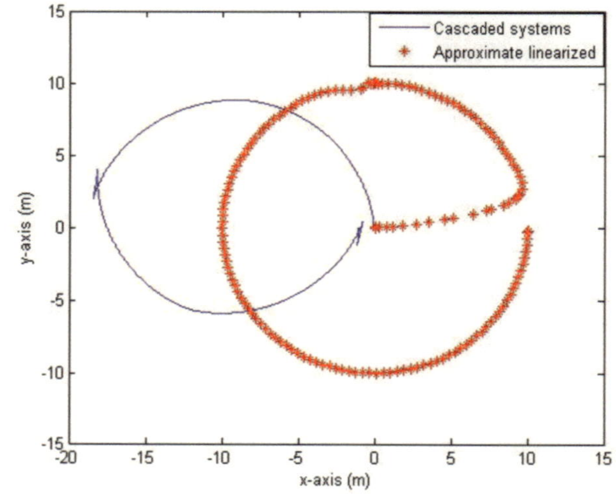

Fig. 7. Actual trajectory for Eq. (46) using approximate linearized and cascaded systems controller

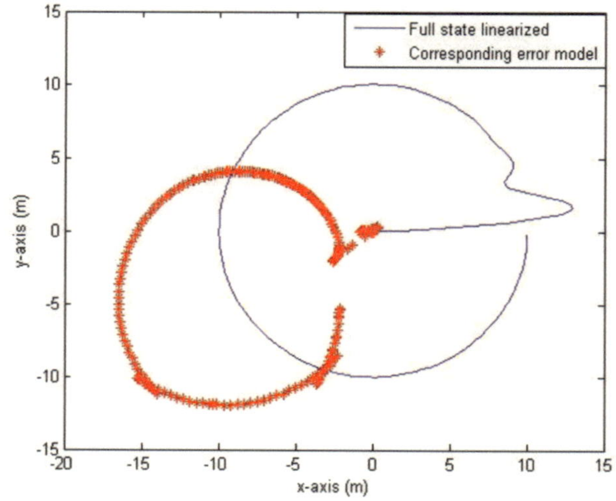

Fig. 8. Actual trajectory for Eq. (46) using linearization of corresponding error model & full state dynamic feedback linearized controller

Based on the above simulation results for the leader robot, it is observed that the full state linearized via dynamic feedback controller minimizes the mean of error more rapidly for the given trajectories. The cascaded systems and linearization of corresponding error model controllers fail to track the correct trajectory of Eq. (46). The reason for failure to track the correct trajectory using cascaded systems controller is that one of the conditions for stability using cascaded systems controller is that ω_d should be persistently exciting. As in trajectory of Eq. (46), ω_d is not persistently exciting, so the controller can not correctly track the desired trajectory. Using the controller based on linearization of corresponding error model, the system is stable provided $\dot{\omega}_d$ is sufficiently small, which is not the case here. Therefore, the cascaded systems controller and controller based on linearization of corresponding error model fail to track the desired trajectory of Eq. (46). Therefore, it can be concluded for the leader robot, that the full state linearized via dynamic feedback is the preferred control strategy for the given trajectories.

7.2 Trajectory tracking controllers for the follower robots

For the follower robots using the separation bearing controller, the following parameters were considered.

$$\begin{aligned} l_{lf}^d &= 2 \\ \varphi_{lf}^d &= \pi / 3 \\ k_1 &= k_2 = 1 \\ d &= 1 \end{aligned} \tag{47}$$

The trajectory of Eq. (44) (eight shaped) and Eq. (46) (circular shaped) were used as the desired reference trajectory for the leader robot. The full state linearized via dynamic feedback controller was used by the leader robot. The actual trajectories for the leader-follower formation using Eq. (44) and (46) for separation bearing controller are shown in Figs. 9 and 10, respectively.

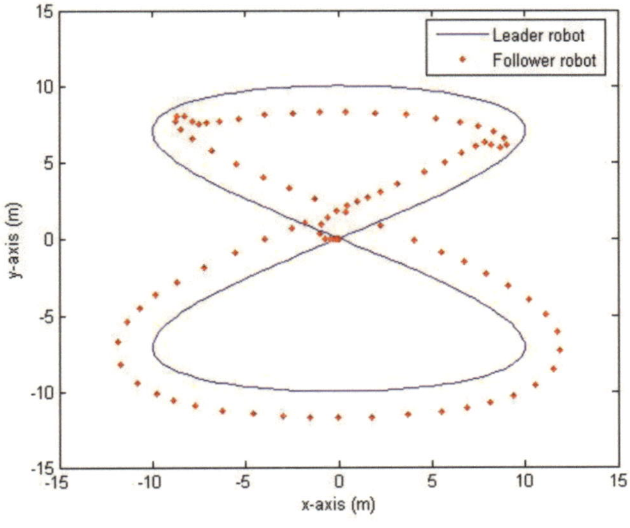

Fig. 9. Actual trajectory using separation bearing controller for Eq. (44)

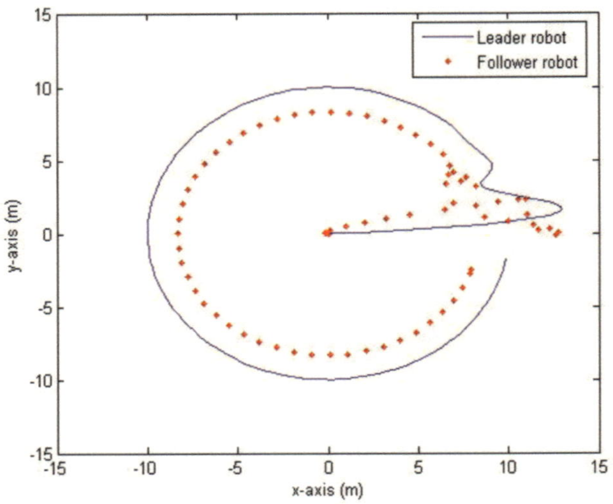

Fig. 10. Actual trajectory using separation bearing controller for Eq. (46)

In another set of simulation, the separation bearing angle was changed as follows.

$$\begin{aligned} \varphi_{lf}^{d} &= \pi/3 \quad \text{for } t < 100 \\ \varphi_{lf}^{d} &= \pi + \pi/3 \quad \text{for } t \geq 100 \end{aligned} \tag{48}$$

The actual trajectory for the leader-follower formation using Eq. (48) is shown in Fig. 11.

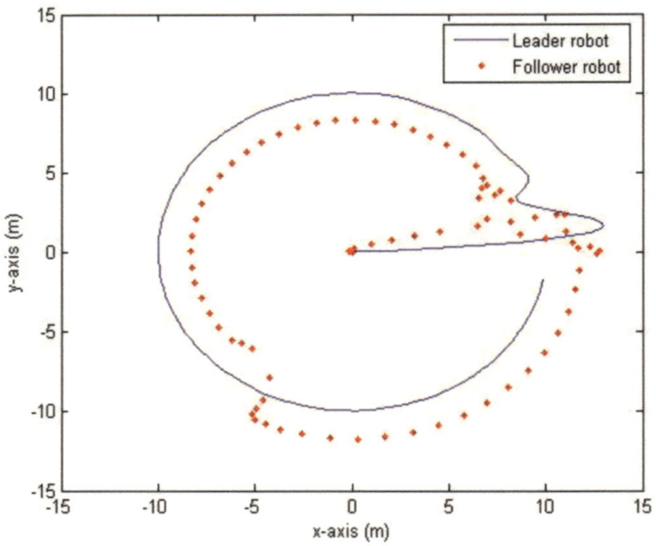

Fig. 11. Actual trajectory using separation bearing controller for Eq. (46)

For the follower robots, using the separation-separation controller, the following parameters were considered.

$$
\begin{aligned}
&l_{1f}^{d} = 2 \\
&l_{2f}^{d} = 2 \\
&\varphi_{1f}^{d} = 3\pi / 2 = (240°) \\
&\varphi_{2f}^{d} = 2\pi / 3 = (120°) \\
&k_1 = k_2 = 1 \\
&d = 1
\end{aligned}
\tag{49}
$$

The actual trajectory for the leader-follower formation using the trajectory defined by Eq. (44) and (46) for separation-separation controller is shown in Figs. 12 and 13, respectively.

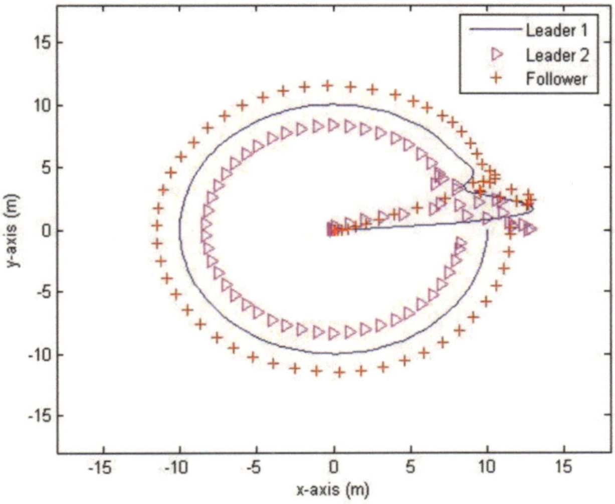

Fig. 12. Actual trajectory using separation-separation controller for Eq. (44)

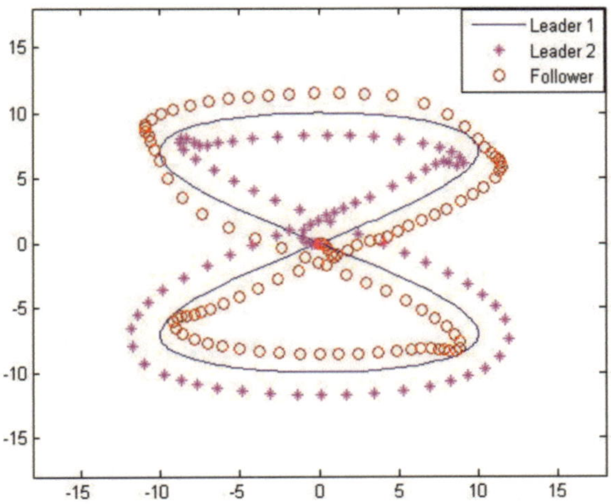

Fig. 13. Actual trajectory using separation-separation controller for Eq. (46)

Based on the simulation results, it is observed that the input-output feedback linearization for the follower robot minimizes the error between the desired and actual formation. Even, if the parameter values of the separation bearing and separation-separation controllers are changed dynamically at run time, the feedback linearized control strategies successfully minimizes the error between the desired and actual trajectory. Hence, the input-output linearized feedback controller is the preferred controller for separation bearing and separation-separation formation control.

7.3 Posture stabilization controllers for the multi agent robots

For posture stabilization, two different goal points were selected as follows. The initial starting position of the leader and follower robots is (-10,-10). The first goal point was defined to reach the origin point (0, 0). The second goal point was to reach the point (-10, 10). The trajectory for the leader robot is not defined. The objective of the leader robot is to move towards the goal point. The goal of the follower robots is to follow the leader robot. The simulation results are provided for the leader robot and finally, using the dynamic feedback linearized controller, the follower robots are also considered. The results of the posture stabilization controllers are as follows.

7.3.1 Smooth time-varying feedback controller

The following parameters were used for the smooth time-varying posture stabilization feedback controller of Eq. (16).

$$\begin{aligned} y_d(t) &= 0 \\ \theta_d(t) &= 0 \\ \omega_d(t) &= 0 \\ v_d(t) &= \dot{x}_d(t) = -k_5 x_d(t) + g(e,t) \end{aligned} \tag{50}$$

where

$$g(e,t) = \frac{\exp(k_6 e_2) - 1}{\exp(k_6 e_2) + 1} \sin t$$

The following values of the gains are used.

$$\begin{aligned} k_1 &= 0.5 \\ k_4 &= 2 \\ k_3 &= 1 \\ k_5 &= 1 \\ k_6 &= 50 \end{aligned} \tag{51}$$

The leader robot is assumed to be at the point (-10, -10). The results of smooth time-varying posture stabilization controller for the first and second goal points are shown in Fig. 14 and 15, respectively.

7.3.2 Polar coordinates feedback controller

The following parameters were used for the polar coordinates posture stabilization controller.

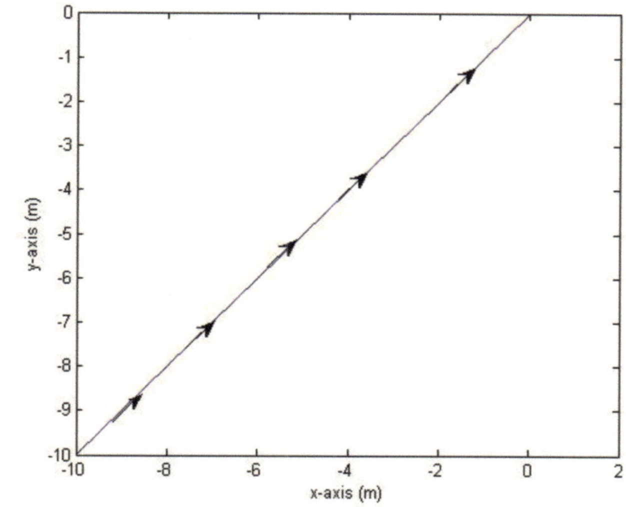

Fig. 14. Actual point to point motion using time-varying feedback controller for the first goal point.

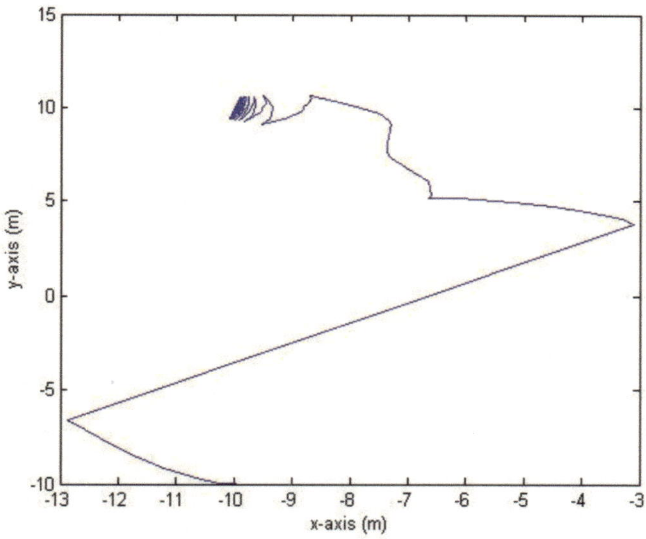

Fig. 15. Actual point to point motion using time-varying feedback controller for the second goal point.

$$\begin{aligned} k_1 &= 1 \\ k_2 &= 3 \\ k_3 &= 2 \end{aligned} \tag{52}$$

The robot is assumed to be at the point (-10, -10). The results of point to point motion using this controller for the first and second goal points are shown in Figs. 16 and 17, respectively.

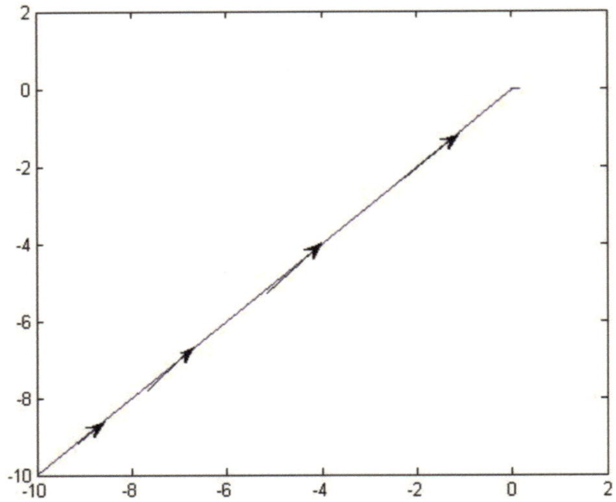

Fig. 16. Actual point to point motion using polar coordinates feedback controller for the first goal point

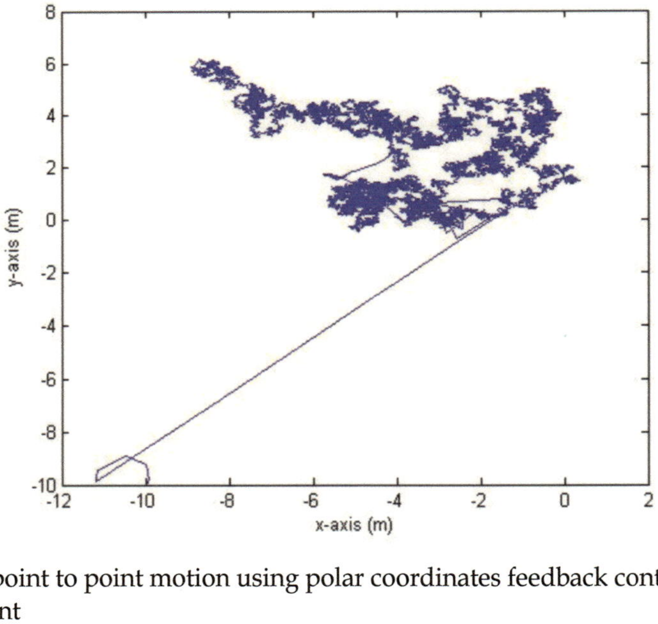

Fig. 17. Actual point to point motion using polar coordinates feedback controller for the second goal point

7.3.3 Full state linearized feedback controller

The following parameters were used for the full state linearized dynamic feedback controller.

$$\begin{aligned} k_{p1} &= 2 \\ k_{d1} &= 3 \\ k_{p2} &= 12 \\ k_{d2} &= 7 \end{aligned} \tag{53}$$

The robot is assumed to be at the point (-10, -10) and the goal point is origin. The results of point to point motion using this controller for the first and second goal points are shown in Figs. 18 and 19, respectively.

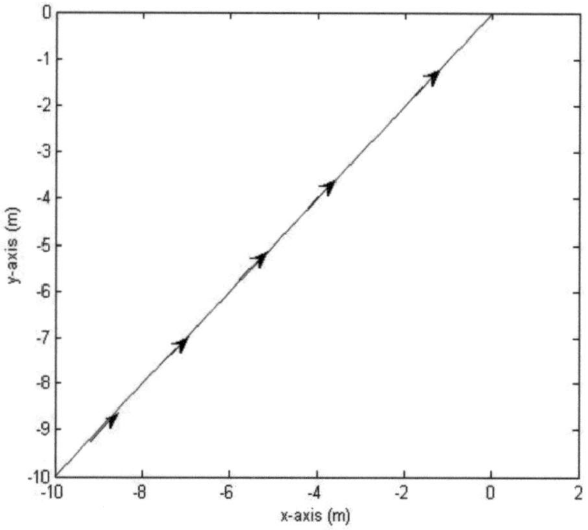

Fig. 18. Actual point to point motion using full state linearized via dynamic feedback controller for the first goal point

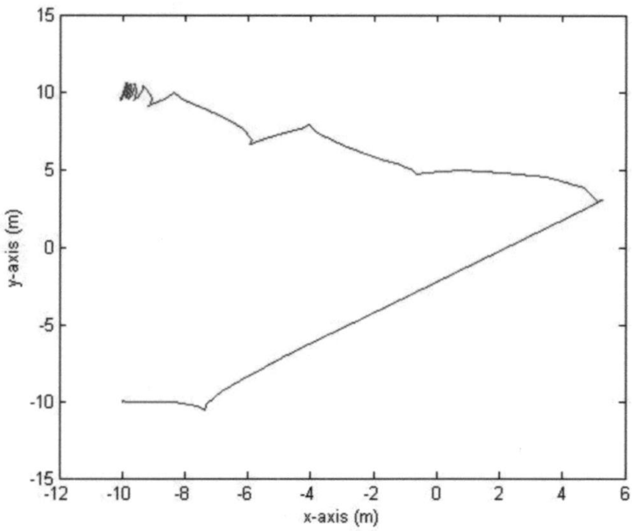

Fig. 19. Actual point to point motion using full state linearized via dynamic feedback controller for the second goal point

Based on the above results, it is found that the posture stabilization feedback controller based on polar coordinates fails to eliminate the error between the desired and the actual goal point. This can be seen in Fig. 19 where the desired goal point is (-10, 10). Although the robot is near to the goal point, still it does not converge to the goal point. The robot achieves the correct goal configuration using the smooth time-varying and dynamic feedback linearized controller. For the follower robots, using SBC the result is shown in Fig. 20.

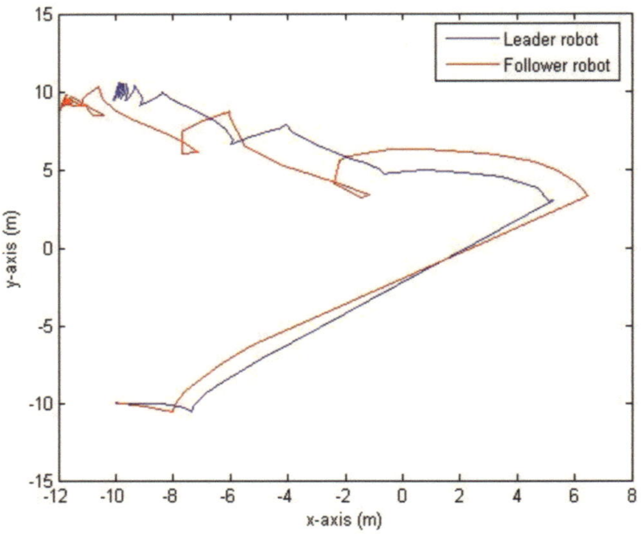

Fig. 20. Actual point to point motion using feedback linearized controllers for SBC formation

8. Conclusions & future work

In this paper, a simulation framework based on the kinematic model for the multi agent robots using the leader-follower formation was presented. The design of feedback controllers for leader-follower formation using feedback linearization techniques was also presented. The follower robots derived their inputs based on the control inputs sent by the leader robot. The leader robot transmitted its control inputs to the follower using the Bluetooth piconet profile.

The posture stabilization controllers using smooth time-varying, polar coordinates and dynamic feedback controller were simulated for the leader robot. For trajectory tracking, the reference trajectory was generated using the feedforward command controller. The multi agent nonholonomic robotic system was modeled using MATLAB/Simulink and the feedback strategies were simulated for a given set of reference trajectories. Based on the simulation results for the various trajectories, the following conclusions are made:

- For the leader robot, the full state linearized controller via dynamic feedback minimizes the mean of error more rapidly than the other feedback strategies.
- The full state linearized dynamic feedback controller for the leader robot achieves posture stabilization.
- The feedback strategies designed using cascaded systems theory and using linearization of corresponding error model fail to track the trajectory if the leader robot's starting point and the trajectory starting point is not the same (circular shaped trajectory).

- The feedback strategy designed using approximated linearization results in a time-varying controller. Hence, asymptotic stability is not guaranteed.
- For the follower robot, the input-output feedback linearized controllers minimize the error between the actual and the desired trajectory.
- If the formation structure is changed dynamically at run-time, the input-output linearized feedback controllers minimize the effect of disturbances and errors.

In summary, the feedback linearized techniques for multi agent nonholonomic robots can more rapidly minimize the error for trajectory tracking and achieve posture stabilization. For a given feasible trajectory, the full state feedback linearized strategy for the leader robot and input-output feedback linearized strategies for the follower robots are found to be more efficient in stabilizing the system.

For future work, the following work can be considered.

- In this chapter, the kinematic model of the multi agent nonholonomic robots has been considered. However, for massive robots and at high speeds, the nonholonomic constraint may not be realistic. It may happen that the robots wheels may slip due to high speed. Hence, the robots dynamics are necessary to be modeled.
- Current implementation of Bluetooth piconet profile does not support roaming protocol; hence the leadership in the formation is always static. To make the leadership more dynamic, a roaming protocol for Bluetooth can be designed.
- The leader and the follower robots are observable. Based on feedback linearized control strategies, observer based feedback laws can be designed for the leader-follower formation.

9. Acknowledgements

The authors would like to thank the Malaysian Ministry of Science, Technology and Innovation for funding this research project through IRPA grant 04-99-02-0003-EA001.

10. References:

Aicardi, M., Casalino G., Balestrino, A. and Bicchi, A. (1995). Close loop steering of unicycle like vehicles via Lyapunov techniques, *IEEE Robotics and Automation Magazine*, pp. 27- 35, vol. 2, issue 1.

Balch, T. and Arkin, R. C., (1998). Behavior-based formation control for multi-robots teams, *IEEE Transactions on Robotics and Automation*, pp. 926-939, vol. 14, no. 6.

Bichhi A., and L. Pallottino, L., (2000). On optimal cooperative conflict resolution for air traffic management systems, *IEEE Transactions on Intelligent Transportations Systems*, vol. 1, no. 4.

Clark, C. M. (2004). *Dynamic Robots Network: A Coordination Platform for Multi-robot Systems, PhD Thesis*, Department of Aeronautics and Astronautics, Stanford University.

Das, A. V. et. al (2002), A vision-based formation control framework, *IEEE Transactions on Robotics and Automation*, pp. 813-825, vol. 18, no. 5.

Desai, J. P. (1998). *Motion Planning and Control of Cooperative Robotic Systems, PhD Thesis*, Mechanical Engineering and Applied Mechanics, University of Pennsylvania.

Desai, J. P., Ostrowski, J. and Kumar, V. (1998). Controlling formations of multiple mobile robots, *IEEE International Conference on Robotics & Automation*, Belgium.

Ferber J., (1999). *Multi Agent Systems: An Introduction to Distributed Artificial Intelligence,* Addison Wesley Longman, England.

FIPA Agent Communication Language Specifications, (2002) [online]. [Accessed 15 Sept. 2008]. Available from World Wide Web: <http://www.fipa.org/repository/aclspecs.html>

Kanayama, Y., Kimura, Y., Miyazaki F. and Noguchi, T. (1991). A stable tracking control method for a nonholonomic mobile robot, *IEEE International Workshop on Intelligent Robots and Systems,* pp. 1236-1241, Japan,.

Khalil, H.K. (2002). *Nonlinear Systems,* 3rd edition, Prentice Hall.

Kolmanovsky, I. and McClamroch, N. H. (1995). Developments in nonholonomic control problems, *IEEE Control Systems Magazine,* pp. 20–36, vol. 15, issue 6.

Langer, D., Rosenblatt, J. K. and Hebert, M. (1994). A behavior-based system for off-road navigation, *IEEE Transactions on Robotics and Automation,* vol. 10, no. 6.

Lefeber, E., Jakubiak, J., Tchon, K. and Nijmeijer, H. (2001). Observer based kinematic tracking controllers for a unicycle-type mobile robot, *IEEE Conference on Robotics & Automation,* May 2001, Seoul, Korea.

Luca, A. D., Oriolo, G. and Vendittelli, M. (2000). Stabilization of the unicycle via dynamic feedback linearization, *IFAC Symposium of Robot Control,* pp. 397-402.

Luca, A. D., Oriolo, G. and Vendittelli, M. (2001). *Control of Wheeled Mobile Robots: An Experimental Overview, Lecture Notes,* Diapartimento di Informatica e Sistemistica, Universita degli Studi di Roma, Itlay.

Morrow, R. (2002). *Bluetooth Operation and Use,* McGraw-Hill, New York.

Nise, N. S. (2004). *Control Systems Engineering,* 4th Edition 2004 John Wiley & Sons, New York.

Oriolo, G., Luca, A. D. and Vendittelli, M. (2002). WMR control via dynamic feedback linearization: design, implementation and experimental validation, *IEEE Transactions on Control Systems Technology,* vol. 10, no.6.

Parker, L. E., (1994). *Heterogeneous Multi-robot Cooperation, PhD Thesis,* Department of Electrical and Computer Engineering, Massachusetts Institute of Technology.

Rydesater, P., MATLAB Central File Exchange, [Last accessed 18th Sept, 2008], http://www.mathworks.com/matlabcentral/fileexchange/loadAuthor.do?objectType=author&objectId=483407

Slotine, J-J. E. and Li, W. (1991). *Applied Nonlinear Control,* Prentice Hall.

Tabuada, P., Pappas, G. J. and Lima, P. (2005). Motion feasibility of multi-agent formations, *IEEE Transactions on Robotics,* pp. 387-392, vol. 21.

Tan, K. H. and Lewis, M. A. (1997). Virtual structures for high-precision cooperative mobile robot control, *Autonomous Robots,* pp. 387-403, vol. 4.

Wit, C. C., Khennouf, H., Samson C. and Sordalen, O. J. (1994). Nonlinear control design for mobile robots", *Recent Trends in Mobile Robots,* , pp. 121-156, World Scientific Publisher, vol. 11.

6

Scalable Coordination Mechanism to Maintain Throughput of Dynamic Multiagent Networks

Rajesh Gautam[1] and Kazuo Miyashita[2]
[1]*DInSys Technologies,*
[2]*AIST,*
[1]*India,*
[2]*Japan*

1. Introduction

Many real-world systems are a manifestation of queuing networks. The queueing theory (Allen 1990) has addressed analysis and control of such networks in a steady state. Nevertheless, to understand and control their dynamic behavior in unstable situations is considered critically important for realizing smooth operations of today's complicated network systems. Transportation, communication and manufacturing are typical examples of such large networks, for which uninterrupted and stable operations are highly required. Influences of failures propagate unexpectedly in a complex network system. Network systems have multiple resources (i.e. nodes) that collectively perform tasks that are not atomic but rather comprise a set of steps to be accomplished in a specific sequence by different resources. As each resource of network is involved in intricate interactions with other resources, even a small failure at a single resource can make ripple effects and damage operations of the entire network. Heavy traffic jams in a transportation network and large-scale blackouts in a power-transmission network are typical outcomes of such cascading phenomena. Therefore, a robust method for controlling behaviors of the network to avert catastrophe caused by failures and maintain smooth operations is of keen interest among many researchers (Barabási 2002).

Manufacturing processes are examples of such networks which have become increasingly complex over time. Due to globalization of economy, manufacturing industry has also become very competitive and has to face new challenges. In addition to the persistent challenge of reducing manufacturing costs, same manufacturing infrastructure is utilized to simultaneously produce numerous customized products which have aggressive time to market and short life cycles. Simultaneously, in order to avoid technological obsolescence and remain competitive, parts of manufacturing infrastructure constantly get modified which adds to the volatility of manufacturing process. In such large, complex and dynamic systems, unexpected failures can have unanticipated effect throughout the system. Because of the size and complexity of problem, analysis and provisioning of preventive measures for the huge number of possible conditions is not possible during the planning phase. To maintain desired performance of such time-critical systems in the face of unexpected failures, developing robust control mechanisms is an active area of research. As a benchmark for controlling large-scale network systems, we have used the semiconductor manufacturing process which is among the most complicated and capital-intensive manufacturing processes in the world.

Semiconductor fabrication processes (*fabs*) consist of complex sequence of process steps, with the number of operations typically in hundreds and lead times extending over a couple of months (Pfund et al., 2006). The various steps of sequence are to be processed at different workstations in a given order. The process routes contain numerous cycles and *fab* produces a diversity of products (having different process routes) simultaneously which result in complex flow of jobs through the system. The capital cost to build and equip a semiconductor fabrication facility runs into billions of (US) dollars[1]. This requires the manufacturer to utilize every opportunity to increase the utilization and throughput of *fab* in order to maximize the return on investment (RoI). Besides increasing the throughput of manufacturing system, another objective of manufacturers is to simultaneously minimize the leadtime of jobs. With shorter leadtimes, a manufacturer can meet the dynamic customer orders more quickly and be more responsive to the market by reducing the time to market for new products. Furthermore, the fierce competition in the global market place and short technology life cycles require manufactures in the semiconductor industry to always deploy state-of-the-art manufacturing technologies. It causes their manufacturing processes to be unstable and unpredictable because they most of the time operate in the early part of the experience curves of manufacturing.

In queueing theory, Little's Law (Little 1961) states that the expected inventory of work in process (WIP) equals the average lead time multiplied by the average throughput. Therefore, with a fixed throughput, reducing the lead time requires WIP to be reduced. However, with a variable and unpredictable manufacturing environment, it is difficult to achieve the desired performance. The network systems usually have multiple and overlapping flows of tasks. When a failure occurs at a resource in the system, the flows using that resource are blocked in the middle and their tasks are delayed. As a result, workloads from the failed resource and downstream resources of its tasks are reduced during the failure and throughput of the affected tasks decreases. After recovery of the failure, for restoring throughput of the affected tasks, downstream resources of the failed resource must process excess flows of these tasks. If those resources should also process other tasks that are not affected by the failure as usual, the resources get congested and deteriorate throughput of those tasks as well. Besides degrading the throughput, the failure causes the lots to be held up for longer duration in the queues which adds up to their leadtimes of completed lots.

1.1 Conventional control approaches

In a manufacturing system, because of connectivity of the steps to be processed, even if a system might have many overcapacity resources, final throughput of system is limited by the resource that has the smallest capacity (called a *bottleneck*). Maximizing throughput of system therefore means keeping maximum utilization of the bottleneck resource. High utilization of the bottleneck resource is ensured by maintaining a sufficient amount of jobs before it as a safety buffer against random events that might cause its starvation. Hence, to improve the tradeoff between leadtime and throughput of a manufacturing system, several

[1] http://www.icknowledge.com/economics/fab costs.html

methods have been developed to regulate WIP at the lowest safe level that prevents starvation of bottleneck machines (Fowleret al., 2002). However, those methods subsume that the bottleneck machines in system are identifiable by preliminary static analyses of problem and do not evolve over time. However, in the course of manufacturing, bottleneck machines might shift temporarily because of unexpected random events such as machine failures that disturb the smooth flow of jobs. This phenomenon is called *wandering* bottlenecks. Most existing solutions to the problem are rather philosophical and managerial (such as Kaizen (Imai 1997) and Theory of Constraint (TOC) (Goldratt & Cox 1992) with a few exceptions of identifying wandering bottlenecks (Roser et al., 2002).
To prevent starvation of bottleneck machines, *lot release control* to regulate workload in front of bottleneck machines by controlling the entry of jobs in system (Glassey & Resende 1988) has been widely used in practice. Nevertheless, it has achieved limited success because its centralized decision-making mechanism at the job entry point cannot respond to the dynamics of manufacturing systems (such as wandering bottlenecks). Rather than controlling the job entry, it is desired that jobs are processed and requested dynamically by every machine in system as to maintain a steady flow of jobs leading to the bottleneck machines. The desired control (*lot flow control*) is possible only through coordinated operations of machines. Centralized control of all machines shares the same weak point with the lot release control (Miyashita et al., 2004). A decentralized coordination method is required so that every machine decides its job request and job processing in harmony with other machines as an intelligent agent.

1.2 Multiagent based coordination approaches

In a time-critical manufacturing environment, no machine (i.e., agent) can afford to search and gather all necessary information of other machines for deciding its actions. Consequently, many coordination techniques proposed in multiagent systems (Jennings et al., 2001, Sandholm 1999, Faltings & Nguyen 2005, Durfee 1996) are inappropriate for our purpose. In a stable and leveled manufacturing system, a *pull control* method (Liberopoulos & Dallery 2000), in which an upstream machine starts processing a new task only when it receives a request from its downstream machine, has been investigated and shown to be efficient. Just-In-Time (JIT) (Ohno 1988) and CONWIP (Hopp & Spearman 2000) are the best-known examples of such pull control methods. In JIT, a machine exchanges tokens (*Kanban* cards) between its adjacent machines to control flows and amounts of WIP in the system. In fact, JIT and its extensions such as CONWIP are instances of *token-based* coordination (Wagner et al., 2003, Xu et al., 2005, Moyaux et al., 2003) and widely used in manufacturing and other related fields. However, because of their simplicity, they cannot correspond smoothly to changes of the environment such as demand fluctuations and machine failures. Hence, as a key of their successful application, emphasis was put on eliminating such deviations, which are inherent and inevitable in the semiconductor manufacturing process.
Although multiagent technology is an active area of research, its success in large complicated systems such as semiconductor fabrication has been limited. Coordination among agents is the cornerstone of distributed multiagent systems and new coordination algorithms are constantly being developed. The sophisticated coordination algorithms that require extensive interaction among large number of agents for making globally optimal decisions cannot work for large complex networks due to high messaging and computations requirements. On the other hand, the coordination algorithms which use simple interactions between small number of agents are although scalable, their efficiency is poor and the

resulting emergent system behavior can deviate greatly from desired behavior. Although multiagent framework suits well to the distributed nature of manufacturing systems, it is still a challenge to develop autonomous and distributed manufacturing control which is robust against unpredictable failures and achieves desired global optimization from today's dynamic manufacturing systems.

We view a manufacturing system as a network of agents that are in charge of processing specific steps of products. Thus each agent represents a machine and its buffers in the manufacturing system. In the manufacturing system, routing of tasks is partially fixed at a product design phase, but dispatching of tasks can be fully and dynamically controlled during manufacturing process. We have proposed an extension of the token-basedcoordination method: Coordination for Avoiding Bottleneck Starvation (CABS) for improving a tradeoff between leadtime and throughput in a large-scale and uncertain network system (Gautam & Miyashita 2007*a*, Gautam & Miyashita 2007*b*). In CABS, agents coordinate with other agents to maintain the adequate flow of jobs to satisfy the various demands by preventing starvation of bottleneck agents. That coordination is achieved by efficient passing of messages in the system. The message includes information that enables agents to identify the bottleneck agents and hence coordinate with other agents to maintain desired flow of jobs to the bottleneck agents.

In this paper, we show that CABS can be effectively applied to the production control of the semiconductor fabrication process. In Section 2, we explain a generic manufacturing problem and the details of coordination algorithms in CABS. Section 3 illustrates how CABS compensates for production loss caused by machine failures using a simulation result of a single failure scenario. Section 4 explains the distributed deadlock avoidance mechanism of CABS. Section 5 empirically validates that CABS succeeds to achieve desired throughput with shorter leadtime than a wellknown conventional manufacturing control method, CONWIP. Finally, Section 6 concludes the paper.

2. Coordination mechanisms in CABS

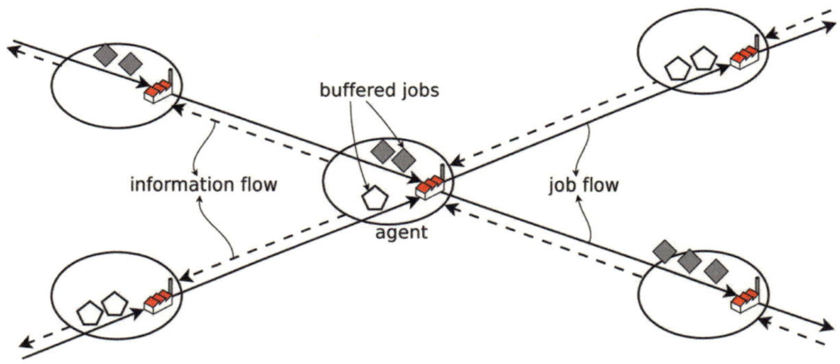

Fig. 1. Agent interactions in CABS

In this section, we first describe a general model of manufacturing problem and then introduce the coordination method developed for mitigating the affect of failures and maintaining throughput of network. In CABS actions of agents are coordinated using the messages transmitted among agents. As shown in Figure 1, an agent uses requirement information in the incoming messages from succeeding agents for making task processing decisions and for generating messages to send to its preceding agents.

2.1 Problem definition

The manufacturing problem requires processing a set of jobs $J = \{J_1, ..., J_n\}$ by a set of workstations, which are modeled as agents $A = \{A_1, ...,A_m\}$ in this paper.

Each job J_l consists of a set of steps $S^l = \{S^l_1, ..., S^l_{s_l}\}$ to be processed according to its process routing that specifies precedence constraints among these steps. Lots of a job flow through agents according to the job's process route. Each agent A_j has identical p_j machines to process its t_j tasks $T^j = \{T^j_1, ..., T^j_{t_j}\}$. Each job J_l has a demand rate dr_l, which is the number of lots of J_l to be completed in one hour. Furthermore, when an agent A_j processes its task T^j_i, it takes a process time pt^j_i.

A task of the agent corresponds to a step in the jobs. Hence, precedence constraints among steps in jobs create a complicated directional network of agents. Presume an agent A_j's task T^j_q is a step S^l_i. A preceding agent of the agent A_j in terms of the task T^j_q, $A_{pre(j,q)}$, is in charge of a step S^l_{i-1} and a succeeding agent of A_j, $A_{suc(j,q)}$, processes a step S^l_{i+1}.

In addition to the agents that model the workstations, two types of synthetic agents exist. One is a *sink-agent* for each kind of job, which receives the completed lots from the last agent of the job's process route. Another synthetic agent, a *source-agent*, releases every job in the system by transferring it to the agent processing the first step of the job.

2.2 Action selection

Algorithm 1 selectTask(message $im[\,]$) of agent A_j

set ET as $\emptyset$
for all $i \in \{1, \cdots, t_j\}$ **do**
  set W_i as current WIP of task T^j_i
  if $(W_i > 0)$ **then**
    add T^j_i to ET
  end if
end for
sort ET according to time limit (i.e., $im[\,].tl$) of tasks
set FET as the first task in ET
delete FET from ET
loop
  set start time of FET at *current time*
  set OFT as $\emptyset$
  for all $ET_i \in ET$ **do**
    // $im[\,].cr$ decides criticality of a task
    if $(criticality(ET_i) > criticality(FET))$
    $\wedge$ $(FET\ delays\ ET_i)$ **then**
      add ET_i to OFT
    end if
  end for
  if $OFT \neq \emptyset$ **then**
    set FET as the first task in ET
    // i.e. next task with earliest $im[\,].tl$
    delete FET from ET
  else
    return FET
  end if
end loop

CABS utilizes token-based coordination so that an agent selects its lot-processing actions based on requirements from its succeeding agents in the process flow. Thus, CABS realizes a *pull mechanism* like a JIT system that does not process jobs until they are "pulled" by downstream agents.

Each agent A_j periodically receives a requirement for processing a task T_q^j from a corresponding succeeding agent $A_{suc(j,q)}$. The requirement consists of the following three types of information (detailed definitions will be given later in Section 2.3):

1. `time limit`: time by which agent $A_{suc(j,q)}$ needs another lot for the next step of the task T_q^j.
2. `request rate`: rate at which agent $A_{suc(j,q)}$ needs the lots for the next step of the task T_q^j, starting at `time limit`.
3. `criticality`: criticality of the agent $A_{suc(j,q)}$.

In addition to the requirement information from succeeding agents, for each task $T_q^j \in T^j$, an agent A_j is assumed to have local information such as the demand rate, its current WIP and the total number of lots it has already produced.

Agent A_j uses the requirement information from its succeeding agents for choosing the next lot to process (i.e. *dispatching*) when any machine of the agent A_j becomes free. Algorithm 1 describes the dispatching algorithm for the agent A_j. It returns a task with the earliest `time limit` whose dispatching will not delay any other task with higher `criticality` beyond its `time limit`. In algorithms of the paper, *im*[ ].*tl*, *im*[ ].*rr* and *im*[ ].*cr* respectively denote requirement information of `time limit`, `request rate` and `criticality` for the corresponding tasks in the incoming messages of the agent. In addition, a task t_1 **delays** task t_2 if processing t_1 before t_2 at current time (t_{curr}) delays the completion of t_2 beyond its `time limit`, $im[t_2].tl$.

$$t_1 \textbf{ delays } t_2 = \begin{cases} true & \text{if } (t_{curr} + pt^j_{t_1}) > \\ & \quad (im[t_2].tl - pt^j_{t_2}) \\ false & \text{otherwise} \end{cases}$$

2.3 Message passing

Dispatching of agents in CABS is decided solely on requirements from succeeding agents. Hence, information in the requirement is a key to coordination among agents.

An agent tries to meet the requirements of succeeding agents for all of its tasks. Aside from meeting those requirements, the critical agents must also minimize their *workload deficit* at all times for satisfying the demand rates of jobs. For example, A_j's workload of a single lot of task T_q^j is the time required to process it (i.e., pt_q^j). Each agent has aggregated workloads of all of its tasks based on the demand rates of jobs (i.e., dr_l). The difference between the workloads and total processing time of tasks that have already been processed is the current workload deficit of an agent.

An agent can recover its workload deficit by processing more lots of any task than the corresponding demand rate. The time needed to recover the deficit depends on the amount of deficit and surplus capacity available to agent. Algorithm 2 calculates an agent's *criticality* as a ratio of its workload deficit and available surplus capacity. In CABS, an agent with a large criticality is considered a bottleneck agent. Dynamic change of an agent's criticality represents *wandering* of bottlenecks.

Algorithm 2 calcCriticality( ) of agent A_j

$\forall i \in \{1, \cdots, t_j\}$ set W_i as current WIP of task T_i^j
$FT \leftarrow current\_time+$
$\quad \sum_{\forall i \in \{1,\cdots,t_j\}} (W_i pt_i^j / p_j)$
// earliest time to finish current WIP
$\forall i \in \{1, \cdots, t_j\}$ set TD_i
as total demand of task T_i^j until FT
$\forall i \in \{1, \cdots, t_j\}$ set TP_i
as total production of task T_i^j until now
$WLD \leftarrow \sum_{\forall i \in \{1,\cdots,t_j\}} (TD_i - (TP_i + W_i)) pt_i^j$
// current estimated workload deficit of A_j
$SC \leftarrow p_j(1.0 - \sum_{\forall i \in \{1,\cdots,t_j\}} dr_{job(T_i^j)} pt_i^j / p_j)$
// surplus capacity of A_j
return WLD/SC

Algorithm 3 makeRequest(message $im[\,]$) of agent A_j

$\forall i \in \{1, \cdots, t_j\}$ set W_i as current WIP of task T_i^j
$ST \leftarrow current\_time+$
$\quad \sum_{\forall i \in \{1,\cdots,t_j\}} (W_i^j pt_i^j / p_j)$
// earliest time when A_j gets starved
$CR \leftarrow calcCriticality()$
// current criticality of A_j
for all $i \in \{1, \cdots, t_j\}$ **do**
 $RT_i \leftarrow im[i].tl - pt_i^j + W_i / im[i].rr$
 // time to replenish T_i^j based on request from $A_{suc(j,i)}$
 if ($im[i].cr >= CR$) **then**
  $om[i].tl \leftarrow max(ST, RT_i)$
  $om[i].rr \leftarrow min(im[i].rr, p_j/pt_i^j)$
 else
  $om[i].tl \leftarrow ST$
  $om[i].rr \leftarrow p_j/pt_i^j$
 end if
 $om[i].cr \leftarrow max(im[i].cr, CR)$
 if (A_j is in failure) **then**
  $om[i].tl \leftarrow \infty$
  $om[i].rr \leftarrow 0.0$
  $om[i].cr \leftarrow 0.0$
 end if
end for
return $om[\,]$

To maintain a continuous lot flow of task T_i^j to $A_{suc(j,i)}$ at the requested rate $im[i].rr$, the agent requires an incoming lot flow at same rate from the corresponding preceding agent $A_{pre(j,i)}$. However, the agent itself might be critical and need the jobs earlier and at a higher rate in order to recover its workload deficit. The agent requires jobs immediately and at the maximum rate at which it can process to recover the deficit rapidly. Based on the requirement from succeeding agent and its current workload deficit, the agent generates a consolidated outgoing requirement for its preceding agent. Algorithm 3 describes the calculation of outgoing requirement messages by agent A_j. For each $T_i^j \in T_j$, a requirement tuple (*om*[*i*].*tl*, *om*[*i*].*rr*, *om*[*i*].*cr*) is generated and sent to the preceding agent $A_{pre(j,i)}$.

The agents use `criticality` of incoming requirements to identify the location of current bottlenecks in the system. If `criticality` of $A_{suc(j,i)}$ is higher than that of A_j, it means that $A_{suc(j,i)}$ is more likely to be a bottleneck in the system. In such a case, A_j acts to recover the deficit of $A_{suc(j,i)}$ and generates the outgoing requirements based on the incoming requirements from $A_{suc(j,i)}$. The agent postpones `time limit` in the outgoing requirements to the time when the current WIP is emptied (i.e., *ST* in Algorithm 3). This realizes *lean manufacturing*, which is intended to reduce the amount of WIP and shorten leadtime. `Request rate` is truncated only when the requested value is greater than the maximum capacity of agent A_j.

The agent prioritizes recovering its workload deficit over satisfying the succeeding agent's requirement when agent A_j is more critical than $A_{suc(j,i)}$. In order to recover its own deficit at the earliest, A_j sends the time when its own WIP is used up as `time limit` and its maximum production rate as `request rate` in requirements to its preceding agent. By sending high `request rate` and short `time limit` to all the preceding agents, the agent tries to expedite the production of all the available jobs for recovering the workload deficit caused by delayed jobs.

As for `criticality`, agent A_j intends to pass the highest `criticality` along the process route by choosing a higher value of itself and its succeeding agent. This enables the preceding agents to identify a location of a current bottleneck in the system along the process routes.

When an agent is in failure, it cannot process any job. Therefore, the agent during the failure period stops requesting jobs to its preceding agents by sending the requirements accordingly (i.e., setting `time limit` as ∞ and `request rate` as zero). `Criticality` of the failed agent is set to zero so that preceding agents can avoid responding to the requests from the failed agent.

3. Covering capacity loss caused by machine failures

In this section, we explain how CABS can cover the capacity loss of failed agents using a simplified scenario of a single failure. A simulation system is developed to model a manufacturing process with agents to test the proposed algorithms in CABS. The system is built using SPADES (Riley & Riley 2003) middleware[2], which is an agent-based discrete event simulation environment. It provides libraries and APIs to build agents that interact with the world by sending and receiving time-based events.

3.1 Test problem

For empirical validation, we used the Measurement and Improvement of Manufacturing Capacity (MIMAC) testbed datasets of the wafer fabrication processes (Fowler & Robinson 1995) from Arizona State university3[3]. The dataset specifies the production steps of semiconductor manufacturing.

---

[2] Available online at: http://spades-sim.sourceforge.net.

[3] Available online at: http://www.was.asu.edu/~masmlab/home.htm.

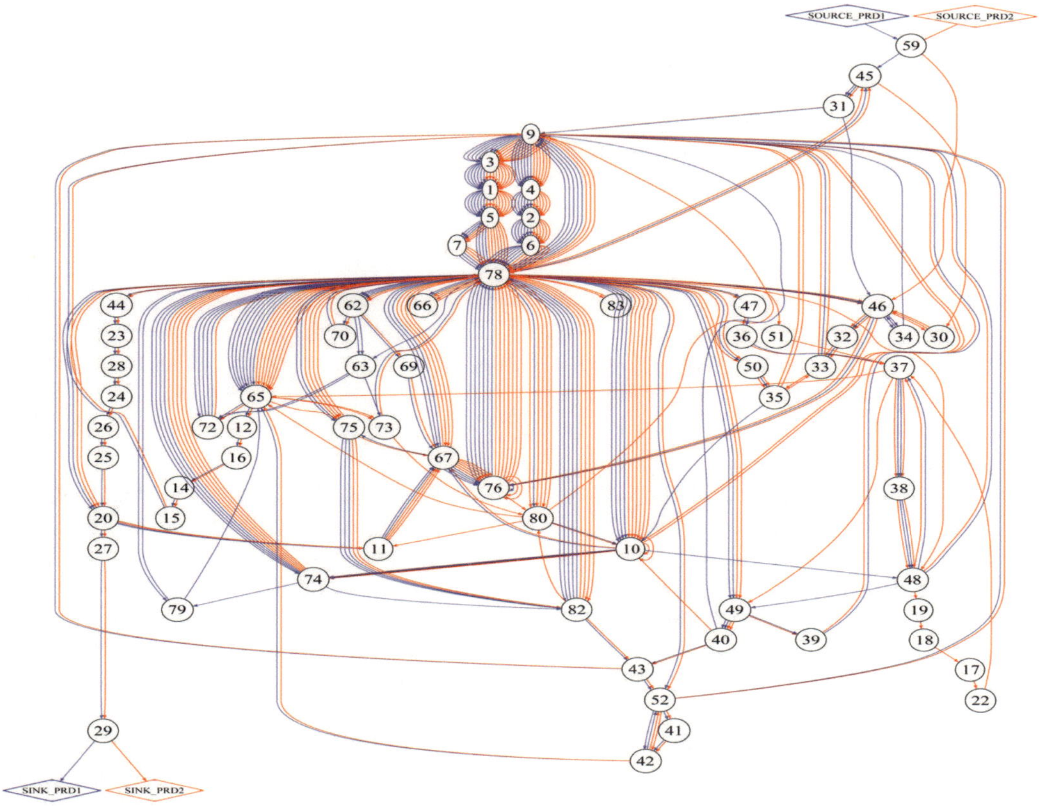

Fig. 2. Process flows of test problem; 83 agents represent workstations and process 455 steps of two types of products.

Table 1 shows the properties of the test problem we chose from the MIMAC datasets. It has basic characteristics of a semiconductor manufacturing process such as lengthy process flow with many repetitive reentrant loops and a couple of bottleneck workstations.

Type of product	Non-volatile memory
Process flows	2
Products	2 (i.e., 1 per process)
Workstation groups	83
Workstation	265
Steps	210 (Product 1) 245 (Product 2)
Raw processing time (hour)	313.4 (Product 1) 358.6 (Product 2)
Demand rate (wafer/day)	336.0 (Product 1) 168.0 (Product 2)
Lot size (wafers)	48(Product 1,2)

Table 1. Specification of test problem

In the experiments, we made the following assumptions to focus our investigative attentions to the basic properties of CABS: (1) there is no variabilities in processing times of operations,

(2) no setup time is considered, (3) operators are not considered in the model, (4) there is neither product rework nor scrap, (5) stochastic machine failure is modeled using exponential distribution, and (6) the demand rates are tuned to realize 87% resource utilization for the most heavily loaded workstation in the steady state.

Figure 2, which depicts the process flows of products through the workstations in the test problem, can be viewed as a "complex network" (Barab´asi 2002). Each node in the network represents a workstation group, which may consist of multiple workstations. Three workstation groups (i.e, No.67, 76 and 78) have average utilization which is higher than 80% and can easily become bottlenecks when unexpected events occur in the manufacturing process. It is noteworthy that, although the number of nodes in the network is moderate (less than one hundred nodes), because they are connected with directional, weighed and multiple links, analysis of the network's behavior is far more intractable than that of networks, which is a current research subject in the area of complex networks.

3.2 Single failure scenario

In this simplified scenario, a single failure occurs at time 50,000 and recovers at time 90,000 on an agent (Workstation group No.19 in Figure 2) that is processing only the 105th step of $Product_2$. To emphasize characteristic behaviors of CABS, we compared the results of CABS with those of a benchmark system using a constant releasing rule and an EDD (i.e., the earliest due date first) dispatching rule. The behaviors of CABS and the benchmark system are shown in Figures 3 - 5 and Figures 6 - 8 in terms of finished product inventory, production rate and WIP levels respectively. The failure duration is shown by the shaded zone in the graphs.

We first explain the behavior of CABS in detail. During the failure, the flow of $Product_2$ is stopped after the failed agent and its production starts to drop (shown as concave lines of $Product_2$ in Figure 3 and Figure 4). Due to unavailability of $Product_2$, the succeeding agents to the failed agent begin to starve, and their workload deficit increases. Consequently, as explained in Algorithm 2, `criticality` of those agents increases during the failure. Among the succeeding agents, some agents are processing both $Product_1$ and $Product_2$. In order to compensate for the shortage of $Product_2$, these agents start to request $Product_1$ early at their maximum rate (see Algorithm 3: lines 10 - 11). This behavior of agents increases the production rate and finished inventory of $Product_1$ during the failure (see rising $Product_1$ lines in Figure 3 and Figure 4).

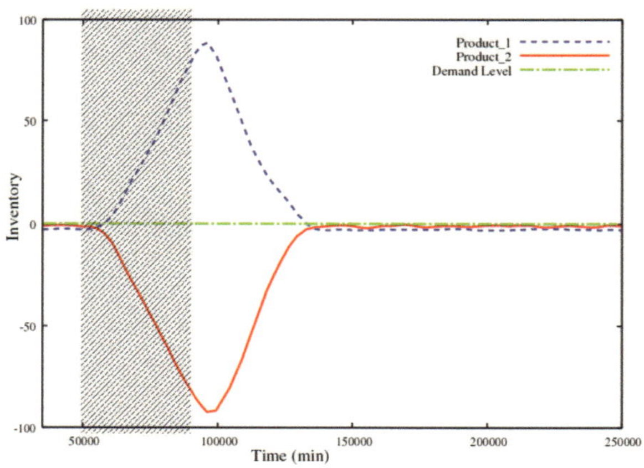

Fig. 3. CABS: Finished Product Inventory

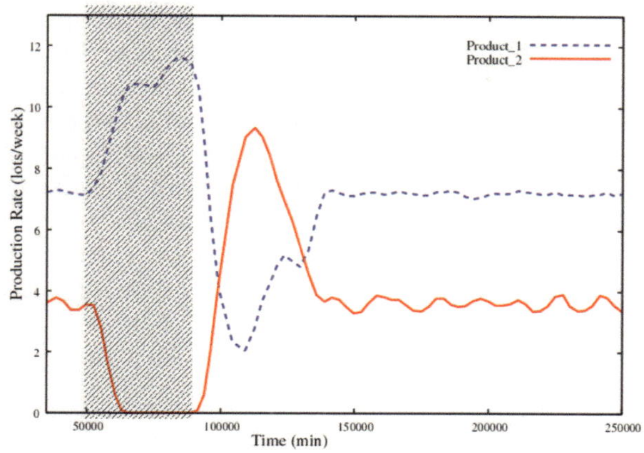

Fig. 4. CABS: Production Rate

In order to recover workload deficits, the agents pull both *Product*$_1$ and *Product*$_2$ at high rates during the failure. But due to the failure, *Product*$_2$ cannot be processed and its WIP is accumulated as shown in Figure 5. When the failure is recovered, the agents increase production rate of *Product*$_2$ by utilizing the extraWIP accumulated during the failure (see rising of *Product*$_2$ lines after the failure recovery in Figure 4 and Figure 3). The production rate of *Product*$_1$ is reduced after the recovery to bring the finished inventory of both the products to the desired demand level by time 130,000 (see Figure 4 and Figure 3). This is achieved by the dispatching rule shown in Algorithm 1, which exploits `time limit` information of different kinds of tasks to pick the next task for processing. Since *Product*$_1$ is produced in excess during the failure, `time limit` in the requirement from *sink-agent* of *Product*$_1$ rises during the failure. `Time limit` of *Product*$_2$ remains low because of its deficit from the demanded production.

Thus, by using the coordination mechanism of CABS, the agents are able to maintain their utilization during failures by processing alternative tasks. This enables them to recover throughput of failed tasks quickly by producing more of them after the resolution of failures.

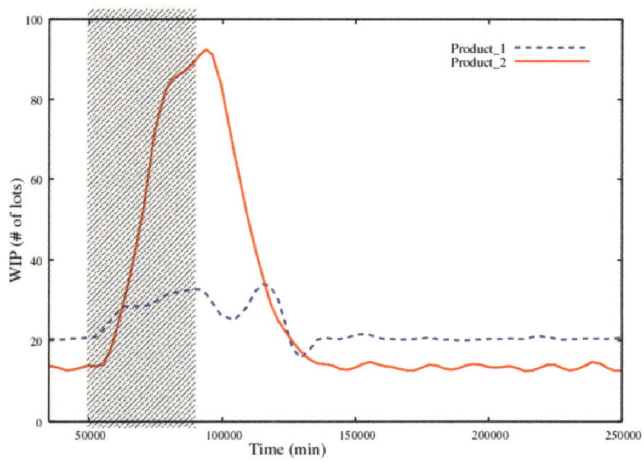

Fig. 5. CABS: WIP

The benchmark system, on the other hand, does not handle failures with a special care. It continues production of $Product_1$ at the same demand rate during the failure (see Figure 7). Thus, due to the suspension of the flow of $Product_2$, the bottleneck agents suffer a capacity loss and the system takes long time to recover the production shortage incurred during the failure. The failure adversely affects production of $Product_1$ as well. Since the EDD dispatching rule tries to balance the deficit of both products, the finished inventory of $Product_1$ also drops after the resolution of failure (see Figure 6). Comparison of Figures 3 and 6 shows that the recovery to the desired product inventory level of both the products is much slower (about at time 220,000) than CABS. More importantly, if the demand rates of the products are higher (or the failure sustains longer), it is more likely that the benchmark system cannot make up for the production loss caused by the failure permanently.

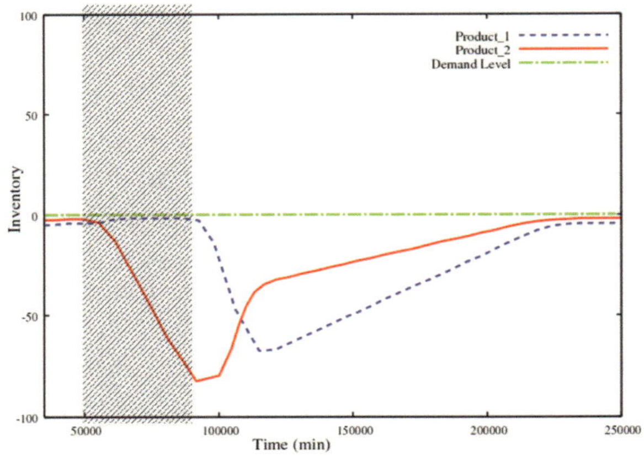

Fig. 6. Benchmark: Finished Product Inventory

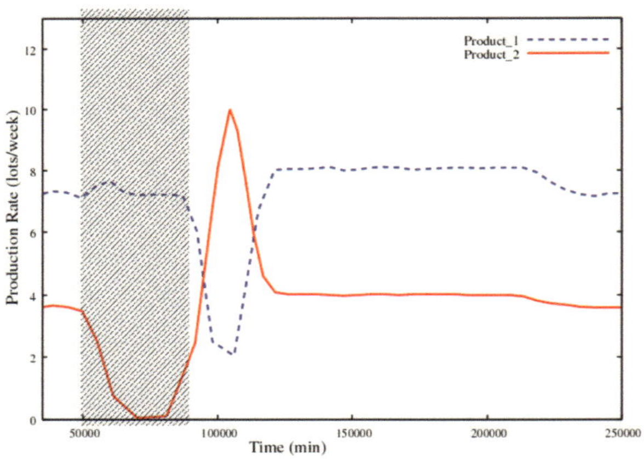

Fig. 7. Benchmark: Production Rate

In the above experiments, we assumed no upper limitation of WIP size in the system. As a result, in both CABS and the benchmark system, WIP was increased up to more than 90 lots during the failure. In realistic manufacturing situations, WIP size should be suppressed under certain level due to physical and economical reasons. Figures 9 - 11 show the behaviors of CABS with a limited WIP size. In the experiment, we limit the total WIP size of the system as 38 lots at its maximum. Figures 9 - 11 show that by limiting the WIP size CABS still performs similarly to CABS with unlimited WIP size but takes more time to compensate for the production loss caused by the failure. However, to be noted is that CABS with limited WIP is still much faster to recover production loss (about at time 150,000) than the benchmark system and the quick recovery of CABS requires less than half of WIP used in the benchmark system (see Figure 11 and Figure 8).

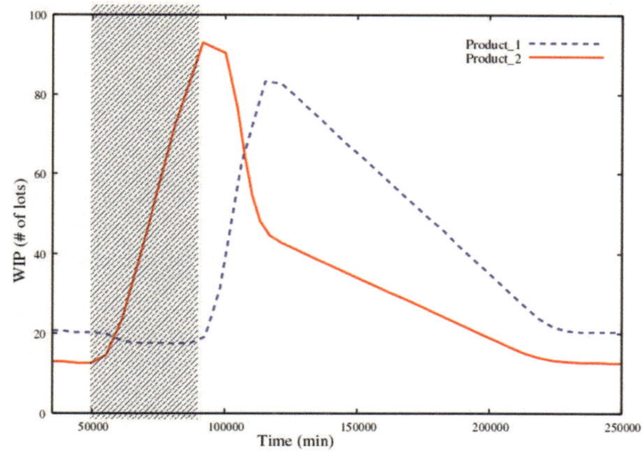

Fig. 8. Benchmark: WIP

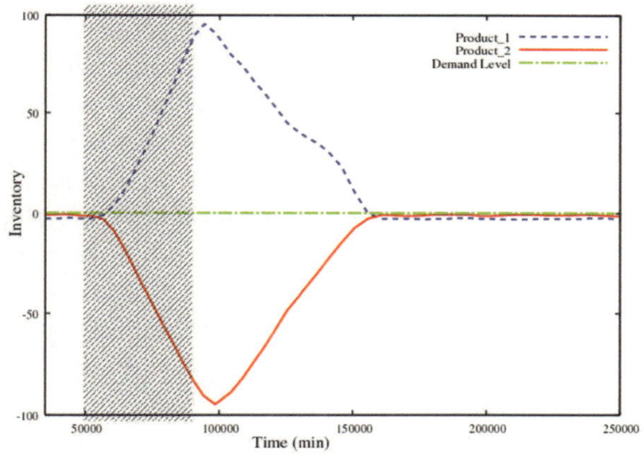

Fig. 9. CABS w/ limited WIP size: Finished Product Inventory

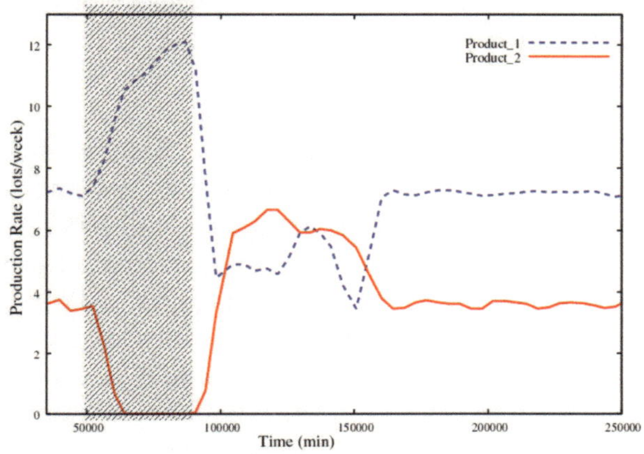

Fig. 10. CABS w/ limited WIP size: Production Rate

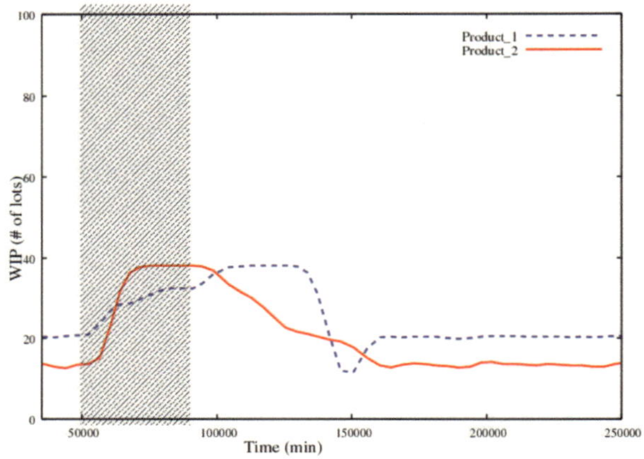

Fig. 11. CABS w/ limited WIP size: WIP

4. Distributed deadlock avoidance

Unlike many other network systems, semiconductor fabrication processes are characterized by existence of large number of re-entrant cycles in their process routes (Figure 2). Although deadlocks can occur in other systems also due to limitation of buffers, semiconductor fabrication processes are more prone to them due to large number of cycles. Deadlocks can be of two types, *permanent* and *transient* deadlock. A permanent deadlock cannot be resolved without external intervention, whereas a transient deadlock resolves itself over time (Venkatesh & Smith 2005). The probability of having deadlocks increases when capacity of buffers in system is reduced. As permanent bottlenecks bring the system to standstill, issue of bottlenecks has to be addressed in order to have an autonomous system that can work with limited buffer capacities. Because of the complexity of system, avoidance, identification and resolution of deadlocks in semiconductor manufacturing processes is a difficult problem and various sophisticated techniques are being investigated under current research (Venkatesh & Smith 2005).

As the techniques for managing deadlocks in semiconductor fabrication processes are still under investigation, in order to focus our attention on behavior of CABS, we have developed an distributed algorithm that avoids permanent deadlocks in system. Our deadlock avoidance algorithm avoids permanent deadlocks by:

- introducing a mechanism of reserved buffers
- utilizing an additional parameter in CABS message

We first explain the concept of our reserved buffers by using an example. Figure 12 describes a permanent deadlock that occurs in the part of system that has a small cycle involving two agents. *PROCESS ROUTE* describes a cycle in process flow of job through *AGENT1* and *AGENT2*, where *AGENT1* is processing two steps of process. As succeeding agent should have a free buffer to park incoming job, agents in system wait for authorization from their succeeding agent before they can start processing a new job. We have used the token based mechanism (similar to *Kanban* (Ohno 1988)) for realizing such authorization. Agents in this example have a shared buffer of size three, which can hold any type of incoming job.

In Figure 12 we first show the occurrence of permanent deadlock in a system that is not using specific buffers, i.e. only has shared buffers. *STAGE0* in Figure 12 shows that *AGENT1* is processing *stepP* as it is authorized by a free buffer of *AGENT2* (shown by directed solid line). Because all buffers of *AGENT1* are full, *AGENT2* cannot process its jobs and is awaiting its authorization from a free buffer of *AGENT1* (shown by directed dashed line). *STAGE1* shows the permanent deadlock that occurs when buffers of *AGENT2* also get full after receiving the additional job from *AGENT1*. As both agents now wait for authorization from each other indefinitely, this deadlock is *permanent* and cannot be resolved without external intervention.
We now explain our mechanism of specific buffers and how it avoids the occurrence of permanent deadlock during the same scenario. In CABS, each agent has two types of input (WIP) buffers: one is a single-sized buffer specific to the WIP of each product step and the other is a buffer shared by any WIP incoming to the agent. Hence, each agent in CABS has (1) multiple single-sized specific buffers whose number is equal to that of the product steps that are processed by the agent, and (2) a shared buffer whose size is not fixed.

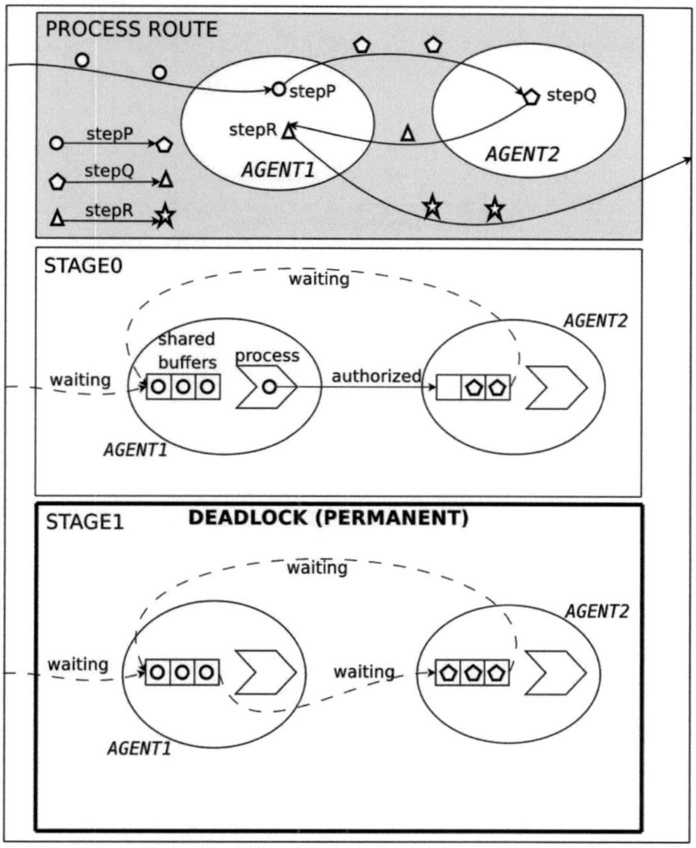

Fig. 12. Deadlock: without specific buffers

We now explain our mechanism of specific buffers and how it avoids the occurrence of permanent deadlock during the same scenario. In CABS, each agent has two types of input (WIP) buffers: one is a single-sized buffer specific to the WIP of each product step and the other is a buffer shared by any WIP incoming to the agent. Hence, each agent in CABS has (1) multiple single-sized specific buffers whose number is equal to that of the product steps that are processed by the agent, and (2) a shared buffer whose size is not fixed.

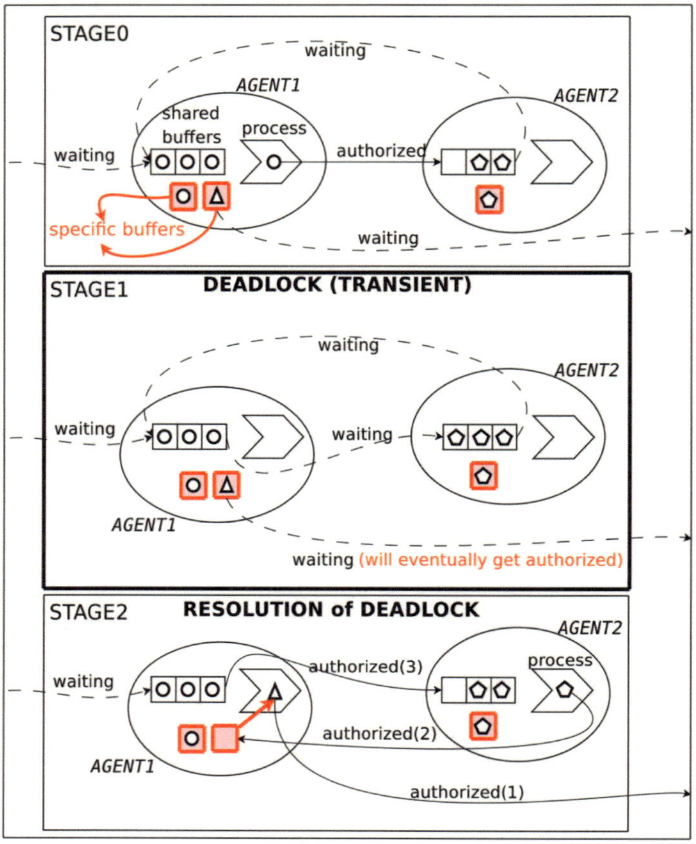

Fig. 13. Deadlock: with specific buffers

We now explain the details of additional message parameter that is used to avoid deadlocks. The additional message parameter, ETA (Estimated Time to Approval), is included in CABS message and is utilized to control the flow of buffers when buffers get occupied. Along with `time limit`, `request rate` and `criticality`, `ETA` is also sent in all the requirement messages of a process step. `ETA` defines the time (in future) at which agent will be able to accumulate a new coming lot of corresponding process step. When an agent has a (shared of specific) free buffer to accommodate a lot, it can immediately authorize the preceding agent to process new lot. However, when the agent does not have any free buffers to accommodate new lot, it sends the ETA (a time in future) when it can accommodate a new lot from its preceding agent. According to the received ETA, the agents plan their dispatching and defer processing of lots accordingly.

If a shared buffer or the reserved buffer of a process step is free, agent sends a value 0 for `ETA` in requirement message to preceding agent. If all shared buffers of agent including the reserved buffer of a process step are occupied, agent calculates the time (`ETA`) at which a buffer will become free according to its dispatching plan.

$$\text{ETA} = \begin{cases} \mathbf{0}, & \text{if a shared buffer or reserved buffer of process is free} \\ \textbf{when a buffer will become free according to plan based on dispatching} & \text{if all shared buffers including reserved buffer of process step are occupied} \end{cases}$$

In order to calculate ETA, agent uses the CABS dispatching algorithm (Algorithm 1) to make dispatching plan of its buffered WIP. A new lot can be accommodated when any shared buffer or the reserved buffer of process step becomes free. When all the buffers are occupied, ETA will be a positive time in future and preceding agents should not send lot before that time. In order to honour the ETA of their succeeding agents, agents defer dispatching of their lots accordingly. The dispatching mechanism of CABS is modified to incorporate ETA by addition of the following rule:

RULE: The lot picked for dispatching should have minimum ETA

This additional rules implies that irrespective of other requirements (`time limit` and `criticality`), the lots are dispatched in order of their ETA. Alternatively, rather than sitting idle to honour the (late) ETA of a high `criticality` lot, agent will dispatch a lower `criticality` job which has earlier ETA. To realize the desired working of ETA mechanism in CABS, Algorithm 4 is called before CABS dispatching algorithm (Algorithm 1).

Algorithm 4 **pruneTasksETA**(message $im[\,]$) of agent A_j

1: $t_{min} \leftarrow$ among $\forall i \in \{1, \cdots, t_j\}$ find i with minimum $im[i]$.**ETA** // i.e. among all tasks, task t_{min} has the earliest ETA
2: **for all** $i \in \{1, \cdots, t_j\}$ **do**
3: **if** ($im[i]$.ETA $>$ $im[t_{min}]$.ETA) **then**
4: delete $im[i]$ from $im[\,]$
5: **end if**
6: **end for**

Algorithm 4 removes tasks with higher ETAs, and dispatching algorithm (Algorithm 1) then chooses a lot to dispatch from the remaining tasks. In case there are multiple tasks with minimum ETA, dispatching works as usual by considering their other requirement parameters. Most of the times, when free buffers are available at agents, ETAs of tasks remain 0 and Algorithm 4 has no effect. In such normal cases, all tasks are considered for dispatching and execution of CABS takes place according to their requirement parameters. However, when buffers become full, agents in CABS prioritize processing of lots with lower ETAs. The last agent of process route assumes a static incoming ETA of 0. The agents towards the end of process generally will have lower ETAs and reserved buffers ensure availability of jobs of all process steps at agents. Hence, by prioritizing lots that will complete earlier and propagating the ETA to remote agents, the flow of lots is perpetually maintained which autonomously avoids the occurrence of permanent bottlenecks.

5. Empirical validation of CABS

In the experiments, using the same semiconductor fabrication problem as in Section 3.1, we evaluate the performance of CABS when there are repeated failures at all agents in the system. Failures occur randomly based on the exponential distribution. MTBF of agents ranges from 951.6 min to 47, 899.0 min with average of about 6, 900 min. And MTTR of agents is between 0.0 min and 4, 009.0 min with average of about 500 min. Exact data of failure patterns (MTBF and MTTR of all workstations) can be found in the MIMAC datasets.

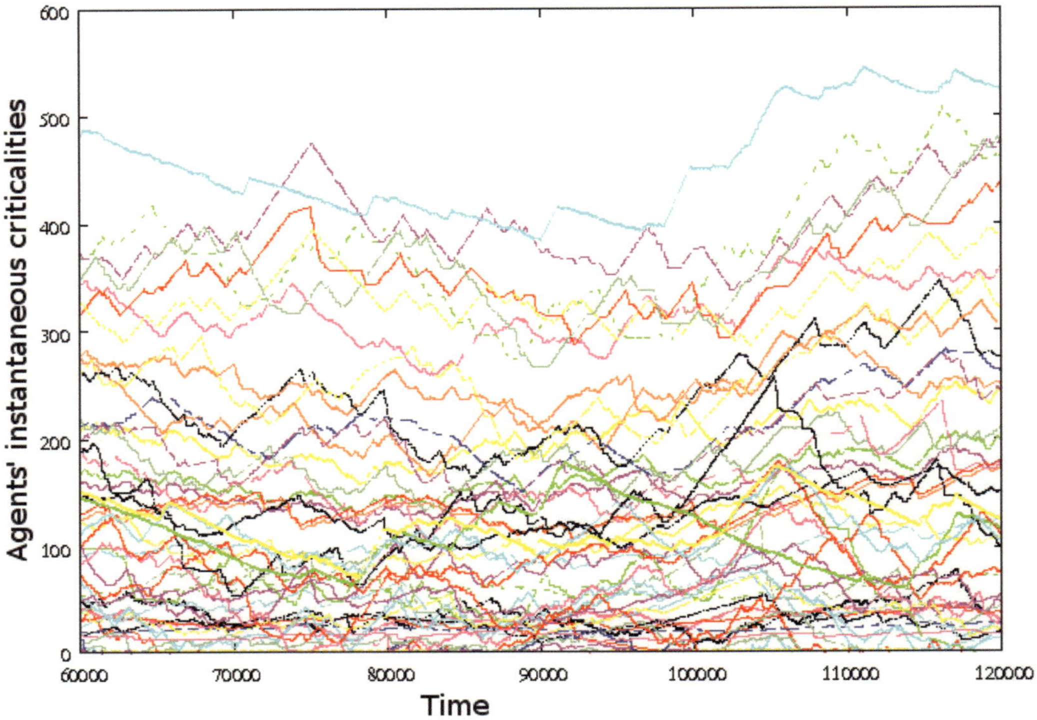

Fig. 14. CABS: Agents' instantaneous `criticality`

Because of dynamic changes of workstations' capacity and disruptions in product flows due to failures, bottleneck workstations shift with time. In CABS we consider the dynamic `criticality` of individual agents as their bottleneck factor. Figure 14 shows how `criticality` values of different agents change in one of the experiments. Figure 14 gives an idea of system's dynamism and shows how different agents can become bottlenecks during the course of execution.

As a criteria to evaluate performance of CABS, we exploit leadtime that achieves the same level of throughput. In queueing theory, Little's Law (Little 1961) states that the expected WIP equals the average leadtime multiplied by the average throughput. Therefore, with fixed throughput, reducing leadtime requires WIP to be reduced. However, with a variable and unpredictable manufacturing environment, reducing WIP tends to decrease throughput by cutting back job stocks of machines so that machine downtimes have a high probability of forcing an idle time of machines due to lack of jobs to process. The system should strike a suitable balance between leadtime (or WIP) and throughput in the face of failures. Hence, the system that requires less leadtime to achieve the same throughput is considered more efficient and robust against failures.

To integrate system's performance on multiple types of products with different manufacturing processes, we calculate the aggregated processing time of all the products as

$$\sum_{i \in ProductSet} Process\_Time_i Throughput_i$$

for representing overall throughput of the system and calculate the aggregated leadtime as

$$\sum_{i \in ProductSet} Leadtime_i Throughput_i$$

for representing overall leadtime of the system. Because

$$Leadtime = Process\_Time + Wait\_Time$$

a system with a smaller aggregated leadtime corresponding to the same aggregated processing time is more efficient and robust against failures.

5.1 Comparison with CONWIP

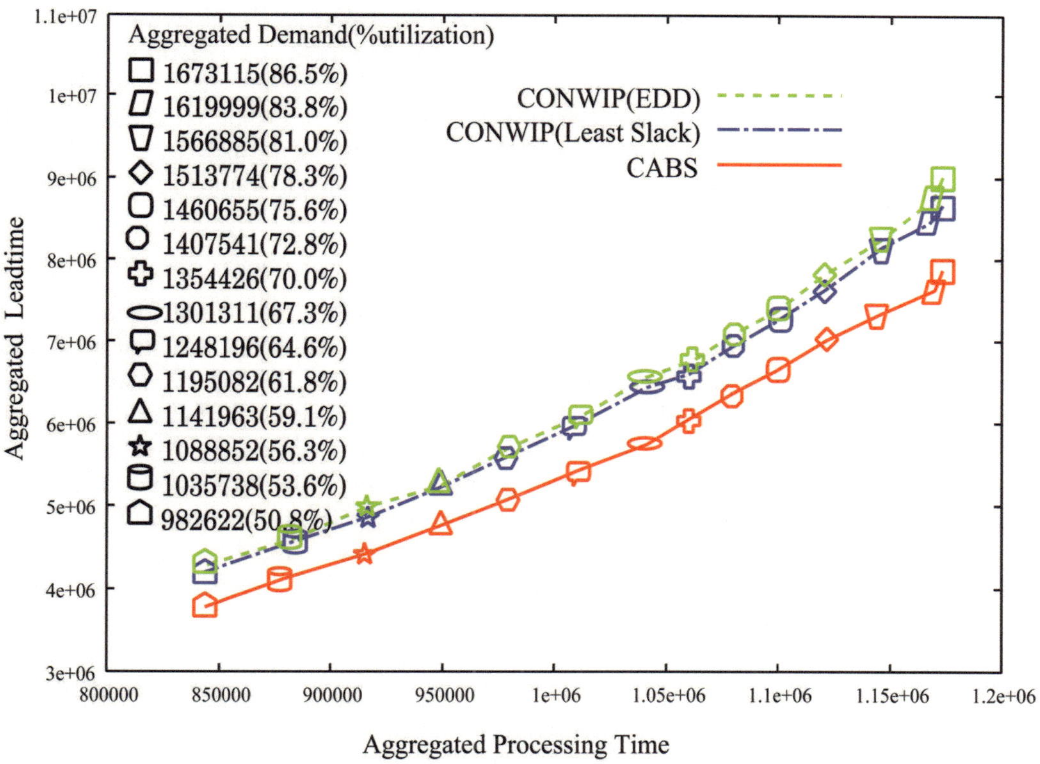

Fig. 15. Comparison of CABS and CONWIP in terms of tradeoff between leadtime and processing time

We compared the performances of CABS with those of conventional manufacturing control methods: CONWIP using the earliest due date first (EDD) dispatching rule and CONWIP using the Least Slack rule[4]. CONWIP processes jobs at the maximum speed as long as there are jobs waiting to be processed and attempts to maintain a constant level of WIP throughout a manufacturing system by introducing a new task into the system only after a processed task has left the system. Since CONWIP is more flexible than JIT, it is supposed to be more tolerant against instability of systems.

In the experiment, we compare performance of CABS and CONWIP based on more than ten demand rates in which utilization of a bottleneck agent ranges from 50.8% to 86.5%. Since the optimal WIP level for CONWIP can be decided only through trials and errors, we have conducted extensive search (i.e., more than 1,000 runs of CONWIP simulation) of the optimal WIP level for CONWIP at each demand rate of the experiments. Then we compare the best result of CONWIP with the result of CABS. To be noted is that CABS determines its WIP level autonomously in realtime without any input from users.

For both CABS and CONWIP, we conducted five independent runs of the system with different random failures. The average of those results is shown as a single datapoint in Figure 15. The experiments simulated over two months of operation after the system's initial stabilization at its startup.

Unlike to a single failure scenario in Section 3.2, in the experiments, since failures occur randomly at all the agents, CABS may not be able to fully exploit its flexibility of controlling flows of tasks to increase production of the appropriate products during failures and after their resolutions. However, Figure 15 shows that CABS performs better than CONWIP with EDD rule and Least Slack rule, succeeding to achieve higher throughput with shorter leadtime, especially in the region of high demand rates. Figure 15 also shows that both CABS and CONWIP fail to achieve the desired high demands due to failures.

5.2 Effects of buffer size limitations

In this section, we evaluate effects of each agent's buffer size to the overall behaviors of CABS. By using its messaging in conjunction with the specified buffer mechanism, CABS can autonomously avoid deadlocks in a distributed manner. In the experiments, we investigate how the size of shared buffers has effects on the performance of CABS.

In order to see the effectiveness of deadlock avoidance mechanism, we have conducted experiments with different buffer capacity at agents. Figure 16 shows the performances of CABS with the different shared buffer sizes. Each line shows the performance of CABS with a certain shared buffer size for various demand rates. In the experiment, each agent of CABS has the same size of shared buffer as depicted in a graph. From the graph it is clear that as we decrease the buffers the performance of CABS degrades. The drop in performance is logical and we have verified that even with minimal shared buffers (size 0), the system continues to function and does not get stalled due to permanent deadlocks. In absence of our deadlock avoidance mechanism, the system comes to a standstill after executing for some time. The probability of deadlocks increases as we reduce the number of buffers.

The performance drop that is caused by reduction of buffer capacity is logical and is also explained in Section 3.2 for hypothetical system-level buffer capacity (Figures 9 -11). In

[4] See (Blackstone, Phillips & Hogg 1982) for detailed presentation of the rules.

order to maintain utilization, agents need to process alternative jobs when some jobs are unavailable due to failures. In the experiment there are many agents who are not processing both kinds of jobs. Utilization of those agents cannot be maintained by increasing the production of alternative products during failures. In order to maintain utilization, those agents need to keep on processing the products that may not be finished because of failures and utilize the shared buffers to keep WIP of those products. Therefore, CABS with smaller buffer sizes has more chances of losing its agents' capacity, and is more likely to degrade the tradeoff between leadtime and throughput.

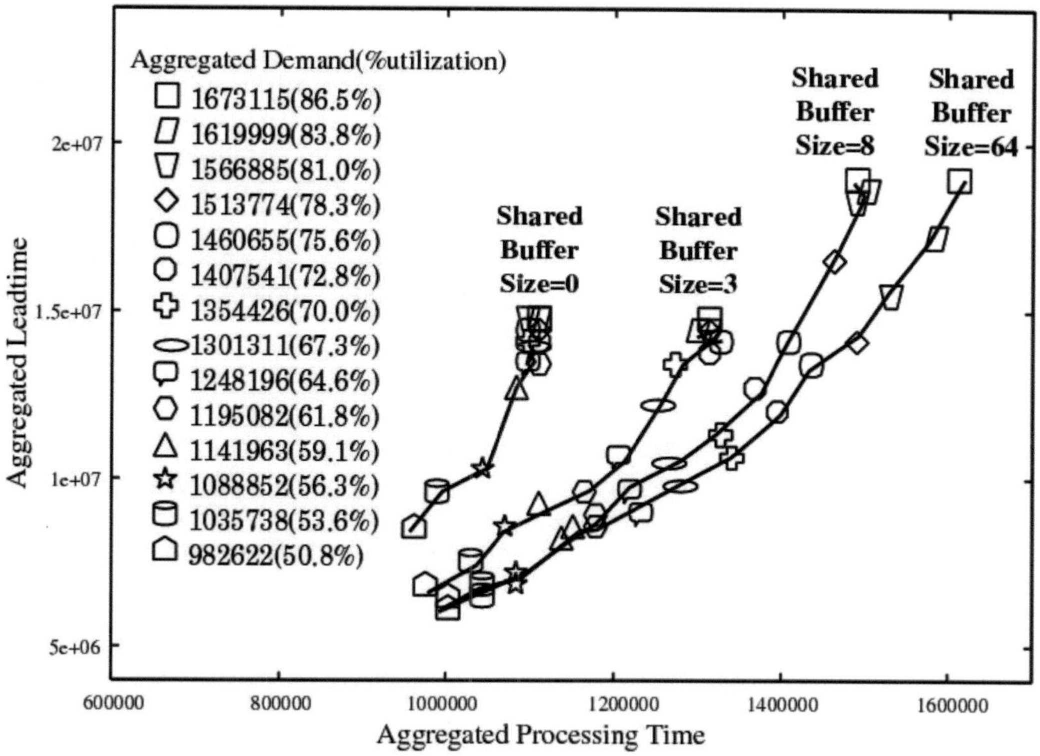

Fig. 16. Effect of buffer size limitations in CABS in terms of tradeoff between leadtime and processing time

6. Conclusion and future works

In this paper, we investigated coordination techniques for maintaining desired throughput of a semiconductor manufacturing system in the face of machine failures. The proposed system, CABS, coordinates the action of agents (i.e., workstations) through a message-passing mechanism that is similar to other token-based coordination methods. Among other methods, what is unique in CABS is the contents of the message and the ways to use them. By passing and utilizing the information of criticalities and job requirements of downstream agents, CABS can sustain high throughput by preventing starvation of wandering bottleneck agents and, simultaneously, achieve short leadtime by reducing the amount of inventories in the system.

In experiments using data of a semiconductor fabrication process, we have shown that CABS can compensate for capacity loss caused by a machine failure efficiently and validated that CABS achieves a better tradeoff between throughput and leadtime than a conventional manufacturing control method CONWIP. We believe that the coordination mechanism of CABS is suitable not only for semiconductor manufacturing, but also for other complex and unstable network systems such as transportation and communication.

We also proposed our new distributed deadlock avoidance mechanism. The deadlock avoidance algorithm works independently and can be therefore used with other dispatching and control mechanisms, other that CABS. We have shown that the proposed deadlock avoidance mechanism is distributed and it autonomously avoids the occurrence of permanent deadlocks. However, the present mechanism requires marking and reserving of some buffers (specific buffers). This additional constraint may lead to underutilization of reserved buffers which may not get utilized optimally. As another future work we want to investigate if and how this requirement of permanent reserved buffered can be avoided. But dynamically reserving the buffers on need basis, more buffers can be used as shared buffers and overall buffer occupancy and system's efficiency can be improved.

7. References

Allen, A. O. (1990), Probability, Statistics, and Queueing Theory, Academic Press.

Barabási, A.-L. (2002), *LINKED: The New Science of Networks*, Perseus Books Group.

Blackstone, J. H., Phillips, D. T. & Hogg, G. L. (1982), 'A state-of-the-art survey of dispatchin rules for manufacturing job shop operations', *International Journal of Production Research* 20, 27–45. URL: http://www.informaworld.com/10.1080/00207548208947745

Durfee, E. H. (1996), Planning in distributed artificial intelligence, *in* G. O'Hare & N. R. Jennings, eds, 'Foundations of Distributed Artificial Intelligence', John Wiley & Sons, New York, NY, chapter 8, pp. 231–245.

Faltings, B. & Nguyen, Q. (2005), Multi-agent coordination using local search, *in* 'Proceedings of IJCAI-05', pp. 953–958.

Fowler, J., Hogg, G. & Mason, S. (2002), 'Workload control in the semiconductor industry', *Production Planning & Control* 13(7), 568–578.

Fowler, J. & Robinson, J. (1995), Measurement and improvement of manufacturing capacities (MIMAC): Final report, Technical Report Technical Report 95062861A-TR, SEMATECH.

Gautam, R. & Miyashita, K. (2007*a*), Coordination to avoid starvation of bottleneck agents in a large network system, *in* M. M. Veloso, ed., 'IJCAI', pp. 1281–1286. URL: *http://www.ijcai.org/papers07/Papers/IJCAI07-207.pdf*

Gautam, R. & Miyashita, K. (2007*b*), Robust coordination to sustain throughput of an unstable agent network, *in* 'AAMAS '07: Sixth international joint conference on autonomous agents and multiagent systems'.

Glassey, C. & Resende, M. (1988), 'Closed-loop job release control for vlsi circuit manufacturing', *IEEE Transactions on Semiconductor Manufacturing* 1(1), 36–46. URL: *http://ieeexplore.ieee.org/xpls/abs all.jsp?arnumber=4371*

Goldratt, E. & Cox, J. (1992), The Goal: A process of Ongoing Improvement (2nd rev edition), North River Press.

Hopp, W. J. & Spearman, M. L. (2000), *FACTORY PHYSICS*, second edn, McGraw-Hill.

Imai, M. (1997), Gemba Kaizen: A Commonsense, Low-cost Approach to Management, McGraw-Hill.

Jennings, N. R., P. Faratin, A. R. L., Parsons, S., Sierra, C. &Wooldridge, M. (2001), 'Automated negotiation: Prospects, methods, and challenges', *International Journal of Group Decision and Negotiation* 10(2), 199–215.

Liberopoulos, G. & Dallery, Y. (2000), 'A unified framework for pull control mechanisms in multi-stage manufacturing systems', *Annals of Operations Research* 93, 325–355.

Little, J. D. C. (1961), 'A Proof of the Queueing Formula $L = \lambda W$', *Operations Research* 9, 383–387.

Miyashita, K., Okazaki, T. & Matsuo, H. (2004), Simulation-based advanced wip management and control in semiconductor manufacturing, *in* 'WSC '04: Proceedings of the 36th conference on Winter simulation', Winter Simulation Conference, pp. 1943–1950.
URL: http://www.ingentaconnect.com/content/tandf/tprs/2000/ *00000038/00000008/art00010*

Moyaux, T., Chaib-draa, B. & D'Amours, S. (2003), Multi-agent coordination based on tokens: Reduction of the bullwhip effect in a forest supply chain, *in* 'Proceedings of AAMAS-03', pp. 670–677.

Ohno, T. (1988), *Toyota Production System: Beyond Large-Scale Production*, Productivity Press.

Pfund, M., Mason, S. & Fowler, J. (2006), Dispatching and scheduling in semiconductor manufacturing, *in* J. W. Herrmann, ed., 'Handbook of Production Scheduling', Springer.

Riley, P. & Riley, G. (2003), SPADES – a distributed agent simulation environment with software-in-the-loop execution, *in* P. J. S. Chick, S., D. Ferrin & D. J. Morrice, eds, 'Winter Simulation Conference Proceedings', Vol. 1, pp. 817–825.

Roser, C., Nakano, M. & Tanaka, M. (2002), Productivity improvement: shifting bottleneck detection, *in* J. L. Snowdon & J. M. Charnes, eds, 'Winter Simulation Conference', ACM, pp. 1079–1086. URL: *http://doi.acm.org/10.1145/1030453.1030609*

Sandholm, T. W. (1999), Distributed rational decision making, *in* G. Weiss, ed., 'Multiagent Systems: A Modern Approach to Distributed Artificial Intelligence', The MIT Press, Cambridge, MA, USA, chapter 5, pp. 201–258.

Venkatesh, S. & Smith, J. (2005), 'An evaluation of deadlock handling strategies in semiconductor cluster tools', *IEEE Transactions on Semiconductor Manufacturing* 18(1), 197–201.

Wagner, T., Guralnik, V. & Phelps, J. (2003), A key-based coordination algorithm for dynamic readiness and repair service coordination, *in* 'AAMAS '03: Proceedings of the second international joint conference on Autonomous agents and multiagent systems', ACM Press, New York, NY, USA, pp. 757–764.

Xu, Y., Scerri, P., Yu, B., Okamoto, S., Lewis, M. & Sycara, K. (2005), An integrated token-based algorithm for scalable coordination, *in* 'Proceedings of AAMAS-05', pp. 407–414.

7

Requirements Driven Service Agent Collaboration

Liwei Zheng, Jian Tang and Zhi Jin
Academy of Mathematics and Systems Science, CAS
China

1. Introduction

Composition of Web services has received many attentions. On the one side the business world has developed a number of XML-based standards to specify Web services and the flow-based composition of Web services, such as WSDL (Christensen, 2001) and BPEL4WS (BPEL, 2007). On the other side, the semantic web community focuses on reasoning about web resources by explicitly declaring the preconditions and effects of Web services with terms precisely defined in ontologies, e.g. the Resource Description Format (RDF), and OWL-S (OWL-S, 2004) etc. Based on these, many efforts have been done for retrieving, discovering, and composing Web services. However, most of efforts assume that the Web services are passive computation entities. They are published and recorded as entries in the service registration centres managed by Service Agency (Kreger, 2001). They just wait there for service requesters, normally a human at present, to discover and invoke them. Some work (Paolucci & Sycara, 2003; Roman & Lausen, 2005; Roman & Scicluna, 2005) on automatic discovery of Web services have also been done by using various matchmaking algorithms according to the similarity between inputs/outputs and even preconditions /effects of Web services (Paolucci et al., 2003).

However, what will go on if the service entities are active to become autonomous Web services, namely the service agents? In fact, there are already some works which have touched this topic. DAML-S (Ankoleka et al, 2002) gives the description that allows web service to connect and interact autonomously with little intervention from the programmers. Web service architecture (Ankolekar et al, 2002a; Ankolekar et al, 2002b) has also been proposed to take advantage of DAML-S description to support automatic discovery and interaction between web services. In our previous work (Zheng & Jin, 2007a; Zheng & Jin, 2007b), web services are considered as active entities distributed in Internet which can autonomously recognize the service requests and compete or cooperate with others for fulfilling the requirements. The principle behind these works is to assume that the web services are active rational agents.

An example of rational agents is BDI agents (Wooldridge, 2000). It is an agent which can take actions based on information and knowledge from its environment. The action a rational agent takes also depends on the estimated benefits and the chances of success of the actions. With this kind of rational agents as the carriers of Web services, the service computing world will become more active, autonomous and dynamical which can be figured out as follows. Service providers design service agents which normally have specific functionalities and deploy them onto Internet. These are available service agents. Service requesters submit their service requests, normally attached with payments, which are virtual and needed-to-be-fulfilled service agents with some desired functionalities. When there is a service request, service agents negotiate with the service request for deciding if they can make contribution and get benefits from the contribution. When a service request can be satisfied by a group of service agents, these service agents form a feasible coalition to fulfil the service request. That has been called on-demand collaboration of service agents (Zheng & Jin, 2007a; Zheng & Jin, 2007b).

This chapter presents the computing mechanism for on-demand collaboration of service agents. There are several functional parts in this computing mechanism. First of all, for allowing the negotiation among the service requests and the available service agents, function ontology has been designed to provide the sharable terminology and serve as the background knowledge for both the available service agents and the service requests. After the service requests and the available service agents make agreement on their contribution relationship, these service agents form candidate feasible coalitions based on the strategy of automated mechanism design (Sandholm, 2003) for fulfilling the service requests. Normally, several feasible coalitions can be formed for one service request. Then after a negotiation process between the service request and its candidate coalitions, one of them can be chosen out and a model of a multi-agent system consisting of the service agents in the chosen coalition can be derived as the specification of the service request.

The strategies adopted in our approach are reasonable and feasible. First of all, Ontology (Sycara & Paolucci, 2003) is often used for providing common knowledge in application domain. We use function ontology for allowing the service requests and the available service agents can understand each others' functionalities. So that they can match the required functions and the provided functions. In terms of the functional matchability between a service request and a set of service agents and the satisfiability of the service request, the set of service agents forms a coalition which can satisfy the service request. Secondly, automated mechanism design is a feasible technique for preventing agents from misreporting information and quitting an established coalition which would make the coalition unstable. That will guarantee those coalitions are feasible and stable. Thirdly, the service request needs to select a suitable coalition based on some criteria, such as the service quality. And on the other hand, the service agents need to decide what they are going to serve based on what they can earn for the contribution. A negotiation framework is designed for them to make the final decision and to build a solution for the service request.

The rest of this chapter is organized as follows. Section 2 presents the function ontology. In section 3, the coalition formation of service agents has been given. And the coalition stability has been analyzed, and how to generate coalition constraints based on automated mechanism design has been discussed. Section 4 formulates the solution selection as a negotiation process and gives a negotiation framework to generate a good enough solution. A case study is given in section 5 for illustrating the whole idea for the service agent coalition formation and the negotiation-based decision-making. Section 6 presents some related works and concludes the chapter.

2. Function ontology

2.1 Ontology concepts and associations

For enabling the requirements driven agent collaboration, service agents have to understand the service requests. ***Function Ontology*** is constructed for this purpose. This ontology gives the terminology for describing the capability provided by service agents as well as the required capability submitted by service requesters. The Function Ontology is represented in a hierarchy of controllable ***resources*** together with the effects on them. For expressing the effects imposed on resources by service agents, concept *state* has been used. So the effect imposed on a resource by a service agent is characterized as the state change of the resource. These effects are caused by the *behaviours* of a service agent. Using the effect, the capability of service agents is grounded onto the state changes of the resources.

Resource. Generally speaking, anything that can be identified and can be operated by service agents is a kind of resource, e.g., information (value, date, etc.), physical entities (Hardware, people, etc.), and software systems and so on. All of these resources are described by a set of attributes, each of which features some aspect of one resource. The attributes of a resource are classified into static ones and dynamic ones. A static attribute is irrespective of time and keeps its value through its whole lifecycle. A dynamic attribute may change its value when some external behaviour happens.

Definition 2.1 (Resource) Resource is described as a 6-tuple:

$$Res:=\langle SAttr, DAttr, SARan, DARan, ValFuncofSAttr, ValFuncofDAttr\rangle$$

In which,

- $SAttr=\{sa_1,\ldots,sa_n\}$ is a finite set of static attributes of the resource;
- $DAttr=\{da_1,\ldots,da_n\}$ is a finite set of dynamic attributes of the resource;
- $SARan=\{sv_1,\ldots,sv_m\}$ is a finite set of static attribute values of the resource;
- $DARan=\{dv_1,\ldots,dv_m\}$ is a finite set of dynamic attribute values of the resource;
- $ValFuncofSAttr:SAttr\rightarrow SARan$ is a value function of static attributes; and
- $ValFuncofDAttr:DAttr\rightarrow P(DARan)$ is a value function of dynamic attributes. $P(DARan)$ is the power set of $DARan$.

For the convenience of description, we use '@' as a general separator which means 'of', e.g. *'sa@res'* means a static attribute *sa* of resource *res*, *'da@res'* means a dynamic attribute *da* of resource *res;*

State. A state of a resource is the attribute-value pair of its dynamic attribute. So we may also call the dynamic attributes the state attributes. The value of the dynamic attributes of a resource may change when some external event happens. That is the state change of a resource.

Definition 2.2 (State) Let *res* be a resource and $da_1,\ldots,da_n$ be dynamic attributes of *res*. The set of states of *res* is $state@res=(val_1,\ldots,val_n)$, in which, $val_i=ValFuncofDAttr(da_i), i=1,\ldots,n$.

Behaviour. Any possible state transition of a resource can be viewed as an effect imposed by an external behaviour. That is our essential idea by mapping behaviour to state changes.

Definition 2.3 (Behaviour) A behaviour is defined as a triple: $beh:=\langle res,s_0,s_1\rangle$, *res* is the resource operated by *beh*. $<s_0, s_1>$ is a state transition of *res*. That means that *beh* is a behaviour which makes *res* changing its state from s_0 to s_1.

If $beh_1=<res,s_1,s'_1>$ and $beh_2=<res,s_2,s'_2>$ and $s'_1= s_2$, then beh_1 and beh_2 are sequential, i.e. beh_1 is a direct precedent of beh_2, and beh_2 is a direct successor of beh_1

Function. Behaviours impose the finest-grain effects on resources. Functions could be fine- or course-grain effects. More importantly, functions can be used to claim patterns for decomposing a course-grain effect into a set of finer-grain effects (sub-functions). It tells how to decompose the function and which constraints should be followed when making the decomposition. Two function structures, i.e. the primitive function and the function decomposition mode, have been used in our function ontology. These two are not exclusive. Using the primitive function structure means that any function can implemented by a set of behaviours, while using the function decomposition mode means some function can be decomposed into a set of sub-functions via the decomposition pattern. Function decomposition modes explicitly capture the hierarchy of function decomposition.

Definition 2.4 (Primitive Function) A primitive function is a 7-tuple:

$$Fun{:=}\langle Beh, Res, Cond, CondFuncofBeh, Prop, PropFuncofBeh, Dependency\rangle$$

In which,

- *Res* is a set of resources operated by the function;
- *Beh* is a set of behaviours which constitute the function;
- *Cond* is a set of the logic expressions on the resource states;
- $CondFuncofBeh{:}Beh \to P(Cond)$ maps behaviour into a set of conditions. It gives the invokable condition for each behaviour. *P(Cond)* is the power set of *Cond;*
- $Prop=\{p_1,p_2,\ldots\}$ is a set of payoff distribution proportions;
- $PropFuncofBeh{:}Beh \to Prop$ is the proportion mapping function of behaviours so that $\sum_{i=1}^{|Beh|} p_i = 1$.
- Dependency:=⟨DirecBehDepen,CondBehDepen⟩ in which,
    - $DirecBehDepen{:}Beh \times Beh$ is a set of direct behaviour dependency relations. For any $beh_i, beh_j \in Beh$, $(beh_i, beh_j) \in DirecBehDepen$ iff beh_i is a successor of beh_i and $CondFuncofBeh(beh_j)=\varnothing$;
    - $CondBehDepen{:}Beh \times Beh$ is a set of conditional behaviour dependency relation. For any $beh_i, beh_j \in Beh$, $(beh_i, beh_j) \in CondBehDepen$ iff beh_j is a successor of beh_i and $CondFuncofBeh(beh_j) \neq \varnothing$.

Here, *Cond* is defined as a logic expression set of resource state. Suppose *r* is a resource, $state@res=(val_1,\ldots,val_n)$ is a logic expression of resource state. That means the current state of *r* is $(val_1,\ldots,val_n)$. Any composite logic expressions composed by logic connectors such as $\neg$, $\wedge$ and $\vee$ are also logic expressions of resource state.

Definition 2.5 (Function Decomposition Mode) A function decomposition mode of function *func* is described as a 6-tuple,

$$FuncDecMod(func){:=}\langle SubFuncs, Cond, CondFuncofSubFuncs,\\ Prop, PropFuncofSubFuncs, Dependency\rangle$$

In which,

- $SubFuncs=\{func_1,\ldots,func_n\}$ is a set of functions, each $func_i (1 \le i \le n)$ is a sub-function of *func;*
- *Cond* is a set of logic expressions on resource states of *func;*
- $CondFuncofSubFuncs{:}SubFuncs \to P(cond)$ maps a sub-function into a set of conditions. It gives the invokable conditions for each sub-functions;
- $Prop=\{p_1,p_2,\ldots\}$ is a set of payoff distribution proportions;
- $PropFuncofSubFuncs{:}SubFuncs \to Prop$ is a proportion mapping function so that $\sum_{i=1}^{|SubFuncs|} p_i = 1$;
- *Dependency:=⟨DirecFuncDepen,CondFuncDepen⟩* in which,

- *DirecFuncDepen:SubFuncs×SubFuncs* is a set of direct function dependency relations. $(func_i, func_j) \in DirecFuncDepen$ iff $func_j$ is a direct successor of $func_i$ and $CondFuncofSubFuncs(func_j)=\varnothing$;.
- *CondFuncDepen:SubFuncs×SubFuncs* is a set of conditional function dependency relations. $(func_i, func_j) \in CondFuncDepen$ iff $func_j$ is the direct successor of $func_i$ and $CondFuncofSubFuncs(func_j) \neq \varnothing$.

Table 1 summarizes the concepts and associations of the function ontology.

Concept class	Description	Super class
owl:thing	The root class.	without
Resource	The concept class of resource, including all the resource instances.	owl:thing
Attribute	The concept class of attribute.	owl:thing
Static attribute	The static attribute concept of resource.	Attribute
Dynamic attribute	The dynamic attribute concept of resource.	Attribute
State	A valid value of the dynamic attribute vector.	owl:thing
Behaviour	The concept for describing the state transition of resource.	owl:thing
Composite behaviour	The composition behaviour concept of two additive behaviours.	Behaviour
Function	The function concept, including all the function instances.	owl:thing
Sub-function	The sub-function concept.	Function
Function decomposition mode	The concept of function decomposition mode.	owl:thing
Execution condition	A group of logic expressions defined in resource states.	owl:thing
Execution condition of behaviour	The execution condition of behaviours in functions.	Execution condition
Execution condition of sub-function	The execution condition of sub-functions in function decomposition modes.	Execution condition
Payoff distribution proportion	The concept of payoff distribution proportion.	owl:thing
Payoff distribution proportion of behaviour	The Payoff distribution proportion concept of behaviours in functions.	Payoff distribution proportion
Payoff distribution proportion of sub-function	The Payoff distribution proportion concept of sub-functions in function decomposition modes.	Payoff distribution proportion

Table 1. Concept classes of function ontology

2.2 An example of function ontology in the domain of E-Learning

Function ontology for E-Learning domain introduced in CELF (CELF, 2005) has been developed as illustration. In this domain, an important resource is the question base. It provides various question data in the learning process, and helps teachers or students finishing their teaching or learning tasks. The attributes of the question base include its name (a static attribute) and a state variable (a dynamic attribute). And its state can be opening, closing, reading or writing. The question base can be described as:

QuestionDatabase:={{databasename},{databasestate},{"QuestionData"},

{"open","read","write","close"},funSA,funDA}

That means that the name of *QuestionDatabase* is *QuestionData* and the value of the dynamic attribute could be *open, read, write,* or *close*, i.e. the state space of resource *QuestionDatabase* is *{Open,Read,Write,Close}*. When the value is *Open*, *QuestionDatabase* is in state *"open"*.
Table 2 lists some resources of this domain and their state spaces.

Resource	State space
QuestionDatabase	{Open, Read, Write, Close}
QuestionBuffer	{NoQuestion, HasQuestions}
AnswerBuffer	{NoAnswer, HasAnswers}
StandardAnswerBuffer	{NoStandardAnswer, HasStandardAnswers}
CompareResultBuffer	{DataInvalid, ResultDataInitiated , HasResultData}
TestPointBuffer	{NoTestPointInfo, HasTestPointInfo}
TestPaper	{NoTestInfo, HasTestInfo, NotEvaluated, HasScore, Evaluated}

Table 2. Resources and their state space

Here we use behaviour *OpenDatabase* operated on resource *QuestionDatabase* as an example for showing the representation of the behaviour. This behaviour is to open a database, which will change the state of resource *QuestionDatabase* from *close* to *open*. According to the representation of behaviours, *OpenDatabase* can be described as:

OpenDatabase:=⟨QuestionDatabase,Close,Open⟩.

Table 3 gives some of the behaviours in the domain.

Behaviour	Resource	Starting state	Ending state
OpenDatabase	*QuestionDatabase*	*Close*	*Open*
ReadFromDatabase	*QuestionDatabase*	*Open*	*Read*
GetQuestions	*QestionBuffer*	NoQuestion	HasQuestions
CreateTestPaper	*TestPaper*	NoTestInfo	HasTestInfo
DisplayTestPaper	*Monitor*	*DisplaybuffEmpty*	*DisplaybuffNotEmpty*
GetStandardAnswer	*StandardAnswerBuffer*	NoStandardAnswer	HasStandardAnswers
GetAnswerFromUser	*KeyBoard*	*InputbuffEmpty*	*InputbuffNotEmpty*
RecordAnswer	*AnswerBuffer*	NoAnswer	HasAnswers
CompareAnswer	*CompareResultBuffer*	DataInvalid	HasResultData
CalculatePoint	*TestPointBuffer*	NoTestPointInfo	HasTestPointInfo
WritePointToPaper	*TestPaper*	*NotEvaluated*	*HasScore*
WriteCommentToPaper	*TestPaper*	*HasScore*	*Evaluated*
EvaluateTestPaper	*TestPaper*	*NotEvaluated*	*Evaluated*

Table 3. Behaviours and their state transitions

To illustrate the representation of the function, we use function *CreateTestPaper* as an example. Function *CreateTestPaper* gets question data from *QuestionDatabase*, and outputs question data in the form of test paper. It consists of two behaviours: *GetQuestion* and *GreateTestPaper*. In this function, each behaviour has a 50% payoff proportion. The invokable condition of *GetQuestion* is that *QuestionDatabase* is in state *Read*. The invokable condition of *CreateTestPaper* is that *QestionBuffer* is n state *HasQuestions*. According to the representation of function, *CreateTestPaper* can be described as follows.

$$CreateTestPaper{:=}\langle\{GetQuestions,CreateTestPaper\},\{QestionBuffer,TestPaper\},$$
$$\{Stateof(QuestionDatabase)=Read,Stateof(QestionBuffer)=HasQuestions\},$$
$$fun^{C},\{50\%,50\%\},fun^{P}\rangle.$$

Similar representation can be obtained for the function decomposition mode of function *GetQuestionPoint*. Function *GetQuestionPoint* obtains the point value of each question in a given test paper. It can be decomposed into two sub functions: *GetQuestionsFromPaper* and *GetDataFromDatabase*. The function decomposition mode of function *GetQuestionPoint* can be described as follows.

$$FuncDecMod(GetQuestionPoint){:=}\langle\{GetQuestionsFromPaper,GetDataFromDatabase\},$$
$$\{\},fun^{SC},\{40\%,60\%\},fun^{SF}\rangle.$$

3. Coalition formation

3.1 Coalition formation of service agents

A service requester submits a service request. To recognize the service request, the service agents have to understand the service request. Function Ontology provides the sharable terminology. A service requester should offer enough information about the request in the publication. These information includes the required functions, the payments which can be payed for the functions, and the assignment of the payments for the different functions. Formally, the structure of the service request can be given as follows.

Definition 3.1 (Service Request) A service request is described as a triple:

$$Req{:=}\langle Funcs,Payment,PayFuncofFuncs\rangle$$

in which,

- *Funcs* is a set of required functions;
- $Payment=\{p \mid p\in\mathbf{R}\}$ is a set of payments for the functions in *Funcs*; and
- $PayFuncofFuncs{:}Funcs\rightarrow Payment$ is the cost function of *Funcs*.

A service agent knows its provided functions and the prospective minimum payoff. And these information will be also needed by service requesters and other service agents. Accordingly, a service agent takes the following structure for self-description.

Definition 3.2 (Service Agent) Service Agent can be described as a triple:

$$SAgent{:=}\langle Beh,MinPay,MinPFuncofBeh\rangle$$

in which,

- *Beh* is a set of the behaviours which the service agent possesses;
- *MinPay* is a set of the minimum prospective payoffs of each behaviour in Beh; and

- *MinPayFuncofBeh:Beh→MinPay* is a minimum prospective payoff function of *Beh*.

As we have seen, the service requests and the service agents use the same terminology. That is the basis for service agents to understand the service requests. Service agents can match its behaviours with the functions' required by the service request.

Let *agt* be a service agent, *req* a service request and $func \in Funcs@req$ a required function of *req*. If $\exists beh \in Beh@func \cap Beh@agt$, then *agt* can contribute behaviour *beh* to *req*. If *agt* takes *beh* for *req*, it can get payment $Pay_{beh_k} = CostFuncofFuncs(func_j) \times PropFuncofBeh(beh_k)$. If there exists a set of service agents *C*, for $\forall beh \in Beh@func$, $\exists agt \in C$ so that $beh \in Beh@agt$, then we say that *func* can be satisfied by *C*, which is denoted by *cando(C,func)*.

For a given service request, a **service agent coalition** will be established, that is driven by payoff which the service agent might obtain from the requester. We defined the coalition structure as follows.

Definition 3.3 (Feasible coalition for service request *req*)

Let *req* be a service request and *FC* a service agent coalition. If forall $func \in Funcs@req$, $\exists C \subseteq FC$ such that *cando(C,func)*. Then *FC* is a feasible coalition for *req*.

To establish the feasible coalition is based on the prospective advantages of the service agents for the service request. With different function decomposition modes in function ontology, a service agent will receive different payoffs in different coalitions. Service agents need to decide in which coalition they can get more payoff so to decide which coalition they shoud take part in.

Let *req* be a service request and *FC* a feasible coalition of *req*. Let $agt \in FC$ be a service agent. The prospective payoff of *agt* in *FC* is

$$ProsPay_{agt} = \frac{1}{|FC|}\sum_{k=1}^{n} Pay_{beh_k}, beh_k \in FeasiBeh_{agt}$$

In which, $FeasiBeh_{agt}$ is a behaviour set for $\forall beh_j \in Beh@agt$, if $\exists func \in Funcs@req$ and $beh_j \in Beh@func$ then $beh_j \in FeasiBeh_{agt}$. $|FeasiBeh_{agt}| = n$.

As service agents can by themselves obtain the prospective payoffs they can get from different coalitions, they might "jump" from one coalition to another just for getting better payoff. For grarantteeing that the service request can be fulfilled, we need stable feasible coalitions in which all the agents have no "jumping" will.

Definition 3.4 (Stable feasible coalition) For an arbitrary feasible coalition C of service request *req*, C is a stable feasible coalition if:

1. $\forall agt \in C$, $Prospay_{agt} \geq \sum_{k=1}^{n} MinPFuncofBeh(beh_k), beh_k \in FeasiBeh_{agt}$;and
2. $\neg\exists C^*, C^*$ is a FC and if $agt \in C^*$, $Prospay^{c^*}_{agt} \geq Prospay^{c}_{agt}$

However, as the stability of coalition is just based on prospective payment, the final coalition could be unstable because there are not constraits for preventing service agents tell lies when forming the coalition which will leads to destroyable coalition. Automated Mechanism Design (Sandholm, 2003) gives solutions to this situation.

3.2 Automated mechanism design for feasible coalition

Mechanism design is the art of designing the mechanism (i.e., rules of the game) so that the service agents are motivated to tell their preferences truthfully and a desirable (according to a given objective) outcome is chosen. In this paper, the objective is to select the solutions which are not destroyable for a given feasible coalition and guarantee the service agents telling truth.

Automated Mechanism Design (AMD) is an approach, where the mechanism is computationally created for the specific problem instance at hand. For conducting automated mechanism design for the coalition of service agents, we need:

- a finite set of outcomes *O*;
- a finite set of *N* service agents which are both in the same feasible coalition *FC* of a given service request *req*;
- for each service agent agt_i,
  - a finite set of types Θ_i, a probability distribution γ_i over Θ_i (in the case of correlated types, there is a single joint distribution Γ over $\Theta_1 \times \ldots \times \Theta_N$);
  - an utility function $u_i: \Theta_i \times O \rightarrow \mathbf{R}$;
  - an objective function whose expectation the designer wishes to maximize.

Further, we need to determine the outcome set and the type set of service agents.

Definition 3.5 (Type Set) Let FC be a coalition of service agents. The type set of a service agent in FC is a vector set whose elements are all the permutations of the functions the service agent can do for *FC*.

Definition 3.6 (Outcome Set) The outcome set is a vector set whose elements are vectors like $(FDM_1^1,\cdots,FDM_{i1}^1,FDM_1^2,\cdots,FDM_{i2}^2,\cdots,FDM_1^s,\cdots,FDM_{is}^s)$, $s \in \mathbf{N}$, satisfying the following two conditions:

- Each element of a vector is a function decomposition mode.
- Every Vector denotes one unique path to accomplish a function of *req*.

This AMD process generates deterministic mechanisms automatically. A deterministic mechanism consists of an outcome selection function $\mathbf{o}: \Theta_1 \times \ldots \times \Theta_N \rightarrow O$.

Two types of constraints are used in the AMD process, IR (individual rationality constraints) and IC (incentive compatibility constraints). IR constraints ensure that every service agent would gain its lower limit of payment at least. IC constraints are to ensure that the service agents will never misreport their type.

Ex interim IR is the IR constraints used in this paper. It means that the service agent would always participate if it knows only its own type, but not those of the others.

Definition 3.7 (Ex interim IR for a deterministic mechanism)

A deterministic mechanism is ex interim IR if for any service agent agt_i, and any type $\theta_i \in \Theta_1$, we have $E_{(\theta_1,\ldots,\theta_{i-1},\theta_{i+1},\ldots,\theta_n)|\theta_i}[u_i(\theta_i, o(\theta_1,\ldots,\theta_n)) - \pi_i(\theta_1,\ldots,\theta_n) - \delta] \geq 0$, in which $\delta = \sum MinPFuncofBeh(beh_k)$, $beh_k \in FeasiBeh_i$, $FeasiBeh_i$ is the behaviour set composed of all the effective behaviours of service agent agt_i in outcome $\mathbf{o}(\theta_1, \theta_2, \ldots, \theta_N)$.

The IC constraint used in this paper is based on Bayesian Nash equilibrium. A mechanism is said to implement its outcome and payment functions in Bayesian Nash equilibrium if truth telling is always optimal to any service agent when that service agent does not yet know anything about the other service agents' types, and the other service agents are telling the truth.

Definition 3.8 (IC based on Bayesian Nash equilibrium)

IC based on Bayesian Nash equilibrium is defined as: for any service agent agt_i, any type $\theta_i \in \Theta_1$, and any alternative type report $\hat{\theta}_i \in \Theta_1$, we have:

$$E_{(\theta_1,\ldots,\theta_{i-1},\theta_{i+1},\ldots,\theta_n)|\theta_i}[u_i(\theta_i,o(\theta_1,\ldots,\theta_i,\ldots,\theta_n))-\pi_i(\theta_1,\ldots,\theta_i,\ldots,\theta_n)]\geq$$
$$E_{(\theta_1,\ldots,\theta_{i-1},\theta_{i+1},\ldots,\theta_n)|\theta_i}[u_i(\theta_i,o(\theta_1,\ldots,\hat{\theta}_i,\ldots,\theta_n))-\pi_i(\theta_1,\ldots,\hat{\theta}_i,\ldots,\theta_n)]$$

This AMD process finds all the mechanisms which can satisfy all the constraints. That is an optimal problem which can be solved by existing optimizing algorithm packages e.g. CPLEX (CPLEX,2007). The complexity of such optimizing has been analyzed by Conitzer and Sandholm in 2002 (Conitzer & Sandholm, 2002).

4. Solution selection and negotiation

For service agents, different solutions mean different payoffs. But for service requester, different solutions mean different costs and service quality. Service agents always concentrate on the payoffs, while service requester pays more attention on service quality. A QoS ontology has been used for evaluating service quality, which includes quality evaluation items, such as responding time, throughput, latency, Load-Balancing, and etc (Maximilien & Singh, 2004). This Ontology can also be used to evaluate service agent. With this QoS Ontology, service requester is able to evaluate the candidate service agent in each quality item. We could define a quality evaluation function for deciding the quality of a service agent *agt* doing a particular function *Func*. Suppose that *n* quality items are considered in a unique evaluation interval $[0,M]$, $M\in\mathbf{R}$, the evalutaion function is as follows.

$$Q(agt,Func)=\frac{1}{n}\sum_{i=1}^{n}\omega_i\sigma_i$$

In which, $\sigma_i\in[0,M]$ is the evaluation value for the i_{th} quality item, ω_i is a preference value for the i_{th} quality item of the requester. Then the solution selection problem can be expressed as follows.

Definition 4.1 (Solution) Suppose there are n service agents $agt_1,agt_2,\ldots,agt_n$ in a given feasible coalition *C*, and *m* functions $Func_1,Func_2,\ldots,Func_m$ in a given service request *req*. p_i is the weight of $Func_i$ and $\sum_{i=1}^{m}p_i=1$. Service agent agt_i has ability to fulfil $Func_j$, and the quality is $Q(agt_i,Func_j)\in[0,M]$. Suppose $W_i\subseteq F$, $F=\{Func_1,Func_2,\ldots,Func_m\}$ is the set of functions which agt_i has the ability to fulfil. A ***solution*** is a vector $(T_1,T_2,\ldots,T_n)$ requiring $\{T_1,T_2,\ldots,T_n\}$ to be a partition of *F*. $T_i\subseteq W_i$ is the set of functions fulfilled by agt_i in solution *S*.

Based on this, we can introduce more notations. Let $Q(S)$ be the quality of solution *S*, then $Q(S)=\sum_{i=1}^{n}\sum_{j\in T_i}p_jQ(agt_i,Func_j)$. Let $P_i(S)$ be the payment of service agent agt_i in solution *S*, then

$P_i(S)=\frac{\sum_{j\in T_i}p_jQ(agt_i,Func_j)}{Q(S)}P(S)$. Here, $P(S)$ is the payment function that requester is willing to pay for solution *S*. $Q(C)$ is the value that each function be assigned to the service agent who has the best quality value of doing it, and $Q(C)=\sum_{j=1}^{m}p_j\max_i Q(agt_i,Func_j)$. $P_i(C)$ is service agent agt_i's maximal payment that it is assigned all the functions in W_i, and $P_i(C)=\frac{\sum_{j\in W_i}P_jQ(agt_i,func_j)}{Q(S)}P(S)$.

Definition 4.2 (Solution Selection Problem) Given the reservation service quality request of the requester *MinQ* and the reservation payoff, $MinPay_i$, of each service agent agt_i, we want to find a solution S^* which satisfies:

- $\frac{Q(S^*)}{Q(C)}+\sum_{i=1}^{n}\frac{P_i(S^*)}{P_i(C)}=\max_S\left(\frac{Q(S)}{Q(C)}+\sum_{i=1}^{n}\frac{P_i(S)}{P_i(C)}\right)$;
- Q(S*)≥MinQ, Pi(S*)≥MinPayi, i=1,2,…,n;

We call $\frac{Q(S^*)}{Q(C)}$ the satisfaction degree of the requester, and $\frac{P_i(S^*)}{P_i(C)}$ the satisfaction degree of service agent agt_i. The two constraints in Definition 4.2 means a solution which maximizes both the requester's satisfaction degree and the service agents' satisfaction degree under the condition of every minimal expectant benefit being satisfied.

Theorem 4.1. The solution selection problem is an optimization problem and the complexity is NP-complete.

Proof. Consider a special case of the problem. Let $n=2$; agt_1, agt_2 be identical and they can fulfil all the functions. For any solution S, $Q(S)=\sum_{j=1}^{m}p_jQ(Func_j)$ is a constant. Let $MinPay_1=MinPay_2=\frac{f(Q(S))}{2P_1(C)}=\frac{f(Q(S))}{2P_2(C)}$, then we should assign proper functions to each service agent such that $P_1(S)=P_2(S)$. That is the 2-partition problem, which is an NP-complete problem.

For solving this problem, we define a negotiation process among service agents and service requester. In this process, each service agent strives to get more payment, and the service requester tries to choose a solution which could get the service quality of as high as possible. Figure 1 shows the negotiation process which can be explained as follows:

step 1. The requester proposes a solution S_0 which he prefers the most. Let S_0 be the current candidate solution S_p.

step 2. Each agt_i, $i=1,2,\ldots,n$ accepts or refuses S_p according to their preference. If all the service agents accept S_p, the negotiation process stops; if not, the service agent who refuses S_p should modify the solution and propose the modified solution. The negotiation process stops if there are service agents who fail to propose a modified solution.

step 3. The requester chooses one solution S from the modified solutions proposed by the service agents. Let S be the current candidate solution S_p and go back to step 2 to enter a new round negotiation..

In the first step, the requester can propose the solution S_0 simply by assigning each function $Func_i$ to the service agent which has the max $Q(agt,Func_i)$. Moreover, there should be $Q(S_0)\geq MinQ$. The candidate solution S_p is referred to be the current considered solution. In the second step, agt_i modifies the candidate solution S_p according to its preference. For example, in solution S_p, agt_1 is assigned to fulfil $Func_1$, but agt_1 prefers to fulfil $Func_1$ and $Func_2$. In this case, agt_1 will modify solution S_p to let agt_1 fulfil $Func_1$ and $Func_2$, and keep the other part of S_p unchanged. Service agent agt_i accepts a solution S when $P_i(S)\geq MinPay_i$. The modified solution by a service agent should be acceptable; otherwise this modification fails. Additionally, the service agents never propose a solution that has been proposed by the requester before. In the third step, the requester chooses one among all the modified solutions. If the best solution S does not meet $Q(S)\geq MinQ$, the negotiation ends without any agreement on the final solution.

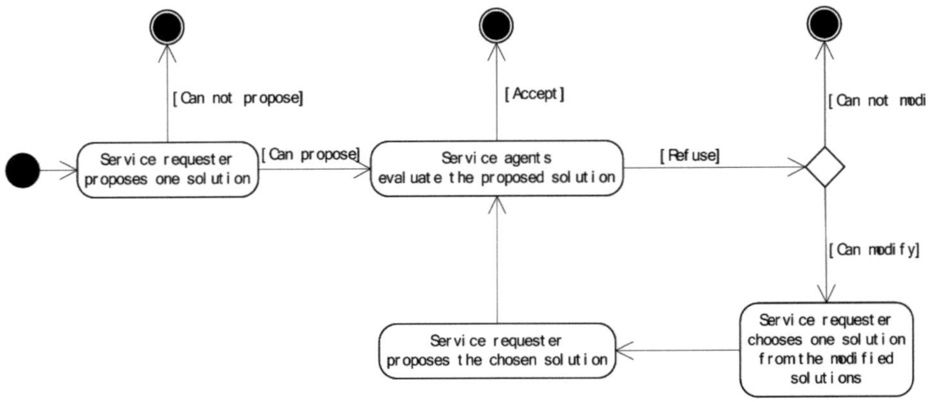

Fig. 1. Process of Negotiation

After the final solution has been chosen, we get a model of a multiple agent system which is able to implement the required service.

5. Case study

Based on the E-Learning domain function ontology in Section 2, a case study in on-demand e-learning domain is illistrated in this Section.
Firstly, the service agents and the service request should be given. For example,

$$DatabaseSearcher{:=}\langle\{OpenDatabase,ReadFromDatabase\},\{1,5\},fun^{BP}\rangle$$

Service agent *DatabaseSearcher* has the ability of searching certain data in database. It has two behaviours, *OpenDatabase* and *ReadFromDatabase.* Its expected minimum payoff for behaviour *OpenDatabase* is 1 and for behaviour *ReadFromDatabase* is 5.

$$OnlineTest{:=}\langle\{CreateTestPaperWithDatabase,Test,Evaluate\},\{40,30,30\},funFC\rangle.$$

That is a service request. It includes three functions: *CreateTestPaperWithDatabase, Test,* and *Evaluate.* The function *CreateTestPaperWithDatabase* creates a test paper based on the data from question database. Function *Test* manages the whole process of test and receives testees' answers from the test terminals. Function *Evaluate* grades the answers and gives comments about the test.
Service agents compute their expected payoff for this service reqest in the domain. For example, the service agent *DatabaseSearcher* has a behaviours *OpenDatabase* which is included in the behaviour set of request function *CreateTestPaperWithDatabase.* The payoff for fulfilling function *CreateTestPaperWithDatabase* is 40. The payoff propotion of behaviour *OpenDatabase* in function *CreateTestPaperWithDatabase* is 10%. So service agent *DatabaseSearcher* will gain 4 for contributing behaviour *OpenDatabase.* As *DatabaseSearcher*'s expected minium payoff for this behaviour is 1, it would participate the coalition for fulfilling the service request.
According to the expected payoff, a service agent coalition is established for the service request. In this case, a coalition includes four service agents is established for service request *OnlineTest.* Besides *DatabaseSearcher,* there are three service agents, *TestPaperCreater, InterfaceAgent,* and *Evaluater.* Table 4 gives the detail information of them.

Agent	Behaviours	*MinimumExpectedPayoff*
TestPaperCreater	*GetQuestions*	10
	CreateTestPaper	10
InterfaceAgent	*DisplayTestPaper*	5
	GetAnswerFromUser	5
	RecordAnswer	5
Evaluater	*EvaluateTestPaper*	10
	GetStandardAnswer	1
	CompareAnswer	5
	CalculatePoint	5
	WritePointToPaper	1
	WriteCommentToPaper	1

Table 4. Agent *TestPaperCreater, InterfaceAgent,* and *Evaluater*

Automated mechanism design is used to guarantee the stability of the coalition. The service agent type and the outcome set must be given firstly in AMD.
In service request *OnlineTest*, the appropriate functions of each service agent includes:

- *DatabaseSearcher* can participate to fulfil functions *GetDataFromDatabase, CreateTestPaperWithDatabase,* and *GetQuestionPoint.*
- *TestPaperCreater* can participate to fulfil functions *CreateTestPaper, GetQuestionsFromPaper,* and *CreateTestPaperWithDatabase.*
- *InterfaceAgent* can participate to fulfil only one function *Test.*
- *Evaluator* can participate *Evaluate, JudgeWongOrRight, CalculateFinalPoint,* and *GiveComment.*

The possible types of *DatabaseSearcher* include 6 different permutations of its appropriate functions. Different permutation means different preference of the service agent. A service agent prefers the functions which could bring it more payoff than others. The expected payoffs from the three appropriate functions of *DatabaseSearcher* are given as follows. Function *GetDataFromDatabase* is a sub-function of request function *CreateTestPaperWithDatabase,* and its payoff proportion is 50%. Function *CreateTestPaperWithDatabase* is one of the requested functions of service request, and its reward is 40. So the expected payoff of function *GetDataFromDatabase* is 20. Similarly, the expected payoff of function *CreateTestPaperWithDatabase* is 20. The expected payoff of function *GetQuestionPoint* is 1.8. Then the type of service agent *DatabaseSearcher* is θ_1=(*GetDataFromDatabase,CreateTestPaperWithDatabase,GetQuestionPoint*), or θ_2=(*CreateTestPaperWithDatabase, GetDataFromDatabase,GetQuestionPoint*).
According to definition 3.6, there are three outcomes for service request *OnlineTest.* They are o_1=(*FuncDecMod*(*GetQuestionPoint*), *FuncDecMod*(*Evaluate*)) for function *Evaluate,* o_2=(*FuncDecMod*(*CreatePaperwithDatabase*)) for function *CreatePaperwithDatabase,* and $o_3 = \Phi$ for function *Test.* Utility function gives the payoffs of each type of service agent for all the outcomes. For example, table 5 gives the utility function of service agent *DatabaseSearcher.*

U_1	O_1	O_2	O_3
□θ_1	1.8	20	0
□θ_2	1	25	0

Table 5. Utility function u_1 of *DatabaseSearcher*

Similarly, we can give all the type sets of other service agents and their utility function. The type set of service agent *TestPaperCreater* includes permutation θ_3=(*CreateTestPaper, CreateTestPaperWithDatabase, GetQuestionsFromPaper*), and θ_4=(*CreateTestPaperWithDatabase, CreateTestPaper, GetQuestionsFromPaper*). The type set of service agent *InterfaceAgent* includes only one permutation θ_5=(*Test*). The type set of service agent *Evaluator* includes permutation θ_6=(*Evaluate, CalculateFinalPoint, JudgeWongOrRight, GiveComment*), and θ_7=(*Evaluate, CalculateFinalPoint, GiveComment, JudgeWongOrRight*). Table 6 lists the utility functions of the three service agents.

U	O_1	O_2	O_3
□θ_3	1.2	25	0
□θ_4	1	20	0
□θ_5	0	0	30
□θ_6	36	0	0
□θ_7	36	0	0

Table 6. Utility values for different service agent types

According to the definition of mechanism, the mechanisms satisfying all the IR and IC constraints could be obtained by using some optimizing algorithms. In this case we use the optimal algorithm package provided by Lingo (Lingo, 2008). The computing result is as follows.

- $\{\theta_1,\theta_3,\theta_6\}\rightarrow o_1$
- $\{\theta_2,\theta_4,\theta_7\}\rightarrow o_1$
- $\{\theta_5\}\rightarrow o_2$
- $\{\theta_1,\theta_3\}\rightarrow o_1$
- $\{\theta_2,\theta_4\}\rightarrow o_1$

With the above mechanisms, the feasible coalitions for service request *OnlineTest* include:

- Coalition 1: *DatabaseSearche* and *TestPaperCreater* cooperate to fulfil function *CreateTestPaperWithDatabase*, *InterfaceAgent* fulfils function *Test*, and *Evaluator* fulfils function *Evaluate* by itself.
- Coalition 2: *DatabaseSearche* and *TestPaperCreater* cooperate to fulfil function *CreateTestPaperWithDatabase*, *InterfaceAgent* fulfils function *Test*, *DatabaseSearche* and *TestPaperCreater* cooperate to fulfil function *GetQuestionPoint*, and *Evaluater* fulfils function *JudgeWrongOrRight*, *CalculateFinalPoint*, and *GiveComment.*

The functions and function decomposition modes used in coalition generation are:

Evaluate:=⟨{EvaluateTestPaper},{TestPaper},{Stateof(TestPaper)=NotEvaluated},funC,{100%},funP⟩.

FuncDecMod(Evaluate):=⟨{GetQuestionPoint,JudgeWrongOrRight,CalculateFinalPoint,GiveComment},{},fun^{SC}*,{10%,20%,50%,20%},*fun^{SF}*⟩.*

CreateTestPaperWithDatabase:=⟨{OpenDatabase,ReadFromDatabase,GetQuestions,CreateTestPaper},{QuestionDatabase,QuestionBuffer,TestPaper},{Stateof(QuestionDatabase)=Read,Stateof(QestionBuffer)=HasQuestions}, funC,{10%,20%,30%,40%},funP⟩.

FuncDecMod(CreateTestPaperWithDatabase):=⟨{GetDataFromDatabase,CreateTestPaper},{},funSC,{50%,50%},funSF⟩.

GetQuestionPoint:=⟨{*GetQuestions,OpenDatabase,ReadFromDatabase*},{*QestionBuffer,QuestionDatabase*},{*Stateof(TestPaper)=HasTestInfo,Stateof(QestionBuffer)=HasQuestions*}, *funC*,{50%,20%,30%},*funP*⟩.

FuncDecMod(GetQuestionPoint):=⟨{*GetQuestionsFromPaper,GetDataFromDatabase*},{},fun^{SC},{40%,60%},fun^{SF}⟩.

We simulate the negotiation process to test the negotiation. In the numerical experiment, there are 4 groups: 10 service agents and 20 functions; 3 service agents and 21 functions; 4 service agents and 20 functions; 5 service agents and 20 functions. Each group is simulated for 100 times and each time we randomly generate the information of service agents and service requester, i.e. the quality of service of service agents, reservation payoff of service agents, and reservation quality requirement of service request. Five statistic data is concerned: the successful rate of negotiation, the result of negotiation comparing with optimal result in theory, the negotiation rounds when the negotiation process is terminated, the satisfaction degree of service requester, and the satisfaction degree of service agents.
Take the group with 10 service agents and 20 functions for example, the statistic data is explained as following.

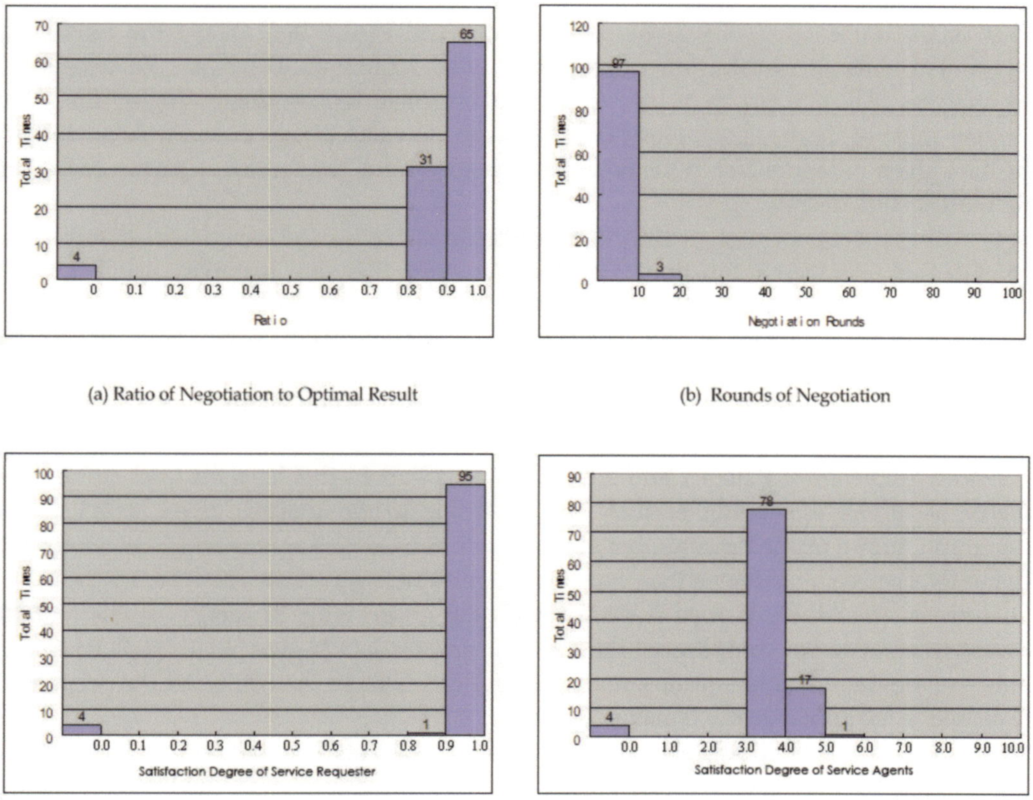

(a) Ratio of Negotiation to Optimal Result

(b) Rounds of Negotiation

(c) Satisfaction Degree of Service Requester

(d) Satisfaction Degrees of Service Agents

Fig. 2. Statistic Data of 10&20

First, within 100 simulations, they all have solution with optimal total satisfaction degree. By negotiating, 4 of them fail. That is to say, there is 4 times that service requester and service agents could not get consensus but there is a solution which could satisfy every one. So the successful rate of the negotiation is (100-4)/100=96%.
Second, the result of negotiation comparing with optimal result in theory is concerned. Denote the total satisfaction degree of negotiation σ^* and optimal total satisfaction degree σ. Figure 2(a) shows the statistic data about $\tau = \sigma^* / \sigma$. Except for that 4 times negotiation fails, τ is no less than 0.8. Further, most of them (65 in 96) are more than 0.9.
Third, we want to know when the negotiation terminates, i.e. how many rounds of the negotiation. Every time service requester chooses one solution and proposes it(first time service requester proposes one) in the modified solutions proposed by service agents, we say that the negotiation passes one round. In our numerical experiment, we tolerate the negotiation round no more than 100 or we stop it without waiting for its terminating. The numerical experiment data of negotiation round is given in Figure 2(b). In the Figure, there are 3 times those negotiation rounds are more than 10, but 97 times that are less than 10. So no matter the negotiation is successful or not, the negotiation is easy to be convergent.
Next is the satisfaction degree of service requester. Figure 2(c) shows the numerical experiment data of satisfaction degree of service requester. There are 96 successful negotiations. All of them have the service requester satisfaction degree higher than 0.8. Further, most of these negotiations (95 in 96) have the value higher than 0.9. According to the data given in Figure 2(c), if the negotiation is successful, the service requester could get high satisfaction degree.
How about the service agents' satisfaction degree? In our numerical experiment setting, each agent can do averagely 6 functions. On the other hand, there are 10 service agents and 20 functions; so the average number of functions that each agent could be assigned is that 20/10=2. Then the average expect satisfaction degree could be calculated by 2/6=0.33. So the total satisfaction degree of 10 service agents is $0.33 \times 10 = 3.3$.
We record the total satisfaction degree of 10 service agents and show them in the Figure 2(d). Within 96 negotiation that are successful, 20 of them have the total satisfaction degree of service agents lower than 3.3, and there are 76 negotiations that have the total satisfaction degree of service agents higher than 3.3. According to the analysis given in the above paragraph, such a result indicates that in the negotiation, service agents could frequently get higher total satisfaction degree than expect average value.
Analysis of other three groups is similar with the group with 10 service agents and 20 service requesters. For comparison, the concrete statistic data is given in Table 7. From the table, we see that in all the groups, the successful rate is more than 90%. All the properties discussed in the 10&20 group remain.
According to the statistic data above, we can conclude that our negotiation framework has a high successful rate and the negotiation result is close to the optimal. Additionally, negotiation process is easy to be convergent. Moreover, service requester could expect high satisfaction degree (higher than 0.8) and mostly, service agents could get higher total satisfaction degree than expect average value. These all confirm that our negotiation framework generates good result.

Agent& Function	Successful Rate	Result Ratio		Negotiation round		Requester Satisfaction		Agents Satisfaction	
		0	4	0	0	0	4	0	4
		0.0-0.1	0	0-10	97	0.0-0.1	0	0.0-1.0	0
		0.1-0.2	0	11-20	3	0.1-0.2	0	1.0-2.0	0
		0.2-0.3	0	21-30	0	0.2-0.3	0	2.0-3.0	0
		0.3-0.4	0	31-40	0	0.3-0.4	0	3.0-4.0	78
10&20	96%	0.4-0.5	0	41-50	0	0.4-0.5	0	4.0-5.0	17
		0.5-0.6	0	51-60	0	0.5-0.6	0	5.0-6.0	1
		0.6-0.7	0	61-70	0	0.6-0.7	0	6.0-7.0	0
		0.7-0.8	0	71-80	0	0.7-0.8	0	7.0-8.0	0
		0.8-0.9	31	81-90	0	0.8-0.9	1	8.0-9.0	0
		0.9-1.0	65	91-100	0	0.9-1.0	95	9.0-10.0	0
		0	9	0	0	0	9	0	9
		0.0-0.1	0	0-10	89	0.0-0.1	0	0.0-1.0	0
		0.1-0.2	0	11-20	4	0.1-0.2	0	1.0-2.0	0
		0.2-0.3	0	21-30	2	0.2-0.3	0	2.0-3.0	61
		0.3-0.4	0	31-40	0	0.3-0.4	0	3.0-4.0	30
7&21	91%	0.4-0.5	0	41-50	0	0.4-0.5	0	4.0-5.0	0
		0.5-0.6	0	51-60	2	0.5-0.6	0	5.0-6.0	0
		0.6-0.7	0	61-70	1	0.6-0.7	0	6.0-7.0	0
		0.7-0.8	1	71-80	1	0.7-0.8	0	7.0-8.0	0
		0.8-0.9	4	81-90	0	0.8-0.9	3	8.0-9.0	0
		0.9-1.0	86	91-100	1	0.9-1.0	88	9.0-10.0	0
		0	8	0	0	0	8	0	8
		0.0-0.1	0	0-10	87	0.0-0.1	0	0.0-1.0	0
		0.1-0.2	0	11-20	2	0.1-0.2	0	1.0-2.0	0
		0.2-0.3	0	21-30	2	0.2-0.3	0	2.0-3.0	90
		0.3-0.4	0	31-40	2	0.3-0.4	0	3.0-4.0	2
5&20	92%	0.4-0.5	0	41-50	1	0.4-0.5	0	4.0-5.0	0
		0.5-0.6	0	51-60	0	0.5-0.6	0	5.0-6.0	0
		0.6-0.7	0	61-70	2	0.6-0.7	0	6.0-7.0	0
		0.7-0.8	0	71-80	0	0.7-0.8	0	7.0-8.0	0
		0.8-0.9	1	81-90	1	0.8-0.9	2	8.0-9.0	0
		0.9-1.0	91	91-100	3	0.9-1.0	90	9.0-10.0	0
		0	6	0	0	0	6	0	6
		0.0-0.1	0	0-10	92	0.0-0.1	0	0.0-1.0	0
		0.1-0.2	0	11-20	2	0.1-0.2	0	1.0-2.0	0
		0.2-0.3	0	21-30	3	0.2-0.3	0	2.0-3.0	93
		0.3-0.4	0	31-40	0	0.3-0.4	0	3.0-4.0	1
4&20	94%	0.4-0.5	0	41-50	1	0.4-0.5	0	4.0-5.0	0
		0.5-0.6	0	51-60	1	0.5-0.6	0	5.0-6.0	0
		0.6-0.7	0	61-70	0	0.6-0.7	0	6.0-7.0	0
		0.7-0.8	0	71-80	0	0.7-0.8	0	7.0-8.0	0
		0.8-0.9	2	81-90	0	0.8-0.9	2	8.0-9.0	0
		0.9-1.0	92	91-100	1	0.9-1.0	92	9.0-10.0	0

Table 7. Statistic Data of Negotiation

6. Conclusions

This paper proposes a feasible strategy for agent-based service computing. The main contributions of this paper may fall into two points.

Firstly, we figure out the vision of agent-based service computing. In which, both the service requests and the available services are agents. The service requests are virtual agents which need the available service agents or their composition to implement the required functionalities and give out the payoffs as rewards. And the available services are service agents which offer their capabilities to implement required functionalities and gain necessary payments. With some constraints, the agent society can form stable coalitions.

Secondly, we design a process for enabling the agent-based service computing. A function ontology has been introduced to allow the understanding between the required service requests and the available service requests so that the required service requests can know which available service agents they need and the available service agents can know which required service requests they can make contributions to. Then those available service agents who can fulfil one required service agent when they form a group form a stable coalition by using automated mechanism design. Finally, the required service agents negotiate with that candidate stable coalition to select the final solution via a negotiation process on the criteria of service quality as well as the payoff.

One of the future directions is extending this work by integrating the widely-used Web service description standards. For example, generating a BPEL-based specification of the multiple agent system for fulfilling the required service agent from the coalition of service agents will allow the agent-based composite service to be executable. That will help to combine this approach with the current efforts in industry.

7. References

ABNF. (2005). Augmented BNF for Syntax Specifications: ABNF, http://tools.ietf.org /html/rfc4234, 2005.

CPLEX. (2007). ILOG Mathematical Programming Optimizers, http://www.ilog.com/ products/cplex/, 2007.

BPEL. (2007). Ws-BPEL2.0(OASIS), http://docs.oasis-open.org/wsbpel/2.0/, 2007.

SOAP. (2004). SOAP version 1.2. http://www.w3.org/TR/soap/,2004.

OWL-S. (2004). OWL-S: Semantic markup for Web services. http://www.daml.org/ services/owl-s/1.0/, 2004.

Jaeger, M.; Engel, L.; Geihs, K. (2005). A Methodology for Developing OWL-S Descriptions. *Proceedings of First International Conference on Interoperability of Enterprise Software and Applications Workshop on Web Services and Interoperability,* pp. 13–31. ISBN1846281512, Geneva, Switzerland, Feb, 2005, Springer Berlin, Heidelberg.

Roman, D.; Lausen, H.; Keller, U. (2005). The Web Service Modeling Ontology WSMO. *WSMO Working Draft D2, final version 1.2.* www.wsmo.org/2004/d2/, April 2005;

Roman, D.; Scicluna, J.; Feier, C. (2005). Ontology-based Choreography and Orchestration of WSMO Services. *WSMO Working Draft D14.* www.wsmo.org/2004/d14/, March 2005.

Conitzer, V. ; Sandholm,T. (2002). Complexity of mechanism design, *Proceedings of the 18th Conference on Uncertainty in Artificial Intelligence (UAI02),* pp. 103-110,ISBN978-1558608979,Edmonton,Canada,Aug.2002,Morgan Kaufmann, San Fransisco.

Christensen, E.; Curbera, F. (2001). Web services description language (WSDL)1.1,http://www.w3.org/tr/wsdl.

Maximilien, E. M.; Singh, M. P. (2004). A framework and ontology for dynamic web services selection. *IEEE Internet Computing,* Vol 8,No. 5, Sept.-Oct. 2004, 84–93, ISSN1089-7801.

Paolucci, M. ; Sycara, K.; Kawamura, T. (2003). Delivering semantic web services. Technical Report CMU-RI-TR-02-32, Robotics Institute, Carnegie Mellon University.

Sandholm, T. (2003). Automated mechanism design: A new application area for search algorithms. *Proceedings of the International Conference on Principles and Practice of Constraint Programming(CP03) LNCS2833,* pp.19-36,ISBN3540202021, Kinsale, Ireland, Spet.2003,Springer,Heidelberg.

Ankolekar, A.; Burstein, M. et al. (2002a). DAML-S:Web Service Description for the Semantic Web, *Proceedings of The First International Semantic Web Conference (ISWC) LNCS2342,* pp. 348-363,ISBN978-3540437604, Sardinia, Italy, June, 2002, Springer, Heidelberg.

Ankolekar, A.; Huch, F.; Sycara, K. (2002b). Concurrent Semantics for the Web Services Specification Language Daml-S. *Coordination Models and Languages LNCS2315,* pp. 567-577, ISBN9783540434108, Jan. 2002, Springer, Heidelberg.

Wooldridge, M. (2000). *Reasoning About Rational Agents.* TheMIT Press,ISBN978-0262232135,Cambridge, MA.

Zheng, L.; Jin, Z. (2007a). Requirement driven agent collaboration. Proceedings of the 2007 International Conference on Autonomous Agents and Multiagent Systems, AAMAS 2007, pp. 446–448,ISBN978-8190426275, Honolulu, Hawaii, May 2007,ACM New York, USA .

Zheng, L.; Jin, Z. (2007b). Requirement driven agent collaboration based on functional ontology and AMD. *Proceedings of 11th IEEE International Workshop on Future Trends of Distributed Computing Systems,* pp. 189–198. ISBN0769528104, Sedona, AZ, April, 2007, IEEE Computer Society, New York, USA .

Kreger, H. (2001). Web services conceptual architecture (WSCA 1.0). IBM Software Group Note.http://www-306.ibm.com/software/solutions/webservices-pdf/WSCA.pdf, 2001.

CELF. (2005). Computing Research Association. Cyberinfrastructure for education and learning for the future: A vision and research agenda. http://www.cra.org/reports/cyberinfrastructure.pdf, 2005.

Sycara, K.; Paolucci, M. (2003). Automated discovery, interaction and composition of semantic Web services. *Journal of Web Semantics.* Vol 1,No.1,Dec. 2003, 27–46, ISSN 1570-8268.

Sycara, K.; Paolucci,M. (2004). Ontologies in agent architectures. *Handbook on Ontologies in Information Systems.* Springer-Verlag, 2004, 343-364, ISBN3540408347, Berlin.

Paolucci, M.; Sycara, K. (2003). Autonomous Semantic Web services. *IEEE Internet Computing.* Vol 7, No.5, Sept.-Oct. 2003, 34 - 41, ISSN1089-7801.

Lingo. (2008). An Overview of LINGO. www.lindo.com, 2008.

Casati, F.; Ilnicki, S ; Jin, L. (2000). Adaptive and dynamic service composition in eflow. *Proceedings of 12th International Conference on Advanced Information System Engineering LNCS1789*, pp. 13-31. ISBN9783540676300, Stockholm, Sweden, June, 2000, Springer Berlin, Heidelberg.

8

Coordination Control and Fault Diagnosis of Production System Using Multi-agent Technology

Li Tiejun[1], Peng Yuqing[1] and Wu Jianguo[2]
[1]Research Institute of Robotics and Automation, Hebei University of Technology,
[2]School of Mechanical Engineering, Tianjin University,
Tianjin, China

1. Introduction of multi-agent and Petri net

1.1 Introduction of multi-agent

1.1.1 The conception of multi-agent

The so-called multi-agent system is the collection of many calculable agents, and every agent is a physical or abstract entity, which can effect both itself and the circumstance and correspond with other agents.

The main idea of multi-agent is that a complicated problem should be divided and the portions should be contributed to every independent agent, then they compose of the answer to the question. Agent can resolve some local problems independently, and finish the whole answer by collaboration.

The incompact network is composed of many agents, these agents interact with each other to resolve the problems that single agent cannot solve because of its insufficient in ability or knowledge. Its main feature is every agent hasn't sufficient ability or knowledge to resolve the problems, when these agents operate at the same time, not only the data is incompact, but also there's no whole control system.

1.1.2 Control structure of multi-agent system

Multi-agent is composed of many agents which have the function of circumstance observation, task layout and operation. In order to make these agents into a big complicated system to fulfill some stated tasks efficiently, a proper control system is needed. Therefore, the main research problem of control structure is to design a correct proper local control plan to guarantee that multi-agent system can resolve the given problems efficiently, including relevant task distribution, correspondence and conflict solution. According to agents' relative relations in the system, generally, there are some kinds of structures[1,2]:

(1) Architecture of fully connected networks

In this system structure, as shown in Fig.1.1, every agent is in an equal relation, every two agents can correspond directly. Equal correspondence and locality of information are the main feature of this kind of structure. This structure demands that every agent should have the function module of correspondence and control, and save all the agents' information and knowledge in the system.

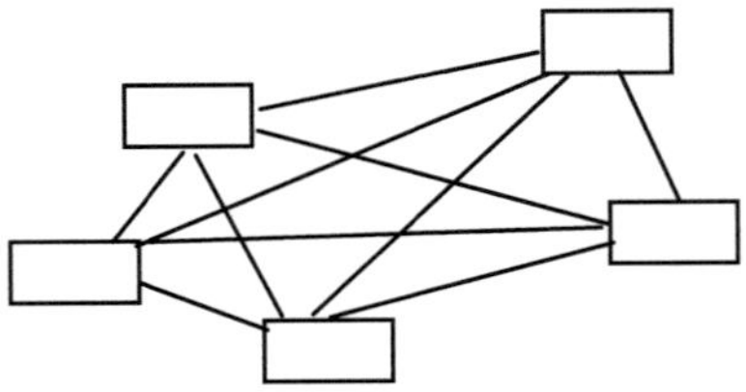

Fig. 1.1 Architecture of fully connected networks

(2) Architecture of fully layered networks

In this system, as shown in Fig.1.2, agents are divided into different layers, the agents at the same layers cannot correspond directly, but have to be finished by the upper layers. The agents of upper layer take charge of decisions and controls of agents at the under layers. Each agent in this structure needn't save all the agents' information in the system, just save the under layers' agents' related information and knowledge, but it is inferior to the structure of fully connected networks in correspondence.

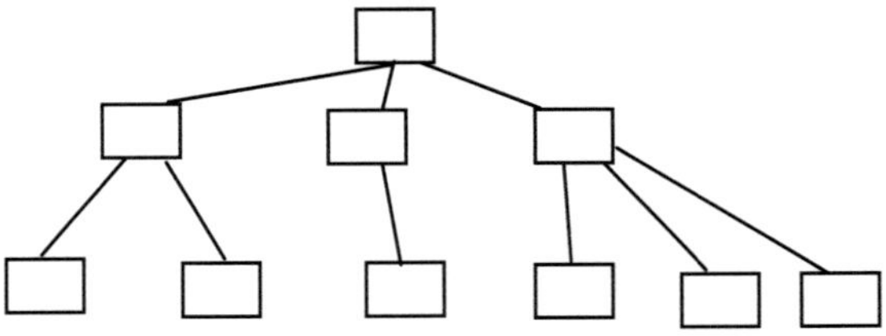

Fig. 1.2 Architecture of fully layered networks

(3) Architecture of allied networks

Agents in the system are divided into different agents allies according to some way (generally according to distance , functions and so on). There's a assistant agent in the inner of every ally, it is in charge of different allies' correspondence. Different allies are in the opposite relation, similar to the relations of every agent in fully connected networks.

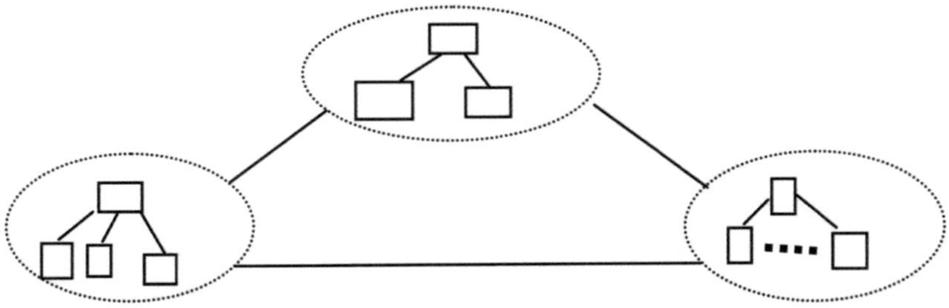

Fig. 1.3 Architecture of allied networks

1.1.3 Correspondence in the multi-agent system

In the system of multi-agent, correspondence means the information exchange between different agents and agents and the circumstance, then they can negotiate and collaborate to fulfill the goal. There are four kinds of ways of agents' information exchange. [3,4]

(1) Direct correspondence

Agents have its own physical connection and send information to the target agent directly by certain protocol, such as TCP/TIP . In this way, agent sends information to the target agent with its own address.

(2) Combine into allies freely, then correspond by Correspondence server

When there are too many agents, the cost is expensive by wholly direct correspondence. One solution is to combine multi-agent into allies, every ally has a correspondence server to fulfill correspondence function, that is there's no direct correspondence among agents, but correspondence server as the media. Structure of allied system is as Fig.1.4.

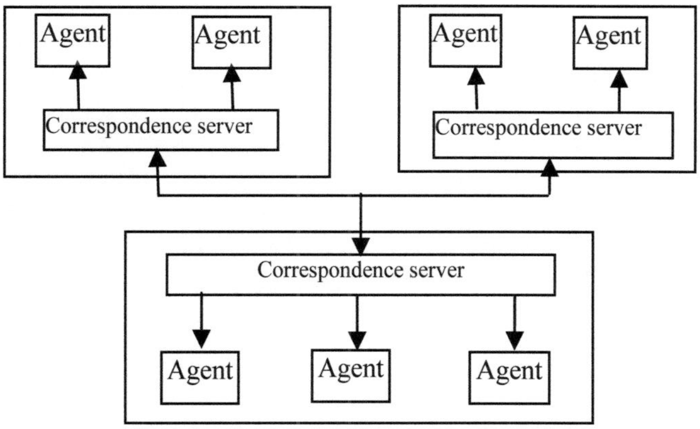

Fig. 1.4 allied system [4]

(3) Broadcast correspondence

If an agent need send information to all the agents in the circumstance, or it doesn't know which agent it should sent to, it has two choices: sends the message by broadcast; or sends it directly to every agent by correspondence. When the message is longer, it will burden the internet largely by direct correspondence. As broadcast correspondence needn't copy many shares of the message and send them separately, therefore, it can avoid the big burden of the networks.

(4) Blackboard Correspondence

This way is the traditional correspondence in the field of artificial agents. All the agents give away and read information in the share area (or blackboard) In order to realize the secrecy of part of information, the problems are generally divided into different abstract layers, agents in different layers have different visited rights.

1.1.4 Multi-agent cooperation and harmony

Harmony and Cooperation among multi-agents are the basic conception of multi-agent system. Harmony means that every agent continuously ratiocinates its behavior purpose and makes decisions to realize a harmonious work process. Generally the cooperation among agents is for fulfilling the common task[5]. Correspondence is very important to the operation and harmony of multi-agent system, agents must share their plans, goals and data to fulfill their cooperation and solution[5]. The ways of cooperation among multi-agent are mainly contract net, blackboard model and the consequence share model.

1.2 Basic knowledge about Petri net

1.2.1 The introduction of Petri net model[6]

System model is an abstract show of the factual system. Petri Net aims at researching the organized structure and dynamic behaviors of the system, with an eye to the possible changes and their relations in the system, it describes the various dependent relations in the accidents,

such as orders, subsequence and so on. It is fit for describing the system which has rules and is featured by flowing behaviors, such as substance flows, information flows and so on.
The structure factors of a Petri Net mainly include place, transition and arc. Place mainly describes the possible local status of the system, for example, fault symptom and phenomenon in the fault diagnose or buffer in the computer and so on. Transition is used to describe the incident of modifying the system status, such as the information process and transmission in computers or correspondence system. Arc is factor to connect place and transition, describing the direction of the system status change .
In Petri Net model, signs are included in the place, their dynamic changes in the place represent the different status of the system. If one place describes one resource, it may include some signs or zero, the amount of the signs represents the amount of the resources. If one place describes one proposition, it can include one sign or no sign, when it has one sign, that shows the proposition represented by the place is true, or that is false. Just as Fig. 1.5, the circles represent the place, the thin sticks represent the transition, and the directed lines represent the arc, and the black dots in the place represent the signs.

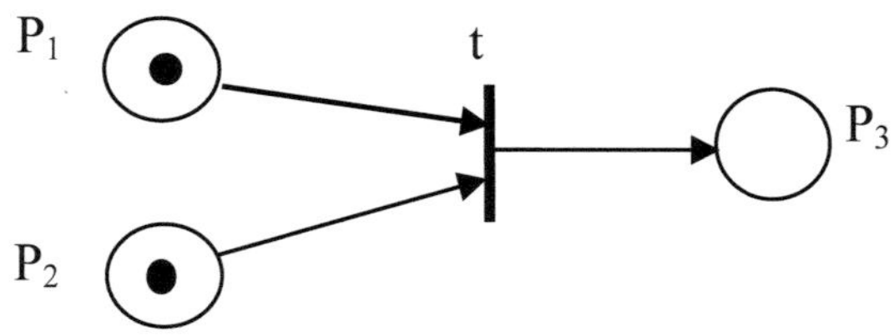

Fig. 1.5 Petri Net

1.2.2 The definition of Petri Net

Definition 1-1 A three tuple $N = (P, T; F)$ is called directed net, shortened form Petri, its sufficient and necessary conditions are:

1. $P \cap T = \Phi$;
2. $P \cup T \neq \Phi$;
3. $F \subseteq (P \times T) \cup (T \times P)$;
4. $dom(F) \cup cod(F) = P \cup T$.

there, $\mathrm{dom}(F) = \{x \mid \exists y : (x, y) \in F\}$, $\mathrm{cod}(F) = \{x \mid \exists y : (y, x) \in F\}$ are defining region and value region of F.
In the net, P and T are two no-intersectant set, called basic factors set of net N, P is places set of net N, T is transitions set of net N, F is the flows relations of net N. One net can be represented by a directed dimidiate figure: generally little dots represent place P, a length of black line represents transition T, the arrows from x to y represent the (x,y) in the flow relationship, its description is shown in Fig.1.6.

Definition 1-2 Prepositive set and postpositive set. Set $N = (P, T; F)$ is a Petri Net, $X = P \cup T$ are elements set, then

$$^{\circ}x = \{y \mid (y, x) \in F\} \text{ is called Prepositive set of } x;$$

$$x^{\circ} = \{y \mid (x, y) \in F\} \text{ is called postpositive set of } x.$$

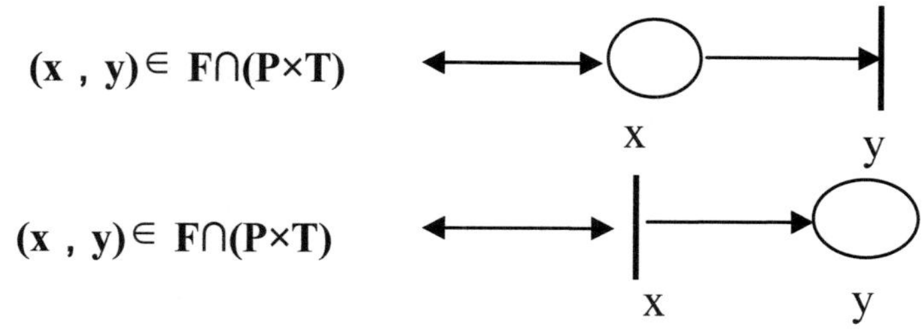

Fig. 1.6 Flow relationship

If place $p\in P$ and transition $t\in T$, makes $p \in t^{\circ} \cap {}^{\circ}T$, then when t happens, p will lose and get token. This feature in the structure shows that the resources in p affect t similar to the activator in chemical reaction. The net which hasn't this structure is called pure net.

On the other hand, if $x,y\in X$, $x\neq y$, *but* ${}^{\circ}x={}^{\circ}y \wedge x^{\circ}=y^{\circ}$, then no matter in structure or in behavior, x cannot distinguishes from y, the net which hasn't this structure is called simple net, the feature of simple net is there's no two transitions which have the same input and output place set.

Definition 1-3 If $\forall x\in X: x^{\circ}\cap{}^{\circ}x=\Phi$, then N is called pure net.

If $\forall x,y\in X: {}^{\circ}x={}^{\circ}y \wedge x^{\circ}=y^{\circ} \Rightarrow x=y$, then N is called simple net.

1.2.3 Petri Net system

Net is different from system. Net just includes place, transition and arc, while system means nets and the original sign related to net. In the circumstance without special introduction, the Petri Net is Petri Net system. In the process from net to net system, the original distribution of resources has to be demonstrated, the activity rule on the frame has to be regulated.

Definition 1-4 the conditions which a six tuple $\sum=(P , T , F , K , W , M_o)$ is a Petri Net system are:

1. $N=(P, T, F)$ is a Petri Net, is called basis net of $\sum$.
2. $K: P\rightarrow N^{+}\cup\{\infty\}$ is capacity function of place.
3. $W: F\rightarrow N^{+}$ is right function.
4. $M_0: P\rightarrow N_o$ is original mark, it satisfied : $\forall p\in P: M_0(p)\leq K(p)$.

$N^{+}=\{1,2,3 , \ldots\}$, $N_o=\{0,1,2,3,\ldots \}$. In the figure show of the net system, to arc $f\in F$, when $W(f)>1$, labels $W(f)$ on the arc. When the capacity of place is limited, generally writes $K(p)$ on the side of the circle of place p, and when $K(p)=1$, the sign is generally omitted. The black dots of place represent the original sign which represents a kind of resource distribution in place.

Definition 1-5 The condition of transition.

1. $t^{\circ}={}^{\circ}t\cup t^{\circ}$ is called the expansion of t.
2. The condition that t has friable in m:

$$\forall s\in {}^{\circ}t: M(s)\geq W(s,t) \wedge \forall s\in t^{\circ}: M(s)+W(t,s)\leq K(s)$$

Labels that t has friable in m $M[t>$, and M enables t happen or t enabled happens by M. Here ${}^{\circ}t$ represents all the input place's set of t. $|{}^{\circ}t|$ represents the amount of input place of t; t° represents all the output place's set of t. $|t^{\circ}|$ represents the amount of output place of t.

Definition 1-6 The consequence of transition
If $M[t>$, then t can happen in M, changes labeled M to M's successor M', the definition of M' is any $s \in S$:

$$M'(p) = \begin{cases} M(p) - W(p,t) & \text{if } p \in {}^{\cdot}t - t^{\cdot} \\ M(p) + W(t,p) & \text{if } p \in t^{\cdot} - {}^{\cdot}t \\ M(p) - W(p,t) + W(t,p) & \text{if } p \in {}^{\cdot}t \cap t^{\cdot} \\ M(p) & \text{if } p \notin {}^{\cdot}t^{\cdot} \end{cases}$$

M° is M's successor, the truth can be labeled $M[t>M^{\circ}$.

1.2.4 The basic relationship of incidents

Petri Net has description abilities of various structures, these structures are the basis to construct other net system of all levels, and also instruments in the basic phenomenon and related theories research. Here are the most basic structures:

1. Order: Transition t_2 must happen after t_1;
2. Conflict: One of transition happens in the transitions of t_1, t_2, t_3, other two can't happen, the substance of conflict is the competition of resources, t_1, t_2, t_3 compete for the share resources;
3. Subsequence: Transition t_1, t_2, t_3 can happen at the same time;
4. Synchronization: Transition can happen just in the circumstance of having all the resources;
5. Union: The happens of transition t_1, t_2, t_3 affect the same resource, if one of transition t_1, t_2, t_3 happens, t_4 will happen;
6. Mixed: The concomitant status of subsequence and conflict.

2. The task allocation of multi-produce line

The problem of the task allocation is a kind of typical problem in combined optimization, it is applied in production, plan and flexible manufacture system, such as mode classification, work allocation, equipment collocation, production arrangement and printed circuit board design and so on.

In the system of multi-agent, the task allocation's mechanism is one of the research hotspots. The reason is that in one aspect whether or not it can make the ability of each agent maximal and avoids taking more resources, and in another aspect task allocation relates to how to complete the tasks together through the effective dialogue and the negotiation if one of the agents did not has the ability to complete its task. Task allocation mechanism establishment is the foundation of studying the multi-agent cooperation [7]. There are four steps in the multi-agent task allocation: task decomposition, task allocation, task solution and result synthesis [8].

2.1 The ways and mechanism of task allocation

2.1.1 The ways of task allocation

Task allocation mainly has two ways: concentration and distribution. In the way of concentration, there are two means: one is man-made allocation in advance, which the task is arranged by personnel in advance to agent in the system. The other is one agent is in charge of task decomposition (which is called Trader), this agent saves the ability table of every agent in the present MAS system. When there is a task to be finished, Trader inquires the able agent whether accepts this task, if it receives the agreeable information, Trader will tell the promulgator of the task, or tell that no agent can fulfill the task at present. In the way of distribution, there are also two means: acquaintance and contract net.

2.1.2 The mechanism of task allocation

The mechanism of task allocation mainly has:

1. General market balance[8]: general market balance furnishes a structure of distributing task and resources to agents efficiently by market mechanism. In this structure, resources are dominated by market with some commodities, and these commodities are the resources that can deal with the task. Every commodity is thought limitless and successive. There are two kinds of agents in market: manufacturers and consumers; the agents which have resources are considered as manufacturers, while the agents which have tasks to resolve are considered as consumers. Manufacturers and consumers balance the market by bargain.
2. Auction: The way of auction is widely used in the task allocation of multi-agent. Auction is a market mechanism, it decides resources allocation and price by a series of clear rules. Price decision is based on the huckster of market anticipants[8].
3. Contract net: Contract net is an important mechanism of task allocation; it is widely used in the arithmetic of task allocation. The basic ideas are: when the manager has some tasks to be solved by other agents, it broadcasts the messages which relate to the tasks to other agents, agents who have received the messages will examine the ability to solve the problem; and then send out its value of bidding and become the bidder; finally, the manager evaluate those values and elect the most appropriate bidder to award the task, that is to say, it fulfill the negotiation process according to the mechanism of tender-bidding–selected as it does in the market[9]. The task allocation negotiation process is given as the Fig. 2.1.

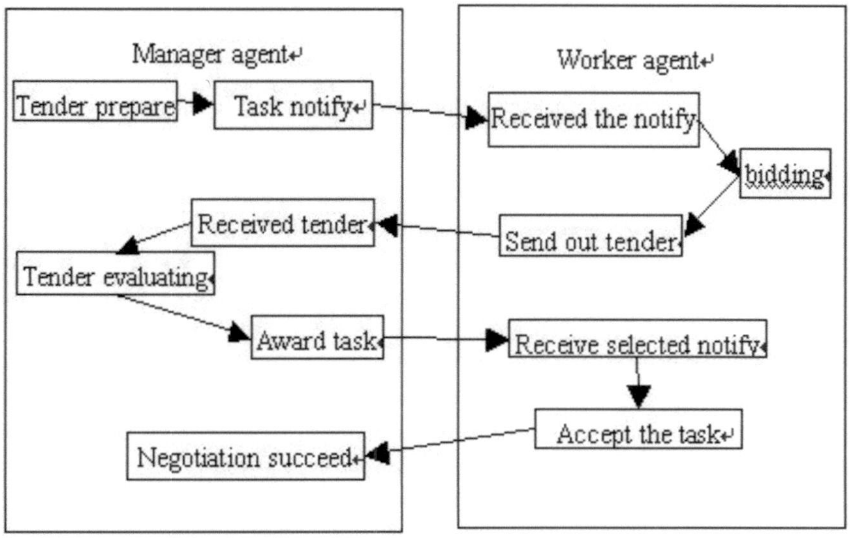

Fig. 2.1 The negotiation process based contract net

2.2 The goal and principles of task allocation and some simplification to the system

2.2.1 The goal of task allocation

The goal of task allocation is to find a feasible way of allocating tasks to the agents, and make the system achieving the set goal and minimize the sum-dissipation after allocating the tasks. The dissipation needs to synthesize factors of the time consumption to complete the task, the reliability of the system, the energy consumption of the system and the effect to the environment of the system.

2.2.2 Principles of task allocation

1. Minimize the consumption time

To minimal the overall time of completing the task, that is, request for $T^*=min(\Sigma Tij)$, and Tij represents the time agent i finish the task j. It contains two parts of the time to fulfill the task: the cost of executing and the cost of communication.

2. Equilibrated the load of each agent

Suppose the load of agent i is Li, that is, it need to satisfy $L1=L2=......=Ln$, this means each agent work with same load, avoiding the phenomena that some of the agents overload longtime but some of agents work with relatively little load. The load of each agent needs to be equilibrated as possible as we can in the process of task allocation

3. Maximize the reliability

The reliability needs to be maximized in the task allocation. The reliability needs synthesize those influence factors: rate of average failure of system, the working time of system and the working environment of system. The system which a person has joined must consider men's factor. Here, we did not consider the incredible because of cheating of agents; the reliability here is focus on the reliability caused by the failure, the working time and the environment of the system. Task allocation should assign the task for the equipment which has the highest reliability.

4. Minimize the energy consumption

Different quantity of energy may be consumed when accomplish a particular task by different agents, task should be allocated to the agent who with minimal energy consumption when accomplish the task.

5. Minimize the influence to the environment

Different systems will cause the different influence to the environment, we should allocate more tasks to the system which with the minimal influence to the environment.

2.2.3 Assumptions and simplification to the practical system

The agents in the system are heterogeneous, that is, a particular task may take a different mounts of running time, rate of fault and influence to the environment if executed on different agents. But we consider it is same for an agent to deal with different type of tasks with same quantity except for the difference at ability, that is, if an agent can solve different types of tasks, the efficiency is same while executing those tasks.

Deeming the communicate costs are zero. Speaking strictly, two parts of the time are cost to finish the task: the time is used for executing and the time is used for communication[10]. The time used in the communication occupied only a very small part then the execution, so we ignore the costs of communication in the article and deem the overall costs of time only used for execution; it is accord with the practical system and can make the discussion simplified.

The tasks needed to be allocated are independent, that is, there are not dependent relationships between tasks, i.e. the tasks *T={t1,t2.........tm}*, it did not need to finish t_j firstly if we want to finish $t_i(i \neq j)$.
The agents are absolutely honest. That is, deeming the values of state which are returned by agents are absolutely believable in the article. There is no cheating when send the values of state for all the agents (include person).
The tasks which need to be allocated have been decomposed. Task decompose is a very important step in the task allocation, but we will not take the task decompose into account in the article and think the task have been decomposed, it can be done by the former agent or the person.

2.3 Factors influence on task allocation and its computinon[11]

There are three factors influence on the task allocation: the integrative reliability of agent; the average energy consumption of agent; the factor influence on the environment; let λ_i be the integrative reliability of agent *i*; let δ_i be the average energy consumption of agent *i* and let $f(\delta_i)$ be the factor of energy consumption; let ζ_i be the influence level to the environment of agent *i*. The computational methods are as follows:

2.3.1 The integrative reliability computation

λ is a set of integrative reliability of agents and the dimension is equal to the number of agents. The value of λ_i fall into [0,1]. It means completely credible of the system when $\lambda_i=1$ and unbelievable when $\lambda_i = 0$.
Let λ_{ifr} be the reliability related to faults; let λ_{iwt} be the reliability related to the working time and let λ_{iwe} be the reliability related to working environment. All the values of that variable are fall into [0,1].
The computation of integrative reliability λ_i is given by (1).

$$\lambda_i = \frac{1}{3}\times\lambda_{ifr}+\frac{1}{3}\times\lambda_{iwt}+\frac{1}{3}\times\lambda_{iwe} \tag{1}$$

Assuming agent *i* has gone wrong *N* times and its maximal allowed number is *M*, then λ_{ifr} can be computed as

$$\lambda_{igz} = \begin{cases} \dfrac{M-N}{M}, \ldots\ldots N \le M \\ 0, \ldots\ldots\ldots\ldots N > M \end{cases} \tag{2}$$

The reliability is the highest when $\lambda_{igz} = 1$ and is the lowest when $\lambda_{igz} = 0$. The computation of *M* is given by (3) and (4) based on the relationship between rate of equipment faults and the working time, as in Fig. 2.2.

$$GZL = \begin{cases} c \; -k_1 T_{wt} + b, \ldots\ldots\ldots\ldots T_{wt} < T_{cs} \\ b \ldots\ldots\ldots\ldots\ldots\ldots\ldots\ldots T_{cs} \le T_{wt} < T_{mh} \\ k_2(T_{wt} - T_{mh}) + b, \ldots\ldots\ldots T_{mh} \le T_{wt} \le T_{sm} \end{cases} \tag{3}$$

$$GZS = \begin{cases} L_1 \ldots\ldots\ldots\ldots T_{sm} < T_{cs} \\ L_2 \ldots\ldots\ldots\ldots T_{cs} \le T_{sm} < T_{mh} \\ L_3 \ldots\ldots\ldots\ldots T_{mh} \le T_{wt} \le T_{sm} \end{cases} \tag{4}$$

Here,

$$L_1 = (c+b)T_{tw} - \frac{1}{2}k_1 T_{wt}^2$$

$$L_2 = (c+b)T_{cs} - \frac{1}{2}k_1 T_{cs}^2 + b(T_{wt} - T_{cs})$$

$$L_3 = (c+b)T_{cs} - \frac{1}{2}k_1 T_{cs}^2 + b(T_{mh} - T_{cs}) + \frac{1}{2}k_2(T_{wt} - T_{mh})^2 + b(T_{wt} - T_{mh})$$

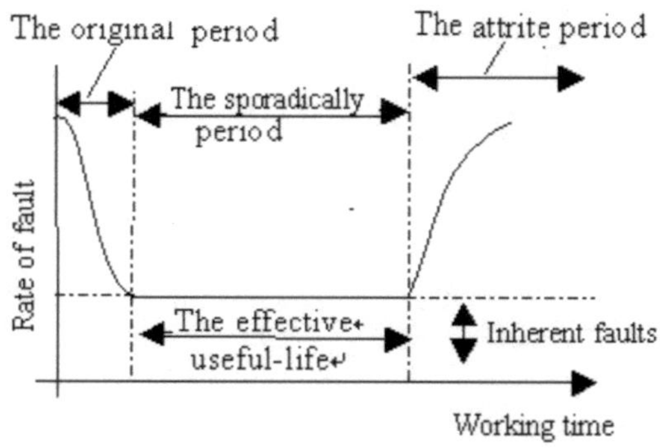

Fig. 2.2 Graph of equipment fault ratio

We simplified it to a linear relationship, as in Fig.2.3. There is not much influence on the practical model after simplified, but it is better for the follow analysis.

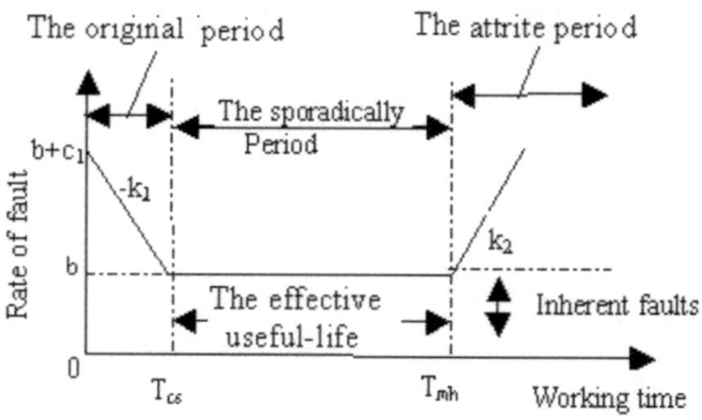

Fig. 2.3 Simplified graph of equipment fault ratio

$$M = Int\,(GZS + 0.5) \tag{5}$$

In (5), Int() denotes to acquire integer for the content in the parenthesis and the GRL in formula (3) denotes the rate of faults. The relationship between the rate of faults and the

working time is expressed by the formula (3), the relationship between the numbers of faults, the working time is represented by the formula (4) and the GZS represent the number of faults. Coefficients k_1, k_2 and c can be given by practical system and experience.
Considering the relationship between the working time and the dependability of normal machine is not linear, we simplified it to linear as the Fig.2.4. The calculation of λ_{iwt} is given as (6).

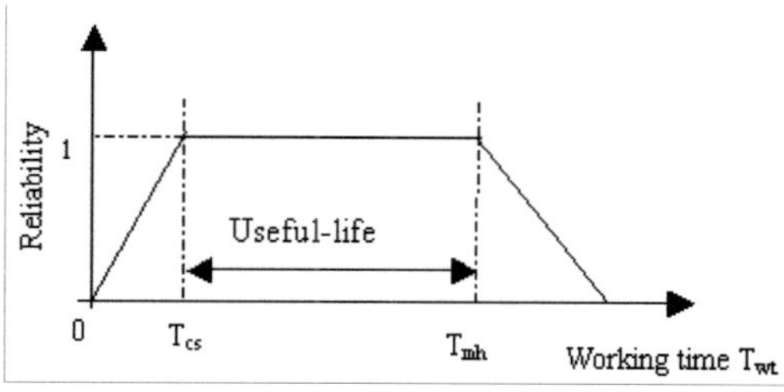

Fig. 2.4 The relationship between reliability and working hours

Let T_{sm} be the life-span of agents; let T_{mh} be the attrite life-span of agent; let T_{cs} be the original life-span of agents; let T_{wt} be the whole working time of agents. The computation of λ_{iwt} is given as (6).

$$\lambda_{iwt}=\begin{cases}\dfrac{1}{T_{cs}}\times T_{wt},\ldots\ldots T_{wt}<T_{cs}\\ 1\ldots\ldots T_{cs}\le T_{wt}\le T_{mh}\\ 1-\dfrac{1}{T_{sm}-T_{mh}}(T_{wt}-T_{mh}),\ldots T_{mh}<T_{wt}\le T_{sm}\end{cases}\qquad(6)$$

The reliability related to the working time of agents is the highest when λ_{iwt}=1 and is the lowest when λ_{iwt}=0.
λ_{iwe} represents the influence to the dependability related to environment and its value, whose range is [0 , 1], depends on the practical environment. It means the working environment of system is of great benefit to the agent when λ_{iwe} =1 and of not benefit when λ_{iwe} =0.

2.3.2 The computation of influencing factors of energy consumption

δ is the set of energy consumption of multi-agent system with n elements and $f(\delta_i)$is also a vector of n dimensions which corresponds with a value of δ_i. The value range of $f(\delta_i)$ is [0,1], here we defined δmax is the maximal energy consumption and δmin is the minimal energy consumption. The consumption of $f(\delta_i)$ is given as (7).

$$f(\delta_i)=\begin{cases}1,\ldots\ldots\delta_i<\delta_{min}\\ \dfrac{\delta_{max}-\delta_i}{\delta_{max}-\delta_{min}},\ldots\ldots\delta_{min}\le\delta_i\le\delta_{max}\\ 0,\ldots\ldots\delta_i>\delta_{max}\end{cases}\qquad(7)$$

It is absolutely fulfilled the demands for the energy consumption when $f(\delta)$=1 and it means energy consumption is too much when $f(\delta_i)$=0.

2.3.3 The factor of influence to the environment

ζ represents the set of influence factors to the environment, and the value range is [0,1]. It is means the smallest influent upon t the environment when ζ_i=1 and is the biggest when ζ_i=0 .the value can be decided by person or the agent based on the practical situation.

2.4 Definitions of some interrelated matrix and its calculation methods

2.4.1 Ability matrix

We consider a system consisting of a set of agent A. The agent can perform different tasks. The set of types of tasks that the agents can perform is denoted by T. Every agent $a_i \in A$ may be able to perform only tasks that are a subset of the overall set of types of tasks in the system. We assume that there is a binary relation $\rho \subset A \times T$ such that for any $a_i \in A$, $t_j \in T$, $\rho_{ij}=1$ if agent ai can carry out a task of t_j and $\rho_{ij}=0$ if agent a_i can not carry out a task of t_j, it can be described as a matrix[12].

For example, suppose there are three agents in the system, $A = (a_1, a_2, a_3)$ and five type of tasks $T = (t_1, t_2, t_3, t_4, t_5)$. The first agent can carry out the tasks of type t_1 and t_4, the second one can carry out the tasks of both types t_1, t_2, t_3, t_4 and t_5, the third agent can carry out tasks t_3 and t_5. The relation ρ can be describes as the Fig. 2.5.

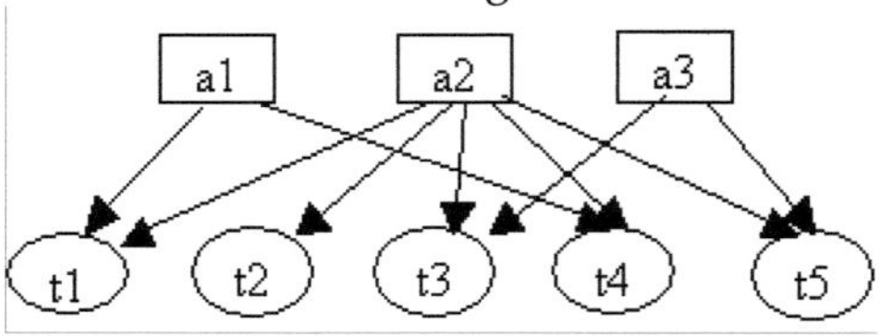

Fig. 2.5 An exmple of the relation between agents and tasks

The relation ρ also can be defined a matrix as

$$\rho = \begin{bmatrix} 1 & 0 & 0 & 1 & 0 \\ 1 & 1 & 1 & 1 & 1 \\ 0 & 0 & 1 & 0 & 1 \end{bmatrix}$$

2.4.2 State matrix

Let the state matrix be $S= \{s_1, s_2, s_3 \ldots s_n\}$, and $S_i= (i, l, \mu_i, \lambda_i, \delta_i, \zeta_i)^T$. The state matrix shows the states of each agent in the system and the meanings of the symbols in the formula are that:

i represents the tab of the agent in the system;

l represents the residual tasks for the agent i;

μ_i represents the average working efficiency of agent i;

λ_i represents the integrative reliability of the agent i;

δ_i represents the average energy consumption of agent i;

ζ_i represents the influence level to the environment of agent i .

2.4.3 The dissipated matrix $C_{n \times n}$

Let the dissipated matrix be $C_{n \times n}$== $\{c_{ij} \mid 1 \le i \le n \ \& \ 1 \le j \le n \}$, c_{ij} represents the integrative consumption that the agent a_i need to accomplish t_j. We define the consumption of time that a agent to accomplish a task to be the basic dissipated matrix, and define the generalized consumption which consider the reliability of agents ,the energy consumption and the factors affect to the environment to be the generalized dissipated matrix. The basic dissipated matrix can be calculated as (8).

$$Cj_{ij} = \frac{l + t_j}{\mu_i + \rho_{ij}} \tag{8}$$

The generalized dissipated matrix can be calculated as (9).

$$C_{ij} = \frac{cj_{ij}}{\lambda_i \times f(\delta_i) \times \zeta_i} \tag{9}$$

When the influencing factors of λ_i, $f(\delta_i)$ and ζ_i equal to 1, the elements in the generalized dissipated matrix do not change, if one of the factors equal to 0 when agent ai to carry out the task t_j, then one of rows correspond with a_i will become infinite and we filled it use INF, in this situation we will consider ai has not the ability to fulfill the task and supposed it did not exist. In the normal situation, the range of λ_i , $f(\delta_i)$ and ζ_i are [0,1], and C_{ij} will be bigger when thinking the influence of those factors.

2.4.4 Task allocation matrix $X_{m \times n}$

The value of x_{ij} is 0 or 1, when x_{ij} = 1, it means to allocate t_j to agent ai; when x_{ij} = 0, it means does not to allocate t_j to agent a_i; A task allocation matrix shows a way which the task can be allocated.

2.5 The limiting conditions and allocation arithmetic of the task allocation

2.5.1 The limiting conditions of the task allocation

Certain conditions should be satisfied when in the task allocation, here we call those conditions as the limiting conditions, when the tasks have been allocated ,each of the agent has to check whether the tasks allocated to them satisfy the limiting condition or not, if the task satisfy the limiting condition, the agent performed it next, if not, the tasks need to be decomposed again.(the work can be done by the agent or the people, and we do not discuss it here),then the agent allocate the tasks again. In the paper, the limiting condition is given as follows (here suppose the task t_j have been allocated to the agent a_i):

$$\begin{aligned} l + t_j &\leq E_{i\max} \\ t_j &= E_{i\min} \end{aligned} \tag{10}$$

Let E_{imax} be the maximal task the agent ai can receive and let E_{imin} be the minimum task the agent a_i can receive; l is the tasks the agent ai is dealing with.

2.5.2 Arithmetic of task allocation

In conclusion, when the task allocation agent receives each agent's status, it can figure out the generalized dissipated matrix based on the above method. And then it deem the generalized dissipated matrix as coefficient matrix in Hungary arithmetic to allocate tasks, the task allocation process is as follows:

Allocating the tasks to the task allocation agent by person;

When the task allocation agent receives tasks, it sends the status request to each agent;
Agent who receives the request sends its status to the task allocation agent;
The task allocation agent figure out the generalized dissipated matrix as the coefficient matrix in Hungary arithmetic based on Equ.(8) and Equ.(9);

1. Judging the relationship between rows (*m*) and columns (*n*) in the matrix, if $m=n$, using the standard Hungary arithmetic to allocate tasks (take the generalized dissipated matrix as the coefficient matrix); if $m \neq n$, then we can translate the coefficient matrix (the generalized dissipated matrix) into a square matrix through adding, then we can allocate tasks through standard Hungary arithmetic takes the square matrix as the coefficient matrix.
2. The task allocation agent send the task allocation information to agents, then agents who received the message check whether the task satisfy the limiting condition or not, if the task satisfy the limiting condition, the agent start to work; if not, it need person to decompose the tasks and assign to the task allocation agent, then go to the step 2.

3. Coordination control of multi-production lines system

3.1 Definition of multi-agent cooperation

Multi-agent cooperation refers to a behavior of multi-agent's assorting of themselves to accomplish a common goal. Most document regard cooperation as a kind of common sense behavior. Some definitions are [13,14,15]:

Definition 3-1: an agent use the goal of another agent. On the assumption that both the agents have been designed , there is no conflict of targets, an agent just accomplishes the other's goal passively.

Definition 3-2: an autonomous agent uses another agent's goal, on the assumption that the cooperation happenes between the agents with capacity of accepting or refusing cooperation.

Definition 3-3: between two autonomous agents, if either meets one of the acquirement, we say that the two agents cooperate.

1. an agent uses another agent's target.
2. Between agents there is conflict, but it can still reach a balance.
3. two or more agents finish their own targets due to their exchange.

We can see that cooperation's goal is to make two autonomous agents get a common target to finish a common task.

Definition 3-4: the so called cooperation is a interaction to make two or more agents exchange information and finish a task together.

Definition 3-5[16]: Multi-agent collaboration means many agents cooperate to finish a common task.

3.2 Definition of multi-agent coordination

Definition 3-6: coordination means each agent infers and disposes its behavior in order to guarantee harmony and consistency in behavior.

Definition 3-7: coordination is the interaction among group of agents taking the same action, is the adaption of the environment. The agent changes its willing to get coordination.

Definition 3-8 [17]: coordination is a procedure that each agent continuously reasons their action desires and makes decision to let all the member get into harmony and consistency.

Typical assorting includes timely delivering messages between agents, guarantying the relating agents synchronism and avoiding redundant solution.
Mintzberg considers the three basic coordination procedures[18]:

1. Mutual adjustment is the most easy form of coordination. It happens when two or more agents agree to share the sources to get a certain common target. Agents always need to exchange information, and continuously modify their behavior according to other agent's behavior.
2. Direct Supervision happens between two or more agents when one of them has the capacity of controlling others, this kind of priority relation usually erects by mutual modify.
3. Standardization is an usual way to assort. In a certain circumstance, the manager assort in a standard way, namely to erect a standard procedure for its subordinate to follow in some circumstance.

3.3 Mechanism of blackboard

The basic idea of blackboard is: when many agent experts solve a question, blackboard is a share work space , all these experts can see the blackboard. The seeking answer begins when question and original data are recorded on the blackboard. All experts see the blackboard and find opportunity to solve question by others' experience knowledge. A solution is recorded on the blackboard when an expert finds enough information to make a answer. Then the new information maybe let other experts continue. Repeat this procedure until the answer is obtained.
There is three basic component in blackboard model. They are:

1. Knowledge Source(KS): the knowledge source means all the knowledge needed to solve problems, each knowledge source accomplishes a complete and independent work , it always use some information on the blackboard to modify the information of another blackboard layer. There are two parts in KS: precondition and action. Precondition is used condition of KS, it is judgement about information change on blackboard. Action describes operation which KS effects blackboard, it is a process. When the information change accords with the precondition of KS, the KS is activated and carries out corresponding action, it adds, deletes or updates solution elements. Each KS is independent and cannot direct call mutually, then only communicate with blackboard. Control mechanism is in charge of monitoring information change on blackboard and checks KS precondition continuously. Once some KS precondition is tenable, the KS is activated and its action is carried out. The information on blackboard is modified which may be activate other KS by control mechanism. Blackboard information changes like this, till find the final solution.
2. Blackboard: solving room for shared problems. It is organized in hiberarchy, it stores information and state data, such as initial data, part solution, substitution solution and final solution, sometimes control data is stored. In the process of seeking solution, KS modifies blackboard continuously. Correspondence among KS only uses blackboard., and the information in blackboard only be added ,deleted and modified through KS.
3. Mechanism of supervise and control : according to the problems on the blackboard and solution skills of KS, adaptive KS is activated which made KS fit for the blackboard change. The design of control mechanism is the most complex task. Its object is to exert pretty KS in context.

3.4 Coordination control of multi-production lines system based on multi-blackboard mechanism

3.4.1 Multi-blackboard mechanism model of multi-production lines system

The traditional blackboard cooperation mechanism applies a public blackboard, which each agent sends messages to and acquire messages from. Here a new model is put forward, in this model, blackboard is classified into there different levels: central blackboard, middle-level blackboard and rock-bottom blackboard. Different hierarchic agent of the system is corresponded to the three different hierarchic blackboards. Every agent has its own knowledge source and control system, and each agent is given a blackboard.

The division among the three-level blackboard and corresponding knowledge source and control mechanism is different. The main responsibility of central blackboard is to manage high-level system administration and coordination, for example, the beginning and ending of system, the overall allocation of resources, and the fault diagnosis. The responsibility of middle-level blackboard lies in the resources allocation and administration of subsystem, the cooperation and fault diagnosis of subsystem, reporting the movement of subsystem to high-level blackboard and resources request. The responsibility of rock-bottom blackboard is to coordinate operation of related agent combination in subsystem, report staggered situation and the corresponded fault code to middle-level blackboard etc.

In this blackboard model, agent of different levels is all considered as an agent. Every agent has its own blackboard. The data produced from each agent is classified into two groups: "result date" and "middle data". Besides added into its own blackboard, result data need to be added into the blackboard of upper agent at the same time in order to make decisions for the upper agent. Middle data need not be added into upper agent blackboard and only need be added into its own blackboard. Thus the quantity of data stored and processed by middle-level blackboard and high-level blackboard will reduce significantly, and in particular when the amount of data in system is large the efficiency of the whole of system will be improved. The multi-blackboard cooperation model is established in Fig.3.1.

3.4.2 Multi-agent coordination Petri Net model based on multi-blackboard mechanism

Each agent owns blackboard in the system and different levels' agent is corresponded to different levels' blackboards. Each agent in the system can reason independently, so there must be have a coordination mechanism to complete the coordination among different levels' agent and different agent at the same level, in order to assure the coordination of the overall system. The qualitative analysis and quantitative analysis of the system and dynamic analysis to agent system can be accomplished by applying Petri Net to describe the complex multi-agent system, which time factor is added into Petri Net and Petri Net coordination simulated model is established.

1. Coordination model of multi-agent system in synchronous forms

For different levels' blackboard, there are agents in three different levels, which are center management decision agent, production lines agent and stand-alone agent. They work at the same clock signal which called in synchronous forms. In conveniency, there are three stand-alone agents and two production lines agents. The Petri Net coordination model of multi-agent system is shown as Fig.3.2.

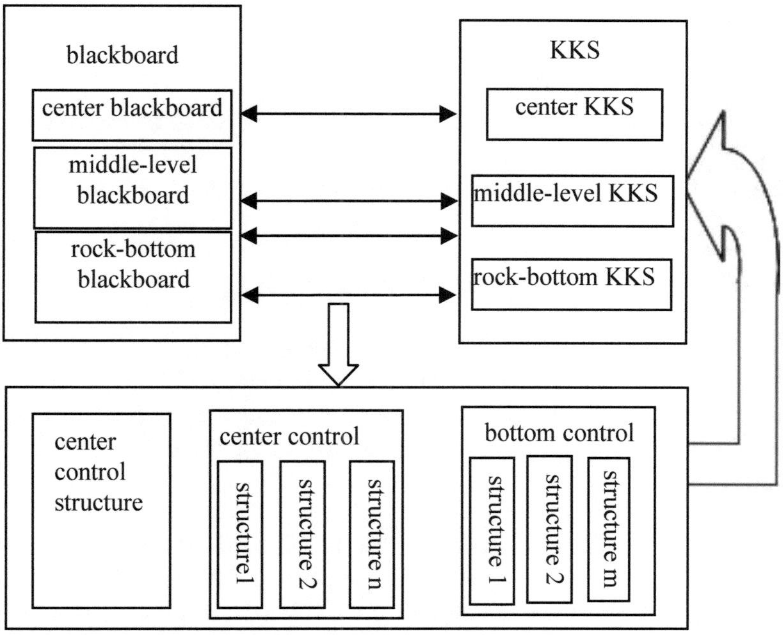

Fig. 3.1 Multilevel blackboard model of packing line system

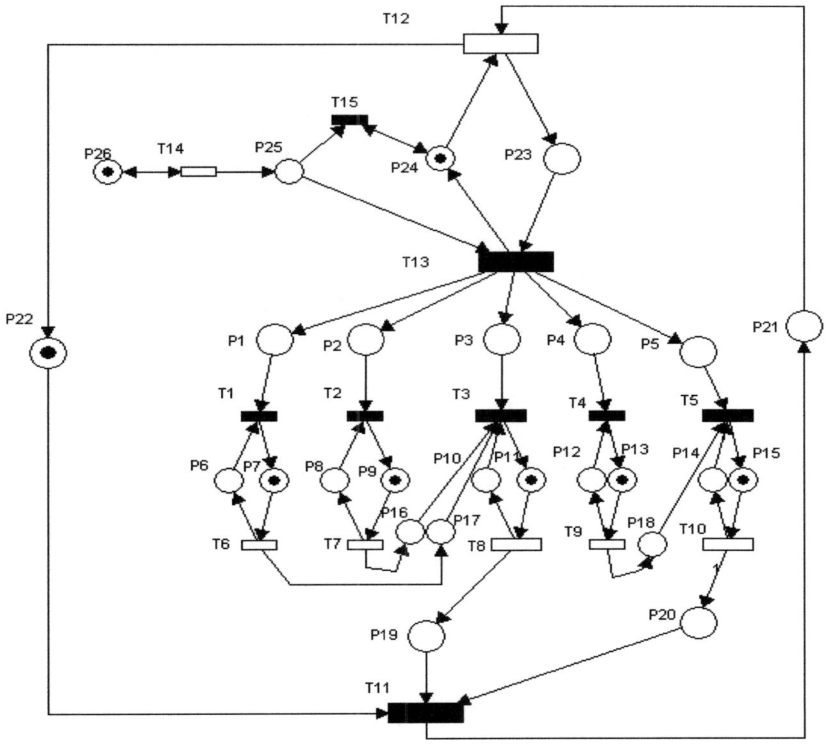

Fig. 3.2 Petri Net coordination model of multi-agent system

The meanings of transition in Fig. 3.2 are:
T1: stand-alone agent 1 begins to work;
T2: stand-alone agent 2 begins to work;
T3: blackboard scheduler of production lines management agent 1 begins to work;
T4: stand-alone agent 3 begins to work;
T5: blackboard scheduler of production lines management agent 2 begins to work;
T6: stand-alone agent 1 fulfills work;
T7: stand-alone agent 2 fulfills work;
T8: blackboard scheduler of production lines management agent 1 fulfills work;
T9: stand-alone agent 3 fulfills work;
T10: blackboard scheduler of production lines management agent 2 fulfills work;
T11: blackboard scheduler of center decision-making management agent begins to infer ;
T12: blackboard scheduler of center decision-making management agent fulfills inference;
T13: blackboard scheduler of center decision-making management agent sends starting sign;
T14: clock sign reached;
T15: waiting for the starting sign;
The harmony process is: P22 expresses that the blackboard scheduler of center decision-making management agent is in free state, P21 expresses that the blackboard scheduler of center decision-making management agent is in transacting state, P19 and P20 means incident signs from production lines management agent to center decision-making management agent. When P22, P19 and P20 all have token, transition T11 happens, and token center decision-making management agent is in place P21 with working state. Center blackboard scheduler begins inference. T12 is a time-lapse transition. Time-lapse means times of blackboard scheduler transacting task. When center blackboard scheduler finishes inference, token transfers to P23, and the system state information is stored in buffer.T13 is starting command and clock sign of synchronization blackboard scheduler. P26 is clock which is timing. P25 is arrived clock sign. When P25 and P23 both have token T13 happens. Each agent receives starting sign sent from blackboard scheduler, token transfers to P1, P2, P3, P4, P5.
Take the production lines agent as an example, the work process of each agent is described as follows. P11 and P12 expresses production lines agent 1 is in free or working state respectively, P3 is the starting sign from center blackboard scheduler.P16 and P17 are information from stand-alone agent 1 and agent 2. When P3,P10,P16,P17 all have token, T3 happens, and blackboard scheduler of production lines agent 1 begins work, token transfers to P11, after a period of time, T8 happens, token transfers to P19,P11, then blackboard scheduler of production lines agent 1 finishes its inference.
2. The working process of multi-production lines system
The actual working process corresponded to the model is shown as follows:

- After the system starting, rock-bottom starts initialization. Then the middle-level agent starts the process of initialization and decision making according to the information preserved last close-down.
- After the middle-level agent finishing initialization and decision making, firstly the basic decision-making information is delivered to rock-bottom agent for the necessary of the next initialization and operation of rock-bottom agent, simultaneity essential information is delivered to central management decision agent, then central management decision agent starts initialization and calculation of task allocation based on entered task data.

- After bottom stand-alone agent finishing initialization, the information is delivered to middle-level administration agent.
- When central management decision agent finishes initialization and calculation and the clock signal arrives, the central management decision information is delivered to corresponding middle-level agent and rock-bottom agent by central management decision agent and starting signal is sent.
- After the rock-bottom agent receives starting signal and the basic information of middle-level agent, it begins running, and middle-level agent starts administration and inference according to decision information from central agent and rock-bottom information from middle-level agent.
- After the middle-level agent finishes the process, it sends decision information to rock-bottom agent and sends essential information to central agent. The central agent begins making decision and turns into step 4.

4. Study on distributed intelligence diagnosis illation mechanism based on Petri Net

The multi-agent system is a complex system, where there are inter current, synchronism, asynchronism, resources competition and coordination etc. System fault is inevitable, when it happens the reasons must be found as soon as possible. The former fault diagnosis only enumerates fault reasons but does not have the function of fault inference, which results in the situation that the fault reasons is undefined, the faults seeking time is overlong, so the fault of early warning can not be realized after the system fault happens. It is imperative to find a powerful tool of fault inference to solve these problems.

Petri Net theory is a kind of newly developed modeling and simulation tool combined "figure" and "shape". It is a theory related to distributed system theory which has the ability of processing supervention phenomena and nondeterminacy, and deducing the matter. If token and a actual value between 0-1 of traditional Petri Net denotes the credibility of event , transition and the probability between 0-1 denotes the possibility of events, thus fuzz Petri Net is formed, which can describe the dynamic process and dissemination process of fault phenomena , and it is an excellent tool used for fault diagnosis.

4.1 The structure of distributed intelligent fault diagnosis

There are two main task of fault diagnosis for the equipment: state monitoring and fault diagnosis. There is a close relationship between the two tasks that state monitoring is the foundation and prerequisite of diagnosis, but their discrepancy is obvious in task, objection, function and implement method etc. Monitoring agent and diagnosis agent is two different agents. Considered both the construction complexity of the diagnosis object and the variety of fault diagnosis methods, we can integrate these different systems and methods in the thought of distributed artificial agent.

The distributed agent diagnosis system is composed of some agents and two system interfaces. The agents are knowledge process entities and each agent has autonomy, so it can make inference, plans and communication according to its knowledge and surrounding events. Agents are independent from each other, they coordinate and solve problems through sharing knowledge, task and middle results. Agents are classified into three types: monitoring agent, diagnosis agent and coordination management agent, and there are two interfaces: equipment system interface and man-machine conversation interface. The structure is shown in Figure 4.1.

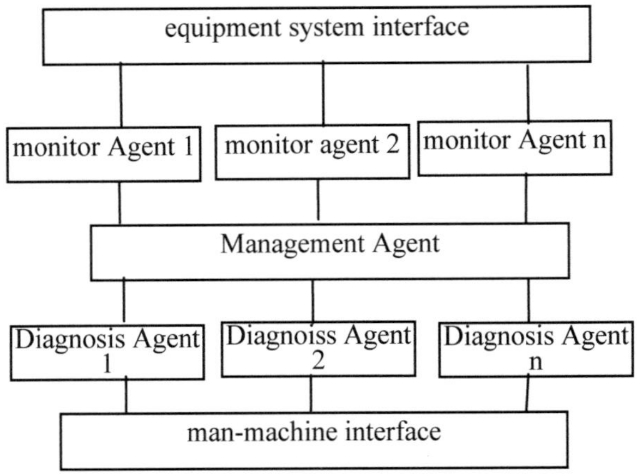

Fig. 4.1 Distributed intelligence diagnosis system structure based on multi- Agent

Monitoring agent is organized based on the equipment structure and function. The distributed state monitor and alarm processing system are used to concurrently acquire parameters reflected the system operation state on line. It can take different approach on different monitoring targets when some parameters go out of normal.

Diagnosis agent can use different methods on different diagnosis targets. Each agent has different knowledge sources and knowledge processing methods, so it can exert respective advantages of different diagnosis methods, and improve the ability of processing problems of the whole system.

Management agent mainly completes the task administration, coordination control and correspond among the distributed agents, which include task allocation, exchange of data and knowledge, conflict process, result colligation and so on.

4.2 Organization and coordination of distributed fault diagnosis system

4.2.1 Multilevel blackboard structure of distributed fault diagnosis system

In the distributed intelligence diagnosis system the agents are organized and administrated by level structure. In this section, the coordination control policy of multi-level blackboard structure is constituted, shown as Figure 4.2, and the policy of multi-level blackboard mechanism are corresponded with the multi-agent coordination mechanism mentioned earlier.

Multi-level blackboard structure is suitable for multi-level mixed decomposition policy and parallel process of equipment fault diagnosis, it can meet the solving needs of real-time and complex , avoid some correspondence bottleneck problems caused by single blackboard, reduce the complexity of diagnosis problems, it is propitious to process of complex information. Different information is distributed into different blackboards so that the quantity of information contained in each blackboard is very small, which can improve system efficiency, make it easy to extend and reduce the complexity of blackboard management. This agent diagnosis structure not only makes the exchange between distributed diagnosis and distributed information possible but also has a good openness.

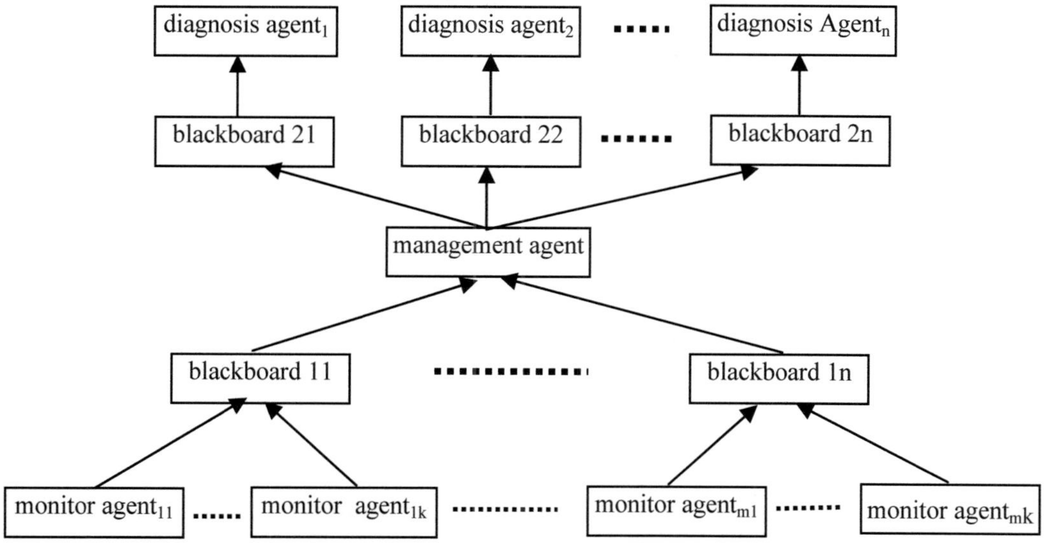

Fig. 4.2 Multilevel blackboard structure of distributed intelligence diagnosis system

4.2.2 A diagnosis process of distributed fault diagnosis

Taking the multi-packing production lines as the example, its stand-alone agent has the function of fault diagnosis and monitoring. In order to form more reliable fault diagnosis system, part of necessary sensors are added on stand-alone agent to form monitoring agent with more powerful functions. Middle-level management agent and the corresponding fault diagnosis functions are composed of fault diagnosis agents. The fault diagnosis process corresponding with the multi-blackboard of distributed intelligence fault diagnosis system above is shown as follows:

- some component has a fault;
- corresponding monitoring agent generates fault code, and sends it to the blackboard opened by corresponding middle-level administration agent;
- middle-level administration agents reports to high-level administration agents after it receiving fault code;
- high-level administrator chooses a suitable middle-level diagnosis agent to start fault diagnosis;
- the result produced by fault diagnosis agent is sent to high-level administration and decision agent for decision-making and display.

4.3 Study on fuzzy Petri Net

Fuzzy Petri Net (FPN) is expanded from Petri Net. Like Petri Net, FPN is a bidirectional directed graph composed of two kinds of nodes that is place and transition. But what is different is that in FPN token included in place is connected with a true value from 0 to 1 while transition is connected with a CF from 0 to 1. Enable and stimulate rules of transition are modified too.

Definition 4-1: Fuzzy Petri Net structure

The structure of Fuzzy Petri Net is defined into a eight-element:

$$FPN = (P, T, D, I, O, f, a, \beta)$$

Where:
$P=\{p_1, p_2, \ldots, p_n\}$ is a place finite set;
$T=\{t_1, t_2, \ldots t_n\}$is a transition finite set;
$P \cap T = \Phi$;
$D=\{d_1, d_2, \ldots d_n\}$ is a proposition finite set;
$|P|=|D|$.
$I{:}P \times T \rightarrow \{0,1\}$ is the input function, if $I(p,t)=1$, it suggests that p and t are related, p is the input place of t, and all place sets of t is expressed as $\circ t$ or $I(t)$; if $I(p,t)=0$, t and p are not related;
$F{:}T \rightarrow [0,1]$ is a correlation function of T, it denotes the real number mapping from T to a "0-1";
$\alpha{:}P \rightarrow [0,1]$ is a correlation function of P, it denotes the real number mapping from P to "0-1";
$\beta{:}P \rightarrow D$ is the correlation function of P, it denotes the bidirectional mapping from P to proposition set.
Making A a directed arc set, if $p_j \in I(t_i)$, then a directed arc a_{ji} from p_j to t_i exists, $a_{ji} \in A$; if $p_k \in O(t_i)$, then a directed arc a_{ik} from t_i to p_k exists, $a_{ik} \in A$. If $f(t_i)=\mu_i$, $\mu_i \in [0,1]$, then it is said that t_i is related with real number μ_i; if $\beta(p_i)=d_i$, $d_i \in D$, it is said that p_i is related with proposition d_i.
Definition 4-2: the marked Fuzzy Petri Net
If in the FPN structure some place include token, it is called the marked Fuzzy Petri Net. The token of place p_i is expressed as $a(p_i)$, $a(p_i) \in [0,1]$. If $a(p_i)=\gamma_i$, $\gamma_i \in [0,1]$ and $\beta(p_i)=d_i$, then it denotes that the confidence of the proposition d_i is γ_i.
For example: fuzzy rule: R_i : IF d_j THEN d_j $(CF=\mu_i)$ is represented by figures as Fig4.3:

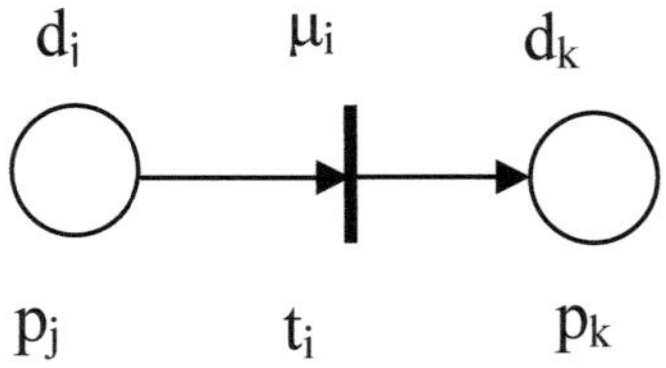

Fig. 4.3 A example of FPN

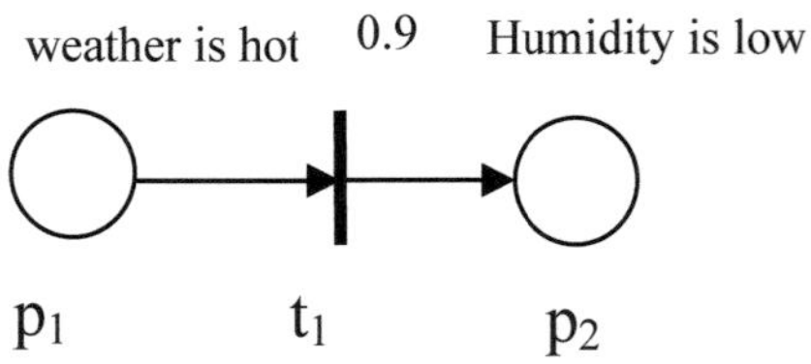

Fig. 4.4 Knowledge expression based on marked FPN

If the fuzzy rule example R_i above is transferred into: IF weather is hot THEN humidity is low ($CF = 0.9$) and the confidence of hot weather is 0.9, it is presented with Petri Net in Fig.4.4, each parameter is defined as follows:
$FPN=(P, T, D, I, O, f, a, \beta)$
$P=\{p_1, p_2\}$;
$T=\{t_1\}$;
$D=\{$*weather is hot, humidity is low*$\}$;
$I(t_i)=\{p_1\}$, $O\{t_i\}=\{p_2\}$, $f(t_i)=0.90$;
$\alpha=\{0.90,0\}$, *namely* $\alpha(p_1)=0.90$, $\alpha(p_2)=0.0$;
$\beta=\{$*weather is hot, humidity is low*$\}$, *namely* $\beta(p_1)=$ *weather is hot*, $\beta(p_2)=$ *humidity is low*;
Definition 4-3: enable and stimulate rules of fuzzy Petri Net

Under the system identification m_1, for transition t_i, if $\forall p_j \in I(t_i)$: $m_1(p_j)=1 \wedge a(p_j)= \gamma_i \geq \lambda$ where $\lambda \in [0,1]$ is the threshold of t_i, $m_1(p_j)$ is the token amount of p_j under the system identification m_1, which is called t_j enable. If the enable t_j simulates, new system identification m_2 will happen:

1. $\forall p_j \in I(t_i) : m_2(p_j) = m_1(p_j)-1$;
2. $\forall p_k \in O(t_i) : m_2(p_k) = m_1(p_k)+1 \wedge a(p_k)= \gamma_k=\gamma_i \times \mu_i$, *where* $\mu_i = f(t_i)$ is the correlation function of t_i.

Definition 4-3 can be presented by Figure 4.5. what must be noticed is that , different from PN, it is not allowed to exist any more than 2 token in FPN. So it is required $m_1(p_j) = 1$ but not $m_1(p_j) \geq 1$ in the transition enable rule.

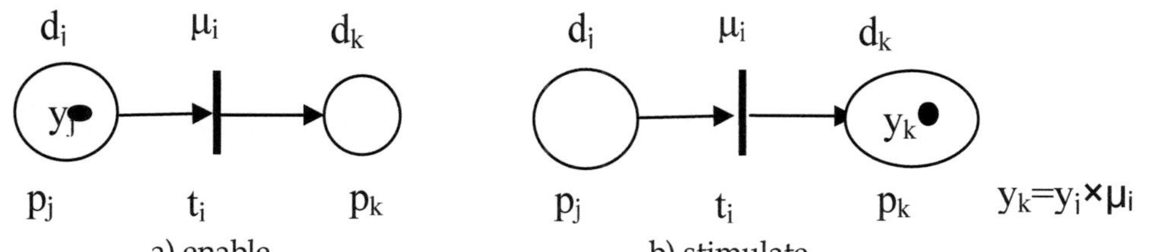

Fig. 4.5 The process of FPN enable and stimulate

4.4 Establishment of production lines fault diagnosis

4.4.1 Conception of Petri Net fault diagnosis model

Definition 4-4: the unit of the system with input and output behaviors is called components. According to the definition above, these, as big as system and subsystem and as small as module and organ, are all belonged to components.

Definition 4-5: the measurement for identifying the system behaviors at the input ends and out ends of the system is called observation.

Definition 4-6: if the fault output of C_A can result in the fault output of C_B, it is said that there is fault transmission relationship between C_A and C_B ,represented with R_J.

Therewithal suppose that the fault transmission relationship has the characteristic of transmission.

Definition 4-7: denoted the structure or behavior state of components with place, denoted changes in state or behaviors of the component with transfer, denoted changes in trends or the operation process of a behavior through connecting place node and transfer node with the directed arc, the fundamental Petri Net model of the system is established as $N=(P,T,F)$.

4.4.2 The steps of Petri Net model establishment

Step 1: Analyze minutely Petri Net model system to be established, find all components of the system from the high-level;

Step 2: Analyze the fault transmission relationship between components from high-level components to the low-level, and find the next lower-level component that causes the high-level possibly until to the lowest-level;

Step 3: Denote the structure or behavior state of components with place, denote changes in state or behaviors of the component with transfer, denote changes in trends or the operation process of a behavior through connecting place node and transfer node with the directed arc to establish the fundamental fault Petri Net model.

Step 4: Confirm the transition reliability of fundamental fault Petri Net model and determine blur measurement table of system events (it is unnecessary if the event reliability is given by the system when asked, but it is necessary to establish system reliability professional system).

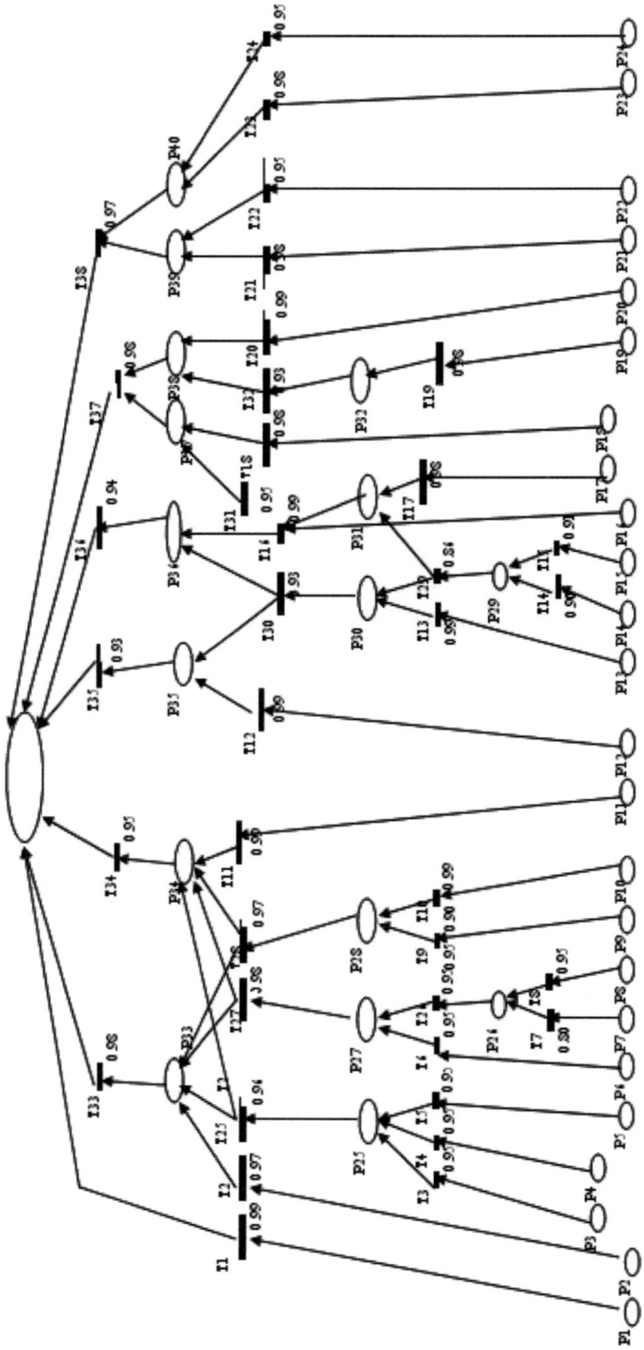

Fig. 4.6 Fault diagnose Petri Net model of sucking and pressing cover machine

4.4.3 Production lines fault diagnosis model

Taking sucking and pressing cover machine as an example to establish its fault diagnosis model, because the concrete structure and establishment methods are the same as the establishment methods of the model in the example, it will not narrate. The Petri model of the system is the basis to make fault diagnosis inference. The model adopts HPSim plotting analysis tool to plot. Fault diagnose Petri Net model of sucking and pressing cover machine is shown in Figure 4.6.

4.4.4 Fault diagnosis inference algorithm based on Fuzzy Petri Net

Petri Net is used to describe two important elements of the dynamic system, which are condition and transition. Condition is the logic description to the system and transition denotes the production process of event or behavior of the system, activation of transition is decided by the condition. Once a transition is evoked, its precondition cannot stand any longer and some examination conditions will be formed and established. The original identification of the net marks the original state of the system, the activity process of transition is the process of moving identifications in the net, which simulates the state exchange process of the system. The transition's activity characteristics of Petri Net makes it describe conditional events and transition activity rules very well. In the process of transition activity, one or more conditions of transition set can be satisfied at the same time, namely that one or more state represented by transition can happen simultaneously. This is one of the important characteristics of Petri Net to describe multi faults happen simultaneously, namely "concurrent".

Fault diagnosis and fault transmission are a reverse process. The process of fault diagnosis refers to, according to a fault phenomena observed, seek for the fault reasons. In the FPN, if there is only input function but no output function in a position, that means the diagnostic fault phenomena is object position. If there is only output function but no input in a position, that means the diagnostic fault reason is original position. The fault diagnosis is the process of seeking for the original position by target position. This process generally adopts reverse inference policies. First of all defined the fault phenomena, namely that selecting a target, then seek for the rule sets that can infer the fault from the fault repository, then selected these rules one by one according to the rule reliability. If the prerequisite of a rule is consistent with the fact in diagnosis database, the rule is active and produce new facts; or takes the prerequisite of the rule as the sub target, enforces the process recursively until to find the fault reasons or not to find a rule producing the fault phenomena.

1 Fuzzy Petri Net fault diagnosis inference algorithm

Fuzzy Petri Net fault diagnosis inference algorithm is shown as follows:

Step 1: establish the reachability set $RS(p_i)$, immediate reach set $IRS(p_i)$, and adjacent place set AP_{ik};

Step 2: according to the fault phenomena, choose the corresponding fault repository and find the corresponding omen place p_o ;

Step 3: for any place, if $p_o \in IRS(p_k)$, compare the reliability of all p_k , choose the most reliable place which is supposed to be p_j, if some place, whose reliability is the same and is the most, exist at the same time, choose one of the most reliable place arbitrarily. The mark υ=1 on p_j suggests that the system has visited the place in searching for the fault reasons, which can avoid repeated searching in depth priority;

Step 4: search for all place in IRS including p_j and compare the corresponding reliability, choose the most reliable one and turn to Step 3 until find the fault place, which is supposed p_f;

Step 5: the system inquires the severity of p_f by its corresponding proposition, a is calculated according to blur measurement table enacted by the system in advance or input by experts directly. If a is more than pre-set threshold, the corresponding proposition to p_f is regarded as an active event, and according to the path finding p_f, calculates its reliability and the reliability of all place from p_f to p_o at the same time, so that finds the reliability of the fault omen corresponding to p_o which is gotten from the fault origin corresponding to p_f. Reliability = the reliability of input place * the confidence of corresponding rules, turn to Step 7;
Step 6: in Step 5 if α is less than pre-set threshold, the corresponding proposition to p_f is not active, then continued to search for other place according to depth priority principle till to find fault reasons and calculate the reliability of the omen place;
Step 7: inference ends. In the process of inference, seek for all the possible paths triggering the omen in repository, select these paths one by one according to the reliability of transition and the depth priority principle. If the input place of a transition matches the fault fact, startup the transition; or repeat the process above until to find fault place or not to find the fault place that can trigger the omen.

4.4.5 An example of production lines fault diagnosis system inference

Now taken the fault of sucking and pressing cover machine at loading position as an example to illuminate the application of fuzzy Petri Net fault diagnosis inference algorithm. The establishment rules are shown as follows:

R1 : IF A THEN B (CF = 0.90)
R2 : IF C THEN D (CF = 0.95)
R3 : IF E THEN D (CF = 0.93)
R4 : IF F THEN D (CF = 0.80)
R5 : IF D THEN B (CF = 0.98)
R6 : IF G THEN H (CF = 0.98)
R7 : IF I THEN J (CF = 0.92)
R8 : IF K THEN J (CF = 0.90)
R9 : IF L THEN B (CF = 0.98)
R10 : IF M THEN N (CF = 0.95)
R11 : IF O THEN N (CF = 1)
R12 : IF P THEN B (CF = 0.98)
R13 : IF Q THEN B (CF = 0.95)

Here,
A: Q230 occurs fault
B: action abnormity on encasement position
C: coupling becomes flexible
D: lead screw doesn't run
E: lead screw is distortion
F: there is eyewinker on lead orbit
G: driver faults
H: servo motor faults
I: motor is over pressure
J: motor is over hot
K: motor is over loading
L: servo motor faults
M: l control card is loose

N: fault on pulse card
O: pulse card is demolished
P: pulse card faults
Q: program faults
Shown with FPN as follows:

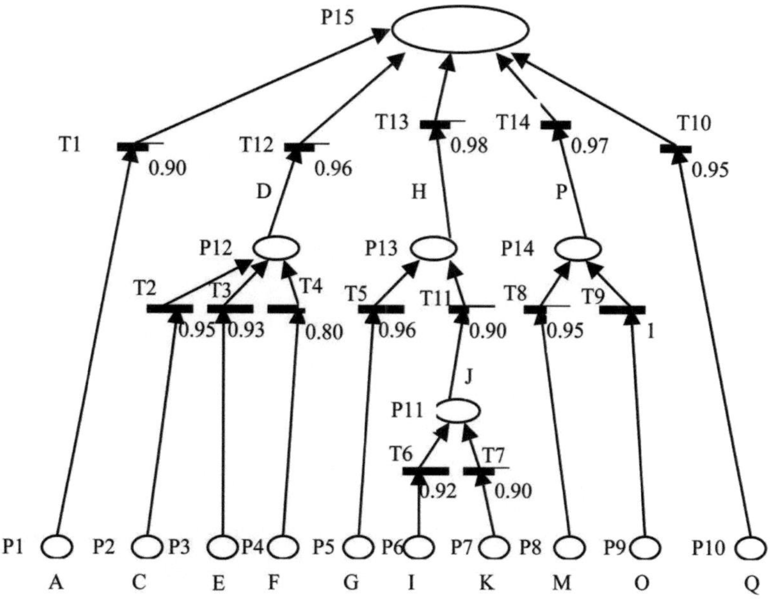

Fig. 4.7 FPN model of sucking and pressing cover machine at loading position

Known from Fig. 4.7, the origination place set is $P_s = \{P_1, P_2, P_3, P_4, P_5, P_6, P_7, P_8, P_9, P_{10}\}$, the target place is $P_g=\{P_{15}\}$. The process of inference diagnosis is to infer in reverse direction from the target place to find the original place that can lead fault in target place. The detail process is shown as follows:

place p_i	IRS(p_i)	RS(p_i)
p_1	$\{p_{15}\}$	$\{p_{15}\}$
P_2	$\{p_{12}\}$	$\{p_{12}, p_{15}\}$
p_3	$\{p_{12}\}$	$\{p_{12}, p_{15}\}$
p_4	$\{p_{12}\}$	$\{p_{12}, p_{15}\}$
p_5	$\{p_{13}\}$	$\{p_{13}, p_{15}\}$
p_6	$\{p_{11}\}$	$\{p_{11}, p_{13}, p_{15}\}$
p_7	$\{p_{11}\}$	$\{p_{11}, p_{13}, p_{15}\}$
p_8	$\{p_{14}\}$	$\{p_{14}, p_{15}\}$
p_9	$\{p_{14}\}$	$\{p_{14}, p_{15}\}$
p_{10}	$\{p_{15}\}$	$\{p_{15}\}$
p_{11}	$\{p_{13}\}$	$\{p_{13}, p_{15}\}$
p_{12}	$\{p_{15}\}$	$\{p_{15}\}$
p_{13}	$\{p_{15}\}$	$\{p_{15}\}$
p_{14}	$\{p_{15}\}$	$\{p_{15}\}$
p_{15}	$\{\Phi\}$	$\{\Phi\}$

Table 4.1 The immediate reachability and reachability set of place

place p_i	place p_k	AP_{ik}
p_1	p_{15}	Φ
P_2	p_{12}	Φ
p_3	p_{12}	Φ
p_4	p_{12}	Φ
p_5	p_{13}	Φ
p_6	p_{11}	Φ
p_7	p_{11}	Φ
p_8	p_{14}	Φ
p_9	p_{14}	Φ
p_{10}	p_{15}	Φ
p_{11}	p_{13}	Φ
p_{12}	p_{15}	Φ
p_{13}	p_{15}	Φ
p_{14}	p_{15}	Φ
p_{15}	Φ	Φ

Table 4.2 The adjacent place of places

1. Established the reachability set $RS(p_i)$, immediate reach set $IRS(p_i)$, and adjacent place set AP_{ik}, shown in table 4.1, table 4.2.
2. Suppose the known fault "action abnormity when marching encasement position", namely p_{15} in the figure. Check table 4.1, table 4.2 to find there are five paths triggering p_{15}; $p_1 \rightarrow p_{15}$, $p_{12} \rightarrow p_{15}$, $p_{13} \rightarrow p_{15}$, $p_{14} \rightarrow p_{15}$, $p_{10} \rightarrow p_{15}$; then inquire the reliability of p_1, p_{12}, p_{13}, p_{14}, p_{10}, of which $p_{13} \rightarrow p_{15}$ is the most reliable. Choosing this path and marking p_{13} suggests that this place has been visited. Then seek in reverse direction, there are two paths triggering p_{13}: $p_5 \rightarrow p_{13}$, $p_{11} \rightarrow p_{13}$; according to the principle of the greatest reliability, the system prefers t_5 and find the input place p_5;
3. Because place p_5 is the original place, the diagnosis system inquires when it enters man machine interface: "servo drivers a fault?". if the answer is "yes" the system will calculates the fuzziness of p_5, where suppose the result of calculation is $a(p_5)=0.93$, because $a(p_5)$ is more than the pre-set threshold 0.7, the corresponding rule to p_5 is considered to be active, calculate the reliability of p_{13}, $a(p_{13}) = a(p_5)\times 0.98 = 0.9114>0.7$, because the proposition corresponding to p_{13} is to be active, calculate the reliability of p_{15} is $a(p_{15}) = a(p_{13})\times 0.98 = 0.8932>0.7$ and endow the mark of p_{15} with 1, which suggests that the fault reason is found that is the proposition "servo drivers fault" corresponding to p_5 and the reliability of the fault is $a(p_{15}) = 0.8932$.
4. If the answer to the inquiry "servo drivers a fault?" is "no", the system sets the proposition $a(p_5)=0.2$, which is less than threshold 0.70, then the corresponding proposition will not be active. But there is another path triggering p_{13}: $p_{11} \rightarrow p_{13}$; and there are two paths triggering p_{11}: $p_6 \rightarrow p_{11}$, $p_7 \rightarrow p_{11}$. According to the size of reliability of transition, the system carries over the inference process above. Only if the fact inquired is defined, namely that the reliability of the proposition is more than threshold 0.70, the reliability of p_{11} is $a(p_{11})$ and set the mark of p_{15} 1 and find the fault reason paths.

5. If the traversal path: $p_6 \rightarrow p_{11} \rightarrow p_{13} \rightarrow p_{15}$, $p_6 \rightarrow p_{11} \rightarrow p_{13} \rightarrow p_{15}$ still failed, the diagnosis system seeks for other path $p_{14} \rightarrow p_{15}$, and carries over the process above until to find the fault reason and calculate the reliability of the target place.

5. Referrence

[1] Tang Zhiqiang. The System Architecture of Multiagent Faced to Road Construction and Its Communiction Mechanism: [master's degree dissertation], Hebei University of Technology, 2005.3

[2] Yu Hongyan. Research of Multi-agent System's Correspondence Mechanism Based on KQML: [master's degree dissertation], Central-South University of Technology, 2001.1: 13~17

[3] Li Ying. Multi-agent system and application in forecast and intelligent traffic system. East China University of Science and Technology Press, 2004.11: 5~7 18~0

[4] Jing Yuehua. Study on Communication System of Road Construction Based on Multi-Agent: [master's degree dissertation],Hebei University of Technology, 2005.3

[5] Cheryl Elizabeth Duty Martin, B. S.; M. S. E. Adaptive Decision-Making Frameworks for Multi-Agent Systems. Dissertation of the University of Texas at Austin in Partial Fulfillment of the Requirements for the Degree of Doctor of Philosophy, 2001.5:21~22

[6] Liang Quan, Xu Xiaomin, Zhang ZHongjun. Analysis of the Machanism of Cooperation and Control and the Foundamental Problems in Multi-agent System. Control and Decision, 1996.09.11(5)

[7] Gao Zhijun,Yan Yan Guozheng, Ding Guoqing. Task Distribution of Multi-agent Systems Based on Network. Computer Engineering, 2005.5, 31(11):19~21.

[8] Krothapalli, Naga K. Dynamic Task Allocation In Multi-agent Systems. A Dissertation of the University of Massachusetts Amherst in Partial fulillment of the requirement for the degree of doctor of philosophy, 2003.3.

[9] Guo Ruifeng,Yu Dong,Liu Minglie.ect. Research Of Task Allocation Based On Contract Net. Mini-Micro Systems,1999.10,20(10):740~743

[10] Ajith, Tom P, C.Siva Ram Murthy. Optimal task allocation in distributed systems by graph matching and state space search 1999, 46:57~75

[11] Li Tiejun, Wu Jianguo, Peng Yuqing. Study on Multi-agent Task Allocation Based on the Contract Net. 2007 IEEE International Conference on Control and Automation, p 2317-2321

[12] Sarit Kraus, Tatjana. Plotkin. Algorithms of distributed task allocation for cooperative agents. Theoretical Computer Science. 2000,242 :1~27

[13] R.G.Smith,R.Davis.Frameworks for cooperation in distributed problem solving.IEEE Transations on Systems,Man and Cybernetics, 11(1):61-70,1981

[14] M.Luck,M dInverno Engagement and Cooperation in Motivated Agent Modeling, Distributed Artifical Intelligence Architecture and Modeling: Proceedings of the Frist Australian Workshop on Distributed Arificial Intelligence,Zhang and Lukose, pages 70-84,Spring-Verlag,Berlin Germangy,1996

[15] Li Changhong. Study on Multi-agent Cooperation Mechanism and Cooperation Structure: [doctor's degree dissertation], Tianjin University, 2002.10.1:20~23

[16] Liu Jinkun. Research of Intelligent Control for Complex Industrial Process: [postdoctor's degree dissertation], Zhejiang University, 1998.12:8~48
[17] M. Luck, M dInverno Engagement and Cooperation in Motivated Agent Modeling, Distributed Artifical Intelligence Architecture and Modeling: Proceedings of the Frist Australian Workshop on Distributed Arificial Intelligence, Zhang and Lukose, pages 70-84, Spring-Verlag, Berlin Germangy, 1996
[18] O'Hare G M P, Jennings N R. Foundation of Distribution and control in a distributed Artificial Intelligence. New York: John Willey & Sons,1996

9

Evolutionary Game Theory based Cooperation Algorithm in Multi-agent System

Yuehai Wang
North China University of Technology
China

1. Introduction

A multi-agent system (MAS) that composed of multiple interacting intelligent agents can be used to solve problems which are difficult or impossible for an individual agent or monolithic system to solve. Since the agent is autonomous and intelligent, it is reasonable to assume that it choice the behavior to bring itself the maximal benefit. Thus, the cooperation and coordination can be achieved successfully if we can wisely design the utility function for every agent so that every agent can get the maximal reward from the cooperation to accomplish a given task.

However, the utility function of one agent usually involves those of others for most "real-world" cooperation needed tasks. Moreover, it is not uncommon that the conflicts between the gains of these agents arise. In other words, the individual optimality is not always consistent with collective optimality in MAS. These conflicts will reduce the collective utility if there is no coordination among these decentralized, autonomous agents.

This paper addresses the essential that in MAS the action of one agent may influence the action of others and there usually be conflicts among the payoff of one another. We investigated the optimal coordination approach for multi-agent foraging, a typical MAS task, from the point view of game theory. After introduced several concepts, we built the equivalence between the optimal solution of MAS and the equilibrium of the game corresponding to that situation, and then we introduced evolutionarily stable strategy into the approach hope that it maybe be of service in addressing the equilibrium selection problem of traditional game theory.

Finally, based on the hawk-dove game model, an evolutionarily cooperation foraging algorithm (ECFA) is proposed to evolve a stable evolutionarily stable strategy (ESS) and bring the maximal reward for the group. If there be some change in the configuration of the environment, ECFA can, then, evolve to the new ESS automatically. And we also proposed a reinforcement factor to accelerate the convergence process of ECFA and thus make a new algorithm Accelerated ECFA (AECFA). These techniques were shown to be successful by the multi-agent foraging simulations.

2. Rationality

2.1 The concept of rationality

Rationality is an important property we imposed upon the players of a game. It is a central principle for agent to respond optimally by selecting its action based on the beliefs he might have about the strategies of his opponents and the structure of game, i.e. payoff matrix of the game. Sometimes rationality, also called "hyper-rationality", implies having complete knowledge about all the details of a given situation. Under this concept, a player can calculate its best action of the current situation, and, furthermore, it can also calculate the best response of its opponents' to his action on the flawless premise that no one will make a mistake. However, perfectly rational decisions are not feasible in practice due to the finite computational resources. In fact, if an agent uses finite computational resources to deduce, we say it is bounded rational.

Of course, we assume all the players are honest and flawless weather he is rational or bounded rational when he selects his action. In other words, he never makes mistakes by choosing sub-optimal action intentionally to confuse his opponents.

2.2 Autonomous agent and rational player

Autonomous agent is the description of the player in a MAS. Autonomous means it can sense the environment and act on it over time in pursuit of its own goal. If the agent was equipped with learning ability, it can find the optimal way in accomplishing the same or similar job by machine learning techniques such as try-and-error, neutral network, and so on. Agent is egocentric during the selection and improvement of its action.

A rational agent is specifically defined as an agent who always chooses the action which maximizes its expected performance, given all of the knowledge it currently possesses, and this may involve "helping" or "hurting" the other players. This time, the agent is game-centric and the action selection is after a careful consideration about the payoff function of other players as well as game structure.

2.3 Rational and selfish

A rational agent always maximizes its payoff function based on the game structure and the common knowledge "other players are rational". But it is not always selfish although it may choice selfish action more often than not. If the game structure shows that cooperation with other player can obtain more benefits for all, it has the incentive to choice this action since both of them are rational and, therefore, they all know these win-win actions. Another exception is repeated game since the Nobel Prize winner Robert Aumann had already shown rational players repeatedly interacting for indefinitely long games can sustain the cooperative outcome in his 1959 paper (Aumann R.J. 1959).

3. Individual rationality and collective rationality

Individual rationality indicates that the choices made by individuals are to maximize their benefits and minimize their costs. In other words, agents make decisions about how they should act by comparing the costs and benefits of different courses of action (Sen, A. 1987). And the collective rationality stand for the group as a whole, to maximize the utility of the entire group which is composed every single agent.

As been stated before, usually there exist conflicts between actions that can make individual benefit or collective gains. Let's take the famous classical prisoner's dilemma as an example. In this game, as in all game theory, the only concern of each individual player ("prisoner") is maximizing his/her own payoff, without any concern for the other player's payoff. The unique equilibrium for this game is a Pareto-suboptimal solution—that is, individual rational choice leads the two players to both play defectly even though each player's individual reward would be greater if they both played cooperately, which is collective rational and Pareto optimal (Poundstone, W. 1992).

4. Game theory based cooperation approach for multi-agent system

4.1 The relationship between the optimal cooperation solution of MAS and Nash equilibrium of the corresponding game

To accomplish a mission is only the preliminary requirement of a MAS. In fact, the MAS are required to complete the given task efficiently, and finally, optimally. It needs all the actions selected by the agent during every step of the procedure should be optimal. Of course, this is a very hard, if not impossible, problem.

But if we regard the procedure of accomplishing the given task as a Markov game composed by multiple stage games which corresponding to every step that constitute the cooperating work, we can find a optimal solution given that we find the best equilibrium of every stage game of the Markov game. Game theory provides several feasible approaches to find an equilibrium, the most popular one among which is Nash equilibrium.

Nash equilibrium is proven to exist for any game and it also is the only "consistent" prediction of how the game will be played in the sense that if all players predict that a particular Nash equilibrium will occur then no player has an incentive to play differently. Thus, a Nash equilibrium, and only a Nash equilibrium, can has the property that the players can predict it, predict that their opponents predict it, and so on (Fudenberg,D. & Tirole,J. 1991). Therefore, it is reasonable for us to choice Nash equilibrium as the optimal solution for each stage game although a Nash equilibrium can not always be Pareto-optimal.

4.2 Fundamental equilibria of the game and their relationship

From different viewpoints and based on different solution approaches, a game have multiple kinds of solution equilibria, among which Nash equilibrium, Iterative deletion of strictly dominated strategies, strictly dominance strategies, risk-dominant equilibrium and Pareto-optimal equilibrium are commonly used for static game of complete information. Here gives a very short description of and the relationship among these equilibria, please refer *game theory* (Fudenberg,D. & Tirole,J. 1991) for the details.

Informally, a set of strategies is a Nash equilibrium if no player can do better by unilaterally changing his or her strategy. Thus, Nash equilibrium is a profile of strategies such that each player's strategy is a best response to the other player's strategies. By best-response, we mean that no individual can improve her payoff by switching strategies unless at least one other individual switches strategies as well. There are two kinds of Nash equilibrium: mixed-strategy Nash equilibrium and pure-strategy Nash equilibrium.

Dominance occurs when one strategy is better than another strategy for one player, no matter how that player's opponents may play. The iterated deletion of dominated strategies is one common technique for solving games that involves iteratively removing dominated strategies. Eventually all dominated strategies of the game will be eliminated. Iterative deletion of strictly dominated strategies are those strategies survived.

Strictly dominance strategies are those strategies that can never be dominated by any strategy. They are the subset of iterative deletion of strictly dominated strategies since it also include the weakly dominated strategies. The idea of a dominant strategy is that it is always your best move regardless of what the other guys do. Note that this is a stronger requirement than the idea of Nash equilibrium, which only says that you have made your best move given what the other guys have done.

Risk-dominant equilibrium (Harsanyi, J.C. & Selten, R. 1988): In a symmetric 2×2 game — that is, a symmetric two-player game with two strategies per player—if both players strictly prefer the same action when their prediction is that the opponent randomizes 1/2-1/2, then the profile where both player play that action is the risk-dominant equilibrium.

Pareto-optimal equilibrium is the equilibrium that has the property that can bring the maximum utilities for all players of the game.

The relationship between these equilibria is depicted in the fig. 1(Li, G.J. 2005).Note that risk-dominant equilibrium may be, or may not be a Nash equilibrium. And also note that a Pareto-optimal equilibrium may be, or may not be a Nash equilibrium.

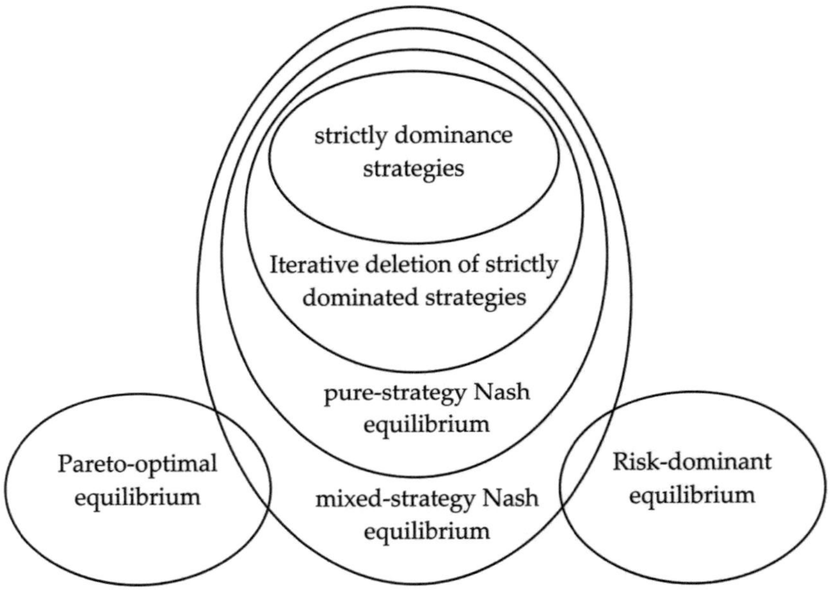

Fig. 1. The relationship between some equilibria

4.3 The type of the non-cooperative game and its equilibrium

A non-cooperative game is a one in which players can cooperate, but any cooperation must be self-enforcing, i.e. without the help through third parties by binding commitments or enforcing contracts. According to different standards, there are many categories of games. Fudenberg and Tirole (Fudenberg,D. & Tirole,J. 1991) use complete information and sequence of the players' move as the category standards. Complete information requires that every player knows the structure of the game, the strategies and payoffs of the other players. Static games (or simultaneous games) are games where both players move simultaneously, or if they do not move simultaneously, the later players are unaware of the earlier players' actions (making them effectively simultaneous), whereas the games where later players have some knowledge about earlier actions are called dynamic games (or sequential games). Therefore, there are four category of games: static games of complete information whose equilibrium is Nash equilibrium, dynamic games of complete information whose equilibrium is subgame prefect equilibrium, static games of incomplete information whose equilibrium is Bayesian equilibrium and the last, dynamic game of incomplete information whose equilibrium is perfect Bayesian equilibrium. Please refer corresponding text for the details.

4.4 Equilibrium selection problem in game theory based cooperation approach

Equilibrium is a profile of strategies such that each player's strategy is an optimal response to the other player's strategies. Nash equilibrium is a most frequently used equilibrium among all kinds of equilibria. The fact that a game may exists several, even infinite, Nash equilibria bring about the trouble for the players to predict the outcome of the game. When this is the case, the assumption that one specific Nash equilibrium is played relies on there being some mechanism or process that leads all the players to expect the same equilibrium. However, game theory lacks a general and convincing argument that a Nash equilibrium outcome will occur (Fieser, J. & Dowden, B. 2008). As a result, it is not surprise that different player predict different equilibrium and so as to lead a non-Nash equilibrium come into exists since there is no common acknowledged doctrines for the player to predict and select. This is the equilibrium selection problem that addresses the difficulty for players to select certain equilibrium over another.

The researchers had already proposed several approaches and advices to make a reasonable selection for the player. Next list the some most frequently used approaches. The "focal points" theory of Schelling (Schelling, T. C. 1960) suggests that in some "real-life" situations players may be able to coordinate on a particular equilibrium by using information that is abstracted away by the strategic form of the game that may depend on players' culture background, past experiences, and so forth. This focal-point effect opens the door for cultural and environmental factors to influence rational behavior. Correlated equilibrium (Aumann R. 1974) between two players and coalition-proof equilibrium in games with more than two players (Bermheim, B.D., Peleg,B.& Whinstion,M.D. 1987a,1987b) that engage in a preplay discussion and then act independently is another approach. Risk-dominant principle first introduced by Harsanyi and Selten (Harsanyi, J.C. & Selten, R. 1988) is still another. However, please note that the selected Nash equilibrium is not necessarily Pareto-optimal equilibrium.

5. Evolutionary game theory approach

5.1 Introduction and advantages

Till now, we have motivated the solution concept of Nash equilibrium by supposing that players make their predictions of their opponents' play by introspection and deduction, using their knowledge of the opponents' payoffs, the knowledge that the opponents are rational, the knowledge that each player knows that the others know these things, and so on through the infinite regress implied by "common knowledge".

An alternative approach to introspection for explaining how players predict the behavior of their opponents is to suppose that players extrapolate from their past observation of play in "similar games," either with their current opponents or with "similar" ones. The idea of using learning-type adjustment process to explain equilibrium goes back to Cournot, who proposed a process that might lead the player to play the Cournot-Nash equilibrium outputs(Fudenberg,D. & Tirole,J. 1991).

If players observe their opponents' strategies at the end of each round, and players eventually receive a great many observations, the one natural specification is that each player's expectations about the play of his opponents converge to the probability distribution corresponding to the sample average of play he has observed in the past. In this case, if the system converges to a steady state, the steady state must be a Nash equilibrium (Weibull, J.W. 1995).

We can use this large-population model of adjustment to Nash equilibrium to discuss the adjustment of population fractions by evolution as opposed to learning. In theoretical biology, Maynard Smith and Price (Smith, J.M. & Price, G. 1973) pioneered the idea that the genes whose strategies are more successful will have higher reproductive fitness. Thus, the population fractions of strategies whose payoff against the current distribution of opponents' play is relatively high will tend go grow at a faster rate, and, any stable steady state must be a Nash equilibrium.

To conclude this section, we know that we can use evolutionary game theory and evolution stable strategies to explain the Nash equilibrium. The advantages of this explanation are if the players play one another repeatedly, then, even if players do not know their opponents' payoffs, they will eventually learn that the opponents do not play certain strategies, and the dynamic of the learning system will replicate the iterative deletion process. And for an extrapolative justification of Nash equilibrium, it suffices that players know their own payoffs, that play eventually converges to a steady state, and that if play does converge all players eventually learn their opponents' steady state strategies. Players need not have any information about the payoff functions or information of their opponents.

5.2 Evolutionarily stable strategies and evolutionary game theory

In game theory and behavioral ecology, an evolutionarily stable strategy (ESS) is a strategy which once adopted by an entire population is resistant to invasion by any mutant strategy that is initially rare. ESS was defined and introduced by Maynard Smith and Price (Smith, J.M. & Price, G. 1973) which is presumed that the players are individuals with biologically encoded, heritable strategies who have no control over the strategy they play and need not even be capable of being aware of the game. The individuals reproduce and are subject to the forces of natural selection (with the payoffs of the game representing biological fitness).

Evolutionary game theory (EGT) is the application of population genetics-inspired models of change in gene frequency in populations to game theory. Now it is one of the most active and rapidly growing areas of research. It assumes that agents choose their strategies through a trial-and-error learning process in which they gradually discover that some strategies work better than others. In games that are repeated many times, low-payoff strategies tend to be weeded out, and equilibrium may emerge (Smith, J. M. 1982).

5.3 Evolution stable strategies and Nash equilibrium

As we already known, Nash equilibrium is a profile of strategies such that each player's strategy is an optimal response to the other player's strategies as a result of the rational agent's introspection and deduction based on the "common knowledge", such as the opponents' payoffs, while ESSes are only evolutionarily stable result of the simple genetic operation among those agents who even not knows any information about the payoff functions or information of their opponents. Given the radically different motivating assumptions, it may come as a surprise that ESSes and Nash equilibria often coincide. In fact, every ESS corresponds to a Nash equilibrium, but there are some Nash equilibria that are not ESSes. That is to say, an ESS is an equilibrium refinement of the Nash equilibrium --

it is a Nash equilibrium which is "evolutionarily" stable meaning that once it is fixed in a population, natural selection alone is sufficient to prevent alternative (mutant) strategies from successfully invading.

In most simple games, the ESSes and Nash equilibria coincide perfectly. For instance, in the Prisoner's Dilemma the only Nash equilibrium and the strategy which composes it (Defect) is also an ESS. Since ESS is more restrict Nash equilibrium, there may be Nash equilibria that are not ESSes. The important difference between Nash equilibria and ESSes is Nash equilibria are defined on strategy sets (a specification of a strategy for each player) while ESSes are defined in terms of strategies themselves.

Usually the game have more than one ESS, we have to choose one as the solution. To most game, the ESS is not necessary Pareto optimal. But for some specific game, there is only one ESS, and it is the only equilibrium whose utility is maximal for all the players.

5.4 Symmetric game and uncorrelated asymmetry

A symmetric game is a game where the payoffs for playing a particular strategy depend only on the other strategies employed, not on who is playing them (Smith, J. M. 1982). If one can change the identities of the players without changing the payoff to the strategies, then a game is symmetric. Symmetries here refer to symmetries in payoffs.

Biologists often refer to asymmetries in payoffs between players in a game as correlated asymmetries. These are in contrast to uncorrelated asymmetries which are purely informational and have no effect on payoffs. Thus, uncorrelated asymmetry only means "informational asymmetry", not "payoff asymmetry".

If uncorrelated asymmetry exists, then the players know which role they have been assigned. i.e. the players in a game know whether they are Player 1, Player 2, etc. If the players do not know which player they are then no uncorrelated asymmetry exists. The information asymmetry is that one player believes he is player 1 and the other believes he is player 2. Let's take the Hawk-Dove game (HDG hereafter), which will be presented in the next section, as an example. If player 1 believes he will play hawk and the other believes he will player dove, then uncorrelated asymmetry exists.

5.5 Hawk-Dove Game (HDG)

The game of Hawk-Dove, a terminology most commonly used in evolutionary game theory, also known as the Chicken game, is an influential model of conflict for two players in game theory. The principle of the game is that while each player prefers not to yield to the other, the outcome where neither player yields is the worst possible one for both players. The name "Hawk-Dove" refers to a situation in which there is a competition for a shared resource and the contestants can choose either conciliation or conflict.

The earliest presentation of a form of the HDG was by Smith and Price (Smith, J.M. & Price, G. 1973) but the traditional HDG payoff matrix for the HDG, given as Fig. 2, is given in his another book, where v is the value of the contested resource, and c is the cost of an escalated fight. It is (almost always) assumed that the value of the resource is less than the cost of a fight is, i.e., $c > v > 0$. If $c <= v$, the resulting game is not a HDG (Smith, J. M. 1982).

The exact value of the Dove vs. Dove playoff varies between model formulations. Sometimes the players are assumed to split the payoff equally ($v/2$ each), other times the payoff is assumed to be zero (since this is the expected payoff to wait, which is the presumed models for a contest decided by display duration).

While the HDG is typically taught and discussed with the payoffs in terms of v and c, the solutions hold true for any matrix with the payoffs in Fig. 3, where W > T > L > X (Smith, J. M. 1982).

	Hawk	Dove
Hawk	$(v-c)/2, (v-c)/2$	$v,0$
Dove	$0, v$	$v/2, v/2$

Fig. 2. Payoff matrix of traditional Hawk-Dove game

	Hawk	Dove
Hawk	X, X	W, L
Dove	L,W	T, T

Fig. 3. Payoff matrix of a general Hawk-Dove game

5.6 Using Hawk-dove game to model multi-agent foraging

Foraging is a popular, typical, as well as complex, multi-agent cooperation task which can be described as, plainly, a search for provisions (food). How to forage food in an unforeseen environment and evolve coordination mechanisms to make the process effectively and intelligently in itself spans a number of sub tasks. Equipping agents with learning capabilities is a crucial factor to improve individual performance, precision (or quality) and efficiency (or speed) and to adapt the agent to the evolution of the environment.

Generally, there are two kinds of food sources. One type is lightweight and can be carried by a single agent alone which is a metaphor for simple task that can be achieved by single robot, the other is heavy and need multiple agents to work simultaneously to carry it. This heavy food is a metaphor for complex task that must be accomplished by the cooperation of multiple robots (Hayat, S.A. & Niazi, M. 2005). Although coordination of multiple robots are not essential in collecting the lightweight food, the utilities can be increased when coordination indeed appear. Only lightweight foods are considered in this paper to simplify the complexity. In this case, the key to improve the collective utilities lies in how to make a feasible assignment of the food source to every agent so as to the goal for every agent is different since the same food source means there are conflicts between individual optimal assignment and collective optimal assignment in the MAS.

But it is nearly impossible to make an optimal assignment under any situation where there exits lots of agents and foods which scattered randomly. Let's start from an extremely simple situation to illustrate the difficulty. As depicted in Fig. 4, there are two agents A and B (red circle) pursuit two static foods F1 and F2 (two black dots) in a one-dimension world which only permit agent to move left or right and the food will be eaten whenever the agent occupy the same grid as a food. It is obvious that the optimal food for both A and B is F2 since it is nearer than to F1. It is also obvious that if both A and B select F2 as their pursuit target, then utilities of A was sacrificed since it can not capture F2. Thus, it will cause low efficiency as far as the collective utility is considered. In this case, the optimal assignment is B pursuits for F2 while A trying to capture F1. This assignment can be regarded as agent A and B select different policy when confront same food, one is to initiate an aggressive behavior (B), just like hawk in HDG, the other is to retreat immediately (A), like a dove in HDG.

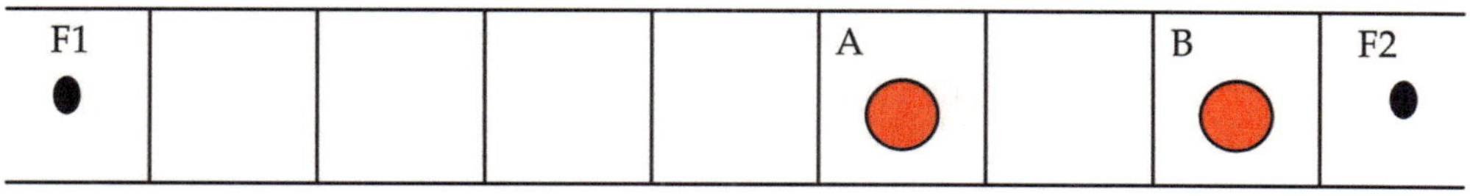

Fig. 4. Simple foraging task in one-dimensional world

And this is only a extremely simple case, if we extend it to two-dimension where the move also extend to {up, down, left, right}, to large number of agents and foods scattered randomly, it will be very hard to make a wise assignment. If we use HDG to model the agent, then we can let the agent select a food by certain doctrine, such as nearest first, and then revise it if the target of multiple agents is the same. In this case, we can let those agents play a HDG to decide who will give up.

As a conclusion, we can abstract the strategies of agents to two categories: one is always aggressive to the food, the other is always yield. The yield agent is dove, and the aggressive one is hawk. In this paper, this HDG model was used to model the strategy of pursuit agents to give the multi-agent foraging a feasible approach.

5.7 Evolution dynamics – replicator dynamics

Replicator dynamics is a simple model of strategy change in evolutionary game theory. Shown in equation (1), it describes how the population with strategy ***i*** will evolve.

$$\dot{x}_i = [u(i,x) - u(x,x)]x_i \tag{1}$$

In the symmetric 2×2 hawk-dove game, a strategy which does better than the average increases in frequency at the expense of strategies that do worse than the average. There are two versions of the replicator dynamics. In one version, there is a single population which plays against itself. In another, there are two population models where each population only plays against the other population (and not against itself).

In the one population model, the only stable state is the mixed strategy Nash equilibrium. Every initial population proportion (except all Hawk and all Dove) converge to the mixed strategy Nash Equilibrium where part of the population plays Hawk and part of the population plays Dove. (This occurs because the only ESS is the mixed strategy equilibrium.) This dynamics of the single population model is illustrated by the vector field pictured in Fig. 5 (Cressman, R. 1995).

Fig. 5. Vector field for single population replicator dynamics

In the two population model, this mixed point becomes unstable. In fact, the only stable states in the two population model correspond to the pure strategy equilibria, where one population is composed of all Hawks and the other of all Doves. In this model one population becomes the aggressive population while the other becomes passive.

The single population model presents a situation where no uncorrelated asymmetries exist, and so the best players can do is randomize their strategies. The two population models

provide such an asymmetry and the members of each population will then use that to correlate their strategies, and thus, one population gains at the expense of another.
Note that the only ESS in the uncorrelated asymmetric single population hawk-dove model is the mixed strategy equilibrium, and it is also a Pareto optimal equilibrium (Smith, J. M. 1982). If some problem can be solved by this model, including our HDG modeled multi-agent foraging, and then the evolutionarily stable strategy is the only Pareto-optimal Nash equilibrium of the system.

6. Evolutionarily cooperation foraging algorithm for MAS

Multi-agent foraging is popular to verify the effectiveness of different cooperation algorithms. In evolving game theory, equilibrium is the result of long process in which the bounded-rational players are trying to optimize their payoff by a natural-selection like mechanism. From the learning process based on replicator dynamic, every player can obtain enough information of personalized equilibrium selection pattern of other agents, and then attain an optimal unanimous equilibrium for the whole MAS. For HDG, the sole evolutionarily stable strategy is also the sole Pareto-optimal Nash equilibrium and thus give a solution to the equilibrium selection of the traditional game theory.
Using evolutionarily stable strategy as optimal solution, we built a HDG model to simulate the interaction between agents, and then proposed a evolutionarily coordinating foraging algorithm (ECFA) to find certain consistent maximal reward equilibrium for the group. Finally, we also add an accelerating factor to make ECFA converge faster, and thus make a new Accelerated ECFA (AECFA). The simulation verified the efficiency of the proposed algorithm.

6.1 Description of problem

Suppose a group of agent (*n* agents) were to capture as much as possible random moving preys (*m* preys) in a bounded rectangle field during a fixed period of time. The agents, having same bounded visual field, start at WANDER state to find a prey. Once it found the food, the agent change its state to GETIT to capture till it eat the food and change its state back to WANDER.
If the agent is the sole pursuer for its target food, it just eats it by moving near to it. Eating occurs when the distance between the food and agent is less than a threshold distance. Another food will be generated at a random position right after to mimic a food abundant environment.
But if the agent find another agent who pursuit the same food (suppose all agent know the goal of other agents), these two agents will play a HDG to determine the rewards they can get. As described in the previous part, two hawks compete for the food with sufficient large cost, while two doves both give up the food and get nothing. If a hawk meet a dove, the hawk eat the food and the dove give up.
Agent can change its strategy to be hawk or dove. As stated in the replicator dynamics, a strategy which does better than the average increases in frequency at the expense of strategies that do worse than the average. Thus, the average reward of the whole system produced by the replicator dynamic is monotonically increasing with time for the symmetric HDG (Losert, V. & Akin, E. 1983). And as a result, the agent with worse strategy would change his strategy to better one and thus lead the whole system to a dynamic stable state with best reward for the agent group (Smith, J. M. 1982).

6.2 Introduction of evolutionarily coordinating foraging algorithm-ECFA

This part describes how the replicator dynamics works so that the system evolves to the sole ESS. In replicator dynamics, the increasing quota of certain strategy is in proportion to the ratio of its average payoff to the average payoff of the population (Weibull, J.W. 1995). Therefore, a strategy which does better than the average increases in frequency at the expense of strategies that do worse than the average. The agent select its strategy based on the accumulated experience or on the observation and imitation of the strategies adopted by opponents. The more popular of a strategy, the more possibility it would be imitated.

During the learning process, agent makes introspection to its strategy from time to time and this gives the possibility that it may change its strategy. Suppose those agents using less successful strategy are more likely to introspection and let $r_i(x)$ be the average rate of introspection of agent using strategy $\boldsymbol{i} \in K$, where K is the strategy set and $\boldsymbol{e^i}$ are strategies of agent $\boldsymbol{i}$ in K.

$$r_i(x) = 1 - \frac{u(e^i, x)}{\sum_{h \in K} u(e^h, x)} \tag{2}$$

Next, we use $p_i^j(x)$ denote the probability that agent $\boldsymbol{i}$ will change to use strategy $\boldsymbol{j}$ and let $p_i^j(x)$ is proportion to the popularity of strategy $\boldsymbol{j}$ and its rewards.

$$p_i^j(x) = \frac{\omega[u(e^j, x), x]x_j}{\sum_{h \in K} \omega_i[u(e^h, x), x]x_h} \tag{3}$$

here ω is continuous Lipschitz function that non-decrease in its first independent variables. Also, to show the agents using less successful strategy are more likely to introspection we suppose $r_i(x) = \phi[u(e^i, x), x]$ and ϕ is continuous Lipschitz function that strictly decreases in its first independent variables.

And at last we get the replicator dynamics of this symmetric revised Hark-Dove game as

$$\dot{x} = \sum_{j \in K} x_j r_j(x) p_j^i(x) - r_i(x) x_i \tag{4}$$

which will lead to the average fitness of the whole system increase monotonically with the time until the system evolve to an Pareto-optimal ESS, the sole evolutionarily stable state(Wang,Y.H., Liu, J., & Meng, W. 2007).

6.3 Description of ECFA

Initialization:

Generate all preys and agents.

Assign random strategy (hawk or dove) to each agent.

Set the state of agent to WANDER to enable the agent looking for food.

Let $RAND \in (0,1)$ is a random generated threshold.

Main:

for every agent, run Step1 to Step3 infinitely until the MAS converge to ESS.

Step 1: //Agent pursues food

if (prey found) {
  Agent change its state to GETIT; goto Step 2;
}
else goto Step 1;

Step 2: //Single pursuer

If (the agent is the only pursuer of the prey) {
  Eat the prey and get reward;
  Generate a new prey at random position;
  goto Step1;
}
else goto Step 3.

Step 3://Multiple pursuer executing introspection - imitation

Play the hawk-dove game and get reward;

Update its environment model $x(x_i,x_j)$, where x_i and x_j are the proportion of encountered hawks and doves.

Compute the utilities $u(i,x)$; $i \in K$={Hawk,Dove}

Using equation (3) to compute the introspective probability of agent who execute strategy i:

If ($r_i(x)$> *RAND*){

Compute the strategy change probability p_{Dove}^{Hawk} and p_{Hawk}^{Dove}; here p_i^j denotes the probability that agent change its strategy from i to j.

if(p_{Dove}^{Hawk} > *RAND*)) strategy = Hawk;

if(p_{Hawk}^{Dove} >*RAND*)) strategy = Dove;

}

6.4 Simulation results of ECFA

Several simulations had been done to verify the efficiency of ECFA. The following parameters were used for the simulations: agent number n =50, prey number m = 130, the benefits of capture prey v =4, the cost to injury to self c = 6. The environment is defined as an 1150*650 grid. Each grid location represent an x and y location which can be occupied by one or more agents at the same time. Preys were randomly disposed in the field before the simulation start. They can move randomly with a lower velocity than that of agents (70%). Right after a prey was eaten, a new prey would be regenerated at a random chosen grid.

The first group of simulation is to test the validity and efficiency of the ECFA, we compare ECFA with another three algorithms, namely random forage, fixed strategy 1 forage with 30% hawk and 70% dove, fixed strategy 2 forage with 70% hawk and 30% dove. While a random forage agent will try to eat every food it found, a fixed strategy forage agent will play the HDG when two agents compete for the same food, but the number of hawk agent and dove agent remains unchanged. In ECFA, however, the number of hawk and dove agent will evolve until they finally converge to a stable state. The performance index is the average number of the preys captured by the agent group in a given span of time.

In either situation, the four algorithms were tested for 10 times respectively, and fig. 6 gives the graphic depiction of simulation results.

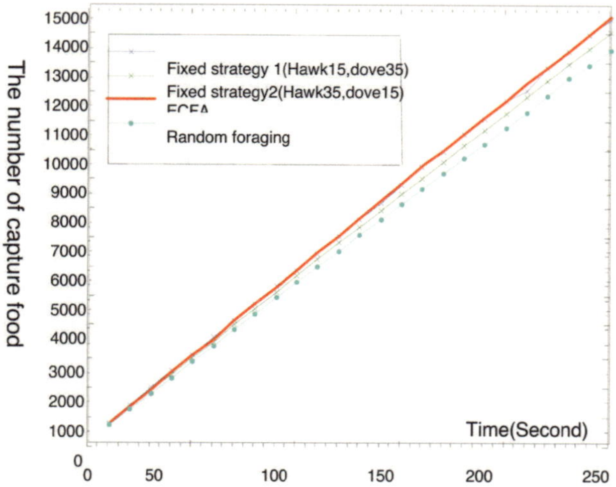

Fig. 6. The average number of preyscaptured by different foraging algorithm

These results show that ECFA captured more foods than other three algorithms averagely. If we investigate the results more carefully, we can see fixed strategy 1 foraging with 30% hawk and 70% dove outperforms fixed strategy 2 that forage with 70% hawk and 30% dove. It is easy to see that the agents with different hawks and doves have different performance. Then, it would be natural to ask how much hawk and dove will be evolved in ESS in various HDG model. That is what we want to show in the second group of simulation.

The second group of simulation is to find how many hawk agents in the evolutionarily stable state for different configuration of the hawk-dove games. Here we suppose $v+c=10$ and we and we test 6 situations from ($c=4,v=6$), ($c=5,v=5$),…, to ($c=9,v=1$). Note that even it is not HDG when ($c=4,v=6$) and ($c=5,v=5$) since $c < v$, we are also eager to know the result. Each situation was test for 10 times and table 1 lists the simulation result as well as the corresponding theoretical result of the average number of hawk agent in the ESS of every situation. Fig. 7 is the corresponding graph.

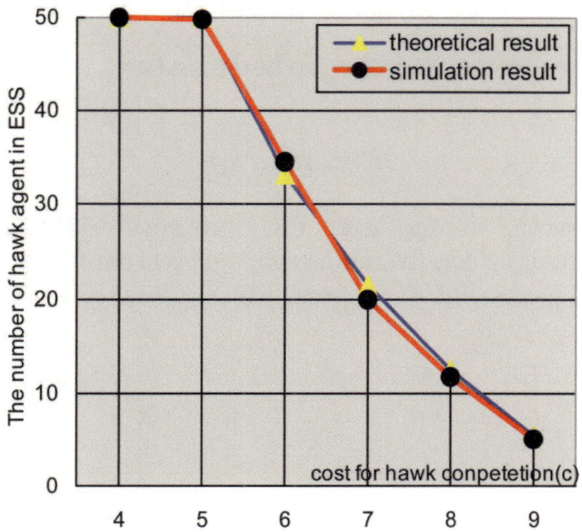

Fig. 7. The average number of hawk agents in convergent ESS of different game model

From these simulations, we can see that the number of hawk agent in the convergent ESS is decreasing with the increasing of the cost for two hawk competition. And it also shows that the simulation results are close to their theoretical values. The error between these two values is probably because the convergent threshold value for our simulation and the theoretical value is limit point which hardly achieved in finite trials.

cost	*4*	*5*	*6*	*7*	*8*	*9*
theoretical result	50	50	33.3	21.4	12.5	5.5
simulation result	50	49.8	34.6	20	11.8	5

Table 1. The number of hawk agent and corresponding theoretical result in different ***c,v***

6.5 Improving of ECFA

As stated in replicator dynamics of this symmetric HDG, a strategy better than the average increases in frequency at the expense of strategies that worse than the average. And the changing quota of certain strategy is in proportion to the ratio of its average payoff to the average payoff of the population. But because the difference between strategies in the early evolutionarily stage is small, the better strategies or worse strategies can only impose a little impact on the agent group. Thus the evolution to the ESS of agent adopted ECFA is slow. Moreover, just as this evolving is a dynamic process and the strategies adopted by the agents are keep changing, which would make the system is not stable enough.

For these deficiencies, we added a reinforcement factor to ECFA to make an Accelerated ECFA (AECFA) to strengthen the outstanding strategies and weaken inferior strategies. The process of convergence will be accelerated and the convergent ESE will be more stable for the impact of the worse mutation strategies is weakened.

6.6 Reinforcement factor and the description of AECFA

Let $\theta_{i,t}^{e^j}$ be the reinforcement factor of agent $\boldsymbol{i}$ with respect to strategy $e^k \in K$ at time $\boldsymbol{t}$ and $\Delta\theta_{i,t}^{e^k}$ be a degree that the reinforcement factor is changed at time t. When t=0, $\theta_{i,t}^{e^j}$ =0 and $\sum_{e^k \in K} \theta_{i,t}^{e^j} = 0$. Then the reinforcement factor can be defined as

$$\theta_{i,t+1}^{e^k} = \theta_{i,t}^{e^k} + \Delta\theta_{i,t}^{e^k} \tag{5}$$

which means the better the strategy does, the more positively it is reinforced. And vice versa, the worse the strategy does, the more negatively it is reinforced.

Now let $q_{i,t}^{e^k}$ denote the probability that agent i execute strategy e^k at time $\boldsymbol{t}$ and let

$$\Delta\theta_{i,t}^{e^k} = \frac{q_{i,t}^{e^k} - \frac{1}{n}}{\frac{1}{n}} = n \cdot q_{i,t}^{e^k} - 1 \tag{6}$$

where $\boldsymbol{n}$ denote the number of the set of strategies K. Then, there is positive correlation between $q_{i,t}^{e^k}$ and the utility of e^k . And we let

$$q_{i,t}^{e^k} = \frac{u(e^k, x)}{\sum_{h \in K} u(e^h, x)} \tag{7}$$

At time *t*, let the agent ***i*** executes the strategy whose reinforcement factor is maximal. If the number of maximal reinforcement factor is more than one, the agent executes one of them according to some probability. At any time, each strategy in the set of agent-strategies is reinforced positively or negatively with respect to its current utility (Wang,Y.H., Liu, J. 2008). The algorithm description of this accelerated ECFA is given in Fig. 8.

```
Step 1:
  Compute the utilities u(e^k, x), e^k ∈ K = {Hawk, Dove}
  Using (2), Computing the reflecting probability of agent i
Step 2:
  IF (r_i(x) >RAND){
    Compute θ_{i,t}^{hawk} and θ_{i,t}^{dove};
    IF (θ_{i,t}^{hawk} > θ_{i,t}^{dove})
    {
        STRATEGY=Hawk;
        Update its environment model;
    }
    ELSE IF (θ_{i,t}^{hawk} < θ_{i,t}^{dove})
    {
        STRATEGY=Dove;
        Update its environment model;
    }
    ELSE
        Keep the strategy as it is;
}
```

Fig. 8. The algorithm description Accelerated ECFA

6.7 Simulation results of AECFA

To verify effectiveness of the reinforcement factor for the algorithm, we use multi-agent foraging task to test the difference of the stability and the time of convergence between AECFA and ECFA.

The parameters: agent number n =64, prey number m =30, c=8, v=2. Theoretically, the number of hawk agent should be 16 in ESE on the condition of this simulation; the simulation sampled the number of hawk once 500 seconds (Liu, J. 2008).

The performance index: the number difference between the number of hawk and the number of hawk in the equilibrium. Here is an example to make it clear. Suppose at certain time, the sampled hawk agent is 18, then the number difference is |18-16|=2 and the performance ratio is 2/64=3.1%. Here 2 and 64 denote the number difference and total number of the agents respectively.

Considering the size of the MAS, we take the following difference ratio as the criterion to decide weather the system is in the convergent state or not. This threshold is determined to be 5% according to several simulations. If the performance ratio is less than the difference ratio 5%, the system would be considered in the ESE. In this case all these two algorithms had been tested for 10 times respectively; the results are given in Fig.9 and table 2. Fig.9 plots the number difference between the average hawk number and the hawk number of theoretical equilibrium in convergent ESE.

As shown in the Fig.9, in convergent ESE, the stability of the AECFA is less than 2 %(between 15 and 18), yet the stability of the ECFA is only close to 5 %(between 12 and 20).

The AECFA evolved into ESE at average 100 seconds and the ECFA at average 56590 seconds. Thus, AECFA gives a much faster convergence process than the ECFA does.

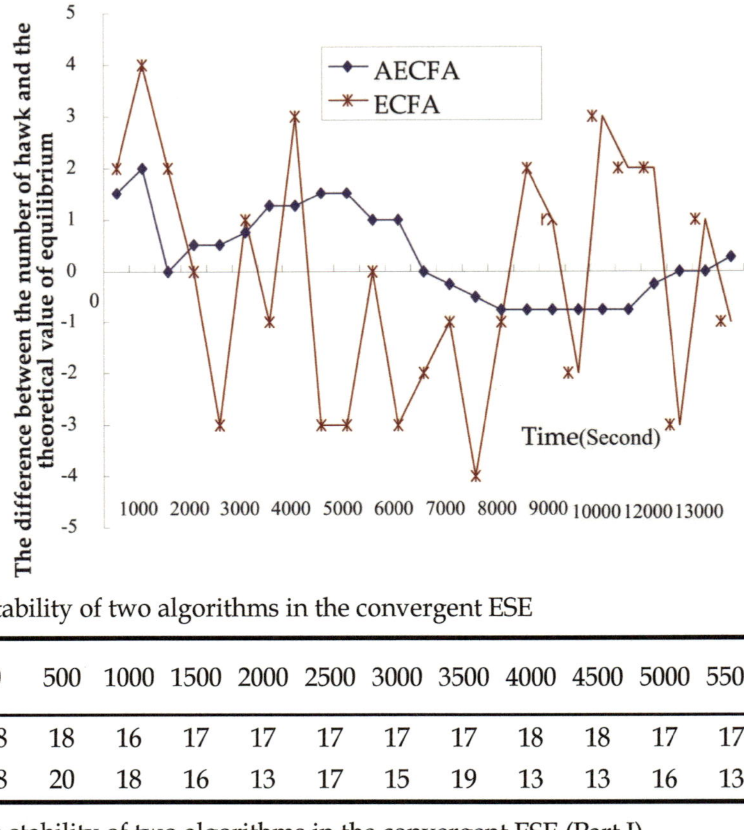

Fig. 9. The stability of two algorithms in the convergent ESE

Time / hawks	0	500	1000	1500	2000	2500	3000	3500	4000	4500	5000	5500	6000	6500
AECFA	18	18	16	17	17	17	17	17	18	18	17	17	16	16
ECFA	18	20	18	16	13	17	15	19	13	13	16	13	14	15

Table 2. The stability of two algorithms in the convergent ESE (Part I)

Time / hawks	7000	7500	8000	8500	9000	9500	10000	10500	11000	11500	12000	12500	13000
AECFA	16	15	15	15	15	15	15	16	16	16	16	15	15
ECFA	12	15	18	17	14	19	18	18	13	17	15	14	19

Table 2. The stability of two algorithms in the convergent ESE (Part II)

7. Conclusion and future works

An evolutionarily stable strategy was adopted to be an optimal solution for the multi-agent foraging task, and hawk-dove game model was used to simulate the interaction between the agents, and finally, an evolutionarily cooperation foraging algorithm (ECFA) that can adapt the environment change, evolve an stable ESS and bring the maximal reward for the group eventually is proposed. Moreover, to the disadvantages such as long convergence process of the ECFA, we imposed a reinforcement factor to accelerate the convergence process.

The technique was shown to successfully apply in the multi-agent foraging task and to increase the efficiency of the agent group. Thus, at least for the domain under study, large population of agents and random moving preys, the technique proposes very fast foraging mechnisms. The simulation shows that the proposed algorithm can convergence to a maximal-reward ESS which in turn give an solution to equilibrium selection problem of game theory based cooperation MAS.

For the second type of preys, a big food that need more than one agent together to capture, and dynamic environments where the value and cost to contest can change due to some reason need to studied in the future work.

8. Acknowledgements

I would like to thank Mr. Liu jie for his early work in experiments, and this study was supported by Science and Technology Developing Plan of Beijing Municipal Education Commission under the grant KM200810009009, and the Funding Project for Academic Human Resource Development in Institutions of Higher Learning under the Jurisdiction of Beijing Municipality.

9. References

Aumann R.J. (1959), Acceptable points in general cooperative n-person games, in: *Contributions to the Theory of Games IV, Annals of Mathematics Study*, Luce, R.D. & Tucker, A.W. (Ed.), pp. 287-324, Princeton University Press, Princeton NJ.

Aumann R. (1974), Subjectivity and correlation in randomized strategies. Journal of Mathematical Economics, Vol. 1, pp. 67–96

Bermheim, B.D., Peleg,B. & Whinstion, M.D. (1987), Coalition-proof Nash equilibria - I. Concepts, Journal of Economic Theory, Vol. 42, pp.1-12

Cressman, R. (1995). Evolutionary stability for two-stage Hawk-Dove games. The Rocky Mountain Journal of Mathematics, Vol. 25, No. 1, Winter 1995. pp.145–155.

Fieser, J. & Dowden, B. (2008), Game theory, in: the Internet encyclopedia of philosophy, http://www.iep.utm.edu/g/game-th.htm, accessed on 8 August 2008

Fudenberg,D. & Tirole,J. (1991), Game Theory, the MIT Press, Cambridge, Massachusetts, London, England

Harsanyi, J. C. & Selten, R. (1988), A General Theory of Equilibrium Selection in Games, the MIT Press, Cambridge, Massachusetts, London, England

Hayat, S. A. & Niazi, M. (2005), Multi-agent foraging – taking a step further Q-learning with search. Proceedings of IEEE international conference on emerging technologies (ICET05), September 2005, Islamabad, pp. 215-220

Li, G.J. (2005), A fundamental course in game theory, the Chemical industry press. Beijing, China, (Feb. 2005), p30-32

Liu, J., The study on multi-agent cooperative algorithm based on game theory. Master thesis, North China University of Technology, Beijing, China, June 2008

Losert, V. & Akin, E. (1983), Dynamics of games and genes: discrete versus continuous time, Journal of Mathematical Biology, 1983

Poundstone, W. (1992), Prisoner's Dilemma: John Von Neumann, Game Theory and the Puzzle of the Bomb, Doubleday, (February 1993). ISBN-13: 978-0385415804

Schelling, T. C. (1960), The Strategy of Conflict, Harvard University Press, Cambridge, Massachusetts.

Sen, A. (1987), Rational behaviour, The New Palgrave: A Dictionary of Economics, Vol. 3,(1987) pp. 68-76.

Smith, J. M. & Price, G. R. (1973), The logic of animal conflict. Nature, Vol. 246. pp.15-18.

Smith, J. M. (1982), Evolution and the theory of games, Cambridge University Press, ISBN 978-0-521-28884-2

Wang,Y.H., Liu, J., & Meng, W. (2007), Cooperative algorithm for multi-agent foraging task based on modified hawk-dove game. Proceeding of International Conference on Computational Intelligence and Security Workshops (CIS07), December 2007, IEEE Computer Society Press, Harbin, China. pp.179-182

Wang, Y.H., Liu, J. (2008), Ponder-reinforcement cooperative algorithm for multi-agent foraging task based on evolutionary stable equilibrium, Proceedings of 7th World Congress on Intelligent Control and Automation (WCICA08), June 2008, Chongqing, China. pp. 4527-4530.

Weibull, J.W. (1995), Evolutionary Game Theory. The MIT Press, Cambridge, Massachusetts. ISBN 0-262-23181-6

10

Indirect Coordination Mechanism of MAS

Satoshi Kurihara, Kensuke Fukuda, Shinya Sato and Toshiharu Sugawara
Osaka University
Japan

1. Introduction

There has recently been a large amount of research on the difficulty of constructing centralized control type systems, such as the next generation intelligent transport systems, artificial market systems, and next generation electronic auction systems, etc, with the expansion of the Internet, ubiquitous information communication infrastructures, complex web services, and grid computing technologies. Usually, the distributed system is constructed by many modules, and it is better that each module be more autonomous. And an agent is an autonomous module, so these systems should be constructed as multi-agent systems (MASs), from the viewpoints of efficiency, adaptability and robustness.

In a MAS, the interaction mechanism between agents, and the range of view of each agent are important factors. For example, in grid computing and the web services, a system works by cooperating agents throughout the Internet, so each agent needs a wide-ranging view.

On the other hand, each car and trader agent, for example, in a next generation intelligent transport system, artificial market system, or next generation electronic auction system basically behave selfishly and interact competitively for their own benefit due to a limited amount of resources. In this competitive situation, each agent does not want give information to other agents and do not interact directly. As a result, the range of view of each agent may narrow.

However, even in a competitive system in which agents scramble for limited resources, the goal of the system itself is to provide higher benefits for all agents (the system must not cause a disparity in wealth). For example, in next generation intelligent transport systems, though the goal of each car navigation agent is to reach a destination faster, the system's goal is for all cars to be able to move both efficiently and faster. In the artificial market systems, though the goal of each trader agent is to get higher benefits, the system's goal is for all agents to benefit and not cause any disparity in wealth.

Most conventional MASs are completely based on cooperated interactions. In the future, however, it is believed that some systems will be based on cooperative, but in which each agent is competitive.

2. Indirect coordination

There have recently been studies on the emergence of intelligence from many simple autonomous agents' cooperation and competition such as collective intelligence, swarm-made architecture, and pheromonal communication model. Cooperation and competition are roughly divided into both direct and indirect types.

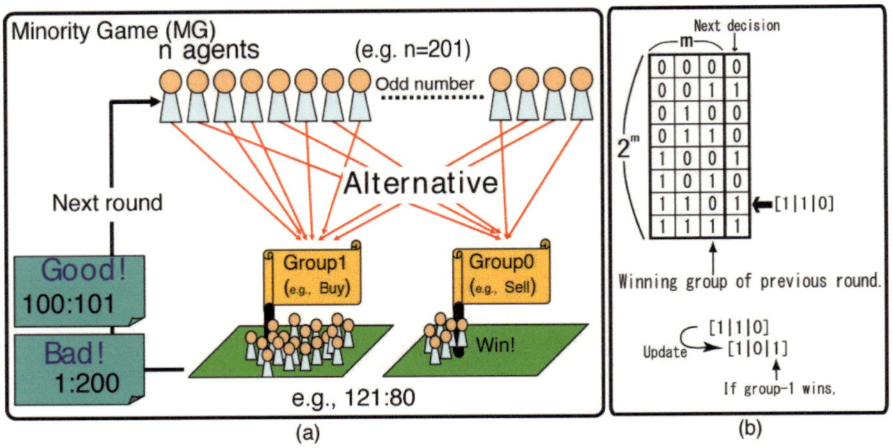

Fig. 1. Rule of MG and detail of strategy table.

The load of interactions between agents may increase in MASs based on direct interaction when the number of agent becomes too large. Moreover, a more complex interaction may be necessary if synchronized interaction is required. Therefore, when the number of agent increases, a MAS based on direct interaction may lose adaptability and robustness when new agents join dynamically and when some agents suddenly become inactive.

In contrast, in a MAS based on indirect interaction, each agent has a relatively narrow range of view and the interaction between agents is indirect through, for example, the environment (the real world). For example, in nature, ants interact with each other by using pheromones. We call this "stigmergy [1]". A typical interaction model based on indirect interaction is the ant colony optimization algorithm (ACO).

The ant colony optimization algorithm is one of the most well-known models of pheromone communication derived from the swarming behavior of ants in nature. Ant colony optimization is recognized as being extremely robust against and adaptable to dynamic changes in the environment, and various kinds of optimization problems have been solved using ACO-based approaches [2] . Another indirect interaction model is particle swarm optimization (PSO) [3]. PSO are population-based optimization algorithms modelled after the simulation of social behavior of bird flocks [4]. In a PSO system, a swarm of individuals (particles) fly through the search space. Each particle represents a candidate solution to the optimization problem. The position of a particle is influenced by the best position visited by itself.

The goal of ACO and PSO is to get higher benefit of all agents as a whole and not to take care about each agent's benefit. In contrast, in newer systems that are larger and more complex, such as next generation intelligent transport systems, the goal is not only to obtain more benefits of all agents as a whole but also focus on obtaining benefits for each individual agent.

The El Farol Bar problem [5] and Minority Game (MG) [6] are good examples of newer MASs. Minority Game is a competitive multi-agent based simulation environment for analyzing the dynamics of social economy. In MG, many agents play a simple competitive binary decision game. Even though they have no range of view and behave selfishly, certain coordinative elements emerge from the viewpoint of the agents as a whole. The most important element of MG is to make coordination a behavior rule of each agent. This rule may not be applicable to other MASs, but it is important to analyse the dynamics of MG and the behavior of each agent to find out the general-purpose behavior rules of agents.

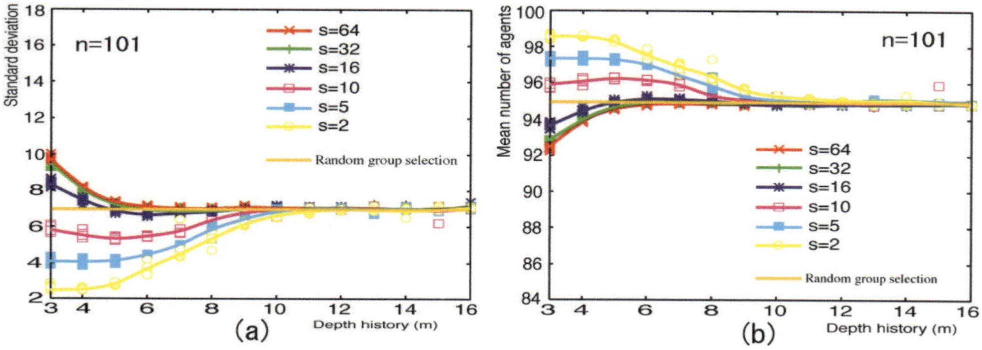

Fig. 2. (a) Standard deviations of the number of winning agents.
(b) Mean numbers of winning agents.

3. Minority Game (MG)

First, we review the rules of MG (see Fig. 1(a)). There are *n* (odd number) autonomous agents, each of which independently chooses between two alternatives (*group-0* or *group-1*) according to its personalized behavioral rules, that is, it does not see other agents' behaviors. After all of the agents choose one or the other, the agents that finish in the minority group are considered to be winners. This is one round of the game.

Each winner agent is awarded one point, and the total number of winner agents is the profit in this round of the game for this multi agent system. Therefore, the more winner agents the better, that is, the smaller the difference between the number of agents in the majority and minority groups, the better.

The each agent makes its selection by using one of multiple strategy tables that it holds (*s* tables). The entities in the table contain all combinations of *m* past history of the minority group choices and next decisions that corresponds to each of the combinations for the next round (see Fig. 1(b)). At the beginning of the game, each agent prepares *s* ($s < 2$) strategy tables, and 0 or 1 is allocated randomly in the next decision entries of each strategy table. After the game starts, we cannot modify the entries of each table.

In the first round of the game, we initially set the past combinations of the winning group at random, for example, [1|1|0], and each agent randomly chooses one of its holding *s* strategy tables and sees the next decision entry corresponding to [1|1|0] (see Fig. 1(b)). In this case, the past combinations of the winning group is [1|1|0], so this agent sees the [1|1|0] entry and select *group-1* in the next round of the game. Then if the agent becomes winner, one point is assigned to the agent and also the selected strategy table. If the agent loses, one point is deducted from the selected tables. After the score of the strategy tables for all agents are updated, the past combinations of the winning group is updated from [1|1|0] to [1|0|1] because *group-1* is the winner-group in this round of the game. In the second and subsequent rounds, each agent selects the strategy table that has the highest score. The round is repeated a predetermined number of times, and the final result of the game is the total number of points acquired by the winner-agents.

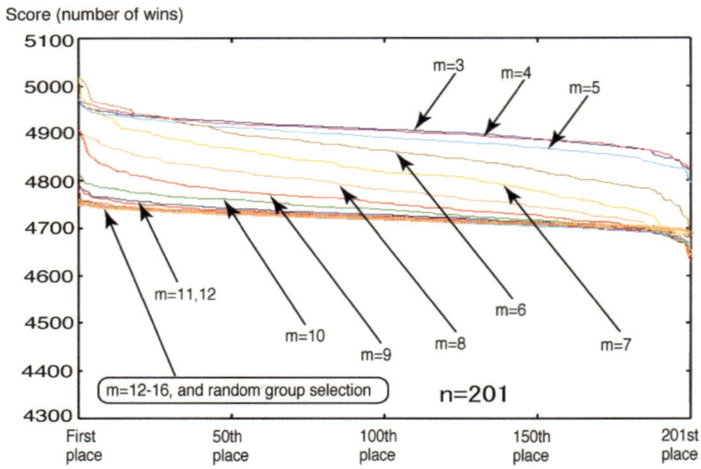

Fig. 3. Rankings of agents for each *m* after 10,000 rounds.

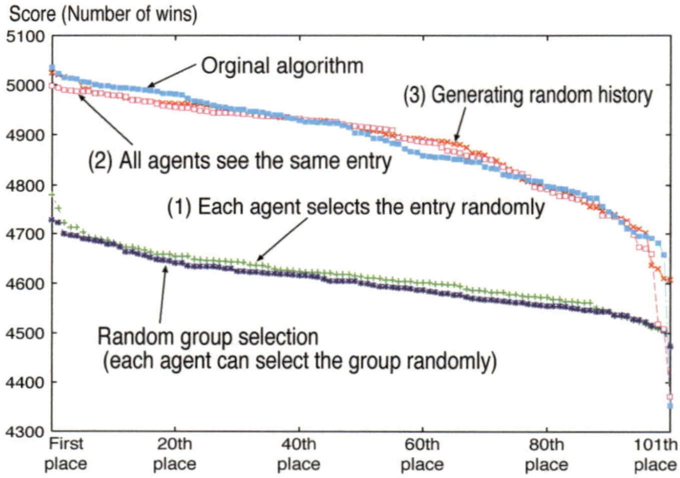

Fig. 4. Ranking of agents for each entry selection rule.

3.1 Coordinated behaviors

The following overall order emerged through such simple rules. First, the standard deviation of the number of winning agents is shown in Fig. 2(a). The game was played for the number of rounds described below with the agents possessing various numbers of strategy tables, $s = \{2, 5, 10, 16, 32, 64\}$ and each strategy table consists of various m, $m = 3$ to 16. One trial for each parameter pair, $\{s, m\}$, is 10,000 rounds of the game; ten trials were conducted for each pair. As for the simulation, we ran the game with 201 agents. Figure 2(b) shows the mean number of winning agents. The horizontal lines in Figs. 2(a) and (b) represent the standard deviation and mean value when all of the agents made random choices at all times. These graphs show that, for the lower values of s, the standard deviation was lowest and the mean number of winning agents was highest when m was from three to six. Figure 3 shows the ranking of the 201 agents by their average score. In the case where each agent randomly selected *group-0* or *group-1*, all of the agents were able to get approximately 4750 points. In contrast, the mean score was especially high when the standard deviation was small (m=3, 4, 5) and, although some differences between agents can be seen in the scores, all or almost all of the agents were able to achieve stable high scores. This means that some kind of coordinated behavior among the agents was driving the winning-group ratio closer to 100:101 in these cases. The most interesting characteristic is that, although we would expect behavior based on longer histories to be more efficient, m larger than ten produced results that were the same as those of random behavior. As for n and m, there is a constant relationship between m and $\sigma^2/2n$ (σ is the standard deviation of Fig. 2(a)). In this chapter, we ran the game with 101, 201, and 301 agents.

4. Key elements for emergence of coordination

In MG, the following two rules are thought to be important elements for coordination to occur: (i) all agent must see the same entry of their strategy tables according to the past combinations of the winning group and (ii) each strategy table's point is changed like a random walk.

4.1 Winner-group history

To verify whether the past combinations of the winning group is necessary or not, we performed the following simulations: In the normal algorithm, when the past combinations of the winning group is [0|1|0], all agents see [0|1|0] entry of their holding strategy tables, and each agent selects one of its holding strategy tables, depending on their points.
At this point, we performed the simulation to answer the following questions:

1. If each agent is allowed to select an entry of strategy tables randomly, can coordinated behavior occur?
2. If only one agent, agent-A, is allowed to select an entry by its own rule and the other agents use the same entry as agent-A, can coordinated behavior occur? In other words, all agents do not obey the past combinations of the winning group, but they see the same entry of their strategy table.
3. If we intentionally generate a random winner group history, can coordinated behavior?

Figure 4 shows the results. The same type of coordinated behavior as with the normal algorithm could be formed in situations (2) and (3). These results show that the past combinations of the winning group itself may not be important for the emergence of coordination. As for (1), when each agent randomly selected a strategy table entry, their behaviors were the same as those based on the random group selection.
Therefore, we can infer that an important point concerning strategy tables is that, in the normal algorithm, the rule that all agents depend on the past combinations of the winning group placing an adequate constraint on agents. In other words, if we can place an adequate constraint on agents like in situation (2) or (3), we may be able to use any kind of rule. Applying an adequate constraint to agents also means decreasing their freedom.

m	3	5	9	13
Average	46.6	46.5	43.2	33.7
σ	2.8	2.9	3.0	4.1

Table. 1. Relation between m and the total number of *0*.

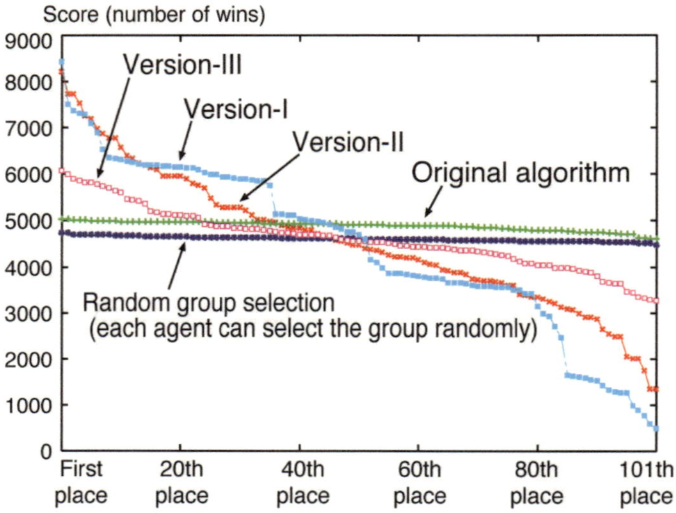

Fig. 5. Ranking of agents for each point rule.

4.1.1 Discussion about *m* value

At this point let's think about why the difference between the number of agents in minority- and majority-group becomes a little in relatively small m. To begin with, since the total of 0 and 1 becomes stochastically equal because 0 and 1 of each strategy table is stored at random, so the total of 0 and 1 that each agent selects corresponding to the past combinations of the winning group must become stochastically equal too. Therefore, in each game, difference between the total of agent in minority-group and majority-group always must become a little, and if the game is repeated many times, almost all agent's winning-ratio will become approximately equal. That is, when m is small it is regarded that the row of 0 and 1 of each strategy table is near to above situation. And in this case, difference between the total of agent in minority-group and majority-group always becomes little and almost all agents' winning-ratio will become equal and high.

On the other hand, when m becomes large the number of entries of strategy tables increases at the rate of 2^m. And at this point, let's think about the following hypothesis: Even if the total of 0 and 1 in each table becomes equal stochastically the existence probability of combination that the difference in the total of 0 and 1 in the next decision of same entry of all the agents becomes large becomes large in big m. So, when m becomes big the difference between the number of agents in minority- and majority-group cannot become a little and result may become as same as random selection case.

To verify this hypothesis, we calculated the average and standard deviation of the total of 0 when each agent would select all the past combinations of the winning group combinations in several m (n = 101). For each m value, we executed the game under 100 kinds of strategy tables and calculated average.

Then, the following relation was confirmed (see Table 1); when m became large the average of total of 0 became low, this means there were big difference between total of 0 and 1 in big m, and the standard deviation became also large, this means the average was not steady in each game in big m. As a result, it can be understood that winning-ratio becomes nearly 50% steady when m is small.

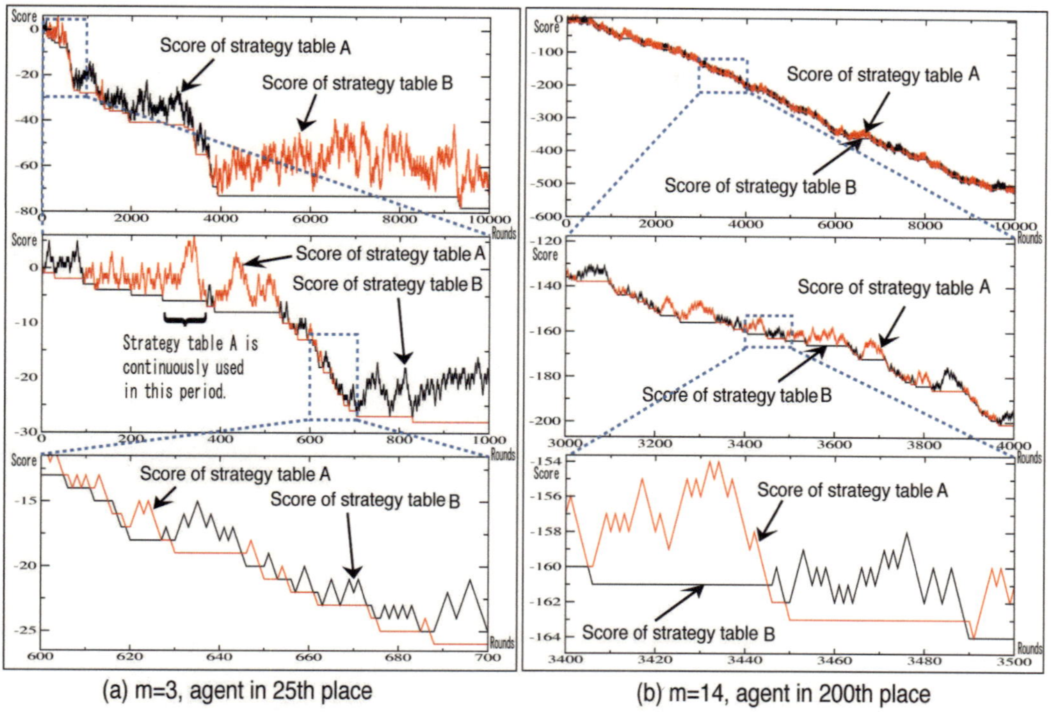

Fig. 6. Scores for (a) m=3, 25th place agent and (b) m=14, 200th place agent in (upper) 10000, (middle) 1000, and (lower) 100 games.

4.2 Importance of indirect coordination

In MG, indirect interaction between agents is also considered to be an important element for coordination to occur. Each agent decides its behavior based on the results of each round, and its decision indirectly influences the behaviors of the other agents. In the algorithm, if the agent wins, one point is added to the selected strategy table, and if it loses one point is subtracted like a random walk. For example let us consider one agent and its two strategy tables, *table-A* and *table-B*. If *table-A* has 4 points and *table-B* has 1 point, *table-B* is not selected until *table-A* has lost at least 4 times in a row.

We verified whether coordinated behavior occurred or not even if we changed the rule for selecting the strategy tables as follows:

(Version I) Agents select the strategy tables sequentially. The interval of the exchange is randomly set up.

(Version II) If it wins, one point is added to the selected strategy table, but if it loses, two points are subtracted.

(Version III) If the agent loses one game, the strategy table is changed even if the points of this strategy table is still higher than the points of the other one.

Figure 6 shows the results of our investigation of this question. Unfortunately, coordinated behavior did not emerge in any of these versions. Therefore, it became apparent that the means of selecting a strategy table is closely related to the initial combinations of the strategy tables of each agent.

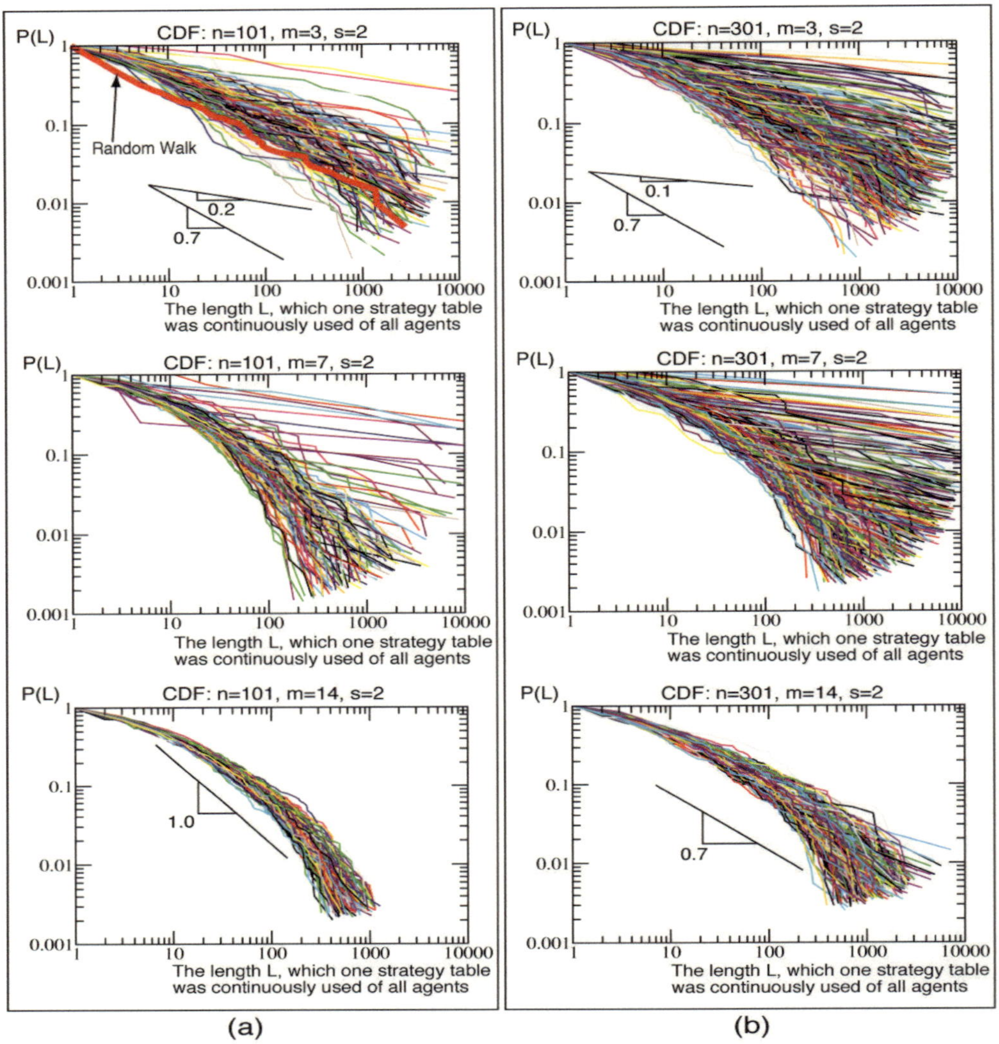

Fig. 7. Histograms of continuously used periods (L) of strategy table of all agents in several kinds of *m* values (m= 3, 7 and 14), for (a) *n*=101 and (b) *n*=301.

4.2.1 Discussion

As mentioned before, the scoring rule for strategy tables is similar to a random walk, that is when an agent wins, the selected strategy table's score is increased by 1 point and in case of losing, 1 point is subtracted. It is known that when a certain value changes, such as a random walk, the probability density histogram of the period when there are *0* or more points follows a power-law.

We investigated how each agent selects strategy tables in detail. Figures 6(a) and (b) show the transitions of the scores for each strategy table held by the 25*th*-place agent of *m* = 3 in a *coordinated situation*, and the 200*th*-place agent of *m*=14 in a *non-coordinated situation* when the game was played with 201 agents (*n*=201) and each agent has two strategy tables (*s*=2). As Fig. 3 shows, the winning percentage goes below 50% for even the best winner agent, so the total score of each strategy table declines.

The 25*th*-place agent in Fig. 6(a) not only used both strategy tables in alternate shifts but also used only one table continuously. An important point is that there is no typical period for continual use of only one table. That is, the "self-similarity characteristic (power-law)" can be seen in the strategy table selection behavior of an agent in a coordinated situation. Figure 7 shows histograms of the continuously used periods of only one strategy table of all agents by log-log scale (for (a) n = 101, and (b) n = 301). The power law can be seen in both cases of m=3 (graphs were nearly straight lines).
In Fig. 6(b), self-similarity cannot be seen in the results for the 200*th*-place agent. This result suggests that some typical continuously used periods by only one table are in the agent in a *non-coordinated situation*. Interestingly, the histograms for agents with m =7 show a mix of *coordinated* and *non-coordinated situations*; some agents were similar to the graphs of m =3, while others were similar to those of m=14.

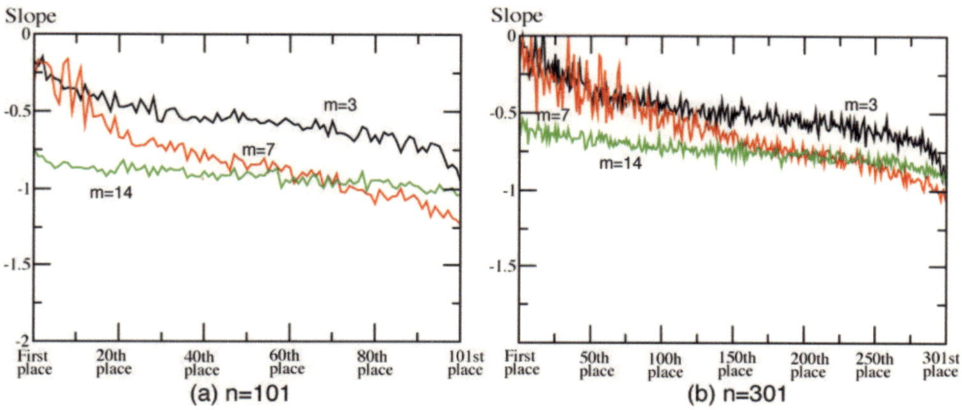

Fig. 8. Slopes of histograms in Fig. 7.

4.3 Consistent constraints and power-law

From 3.1 and 3.2, we can assume that an adequate consistent constraint to all agents and a behavior rule forming a power law feature are both important assumptions for coordination to occur. Note that coordination occurs when m is small. When m is large, the coordination cannot occur due to the construction rule of the strategy table. The rules of MG may not be applied to other MASs. However, these two assumptions may be considered as important general methodologies for coordination, especially the latter assumption. When a system performs most effectively at critical a point, a power law feature can be observed. Therefore, it is necessary to analyze the dynamics of MG more in more detail.

5. Improvement of winning percentage using power-law feature

As shown in Fig. 8, there is a consistent relationship between the slope of the power-law and the score of each agent, and this relationship is maintained regardless of various values of n and m. That is, each agent can know its rough position among the group by seeing whether its own strategy table selection obeys the power-law or not.
A possible ways to change the agent behavior without changing the strategy usage rule and random walk-based point rule is to renew the next decision entries of the strategy tables. The problem is how to decide when each agent renews its strategy tables.

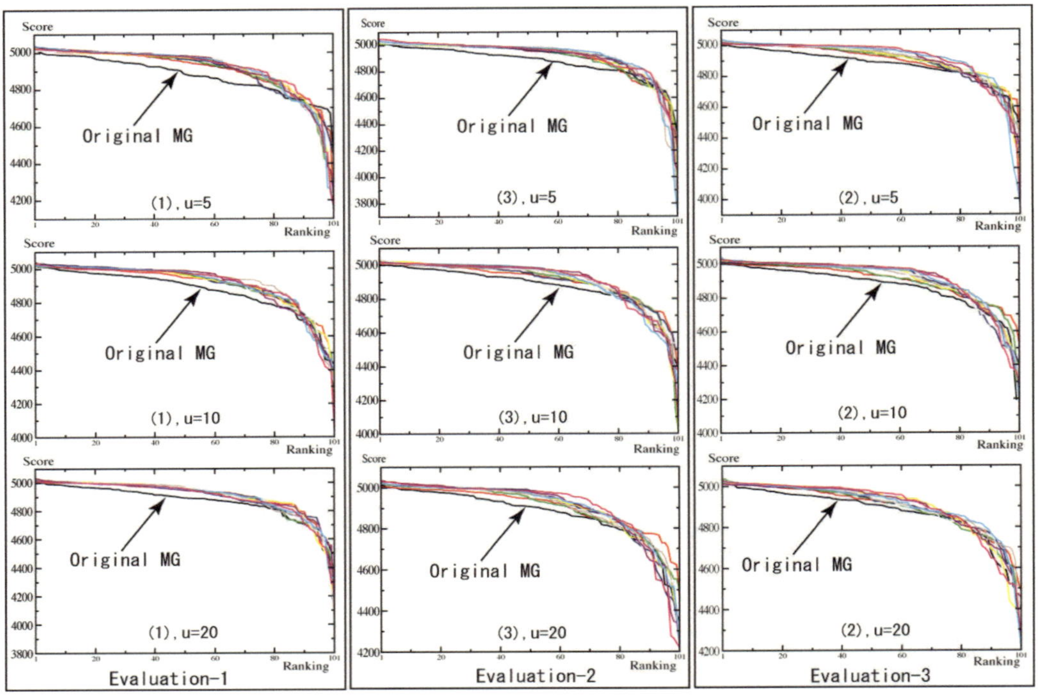

Fig. 9. Scores of three kinds of evaluation-criteria.

We conducted the following are experiment in which each agent renews its strategy tables using three criteria. We executed the game with 101 agents (n = 101, s=2). After 10,000 rounds (10,000 rounds is one turn) of the game were played, each agent's behavior efficiency was evaluated with the following criteria, and each agent, which is identified as inefficient, renews its strategy tables. Then the next turns continue cyclically. In the experiment we repeated the renewing process 10 times, so 100,000 rounds were executed in total. We prepared the three criteria as follows:

1. Since the agent with its power-law slope at nearly 0 has a high winning-ratio, we randomly select u number of agents whose power-law slope is lower than in the previous turn, and they renew their strategy tables. Since the calculation of each agent's power-law is computable only from its behavior, each agent does not need to know global information such as the total number of agents in the game. However, since this criterion uses only the change in slope, even an agent with a high winning-ratio may renew its strategy tables.
2. We randomly select u number of agents whose power-law slope is lower than a certain value (0.75), and they renew their strategy tables. We use the following knowledge that is, there is a consistent relationship between the power-law slope and the winning-ration of each agent (Fig. 8), and this consistent relationship does not depend on the total number of participating agents in the game. Each agent knows its approximate position without knowing the total number of participating agents, and the only agents with low winning-ratios can renew their strategy tables. However, it is necessary to know that the adequate threshold value is 0.75 beforehand.
3. We select u number of agents with low scores, and they renew their strategy tables. It is necessary for each agent to know the following global information, each agent's

score and the number of participating agents. This criterion can be thought of as the best way to select agents to renew their strategy tables. We prepared this criterion for comparing it to (1) and (2).

Figure 9 shows the scores of 101 agents of nine kinds of evaluation settings. We executed three kinds of games (u =5, u =10, and u =20) for each evaluation criterion. As mentioned above, in each situation, the strategy table renewing process was repeated 10 times and the scores of the agents after each renewing process was plotted in the graph of each evaluation setting. As a result, the winning-ratio improved for most agents in all nine evaluations settings. This result means that each agent can know its efficiency by seeing only its behavior without global information. As for u, u=5 was little better than u=10 and u=20. The reason is that if we select too many agents, many renewed strategy tables may destroy the current strategy table's combinations of high winning-ratio agents, and thus the effect of renewing may be lost. While (3) uses some global information and focuses only on the score transition of an agent, (1) and (2) focus on agent behavior. This result shows that focusing on agent behavior is as effective as using the global information.

6. Conclusions

We discussed indirect coordination of MASs. Unlike direct coordination MASs, which are usually constructed from the top-down, indirect coordination MASs are constructed from the bottom-up. It is difficult to design a concrete common coordination algorithm for various applications from the bottom-up, that is, each coordination algorithm is strongly dependent on each application. However, we know that common constraints and the power-law based rule may commonly be the important assumptions for coordination in indirect coordination MASs. Moreover, we have succeeded in improving the efficiency of each agent's behavior in MG by changing the behavior rules within the range where these assumptions were not changed. This game is a competitive game for the acquisition of limited resources, so the rule of MG may be applicable for the other similar problems, but it is necessary to analyze not only individual agent dynamics but also all agents' dynamics of various kinds of indirect coordination MASs to clarify assumptions for coordination to occur.

7. References

[1] PP. Grasse, La reconstruction du nid et les coordinations interindividuelles chezBellicositermes natalensis etCubitermes sp. la théorie de la stigmergie: Essai d'interprétation du comportement des termites constructeurs, Insectes Sociaux, Vol. 6, No.1, pp. 41 - 80, 1959.

[2] M. Dorigo and G. Di Caro, The Ant Colony Optimization Meta-Heuristic, New ideas in optimization, 1999.

[3] A. Abraham, C. Grosan, and V. Ramos (Eds.), Swarm Intelligence in Data Mining (Studies in Computational Intelligence), Springer, 2006.

[4] RC. Eberhart, Y, Shi, and J. Kennedy, Swarm Intelligence (The Morgan Kaufmann Series in Artificial Intelligence), Morgan Kaufmann, 2001.

[5] W. Brian Arthur, "Inductive Reasoning and Bounded Rationality", American Economic Review (Papers and Proceedings), 84, pp. 406 - 411, 1994.

[6] D. Challet and Y.-C. Zhang, Emergence of Cooperation and Organization in an Evolutionary Game, Physica A 246, 40 7 (1997).
[7] RC. Eberhart, Y, Shi, and J. Kennedy, Swarm Intelligence (The Morgan Kaufmann Series in Artificial Intelligence), Morgan Kaufmann, 2001.

11

A Multi-Agent Approach to Bluffing

Tshilidzi Marwala and Evan Hurwitz
University of the Witwatersrand
South Africa

1. Introduction

The act of bluffing confounds game designers to this day. The very nature of bluffing is even open for debate, adding further complication to the process of creating intelligent virtual players that can bluff, and hence play, realistically. Through the use of intelligent, learning agents, and carefully designed agent outlooks, an agent can in fact learn to predict its opponents' reactions based not only on its own cards, but on the actions of those around it. With this wider scope of understanding, an agent can in fact learn to bluff its opponents, with the action representing not an "illogical" action, as bluffing is often viewed, but rather as an act of maximising returns through an effective statistical optimisation. By using a Temporal Difference-lamba (TD(λ) re-inforcement learning algorithm (Sutton, 1988; Sutton, 1989) to continuously adapt neural network agent's intelligence ability, agents are shown, in this chapter, to be able to learn to bluff without outside prompting, and even to learn to call each other's bluffs in a free competative play.

While many card games involve an element of bluffing, simulating and fully understanding bluffing yet remains one of the most elusive tasks presented to the game design engineer (Hurwitz & Marwala, 2005, 2007[a,b]). The entire process of bluffing relies on performing a task that is unexpected, and is thus misinterpreted by one's opponent. For this reason, static rules are doomed to failure since once they become predictable, they cannot be misinterpreted. In order to create an artificially intelligent agent that can bluff, one must first create an agent that is capable of learning. There are many learning algorithms that have been developed and successfully implemented and these include neural networks (Mohamed et al, 2005), support vector machines (Msiza et al, 2007) and neuro-fuzzy systems (Tettey & Marwala, 2006). These learning algorithms have been applied to diverse areas such as civil engineering (Marwala, 2000), mechanical engineering (Marwala & Hunt, 1999), aerospace engineering (Marwala, 2001) and biomedical engineering (Leke et al, 2006). The agent must be able to learn not only about the inherent nature of the game it is playing, but also must be capable of learning trends emerging from its opponent's behaviour, since bluffing is only plausible when one can anticipate the opponent's reactions to one's own actions.

Firstly the game to be modelled will be detailed, with the rationale for its choice being explained. This chapter then details the system and agent architecture, which is of paramount importance since this not only ensures that the correct information is available to the agent, but also has a direct impact on the efficiency of the learning algorithms utilised. Once the system is fully illustrated, the actual learning of the agents is demonstrated, with the appropriate findings detailed.

2. Game of Lerpa

While not a well-known game, Lerpa's rules suit the purposes of this chapter exceptionally well, making it an ideal test-bed application for intelligent multi-agent modelling (MAM) (Mariano et al, 2001; Abramov et al, 2001; van Aardt & Marwala, 2005). The rules of the game first need to be elaborated upon, in order to grasp the implications of the results obtained. Thus, the rules for Lerpa now follow.
MAM has been used successfully in many different areas and these include in modelling the stock market (Marwala et al, 2001), modelling HIV (Teweldemedhin et al, 2004), in modelling electrical systems (Vilakazi & Marwala, 2007) and in developing human capacity development infrastructure (Marivate et al, 2008).
The game of Lerpa is played with a standard deck of cards, with the exception that all of the 8s, 9s and 10s are removed from the deck. The cards are valued from greatest- to least-valued from ace down to 2, with the exception that the 7 is valued higher than a king, but lower than an ace, making it the second most valuable card in a suit. At the end of dealing the hand, the dealer has the choice of dealing himself/herself in - which entails flipping his/her last card over, unseen up until this point, which then declares which suit is the trump suit. Should the player elect not to do this, he/she then flips the next card in the deck to determine the trump suit. Regardless, once trumps are determined, the players then take it in turns, going clockwise from the dealer's left, to elect whether or not to play the hand (to knock), or to drop out of the hand, referred to as folding (if the Dealer has dealt himself/herself in, as described above, the player is then automatically required to play the hand).
Once all players have chosen whether to play or not, the players that have elected to play then play the hand, with the player to the dealer's left playing the first card. Once this card has been played, players must then play in suit - in other words, if a heart is played, they must play a heart if they have one. If they have none of the required suit, they may play a trump, which will win the trick unless another player plays a higher trump. The highest card played will win the trick (with all trumps valued higher than any other card) and the winner of the trick will lead the first card in the next trick. At any point in a hand, if a player has the Ace of trumps and can legally play it, he/she is then required to do so. The true risk in the game comes from the betting, which occurs as follows: At the beginning of the round, the dealer pays the table, three of whatever the basic betting denomination is (referred to usually as 'chips'). At the end of the hand, the chips are divided up proportionately between the winners, i.e. if you win two tricks, you will receive two thirds of whatever is in the pot. However, if you stayed in, but did not win any tricks, you are said to have been Lerpa'd, and are then required to match whatever was in the pot for the next hand, effectively costing you the pot. It is in the evaluation of this risk that most of the true skill in Lerpa lies.

3. Multi-agent modelling of Lerpa

As with any optimisation system (Marwala, 2005 & 2007), very careful consideration needs to be taken with regards to how the system is structured, since the implications of these decisions can often result in unintentional assumptions made by the system created. With this in mind, the Lerpa Multi-Agent System (MAS) has been designed to allow the maximum amount of freedom to the system, and the agents within, while also allowing for generalisation and swift convergence in order to allow the intelligent agents to interact unimpeded by human assumptions, intended or otherwise.

3.1 System overview

The game is, for this model, going to be played by four players. Each of these players will interact with each other indirectly, by interacting directly with the table, which is their shared environment, as depicted in Figure 1.

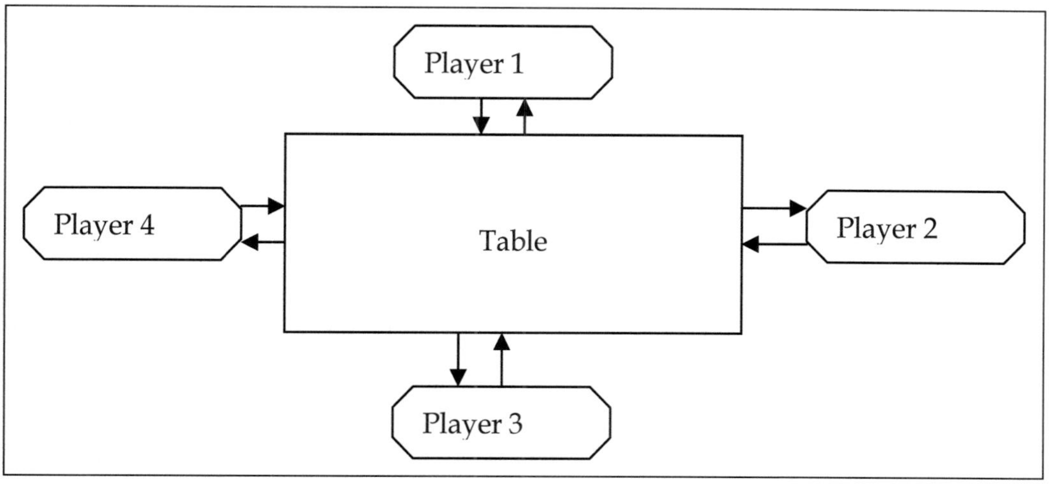

Fig. 1. System interactions

Over the course of a single hand, an agent will be required to make three decisions, once at each interactive stage of the game. These three decision-making stages are:

1. To play the hand, or drop (knock or fold)
2. Which card to play first?
3. Which card to play second?

Since there is no decision to be made at the final card, the hand can be said to be effectively finished from the agent's perspective after it has played its second card (or indeed after the first decision should the agent fold). Following on the TD(λ) algorithm, each agent will update its own neural network at each stage, using its own predictions as a reward function, only receiving a true reward after its final decision has been made. This decision making process is illustrated below, in Figure 2.

There are two fundamental conceptual characteristics of TD(λ) and these are:

1. There is a heuristic error signal described at each time step, which is based on the difference between two successive predictions, that ensures the learning,
2. Granted that a prediction error has been perceived at a specific time step, an exponentially decaying feedback of the error in time exists such that the earlier estimates for preceding states are also corrected.

This time scale of the exponential decay is directed by the lambda parameter.

With each agent implemented as is described, the agents can now interact with each other through their shared environment, and will continuously learn upon each interaction and its consequent result. Each hand played will be viewed as an independent, stochastic event, and as such only information about the current hand will be available to the agent, who will have to draw on its own learned knowledge base to draw deductions not from previous hands.

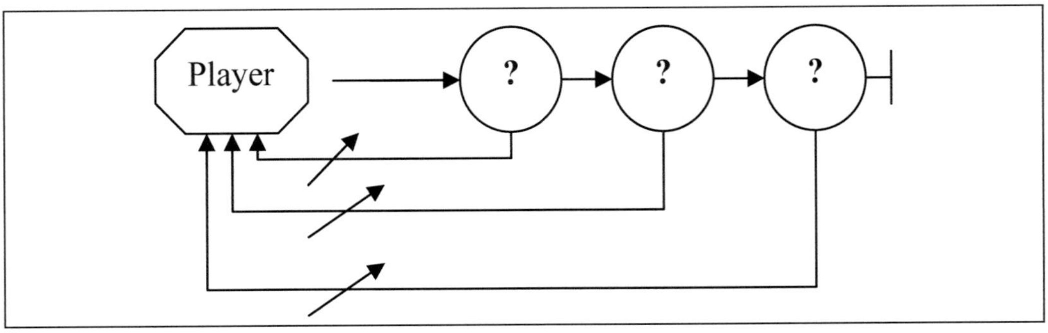

Fig. 2. Agent learning scheme

3.2 Agent AI design

A number of decisions need to be made in order to implement the agent's artificial intelligence (AI) effectively and efficiently. The type of learning to be implemented needs to be chosen, as well as the neural network architecture. Special attention needs to be paid to the design of the inputs to the neural network, as these determine what the agent can 'see' at any given point. This will also determine what assumptions, if any, are implicitly made by the agent, and hence cannot be taken lightly. Lastly, this will determine the dimensionality of the network, which directly affects the learning rate of the network, and hence must obviously be minimised.

3.2.1 Input parameter design

In order to design the input stage of the agent's neural network, one must first determine all that the network may need to know at any given decision-making stage. All inputs, in order to optimise stability, are structured as binary-encoded inputs. When making its first decision, the agent needs to know its own cards, which agents have stayed in or folded, and which agents are still to decide. It is necessary for the agent to be able to determine which specific agents have taken their specific actions, as this will allow for an agent to learn a particular opponent's characteristics, something impossible to do if it can only see a number of players in or out. Similarly, the agent's own cards must be specified fully, allowing the agent to draw its own conclusions about each card's relative value. It is also necessary to tell the agent which suit has been designated the trumps suit, but a more elegant method has been found to handle that information, as will be seen shortly. Figure 3 illustrates the initial information required by the network.

The agent's hand needs to be explicitly described, and the obvious solution is to encode the cards exactly, i.e. four suits, and ten numbers in each suit, giving forty possibilities for each card. A quick glimpse at the number of options available shows that a raw encoding style provides a sizeable problem of dimensionality, since an encoded hand can be one of 403 possible hands (in actuality, only ${}_{40}P_3$ hands could be selected, since cards cannot be repeated, but the raw encoding scheme would in fact allow for repeated cards, and hence 403 options would be available).

The first issue to notice is that only a single deck of cards is being used, hence no card can ever be repeated in a hand. Acting on this principle, consistent ordering of the hand means that the base dimensionality of the hand is greatly reduced, since it is now a combination of cards that are represented, instead of permutations. The number of combinations now

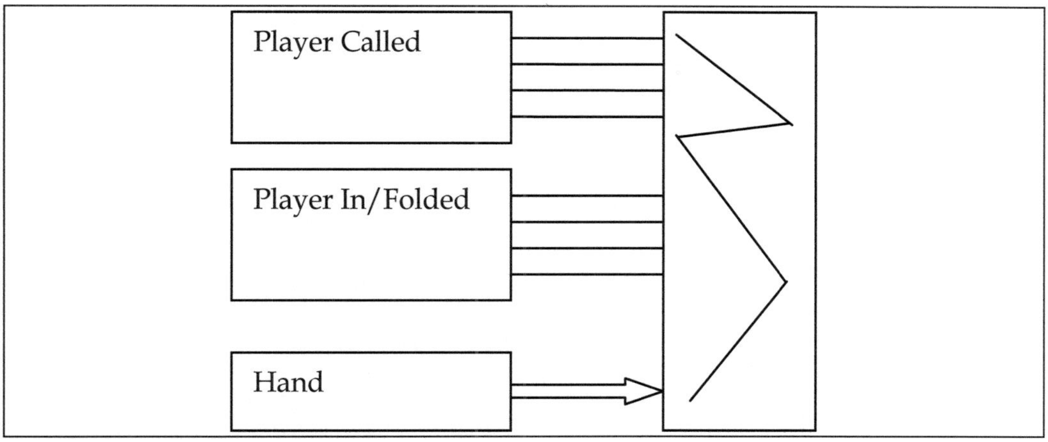

Fig. 3. Basic input structure

represented is $_{40}C_3$. This seemingly small change from $_nP_r$ to $_nC_r$ reduces the dimensionality of the representation by a factor of r!, which in this case is a factor of 6. Furthermore, the representation of cards as belonging to discrete suits is not optimal either, since the game places no particular value on any suit by its own virtue, but rather by virtue of which suit is the trump suit. For this reason, an alternate encoding scheme has been determined, rating the 'suits' based upon the makeup of the agent's hand, rather than four arbitrary suits. The suits are encoded as belonging to one of the following groups, or new "suits":

- Trump suit
- Suit agent has multiple cards in (not trumps)
- Suit in agent's highest singleton
- Suit in agent's second-highest singleton
- Suit in agent's third-highest singleton

This allows for a much more efficient description of the agent's hand, greatly improving the dimensionality of the inputs, and hence the learning rate of the agents. These five options are encoded in a binary format, for stability purpose, and hence three binary inputs are required to represent the suits. To represent the card's number, ten discrete values must be represented, hence requiring four binary inputs to represent the card's value. Thus a card in an agent's hand is represented by seven binary inputs, as depicted in Figure 4.

Subsequently, the information required to make the second and third decisions must be considered. For both of these decisions, the cards that have already been played, if any, are necessary to know in order to make an intelligent decision as to the correct next card to play. For the second decision, it is also plausible that knowledge of who has won a trick would be important. The most cards that can ever be played before a decision must be made is seven, and since the table after a card is played is used to evaluate and update the network, eight played cards are necessary to be represented. Once again, however, simply utilising the obvious encoding method is not necessarily the most efficient method. The actual values of the cards played are not necessarily important, only their values relative to the cards in the agent's hand. As such, the values can be represented as one of the following, with respect to the cards in the same suit in the agent's hand:

- Higher than the card/cards in the agent's hand
- Higher than the agent's second-highest card

- Higher than the agent's third-highest card
- Lower than any of the agent's cards
- Member of a void suit (number is immaterial)

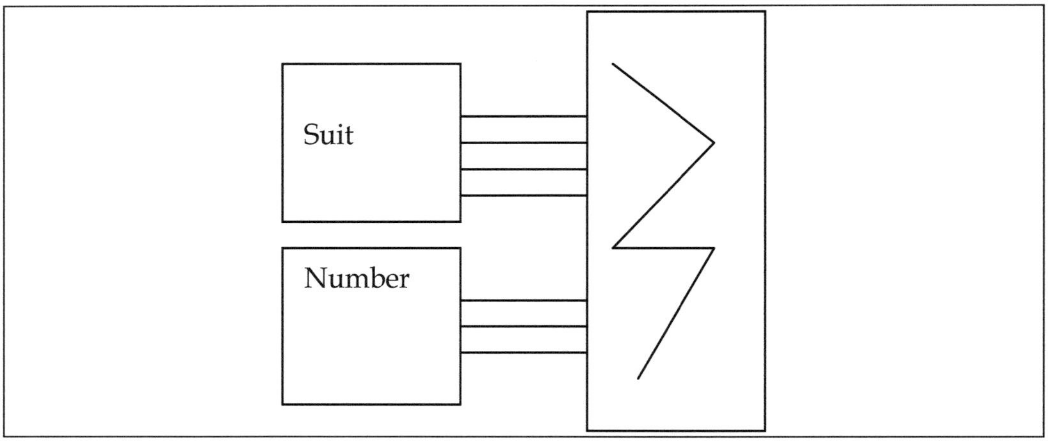

Fig. 4. Agent card input structure

Also, another suit is now relevant for representation of the played cards, namely a void suit - a suit in which the agent has no cards. Lastly, a number is necessary to handle the special case of the Ace of trumps, since its unique rules mean that strategies are possible to develop based on whether it has or has not been played. The now six suits available still only require three binary inputs to represent, and the six number groupings now reduce the value representations from four binary inputs to three binary inputs, once again reducing the dimensionality of the input system. With all of these inputs specified, the agent now has available all of the information required to draw its own conclusions and create its own strategies, without human-imposed assumptions affecting its "thought" patterns

3.2.2 Network architecture design

With the inputs now specified, the hidden and output layers need to be designed. For the output neurons, these need to represent the prediction P that the network is making. A single hand has one of five possible outcomes, all of which need to be catered for. These possible outcomes are:

- The agent wins all three tricks, winning 3 chips.
- The agent wins two tricks, winning 2 chips.
- The agent wins one trick, winning 1 chip.
- The agent wins zero tricks, losing 3 chips.
- The agent elects to fold, winning no tricks, but losing no chips.

This can be seen as a set of options, namely [-3 0 1 2 3]. While it may seem tempting to output this as one continuous output, there are two compelling reasons for breaking these up into binary outputs. The first of these is in order to optimise stability, as elaborated upon in Section 5. The second reason is that these are discrete events, and a continuous representation would cover the range of [-3 0], which does not in fact exist. The binary inputs then specified are: P(O = 3); P(O = 2); P(O = 1) and P(O = -3), with a low probability of all four catering to folding, winning and losing no chips. Consequently, the agent's predicted return is:

$$P=3A+2B+C-3D \quad (1)$$

where

$$A = P(O = 3) \quad (2)$$

$$B = P(O = 2) \quad (3)$$

$$C = P(O = 1) \quad (4)$$

$$D = P(O = \quad 3) \quad (5)$$

The internal structure of the neural network uses a standard sigmoidal activation function, which is suitable for stability issues and still allows for the freedom expected from a neural network. The sigmoidal activation function varies between zero and one, rather than the often-used one and minus one, in order to optimise for stability. Since a high degree of freedom is required, a high number, of hidden neurons is required, and thus fifty have been used. This number is iteratively achieved, trading off training speed versus performance. The output neurons are linear functions, since they represent not binary effects, but rather a continuous probability of particular binary outcomes.

3.2.3 Agent decision making

With its own predictor specified, the agent is now equipped to make decisions when playing. These decisions are made by predicting the return of the resultant situation arising from each legal choice it can make. An ε-greedy policy is then used to determine whether the agent will choose the most promising option, or whether it will explore the result of the less appealing result. In this way, the agent will be able to trade off exploration versus exploitation.

4. The intelligent model

With each agent implemented as described above, and interacting with each other as specified in Section 3, we can now perform the desired task, namely that of utilising a multi-agent model to analyse the given game, and develop strategies that may "solve" the game given differing circumstances. Only once agents know how to play a certain hand can they then begin to outplay, and potentially bluff each other.

4.1 Agent learning verification

In order for the model to have any validity, one must establish that the agents do indeed learn as they were designed to do. In order to verify the learning of the agents, a single intelligent agent was created, and placed at a table with three 'stupid' agents. These 'stupid' agents always stay in the game, and choose a random choice whenever called upon to make a decision. The results show quite conclusively that the intelligent agent soon learns to consistently outperform its opponents, as shown in Figure 5.

The agents named Randy, Roderick and Ronald use random decision-making, while AIden has the TD(λ) AI system implemented. The results have been averaged over 40 hands, in order to be more viewable, and to also allow for the random nature of cards being dealt. As can be seen, AIden is consistently performing better than its counterparts, and continues to learn the game as it plays.

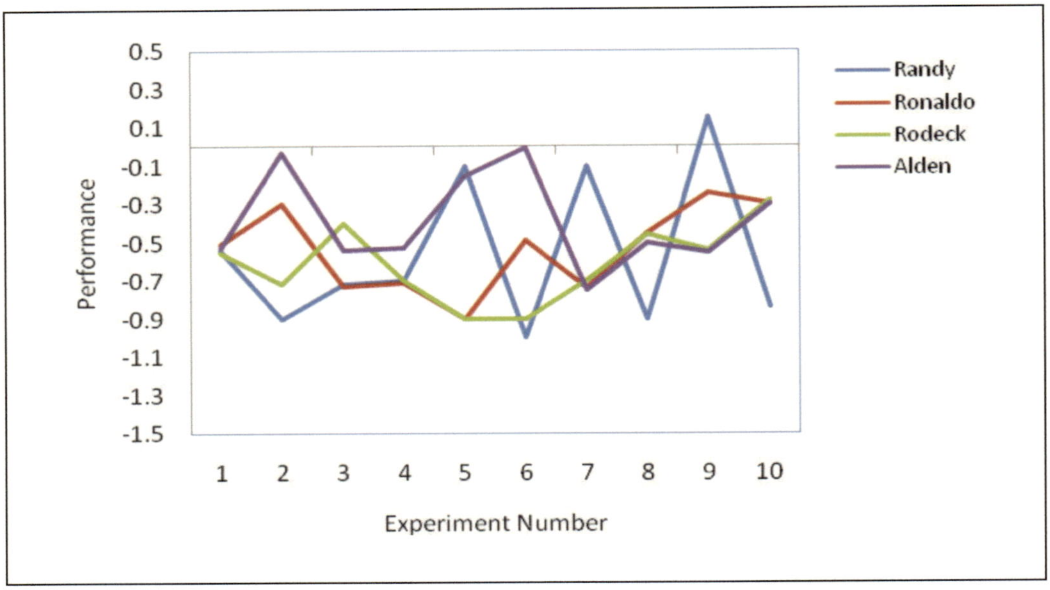

Fig. 5. Agent performance, averaged over 40 hands

4.1.2 Cowardice

In the learning phase of the abovementioned intelligent agent, an interesting and somewhat enlightening problem arises. When initially learning, the agent does not in fact continue to learn. Instead, the agent quickly determines that it is losing chips, and decides that it is better off not playing, and thereby keeping its chips! This is illustrated in Figure 6.

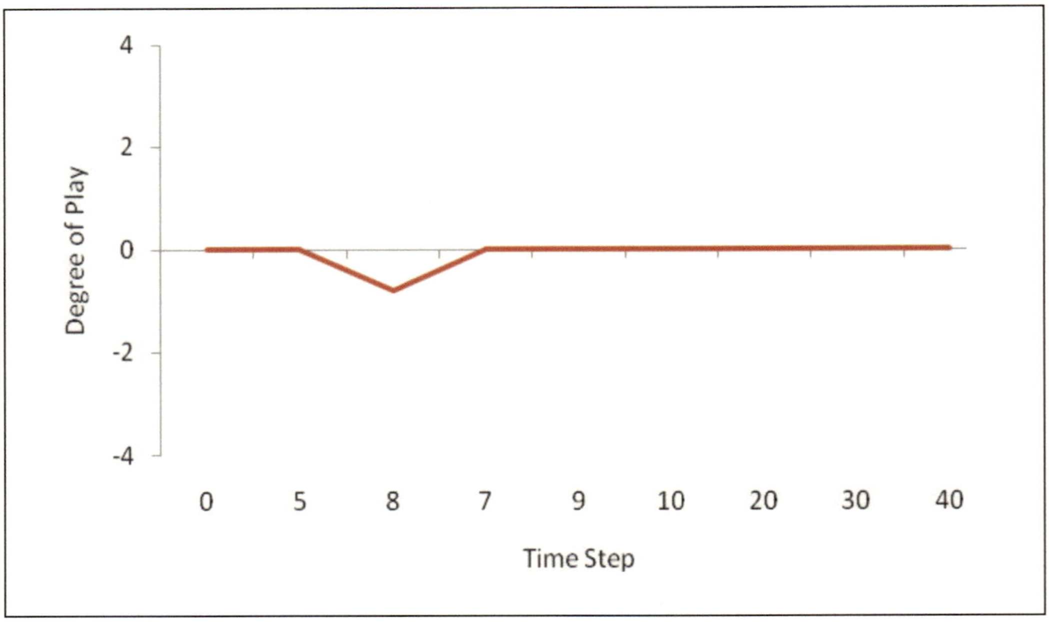

Fig. 6. Agent cowardice. Averaged over 5 hands

As can be seen, AIden quickly decides that the risks are too great, and does not play in any hands initially. After forty hands, AIden decides to play a few hands, and when they go badly, gets scared off for good. This is a consequent of the penalising nature of the game, since bad play can easily mean one loses a full three chips, and since the surplus of lost chips is nor carried over in this simulation, a bad player loses chips regularly. While insightful, a cowardly agent is not of any particular use, and hence the agent must be given enough 'courage' to play, and hence learn the game. In order to do this, one option is to increase the value of ε for the ε-greedy policy, but this makes the agent far too much like a random player without any intelligence. A more successful, and sensible solution is to force the agent to play when it knows nothing, until such a stage as it seems prepared to play. This was done by forcing AIden to play the first 200 hands it had ever seen, and thereafter leave AIden to his own devices, the result of which has been shown already in Figure 5.

4.2 Parameter optimisation

A number of parameters need to be optimised, in order to optimise the learning of the agents. These parameters are the learning-rate α, the memory parameter λ and the exploration parameter ε. The multi-agent system provides a perfect environment for this testing, since four different parameter combinations can be tested competitively. By setting different agents to different combinations, and allowing them to play against each other for an extended period of time (number of hands), one can iteratively find the parameter combinations that achieve the best results, and are hence the optimum learning parameters. Figure 7 shows the results of one such test, illustrating a definite 'winner', whose parameters

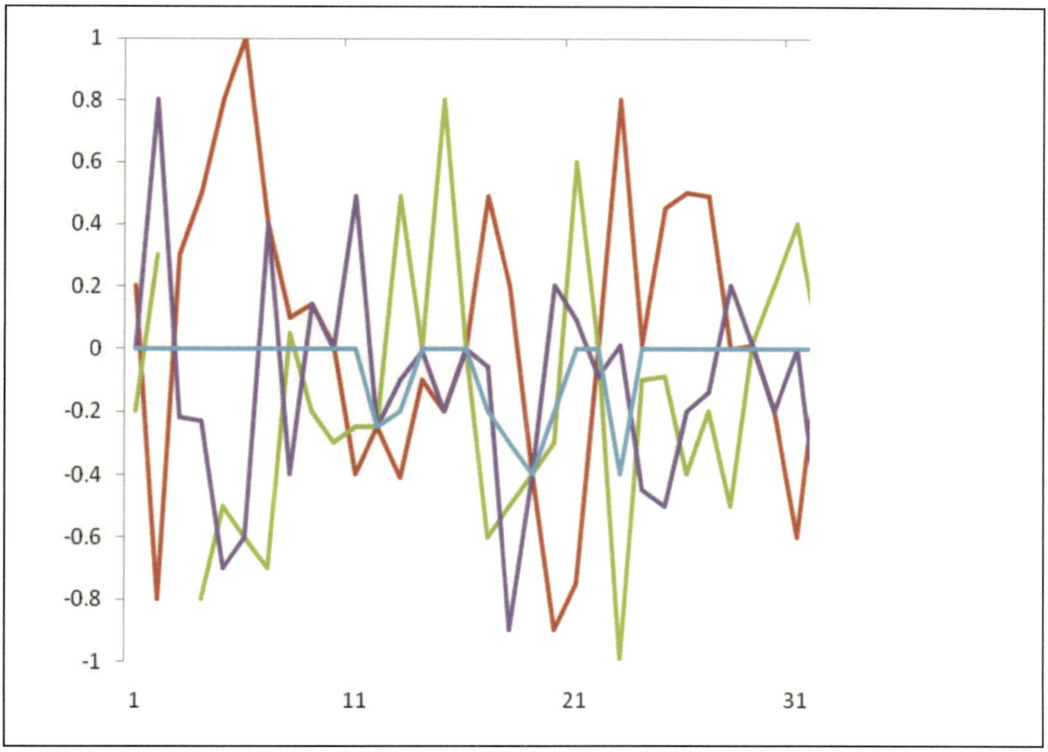

Fig. 7. Competitive agent parameter optimisation. Averaged over 30 hands

were then used for the rest of the multi-agent modelling. It is also worth noting that as soon as the dominant agent begins to lose, it adapts its play to remain competitive with its less effective opponents. This is evidenced at points 10 and 30 on the graph (games number 300 and 900, since the graph is averaged over 30 hands) where one can see the dominant agent begin to lose, and then begins to perform well once again.
Surprisingly enough, the parameters that yielded the most competitive results were $\alpha = 0.1$; $\lambda = 0.1$ and $\varepsilon = 0.01$. while the ε value is not particularly surprising, the relatively low α and λ values are not exactly intuitive. What they amount to is a degree of temperance, since a higher value would mean learning a large amount from any given hand, effectively over-reacting when they may have played well, and simply have fallen afoul of bad luck

4.3 MAS learning patterns

With all of the agents learning in the same manner, it is noteworthy that the overall rewards they obtain are far better than those obtained by the random agents, and even by the intelligent agent that was playing against the random agents. A sample of these results is depicted in Figure 8.

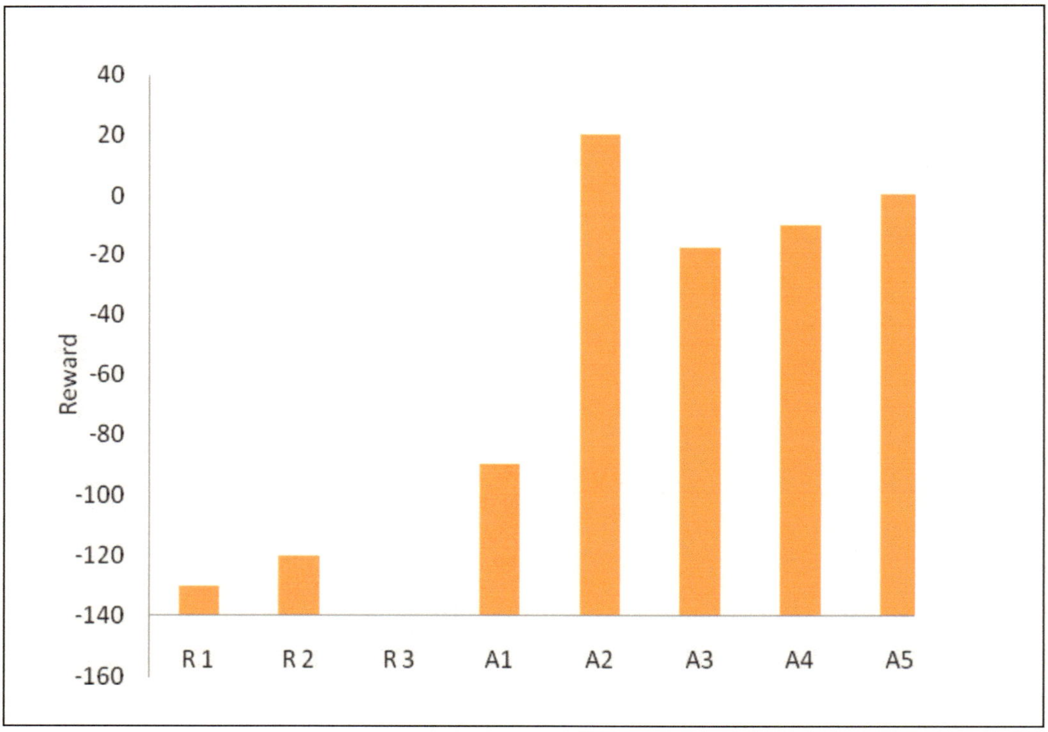

Fig. 8. Competitive agent parameter optimisation. Averaged over 30 hands

R1 to R3 are the Random agents, while AI1 is the intelligent agent playing against the random agents. AI2 to AI 5 depict intelligent agents playing against each other. As can be seen, the agents learn far better when playing against intelligent opponents, an attribute that is in fact mirrored in human competitive learning. The agents with better experience tend to fold bad hands, and hence lose far fewer chips than the intelligent agent playing against unpredictable opponents.

4.4 Agent adaptation

In order to ascertain whether the agents in fact adapt to each other or not, the agents were given pre-dealt hands, and required to play them against each other repeatedly. The results one such experiment, illustrated in Figure 9, shows how an agent learns from its own mistake, and once certain of it changes its play, adapting to better gain a better return from the hand. The mistakes it sees are its low returns, returns of -3 to be precise. At one point, the winning player obviously decides to explore, giving some false hope to the losing agent, but then quickly continues to exploit his advantage. Eventually, at game #25, the losing agent gives up, adapting his play to suit the losing situation in which he finds himself. Figure 10 illustrates the progression of the agents and the adaptation described.

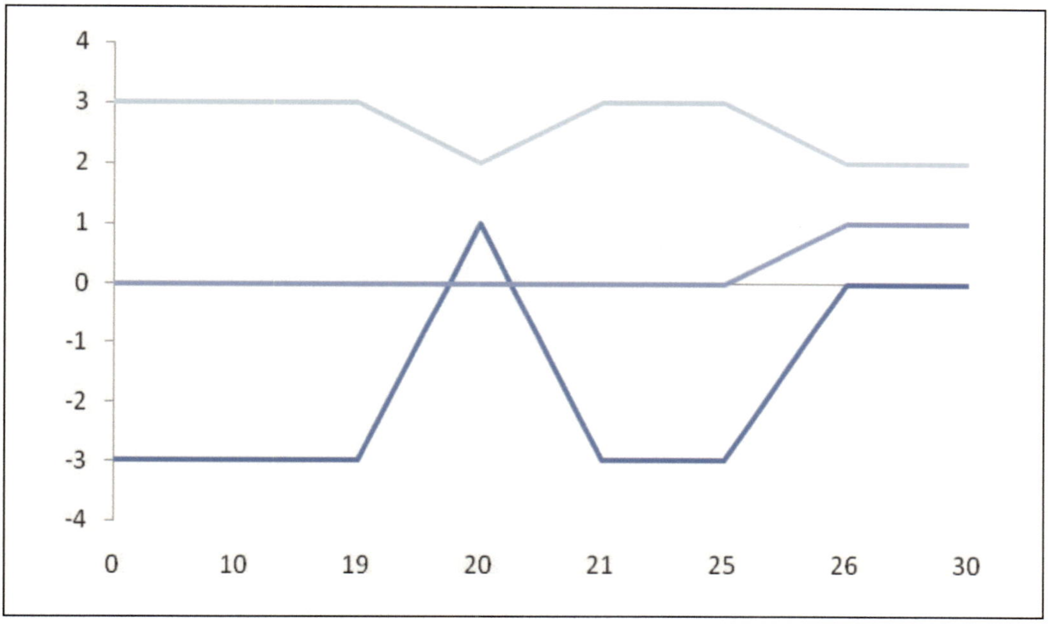

Fig. 9. Adaptive agent behaviour

4.5 Strategy analysis

The agents have been shown to successfully learn to play the game, and to adapt to each other's play in order to maximise their own rewards. These agents form the pillars of the multi-agent model, which can now be used to analyse, and attempt to 'solve' the game. Since the game has a non-trivial degree of complexity, situations within the game are to be solved, considering each situation a sub-game of the overall game. The first and most obvious type of analysis is a static analysis, in which all of the hands are pre-dealt. This system can be said to have stabilised when the results and the play-out become constant, with all agents content to play the hand out in the same manner, each deciding nothing better can be achieved. This is akin to Game Theory's "static equilibrium", as is evidenced in Figure 10.

4.6 Bluffing

A bluff is an action, usually in the context of a card game that misrepresents one's cards with the intent of causing one's opponents to drop theirs. There are two opposing schools of thought regarding bluffing. One school claims that bluffing is purely psychological, while the other maintains that a bluff is a purely statistical act, and therefore no less sensible than any other strategy. Astoundingly enough, the intelligent agents do in fact learn to bluff! A classic example is illustrated in Figure 11, which depicts a hand in which bluffing was evidenced.

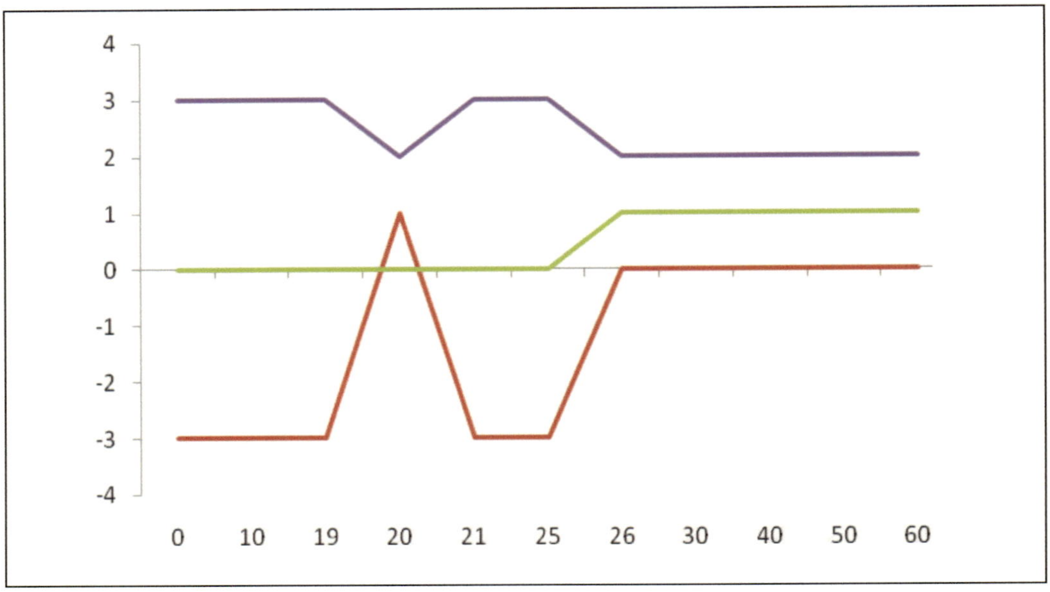

Fig. 10. Stable, solved hand.

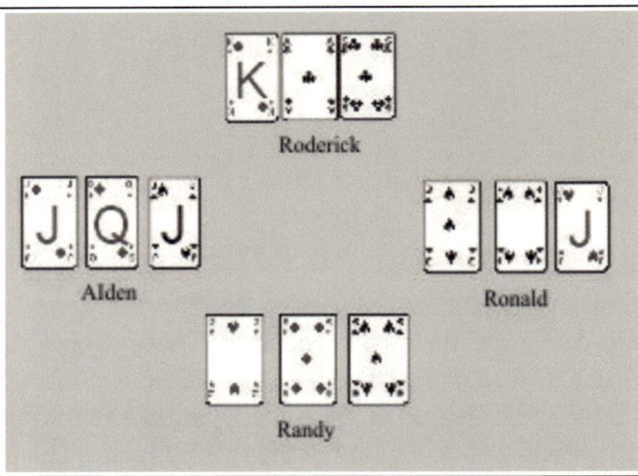

Fig. 11. Agent bluffing

In the above hand, Randy is the first caller, and diamonds have been declared trumps. Randy's hand is not particularly impressive, having only one low trump, and two low supporting cards. Still, he has the lead, and a trump could become a trick, although his risks are high for minimal reward. Nonetheless, Randy chooses to play this hand. Ronald, having nothing to speak of, unsurprisingly folds. Roderick, on the other hand, has a very good hand. One high trump, and an outside ace. However, with one still to call, and Randy already representing a strong hand by playing, Roderick chooses to fold. Alden, whose hand is very strong with two high trumps and an outside jack, plays the hand. When the hand is played repeatedly, Randy eventually chooses not to play, since he loses all three to Alden. Instantly, Roderick chooses to play the hand, indicating that the bluff was successful, that it chased a player out of the hand! Depending on which of the schools of thought regarding bluffing one follows this astonishing result leads us to one of two possible conclusions. If, like the authors, one holds that bluffing is simply playing the odds, making the odds for one's opponent unfavourable by representing a strong hand, then this result shows that the agents learn each other's patterns well enough to factor their opponent's strategies into the game evaluation, something game theory does a very poor job of. Should one follow the theory that bluffing is purely psychological, then the only conclusion that can be reached from this result is that the agents have in fact developed their own 'psyches', their own personalities which can then be exploited. Regardless of which option the reader holds to, the fact remains that agents have been shown to learn, on their own and without external prompting, to bluff!

5. Conclusions

While the exact nature of bluffing is still unknown, it has been shown that a system involving agents capable of learning adaptively not only from the game being played, but also from their opponents, is in fact able to learn to predict its opponent's reactions. This knowledge in turn changes the statistical nature of a game being played, allowing agents to learn to bluff, based purely on rational reasoning, lending strong support to the theory that bluffing is simply playing the odds, and not an illogical, psychologically based action. The use of the Re-enforcement learning paradigm (Sutton & Barto, 1998), along with the TD(λ) algorithm for adaptively training neural networks, has been shown to meet all of the requirements to produce such agents. Lastly, the design of the agent "view", has been seen to be the most important facet of creating bluffing agents, since their view of the game as inclusive of the other players allows for the incorporation of those players into its estimation of the game's outcome. With all of these steps adhered to, artificially intelligent agents can learn to bluff!

6. References

Abramov, V.A., Szirbik, N.B, Goossenaerts, J.B.M., Marwala, T., de Wilde, P., Correia, L., Mariano, P. & Ribeiro, R. (2001). Ontological basis for open distributed multi-agent system, *Proceedings of the Symposium on Adaptive Agents and Multi-Agent Systems,* York, U.K., pp. 33-43.

Hurwitz, E. & Marwala, T. (2005) Optimising reinforcement learning for neural networks. *Proceedings of the 6th Annual European on Intelligent Games and Simulation,* Leicester, UK, 2005, pp. 13-18.

Hurwitz, E. & Marwala, T. (2007a). Multi-agent modeling of interaction-based card games, *Proceedings of the 3rd International North American Conference on Intelligent Games and Simulation,* University of Florida, USA, pp. 23-28.

Hurwitz, E. & Marwala, T. (2007b). Learning to bluff: A multi-agent approach, *Proceedings of the IEEE International Conference on Systems, Man and Cybernetics,* 2007, Montreal, Canada, pp. 1188-1193.

Leke, B.B., Marwala, T., & Tettey, T. (2006). Autoencoder networks for HIV classification. *Current Science*, Vol. 91, No. 11, pp. 1467-1473.

Mariano, P., Correia, L., Ribeiro, R., Abramov, V., Szirbik, N., Goossenaerts, J., Marwala, T., de Wilde, P. (2001). Simulation of a trading multi-agent system, *Proceedings of the IEEE International Conference on Systems, Man, and Cybernetics*, Tucson, Arizona, USA, pp. 3378-3384.

Marivate, V., Ssali, G. & Marwala, T. (2008). An intelligent multi-agent recommender system for human capacity building, *Proceedings of the 14th IEEE Mediterranean Electrotechnical Conference*, pp. 909 – 915.

Marwala, T. (2000). On damage identification using a committee of neural networks. *American Society of Civil Engineers, Journal of Engineering Mechanics*, Vol. 126, pp. 43-50.

Marwala, T. (2001). Probabilistic fault identification using a committee of neural networks and vibration data. *American Institute of Aeronautics and Astronautics, Journal of Aircraft*, Vol. 38, pp. 138-146.

Marwala, T. (2005). Finite element model updating using particle swarm optimization. *International Journal of Engineering Simulation,* Vol. 6, No. 2, pp. 25-30.

Marwala, T. (2007). *Computational Intelligence for Modelling Complex Systems*, Research India Publications, ISBN: 978-81-904362-1-2, New Delhi.

Marwala, T., de Wilde, P., Correia, L., Mariano, P., Ribeiro, R., Abramov, V., Szirbik, N., Goossenaerts, J. (2001). Scalability and optimisation of a committee of agents using genetic algorithm, *Proceedings of the International Symposia on Soft Computing and Intelligent Systems for Industry*, Scotland.

Marwala, T. & Hunt, H.E.M. (1999). Fault identification using finite element models and neural networks. *Mechanical Systems and Signal Processing*, Vol. 13, pp. 475-490.

Mohamed, N., Rubin, D.M. & Marwala, T. (2005). Detection of epileptiform activity in human EEG signals using Bayesian neural networks, *Proceedings of the IEEE 3rd International Conference on Computational Cybernetics*, Mauritius, pp. 231-237.

Msiza, I.S., Nelwamondo, F.V., & Marwala, T. (2007). Artificial neural networks and support vector machines for water demand time series forecasting, *Proceedings of the IEEE International Conference on Systems, Man and Cybernetics*, Montreal, Canada, pp. 638-643.

Sutton, R. S. (1988). Learning to predict by the methods of temporal differences. *Machine Learning*, Vol. 3, pp. 9-44.

Sutton, R. S. (1989). *Implementation details of the TD(λ) procedure for the case of vector predictions and Backpropogation*. GTE Laboratories Technical Note: TN87-509.1.

Sutton, R. S. & Barto, A. G. (2004). *Reinforcement Learning: An Introduction*, MIT Press, ISBN, Cambridge, MA.

Tettey, T. & Marwala, T. (2006). Neuro-fuzzy modeling and fuzzy rule extraction applied to conflict management, *Lecture Notes in Computer Science*, Volume 4234, pp. 1087-1094.

Teweldemedhin, E., Marwala, T. & Mueller, C. (2004). Agent-based modelling: A case study in HIV epidemic, *Proceedings of the IEEE 4th International Conference in Hybrid Intelligent Systems,* Japan, pp. 154-159.

van Aardt, B. & Marwala, T. (2005). A study in a hybrid centralised-swarm agent community, *Proceedings of the IEEE 3rd International Conference on Computational Cybernetics,* Mauritius, pp. 169-174.

Vilakazi, B. & Marwala, T. (2007). Agent and multi-agent system and its application to condition monitoring, *Proceedings of the IEEE International Conference on Systems, Man and Cybernetics,* Montreal, Canada, pp. 644-649.

12

MASL: a Language for Multi-Agent System

Michel Dubois, Yann Le Guyadec and Dominique Duhaut
University of South Britanny. Université Européenne de Bretagne
France

1. Introduction

Our work takes place in the field of Multi-Agent Modular Robotic System. We propose to mix several paradigms of computation to offer a high-level point of view to the programmer into a new language, namely MASL for Multi-Agent System Language. Expressivity of MASL is illustrated on an example applied to a fleet of robots.

A Multi-Robot System (MRS) can be characterized as a set of robots operating in the same environment that operate together to perform some global task. In this chapter, we regard MRS as a particular form of Multi-Agent System (MAS). The main differences between general MAS and MRS are:

- The fact that in MRS direct communication is based on dedicated physical devices, resulting in a much more expensive and unreliable solution to attain coordination with respect to MAS.
- The number of robots acting in the same environment is still quite limited with respect to the number of agents in a MAS.
- Agents architectures in a MAS are usually deliberative (Nilsson, 1984) (Sense-Represent-Plan-Act), reactive (Brooks, 1989; Hudak et al., 2002) (subsumption architecture) or hybrid (Alur et al., 2000; Ingrand et al., 1996; Benjamin et al., 2004) as shown in figure 1 while in MRS we consider only the last two. The pure sense-represent-plan-act architecture, which is used to realize a high level deliberative behaviour, is not currently used in MRS because of its intrinsic limits, while the behaviour-based and the hybrid architectures are quite common, especially when the robot is situated in a highly dynamic environment, where a quick reaction to a new input is very important, being the environment itself uncertain and unpredictable.

Robot programming is a difficult task that has been studied for many years (Lozano-Perez & Brooks, 1986). This particular field often covers some very different concepts such as methods or algorithms (planning, trajectory generation...). Therefore, languages are developed to implement these high-level considerations (Pembeci & Hager, 2001; Zielinski, 2000). Different approaches have appeared through functional (Armstrong, 1997; Atkin et al., 1999; King, 2002), deliberative or declarative (Dastani & van der Torre, 2003; Benjamin et al., 2004; Peterson et al., 1999), synchronous characteristics (Pembeci & Hager, 2001). Nonetheless, the difficulties of robot programming can by schematically summarized by two main characteristics:

- One is that programming a set of elementary actions (primitives) on a robot often leads to (if not always) a program including many processes running in parallel with real-time constraints and local synchronizations.

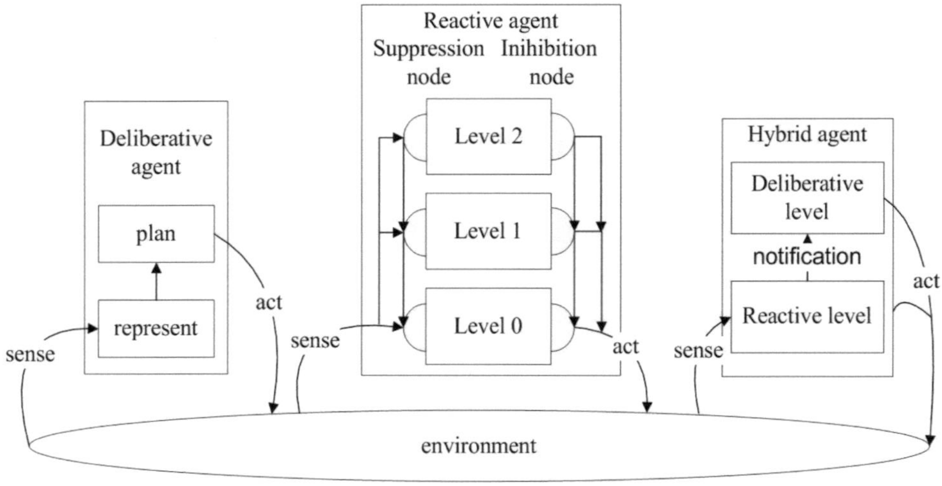

Fig. 1. Different types of agents in a MAS

- The other is that in its interactions with the environment, the program running the robot (i.e. the sequence of primitives) must be able to carry out traditional features: interruption of an event or exception and synchronization with another element.

The recent introduction of teams of robot, where cooperation and coordination are needed, presents an additional difficulty which is that the expression of computation is no longer limited to a single physical system. The problem is then to program the behaviour of a group of robots or even of a society of robots (Klavins, 2003; Klavins, 2004; Mackenzie & Arkin, 1997). In this case (except in the case of centralized control) programming implies loading, in each robot, a program which is not necessarily identical to the others because of the characteristics of the robots: different hardware, different behaviour and different programming languages. These various codes must in general be synchronized to carry out group missions (foraging, patrol movement...) and to have capacities of reconfiguration according to a map of communicative cooperation.

From the human point of view it is then difficult to have a simultaneous overall description of the group of robots. We met this problem in two types of distinct applications: RoboCup and the self reconfigurable robots (Gueganno & Duhaut, 2004; Jorgensen et al., 2004; Yoshida et al., 2004).

Robotic soccer has been considered in the last years as an interesting test-bed for research in multi-agent and multi-robot cooperation. The uncertain dynamics and hostile environment in which the robots operate makes coordination of the multi-robot system a real challenging problem. While in the early years of the robotic league competitions the focus has been on improving the single robot capabilities, only recently coordination in the MRS has become a central issue. The different settings of each of the robotic leagues present several issues for coordination in MRS. In particular, in the Middle-Size league and the Four Legged league, all the robot sensors must be on board; therefore robots are more autonomous and have to deal with high uncertainty in reconstructing global information about the environment. On the other hand in the small size league the robotic agents can take advantage of a top view of the environment provided by a camera on the top of the field, therefore the coordination approaches in this league are mostly centralized. The use of coordination in the soccer domains has demonstrated significant improvement in the performance of the teams. In

Robocup the teams of robots play football (Vu et al., 2003) and the robots players which are on the ground have different types of behaviour according to the dynamics of the environment. It is thus necessary to be able to express when and how an offensive player decides to play defence (and vice versa). Here we look for the "re-evaluation" of the behaviour (new role in the team according to a given goal).

Self reconfigurable robots have been recently studied as swarm intelligence system using self organising and self-assembling capabilities shown by social insects and other animal societies (Mondada et al., 2003). One of the main difference between swarm-robotics and MAS is that MAS also supports deliberative or hybrid controllers for the robots rather than reactive ones. Swarm-robotics strictly discards deliberative and hybrid controllers because of its bias on simplicity. No robot in the swarm has a global knowledge of the environment or of the status of the swarm itself. Instead, each robot exploits only local information and a global behaviour emerges from the interactions among the individuals. Between each member of the swarm, direct communication makes use of some on board dedicated hardware devices, while indirect communication makes use of stigmergy (a mechanism of spontaneous, indirect coordination between agents or actions, where the trace left in the environment by an action stimulates the performance of a subsequent action, by the same or a different agent). The direct communication should be kept limited as much as possible and preferably communication should be done using broadcasting instead of using robot names or addresses or complex hierarchies based on robot addresses. For self reconfigurable robots another problem is that the walking motion implies "synchronisation" in the movement of the robot components. Then, we need to express that all the robots participating in the movement carry out their actions at the same time. We have noted that traditional languages did not provide simple constructions to address this double problem: the expression of an attempt at "re-evalutation" of its behaviour and the nature of the parallel execution of the group of robots.

The main idea of our work is thus to give a definition of a general language, MASL, in order to address 6 constraints:

- Heterogeneous agents,
- Composition of computation,
- Cooperation,
- Dynamic integration of agent,
- Permeability dynamic,
- Scalability.

In this chapter, section 2 will give a brief definition of the aforementioned six constraints, while section 3 will inspect related works in MAS for MRS and section 4 will present some examples of the MASL language to show how it solves these features. Section 5 will provide a simple example to show MASL expressivity. Implementation issues will follow and some future works will end.

2. Our model

First, the six constraints must be defined. And we present after the construction **`entry`** that unifies all these aspects.

2.1 Heterogeneous agents

The program of an autonomous robot is an "agent" in the sense of agent programming. Robots are different. They may be identical at the beginning but become different due to

their dynamics or may be different by construction (leg, wheel, manipulator ...). They also can be running different operating systems with different local programming languages.
MASL addresses all these differences by introducing an abstraction of the robot in which the capabilities of the robots are described. This abstraction will define a "type" of the MASL language. This type will be instantiated to declare a corresponding agent.

2.2 Synchronous/asynchronous computations

A set of robots running their code is usually described following an asynchronous model of execution. This means that all the robots run their code at their own speed. For specific tasks, the team of robots can be asked to execute their code synchronously: after the execution of each instruction, each robot waits for the others to finish their current instruction. An example in human life would be a group of people dancing on music in which each one is following one's own sequence of movement but all are doing it at the same rhythm.
MASL will integrate two descriptions of the parallel composition of sequences of code: synchronous and asynchronous.

2.3 Cooperation

Cooperation is usually made with communication variables, events and synchronous/asynchronous message passing.
Communication variables and events are very classical but needed by the language. It defines the possibility of a set of robots to share variables or events. MASL offers three levels for sharing information: the whole set of robots (global variable), restricted to an agent (local level) and an intermediary level called "group" level in which a specific set of robots can access a piece of information. This set changes dynamically according to the section of the running code.
Synchronous/asynchronous message passing is used when an agent asks another one for a service, there are two ways of managing the dynamics. First, the caller is blocked until the service is delivered by the callee, or the caller receives the result of the service later, but is free to work during the execution of the service. The first call is synchronous (caller blocked) the second one is asynchronous (the result will be given in the future). MASL exploits these two types of message passing.

2.4 Dynamic integration of agent

By this feature we mean that an agent running its code within a group (for instance playing offence on a football team) will be able to change its affiliation and become a member of another group (for instance defence). MASL allows an agent to dynamically quit a group and to join another one.

2.5 Autonomy by dynamic permeability

This original notion is defined to express that an agent cannot always execute its entire set of primitive capabilities. For instance, if the communication is not working then it is not possible to ask for a service. At another time, an agent can communicate, but due to its position in the environment he must remain silent in some emergency cases. The permeability will define a set of roles of the agent and will provide some instruction to manipulate it. These roles define which services are activable in the set of all available services from the agent. The permeability of an agent refers to its autonomy. It can neglect access demands to its interface from other agents because it is not a passive object but an active one or a reactive one.

2.6 Scalability

MASL also respects scalability constraints. This means that the same controller can be applicated on variable sized group. Scalability is one of the desired characteristics of swarm robotics and swarm systems should work with large numbers of system components.
MASL language provides one construct named **entry** that unifies several paradigms of computation to offer a high-level point of view to the programmer.

3. Related works

In this section, we study the existing Multi-Agent Languages in MRS with respect to our six constraints. They are CHARON (Alur et al., 2000) (Coordinated control, Hierarchical design, Analysis, and Run-time mONitoring of hybrid systems), CCL (Klavins, 2003; Klavins, 2004) (Computation and Control Language), MRL (Nishiyama et al., 1998) (Multiagent Robot Language), Tapir (King, 2002), GOLOG (alGOl in LOGic) (Levesque et al., 1997), CDL (Mackenzie & Arkin, 1997) (Configuration Description Language) and XABSL (Lötzsch, 2004) (eXtensible Agent Behavior Specification Language).

	(1)	(2)	(3)	(4)	(5)	(6)
CHARON	+	Not so precise	SV, MP, E-	Not so easy	+	-
CCL	+	Not so precise	SV, MP	Not so easy	+	+
MRL	+	Not so precise	E, SV, MP		+	-
Tapir	+	Not so precise	MP, SV		+	-
GOLOG	+	Not so precise	E, SV		+	-
CDL	+	Not so precise	E, MP	-	-	+
XABCL	+	Not so precise	E, MP	Not so easy	-	+

Table 1. Existing Multi-Agent Languages Features

The legend is: SV (Shared Variable), MP (Message Passing), E (Events), E- (partially implemented), + (feature available), - (feature unavailable), nothing (not documented).

4. Informal semantics

In this section, the agent will be used to indicate the program which runs the primitives of the robot.

4.1 Heterogeneous agents

The objective is to program a set of heterogeneous agents working together. Then the proposed approach is to import the list of capabilities of agents from an XML description.
Example:

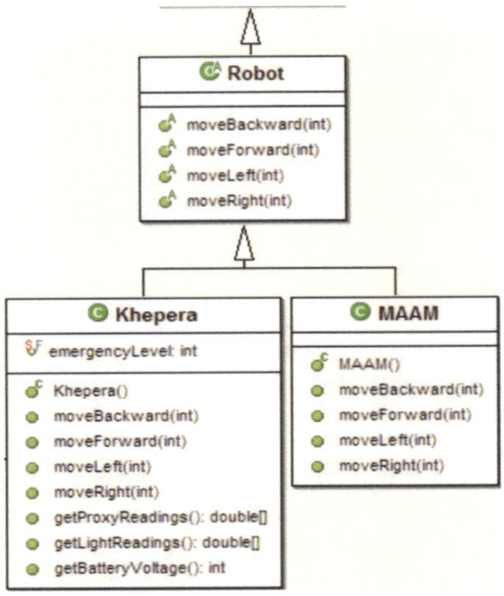

Fig. 2. UML class diagram of the robot primitives

An XML file describes the Khepera robot and MAAM robot. A set of primitives is defined for each of them.

```
01 import Khepera.xml as Khepera;
02 import MAAM.xml    as MAAM;

03 Khepera k1,k2    = newAgent(Khepera);
04 MAAM    m1,m2,m3 = newAgent(MAAM);
```

Here lines 01, 02 define a MASL type referenced by the description of the XML file. Then, lines 03, 04 are the instantiations of 5 agents k1 and k2 of the Khepera type and m1, m2, m3 of the MAAM type.

```
05 asynchronous entry main (true) {
06    .moveLeft(30);
07    .moveForward(10);
08    .moveRight(30);
09    .moveBackward(10);
10 }
```

The `main` is executed by the 5 agents. The semantic of `.moveLeft(30);` is a self execution of the instruction which is the same as the Java **this**`.moveLeft(30);`. Each robot executes its own code independently in this first example (asynchronous entry). From that time, it is not possible to predict the order of execution of these instructions over the 5 agents.

4.2 Synchronous/asynchronous interleaving

The previous example is an asynchronous execution in which all the agents execute their code independently. In the next example, we study the synchronous version.

```
05 synchronous entry main (true) {
06    .moveLeft(30);
07    .moveForward(10);
08    .moveRight(30);
09    .moveBackward(10);
10 }
```

Here the difference is the `synchronous` keyword in the `main entry`. The `synchronous` keyword means that after the execution of each instruction, all agents inside the `entry` (here all agents because the test is `true`) will wait for the end of the execution of all others. In this case the movement of all robots are performed simultaneously. Once again, at that point in time, it is not possible to predict exactly the schedule table of the execution because one agent may take longer in carrying out its action, in which case all others will be waiting. The granularity of synchrony is macroscopic.
The notion of entry is also used to define a section of code to be executed by a subset of agents using an entry condition. For instance

```
05 asynchronous entry example(.isMAAM()) {
06   .moveLeft(30);
07   .moveForward(10);
09 }
```

defines an instruction **entry** named `example` with a test (`.isMAAM()`). The evaluation of this test (`.isMAAM()`) will select the agent authorized to execute the line sequence 6 ,7,8. The agents which don't satisfy the test jump to the next instruction (line 10). The instruction is used to form groups of agents. In this block it is possible to describe the behaviour, the subset, i.e move left or move forward.
MASL also proposes a

```
scalar entry e1(test)
```

to define an entry in which only one agent is allowed to enter. The first agent satisfying the `test` will enter in the `entry` and `lock` this entry so the others will skip this `entry`.
The notion of `entry` can be compared to the entry/accept of Ada language.

4.3 Communication variables, events

The scope of variables or events depends on the place where they are defined and the local/shared modifier expressed.

```
01 asynchronous entry main (true) {
02   shared int sglobalvar=0;
03   synchronous entry e1 (.isMAAM()) {
04     shared int svar=0;
05     local  int lvar=0;
06     lvar++;
07     svar++;
08     .log("lvar="+lvar+"\n");
09     .log("svar="+svar+"\n");
10   }
11 }
```

In this example, all the agents entering the main will share the variable declared in line 2 `sglobalvar`. This means that only one `sglobalvar` exists in the run-time and any modification from any agent will change its value.
Line 03 is an entry where only a subset of robot are selected (`.isMAAM()`). Thus, the variable `svar` defined in line 04 will be shared only for the 3 agents in this section of code. The variable `lvar` defined in line 05 (so 3 different `lvar` will be defined one per agent) instanced locally in each agent in this section of code.
In line 06, each agent will increment its internal variable `lvar`. Therefore, the final value written in line 08 will be 1 (3 times if there are 3 MAAM-type agents). But the `svar` final

value will be 3 because each of the 3 MAAM agents will increment its value. Notice that this value will be written 3 times due to the synchronous scheduling of the **entry** e1.
On the same principle it is possible to define an event. This event can be **global** to all the agents if defined in the main or restricted to a **group** if defined in an entry or a **local** event visible only by the agent itself. The only instruction with events is **emit** (event).

```
01 asynchronous entry main (true) {
02   shared event sevent;
03   asynchronous entry e1 (.MAAM()) {
04     ...
06     react (sevent) {
07       .log("Reaction to an event");
08     }
```

Here, line 02 is the global declaration of the event named sevent in the **entry** main. The agent entering the **entry** e1 will execute the code (line 04). If during its execution, the sevent is emitted by any agent in some other section of the code, then the normal execution stops and jumps to the section **react**. Here the event sevent will be searched in the list and the corresponding code will be executed.
If the code (line 08) includes the MASL instruction **resume** then the agent jumps back where it was in the code (line 04) when the event was emitted. This construction allows an agent to respond to an event and return to the ongoing work.

4.4 Dynamic integration of agent

Here the problem is to allow an agent to quit a group to join another. To quit the group we can finish the normal execution of an entry using the instruction **break** or use the instruction **reelect** that comes back to the last entry and checks the test again. For instance, if in the previous example the line 08 is **reelect** then the agent will test the **entry** e1 in line 03 again. In fact, it will test if the agent is still a MAAM robot or not. If yes, it will enter the **entry** e1 again, or it will go to the next instruction (line 09).
This construction is useful to extract one agent from a group. However, the problem is then to add the agent to another group. We must thus imagine that it will find another **entry** in which the test will be true.
Notice that we also defined some instructions to lock or unlock an **entry**. This allows some agents to control the number of agents entering an **entry** section.

4.5 synchronous/asynchronous message passing

In the XML definition of the Khepera, the primitive moveLeft is defined. This can be used in two ways.
First, an agent k1 wants to move left, its code will then include:

```
01 : .moveleft(30);
```

expressing that the instruction is applied to agent k1 itself.

Or the code of agent k1 contains:

```
01 : k2.moveleft(30);
```

then k1 is asks agent k2 to move left. In this case we can imagine two scenarios.

- The execution of k1 is blocked until the move-left execution of agent k2 is done.

- The execution of k1 can continue during the execution of the move left of k2.

This depends on the definition of the primitive action `.moveleft()`.
The XML file defining the services of the robot can describe two types of primitives depending on the value of the field `synchronous_call`. When it is true, k1 is blocked and it is called a synchronous message passing.
The problems are with the other kind: asynchronous message passing. The problem is that if you ask for a function producing an integer like `getBatteryVoltage() : int` in the XML file of Khepera. Then the code of k1 could be

```
02 : li= k2.getBatteryVoltage ();
```

expressing that a local variable li of k1 will receive the value of the voltage of the battery of k2. In the case of an asynchronous call, k1 will continue its work. If at some location in the code, k1 wants to use the value `li` then it must be sure that the assignment of `li` is accomplished.

To solve this problem we introduce in MASL the synchronisation utility named Label, inspired from the Java interface `java.util.concurrent.Future`.

```
01 : Label llabel;
02 : llabel.li= k2.getBatteryVoltage ();
...
06 : if (isFinished(llabel)){...}
```

Here, line 01 declares a new label `llabel`. Line 02 attaches an asynchonous message passing instruction to this label `llabel`. It is then possible for line 06 to test the label `llabel` to know whether the instruction attached to it is completed or not. Note that it is possible to attach more than one instruction from an agent to a label, as well as different instructions coming from different agents.

4.6 Dynamic permeability

The permeability notion is completely connected to the previous message passing notion. It is used to express that some agents might not be able to answer a primitive call at some time during the execution.
The permeability is defined in the XML file of the robot. It defines a set of states of the robot and the list of primitives that can be executed in each of these states.
For instance, a permeability state: `standard` would determine if it is possible for a MAAM agent to execute all the 4 primitives defined in Figure 1. But for a second permeability state: `damage`, only the `moveForward(int)` primitive could be called. This state would correspond to a robot having some problems.
Moreover, for all permeability states the allowed primitives are protected from execution in virtue of the levels: global, group, local. This means that depending on the permeability state a primitive can be executed: by all agents of the main, only by the members of the group (in the same `entry`) or only by the agent itself.
The permeability state can be dynamically changed only by the agent itself by the execution of a specific MASL instruction **`setAcceptState`**`(string)`, where `string` is the name of the permeability state.
The MASL language also provides a **`wait`**`(string)` instruction. This instruction is used to put an agent in a waiting mode until its activation by a call from one of the primitives visible in the permeability state defined by `string`. Them this agent behaves as a passive agent but constrained by this permeability state until its activation.

5. MASL expressivity in a RoboCup application

To show an example of the MASL language, we propose here a small sample in which we will distinguish three groups of robots: one is an attacker and the second is a defender and one is the coach.

```
05 asynchronous entry main (true) {
06   shared event mvBack, mvForward, move;
07   scalar entry coach (true) {
08     local  int lv, li=0;
09     loop
10       lv=.analyseSituation(); li++;
11       if (lv<0) emit mvBack;
         else emit mvForward;
12       if (li==100) {li=0; emit move;};
13     endloop
14   }
15   asynchronous entry attack(.isFast()) {
16     loop .playAttack(); endloop;
17     react(mvForward)
       {.moveForward(20);resume;};
18     react(mvBack)
       {.moveBackward(20);resume;};
19   }
20   asynchronous entry defense (true) {
21     loop .playDefense(); endloop;
22     react(mvForward)
       {.moveForward(5);resume;};
23     react(mvBack)
       {.moveBackward(5);resume;};
24     react(move)
       {.setRandomFast();reelect(2);};
25   }
26 }
```

This example is built to show some features:

- definition of groups of robots,
- scalability,
- dynamic change of group,
- how to control a group from a supervisor.

The instantiation of the agents is not shown here. We assume that it is a set of agents for identical robots. All these agents will share 3 events (line 6).

During the execution the first agent to execute line 7 will become the coach (because it is a `scalar entry` only one can enter). The next agents will skip instruction line 7 and move to execute line 15. If the test performed on themselves `(.isFast())` is true, then they will enter and go to line 16 to play in attack mode, the other ones will move to line 20 where they will enter (because the test is `true`) and run line 21 to play in defence mode.

We can see here that the initial group of agents is separated into 3 groups: one (alone) in the `entry coach`, a set of agents in the `entry attack` and the rest in the `entry defense`. Notice that this is independent of the number of robots.

Now the dynamic evolution will develop through the coach's behaviour. He analyses the situation (line 10) and decides of the actions of the two groups of attackers and defenders. So, in line 11 he emits the event `mvBack` (resp. `mvForward`). This event is global to all agents and they can react to it.

The attackers will `react` (line 17 (resp. 18) by a `moveForward(20)` (resp. `moveBackward(20)`) and then go back to their offence behaviour in line 16 when executing `resume`.
The defenders will `react` (line 22 (resp. 23) by a `moveForward(5)` (resp. `moveBackward(5)`) and then go back to their attacking behavior line 21 when executing `resume`.
We can see here how one group is asked to make big amplitudes? (20), while the other one is not (5).
The coach can also force defenders to become attackers. Every 100 loops (line 12) the coach emits an `event move`. In this `event` only the defenders `react` (line 24). Their reaction is to randomly decide whether they are `Fast` or not. After which they will reenter the program line 5 by the execution of the **`reelect`**`(2)` instruction. They will enter again in the `main`. Because the `coach entry` is locked they will move to line 15 to decide whether they become attackers (if yes, they enter line 16) or not (they move to line 20) or become defenders again.
Here we can see all groups of agents reevaluating their behaviour. It is, of course, possible in MASL to refine? to a specific agent.

6. Toward centralized execution model

In this section, we present the basic algorithm of the execution of a MASL instruction. It is divided into 4 steps:

1. Execution of the instruction, it is the execution of the primitive by the agent
2. Ask MASL runtime for the list of events. At this level the call to the basic primitive is finished and the agent checks if there is some events emitted. If so, it will jump to the **`react`** part of the code and search for the first instruction to execute, then go back to step one
3. Ask MASL runtime for the list of primitive calls. Here, the agent according to the permeability state will execute the primitive calls. The calls that are not allowed due to the permeability will be neglected.
4. Wait for synchronization. If the agent is in a **`synchronous entry`** then it will wait for the end of the group before looping to step 1.

From agent architectural point of view, only some MASL features have a deliberative nature (shared variables for example). Broadcasted shared events have a reactive nature in contrast. MASL Controllers with shared variables will produce a deliberative loop. MASL Controllers without any deliberative feature will produce reactive loop. In this particular case, please replace in figure 3 hybrid/deliberative worlds by reactive one.
From MASL it is possible to define a rewriting algorithm to produce a source code for a specific robot programming language. This algorithm is under development. The MASL to Java translator use XML files and MASL program to generate the reactive/deliberative loop in java. We plan also to develop the MASL to C++ translator.
We have studied some deployment cases and some different execution models shown in figure 3. Only the simulated MASL agents (in the far right) are working for now. The implementation of some MASL concepts (**`synchronous entry`**, broadcast of `events`, shared variables, **`react`**, **`resume`**, **`reelect`**) depends on the target execution model (centralized or distributed). Outside the remotely connected agent case, the MASL program

is replicated into each agent. In case of a distributed execution model, broadcasted events, access to (virtually) shared variables (physically replicated) and synchronisation mechanisms have to be implemented on top of the network. Consistency of access to shared variables has to be ensured in this case. We have defined features that are in all cases into each agent. They are managed by the local runtime. Other features are managed by centralized MASL runtime or distributed MASL runtime in respect to deployment case. The deliberative loop communicates only with local runtime that optionally uses shared services. This rule prevents to have to modify the MASL to Java translator nor the MASL to C++ translator to produce the source code for real or simulated agents for specific deployment case.

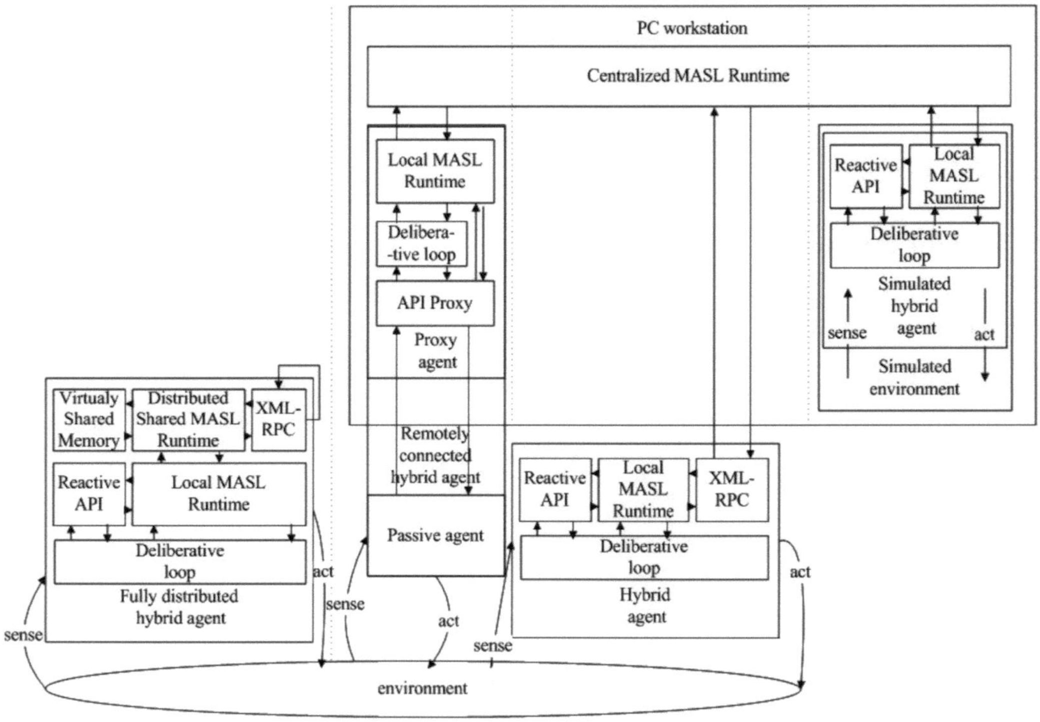

Fig. 3. Different deployment cases for MASL agents

Remote Procedure Calls (RPC) is a technique for constructing distributed, client-server based applications. It uses the notion of conventional local procedure calls, so the called procedure need not exist in the same address space as the calling procedure.

XML-RPC (de Rivera et al., 2005) is a specification and a set of implementations that extend RPC to allow procedure calls to be made over the Internet to machines with potentially different execution environments and operating systems. This makes use of HTTP as the transport and XML as the encoding. XML-RPC is designed to be simple, but also be powerful enough to allow complex data structures to be transmitted, processed, and returned. There are many XML-RPC implementations in various computer languages, e.g., C/C++, Java, Perl, and Python, and for various operating systems, e.g., GNU/Linux, Microsoft Windows, and Sun Solaris.

7. Conclusion and future works

The MASL language proposed here allows for the description of multi-agents, multi-robot behaviour at three different levels: global, group, and local. The originality of MASL is the definition of the instruction entry to create groups of robots. This instruction can run dynamically in two modes: asynchronous or synchronous. Another particularity of MASL is the message passing construction which allows asynchronous or synchronous calls to be defined under a permeability state.

Future works are:

- We want to implement MASL to C++ translator,
- We want to test real robots controllers,
- We want to define some good principles in MASL programming,
- We want to provide GUI (Graphical User Interface) for MASL mission specification,
- We want to express the formal semantic to allow us to prove several properties in our controllers,
- We want to provide FIPA compliant services to our agents.

8. Acknowledgement

This work is a part of the MAAM project that is supported by the Robea project of the CNRS.

9. References

Alur, R.; Grosu, R.; Hur, Y.; Kumar, V. & Lee, I. (2000). Modular specification of hybrid systems in CHARON. *In HSCC*, pp. 6-19.

Armstrong, J. (1997). The development in Erlang, *ACM sighpla international conference on functional programming*, pp. 196-203.

Atkin, M.; Westbrook, D. & Cohen, P. (1999). HAC : a unified view of reactive and deliberative activity, *Notes of the European conf on artificial intelligence.*

Benjamin, P.; Lonsdale, D. & Lyons, D. (2004). Integrating perception, language an problem solving in a cognitive agent for mobile robot, *AAMAS'04*, July 19-23 2004, New York

Brooks R. (1991). Intelligence without Reason, *Proceedings of the IJCAI'91*, Sydney (Australie), Morgan-Kaufmann, pp. 569-595.

Dastani, M. & van der Torre, L. (2003). Programming Boid-Plan agents deliberating about conflicts along defeasible mental attitudes and plans, *AAMAS 2003*

Gueganno, C. & Duhaut, D. (2004). A hardware/software architecture for the control of self reconfigurable robots, *DARS 04*, 7th symposium on distributed autonomous robotics systems, June 23-25, Toulouse France.

Hudak, P.; Courtney, A.; Nilsson, H. & Peterson, J. (2002). Arrows, robots, and functional reactive programming, *lecture note in computer science* 159-187 Springer Verlag 2002

Ingrand, F.; Chatila, R.; Alami, R. & Robert, F. (1996). PRS : a high level supervision and control language for autonomous mobile robots, *IEEE int cong on robotics and automation*, Minneapolis.

Jorgensen, M.W.; Ostergaard, E.H. & Hautop, H. (2004). Modular ATRON: modules for a self-reconfigurable robot, *IEEE/RSJ int conf on intelligent robots and systems IROS 2004* Sendai Japan

King, G. (2002). Tapir: the evolution of an agent control language, *American association of artificial intelligence.*

Klavins, E. (2003). A formal model of a multi-robot control and communication task, *IEEE conf on decision and control.*

Klavins, E. (2004). A language for modeling and programming cooperative control systems, *Int conf on robotics and automation ICRA.*

Levesque, H.; Reiter, R.; Lespérance, Y.; Lin, F. & Scherl, R. (1997). Golog: A logic programming language for dynamic domains, *Journal of Logic Programming.*

Lötzsch, M. (2004). XABSL - A Behavior Engineering System for Autonomous Agents. *Diploma thesis.* Humboldt-Universität zu Berlin.

Lozano-Perez, T. & Brooks, R. (1986). An approach to automatic robot programming, *Proceedings of the 1986 ACM fourteenth annual conf on computer sciences,* ACM Press

Mackenzie, D.C. & Arkin, R. (1997). Multiagent mission specification and execution, *Autonomous robot vol 1 num 25.*

Mondada, F.; Guignard, A.; Bonani, M.; Bar, D.; Lauria, M. & Floreano, D. (2003). Swarm-bot : for concept to implementation, *IEEE/RSJ int conf on intelligent robots and systems IROS.*

Nilsson, N. J. (1984). Shakey the robot. *Technical Report 323,* SRI Artificial Intelligence Center.

Nishiyama, H.; Ohwada, H. & Mizoguchi, F. (1998). A Multiagent Robot Language for Communication and Concurrency Control. *Proceedings of the International Conference on Multiagent Systems,* pp. 206–213.

Pembeci, I. & Hager, G. (2001). A comparative review of robot programming languages, *report CIRL* – Johns Hopkins University.

Peterson, J.; Hager, G.D. & Hudak, P. (1999). A language for declarative robotic programming, *Int conf on robotics and automation ICRA.*

de Rivera, G.G.; Ribalda, R.; Colas, J. & Garrido, J. (2005), A generic software platform for controlling collaborative robotic system using XML-RPC, *Advanced Intelligent Mechatronics. Proceedings, 2005 IEEE/ASME International Conference on,* Volume , Issue , 24-28 July 2005, pp. 1336 - 1341

Vu, T.; Go, J.; Kaminka, G.; Veloso, M. & Browning, B. (2003). Monad: a flexible architecture for multi-agent control, *AAMAS'03.*

Yoshida, E.; Kurokawa, H.; Kamimura, A.; Murata, S.; Tomita, K. & Kokaji, S. (2004). Planning behaviors of modular robots with coherent structure using randomized method, *DARS 04 7th symposium on distributed autonomous robotics systems,* June 23-25, Toulouse France.

Zielinski, C. (2000). Programming and control of multi-robot systems, *Conf. On control and automation robotics and vision ICRARCV'2000 Dec. 5-8,* Singapore.

13

Agent-Oriented Novel Quantum Key Distribution Protocol for the Security in Wireless Network

Xu Huang, Shirantha Wijesekera and Dharmendra Sharma
University of Canberra
Australia

1. Introduction

Wireless security is becoming increasingly important as wireless applications and systems are widely adopted. Numerous organizations have already installed or are busy in installing "wireless local area networks" (WLANs). These networks, based on the IEEE 802.11 standard, are very easy to deploy and inexpensive. Wi-Fi allows LANs to be deployed without cabling for client devices, typically reducing the costs of network deployment and expansion. As of 2007 wireless network adapters are built into most modern laptops. The price of chipsets for Wi-Fi continues to drop, making it an economical networking option included in ever more devices. Wi-Fi has become widespread in corporate infrastructures, which also helps with the deployment of RFID technology that can piggyback on Wi-Fi. Wi-Fi is a global set of standards, unlike mobile telephones, any standard Wi-Fi device will work anywhere in the world. Other important trends in wireless adoptions are including the introduction of wireless email with devices such as the Blackberry and The Palm VII, rampant digital cell phone use, including the use of short message service (SMWS), and the advent of Bluetooth devices. But the risks associated with the adoption of wireless networking are only now coming to light. A number of impressive attacks are possible and have been heavily publicized, especially in the IEEE 802.11b area. As far as base technology is concerned, wireless security appears to be following the usual "penetrate and path" route. Early wireless security focused almost exclusively on cryptography and secure transmission-with unfortunate results thus far. Wired Equivalency Privacy (WEP) security, the cryptography built in to 802.11b, for example, is completely broken and offers very little real security. In fact, one might argue that using WEP is worse than using no cryptography at all, because it can lull users into a completely unfounded sense of security. For every time one introduces new technologies one can rest assured that exploits for it are soon to follow. So with this in mind it was no great surprise that 64 bit WEP was quickly found to be lacking in terms of its implementation. So the vendors upped the ante and came out with 128 bit WEP, and this in turn was also found to be lacking. Wi-Fi hacking has been around for some time now, and oddly enough has really received little press. Since 2001, 64 bit WEP has been breakable [Park, Don 2006]. That was also around the time that well known tools such as Airsnort gave the ability to break into wireless network to the masses. In fact we looked at some of the tools that exist today which will allow user to discover wireless access points (WAP). It is obviously to face the fact that wireless network have become very popular over the past few years for not only business, but also the home market. In all likelihood user's neighbors are probably running a wireless router for their home computer network even though it is not using a wireless card. The wireless communication revolution has been bringing fundamental changes to data networking, telecommunication, and has been making integrated networks a reality. By freeing the user from the cord, personal communications networks, wireless LAN's [IEEE Standard for Local Metropolitan area networks], wireless MAN's, mobile radio networks and cellular systems, harbor the promise of fully distributed mobile computing and communications, any time, anywhere.

There are number of such wireless services widely in use at the moment. Wi-Fi (IEEE 802.11) [Chip Elliott, 2002] [Hasan Jamshed 2006], WiMAX (IEEE 802.16) [Bennett, C.H. 1984] and Mobile device networks such as GSM, 3G are now cater users across the globe.

Without physical boundaries, a wireless network faces many more security threats than a wired network does. For an example, WEP (Wired Equivalent Privacy) the authentication and data confidentiality definition of IEEE 802.11 standard was found to be vulnerable to security attacks, hence IEEE later came up with its 802.11i [IEEE Standrad 802.11i] to rectify the flaws of WEP. Likewise security flaws of IEEE 802.16 standard too have been exposed [Sen Xu, et.al. 2006], [Hasan Jamshed 2006]. This indicates how important the authentication and data encryption of these wireless networks. Given the tremendous growth in WLAN usage, and the weakness of current security protocols, new and better security mechanisms are required to protect wireless transmissions. One of these is the IEEE 802.1x standard [Craiger, J. Philip 2002]. 802.1x was intended to provide strong authentication, access control, and key management and allow WLANs to scale by allowing centralized authentication of wireless users or stations. It is well known that 802.1x is based upon an existing authentication protocol known as the extensible authentication protocol (EAP) which in itself is an extension of PPP (point-to-point protocol). It is also noted that 802.1x maps EAP to the physical medium, regardless of whether it is Ethernet, Token Ring or wireless LAN. In fact, it is necessary to note that the 802.1x standard provides for authentication only. The standard does not specify the specific types of authentication or any type of encryption. In fact, it is reported that 802.1x is susceptible to session hijacking as well as man-in-the-middle attacks [Connolly, P.J., 2002], [Schwartz, E. 2002].

One area that hasn't got much attention, which has shown a great future, on wireless security is the use of quantum cryptography for encryption of data. The uncertainty principle in quantum mechanics created a new paradigm for Quantum Key Distribution (QKD) [Bennett & Charles H., 1992], [Lenz & Moritz, 2007], [Buttler et al., 1998]. The uncertainty principle in quantum mechanics created a new paradigm for cryptography: Quantum cryptography, or more specifically QKD. Unlike the classical cryptography which relies on mathematical complexity, quantum cryptography is based on the laws of quantum theory in physics. The laws of quantum physics showed that nobody can measure a state of arbitrary photon carrying information without introducing disturbances to the transmission. Since all these eavesdropping can be detected, quantum cryptography is considered as providing unconditional security. In fact this is called "No-Cloning" Theorem [Wootters, W. and Zurek, W., 1982] and implies that a possible eavesdropper cannot intercept, measure and re-emit a photon without introducing a significant and therefore detectable error in the re-emitted signal. In this chapter we shall introduce some updated research results of our current projects [Huanget al., Feb 2008] and [Huang et al., May 2008]. The next section describes wireless 802.11 and quantum cryptography. In section 3, we shall discuss the system implementation for QKD in a wireless communication. In section 4 we present our new developed protocol for wireless networks and in section 5 we present our conclusion.

2. Wireless 802.11 and quantum cryptography

As we described above that 802.11 security defines WEP [Edeny, J. & Arbaugh, W.A., 2004] for the authentication and data confidentiality of user data over the wireless link. However, WEP was not well designed and presents serious vulnerabilities as a new standard for the 802.11 security. In this context, 802.11i is defined to rectify the flaws of WEP. 80211i received much attention from specialists in cryptography and network security.

Regarding the 802.11i authentication and key management, we knew that 802.11i defines two authentication and key management methods, namely 802.1X authentication and preshared key. The former is for large network having an important number of access points and the later is suitable for small network.

Therefore, the former has three elements participating to the authentication and key management are the supplicant (or mobile terminal), authenticator (or access point), and the authentication server. Once having the pairwise master key (PMK), the access point starts the four -way handshake for the mutual authentication and the derivation of the pairwise transient key (PTK) with the mobile terminal.

In contrast to the 802.1X, the preshared key is involved in the authentication and key management using preshared key without "authentication server" and no extensible authentication protocol (EAP)-based authentication.

Following [Thi Mai Trang Nguyen et al., 2006], we are using Figure 1 shows the pairwise key hierarchy containing the keys related to the encryption of unicast traffic.

It is noted that 802.11i has many keys at different levels, which becoming a key hierarch as shown Figure 1. At the top level there is the master key titled pairwise master key (PMK) that is used to derive the other keys.

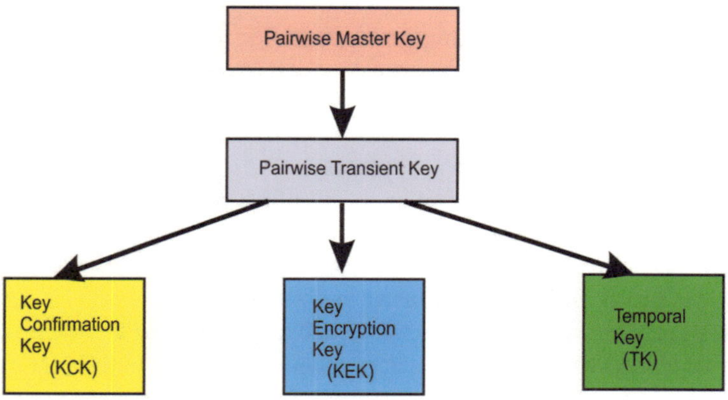

Fig. 1. Pairwise key hierarchy

It is noted that 802.11i has many keys at different levels, which becoming a key hierarch as shown Figure 1. At the top level there is the master key titled pairwise master key (PMK) that is used to derive the other keys.

The pairwise transient key (PTK) is created between the access point and the mobile terminal during the 4-way handshake. The PTK is split into three final temporal keys, namely key confirmation key (KCK), key encryption key (KEK), and temporal key (TK).

Quantum Key Distribution systems transmit the secrete key, which are derived from random numbers, one photon (one bit) at a time in a polarized state. If intercepted by an eavesdropper or due to other atmospheric interferences etc, this state will change, and an error will be detected at the receiving side [Bennett et al., 1992].

Quantum cryptography aims at exploiting the laws of quantum physics in order to carry out a cryptographic task. For the moment, the use of quantum physics at cryptographic ends is limited mainly to the distribution of secret keys.

There are several QKD protocols available. Most widely used is being the BB84 [Bennett, C.H. & Brassard, G, 1984]. B92 (Bennett, Charles 1992), a slight variation of BB84, is another well known QKD protocol [Bennett, C.H., 1992]. B92 can be used two non-orthogonal states which represent the bit values 0 and 1 as shown below:

$$
\begin{aligned}
&| u_0 >, \\
&| u_1 >,
\end{aligned}
\tag{1}
$$

BB84 coding scheme, invented by Charles Bennett and Gilles Brassard, is the first quantum cryptography communication protocol. There are four different quantum states. The corresponding four quantum states can be expressed as below:

$$
\begin{aligned}
&| 0 >, \\
&| 1 >, \\
&| \overline{0} >= \frac{1}{\sqrt{2}}(| 0 > + | 1 >), \\
&| \overline{1} >= \frac{1}{\sqrt{2}}(| 0 > - | 1 >),
\end{aligned}
\tag{2}
$$

As an example, this coding system uses four non-orthogonal polarization states identified as *horizontal*, *vertical*, 45° and *135°*.

This protocol operates with transmitting party (say, Alice) sending polarized quantum bits (qubits) to the receiving party (call, Bob) via the quantum channel.

Once the quantum transmission finishes, Bob publicly communicates to Alice which measurements operators he used for each of the received bit. Alice then informs Bob which of his measurement operator choices were correct.

The B92 quantum coding scheme is similar to the BB84, but uses only two out of the four BB84 non-orthogonal states, as shown in equation (1). It encodes classical bits in two non-orthogonal BB84 states. In addition to this, Bob simply sends the positions of the bases to retain, keeping the protocol simpler and faster to operate.

In out current paper, we decided to implement B92 protocol as a case study, the whole processing can be easily extended to four states, where BB84 used, and therefore from now on in this paper we are focusing on two quantum states, namely B92 protocol unless otherwise.

The Quantum key transmission happens in two stages that can be shown in Figure 2. It is noted that in Figure 2 the Wi-Fi connections are classical channels and the "optical Fiber" channels are quantum channels.

Those two stages are as follows:

Stage 1: Quantum Channel (One way communication)

This transmission could happen in either through free space or optical fiber. At present this implementation is being done at the Monash University, Australia.

Stage 2: Classical Channel (Two way communication)

This phase deals with recovering identical secrete keys at both ends.

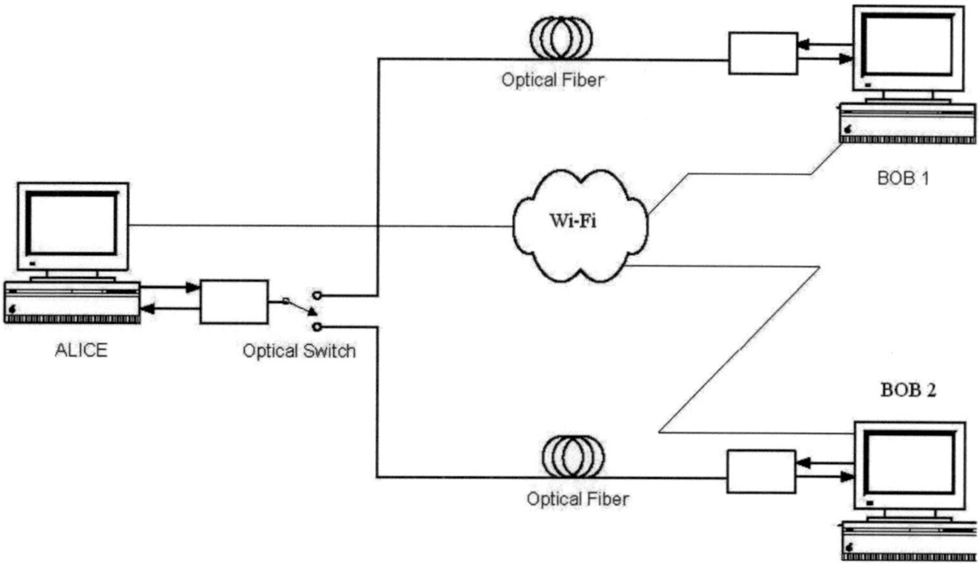

Fig. 2. Simplified block diagram of a point-to-point QKD link in concept, where SS is denoted "subscriber station" and the BS standing for "base station"

During the stage Alice & Bob communicate over a Classical channel that can be divided further in 4 main phases as shown below:

a. Raw key extraction (Sifting)
b. Error Estimation
c. Reconciliation
d. Privacy Amplification

It is noted that there are, in terms of physics concepts, two different channels one is classical channel another is quantum channel. For the implementation that we are going to present the wireless Wi-Fi is chosen as the classical channel (Figure 2). The quantum channel is the line of sight (LOS) optical path running by the polarization photon.

We can find, in Figure 2, that the classical channel forms by the standard Wi-Fi wireless and the quantum established by the optical photos. In Figure 2, in order to discuss our implementation more generally, SS is denoted "subscriber station" and the BS standing for "base station".

The Quantum channel is taking the task that using quantum cryptography to establish the key used for the encryption of user data in 802.11i, which is the TK. It is noted that TK is part of the PTK, as shown in Figure 1, which is established during the four-way handshake, we shall modify the four-way handshake to integrate the B92 protocol, as a case study, and make it as quantum handshake.

When the quantum handshake completion the wireless Wi-Fi will either refuse the subscriber station to communicate data via the classical channel or take the subscriber station to access the Wi-Fi and the system becomes "normal" Wi-Fi working states, which will run the communications in the defined classical channels.

The quantum channel between Alice and Bob1 is shown in Fig. 3, the channel between Alice and Bob2 is similar. At Alice, laser pulses are generated by vertical cavity surface emitting lasers (VCSELs) and attenuated into single photon level. The polarization states of photons are set by polarizers according to corresponding protocol (B92 or BB84). Then photons are combined and sent into a fiber through a non-polarizing beam splitter (NPBS). The polarizers Pol. 0A, 0B, 1A, and 1B are oriented to 0°, 90°, +45°, and -45° respectively. Only two channels, 0A and 1A, are used for B92, while all four channels are used for BB84. At Bob, polarization controllers recover the polarization state of photons to their original state at Alice. The 3-dB coupler randomly chooses the detection base and the polarization beam splitter (PBS) helps to determine the key value via the an agent-ortened. Finally the photons are detected by single photon detectors (APDs). Two APDs, 0A and 1A, are used for B92, while four APDs are all used for BB84.

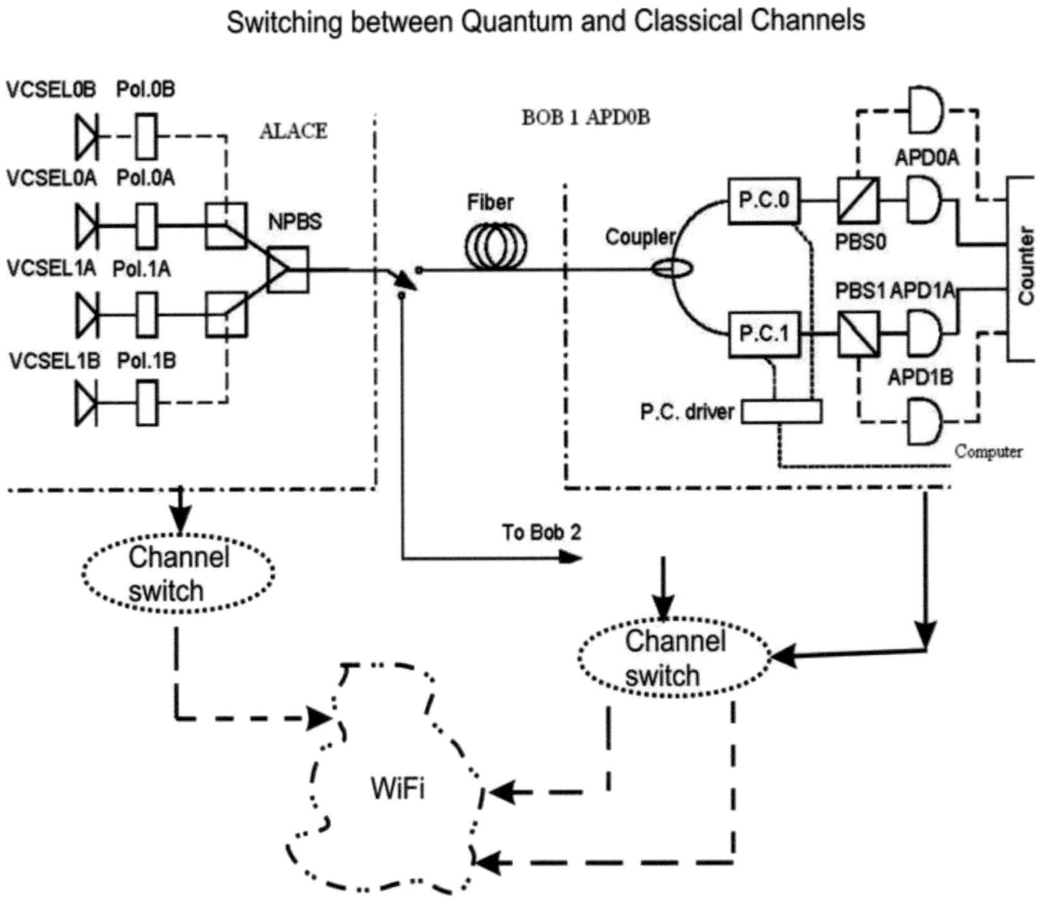

Fig. 3. Quantum channel implementing by optical fibers: schematic diagram of the QKD system with PRAC sub-systems. VCSEL: Vertical Cavity Surface Emitting Laser ; Pol.: Polarizer; NPBS: Non-Polarizing beam splitter; P.C.: Polarization Controller; PBS: Polarizing beam splitter; APD: Silicon avalanche photodiode.

2.1 Quantum network

Quantum Key Distribution techniques are emerging as useful building blocks in highest secure networks. The quantum network marries a variety of QKD techniques to well established internet technology in order to build a secure key distribution system employed in conjunction with the public internet or, more likely, with private networks that employ the internet protocol suite [2]. At present there are large numbers of such private networks in widespread use around the world with customers' desire secure and private communications.

The merge of QKD technologies to these networks proves feasible and appealing in certain contexts.

Free space QKD uses the air as the medium for the transmission of photons between the quantum sender and receiver. The feasibility of QKD over the air is considered problematic because of a medium with varying properties and a high error rate. In particular for the limited distance and indoor environment the quantum channel would be realized at the reasonable level.

2.2 Agent society

Computer systems no longer stand along, but are networked into large distributed systems. The movement away from machine-oriented views of programming toward concepts and metaphors that more closely reflect the way we ourselves understand the world. Programmers conceptualize and implement software in terms of ever higher-lever more hunan-oriented.

An agent is a computer system that is capable of independent (autonomous) action on behalf of its user or owner (figuring out what needs to be done to satisfy design objectives, rather than constantly being told)..

Normally there are two key problems need to be noted for agnet society designs, namely (a) How to we build agents that are capable of indendent, autonomous action in order to successfully carry out the tasks that we delegate to them? (b) How do we build agents that are capable of interacting (cooperating, coordinating, negotiating) with other agents in order to successful cary out the tasks that we delegate to them, particularly when the other agents cannot be assumed to share the same interests/goals?

It is well known that an intelligent agent is a computer system capable of flexible autonomous action in some environment. Here "flexible" means (a) reactive (b) pro-active and (c) social.

A reactive system is one that maintains an ongoing interaction with its environment, and responds to changes that occur in it (in time for the response to be useful).

Pro-activeness is generating and attempting to achieve goals; not driven solely by events; taking the initiative.

Social ability in agents is thew ability to interact with other agents (and possibly humans) via some kind of agent-communication language, and perhaps coopewrate with others.

There are other properties of agency somethimes to be discussed depend on the indivical cases, such as mobility, which shows an agent to move around an electronic network; veracity, showing whether an agent will knowingly communicate false information; benevolence, showing whether agents have conflicting goals, and thus whether they are inherently helpful; rationality, showing whether an agent will act in order to achieve its goals, and will not deliberately act so as to prevent its goals being achieved.

In fact, for the channle switching shown in Figure 3 it can be expressed as in block diagram shown in Figure 4.

The design for the implemation of the switching will be run by the "operational agent society" shown in Figure 5.

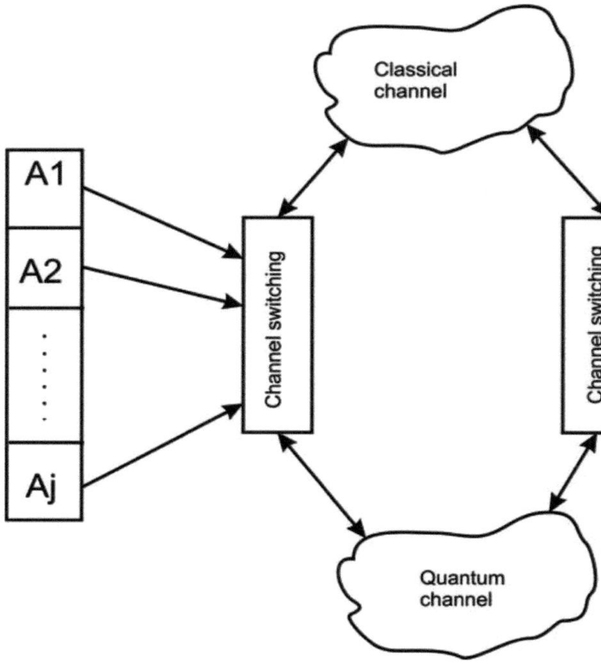

Fig. 4. A block diagram for QKD channels' switching

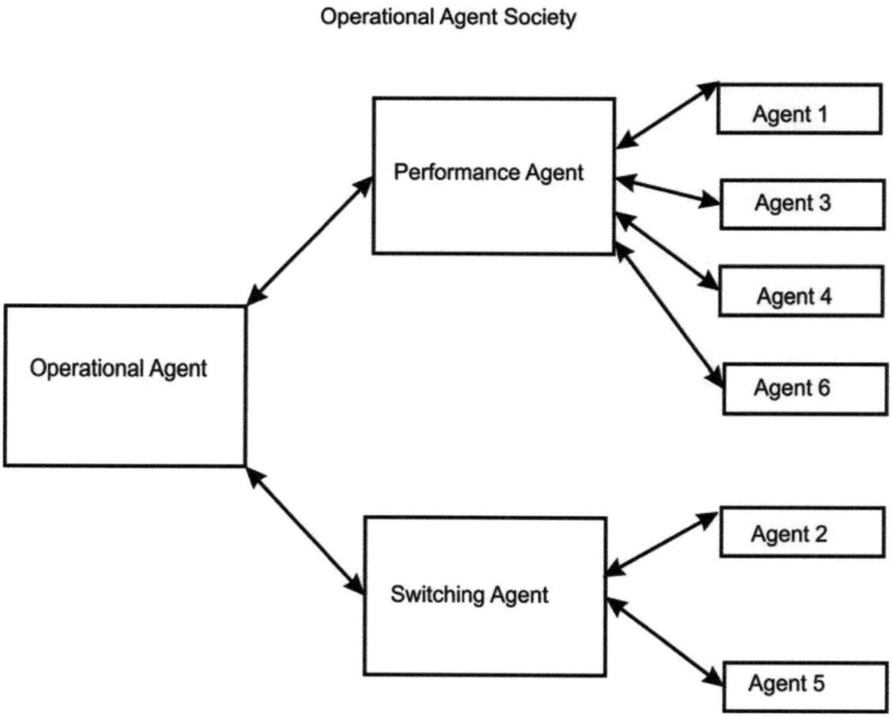

Fig. 5. A block diagram for "Operational Agent Society".

We design two types agents, switching agent and performance agent. The performance agent looks after the "perfomances" between transmiters and seitching, namely Alace 1 (A1), Alace 2 (A2), etc to channel switch or Bob 1 (B1), Bob 2 (B2) etc to channel switch. The switch agent takes of the channel switching. In Figure 4, we labeled the agent number from left to right between Ai (i≤j) and channel switch (left hand side in Fig 4) as "Agent 1",looking after channel switch is "Agent 2," between channel switch and mediea as "Agent 3", between media and another channel switch (right hand side in Fig 4) is "Agent 4", the rigth hand side channel switch is taken care of by "Agent 5" and between channel switch and receiver Bq (q≤k) is "Agent 6". All the labeled agents are shown in Figure 5 for the Operational Agent Society.

Therefore, agent 1 makes sure the tresmitor Ai (i≤j) is connected to channel switch via the media. Agent 3 ensures the transimitions are connected by quantom channel when the communications are beginning. Agent 4 would play the similar role for the transmitions. Agent 6 will check the the receivers between the switch channel are correctly connected. Angent 2 and agent 5 check the channel situation, either in quantum state (at the beginning for the communications) or classical state (after identifications via quantum channels). The performance agent will cooperatively working with switching agent via operational agent.

3. System implementation

The KCK is generated from the PMK to serve the mutual authentication of the supplicant and the authenticator and protect the B92 protocol from the main-in-the-middle attack as described in [Thi Mai Trang Nguyenet al., 2006].

Once the mutual authentication finished, the supplicant and the authenticator stats the B92 protocol for the establishment of the Q-PTK. The Q-PTK is splits into the KEK and TK.

It is noted that we can use quantum cryptography to establish the PK, therefore all KEK, yKCK, and TK are established using quantum cryptography.

Security provides subscribers with privacy across the broadband wireless network. It achieves security by encrypting connection between BS (Base Station) and SS (Subscriber Station).

The protocol for first 2 stages of QKD

3.1 Index files

The software implementation depends on the key bits recorded at BS and SS. These key bits are to be recorded in set of files, known as "Index Files". Since the original key transmitted by BS in the Quantum Channel could contain many bits (gigabits), there will be multiple index files generated at either ends.

Those index files will act as the input to this software development project.

3.2 Index files at BS

All the key bits that BS transmits in the Quantum Channel are to be recorded into index files at her end. These files hold the original key that BS transmitted to SS.

Examples of the bits recorded in those index files:-

1,0,1,1,0,0,0,1,1,0,0,1,0,1,1,1,0,0,0,1,1,0

where "," being the delimiter

Index files at BS

All the key bits that BS transmits in the Quantum Channel are to be recorded into index files at her end. These files hold the original key that BS transmitted to SS.

Examples of the bits recorded in those index files:-

1,0,1,1,0,0,0,1,1,0,0,1,0,1,1,1,0,0,0,1,1,0

where "," being the delimiter

Index files at SS

During the Quantum transmission, SS too records the key bits that he received from BS in Index files. These bits will not be identical to what BS has transmitted due to the random bases used by SS's photon detector, eavesdropper attacks, channel noise, dark counts of the photon detector etc..

Therefore the index files recorded at SS's end will comprise non-receptions. Non-receptions are the bit positions that SS should have received, but not receive a bit.

Examples of the bits recorded at SS's index files:-

1,1,,,0,0,,0,1,,1,0,0, ,0, ,1,,1,0,0, ,1,1,0

where "," being the delimiter

With the use of delimiter to separate each key bit, it is easy to identify the of non-reception bits.

3.3 Program structure and protocol

Both BS and SS maintain a C++ class to hold individual parameter values of each index file. This class comprises of: Key bits, total number of bits, non-receipt bit positions etc.

At start up, BS and SS reads all the index files and populates the respective parameters in their data structures.

Figure 5 shows the protocol used between BS and SS.

The software has been developed in C++ language using UNIX socket programming.

In order to establish the communication path, BS first *listens* to a specified port. SS sends the *connect* message to the specified port in BS. Upon receiving the *connect* request, BS sends *accept* call to SS establishing the communication path between them.

Raw Key Extraction (Sifting)

During this process, which happens at start up, SS sends the non-erasure bit positions to Alice by running through the index file data loaded into the memory. BS in turn, processes her index files and keeps only those corresponding bits.

At the end of this process, both BS and SS will have index files of identical lengths after removing all non-receipt bits. This process is called *Raw Key Extraction* and the keys recovered after this phase is known as *BS Raw Key* and *SS Raw Key*.

Error Estimation

This process starts with BS requesting SS to send a block of bits of length "L" from a particular index file.

This request has the following format:

<STRAT_ERR_ESTIMATION> <INDEX FILE NUMBER> <START BIT> <LENGTH> <END_ERR_ESTIMATION>

All the above values can be read as configurable parameters to the program.

Upon receiving this message, SS sends the requested block of bits to BS.

BS calculates the Bit Error Rate (**e**) of the Quantum transmission.

$$\mathbf{e} = \frac{\text{Number of bits in error}}{\text{Total number of bits in the block}} \times 100\ \% \qquad (3)$$

BS then compares with the maximum error rate allowed (e_{max}). This value is also known as Quantum Bit Error Rate (QBER).

If $\mathbf{e} <= \mathbf{e}_{max}$ they accept the quantum transmission and proceeds to the next phase called Reconciliation.

Both BS and SS remove those bits which are publicly revealed from their index file(s).
If $\mathbf{e} > \mathbf{e}_{max}$ BS sends ABORT message to SS indicating the quantum transmission contains errors to a level where they cannot recover the key from the bits received. In this case, they seizes the session by terminating the program.

4. Our new developed protocol for wireless networks

Recall IEEE 802.1X offers an effective framework for authenticating, managing keys and controlling user traffic to protect large networks. It employs the Extensible Authentication Protocol (EAP) [11] to allow a wide variety of authentication mechanisms. 802.1X authentication process happen between three main elements. The user or the client that wants to be authenticated is known as Supplicant or Station (STA). The actual server doing the authentication is called Authentication Server (eg: RADIUS, DIAMETER). The Authenticator or the Access Point (AP) allows only the supplicants who are authorized by the authentication server to gain access to the network.
Figure 2 shows the RSN Association, IEEE 802.1X authentication and key establishment process. This assumes the pre-shared key is not used. In Figure 2, flows 1 to 6 illustrate the IEEE 802.11 association and authentication process. Once the IEEE 802.11 association is completed, the IEEE 802.1X authentication starts. This is shown by flows 7 to 13 in Figure 2. During this process "Supplicant" sends "Request Association" to "Authenticator". Authenticator responds with "Association Response" to indicate the supplicant system has associated with the switch. Supplicant then sends EAP-Start message to the Authenticator. This begins a series of message exchanges to authenticate the Supplicant. Having seen the link is active, Authenticator sends "EAP-Request/Identity" packet to Supplicant. The Supplicant sends an "EAP-Response/Identity" packet to the Authenticator, which is then passed on to the Authentication Server. The Authentication Server sends back a challenge to the Authenticator, such as with a token password system. The Authenticator unpacks this from IP and repackages it into EAPOL (EAP over LAN) and sends it to the Supplicant. Different authentication methods will vary this message and the total number of messages. The Supplicant responds to the challenge via the Authenticator, which passes the response onto the Authentication Server. The Authentication Server responds with a success message, if the Supplicant provides proper identity, which is then passed onto the supplicant. Authenticator then allows the Supplicant to access the network with restrictions based on attributes that came back from the Authentication Server. For example, the Authenticator might switch the Supplicant to a particular virtual LAN or install a set of firewall rules. At the end of this stage, the Supplicant and Authentication Server have generated a shared Pairwise Master Key (PMK). The Authentication Server then transmits PMK to the

Authenticator through a secure channel (e.g.: TLS). This PMK is used to derive Pairwise Transient Key (PTK) through an exchange of IEEE 802.1X EAPOL-Key frames, often called as 4-Way Handshake in the IEEE 802.11 standard. Once the 4-Way Handshake is completed, the group key handshake is initiated. It is used to generate and refresh the group key, which is shared between Authenticators (APs) and group of Supplicants. This key is used to securely exchange broadcast and multicast messages in the air.

In our current work, we paid special attention on the stage where mutual authentication employs in 802.11i networks. We take the advantage of EAP types such as EAP-TLS, EAP-TTLS which offer mutual authentication, to merge 802.11i networks with QKD. Our aim is to introduce quantum key transmission soon after the 802.1X authentication is completed. The proposed protocol is shown in figure 7.

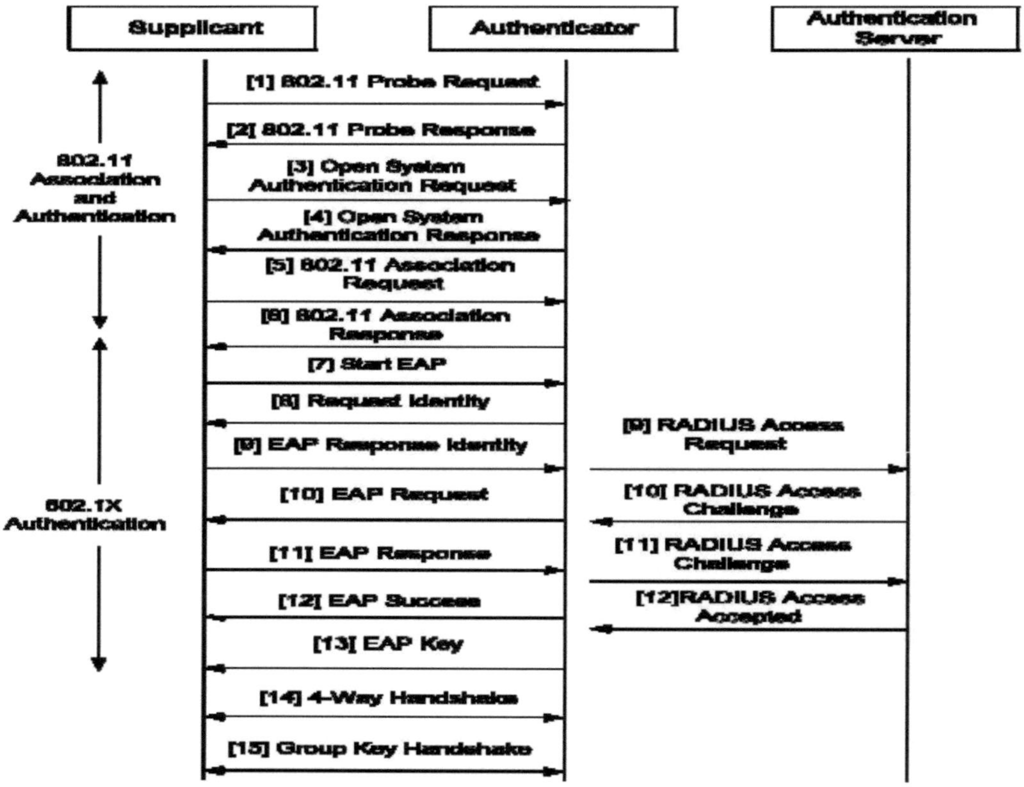

Fig. 7. RSN Association, IEEE 802.1X Authentication and Key Establishment process

At the end of the IEEE 802.1X authentication, both supplicant and authenticator hold PMK. As described in flow 13 of figure 7, the last message of 802.1X protocol is the EAPOL message giving the EAP Key from Authenticator to Supplicant. Since the two parties are mutually authenticated at this stage, we know this message is genuine. We use this message as the starting point of quantum transmission. By this way we can safely start the quantum key exchange as both the Supplicant and Authenticator are mutually authenticated.

As soon as the Supplicant receives the EAP Key message, the communication switches to quantum channel. Supplicant starts BB84 key distribution, by sending series of photons towards the Authenticator. Once the photon transmission finishes, the communication switches back to classical wireless channel. Afterwards they complete the BB84 quantum key exchange as described in previous section. At the end of this process, i.e. at flow 6, both Supplicant and Authenticator hold a common key, which we call as Quantum Key (Q-Key). We get this Q-Key as the PTK. For CCMP, PTK is 256 bits, while TKIP occupies 384 bits for PMK. Once PTK is available, we can retrieve the key hierarchy containing all other keys using the Pseudo Random Function (PRF) as previously described.
From PTK, we can derive KEK, KCK and TK. From KCK, MIC can be calculated. We use this MIC in our subsequent protocol messages to implement mutual authentication. The main reason of performing mutual authentication at this stage is that, BB84 is subjected to man-in-the-middle attacks [IEEE Standard for Local Metropolitan area networks]. Even though the Supplicant and Authenticator are mutually authenticated during the EAP authentication, an eavesdropper can fake a photon transmission towards Authenticator after seen the EAP Key message. At this stage, Supplicant performs XOR operation with the MIC and the first set of bits of equal length in PMK. We call this resulted MIC as Quantum MIC (Q-MIC).

$$Q\text{-}MIC = (MIC)\ XOR\ (\text{first bits of } PMK\text{, same length as } MIC) \quad (4)$$

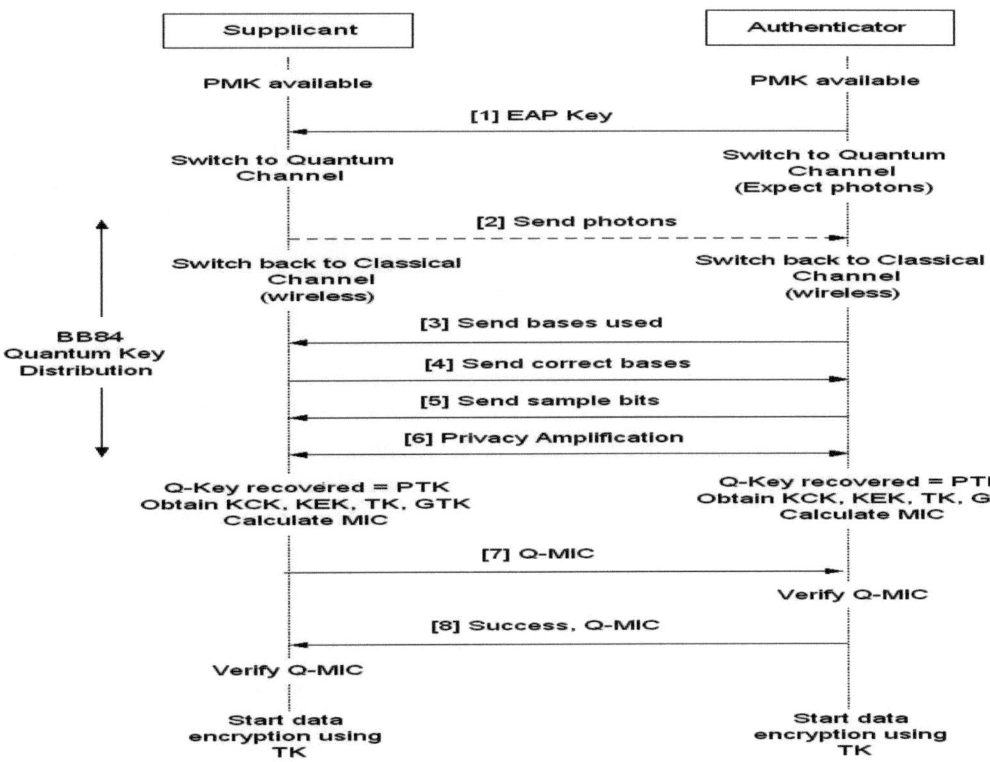

Fig. 8. Novel Proposed Protocol

The Supplicant sends the Q-MIC to Authenticator as shown in flow 7 of Figure 8. Upon receiving Q-MIC, Authenticator verifies the Q-MIC. Since the Authenticator is in possession of all the keys, it can calculate its own Q-MIC and compares with the one came from the Supplicant. If they match, the Supplicant is authenticated. The Authenticator then sends Success message along with Q-MIC to Supplicant as shown in flow 8 of Figure 8. Supplicant verifies the Q-MIC to authenticate the Authenticator, thus achieving the mutual authentication. From now on both parties use TK to encrypt the data and start secure communication and also the GTK for multicast applications.

With this protocol, we can eliminate the use of IEEE 802.11i 4-way handshake. It was shown that the message 1 of 4-way handshake is subject to DoS attacks. Intruders can flood message 1 to the supplicant after the 4-way handshake has completed, causing the system to fail.

5. Conclusion

In this paper we present the implementation of first two stages of an agent-oriented KQD for Wi-Fi. At present, the first two stages of B92 (or BB84) protocol has been implemented in C++ language on Linux platform. The KQD can handle multiuser as it benefits from an agent-oriented mechanism.

This caused a heavy overhead as the program consumes considerable amount of time during bit comparisons etc when doing file processing. To avoid this inefficiency, a STL list structure has been implemented to hold the index file data. Due to this modification, most of the computations and bit comparisons are done in-memory. This has resulted in improving the efficiency by about 60%.

With this set up, the program can be operated by setting different values to suit any requirements. One such parameter is the QBER, where this value is used to calculate the error rate of the quantum transmission. QBER of the quantum transmissions could be impacted by various issues (described earlier) causing it to vary per each transmission. Therefore by having the QBER as a configurable parameter, this software can be used to run even for simulation purposes by setting different values.

6. References

Bennett, C. H. and Brassard, G., Quantum Cryptography: Public Key Distribution and Coin Tossing, *Proceedings of IEEE International Conference on Computers Systems and Signal Processing*, Bangalore India, December 1984, pp 175-179..

Bennett et, C.H. , Bessette, Francois, BBrassard, Gilles, Salvail, Louis, and Smolin, Jojn., Experimental Quantum Cryptography, *J. Cryptology*, vol. 5, no. 1, 1992, pp. 3–28.

Bennett, Charles H. Quantum Cryptography: Uncertainty in the Service of Privacy, *Science 257*, 752-3 (1992) .

Bennett, C. H., Quantum cryptography using any two nonorthogonal states, *Phys. Rev. Lett.* 68, 3121-3124 (1992).

Buttler, W.T., Hughes, R.J., Kwiat, P.G., Luther, G.G., Morgan, G.L., Nordholt, J.E., Peterson, C.G., and Simmons, C.M., Free-space quantum key distribution, at Xiv: quant-ph/9801006 Vo1. 1, Jan. 1998.

Chip Elliott, Building the Quantum Network, BBN Technologies, *New Journal of Physics* 4 (2002) 46.1-46.12, http://www.iop.org/EJ/article/1367-2630/4/1/346/nj2146.html

Craiger, J. Philip 802.11, 802.1x, and wireless security, *GIAC security essentials certification Practical Asssignment*, version 1.4, ©SANS Institute 2002.

Connolly, P.J. "The trouble with 802.1x," InfoWorld. 8March 2002, URL: http://www.infoworld.com/articles/fe/xml/02/03/11/020311fe8021x.xml

Edeny, J., and Arbaugh, W.A., Real 802.11 Security-Wi-Fi protected access and 802.11i, *Addision-Wesle*, 2004.

Hasan, Jamshed , Security Issues of IEEE 802.16 (WiMAX), 2006. http://scissec.scis.ecu.edu.au/conference_proceedings/2006/aism/Hasan%20-%20Security%20Issues%20of%20IEEE%20802.16%20(WiMAX).pdf

Lenz, Moritz, High Bit Rate Quantum Key Distribution Systems 5 *Year Project Report* 2006/2007", Heriot Watt University, Feb. 16, 2007. http://moritz.faui2k3.org/

Lomonaco, Samuel J., A Quick Glance at Quantum Cryptography (1998), http://www.cs.umbc.edu/~lomonaco/lecturenotes/9811056.pdf

Huang, Xu, Wijesekera, Shirantha and Sharma, Dharmendra, Implementation of Quantum Key Distribution in

Wi- Fi (IEEE 802.11) Wireless Networks, *IEEE the 10th International Conference on Advanced Communication Technology*, Feb 17-20, 2008 Phoenix Park, Korea. Proceedings ISSN 1738-9445, ISBN 978-89-5519-135-6, Vol. II, p865.

Huang, Xu and Sharma, Dharmendra Quantum Key Distribution for Wi-Fi Network Security, *IEEE International Conference on Circuits & Systems for communications*, 26-28 May 2008, Shanghai, China. Accepted.

IEEE Standrad 802.11i, Part 11: Wireless LAM Medium Access Control (MAC) and Physical Layer (PHY) specifications - Amendment 6: Medium Access Control (MAC) Security Enhancements, July 2004

IEEE Standard for Local Metropolitan area networks, Part 16: Air Interface for Fixed Broadband Wireless Access Systems

Park, Don, The Lack of WiFi Security (part 1), Dec 07, 2006 http://www.windowsecurity.com/articles/WiFi-security-lack-Part1.html?prontversion.

Schwartz, E. Researchers crack new wireless security spec. *InfoWorld*. 14 February 2002, URL: http://www.infoworld.com/articies/hn/xml/02/02/14/020214hnwifispec.xml

Sen Xu, Manton Matthews, Chin-Tser Huang, Security Issues in Privacy Key Management Protocols of IEEE 802.16, *ACM SE'06*, March 10-12, 2006, Melbourne, Florida, USA, pp113-118.

Thi Mai Trang Nguyen, Mohamed Ali Sfaxi and Solange Ghernaouti-Hélie, 802.11i Encryption key distribution using quantum cryptography, *Journal of Networks*, Vol. 1, No.5, Sepetember/October 2006, pp.9-20

W. Wootters and W. Zurek, A single quantum cannot be cloned *Nature,* vol. 299, pp 802-803, 1982

14

A Framework for Business Process Simulation Based on Multi-Agent Cooperation

Wenan Tan[1,3], Wei Xu[2], Fujun Yang[3], Song Li[3] and Yi Du[1]
[1]*School of Computer and Information, Shanghai Second Polytechnic University, Pudong, Shanghai,*
[2]*College of Arts and Science, Jianghan University, Wuhan, Hubei,*
[3]*Institute of Computer Software and Theory, Zhejiang Normal University, Jinhua, Zhejiang, P.R. China*

1. Introduction

Most enterprise information systems can be viewed as discrete event systems (DES). Workflow is the computerized business processes. Workflow technology is one of key techniques in current enterprise information system. As the analyzing tool for workflow model, process simulation can support business process reengineering (BPR) effectively. Defects and bottlenecks of enterprise processes can be found through process simulation before the deployment of business management system. After the simulation, considerable reduction of cost is achieved as the result of improved workflow model.

Compared with other workflow research areas, process simulation is still underway. Discrete event simulation is the generic method used in process simulation.

Workflow model is the abstract representation of business processes. Some workflow definition languages have been developed, such as WPDL [1], FDL, and PSL [2]. PSL is the abbreviation of Process Specification Language which defines a neutral representation for manufacturing processes.

XPDL (XML Process Definition Language), which inherits WPDL, is a standard for "interface I" defined by the Workflow Management Coalition (WfMC). The WfMC has identified five functional interfaces to a workflow service as part of its standardization program. "Interface I" is specified to support Process Definition Import and Export, which includes a common meta-model for describing the process definition and an XML schema for the interchange of process definitions. The meta-model defines the objects and attributes contained within a process definition. One of key elements of XPDL is its extensibility to handle information used by a variety of different tools.

To support workflow simulation, we define some XML-based elements containing simulation information or facilitating simulation. These elements, such as <TimeDistribution> (containing information on the distribution of activity's duration, e.g. beta distribution, standard distribution), <Utility> (containing information to facilitate utility calculation, used to support activity execution) can be inserted into other XPDL-derived workflow model schema seamlessly.

In this paper, we propose a framework for business process simulation based on multi-agent cooperation. Social rationality of agent is introduced into the proposed framework. Adopting rationality as decision making strategies, flexible scheduling of activities is achieved. On the base of our newly defined XPDL elements, workflow model extended on XPDL can support simulation effectively. WfModel, a prototype application supporting workflow modeling, has been developed. JAXB (Java data binding framework proposed by SUN) and JGraph (an open source Java graphic library) are used to rapidly develop a visual workflow modeling application. The output of MfModel is a XML format compatible to XPDL.

The rest of the paper is organized as follows: Section 2 discusses the discrete event simulation and agent technology. Section 3 proposes a framework for process simulation based on multi-agent cooperation, and discusses the process agent simulation, decision-making strategies, and the multi-agent communication mechanism. A prototype system, namely WfEmulator, has developed to validate the proposed architecture. Section 5 gives a conclusion and discusses future works.

2. Related techniques

2.1 Discrete event simulation for workflow

Discrete event system is a discrete-state, event-driven system, that is, its state evolution depends entirely on the occurrence of asynchronous discrete events over time. Most systems in life are discrete event systems. Such as: traffic system, manufacturing systems.

Discrete event simulation (DES) is one way of building up models to observe the time based behaviors of an enterprise system. The range of application areas is extremely large and there are numerous examples of the use of simulation in service industries, manufacturing (batch and process) and office environments.

Inside the DES model will be a number of important concepts, namely entities:

- *Entities* are the tangible elements found in the real world.
- *Relations* link entities together, e.g. a part may be processed by a machine.
- *Simulation Executive* is responsible for controlling the time advance and executing discrete events.
- *Random Number Generator* helps to simulate different data coming into the simulation model.
- *Result and Statistics* provides the user a means of utilizing the simulation tool to gain meaningful analysis of the model.

The structure of DES is illustrated as figure 1.

Executive is responsible for ordering the events. The executive removes the first event from the list and executes the relevant model logic. Any new events that occur as a result are inserted on the list at the appropriate point. The cycle is then repeated. A central clock is used to keep track of time.

When DES is used in workflow simulation, activity instances are scheduled by execution. The executive will control the logical relationships between the activity instances and advance the clock to the new time. All the activity instances have to be scheduled by executive according to one rule, e.g. FIFO (first in first out), HPFS (high priority first serve). This mechanism is conflicting to the reality. Different departments in organization do not operate in the same manner. For example, in production department, most of activities are scheduled on time basically, sometimes on priority of work order. While in another department, some activities may be scheduled by waiting time (retail department). A DES-based simulation system has to alter its scheduling strategies whenever workflow model is changed. A new mechanism should be introduced to implement dynamic scheduling.

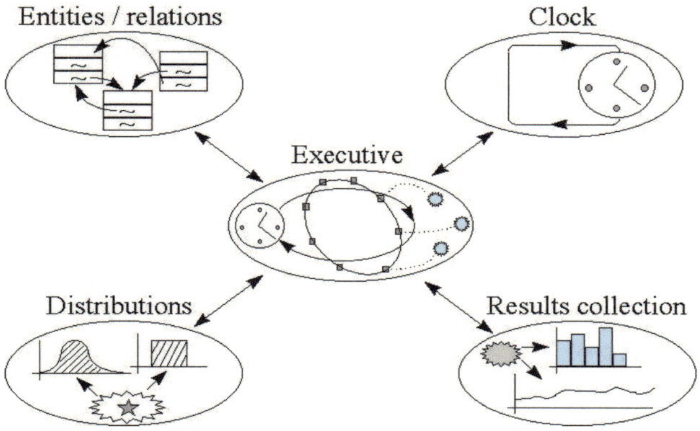

Fig. 1. Structure of discrete event simulation

2.2 Multi-agent theory and agent social rationality

Agent is a software entity which functions are proactive and autonomous in a particular environment. Multi-agent system (MAS) is a kind of intelligent system that interconnects separately developed agents, thus enabling the ensemble to function beyond the capabilities of any singular agent in the set-up [3].

There are two fundamental approaches used in modeling multi-agent systems: qualitative (some form of logic, e.g. BDI) and quantitative (e.g. Bayesian). Utility theory is a quantitative one to model MAS. Utility function is a mapping from states of the world to real numbers, indicating the agent's level of happiness with that state of the world. Agents in the competitive MAS potentially have different utility function.

In MAS, as to bounded resources and capability, agent does not stand alone. In accordance with behavior in reality, agent must take action based on certain strategy or rationality. Traditionally, designers have sought to make their agents rational so that they can "do the right thing". Rationality is how the rational decision is made among multiple strategies in the interaction of multi-agent [4].

The predominant theory of rational decision making in agents is that of the economic principle of maximizing the expected gain of actions [5]. Decision theoretic rationality dictates that the agent should choose an action which will maximize the expected utility of performing that action given the probability of reaching a desired state in the world and the desirability of that state [6]. The action that maximizes individual utility may conflict with overall interest (social utility), or redundant actions could be taken due to local utility preference. Hence rationality needs to be considered not only from the individual's point of view, but also from the social perspective. Jennings and Campos proposed the principle of social rationality [7] as follows:

If a member of a respective society can perform an action whose joint benefit is greater than its joint loss, then it may select that action.

Here, joint benefit is defined as the benefit provided to the individual plus the benefit afforded to society as a result of an action. Similarly, joint loss is the individual plus societal loss of performing an action. Social rationality can be expressed as follows:

$$W_i(a_j) = \lambda_i u_i(a_j) + \lambda_{soc} \sum_{k \in \{1-i\}} u_k^{'}(a_j) \qquad (1)$$

Where $U_i(a_j)$ is the individual utility of agent i when it takes an action a_j,λ_i is the weighting given to the individual utility of agent i; $\Sigma U_k'(a_j)$ is the sum of utilities of other agents in the system when action a_j is taken by agent i , λ_{soc} is the weighting given to the social utility part of the function.
At a coarse level, equation (1) can be rewritten as:

$$U(i,j)=k_1*selfUtility(ps)+k_2*publicUtility(pp). \qquad (2)$$

Where $U(i, j)$ is the utility of agent i when it takes action j; k_1, k_2 are the weighting given to individual utility and public utility respectively. *ps* and *pp* are the key influence parameters for individual utility function and public utility function, e.g. activity's duration, waiting time, priority. The values of k_1, k_2 can be altered to implement a wide range of decision-making strategies [8].
The proposal of social rationality is to ensure the proceeding of task planning when resource competition appears [9]. Social rationality can be used to guide an agent's decisions. In process simulation, when different activity instances could not share limited resources, competition appears. Thus agent social rationality can be introduced into process simulation to represent the decision making strategies of organizations/departments. Related organization will prefer the activity instances which maximize their predefined rationality utility functions.

3. Simulation framework based on multi-agent cooperation

3.1 Process simulation framework

Multi-agent technique is used to address the issues of complex controls and solutions through intelligent behaviors such as cooperation, competition, coordination in a set of autonomous agents under a dynamic distribution-oriented open environment [10]. These features of multi-agents make them suitable to represent the entities in the enterprise environment. Compared to the discrete event simulation, MAS is more natural to build a simulation framework for enterprise process model.
To achieve flexible simulation structure, we model workflow simulation structure as a MAS, in which agent adopts rational utility functions as its scheduling strategies.
The proposed simulation framework consists of Process agent, Sub-Process agent, Activity agent, Resource agent and Organization agent. Relational database is necessary to support data import and export in simulation process. The framework is illustrated as Figure 2.
Due to the complexity of reasoning, intentional agent can not react rapidly to the change, thus it is not suitable in our simulation system. We use a self-controllable thread to represent the weak notation of agent.
The core agent is process agent, in which maintains two lists: ready activity instance list and pre-running activity instance list. When all the former activities are completed, the instance is ready; when all the needed resources can be satisfied, the ready activity instance are pre-running, and awaiting activity agent. Process agent records the information of all activity agents, e.g. binding organization, utility value of running instance.
Activity instance is a plain object, which contains corresponding information of activity, such as activity's state, priority, utility value. Ready activity instance list and pre-running activity instance list store its reference.

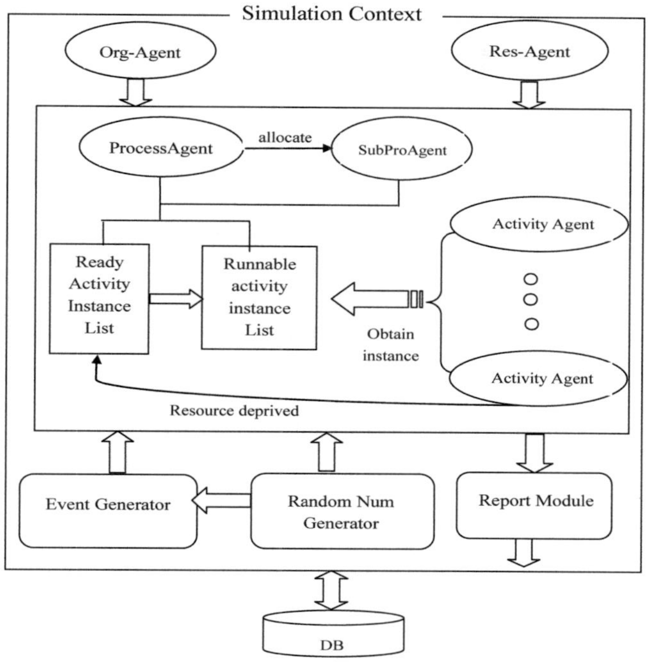

Fig. 2. Workflow simulation framework based on multi-agent cooperation

Activity agent is a continuously-running thread, which obtains activity instance from pre-running activity instance list, simulates the activity, and sends the result data to report module, meanwhile sends message to process agent to inform the end of simulation

Sub-Process agent, who shares the same ready activity instance list and pre-running activity instance list with process agent, is the agent addressing sub-process. If the type of activity instance is sub-Process (XPDL divides activity into three types: plain activity /Implementation, Route, and sub-Process/compound activity), instance will send to this agent. The inner structure of sub-Process agent is similar to process agent.

Resource agent and Organization agent act as infrastructure model in enterprise model. The two agents communicate with process agent and sub-Process agent, and monitor ready activity instance list and pre-running activity instance List. Organization agent understands all the organizational details and is responsible for the calculation of activity instance's utility.

Event Generator is used to create event message, which is sent to *Process agent* to activate simulation. More than one unrelated process could be defined in one process model, and different messages will activate different process.

Random Number Generator is used in the calculation of working time of activity instance. Different time distribution (e.g. Beta, Standard) depends on different random number generation algorithm.

Report Module is a common object collecting statistic information shown in dialog boxes. *Simulation Context* is the body of simulation, which is responsible to create all the agents used in simulation.

The main steps in simulation are shown in Figure 3. The core step, process agent simulation is as follows:

1. Process agent import the data stored in database, which is converted from workflow model formatted in XML.
2. Event Generator creates message to inform process agent that one simulation is activated. Process agent instantiate Start Activity, and put it into Ready Activity instance List. Resource agent and organization agent, which monitor the two lists, will be messaged and put the instance that can be satisfied resource requirements into Pre-running Activity instance List.
3. Activity agent obtain instance from Pre-running Activity instance List, register itself in process agent, and resources are occupied.
4. Activity agent runs simulation on the instance. Random Number Generator gives its working time according to the time distribution defined in the workflow model.
5. When simulation of the instance ends, statistic data are sent to report module, and process agent is informed.
6. Once received end message from an activity agent, process agent queries database to get subsequent activities of the instance, instantiate them and put them into Ready Activity instance List.
7. Event Generator create SIMULATION_START event continuously until predefined end-simulation- condition is satisfied.

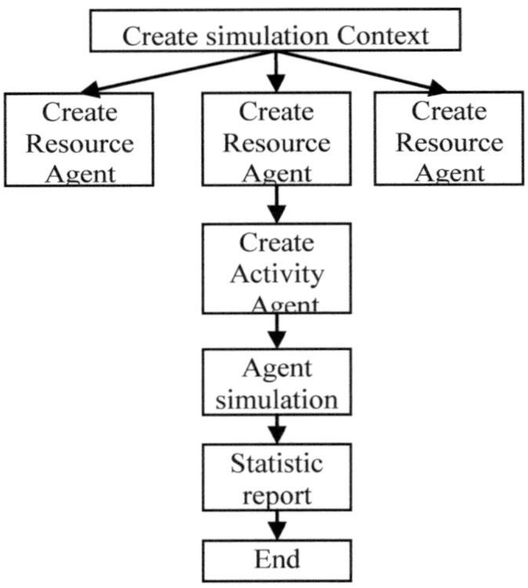

Fig. 3. Main procedure of simulation

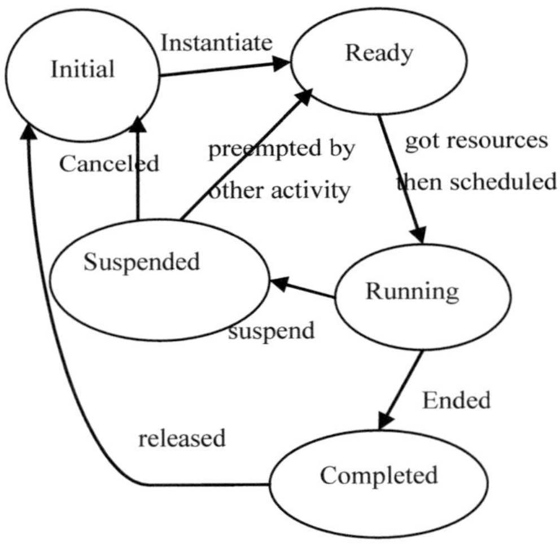

Fig. 4. State transition in process simulation

In the simulation framework, the states of agent include: Initial, ready, running, suspended, complete. States are explained as follows:

- *Initial* is the state after the activity is instantiated. As we mentioned before, activity instance is a plain object containing simulation information of the activity.
- *Ready* is the state that all the former activities of current instance are completed,
- *Running* is the state that an instance is in simulation by an activity agent. A running instance can be switched to ready when it is replaced by a higher-utility instance.
- *Suspended* state is used to support the pause operation during simulation procedure.
- *Complete* is the state that the activity instance finishes its simulation. The instance object will be disposed.

Figure 4 illustrates the relation between them. In workflow management system, there is an activating state (work-item put into working). While in activating, activity instance could not be suspended or completed. In simulation, what we care is the running features, and work-item does not work, therefore activating state is out of consideration.
When an activity instance is running, it can be replaced by another instance whose utility is higher. Then the instance's state will switch to ready, and the instance is put into Ready Activity instance List. Related information (e.g. running time, left working time) are updated in the instance. Process agent maintains the relation between activity agent and organization, as well as the utility value of running instance.
A running activity instance can be replaced, which is similar to the preemptive priority scheduling in computer operation system. When an activity instance (called A) is shifted to *Pre-running Activity instance List*, process agent check its utility value and performer, then query the registered activity agents. If the same performer is found (the two activity instance are performed by the same organization), the instance, which is running by the found activity agent (called B), may be replaced by instance A. The preemptive condition is that A's utility is larger then B's. For example, a production activity can be stopped to a new coming work order with higher priority (utility). Practical influence parameter may be activity's duration, cost, etc., but all these influence parameters are in utility function for different organizations.
In the framework, there is no global clock. Resources and roles are initiated, who maintain their own time. Here we explain the clock management in the framework in the following figure 5.

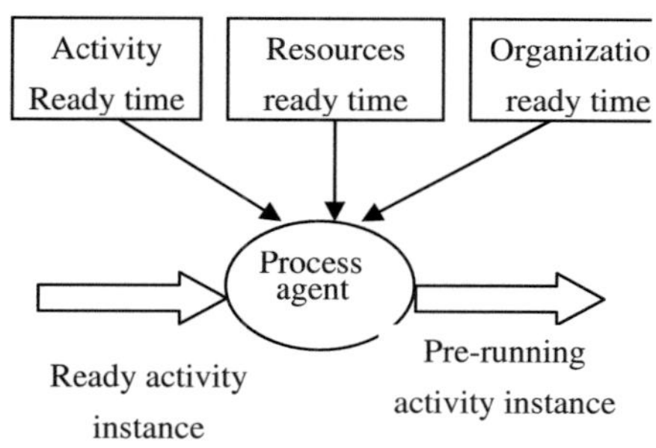

Fig. 5. Time management in the framework

When an activity instance is ready, that is, all the former activities are complete; *Activity Ready Time* is the latest complete time of these former activities. Before running ready activity, the required resources and role/role-set (in the organization) instances have to be free, so that, it can be allocated to the activity. Corresponding start time of resources and organization is the active time of the activity. When an activity is complete, resources and role instances are released, this time is the end time of service of resource agent and organization agent.

3.2 Decision making strategies

It's generally believed that different department has its own interest in an organization. Sometimes local interest of inner organization conflicts with overall interest of the organization. Therefore organization/ department can be described as a competitive agent, or a self-interested agent. Utility function defined on social rationality is an appropriate form to represent the decision making strategies of organization.

An agent self-interested neither means that it wants to harm other agent nor means it only cares about things that benefit it. In simulation, resource competition is in evitable because the bounded resource could not satisfy all the needs. Since a resource always belongs to an organization/ department, the allocation of resource is determined by the interest of the organization. When two or more activities competitive on one resource, the organization agent calculates the utility value based on certain index predefined in activity and k_1, k_2 defined in the organization. The parameters k_1, k_2, which represent the orientation of organization, are constants determined through the consultation between simulation engineers and customers, and modified in a few simulation procedures.

In our implemented system, *selfUtility* and *publicUtility* are defined in <ExtendedAttributes> in each <activity> element of workflow model. <ExtendedAttribute>, which contains few <name, value> pairs, is widely used in XPDL. The utility can be a constant, or a key factor affecting the activity radically, such as the number of a specific resource, working time of the activity. For example, in the repertory department, the cubage is bounded, and deliveries should be done in time to contain newly produced products. When the delivery of the day is already scheduled, the repertory department prefers delivery according to the cubage of the delivery products. As a result, delivery priority or delivery time is the key factor in *publicUtility*, and the cubage becomes the key factor in *selfUtility*. Combined with k_1, k_2 defined in repertory, the utility of delivery activity can be calculated.

Once there is no conflict between local interest and overall interest, social rationality of agent degenerates into a singular-parameter utility function. For example, in a sale department, employee's salary is affected by sale amount directly. Receiving more customers is the same preference of local interest and overall target. Thus activities can be scheduled based on working time or customer priority.

In our simulation framework, organization agent is responsible to calculate utility. When the two conflicting instances' utility values are equal, maximum waiting time first serve or random choice can be used to determine the choice.

The steps dealing with resource competition are as follows:

1. When activity instance is put into *Ready Activity instance List*, resource agent and organization agent are informed.
2. Organization agent checks all the ready activity instances in the list and finds out all instances whose requirements in role/organization can be met.
3. Finding out conflicting instances. Only activities need to be supported by same organization or resources, conflict will appear.
4. Comparing the utility values of conflicting instances. We need to choose the instance whose value is maximal.
5. Process agent tries to allocate resource agents to the activity instances in step 4.
6. Instances whose requirements in resource are put into *Pre-running Activity instance List*.

3.3 Multi-agent communication mechanism

Multi-Agent coordination mechanism is achieved through the communications and information sharing between the agents [11]. The main communication mechanism is the basis on collaboration, with the current means of communication blackboard system, which is an expansion system from the agenda systems and artificial intelligence systems of the expert system. The problem solving means of the coordination mechanism is the use of appropriate structural support distributed of the agenda. In the Multi-Agent workflow simulation system, we adopted the blackboard communication mechanism which is the provision of public work area for all agents to communicate with each other in the system. The agents can exchange information, data and knowledge with each other by the public blackboard communication mechanism. A message is written by an agent on the blackboard. The other agents can access the blackboard to read the message. When the message is the service that some agent wants, the agent should send a message to the writer, Meanwhile, a relationship message should be written to the blackboard to show the service used. An agent may access the blackboard at any time. The communication mechanism is complement by the service configuration message shown in Figure 6.

After an agent read a message from the blackboard, the agent core that is the will be activated by the message. The core is the main method or function of the call nested in coordinated inter-related tasks.

```
Struct Service{
Agent ID Source; //The service name of the source
                   agent;
Agent IP SourceIP;   //The service IP address of
                               the source agent;
Unsigned Servicetype; // Service type;
Cstring Servicename; // Service name;
Cstring Servicecontent; // Service content;
Cstring Servicepriority; // Service priority;
Cstring ServiceResource; // Service resource.
......
}
```

Fig. 6. Communication configuration message

Overall, the strengths of this approach are that the finally constructed methodology is highly attuned to system conditions and the agents in the Workflow system. The challenges are to construct the several blackboards, ensuring that a linkages accord to the local situation and that the interfaces of any pair of method fragments to be plugged together are compatible. Both of these can be facilitated by the use of software tools, the former with a process construction tool, both of which we have developed.

3.4 Prototype system –WfEmulator

To validate our framework, a prototype system, WfEmulator, has been designed and developed, which is written in Java. Workflow model generated by WfModel can be simulated in our prototype application. The architecture of prototype system is shown in Figure 7.

In the architecture, Wfemulator is mainly composed of four parties: *User Interface, Process Center, Wfmodel Center,* and *Simulation Engine. Process Center* and *Simulation Engine* form the core of the simulation system.

- *User Interface:* the module shows the Tools Bar and Menu Bar to users, The Tools bar includes many modeling figures, chars and so on to model a working follow of a system. The Menu Bar includes load action, save action, operation action and system setting, and so on.

- *Process Center:* the module is the operation module of the system. Process Agent is the defined many current process rules. When a working following is defined, the Process Agent should creative the relevant relations for the every operation of the working following. Resource Agent manages all of the resource of the system, such as resource assignment, resource statistics, and resource effective use analysis. Activity Agent is created by the sup-process agent. An activity takes charge in one activity from the beginning to the end of the activity.
- *Wfmodel Center:* simulation configuration is the initialization of the simulation job. There are many ex-defined working following models on different operation process in various enterprises. Initially, users are either allowed to open existent working following model or define a new one and save it in the model database.

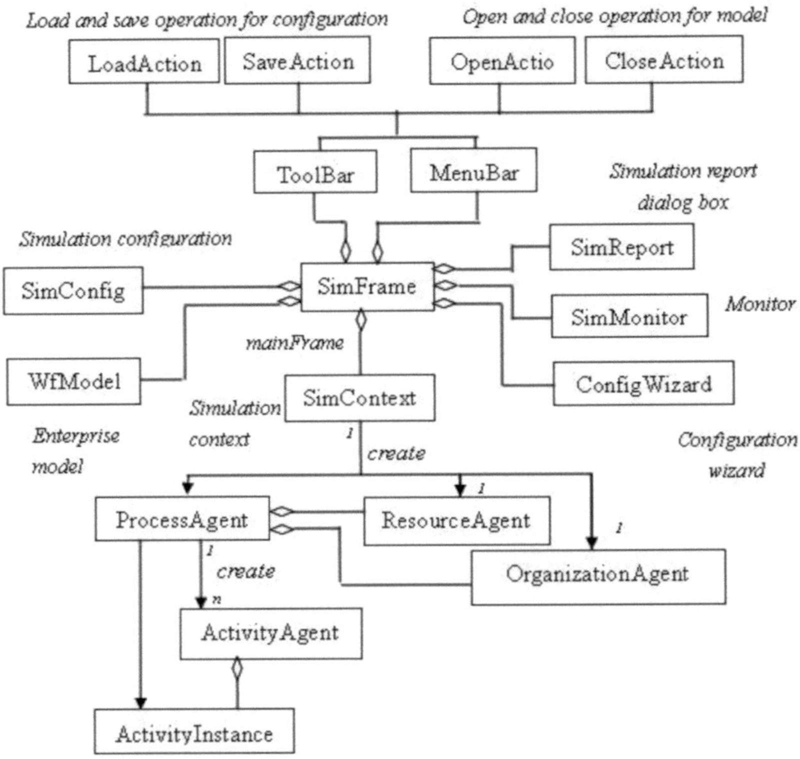

Fig. 7. Architecture of Wfemulator

- *Simulation Engine:* the module is the control center of the system. Many arithmetic, schedule rules, and analysis means are defined in the module which drives the whole of the operation of the simulation process. Simulation Report shows the simulation result and advice to the users. Simulation Monitor cooperates with the operations and communication of the different agents.

Workflow model used in our prototype system is generated by WfModel, which generates a XPDL-compatible model in XML format. Simulation configuration is an XML file containing information on simulation, e.g. halt condition, resource instantiation, activity agent number.

4. Conclusion and future works

We analyze discrete event simulation for workflow, and propose a framework for process simulation based on multi-agent to support flexible activity scheduling. Social rationality of agent is used to represent the utility function as the decision making strategies of organization. Physical elements such as cubage, cost can be imported to schedule activity instances, which makes simulation running in a more flexible and realistic manner. Currently, we have proposed a framework consisting of socially rational agent. If the agent has the ability to learn from previous decision making successes and failures, there is the potential that it could converge towards finding the right balance, depending on the situation, between individual and social needs. Hence a knowledge mechanism can be imported into our simulation framework to accelerate decision making when similar situation appears again.

Furthermore, due to the autonomy of agent, the number of activity agent may be varied and the activities can be distributed to a number of computers, according to the computational resources. Multiple sub-process simulations can run synchronously to hasten complex process simulation. Thus a distributed simulation environment becomes a potential alternative. JNDI and RMI can be used to help the communication among agents in this distributed simulation system.

5. Acknowledgment

This paper was supported by the National Natural Science Foundation of China under Grant No. 60874120 the Zhejiang provincial Natural Science Foundation of China (Grant No. Y106039), and the Science Foundation of Nanjing University of Aeronautics and Astronautics (Grant No.S0777-042).

6. References

[1] Workflow Process Definition Interface— XML Process Definition Language. Workflow Management Coalition Document Number WFMC-TC-1025

[2] Gruninger M., Menzel C.: The Process Specification Language. Principles and Applications, AI Magazine, 24(2003) 63-74

[3] Kary F., Timo A.R., Mikko K., Jan H.: Agent-based model for managing composite product information. Computers in Industry, 57 (2006) 72–81

[4] Russell S.: Rationality and intelligence. Artificial Intelligence, 94 (1997) 55-57

[5] J. Doyle.: Rationality and its role in reasoning. Computational Intelligence, 8 (1992) 376-409

[6] Hogg L.M., Jennings N.R.: Social rational agents- some preliminary Thoughts. Proc. of the 2nd Workshop on Practical Reasoning and Rationality, UK, Manchester, (1997) 160-162

[7] Jennings N.R., Campos J.: Toward a social level characterization of socially responsible Agent, Proc. IEEE Software Eng., 144 (1997) 11-25

[8] Hogg L., Jennings N.R.: Variable Sociability in Agent-Based Decision Making. Proc. of 6th Int. Workshop on Agent Theories Architectures and Languages (ATAL-99), (1999) 305-318

[9] Chen X.Y., Shi C.Y.: Research on Socially Rationality of agent. Journal of Software, 12(12) (2001) 1825-1829
[10] John R., Cathal H.: Process modeling for simulation. Computers in Industry, 57(2006), 437–450
[11] Tan W., Fan Y.: Dynamic workflow model fragmentation for distributed execution. Computers in Industry, 58, (2007) 381-391.

15

Agent Oriented Engineering and Methodologies with Application to Production, Economical and Social Systems

Baltazár Frankovič, Than Tung Dang, Tomáš Kasanický,
Viktor Oravec and Ivana Budinská
Institute of Informatics SAS
Slovakia

1. Introduction

Multi-agent systems paradigm and technologies are known for couple of years. They are applied in real word in many applications, where characteristic features of multi-agent systems (MAS) are useful and can help to handle, e.g. control and coordination problems. Possibilities to use MAS in many different applications are huge. This chapter features some possible alternatives, where and how MAS can be applied and a problem of agents' coalitions creation. The application field of this approach may be a variety and very wide. It is applicable in resolving planning problems in manufacturing (Sandholm, 1999), (Odubyi, 1997). Another applicable field is in creating of virtual and network enterprises (Horvath, 2006) and in marketing for enterprises, where to maximize own profit each manager (considered as one agent) can try to cooperate with another ones (Cantamessa, 2001), (Wellman, 1993). Coalition in this case may have another effect to eliminate execution of agents not belonging to the same coalition. Another problem belongs to the coalition creation for large scale multi-agent systems that adress problem of shceduling and planing in huge manufacturing systems and network enterprises. MAS can be used for modelling and managing social systems and virtual societies, as it is described in this chapter. One of new approaches to the MAS research is inspired by similarity between artificial immune systems and multi-agent systems. A multi-agent control system inspired by immune systems is described by the end of the chapter.

2. Agents and multi-agent systems approach to the modelling, management, and control of production systems.

The problem of scheduling in production process has been discussed in many recent papers. The scheduling process can be static (the schedule is constructed before execution) or dynamic (sometime, a decision has to be made immediately or for a predetermined time), depending on the system requirements. It is clear that the optimal situation in when there is enough time to search an appropriate plan so that all possible plans can be explored. In practice, mostly time is limited and so it is necessary to search for any solution for a shor time. Therefore, all requirements might not be fulfilled and, in some cases, we must content with a plan that is far from the optimal one.

The creation of coalition and coalition structure of agents is one of possible technical way for formulation agents' cooperation to improve plan quality. A coalition of agents essentially may be considered in the framework of multi-agent-system (MAS) as a group of such agents, which are willing to cooperate with all another members in this group and their common cooperative activities aim to reach the optimum of the given criteria, but on other hand, methods for cooperation are collected by these members via negotiation among themselves and they depend on concrete situations. The optimum, which the members in coalition try to reach, does not have to be always a global optimal solution, but in most cases only is optimal from any point of view (criterion) or a Nash optimal solution (Wooldrige, 1996), (Sandholm, 1999).

There exists a lot of possible ways to search for and create an optimal coalition – mainly via negotiation, or sequentially search all possible variants - and several of potential methods that we shall use for finding the solution of such formulated problem are as for example: an application of automata theory, game theory, genetic algorithms or another.

Finding a solution for the above-introduced problem has been the subject of many publications, which tried to obtain a feasible way to resolve a general problem of creating coalition (Dang, 2002), (Wooldrige, 1996), (Sandholm, 1999).

2.1 Coalition formation based on dynamic programming approach

Let $\{A_1,\ldots,A_n\}$ be a set of n agents, and I denote a set of index, I ={1,..,n}. For simplicities we shall use a note I and a mark $K \subseteq I$ denotes a subset created by the agents, whose index belongs to a set K. Let denote $\Re_+^s$ a s-dimensional set of nonnegative real values, which is used to assess an agent's execution. Each option in this set represents one parameter of agent's execution, e.g. cost, payoff, effectiveness, etc.

Definition 1: An agent's value is a function mapping from a set of all possible results that the agent can achieve (independently or via cooperation) to $\Re_+^s$.

Further notations are: for $\forall\ i \in I, K \subseteq I$,

- q_i^* denotes a value if the agent A_i works independently,
- q_i^K denotes a value if the agent A_i joins coalition K ,
- f_i denotes an expected value of the agent A_i .

f_i = s if the agent A_i works independently, or

= q_i^K if the agent A_i joins the coalition K .

- F_K denotes a value of a set of agents $K \subseteq I$ and is defined as:

$$F_K = \sum_{i \in K} c_i * f_i \,.$$

where $\forall i \in K$, c_i is a parameter, which is used to express the priority of the agent A_i in this society (since some agents might be more important than other ones depending on concrete applications, therefore these parameters might be various) and $\sum_{i=1}^{k} c_i = const$.

Generally, all the agents have the same priority; therefore, the function F_K can be defined as:

$$F_K = \sum_{i \in K} f_i \quad (1)$$

In this case $\forall i \in [1,n]$, $c_i = 1$.

In practice, each agent can know what it will get after joining any coalition until the discussion with other ones (about what every member within this coalition has to do regarding their possibilities, aims and willingness, and consequently which results each member can achieve) within this coalition finishes. As a result, in order to know all the values q_i^K the agents need another phase to negotiate with other ones about each possible coalition. It is clear that this process requires very exhausted work. To simplify let assume that these values are defined in advance or taken from historic database. Certainly, the more these values are defined, the larger is a probability to achieve the optimal solution. If the agents' society is too large, and that results an agent cannot explore every possible coalition, in such case all the values $q_i^K |_{i \in K}$, where the coalition K has not been explored, are defined to be zero. In the next part we will show some important definitions and characteristics of the agents' coalition.

General definitions and properties of agents' coalitions

Initially, let consider a following important property of the optimal coalition: for each set $K \subseteq I$ is valid that the set K is an optimal coalition if every experiment trying to separate the set K to a set of smaller coalitions will decrease a value F_K (defined by an equation (1)). This property is derived from the assumption, in which the agents are always willing to remain in the large coalition, if they know that breaking this one to smaller sets will bring the whole party worse results.

Definition 2: A set $K \subseteq I$ is an optimal coalition if

$$\sum_{i \in K} f_i \geq \sum_{K_j} \sum_{i \in K_j} f_i , \quad (2)$$

where $K = \bigcup_j K_j$.

Every agent, in fact, is an optimal coalition itself, because it is impossible to divide it to smaller subsets. From definition 1 the following theorem is deduced.

Theorem 1: Let be any structure of a set *I* for which the value F_I achieves maximum, then, such structure must be only composed from the optimal coalitions.

Proof: Let a set *I* be divided to *m* subsets like coalitions.

$$\mathrm{I} = \bigcup_{j=1}^{m} K_j \text{, and } \forall i \neq j \in [1,m] \text{ is valid } K_i \cap K_j = \{\varnothing\}.$$

If any subset $K_{i \in [1,m]}$ is not an optimal coalition, then, resulting from the definition 1: here must exist such a structure for organization a set K_i, $K_i = \bigcup_r K_r^i$, in which a value F_{K_i} is bigger than an actual value. Afterwards a structure composed as s={ $\bigcup_{j=1, j \neq i}^{m} K_j$ }$\bigcup_r K_r^i$ will have a bigger value than the actual one. Confrontation.

Definition 3: Let S_i denote a set of coalitions, which can bring the agent A_i at least the same or better results than when it works independently.

$$S_i = \{\mathrm{K} \subseteq \mathrm{I} \mid q_i^K \geq q_i^*\} \quad (3)$$

Definition 4: Let S_K denote a set of coalitions, which can bring at least the same or better results for all agents belonging to a set K than when they work independently.

$$S_K = \{Ko \subseteq I \mid \forall\, i \in K,\ q_i^{Ko} \geq q_i^*\} \tag{4}$$

Example 2: In the previous example, if a set $K = \{1,2\}$, then, $S_{\{1,2\}} = \{1,2,3\}$, etc.
From these definitions the following results are derived:
Lemma 1:

1. If $K_1 \subset K_2$, then, $S_{K_1} \supset S_{K_2}$.
2. $S_{K_1 \cup K_2} \subset S_{K_1} \cap S_{K_2}$.
3. $S_{K_1} \cap S_{K_2} \subset S_{K_1 \cap K_2}$.

Proof: see in (Dang, 2002)
Consequences 1:

1. $S_{K_1 \cup K_2} \subset S_{K_1 \cap K_2}$
2. $S_{K_1 \cup .. \cup K_m} \subset S_{K_1} \cap \ldots \cap S_{K_m}$,

where $K_1, \ldots, K_m \subseteq I$.

Certainly, we want to attempt to implement all possible features of the real agent's behavior into our model, however, a mathematical model cannot copy exactly and completely agent's behavior, but one property has to be considered and it is also very often happened in practice. It is that, every agent is willing to join coalition with other ones if and only if this coalition brings it at least the same or better results than when it works independently. Furthermore, a coalition might exist if all the agents creating this one are willing to join.
Assumption 1: the agent A_i joins coalition $K \Leftrightarrow (q_i^K \geq q_i^*)$.
Assumption 2: a set $K \subseteq I$ is an *acceptable coalition* $\Leftrightarrow \forall i \in K : (q_i^K \geq q_i^*)$
With these assumptions it is possible to deduce a following theorem.
Theorem 2: A set $K \subseteq I$ is an *acceptable coalition* (does not have to be optimal) if and only if

$$K \in \bigcap_{i \in K} S_i \tag{5}$$

Proof:

1. If K is an *acceptable coalition*, it means $\forall\ i \in K$ it is valid: $q_i^K \geq q_i^*$. Afterwards, $K \in S_i$ for $\forall\ i \in K$. A result from this is $K \in \{\bigcap_{i \in K} S_i\}$.
2. If $K \in \bigcap_{i \in K} S_i$, it means that the coalition K can bring at least the same or better results for all the agents belonging to this coalition $\Rightarrow$ a set K can be an *acceptable coalition* (does not have to be optimal).

Consequence 2: If $\bigcap_{\alpha_i \in I, i=1,..,m} S_{\alpha_i} = \{\varnothing\}$, then these agents $A_{\alpha_1}, \ldots, A_{\alpha_m}$ cannot be in the same acceptable coalition.
The proof is derived directly from the theorem 2.
Example 3: In the previous example, since $S_1 \cap S_2 \cap S_3 = \{1,2,3\}$, therefore, the set {1,2,3} is a unique possible coalition that all the agents are willing to join.

The main problem addressed here is: to find such a structure of a set I to maximize a function F_I defined by (1). Another way to say: we want to find such a structure $I=\bigcup_{i=1}^{m} K_i$, where $\forall$ i, j $\in$ [1,m] $K_i \cap K_j = \{\emptyset\}$ and $F_I = \sum_{i=1}^{n} f_i$ =max.

To resolve completely this task and to find a maximal value of a function F_I it is necessary to search the whole space of all possible structures of a set I. The complex searching of all possible structures of a set I can be executed in a variety ways, but a complexity of those approaches is the same for every method, because every variant have to be examined and for arbitrary n the problem is known to be NP-hard, thus, it is necessary to turn to heuristic methods to search, which are computationally efficient but which might guarantee only sub-optimal solutions from any point of view, for example: *tabu search, branch and bound, genetic algorithms*, etc.. Generally, a quality of those methods strongly depends on how long the process has repeated and a quality of an initial choice. On the other hand, each agent presents one independent object with own goals and intelligence, and consequently the agent's execution (or choice) will aim to the best results for the agent; therefore, naturally each agent might poll such coalitions, in which its benefit is the best from its point of view.

Furthermore, next property of such formulated problem that is easy to verify is that the mentioned problem might be resolved by a *recursive approach*, sequentially for cases with 1 to n agents, where each new agent will try to join any formulated coalition, afterwards a result of the criterion function F_I will be compared with the best one so far. This approach can guarantee the complex searching of the whole space and the final solution certainly will be the globally optimal one. But, as we have mentioned above, agents' choices might influence the searching process a lot, because on a basis of these choices lots of coalitions might not be necessary to be examined and searching space could be reduced.

A general dynamic programming scheme

For a set $K \subseteq I$ it is assumed: a set K can be decomposed to an amount of independent nonempty subsets. $K = \bigcup_{j=1,..,m} K_j$, where, $\forall$ i, j $\in$ [1,m], $K_i \cap K_j = \{\emptyset\}$. Certainly $m \leq |K|$.

Let us define a function Q_K as follows:

$$Q_K = \arg\max_{\{K_j\}} \{\sum_{K_j} \sum_{i \in K_j} f_i\} \qquad (6)$$

Or by other words, Q_K is a maximal sum of all agents' expected values, which are creating the set K, among all possible structures of the set K.

Furthermore, by comparison an equation (1) and (6) it is possible to derive that $Q_K = \max\{F_K\}$ for $\forall\ K \subseteq I$. Therefore, the main task mentioned in the previous section might be transformed to the task to find a value Q_I and such a structure, which achieves this value.

Because each agent has only two alternatives: to work alone or to join any coalition. From this reason we shall present a general dynamic programming method for resolving problem Q_I. We consider n stages, where in each stage one agent is added and after n-th stage the whole problem will be resolved. For j=1,..,n-1 we denote I_j = {1,..,j}, where every set I_j means we will search an optimal solution (an optimal structure) for j agents {A_1,…, A_j}, which guarantees a maximal value F_{I_j} (= Q_{I_j}). Since each set I_j can be obtained by adding the agent A_j to the set I_{j-1}, we might have the following recursive equation:

$$Q_{I_j} = \arg\max_{K}\{(Q_{I_{j-1}} + q_j^*), (Q_{I_{j-1}\setminus K} + Q_{K\cup j})\} \tag{7}$$

Where $K \subseteq I_{j-1}$ and j={1,..,n-1}, $I_0 = \{\varnothing\}$.
Further, for each j={1,..,n-1}, if we denote

$$h_j = \arg\max_{K\subseteq I_{j-1}}\{Q_{I_{j-1}\setminus K} + Q_{K\cup j}\} \tag{8}$$

The equation (7) could be rewritten as:

$$Q_{I_j} = \max\{(Q_{I_{j-1}} + q_j^*), h_j\} \tag{9}$$

On the basis of these recursive equations we can, in principle, find an optimal solution for Q_I by the following backward scheme:

- Sub-problem in stage n: Search a value h_n in (8) by examining all possible coalitions that the agent A_n is willing to join with using theorem 2 and consequence 2. After that, replace them to (9) to obtain a value Q_I.
- Sub-problem in stage n-1: Analogously as above: it is necessary to examine those coalitions that the agent A_{n-1} is willing to join and do not involve the agent A_n, etc.
- Sub-problem in stage 1: $Q_{I_1} = q_1^*$.

Now we get:
Theorem 3: By solving sub-problem in n stages we will obtain the optimal structure for the given set I and a maximal value of F_I.
Proof: (outline) Since by adding an agent A_n to a set I_{n-1} we obtain the set I, and from these equations (7), (8) it is easy to verify that calculating of a value Q_I can be made from the known values in the previous stages from the first to (n-1), otherwise, these values have been calculated for optimal cases, in which a structure of each subset was optimal. Consequently, a value Q_I from an equation (9) has to be optimal one.
From an equation (8) it is possible to contend that the main complication in the general method presented above is that the process of calculating a function $h_{j\in[1,..,n-1]}$ is huge and complicated, essentially with large values of n. Because, theoretically, the new added agent is able to join every coalition (if there are $j_{j=1,..,n-1}$ agents in the previous set, then, the new $j+1$ agent could join one of 2^j possible coalitions), therefore dimensions of this problem will grow with an exponential speed when n is increased.
To improve the previous approach to computable dimensions, *the first step* that we need to do is to reduce an amount of coalitions that the new added agent can join. To do it, it is necessary to use agents' intelligence and their attributes. Because each agent can own different mechanisms to poll coalitions that it is willing to join. *The second step* is: applying theorem 2 and consequent 2 to remove coalitions that the new added agent cannot join and leave only the *acceptable coalitions,* which are accepted by all the agents creating these ones. Afterward, an equation (8) could be resolvable. Certainly, the results of the first step will hardly depend on each agent's choices even though, these choices might be executed by different ways and they also might be dependent on other agents' decisions too. In the next section we will discuss this problem.
Creating the optimal structure by sequential conceding.
As we have mentioned above, reducing an amount of potential coalitions that the new added agent could join is a necessary thing, which enables to overcome huge complexities of

an equation (8). We assume that, these expected values ($q_{i\in I}^{K\subseteq I}$), which each agent is able to achieve by joining coalition with another ones, are random and known for all the agents creating this coalition. Moreover, any continue function does not exist, which is able to approximate exactly these values (because if it exists, this problem could be solved by different ways as for example: searching global maximum or minimum of any multi-parameters' function). Furthermore, for simplicities we will omit a negotiation part to achieve these values $q_{i\in I}^{K\subseteq I}$ and assume that they are known.

The first step mentioned above: to reduce an amount of coalitions that the new added agent could join, might be made by the following principle:

Because for each agent, a coalition, in which its expected value is maximal, it will have the highest priority in its choice. On other hand, with such choice of each agent, they will with a very high probability never reach an optimal structure. Therefore, each agent will have to concede, however, a new question: which agent has to concede and how much is a further complicated problem, because the agent could prefer one coalition before another from its criteria or on the basis of its deliberations it might consider its choices as the best for its execution. We shall propose three methods, in which the agents are assumed to have the same aim to achieve the global optimal executions of the whole agents' society.

Before that, we have to define some important specifications:

Definition 5: for each agent $i \in I$, let $v_i^0 = \max_{K\subseteq I}\{q_i^K\}$ be a maximal expected value that the agent A_i can receive and for $\forall 0 < \alpha \le v_i^0$ let $\Omega_\alpha^i = \{K \subseteq I \mid q_i^K \ge \alpha\}$ be a set of coalitions in which the expected value for the agent A_i is more or equal than α.

After these preparations we can now formulate our algorithms:

First, each agent states its aim equal a maximal value that it can achieve in all coalitions and collects only these coalitions in which its expected value is more or equal this value. After that, the agents try together to find a solution among these sets, if they cannot find any solution, all the agents sequentially have to concede by decreasing its aim. In an algorithm 1, all the agents sequentially decrease their aim but with the same ratio (ratio between a new aim and present one), in an algorithm 2, a difference between a new aim and the present one is the same for every agent. In an algorithm 3, we consider that in each turn only one agent decreases its aim and it always collects such coalitions, in which its expected value is maximal between remained ones.

An algorithm 1: (based on an *equal ratio* of conceding)

Step 1:

a. $\forall\ i \in I$ Choose coefficient c=1 and $\alpha_i = c * v_i^0$.

b. $\forall\ i \in I$ Search a set $\Omega_{\alpha_i}^i$.

Step 2:

a. Using a general dynamic programming scheme presented above to search a sub-optimal solution among sets $\Omega_{\alpha_i}^i$, $i \in I$.

b. If a solution is not found, decrease a coefficient c and repeat a step 1.

c. If any solution is found, this process is stopped.

To effectively resolve a step 1.b, at first each agent sorts out all possible coalitions accordingly a value q_i^K, $K \subseteq I$ (since each agent could join 2^{n-1} possible coalitions, then, this procedure has a complexity $\cong O(2^{n-1} * (n-1) * \log 2)$). Afterwards, in every time when

the coefficient c is decreased, each agent can choose immediately from its sorted coalitions feasible ones, which satisfy a condition for creating a set Ω^i_α, $\forall\ i \in I$. To solve a step 2.a we could apply the approach based on a dynamic programming scheme presented above.
Similarly, we shall propose further algorithm based on equal regressions of each agent in a searching process.

An algorithm 2: (based on an equal regression of conceding)

Step 1:

a. $\forall\ i \in I$ Choose coefficient c=0 and $\alpha_i = v_i^0 - c$.

b. $\forall\ i \in I$ Search a set $\Omega^i_{\alpha_i}$.

Step 2:

a. Search a sub-optimal solution among sets $\Omega^i_{\alpha_i}$, $i \in I$.

b. If a solution is not found, increase a coefficient c and repeat a step 1.

c. If any solution is found, this process is stopped.

Differences between these both algorithms are not very significant; the results obtained by applying them depend on values q_i^K, for example: when values q_i^K are significantly different (a value var$(q_i^K)_{K\subseteq I}$ is high) for every $i \in I$, then, the first algorithm could achieve better results than the second one, but in another case when these values are nearly similar, the results could be contrary. To improve these algorithms, we shall present the third one, which is modified from the previous methods and differs from them in such point that in each turn only one agent tries to decrease its aim and how much this agent decreases, it depends on its decision. Certainly, if each agent chooses a different way to decide how much it wants to concede, then, this process might be very interesting and immediately occur lots of problems related to agent's decision, negotiation, selecting agent to concede, etc.

In the next method, each agent sequentially will modify its aim in turn and we assume that each will choose immediately the best coalitions from a set of the remained ones. For the next algorithm we define some notations:

Let $\Psi_i = \{\phi_i^j\}_{j=1}^{\lambda_i}$ be a sorted set of values q_i^K for the agent A_i (from top to down). λ_i is a sum of possible coalitions that the agent A_i could join - $\max(\lambda_i) = 2^{n-1}$. Certainly it is valid: $\forall i \in I, \phi_i^1 = v_i^0$. Instead of coefficient c we will use only α_i for simplicity.

After preparations we can present the following algorithm:

An algorithm 3: (modified from *the algorithm 1 and* 2)

Step 1:

a. $\forall\ i \in I$ Choose coefficient $\alpha_i = \phi_i^1 = v_i^0$.

b. $\forall\ i \in I$ Search a set $\Omega^i_{\alpha_i}$.

Step 2:

$i = 1$.

a. Search a sub-optimal solution among sets $\Omega^j_{\alpha_j}$, for all $j \in I$.

b. If a solution is not found,

   1. decrease a coefficient α_i to: $\alpha_i = \max\{\phi_i^k \mid \phi_i^k < \alpha_i\}$,

   2. update a set $\Omega^i_{\alpha_i}$,

3. repeat a step 2.a,
4. if $i < n$, then $i = i + 1$, else $i = 1$.

c. If any solution is found, this process is stopped.

Comparison between these algorithms is implemented in an illustrate example with 11 agents and shown in following graphs and a number of steps of the searching process to achieve the final solution is depicted in a table 1.

In these experiments we have bounded that each value q_i^K lies in an interval [0,100] and is randomly generated. From the obtained results it is possible to conclude that the algorithm presented above have achieved average very good results (average 95 percent of the optimal results, in some cases they even achieved the optimal results) and for a short time (see table 2). The difference between these algorithms is not so significant, in some examples one algorithm could achieve better results than another ones, but both algorithms 1 and 2 are more appropriate for parallel working, since after each round each agent could immediately calculate its value α_i and does not have to wait until its turn. On the other hand, for an arbitrary set of values $\{q_i^K\}$, the algorithm 3 generally produced less complicated sets $\Omega_{\alpha_i}^i |_{i=1,..,n}$ than both first ones, since after each turn only a small number of possible coalitions is added, not massively as in the algorithms 1 and 2. Moreover, the algorithm 3 could be extended and modified for the case when each agent should choose a different way to calculate its value α_i. In a graph (Fig. 1), the results of complex searching always have the maximal values. Another problem that may appear in this graph is that in several points is only one pattern; it means more results have the same value in this point.

In the Table 1 is shown how many steps the searching program has repeated until the final result is found. These values may be used also to point to a time-complexity of each method to achieve the final results. For a genetic algorithm we fixed that the program will finish after certain number of steps.

Order	Complex searching	GA	A1	A2	A3
1	859868	8500	134	173	238
2	900848	8500	112	113	189
3	1025352	8500	359	190	522
4	839476	8500	76	47	135
5	864455	8500	144	125	228
6	904389	8000	86	77	154
7	926803	8000	57	36	89
8	865845	8000	12	24	20
9	886832	8000	164	103	287
10	1112554	8000	152	168	260

Table 1. A case with 11 agents - complexity for searching max(F_I)

The experiment has been repeated with more agents and from the obtained results we can see that: with a small number of agents (up to 8 agents) the complex searching approach can be applied, because a complexity is acceptable and all another reducing algorithms give sufficiently large differences. For cases with more agents (9 agents and more), all reducing methods have an omissible low complexity in comparison with using the complex searching approach or a genetic algorithm; nevertheless the results of these algorithms achieve just about the best results obtained by searching complex space. Better results we can reach by modifying the step 2.b.1 in the algorithm 3, instead of adding only coalitions, which have a value φ_i^k or q_i^K respectively immediately after a coefficient α_i, we can attach more ones at once. By this way a number of satisfied solutions will increase and a chance to reach the best solution will be bigger. Otherwise, for a case with 11 agents, a number of steps that the searching program repeated are about 1 million and this number will continuously increase with an exponential speed, therefore, from a practical point of view it is not possible to apply the complex searching method but more effectively is to use one of some presented reducing mechanisms, which give also average optimal results.

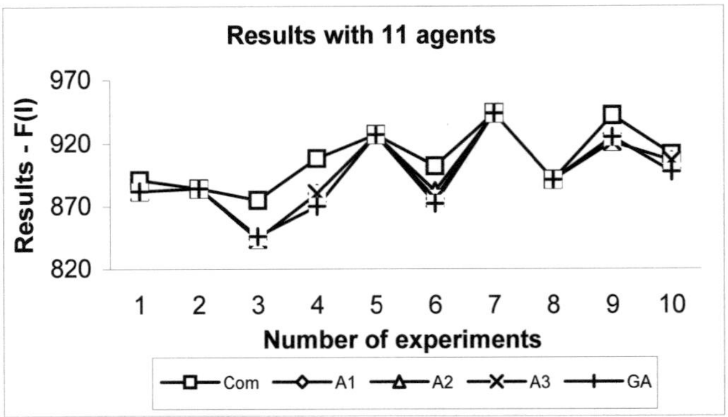

Fig. 1. Results of searching max(F_I) with 11 agents

Notation: in figure 1 and table 1: *com* = complex searching, *GA* = genetic algorithm, *A1* = algorithm 1, *A2* = algorithm 2, *A3* = algorithm 3.

2.2 Coalition formation for large scale multi/agent systems

Recently huge manufacturing systems and network enterprises have been created. There is lack of new theoretical and practical tools for solving upcoming problems such as enterprise integrity, distributed and heterogeneous environment. According to (Nof et al., 2005), previously mentioned problems in huge manufacturing systems can be handled by large-scale multi-agent systems (LSMAS). LSMAS are distributed systems with large number of elements. These systems can easier handle problems such as robustness, flexibility and scalability than centralized systems. Computations and methods used in systems can be distributed among independent parts of the system. These independent parts solve problems with smaller complexity and results are aggregated together. In MAS theory several distributive methods can be found, e.g. agreement reaching methods such as auction, bargaining and coalition formation (Sandholm, 1999), (Woodridge, 2002). Almost every previously mentioned approach has two type methods. The first type is known computational method, which uses more computations than negotiation. The second type is negotiation method, which prefers negotiation before computation.

Another very important topic in a new age manufacturing system is to utilize human knowledge and experience. There are numerous approaches how to store knowledge, for supporting users in manufacturing and production systems as well. Among recently most used approach belongs ontology utilization (Budinská, 2004), (Dang, 2003) and experience management (Bergman, 2002). However, expressions such as near, slightly above or almost cannot be described by numbers and thus it is hard to store them. Fuzzy relations can handle this problem easily and complex. Users' inputs are fuzzy membership functions rather than single values.

Objective function

Huge amount of decisions are made on the basis of some criterions called objective functions. A LSMAS that fulfils enterprise integrity property is divided into dependent or independent subsystems. Decisions made in these subsystems may have different domains. And thus, each decision process should have different objective function. Principle of objective functions should be based on measuring distance between two compared entities, which can be represented by attribute-value pairs, an object or a tree structure and etc (Bergman, 2002). One of these entities is know as a set point and represents desired properties of right decision. An objective function can be Euclidian or hamming distance measure, fuzzy similarity measure and etc. Entities represented by vectors are the most used, hence lots of specialized metrics has been invented to solve this issue. Note that methods that utilize the vector representation of entities do not take into account their structure. For example, in coalition formation problem coalition properties are compared, but the structure of coalition is not considered. If the structure of compared entities is considered, then more sophisticated methods should be used, e.g. social hierarchical entropy (Balch, 2000). These metrics have very crucial assumption; vectors, which represent entities, must have the same dimensions, otherwise vectors could not be compared. This is very important fact, because in LSMAS should occur situations, where two vectors with different dimensions have to be compared. In such situations, standard distance measures, such as Manhattan metric, can be modified by dimension evaluation .

$$f(\overline{x},\overline{y}) = \frac{1-\alpha n}{m_y} \cdot \frac{1}{n} \sum_i |x_i - y_i| \qquad (10)$$

$$\forall i : x_i \notin \{\} \wedge y_i \notin \{\}$$

where $\overline{x} \in X$ is a vector of attribute-values pairs with dimensions $(m_x,1) : m_x \in N$ that describes properties of an entity that is compared with a set point entity represented by a vector $\overline{y} \in X$ with dimensions $(m_y,1) : m_y \in N$, X is the space of all possible vector representations of entities, $n \in N$ is a number of attribute-value pairs, which can be found in both vectors $\overline{x}$ and $\overline{y}$, $\alpha \in (0,1>$ is a coefficient that shorten distances that have bigger n . This heterogeneous modification is based on preferring distances, where two entities with similar sets of attributes are compared. Distances with normalized input vectors are usually defined as functions $f : X \times X \to <0,1>$, where the shortest distance have the lowest value of distance measure f. The most of distance measures fulfil symmetry, reflexivity and triangular inequality properties; previously mentioned heterogeneous modification of Manhattan metric is one of such measures.

Fuzzy voting criterion

Fuzzy voting criterion (FVC), which is depicted in simple scheme on Fig. 2, is based on fuzzy pre-processing of attribute values and on agents voting.

Fuzzy preprocessing includes a set of fuzzy set, which describes the set point entity and transforms attribute values of compared entities into interval $\langle 0,1 \rangle$. Each fuzzy set is defined by its membership function $\mu(x_{ji})$, shown in Fig. 3 where x_{ji} is the value of the jth property of i-th analyzed attribute vector. In this example, fuzzy transformation converts the value of one analyzed property, i.e. single variable transformation is considered. More complicated fuzzy transformations can be defined as well.

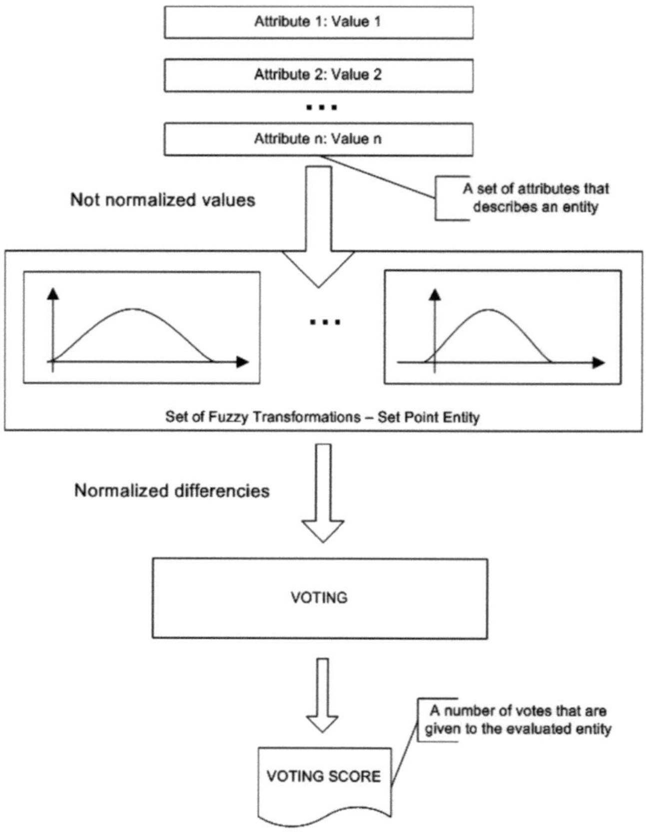

Fig. 2. Illustrative scheme of fuzzy voting criterion.

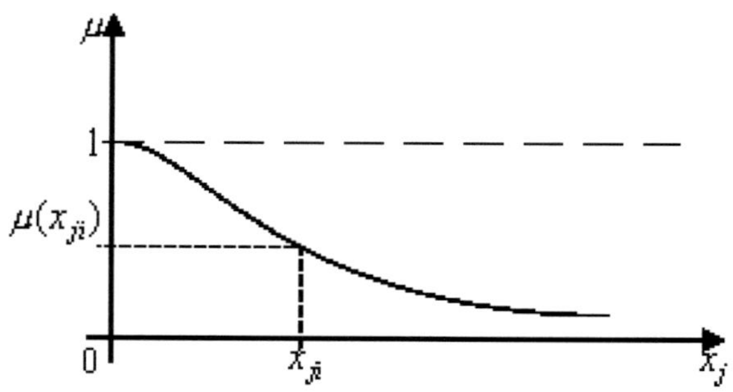

Fig. 3. An example of fuzzy transformation of j-th coalition property.

Fuzzy transformation results are processed by voters that make votes in election. Voters assign votes to each transformed value. Assigning of votes is a simple straightforward algorithm and can be summarized as follows:

1. Each vector that includes analyzed properties is assigned to voter that supports these properties.

2. Each voter evaluates the membership function value of the defined fuzzy transformation for each vector. Note that voters transform only subset of values of the vector.
3. Each voter sorts the set of transformed values in descending order.
4. Each voter assigns particular amount of votes to a vector. The assigned amount of votes is based on the following rule: The first vector gets votes, where is the number of vectors assigned to the w-th voter. In general, can differ from the number of all vectors, because only vectors, whose properties are supported by the w-th voter, are assigned to that voter. The last vector gets one vote. If two or more vectors have the same values, then all of them get votes, where is the amount of votes assigned to the first vector that has higher transformed value.
5. Votes for each vector are summed across voters, i.e. final amount of votes for each vector is the sum of votes from all voters.
6. The best vector is that with the highest number of votes.

The sixth step declares that the best vector maximizes utility.

Mathematical representation of the fuzzy voting criterion

Definition of environment:

- Vector of coalitions is denoted by $C = (c_1, c_2, ..., c_l)^T$, where $l \in L$ is the number of coalitions that are compared in the coalition formation algorithm.
- Vector of voters is denoted by $V = (v_1, v_2, ..., v_w, ..., v_o)^T$.
- Vector of coalition properties is denoted by $X = (\overline{x}_1, \overline{x}_2, ..., \overline{x}_l)^T$.

Definition of fuzzy and voting transformation.

Function $f_i : X \to Z_i$ is called fuzzy transformation function for the *i*-th voter, where vector $Z_i = (z_{i1}, z_{i2}, ..., z_{il})^T, z_{ij} \in \langle 0,1 \rangle$. Function $g_i : Z_i \to W_i$ is called voting transformation function for the *i*-th voter, where $W_i = (w_{i1}, w_{i2}, .., w_{il})^T, w_{ij} \in W$. Function $\overline{f} = (f_1 f_2 ... f_o)^T$ is called voting system fuzzy transformation function. Function $\overline{g} = (g_1 g_2 ... g_o)^T$ is called voting system voting transformation function.

Definition of fuzzy voting criterion.

Vector of fuzzy transformation criterion value for each coalition is $\overline{J} = \left(\overline{g}\left(\overline{f}(Y)\right) \cdot \overline{e}\right)$, where $\overline{e}$ is vector $(1,1,...,1)^T$ of size $(l,1)$. $\overline{J}_i$ is value of fuzzy voting criterion for the *i*-th coalition.

Vector of fuzzy transformation criterion can be rewritten in a more complex way:

$$\begin{aligned} \overline{J} &= \left(\overline{g}\left(\overline{f}(Y)\right) \cdot \overline{e}\right) = \\ &= g_1(f_1(Y)) + ... + g_l(f_l(Y)) \end{aligned} . \tag{11}$$

Note that the above definition looks like linear criterion. In some applications, voters may have different influence on results of the criterion. The definition of FVC can be modified as follows

$$\overline{J} = \left(\overline{g}\left(\overline{f}(Y)\right) \cdot \overline{a}\right), \tag{12}$$

where $\overline{a} \in R^n$ is voters' influence vector. Note that $\overline{a}$ has the same role in FVC as diagonal items in matrix A of the quadratic criterion.

Comparison of fuzzy voting and heterogeneous Manhattan metric

An advantage of FVC is that decisions are made in distributed manner and no preprocessing of properties values is needed. Normalization of input data is performed by the fuzzy transformation.

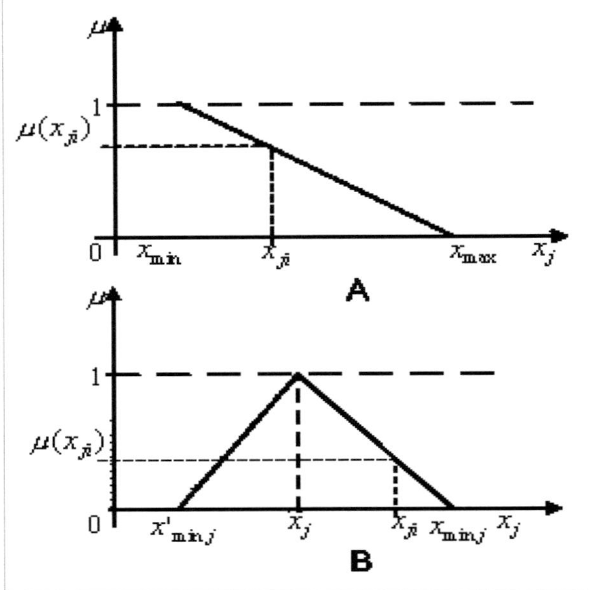

Fig. 4. Examples of normalization performed by fuzzy transformation

In Fig 4 examples of such normalization are given. Note that each entity property is transformed into the interval $\langle 0,1 \rangle$; thus all properties are normalized. In these examples, the normalization is linear (Figure 4A). The linear normalization depends on minimal x_{min} and maximal x_{max} values of the set of considered values. In general however, normalization can be influenced by experts' intentions, i.e. some values of the transformed interval can be preferred.

In Figure 4 B, special type of fuzzy transformation is shown. The maximal normalized value of the j-th analyzed property is $\tilde{x}_j$. This value represents the desired value of the j-th analyzed property. This type of transformation has two minimal values - $x'_{\min j}$ and $x_{\min j}$.

Figure 4 proposes that in general entities have two types of properties, the first (Figure 4A) being a type of properties that is minimized during a evaluation, and the second (Figure 4B) minimizes the difference between the value of property and the desired value of this property $\tilde{x}_j$. In case of heterogeneous Manhattan metric differences have to be evaluated; in case of FVC these differences are evaluated by fuzzy transformation function.

An illustrative example:

FVC is used in a polynomial coalition formation algorithm in a super-additive environment, based on an enhanced distributed generation of a coalition configuration proposed by Shehory and Kraus (1999), where the coalition configuration is a set of coalitions of agents in MAS and This generation algorithm has the following advantages:

- the set of coalitions are polynomial
- the load of computation is distributed among agents

- agents generates only unique coalitions
- the search space (coalition configuration) of the algorithm can be controlled by probability distribution of random choices made by agents.

A multi agent system consists of one hundred agents, which generates 5098 unique coalitions in the coalition configuration. Each agent represents one power plant in an electric grid that is described by three properties, namely cost per time unit (c), resource (r), loading time (lt) and loading cost (lc). Note that engineer units are considered in all measurements. Several agents with properties are presented in the table 2.

power plant	r	lt	c	lc
A31	21	9	1	0.25
A32	10		0.125	
A33	24	2	1.25	1.7
A34	36	2	1	0.57
A35	10	6	1.7	1.7
A36	30		0.8	3.5
A37	20	1	0.5	0.5
A38	8	3	0.5	
A39		5	0.75	
A40	19	5	1	4

Table 2. Values of several analyzed agents' properties. Note that some values are not filled in tables, i.e. attribute values of particular agents are not known or not defined. This is typical situation in LSMAS, which result in heterogeneous environment.

Experiment in a heterogeneous environment

In this subsection comparison of FVC and heterogeneous Manhattan metric is performed, which is made by the experiment based on searching for the best coalition that minimizes the cost per time unit the cost per preparation time, preparation time and to minimize the difference between the value of the coalition's resource property and the desired value of the resource property stored in set point. The force of each property is equal, i.e. each property has the same influence on the criterion value (objective function).

The heterogeneous Manhattan metric is defined as in (Balch, 2000). Definition of the FVC is more complicated. FVC consists of four voters, where each voter is assigned to one property. Each voter has a fuzzy transformation. Each fuzzy transformation is defined as follows

$$f_i(x_{ij}, c_i, \sigma_i) = e^{\frac{(x-c)^2}{2\sigma^2}}, \tag{13}$$

where $x_{ij} \in \bar{x}_j$ is the *i*-th value of the *j*-th property which is assigned to the *i*-th voter, c_i is the desired value of the *i*-th property and finally σ_i is *i*-th coefficient that describes width of Gaussian curve. In this experiment the values of c_i and σ_i for each voter are defined in the following table 3.

Voter	i	c_i	σ_i
r voter	1	30	10
lt voter	2	0	10
c voter	3	0	10
Lc voter	4	0	10

Table 3. Parameters of voters' fuzzy transformations

Note that the value of the parameter c_i is the desired value of a particular property.

In the following two tables 4 and 5, results of the experiment are presented. In the first table, the results of top ten coalitions evaluated by the FVC are given. In the second one, there are results evaluated by the heterogeneous Manhattan metric.

Position	lt	lc	r	c	FVC
1	1,00	0,50	20,00	0,50	20356
2	1,92	0,50	33,00	0,50	20348
3	1,33	0,50	38,00	1,00	20325
4	3,00	1,00	24,00	0,67	20313
5	3,00	1,00	45,00	0,67	20313
6	6,00	0,88	39,00	0,10	20311
7	8,00	0,44	14,00	0,17	20303
8	6,00	0,75	36,00	0,67	20301
9	6,75	1,00	20,00	0,50	20292
10	8,00	0,44	47,00	0,79	20280

Table 4. Results of fuzzy voting criterion in heterogeneous environment

Pos.	lt	lc	r	c	HMM
1	1,00	0,50	20,00	0,50	0,001834
2	1,92	0,50	33,00	0,50	0,002188
3	1,33	0,50	38,00	1,00	0,002718
4	0,33		2	0,8	0,002744
5	3,00	1,00	45,00	0,67	0,003551
6	6,00	0,88	39,00	0,10	0,003681
7	8,00	0,44	14,00	0,17	0,003958
8	6,00	0,75	36,00	0,67	0,004363
9	6,75	1,00	20,00	0,50	0,004748
10	8,00	0,44	47,00	0,79	0,004901

Table 5. Results of heterogeneous Manhattan metric in heterogeneous environment

Note that in the tables, only top ten coalitions are given; the remaining coalitions are omitted. The top ten coalitions are very similar in both cases. In general the best coalition can differ in each criterion, because the best coalition is suboptimal, not optimal. Better

results might be encountered in case of weigthened modification is considered. However, the proof of this subsection is obvious: the FVC is applicable criterion for coalition formation problem.
In the case of multivariable fuzzy transformation, a voter works with more than one property of a coalition. This can be very useful in the case when some subset of properties are dependent or are meaningful as whole only. In situations where several values of some properties are preferred, multi-variable preference by fuzzy transformation can be used, which can be constructed from several fuzzy transformations constructed for each preferred value. This results in performing decision on fuzzy transformation level. One of the most significant issues in economical applications of MAS is cheating. If agents can predict decisions then they can change their properties. Thus, they knowingly lie. Agents, who have same interests or common goal, can interchange knowledge about others to reveal cheating. Afterwards, cheaters should be excluded from next considerations or are penalized.
The main aim of the future work is to implement FVC into management decision support system of national electric grid that utilizes experience management in process of coalition formation.

3. Modelling of social environment in multi/agent systems

MAS are appropriate to model and control huge systems in many different applications. Besides manufacturing, social environment and virtual societies can be modelled via MAS. Suppose that social environment contains, for example, the cultural, educational, business, traffic etc. parts. Each of them may be characterized by certain phenomena, behaviours, properties, etc., and may be considered as an autonomous complex with its own norms, relations, rules, aims, conflicts, communications, working way, etc.
From this aspect their definitions have different meaning in various areas, such as social science, psychology, legal theory, biology, medicine, ecology, education, production etc. To solve their performance requires special tools, which are able to handle the appeared problems. As one of the possible tools multi-agent system (MAS) can be used, because:

- multi-agent systems are evolved as a methodical solution to large complex distributed problems
- an agent is a hardware or more usually software entity that enjoys the properties such as autonomy, social ability, reactivity and pro-activeness,
- each agent in MAS is considered rational and autonomous in making decision for improving its individual benefit.

According to the above considerations the paper will be focused to the application of MAS to handle some special problems of society performance. Each society is characterized by the norms (N) in a population (P), which is defined as a function of beliefs and preference of the P members, if the following conditions hold :

- almost every member of P prefers to conform to N on the condition that almost everyone else also conforms,
- almost every member of P believes that every other member of P conforms to N.

The above conditions may be translated to MAS as follows:

- norms as obligations,
- norms as requirements,
- norms as goals or objectives (deduced from obligations and requirements),
- norms as constraints on behaviour.

Depending on the membership in agent coalition which corresponds to any society in P and its individual requirements and intentions, an agent is confronted with a set of norms, based on the situation of the society, to which the agent belongs. This agent has to strictly abide by norms, and for other norms it has to consider an adoption strategy to decide whether to comply.

In production systems and intelligent engineering research, virtual space can be taken as analogy to the physical intelligent space .

In social research, norms are considered as responsible for regulating the social behaviour of individuals. They prescribe how to interact and resolve issues in conflicting circumstances. In MAS this case is solved by the rules of negotiation. The negotiation form is an important part of social agent: agents need to cooperate and organize their activities to achieve their individual as well as collective goals.

On the basis of this consideration the challenges addressed by this paper can be formulated as follows:

- building the knowledge in the multi-agent system's environment
- incorporating knowledge system into multi-agent system environment
- management of virtual societies
- experience retrieval from the experience base.
- conclusion and future work.

One objective of multi-agent system's environmental engineering is to implement knowledge into environment in order to describe

- world of interest,
- environmental knowledge,
- agent system.

This implementation should have to follow the environmental reference model , which divides environment into several active and passive elements supporting communication between agent system and world of interest. Furthermore, it includes the module for processing internal processes over data repository known as State concluding state of the environment.

In general, the knowledge system model consists of three layers, namely:

- conceptual,
- contextual,
- product layer.

These three layers include the following six models: organizational, task, agent, knowledge, communication and design model. Organizational model describes setting where the knowledge system is deployed. The model is spread over five subsystems of the environment: synchronization, observation, interaction, perception (cover concepts parts of the world of interest, which are taken into account by the knowledge system) and communication.

Task model represents all assignments which have to be done by executive parts of the knowledge system.

Agents defined in agent model are called environmental processes. Each environmental process has one or more tasks assigned, which is/are defined in the task model.

Knowledge represented in knowledge system of environment is described within the knowledge model which partially results in a part of a law model describing principles of the world of interest.

Communication model describes interactions among environmental processes working with knowledge and fulfilling the tasks defined by the task model.
The design model represents implementation of the knowledge system into the settings.

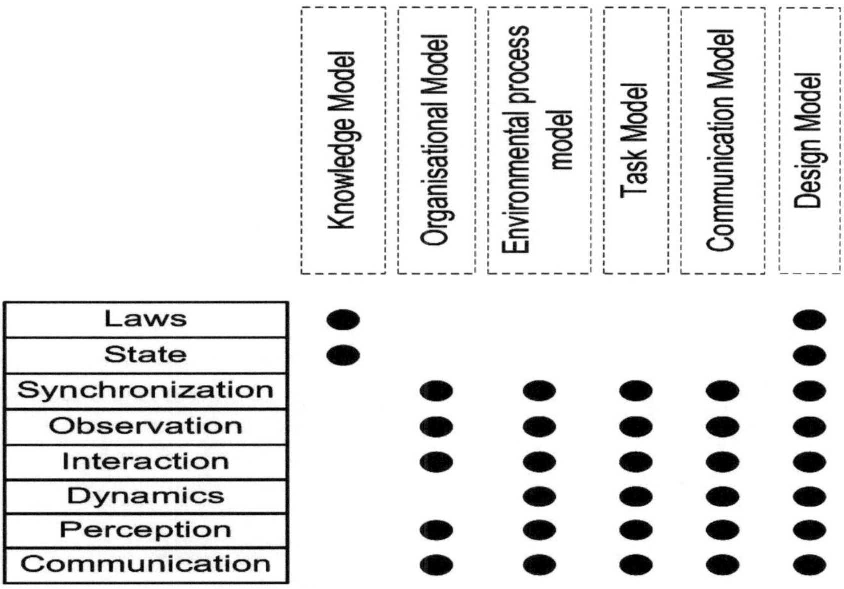

Fig. 5. The relation matrix between reference model of the environment and models of the knowledge system

The knowledge model is distributed over whole MAS environment which is shown in the following figure utilizing interaction matrix. Figure 5 presents two types of boxes, namely solid and dashed ones. Solid boxes represent parts of the environment's reference model. On the other hand, dashed boxes encompass knowledge system models.
The set of executed processes depends on application. Valckenaers et al. in (Valckenaers, 2007) present three types of applications:

- emulation; in emulation application, environment is off line emulator of the world of interest
- interacting information system communicates with the world of interest in real-time
- adaptive information system is interacting information system dynamically adapting upon changes in the world of interest.

From this aspect the main tasks are as follows:

- mapping knowledge into MAS environment through experience management of virtual societies in a multi-agent system,
- addressing three experience management processes, namely:
- experience,
- item representation,
- storing and retrieval.

Management of virtual societies

Agents in multi-agent system form structured virtual societies with different organization and purposes.

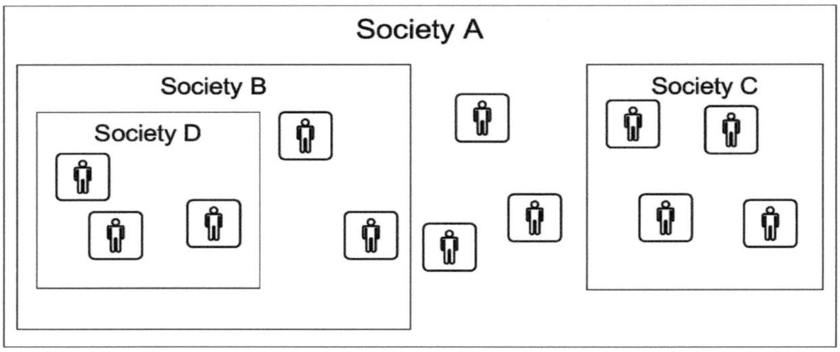

Fig. 6. Conceptual description of structured agent society is presented. Society A is top-level society in this example which encompasses three agents and two societies, namely Society B and Society C. The important result of this description is hierarchical distribution of agents over nested societies.

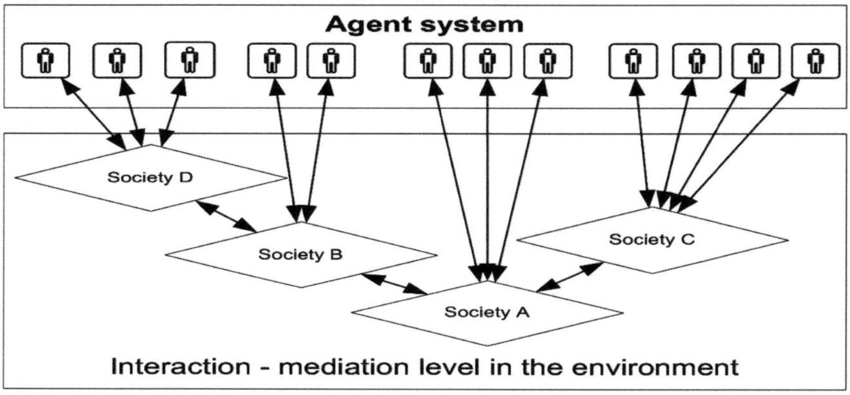

Fig. 7. Vertical section of the multi-agent system of nested agents societies.

The interaction and mediation levels are taken into account in following way:

- virtual societies are distributed over the agent system and its environment has impact on the expansion of functionalities of the environment,
- vertical cut over virtual society shows that it is distributed over agent system and its environment.

This is an important fact, because structure of a society is developed in the environment, not in the agent system, which is just a container encompassing all agents on one place. Developed societies can be registered to the environment; afterwards the environment can manage them. In this point, two approaches to manage societies - free and controlled - can be recognized: Free management of agent society just manages existence of the society and does not control agent behaviour in the agent system. On the other hand, controlled agents' society management can control behaviour of agent through communication among agents and virtual societies. Societies are built according to a precisely defined problem which is the goal of the directive or negotiation formation process. Agents in a society take actions which can be described by a plan, (in negotiation processes actions are usually generated ad-hock) The plan of actions and the plan of outcomes' distribution are properties of the society. Thus, society can be described by a concept with the following properties:

- an activity defining the aim of the society;

- a plan describing sequence of the activities taken by entities in the society, or distribution of the outcomes;
- a set of entities located in the society;
- a relation to upper level society.

The concept entity encompasses both agents and societies. The term activity includes one of the following concepts:

- an objective addressed by societies,
- a task solved by agents,
- an action executed by agents.

For mathematical description of society with action plan, propositional logic can be used. Since societies are oriented towards actions, it is proper to use concurrent dynamic epistemic logic.

For our purposes, the sequential, parallel and conditional execution and testing of proposition are the most important.

According to logic agents, such societies can be described by the following sorted set of four elements:

$$S = \left(\Sigma, F, F^0, \Sigma_S^0\right)$$

Where:

- Σ denotes all agents and societies in the MAS,
- ***F*** represents a set of all formulas in particular propositional logic,
- $\boldsymbol{F^0}$ represents the set of all formulas in the particular propositional logic including $\varnothing$, this means that the society has not defined a plan of actions,
- Σ^0_S defines the set of al societies existing in the MAS and symbol $\varnothing$ denotes that defined society S is the top-level society and has no parent society.

The second and third elements represent activities of society S. However, the former element defines the aim of the society, and the latter introduces an optimal pal, if there s any.

Example of the society description is in the following formula:

$$\left(\{S_2, A_2, A_3\}, [?\,p_1]p_2, [?\,p_1; \alpha_1; \alpha_2]p_2, S_0\right)$$

where society including two agents A_2, A_3 and society S_2 is defined. This society has an objective to satisfy proposition p_2 when p_1 is satisfied. Optimal plan of actions to satisfy the objective of the society is also defined. The parent society is defined as well, using the fourth element of society definition.

The above presented knowledge system distributed over the MAS environment is used to manage virtual societies of agents. The knowledge system includes ontology of the virtual society derived from mathematical representation that presents idea of defining society structure in the environment rather than in agent system. Similar MAS approach may be effectively applied in a framework of extended social field, for example, in business areas because it deals with continuous input of varying information and the maintenance of distributed databases over the intra and inter nets.

4. Multi agents´ control system inspired by immune systems

4.1 Artificial immune systems

Study of biological principal as a new solution in computer science become very popular in last two decades. There are many popular approaches with biological background applied in computer science. One of the most often used algorithms is neural network, which is inspired by neuro-science result. Also genetic algorithm and cellular engineering are used with great success in computer science. Another, in last years very popular area of research, is artificial immune systems (AIS) based on principals of mammal immunology. Artificial immune system imitates the natural mammal immune system that has sophisticated methodologies and capabilities to build computational algorithm that solves engineering problems efficiently. The main goal of the mammal immune system is to protect the internal components of the mammal body by fighting against the foreign elements such as the fungi, virus and bacteria. Mammal immune system can be dividing in to the two basic immune responses:

- Innate immune system
- Adaptive immune system

Innate immune system consists of several barriers that protect organism from infection. Typical barriers are mechanical, chemical and biological barriers. These barriers are the first line of defence against infection.

Artificial immune systems are based on metaphor to adaptive immune system. Adaptive immune systems are composed of a great variety of molecules, cells, and organs spread all over the body. There is no central organ coordinating functions of the immune system, and there are several elements performing complementary roles. The main task of the immune system is to survey the organism in the search for malfunctioning cells from their own body (e.g., cancer and tumour cells), and foreign disease causing elements (e.g., viruses and bacteria) (de Castro & Timmis, 2002).

4.2 Adaptive immune systems and their metaphors

Elements that can be recognized by immune system are called antigens. On the other side, cells that originally belong to our body are harmless to its functioning are termed self antigens and disease causing elements are named non-self antigens. One of the main functions of the immune system is to be capable to distinguish between what is self and what is non-self antigens. There are many types of immune cells but two of them are necessary to know, to understand basic principals B-cells and T-cells. These two types of cells are rather similar, but differ with relation to how they recognise antigens and by their functional roles. B-cells are capable to recognise antigens free in solution (e.g., in the blood stream), while T-cells require antigens to be presented by other accessory cells (de Castro & Timmis, 2002). Four basic metaphors have been taken from the mammal immune systems and applied to the artificial immune systems:

- *Positive and negative selection*
- *Clonal selection*
- *Jerne's idiotropic network*
- *Danger theory*

Positive and negative selection.

The mammal Thymus is pleased where the T-cell maturated. Process of maturating consists of removing T-cells which attack self antigens. If they escape this elimination, they may subsequently react against self antigens, and cause Autoimmune disease. Negative selection was introduced in 1994 (Forrest et al., 1994), and is now often called negative detection. The basic principle of negative selection is to find sets of individual which does not react with any self individuals. So, when in future will be present non-self antigen, some of the individual form set of T-cell will be reacting (eliminate) with it. Positive selection is opposite process. Immune cell will be exposed to the set of non-self antigen and tries to learn their characteristics.

Danger theory.
There appeared, in few experimental observations, cases, which can not be explained by original self-non-self theory. For example, how can be explained the fact that bacteria in our gut, which is clearly non-self pathogen, does not start immune reaction. Matzinger has developed an interesting alterative theory (Matzinger P. (1994).) to explain that phenomen. Immune cell can die in two ways. The first one is normal death that has been requested by the body's internal signaling system, and the second is via unexpected death caused by something going wrong with the cell, which often causes an inflammatory response. Matzinger suggested that the immune system is particularly activated by cell necrosis. It appears that danger theory might help intrusion detection systems by focusing attention only on those internal or external events that are likely to be harmful in general a smaller subset of events than the non-self subset.
Clonal selection
Clonal section focuses on how immune cell can adapt to the new match and how can eliminate invaders. Clonal selection is responsible for the ability of mammal immune systems to adapt its B-cell to new types of non-self antigens. There is more variants of clonal selection in area of artificial immune systems. One of the main algorithm that represents this group of approaches is COLNALG(de Castro and Von Zuben, 2002).The CLONALG algorithm is as follows:

1. Randomly initialise a population of individuals (M);
2. For each pattern of P, present it to the population M and determine its affinity (match) with each element of the population M;
3. Select n1 of the best highest affinity elements of M and generate copies of these individuals proportionally to their affinity with the antigen. The higher the affinity, the higher the number of copies, and vice-versa;
4. Mutate all these copies with a rate proportional to their affinity with the input
5. Add these mutated individuals to the population M and re-select n2 of these maturated (optimised) individuals to be kept as memories of the system;
6. Repeat Steps 2 to 5 until a certain criterion is met, such as a minimum pattern recognition or classification error.

Jerne's idiotropic network
Jerne's idiotropic network deals with the interaction of antibodies. Jerne's network is a network of B cells that communicate the shape of the antigenic epitope amongst them through idiotopes and paratopes. There is few models (Farmer et al., 1986)(Fukuda et al., 1998)(Timmis et al., 2000) of idiotropic network used in artificial immune system.

4.3 Relation between AIS and MAS, case study

There are two basic points of view on interaction between AIS and MAS. The main difference between these two concepts is question which technology could be used as a tool. The basic concept is to use MAS as a powerful modelling tool for AIS simulation. Agents simulate cell of an immune system and interaction between cells are reflected in to the interaction between agents. This concept is used in process of understating some disease. Typical application is simulation of reaction of the immune system on viruses (Bernaschi & Castiglione, (2002)). The second concept is, when metaphors that form mammal immune system are used to solve problem of agent system. Mammal immune system is robust, distributed, decentralized, self-organized and adaptive complex. All these features are very important in multi-agent funkcionality. This is reason, why artificial immune system is more and more applied on multi-agent paradigms.
Security task is one of the common application areas of the artificial immune systems in multi-agent system. The security problem is very similar to the specific immune response of

mammals. There is the same task in the network security and the immune response, to protect system against intruders (pathogen). All types of immune responses principals are tried to be used in the area of security. With the development of the network security technology, there are more an more equipments to protect network systems. Especially for large network system, the network architecture becomes more and more complex and dynamic. In the dynamic network environment, agent is suitable for collecting data information and constructing the complex fusion model. In work (Zhou et al., 2007) authors try to solve problem of the large network security thru the application of the danger theory (Matzinger, 1994). In the paper they show, the Danger Theory can be successfully applied to the field of network security.

Interesting work in this field is Nishyama's research (2001). Authors try to build a system to detect and reject unauthorized intrusion using security technology similar to the flexible structure of an immune system. They applied the recognition mechanism of self and non-self of an immune system and cooperation among immune cells. In such a way they were able to realize a security system that automatically detects and eliminates unauthorized intrusion from inside or outside. Authors extend the multi-agent language MRL (Nishiyama, 1998), which design is based on a parallel-logic programming language and apply it to implementing an immune security system. System is based on B-cells and T-cells functionality and on thir cooperation. When connection is acquired system generate B-cell agent for this connection, so B-cells response to outside connection. The role of B-cell agent is to watch at the input of the connection. When activity comes from inside, some process starts or some file is created and system generates T-cell agent which watch at these processes. When network connection invocateds some process or file creation, then connection between B-cell and T-cell will happen.

Another interesting point of view of artificial immune systems usage in multi agent system is reported in paper (Bakhouya & Gaber, 2007). Authors try to use agent, based on AIS algorithm to create a network for computer-based human interactions. Basic principle of AIS, the affinity is used for representation of relationship between agents. The learning mechanism is used to adjust the affinity relationships between agents representing the services to cope with the user context and provoke or produce emergent services. In this approach, the mechanism of establishing affinity relationships is based on keywords similarities.

One of the parameters which is hard to set in large scale multi-agent systems is population size. It is difficult to estimate the appropriate number of agents allowed to be spawned in the network, when mobile agents operate in a dynamic and distributed environment. Trying to increase robustness and efficient of the MAS in heterogeneous environment through the rising population of agent may cause, on the other hand, increasing resource demands of the network. In work (Bakhouya & Gaber, 2006) authors try to solve population size problem through artificial immune system approach. The main idea is to use life cycles of B-cell in immune network to dynamically set size of population. In this adaptive approach, agent retrieves local information from its environment and makes appropriate decision to either kill, or move without cloning or clone itself and move to another node of the network.

Very interesting work in the area of AIS application in MAS is described in (Sathyanath & Sahin, 2002). There are AIS and MAS applied in interesting field of mine detection problem. All the self-agents work in an agent network similar to Jerne's network. The process of information transfer and communication between the agents is an analogy of the agent network to the immune network. The nature of the agent network is application dependent.

Also in typical application domain of MAS technology are artificial immune system applied. In paper (Lee & Suzuki, 2006) authors present how negative and positive selection in process of improving performance and workload balancing can be used. Authors call the network of agent in this work, which simulate cell of immune system, iNet. Each agent continuously senses a set of current environment conditions as an antigen and examine whether it is self or non-self. A self antigen indicates that the agent adapts to the current environment conditions well, and a non-self antigen indicates it does not. When environment evaluation facility detects a non-self antigen, it activates behaviour selection. Behaviour selection allows each agent to choose behaviour as an antibody that specifically matches with the detected non-self antigen. Antibodies are situated in idiotope Jerene's network. Authors in result describe that iNet artificial immune system, allows each grid service to autonomously sense its surrounding environment conditions to evaluate, whether it adapts well to the conditions, and if it does not, adaptively perform a behavior suitable for the conditions. Also the simulations show that iNet allows agents to autonomously adapt to dynamic environmental changes for improving their performance and balancing workload. Presented case studies show great potential of AIS application in field of MAS. In future AIS can be helpful in a solving of the new challenges in area of multi-agent system. Especially in tasks, which require fault tolerance, self- organizing and self-adapting.

5. References

Balch T. (2000) Hierarchic Social Entropy and Behavioral Difference: New Measures of Robot Group Diversity, NIST Workshop on Metrics for Intelligent Systems, Gaithersburg, July, 2000

Bakhouya, M. and Gaber, J. (2006). Adaptive Approach for the Regulation of a Mobile Agent Population in a Distributed Network. In *Proceedings of the Proceedings of the Fifth international Symposium on Parallel and Distributed Computing* (July 06 - 09, 2006). ISPDC. IEEE Computer Society, Washington, DC, 360-366.

Bakhouya, M.; Gaber, J.,(2007). A Propitient Multi-agent System for Spontaneous Service Emergence in Pervasive Computing environments, *Pervasive Services*, IEEE International Conference on , vol., no., pp.409-414, 15-20 July 2007

Bernaschi, M., Castiglione,(2002). F., Selection of Escape Mutants from Immune Recognition During HIV Infection, *Immunology and Cell Biology Journal*, 80, february 2002, 307–313

Bergman (2002) Experience Management: Foundations, Development Methodology, and Internet-Based Applications, Springer

Budinská I., Dang T.T. (2004) A Case Based Reasoning in a Multi Agents Support System, Proceedings. of the 6th International Scientific - Technical Conference, Process Control 2004, Kouty nad Desnou, Czech Republic, June 8-11, 2004, Eds.: Stanislav Krejčí et.al, Editorial University of Pardubice, pp. 57, ISBN 80-7194-662-1

Cantamessa, M. and Villa, A.: Negotiation Models and Production Planning for Virtual Enterprises. In Proceeding of The IFAC Workshop on Manufacturing, Modeling, Management and Control - MIM 2001, Prague, Czech Republic, 1-5, 2001.

Dang, T-Tung, Frankovic, B. and Budinska, I.: Agents Coalition in Coordination Process. In XV IFAC World Congress b'02, Barcelona, 2002.

Dang T.Tung, Frankovič, B., Budinská, I. (2003) Optimal creation of agent coalitions for manufacturing and control. In Computing and informatics. ISSN 0232-0274, Vol. 22, No.1

de Castro, L. N. and Von Zuben, F. J. (2000). The clonal selection algorithm with engineering applications. *In Proceedings of GECCO'00*, Workshop on Artificial Immune Systems and Their Applications, pages 36–37.

de Castro, L.N & Timmis, J. (2002). Artificial Immune Systems: A Novel Approach to Pattern Recognition, In: *Artificial Neural Networks in Pattern Recognition Corchado, L Alonso and C Fyfe*, 67-84, University of Paisley, ISBN 84-95721-22-8

Farmer, J. D., Packard, N. H., and Perelson, A. S. (1986). The immune system, adaptation, and machine learning. *Phys.* D 2, 1-3 (Oct. 1986), 187-204.

Fukuda, T., Mori, K., and Tsukiyama, M. (1993). Immune networks using genetic algorithm for adaptive production scheduling. *In 15th IFAC World Congress*, volume 3, pages 57–60.

Forrest, S., Perelson, A. S., Allen, L., and Cherukuri, R. (1994). Self-Nonself Discrimination in a Computer. In *Proceedings of the 1994 IEEE Symposium on Security and Privacy*, PP.132-143, May 16 - 18, 1994, SP. IEEE Computer Society, Washington, DC.

Horváth László, Rudas Imre, J.: Virtual Space for Intelligent Engineering in Mechatronics, In Proc. Of IEE Conference ICM 2006, Budapest Hungary, pp. 248-253

Lee C. and Suzuki, J. (2006) Biologically Inspired Design of Autonomous and Adaptive Grid Services In *Proc. of the 2nd IEEE International Conference on Autonomic and Autonomous Systems (ICAS)*, Santa Clara, CA, July 2006.

Matzinger P. (1994).Tolerance "Danger and the Extended Family", Annual Review of Immunology. 1994, pp. 911-1045

Nishiyama, H., Ohwada, H. and Mizoguchi, F. (1998). A Multiaget Robot Language for Communication and Concurrency Control, International Conference on Multiagent Systems, pp. 206–213, 1998.

Nishiyama, H. and Mizoguchi, F. (2001). Design of Security System Based on Immune System. In *Proceedings of the 10th IEEE international Workshops on Enabling Technologies: infrastructure For Collaborative Enterprises* (June 20 - 22, 2001). 138-143,WETICE. IEEE Computer Society, Washington, DC.

Nof, S.Y., G. Morel, L., Monostori, A. Molina, F. Filip, (2005) "Milestone report for CC5 Manufacturing & Logistics Systems: From plant and logistics control to multi-enterprise collaboration," Proceedings of IFAC Congress , Prague , CZ.

Odubiyi, J. B., Kocur, D. J., and Weinstein, S. M.: A Scalable Agent-Based Information Retrieval Engine. In Proceedings of the First Annual Conference on Autonomous Agents. California USA, ACM Press / ACM SIGART, 292-299, 1997.

Sandholm, T. (1999) Distributed Rational Decision Making In the textbook Multiagent Systems: A Modern Introduction to Distributed Artificial Intelligence, Weiß, G., ed., MIT Press. Pp. 201-258

Sathyanath, S., Sahin, F. (2002) "AISIMAM - An AIS based intelligent multi agent model ands its pplication to a mine detection problem", in *Proceedings of the ICARIS 2002 1st international Conference on Artificial Immune Systems*, Canterbury, UK, September 9 - 11, 2002

Shehory, O., Kraus, S. (1999) Feasible formation of coalitions among autonomous agents in non-super-aditive environments, in Computational Intelligens, Vol. 15 (3), August 1999, pp 218-251

Timmis, J., Neal, M., and Hunt, J. (2000). An artificial immune system for data analysis. *Biosystems*,55(1/3):143–150.

Valckenaers P., Sauter J., Sierra C., Rodriguez-Aguilar J. A. (2007) Application and environments for multi-agent systems, Journal of Autonoumous Agents and Multi-Agent Systems, Vol 14, pp. 61-85, DOI 10.1007/s10458-006-9002-5, Springer

Wellman, M. P.: A MarketOriented Programming Environment and its Application to Distributed Multicommodity Flow Problems. In Journal of Artificial Intelligence Research 1, 123, 1993.

Wooldridge, M., Bussmann, S. and Klosterberg, M.: Production Sequencing as Negotiation. In Proceedings of the First International Conference on the Practical Application of Agents and Multi-Agent Technology (PAAM--97), 709-726, 1996.

Wooldridge, M. (2002) An introduction to Multiagent systems, John Willey & Sons, 2002.

16

Effective Multi-Model Motion Tracking Under Multiple Team Member Actuators

Yang Gu and Manuela Veloso
Computer Science Department, Carnegie Mellon University
USA

1. Introduction

Autonomous robot agents need to be able to track moving objects. When tracking is performed by a robot executing specific tasks acting over the target being tracked, such as a Segway RMP soccer robot grabbing and kicking a ball, the motion model of the target becomes dependent on the robot's actions. The robot's tactic provides valuable information in terms of the target behavior. We introduced a play-based motion modeling and tracking in such scenarios (Gu & Veloso, 2006). Observations from the sensors might consist of multiple measurements due to the moving objects and the clutter. Generally the clutter has similar color as the targets we are interested in and it causes multiple hypotheses for the true targets. Our previous approach does not perform well once incorrect measurements originating from clutter or false alarms exist, which causes multiple hypothesis of the tracked target. Recently, a hybrid approach for online joint detection and tracking for multiple targets was proposed (Ng et al., 2005). This approach does not assume the knowledge of true targets (without clutter) is given. It first uses a deterministic clustering method that searches for regions of interest (ROIs) based on the observations and monitors these ROIs for target detection, then performs multi-target tracking by Sequential Monte Carlo (SMC) methods.

In this chapter, we extend the contributed play-based tracking by introducing a multi-target dynamics model. We also take use of an improved proposal function for the PBPF based on the ROIs. We construct two multi-target trackers in the system, for the ball and the team member respectively. We use multi-target tracker instead of single target tracker because we can keep track of the true target and the false positive at the same time without losing any of them and perform ball (or team member) recognition from a pool of tracked objects later.

This chapter is organized as follows. We give a brief description of our robots and two main components of the control architecture. We describe the multi-target dynamics model. We describe the clustering algorithm we used to continuously monitor the appearance and disappearance of regions of interest (ROIs) on the field. The ROIs is used to deterministically obtain the number of targets. The ROIs is further used to get better proposal functions in particle filtering algorithm. We use an improved proposal function for the PBPF based on the ROIs. We contribute the multi-target tracking extension to the PBPF introduced in (Gu & Veloso, 2006).

2. Segway RMP soccer robot

The Segway platform is unique due to its combination of wheel actuators and dynamic balancing (Browning et al., 2005). Segway RMP, or Robot Mobility Platform, provides an extensible control platform for robotics research. It imbues the robot with the novel characteristics of a fast platform and travel long ranges, able to carry significant payloads, able to navigate in relatively tight spaces for its size, and provides the opportunity to mount sensors at a height comparable to human eye level (Searock et al., 2004).
In our previous work, we have developed a Segway RMP robot base capable of playing Segway soccer. We briefly describe the two major components of the control architecture, the sensor and the robot cognition, which are highly related to our multi-model motion tracking.

2.1 Vision sensor and infrared sensors

The goal of vision is to provide as many valid estimates of targets as possible. Tracking then fuses this information to track the most interesting targets (the ball and the team member, in this paper) of relevance to the robot. We use one pan-tilt camera as the vision sensor. We do not discuss the localization of the robot in the sense that a lot of soccer tasks (known as tactics and plays described in section 2.2) can be done by the Segway RMP robot without localization knowledge. Also we use global reference for position and velocity in this paper which means it is relative to the reference point where the robot starts to do dead reckoning.
We have equipped each robot with infrared sensors to reliably detect the objects located in the catchable area of the robot. Its measurement is a binary value indicating whether or not an object is there. In most cases, this is the blind area of the pan-tilt camera. Therefore, the infrared sensor is particularly useful when the robot is grabbing the ball.

2.2 Robot cognition

A control architecture, called Skills-Tactics-Plays, was proposed in (Browning et al., 2005) to achieve the goals of responsive, adversarial team control. The key component of STP is the division between single robot behavior and team behavior.
Play, $\boldsymbol{P}$, is a fixed team plan consisting of a set of applicability conditions, termination conditions, and $\boldsymbol{N}$ roles, one for each team member. Each role defines a sequence of tactics T_1, T_2, ... and associated parameters to be performed by that role in the ordered sequence. Assignment of roles to team members is performed dynamically at run time. Upon role assignment, each robot $\boldsymbol{i}$ is assigned its tactic T_i from the current step of the sequence for that role.
A tactic, $\boldsymbol{T}$, encapsulates a single robot behavior. Each robot $\boldsymbol{i}$ executes its own tactic as created by the current play $\boldsymbol{P}$. A tactic T_i determines the skill state machine SSM_i to be executed by the robot $\boldsymbol{i}$.
A skill, S, is a focused control policy for performing some complex action. Each skill is a member of one, or more, skill state machines SSM_1, SSM_2, ... Each skill S determines what skill it transitions to S' based upon the world state, the time skill S has been executing for, and the executing tactic for that robot.
We construct the robot cognition using a similar architecture. Plays, tactics, and skills, form a hierarchy for team control. Plays control the team behavior through tactics, while tactics

encapsulate individual robot behavior and instantiate actions through sequences of skills. Skills implement the focused control policy for actually generating useful actions. Figure 1 shows the ***SSMs*** and transitions for an example tactic: ***CatchKickToGoal***, which contains six skills. Each node in the figure is a skill and the edges show the transition between skills.

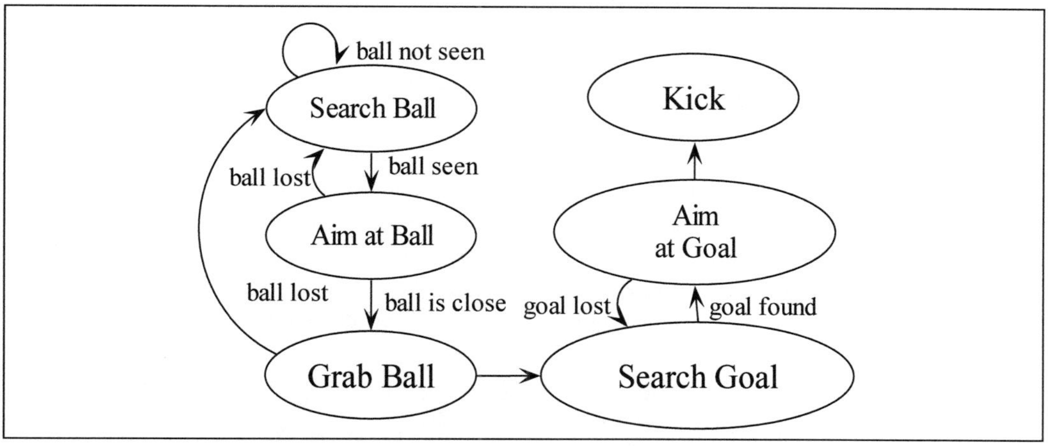

Fig. 1. Skill state machines (SSMs) for an example tactic: ***CatchKickToGoal***.

Segway soccer is a team sport, and therefore the building of our game strategy required not only execution of single robot behaviour, but also coordination with the team member, the human player. The current coordination is simple and basically based upon two fixed plays for offensive and defensive situation respectively. Our offensive play is shown as follows, in which the termination condition is either play aborted or the situation changed (a turn-over of ball possession announced by the referee). There are two roles in this play, one passes the ball to the other who positions down field and waits for receiving a pass. Once the positioning is done (e.g., the other is closer to the opponent goal), the passing is performed.

```
PLAY Naive Offense
APPLICABLE offense
DONE aborted OR !offense
ROLE 1
  pass 2
  none
ROLE 2
  position_down_field
  receive_pass
```

Table 1. The example play: ***Naive Offense***.

Our current coordination is purely observation based. Each player assigns role from his own eyeshot without communication. For example, should the robot think the team member is closer to the ball, the robot (ROLE 2) would choose to position and receive the ball from its team member (ROLE 1). Furthermore, the robot knows which side gains possession of the ball from the referee announcement, therefore it tells offensive from defensive situation clearly and thus it has deterministic idea of which play the team is using. The robot makes an assumption that its team member is performing the same game play as itself. The robot infers what tactic the team member is executing from the team play. For example, after receiving the ball from the team member, as a passer the robot would assume the team member go forward to a tactically advantageous position to receive a pass. The predefined play for team coordination helps motion modeling, which will be further discussed in section 3.

3. Play-based motion modeling

In this section, we take a multi-target tracking problem as a detailed example to show the extension of the tactic-based motion modeling method in general when the team coordination knowledge (play) is incorporated. First we give an introduction of the environment and targets under the Segway soccer setup. Second, we describe detailed motion models for both the ball and the team member. Third, we extend the tactic-based motion modeling to the play level when both the ball and the team member are included into the tracking. We show how we model the play-dependent interactions between the team member, the robot and the ball and set up a base for giving the multi-model tracking algorithm in the next section. Although we present the Segway soccer domain as an example, the formalism is general.

3.1 Tracking scenario

Many tracking scenarios involve multiple moving targets. In a Segway soccer game, we need to track the ball, the human team member and the two opponents. Each team is identified by their distinct color. The ball is orange (Veloso et al., 2005). An observation from the sensors might consist of multiple measurements due to the moving objects and the clutter. Generally the clutter has similar color as the targets we are interested in and it causes multiple hypotheses for the true targets. Therefore, we construct two multi-target trackers in the system, for the ball and the team member respectively. We use two separate trackers instead of one because we can differentiate the ball with the team member thanks to the color-based vision system. We use multi-target tracker instead of single target tracker because we can keep track of the true target and the false positive at the same time without losing any of them and perform ball(or team member) recognition from a pool of tracked objects later.

3.2 State space and dynamics

Let $x_t = [x_{1,t}^T, x_{2,t}^T, \cdots, x_{K_t,t}^T]^T$ denote a combined target state vector for K_t unknown and time-varying number of targets. The general parameterized system process for the kth target $\mathbf{x}_{k,t}$ at time t is given by:

$$x_{k,t} = f_k\,(x_{k,t-1}, u_{k,t-1}, v_{k,t-1}) \tag{1}$$

Where f_k is the parameterized state transition functions for the kth target; **x, u** are the state and input vectors; **v** is the process noise vectors of known statistics. Given the number of targets at ***t-1*** and ***t***, the state transition can be represented as follows:

$$p(x_t \mid x_{t-1}, K_t, K_{t-1}) = \begin{cases} p_0(x_{K_t,t})\prod_{k=1}^{K_{t-1}} p(x_{k,t} | x_{k,t-1}), if \quad K_t = K_{t-1}+1 \\ \prod_{k=1}^{K_t} p(x_{k,t} | x_{k,t-1}), if \quad K_t = K_{t-1} \\ \prod_{k=1,k\neq k^*}^{K_{t-1}} p(x_{k,t} | x_{k,t-1}), if \quad K_t = K_{t-1}-1 \\ 0, otherwise \end{cases} \tag{2}$$

The prior $p(x_{k,t} \mid x_{k,t-1})$ can be evaluated from Equation (1). The function $p_0(x_{K_t,t})$ is the initial distribution of a new target state and k^* is a target that vanishes at t. We assume at most one target appears or vanishes in each time step. The number of targets is obtained deterministically (see section 4.1 for the details).

3.3 Observation model

We assume that measurements are independent of each other and either originate from true targets or clutter. Furthermore, each target generates at most one measurement in each time step but may not be detected by the sensor.

Let $z_{c,t} = [z_{1,t}^T, z_{2,t}^T, \cdots, z_{M_t,t}^T]^T$ denote an observation vector for M_t measurements. The observation equation for modeling the cth measurement originating from the kth target is given as:

$$Z_{c,t} = h_k(x_{k,t}, n_{c,t}) \tag{3}$$

where $\mathbf{n}_{c,t}$ is a zero-mean observation noise with a known covariance Σ_n. The measurement originating from a clutter is modelled to be uniformly distributed within the entire visible region (observation volume V) of the camera. We use a deterministic method to perform measurement-to-target association. Let α_t denote the association vector which indicate the measurement-to-target assignment, whose ith element $\alpha_{i,t}$ is set to j if the ith measurement originates from the jth target, or zero if it originates from clutter. Let N_{Ct} denote the number of clutter points, and Ω_D denote the set of measurements indices corresponding to the detected targets, the likelihood function for measurement $\mathbf{z}_t$ can be written as:

$$p(z_t \mid x_t, K_t, \alpha_t) = \left(\frac{1}{V}\right)^{N_{C_t}} \prod_{l\in\Omega_D} p(z_{l,t} \mid x_{\alpha_{l,t},t}), \tag{4}$$

where $p(z_{l,t} \mid x_{\alpha_{l,t},t})$ is evaluated from (3).

3.4 Ball motion modeling

In our Segway RMP soccer robot environment, we define five models to model the ball motion (for the rest of this paper, for simplicity, we use $\mathbf{x}_t$ to represent the ball state, and use $\mathbf{x}'_t$ to represent the team member state).

- ***Free-Ball, Robot-Grab-Ball, Robot-Kick-Ball.*** We use the same models as ***Free-Ball, Grab-Ball, Kick-Ball*** introduced in (Gu, 2005) respectively.
- ***Human-Grab-Ball.*** The ball is held by the team member. We can infer the ball position similarly if we know the team member position well.
- ***Human-Grab-Ball.*** The ball is kicked by the team member and it is supposed to be either a pass to the robot or a shoot at the goal.

In general, we will have n motion models $m_1, m_2, \ldots, m_n$.

3.5 Team member motion modeling

We define four models to model the human team member's motion.

- ***Random Walk***. The team member is wandering in the field. So the state at the new time is the state at the current time with some additive zero-mean (assumed Gaussian) noise.
- ***Holding Ball***. The team member is holding the ball without moving and waiting for the robot to receive the ball. Should the robot know the ball position well, it can infer the team member position by the ball position in a similar way as ***Robot-Grab-Ball*** for ball motion modeling.
- ***Accelerating (Decelerating)***. The team member dashes (stops) to obtain (lose) a velocity in a short time.
- ***Positioning***. The team member is going to a predefined tactical position with a constant speed. This case happens mostly after the team member passing the ball to the robot and moving down the field toward opponent's goal.

3.6 Play based model transitions

Given the knowledge of the team coordination plan (the play P_{t-1} at time $t-1$), the robot can infer what tactic the team member is executing (T'_{t-1}), which provides valuable information about the motion model of the team member (m'_t). Both the robot and the team member act over the ball in a Segway soccer game. The motion model of the ball (m_t) is therefore affected by what tactic the robot (T_{t-1}) and the team member (T'_{t-1}) are executing.
From the previous subsection, we know that the model index m determines the present model being used. For our team member tracking example, $m'_t = i$, $i = 1, \ldots, 4$$. In our approach, it is assumed that the team member motion model index, m'_t, conditioned on the previous tactic executed T'_{t-1} by the team member, and other useful information v'_t (such as ball state), is governed by an underlying Markov process, such that, the conditioning parameter can branch at the next time-step with probability.

$$p(m'_t = i \mid m'_{t-1} = j, T'_{t-1}, v'_t) = h'_{i,j}, \tag{5}$$

where $i, j = 1, \ldots, N_{m'}$. Since T'_{t-1} can be determined by P'_{t-1}, we get

$$h'_{i,j} = p(m'_t = i \mid m'_{t-1} = j, P_{t-1}, v'_t). \tag{6}$$

Since we can draw $p(m'_t = i \mid m'_{t\ 1} = j)$ in an $N_{m'} \times N_{m'}$ table, we can create a table for Equation (6) with a third axis which is defined by the $\langle P_a, v_b \rangle$ as shown in Figure 2. Here the play P_a, is the primary factor that determines whether m_i transits to m_j and what the transition probability is, while the information V_b determines the prior condition of the transition. Each layer in the graph is conditioned on a particular combination of the tactic executed and the additional information obtained.
For our ball tracking example, $m_t = i$, $i = 1, \ldots, 5$. Similarly,

$$h_{i,j} = p(m_t = i \mid m_{t-1} = j, T_{t-1}, T'_{t-1}, v_t), \tag{7}$$

where $i, j = 1, \ldots, N_m$. Since T_{t-1}, T'_{t-1} can be determined by P_{t-1}, we get

$$h_{i,j} = p(m_t = i \mid m_{t-1} = j, P_{t-1}, v_t) \quad (8)$$

Suppose the current team play is the ***Naive Offense*** in Section 2.2, we can obtain the corresponding motion model transitions for both the ball and the team member using the play-based method (Figure 3).

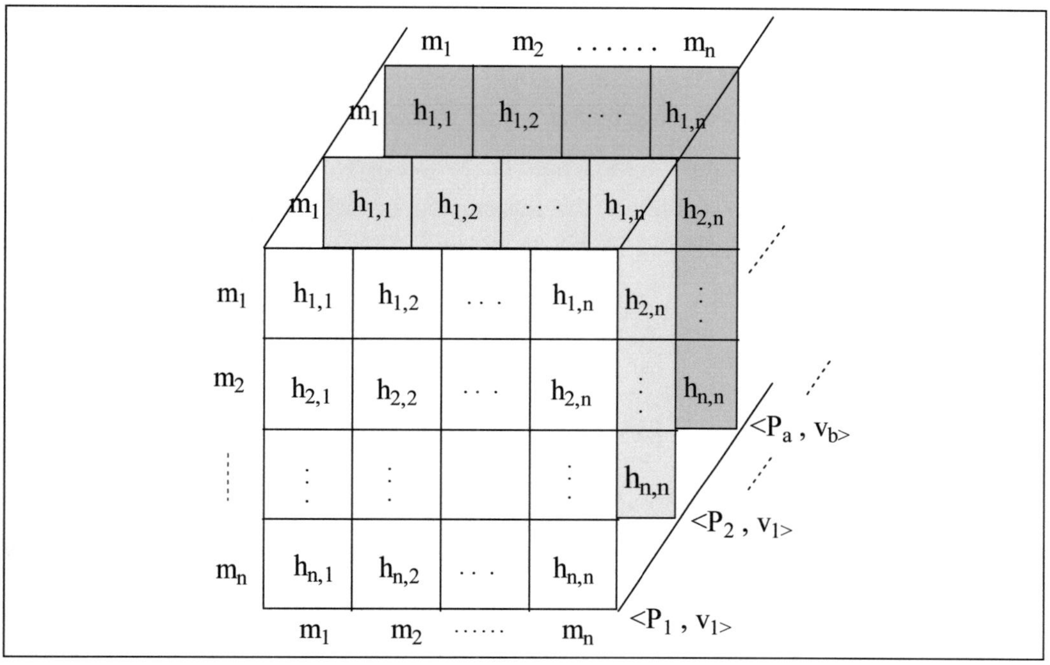

Fig. 2. Play-Based motion modeling. Each layer in the graph is conditioned on a particular combination of the play executed and the additional information obtained.

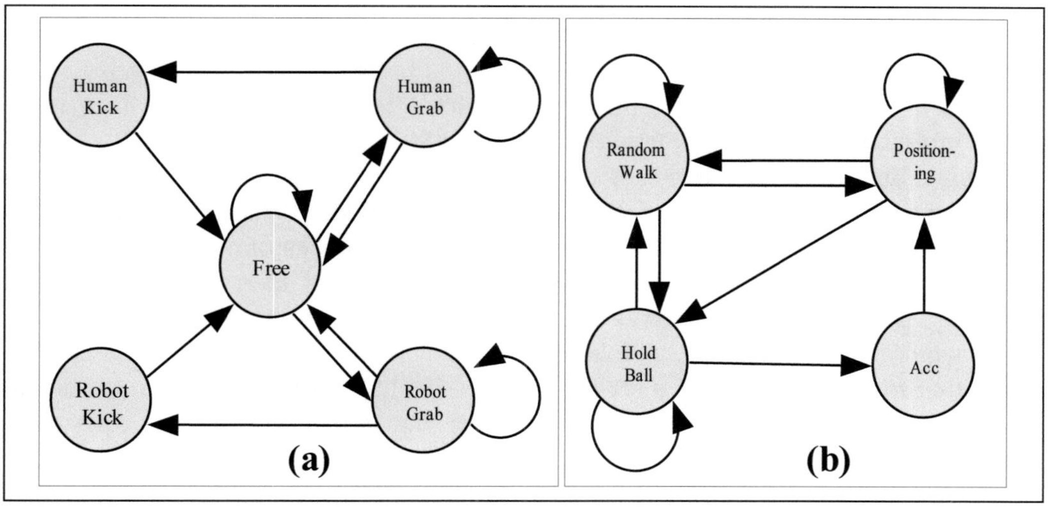

Fig. 3. Object motion modelling based on the play: Naive Offense. Each node is a model. Models transit to one another according to the predefined probabilities (not shown in the figures). (a) Ball motion model. (b) Human team member motion model.

4. Multi-model motion tracking

In this section, we first describe the clustering algorithm we used to continuously monitor the appearance and disappearance of regions of interest (ROIs) on the field. We then use dynamic Bayesian networks to represent the whole system. We give the detailed sequential Monte Carlo methods of tracking in a multi-model multi-hypothesis scheme finally.

4.1 Clustering algorithm

The idea of this algorithm is to group a set of ROIs, $S_t = \{S_t^{(j)}\}_{j=1}^{J_t}$, within a buffer of observations, $Z_t = \{z_{t'}\}_{t-\tau}^{t}$, where τ is the length of the sliding window (Ng et al., 2005). If the current targets are widely separated, the measurements originating from them will be clustered in the locations where the targets had visited from ***t-τ*** to ***t***. Therefore the distance between two measurements within two successive time steps can be taken as the clustering criteria. Let $d_{c,l}(t'+1,t')$ denote the normalized distance between the ***cth*** and ***lth*** measurements of $z_{t'+1}$ and $z_{t'}$.

$$d_{c,l}(t'+1,t') = e_{c,l}^{T}(t'+1,t') \sum_e^{1} e_{c,l}(t'+1,t')\, t \tag{9}$$

where $c \in \{1,\cdots,M_{t'+1}\}$ and $l \in \{1,\cdots,M_{t'}\}$, $e_{c,l}(t'+1,t') = z_{c,t'+1} - z_{l,t'}$ and $\sum_e = 2\sum_n$. For all measurements of $z_{t'+1}$, we have a set of normalized distances $\{d_{c,l}(t'+1,t')\}_{c=1}^{M_{t'+1}}$. The ***c*th*** measurement $z_{c^*,t'+1}$ will be grouped with $z_{l,t'}$ in the same cluster $S_t^{(j)}$ if

$$d_{c^*,l}(t'+1,t') = \arg\min\{d_{c,l}(t'+1,t')\}_{c=1}^{M_{t'+1}} \tag{10}$$

and

$$d_{c^*,l}(t'+1,t') \le \varepsilon_z , \tag{11}$$

where ε_z is a threshold. If none of the measurements of $z_{t'+1}$ can be grouped with $z_{l,t'}$, the search procedure continues and uses $z_{t'+b}$, $1 < b \le \tau$ until (10) and (11) are both satisfied. Meanwhile the algorithm propagates through time to group other measurements in the remaining observations. Since the detected regions obtained via (10) and (11) possibly arise from clutter points, another threshold is set to examine the number of measurements in the region to eliminate the false positives. That is, if the number of measurements in the ***jth*** region $S_t^{(j)}$ is less than τ_{min}, defined as the minimum number of clustered measurements in a region required to identify a target, it is discarded; otherwise, the ***jth*** region is classified as originating from a target. Once a set of ROIs $S_t = \{S_t^{(j)}\}_{j=1}^{J_t}$ is obtained, it is necessary to determine which region belongs to which existing active track or a new track deterministically. Let $\gamma_t = [\gamma_{1,t}, \gamma_{2,t}, \cdots, \gamma_{K_t,t}]^T$ denote the track-to-region association vector. $\gamma_{k,t}$ is used to indicate the association between the ROIs and the active tracks. $\gamma_{K_t,t}$ is evaluated as *j* if track *k* can be associated with $S_t^{(j)}$, otherwise it is zero. Refer to (Ng et al., 2005) for more details of the clustering algorithm.

4.2 DBN representation

Following the play-based motion model, we can use dynamic Bayesian networks (DBNs) to represent the whole system for team member and ball tracking in a natural and compact way as shown in Figure 4 and Figure 5 respectively. In the two graphs, the system state is represented by variables (play P, tactic T, infrared sensor measurement s, ball state $\mathbf{x}$, ball motion model index m, vision sensor measurement of ball $\mathbf{z}$, team member state $\mathbf{x}'$, team member motion model index m', vision sensor measurement of team member $\mathbf{z}$), where each variable takes on values in some space. The variables change over time in discrete intervals, so that e.g., $\mathbf{x}_t$ is the ball state at time t.

Furthermore, the edges indicate dependencies between the variables. For instance, in Figure 5 the ball motion model index m_t depends on m_{t-1}, T_{t-1}, T'_{t-1}, s_t and $\mathbf{x}_{t-1}$, hence there are edges coming from the latter five variables to m_t. For the rest of this section, we give the ball-tracking algorithm following Figure 5. The team-member-tracking algorithm can be obtained similarly following Figure 4.

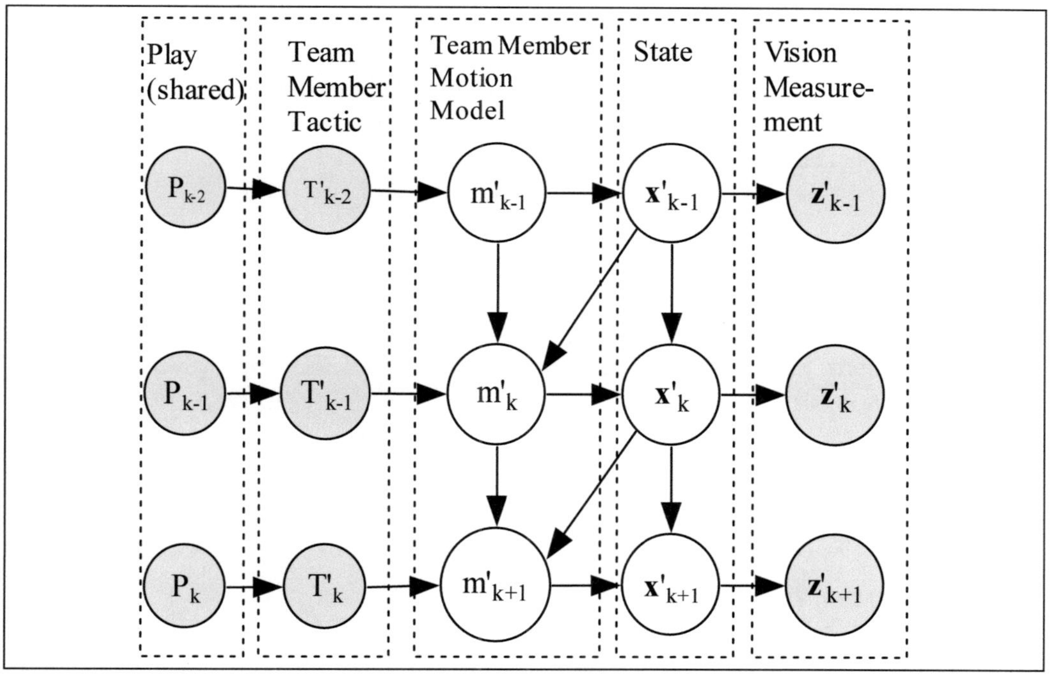

Fig. 4. A dynamic Bayesian network for team member tracking. Filled circles represent deterministic variables with are observable or are known as tactics or plays that the robot is executing.

4.3 Importance sampling function

We use the sequential Monte Carlo method to track the motion model m and the multi-target state $\mathbf{x}$. Particle filtering is a general purpose Monte Carlo scheme for tracking in a dynamic system (Doucet et al., 2001). It maintains the belief state at time t as a set of particles $p_t^{(1)}, p_t^{(2)}, \cdots, p_t^{(N_s)}$, where each $p_t^{(i)}$ is a full instantiation of the tracked variables

$\{p_t^{(i)}, w_t^{(i)}\}$, $w_t^{(i)}$ is the weight of particle $p_t^{(i)}$ and N_s is the number of particles. In our case, $p_t^{(i)} = \langle x_t^{(i)}, m_t^{(i)} \rangle$. To make our notation more concrete, a particular particle $p_t^{(i)}$, which is tracking Kt multi-target state vector xt and motion model mt, is given as (Kreucher et al., 2003):

$$p_t^{(i)} = \begin{pmatrix} m_{1,t}^{(i)} & m_{2,t}^{(i)} & \cdots & m_{K_t,t}^{(i)} \\ x_{1,t}^{(i)} & x_{2,t}^{(i)} & \cdots & x_{K_t,t}^{(i)} \\ y_{1,t}^{(i)} & y_{2,t}^{(i)} & \cdots & y_{K_t,t}^{(i)} \\ \dot{x}_{1,t}^{(i)} & \dot{x}_{2,t}^{(i)} & \cdots & \dot{x}_{K_t,t}^{(i)} \\ \dot{y}_{1,t}^{(i)} & y_{2,t}^{(i)} & \cdots & y_{K_t,t}^{(i)} \end{pmatrix} \tag{12}$$

We sample the ball motion model following the ball-tracking DBN as below:

$$m_{k,t}^{(i)} \sim p(m_{k,t} \mid m_{k,t-1}^{(i)}, x_{k,t-1}^{(i)}, s_t, T_{t-1}, T'_{t-1}) \tag{13}$$

Note that T_{t-1} and T'_{t-1} are inferred deterministically from P_{t-1} instead of sampling. Conditioned on the ball motion model $m_{k,t}^{(i)}$, we then use the importance function introduced in (Ng et al., 2005) to sample ball state $x_{k,t}^{(i)}$:

$$x_{k,t}^{(i)} \sim \begin{cases} q_D(x_{k,t} \mid m_{k,t-1}^{(i)}), k \notin \Psi_{S_t} \\ q_{DS}(x_{k,t} \mid m_{k,t}^{(i)}, x_{k,t-1}^{(i)}, S_t^{(j)}, k \in \Psi_{S_t} \end{cases}, \tag{14}$$

where $k \in \Psi_{S_t}$ are those tracks with $\gamma_{k,t} = j$ and $j \in \Omega_D$, and $q_D(\cdot)$ and $q_{DS}(\cdot)$ are the proposal functions for $x_{k,t}$ without and with an associated ROI $S_t^{(j)}$, given as follows, respectively,

$$q_D(x_{k,t} \mid m_{k,t}^{(i)}, x_{k,t-1}^{(i)}) = p(x_{k,t} \mid m_{k,t}^{(i)}, x_{k,t-1}^{(i)}), \tag{15}$$

$$q_{DS}(x_{k,t} \mid m_{k,t}^{(i)}, x_{k,t-1}^{(i)}, S_t^{(j)}) = \mu p(x_{k,t} \mid m_{k,t}^{(i)}, x_{k,t-1}^{(i)}) + (1-\mu) q(x_{k,t} \mid m_{k,t}^{(i)}, x_{k,t-1}^{(i)}, S_t^{(j)}), \tag{16}$$

where $0 \le \mu \le 1$ and $q(\cdot)$ is a uniform sampling from the associated ROI $S_t^{(j)}$. If $\mu = 1$, the importance sampling function is reduced back to the dynamic prior. If $\mu = 0$, all particles are generated from the data-dependent importance function. If $0 < \mu < 1$, this proposal combines the dynamic prior and the current ROIs to generate representative particles.

4.4 Birth, death and update moves

Assuming that there are K_t^b ROIs that cannot be associated with any existing track, we will initiate a new track in each time step from one of these regions instead of initiating K_t^b tracks simultaneously in order to fit the birth move with the assumed system process model in (2). When an existing track cannot be associated with a region at a given time, the target being tracked by the tracker may have disappeared or temporarily experience a short period of data loss. Thus we may remove the track for the target only if it has failed to associate with any ROI with τ_d time steps. Refer to (Ng et al., 2005) for the detailed algorithm of birth move and death move.

In the update move, there is no change in terms of the number of ROIs. We only need to update the target states with a common value of number of targets $K_t^{(i)} = K_{t-1}^{(i)}$, using the sequential importance sampling method as follows:

$[\{x_t^{(i)}, m_t^{(i)}, w_t^{(i)}\}_{i=1}^{N_s}] = \mathrm{MT\text{-}PBPF}[\{x_{t-1}^{(i)}, m_{t-1}^{(i)}, w_{t-1}^{(i)}\}_{i=1}^{N_s}, z_t, s_t, T_{t-1}, T'_{t-1}]$

for i = 1: N_s

  for k = 1: K_t

    draw $m_{k,t}^{(i)} \sim p(m_{k,t} \mid m_{k,t-1}^{(i)}, x_{k,t-1}^{(i)}, s_t, T_{t-1}, T'_{t-1})$

    if track k has corresponding ROI $S_t^{(j)}$

      draw $x_{k,t}^{(i)} \sim q_{DS}(x_{k,t} \mid m_{k,t}^{(i)}, x_{k,t-1}^{(i)}, S_t^{(j)})$

    else

      draw $x_{k,t}^{(i)} \sim q_D(x_{k,t} \mid m_{k,t}^{(i)}, x_{k,t-1}^{(i)})$

    end if

  end for

  set $w_t^{(i)} = w_{t-1}^{(i)} \quad p(z_t \mid x_t, K_t, \alpha_t)$

end for

calculate total weight: $w = \sum_{i=1}^{N_s} w_t^{(i)}$

for i = 1: N_s

  normalize: $w_t^{(i)} = w_t^{(i)} / w$

end for

resample

Table 2. The Multi-Target Play-Based Particle Filtering algorithm (MT-PBPF).

The inputs of the algorithm are samples drawn from the previous posterior $\langle x_{t-1}^{(i)}, m_{t-1}^{(i)}, w_{t-1}^{(i)} \rangle$, the present vision and infrared sensory measurement z_t, s_t, the robot's tactic T_{t-1}, and the team member's tactic T'_{t-1}. The outputs are the updated weighted samples $\langle x_t^{(i)}, m_t^{(i)}, w_t^{(i)} \rangle$. In the sampling algorithm, first, a new ball motion model index, $m_t^{(i)}$, is sampled according to (13) at line 03. Then given the model index, and previous ball state, a new ball state is sampled according to (14) at line 05/07. According to (4), the importance weight of each sample is given by the likelihood of the vision measurement given the predicted new ball state at line 10. Finally, each weight is normalized and the samples are resampled. Then we can estimate the ball state based on the mean of all the $x_t^{(i)}$. Though we are trying to eliminate the clutter from the beginning of tracking (clustering algorithm), due to the property of the multi-target tracker, further recognition process might be done in order to figure out which tracked target is the true ball. Similarly the state of the team member $\mathbf{x}'_t$ can be obtained from the team member tracker.

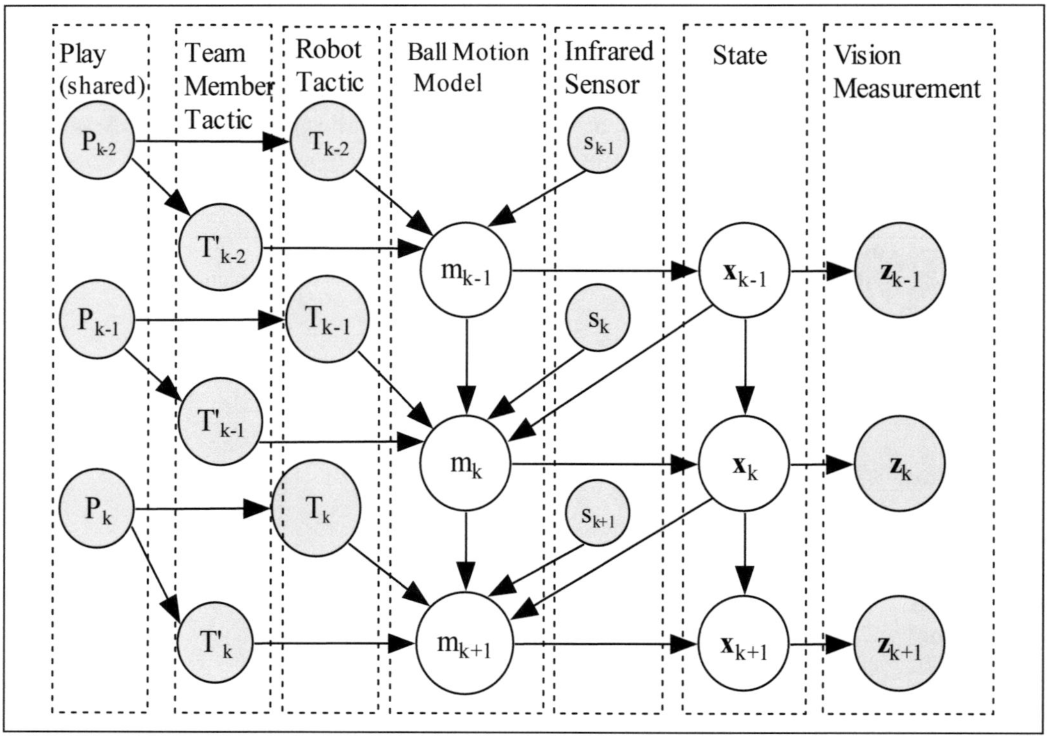

Fig. 5. A dynamic Bayesian network for object tracking.

5. Experimental results

From previous work we knew the initial speed and accuracy of the ball velocity after a kick motion. We profiled the system and measurement noise as well. In this section, we evaluate the effectiveness of our tracking system in both simulated and real-world tests.

5.1 Simulation experiments

Because it is difficult to know the ground truth of the target's position and velocity in the real robot test, we do the simulation experiments to evaluate the precision of tracking.

Motion Model	Single Model	Multi-Model
Human Position Est RMS (m)	0.0030	0.0014
Human Velociy Est RMS (m/s)	0.42	0.025
Ball Position Est RMS (m)	0.0028	0.0017
Ball Velocity Est RMS (m/s)	0.4218	0.0597

Table 3. The average RMS error of position estimation and velocity estimation from human trackers and ball trackers.

Experiments are done following the ***Naive Offense*** play, in which the robot acts as the receiver and the human team member acts as the passer. Noises are simulated according to the model we profiled in previous work. In the beginning, the team member holds the ball. After a fixed amount of time, the ball is kicked towards the robot, and the team member moves forward to a predefined location.

We implement both a single model tracker and a play-based multi-model tracker for the ball and the team member. We simulate the experiment for 50 runs, and then compare the performance of the two trackers with different implementations. The average RMS error of position estimation and velocity estimation are shown in Table 3. The results show that the play-based multi-model scheme performs much better than the single model especially in terms of velocity estimation. Because with the play-based motion model, when the ball is being kicked, most particles evolving using the transition model determined by the play will change its motion model $m_t^{(i)}$ from ***Free-Ball*** to ***Human-Kick-Ball***, and a velocity will be added to the ball accordingly.

5.2 Multi-target tracking test

In this test, one Segway RMP robot is tracking one or more balls on the field with ***SearchBall*** tactic. We would like to compare solely the target detection performance between the proposed method and the IMM tracker. A scenario with K_t $(0 \le K_t \le 3)$ balls appearing and disappearing at different times and there are a set of false positives at fixed position in the surroundings.

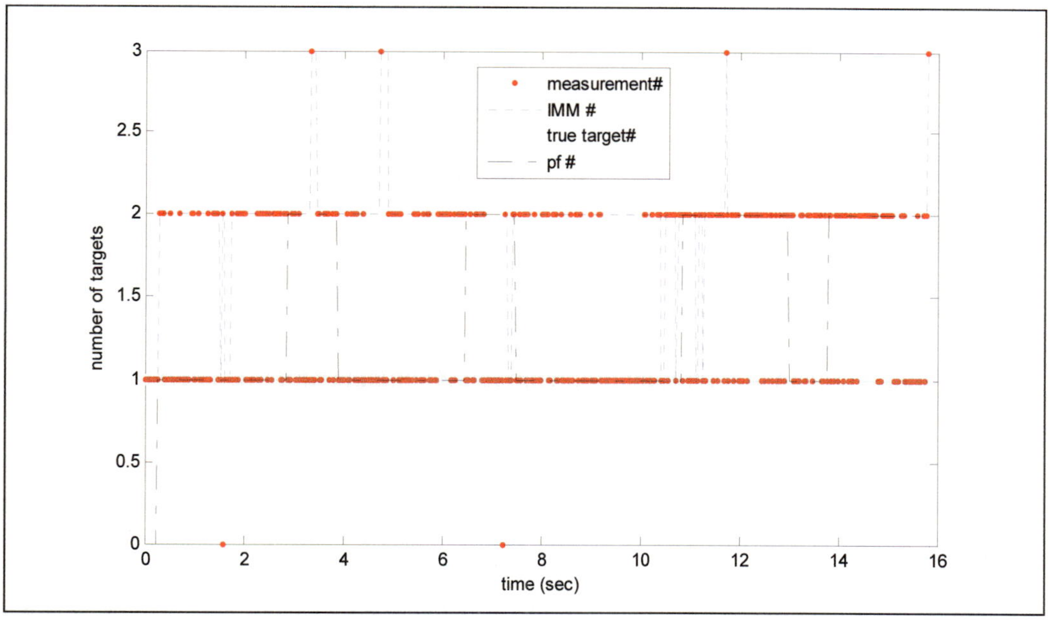

Fig. 6. A comparison of the target detection performance between the proposed method and the IMM tracker when only one target exists with surrounding clutters.

When estimating the number of targets, 3600 particles are used in the proposed method. Figures 6-7 summarize the results. In both figures, the dots show the number of measurements at a given time. The dotted line represents the number of the targets tracked by the IMM tracker. The dash dotted line represents the number of targets tracked by the multi-model multi-target tracker proposed in this paper. The crosses show the true number of the targets at any given time. As shown in the figure, the IMM tracker is sensitive to the number of measurements, while our approach is more robust and consistent to high clutter density. Since the detection is basically performed on the clustering of the observations and the association between the detected ROIs and the existing tracks, it is computational low-cost. Therefore it is also practical for real-time multi-target detection and tracking.

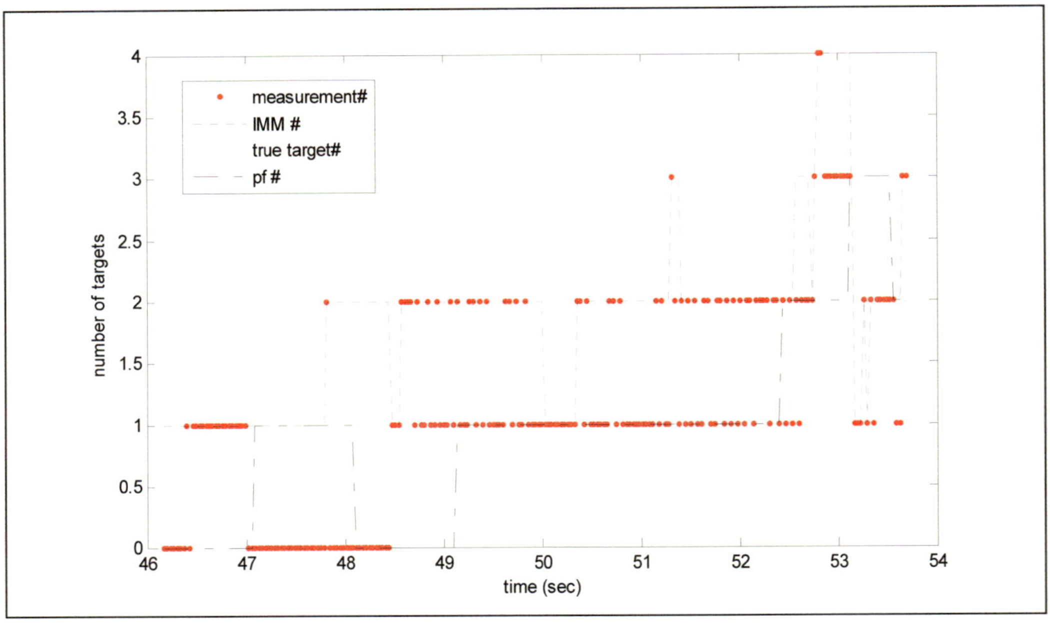

Fig. 7. A comparison of the target detection performance between the proposed method and the IMM tracker when multiple targets exist with surrounding clutters.

5.3 Team cooperation test

We do experiments on the Segway RMP soccer robot executing the offensive play and coordinating with the human team member. The test setup is demonstrated in Figure 8, in which the digits along the lines show the sequence of the whole strategy, the filled circle at position B represents the robot, the unfilled circle at position E represent an opponent player, and the shaded circle represent the human team member.

When each run begins, the human team member is at position A. With this team cooperation plan (play), the robot chooses the tactic ***CatchKickToTeammember*** to execute, in which the robot starts with the skill ***Search-Ball***. When the robot finds the ball, the team member passes the ball directly to the robot and chooses a positioning point to go to either at C or D. The robot grabs the ball after the ball is in the catchable area and is detected by the infrared sensor (skill ***Grab-Ball***). Next the robot searches for the team member holding the ball with its catcher (skill ***Search-Teammember***). After the robot finds the team member, the robot kicks the ball to its team member (skill ***KickToTeammember***) and the team member shoots at the goal, completing the whole offensive play. Each run ends in one of the following conditions.

- Succeed if the human receives the ball from the robot or the human does not receiver the ball but the pass can be considered as a "good" one.
- Fail if the robot is in searching for the ball or the team member for more than 30 seconds.
- Fail if the ball is outside the field before the robot catches it.

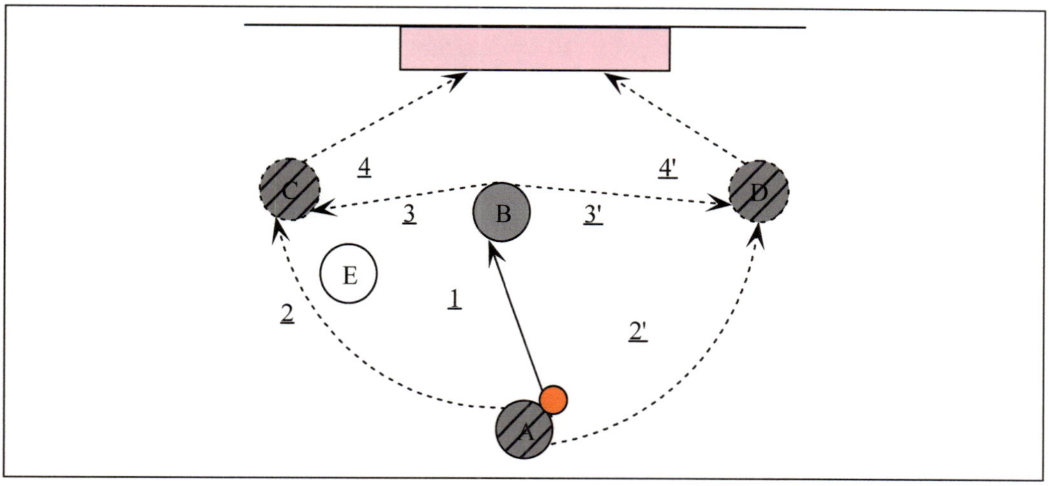

Fig. 7. A comparison of the target detection performance between the proposed method and the IMM tracker when multiple targets exist with surrounding clutters.

In the experiment over 15 runs, the robot with single model trackers fails 5 of the total. While the robot with play-based multi-model trackers fails 2 of the total. We also keep track of the mean time taken in all the successful runs. We list the result in Table 4. Using play-based multi-model tracking saves 32.3% time in terms of completing the whole play over single model tracking. During the experiment, we note that when using the single model tracking, most time was spent on searching the team member. Incorporating the team cooperation knowledge known as play into the team member motion modeling greatly improves the accuracy of the team member motion model and therefore avoids taking time in searching a lost target from scratch.

Motion Model	Single Model	Multi-Model
Mean Time (sec)	33.4	22.6

Table 4. The average time taken over all the successful runs.

6. Related work

Tracking moving targets using a Kalman filter is the optional solution if the system follows a single model, f and h in Equation (1) and (3) are known linear functions and the noise v and n are Gaussians (Arulampalam et al., 2002). Multiple model Kalman filters such as Interacting Multiple Model (IMM) are known to be superior to the single Kalman filter when the tracked target is manoeuvring (Bar-Shalom et al., 2001). For nonlinear systems or systems with non-Gaussian noises, a further approximation is introduced, but the posterior densities are therefore only locally accurate and do not reflect the actual system densities.

Since the particle filter is not restricted to Gaussian densities, a tactic-based motion modeling method is proposed in (Gu, 2005). Based on that approach, we further introduce the play-based motion modeling method when team coordination knowledge is available. Another related approach was proposed to track a moving target using Rao-Blackwellised particle filter (Kwok & Fox, 2004) in which a fixed transition table was used between different models. Our transition model is dependent on the play that the robot is executing and the additional information that matters. This model can be flexibly integrated into our existing STP architecture.

There have been different strategies in multi-target tracking. In order to handle the data association and tracking problem, the classical Joint Probabilistic Data Association Filter (JPDAF) adopts the methods like the extended Kalman Filter (EKF) for multi-target state estimation, whose tracking performance is known to be limited by the linearity of the data models (Bar-Shalom & Fortmann, 1988). Another approach known as sequential Monte Carlo methods is able to perform well even when the data models are nonlinear and non-Gaussian. However, almost all of these methods assume that the knowledge of true targets (without clutter) is given, which is not applicable in the field that Segway RMP soccer robots operates in.

Recently, a hybrid approach for online joint detection and tracking for multiple targets was proposed (Ng et al., 2005). This approach does not rely on the clutter-free assumption. In this paper, based on their approach, we present a play-based multi-target tracking algorithm, which incorporates tactic information to eliminate the false alarms and to improve resampling efficiency. Compared to our method, first, existing techniques consider less complex dynamic systems where only one part of the state space is non-linear. In contrast, our approach estimates a system where multiple components are highly non-linear (Segway RMP robot motion, ball motion, team member motion). Second, most existing techniques examine their performance with simulated experiments, while we test our approach in real robot experiments. Third, our approach goes beyond existing techniques by incorporating team cooperation information into the tracking process which further improves the performance.

7. Conclusions and future work

Motivated by the interactions between a team and the tracked target, we contribute a method to achieve efficient tracking through using a play-based motion model and combined vision and infrared sensory information. This method gives the robot a more exact task-specific motion model when executing different tactics over the tracked target (e.g. the ball) or collaborating with the tracked target (e.g. the team member). Then we represent the system in a compact dynamic Bayesian network and use particle filter to keep track of the motion model and target state through sampling. The empirical results from the simulated and using the real robot agent show the efficiency of the multi-model tracking over single model tracking.

If the teammate is a human, not a robot, the certainty that the teammate is executing the expected play or tactic could be reduced. That is, the human teammate could fail to execute the desired play or tactic. Future work will take such uncertainty into account. A better human team member modeling (for example, include intercepting the moving ball, mark a player, covering the goal) will also help. Another interesting work is to know how the performance of the presented method is affected by the presence of tactics of the team member that are not exactly determined in the team coordination plan.

8. Acknowledgments

We would like to thank the members of the CMBalance Segway soccer team for their help with developing the infrastructure for the Segway robots. This work was supported by United States Department of the Interior under Grant No. NBCH-1040007. The content of the information in this publication does not necessarily reflect the position or policy of the Defense Advanced Research Projects Agency (DARPA), US Department of Interior, US Government, and no official endorsement should be inferred.

9. References

S. Arulampalam; S. Maskell, N. Gordon, T. Clapp (2002). A tutorial on particle filters for on-line non-linear/non-gaussian Bayesian tracking. *IEEE Transactions on Signal Processing,* 50(2):174–188, Feb.2002.

Y. Bar-Shalom & T. E. Fortmann (1988). *Tracking and Data Association.* Academic Press, Inc, 1988.

Y. Bar-Shalom; X.-R. Li, & T. Kirubarajan (2001). *Estimation with Applications to Tracking and Navigation.* John Wiley & Sons, Inc, 2001.

B. Browning; J. Bruce; M. Bowling & M. Veloso (2005). STP: Skills, tactics and plays for multi-robot control in adversarial environments. *IEEE Journal of Control and Systems Engineering,* 219:33–52, 2005.

B. Browning; J. Searock; P. E. Rybski & M. Veloso (2005). Turning segways into soccer robots. *Industrial Robot,* 32(2):149–156, 2005.

A. Doucet; N. D. Freitas & N. Gordon (2001). *Sequential Monte Carlo Methods in Practice.* Springer-Verlag, New York, 2001.

Y. Gu (2005). Tactic-based motion modelling and multi-sensor tracking. *Proceedings of Twentieth National Conference on Artificial Intelligence,* 2005.

C. Kreucher; K. Kastella & A. O. H. III (2003). Multi-target sensor management using alpha-divergence measures. pp 209–222, 2003.

C. Kwok & D. Fox (2004). Map-based multiple model tracking of a moving object. *Proceedings of eight RoboCup International Symposium,* July 2004.

W. Ng; J. Li, S. Godsill, & J (2005). Vermaak. A hybrid approach for online joint detection and tracking for multiple targets. *IEEE Aerospace Conferences,* 2005.

D. Schulz; W. Burgrad & D. Fox (2003). People tracking with mobile robots using sample-based joint probabilistic data association filters. *International Journal of Robotics Research,* 22(2), 2003.

J. Searock; B. Browning & M. Veloso (2004). Turning Segways into Soccer Robots. *In Proceedings of IROS'04,* Sendai, Japan, September 2004.

M. Veloso; B. Browning; P. Rybski & J. Searock (2005). Segwayrmp robot football league rules. Technical report, http://www.cs.cmu.edu/ robosoccer/segway/, 2005.

17

MASDScheGATS - Scheduling System for Dynamic Manufacturing Environmemts

Ana Madureira, Joaquim Santos and Ivo Pereira
Computer Science Department, Institute of Engineering - Polytechnic of Porto
GECAD – Knowledge Engineering and Decision Support Research Group
Portugal

1. Introduction

This chapter addresses the resolution of scheduling in manufacturing systems subject to perturbations. The planning of Manufacturing Systems involves frequently the resolution of a huge amount and variety of combinatorial optimisation problems with an important impact on the performance of manufacturing organisations. Examples of those problems are the sequencing and scheduling problems in manufacturing management, routing and transportation, layout design and timetabling problems.
The classical optimisation methods are not enough for the efficient resolution of those problems or are developed for specific situations (Brucker, 2004) (Blazewicz et al., 2005) (Pinedo, 2005) (Madureira, 2003).
New organizational and technological paradigms are needed to reply to the modern manufacturing systems challenges. The traditional structure of manufacturing industries is constructed upon the three pillars of land, labour and capital. The challenge is to move towards a new structure, which can be described as innovating manufacturing, founded on knowledge and capital. Future manufacturing solutions must identify multiple perspectives and linkages between novel approaches to customization, customer response, logistics and maintenance. The current typically linear approach to research, development, design, construction and assembly will be replaced by simultaneous activity in all areas to satisfying global demand and shorten time-to-market (MANUFUTURE, 2004).
Multi-agent paradigm is emerging for the development of solutions to very hard distributed computational problems. This paradigm is based either on the activity of "intelligent" agents which perform complex functionalities or on the exploitation of a large number of simple agents that can produce an overall intelligent behaviour leading to the solution of alleged almost intractable problems. The multi-agent paradigm is often inspired by biological systems.
Meta-Heuristics (MH) form a class of powerful and practical solution techniques for tackling complex, large-scale combinatorial problems producing efficiently high-quality solutions. From the literature we can conclude that they are adequate for static problems. However, real scheduling problems are quite dynamic, considering the arrival of new orders, orders being cancelled, machine delays or faults, etc. Scheduling problem in dynamic environments have been investigated by a number of authors, see for example (Aytug et al., 2005) (Branke, 2000) (Cowling & Johansson, 2002) (Madureira et al., 2004).

In this chapter we will model a Manufacturing System by means of Multi-Agent Systems (MAS) and Meta-Heuristics technologies, where each agent may represent a processing entity (machine). The objective of the system is to deal with the complex problem of Dynamic Scheduling in Manufacturing Systems. Our approach shows that a good global solution for a scheduling problem may emerge from a community of machine agents solving locally their schedules while cooperating with other machine agents that share some relations between the operations/jobs.

The remaining sections are organized as follows: Section 2 summarizes some works related on Meta-Heuristics and Multi-Agent Systems applications. In section 3 the scheduling problem under consideration is described. Section 4 presents the MASDScheGATS Systems and describes implemented mechanisms. Section 5 present a computational study and puts forward results discussion. Finally, the chapter presents some conclusions that were obtained from our model and puts forward some ideas for future opportunities of research and development work.

2. Related work

The planning of Manufacturing Systems involves frequently the resolution of a huge amount and variety of combinatorial optimisation problems with an important impact on the performance of manufacturing organisations. Examples of those problems are the sequencing and scheduling problems in manufacturing management, routing and transportation, layout design and timetabling problems.

Scheduling can be defined as the assignment of time-constrained jobs to time-constrained resources within a pre-defined time framework, which represents the complete time horizon of the schedule. An admissible schedule will have to satisfy a set of constraints imposed on jobs and resources. So, a scheduling problem can be seen as a decision making process for operations starting and resources to be used. A variety of characteristics and constraints related with jobs and production system, such as operation processing time, release and due dates, precedence constraints and resource availability, can affect scheduling decisions (Brucker, 2004) (Blazewicz et al., 2005) (Pinedo, 2005).

Frequently classical optimization methods are not efficient enough for the resolution of Job-Shop Scheduling problems (Blazewicz et al., 2005) (Pinedo, 2005). In most cases they are good for solving only some specific and small size ones. The interest of new approaches, namely Meta-Heuristics such as Tabu Search, Simulated Annealing, and Genetic Algorithms, based on local search, is that they lead, in general, to good solutions in an efficient way, i.e. short computing time and small implementation effort.

Meta-Heuristics is the set of computing techniques inspired by biologically systems that are derived from nature. The distinction between Nature-inspired techniques and Meta-Heuristics is largely counterproductive. Although surface-level dissimilarities, the central themes underlying these two classes of heuristic are nearly identical, e.g., intensification versus diversification, mechanisms for escaping local optimum, intelligent design of selection/mutation/crossover operators, and the structure of the fitness landscape. The family of Meta-Heuristics includes, but it is not limited, to Tabu Search, Simulated Annealing, Adaptive Memory procedures, Scatter Search, Soft Computing, Evolutionary Methods, Ant Systems, Particle Swarm Optimization and their hybrids. For literature on this subject, see for example (Gonzalez,2007) (Xhafa & Abraham, 2008)

In last decades, there has been a significant level of research interest in Meta-Heuristics approaches for solving large real world scheduling problems, which are often complex, constrained and dynamic. Scheduling algorithms that achieve good or near optimal solutions and can efficiently adapt them to perturbations are, in most cases, preferable to those that achieve optimal ones but that cannot implement such an adaptation. This is the case with most algorithms for solving the so-called static scheduling problem for different setting of both single and multi-machine systems arrangements. This reality, motivated us to concentrate on tools, which could deal with such dynamic, disturbed scheduling problems, even though, due to the complexity of these problems, optimal solutions may not be possible to find.

Considering the complexity inherent to the manufacturing systems, dynamic scheduling is considered an excellent candidate for the application of agent-based technology. In many implementations of MAS systems for manufacturing scheduling, the agents model the resources of the system and the tasks scheduling is done in a distributed way by means of cooperation and coordination amongst agents (Lu & Yih, 2001) (Nwana et al., 1996) (Madureira et al., 2007). When responding to disturbances, the distributed nature of multi-agent systems can also be a benefit to the rescheduling algorithm by involving only the agents directly affected, without disturbing the rest of the community that can continue with their work.

Hybridization of intelligent systems is a promising research field of computational intelligence focusing on combinations of multiple approaches to develop the next generation of intelligent systems. An important stimulus to the investigations on Hybrid Intelligent Systems area is the awareness that combined approaches will be necessary if the remaining tough problems in artificial intelligence are to be solved. Meta-Heuristics, Bio-Inspired Techniques, Neural computing, Machine Learning, Fuzzy Logic Systems, Evolutionary Algorithms, Agent-based Methods, among others, have been established and shown their strength and drawbacks. Recently, hybrid intelligent systems are getting popular due to their capabilities in handling several real world complexities involving imprecision, uncertainty and vagueness (Boeres et al., 2003), (Madureira et al., 2004) (Bartz- Beielstein et al., 2007) (Hasan Kamrul et al., 2007).

3. Extended job shop scheduling problem definition

Real world scheduling problems have received a lot of attention in recent years. In this work we consider the resolution of realistic problems. Most real-world multi-operation scheduling problems can be described as dynamic and extended versions of the classic Job-Shop scheduling combinatorial optimization problem.

In practice, many scheduling problems include further restrictions and relaxation of others (Portmann, 1997). Thus, for example, precedence constraints among operations of the different jobs are common because, often, mainly in discrete manufacturing, products are made of several components that can be seen as different jobs whose manufacture must be coordinated. Additionally, since a job can be the result of manufacturing and assembly of parts at several stages, different parts of the same job may be processed simultaneously on different machines (concurrent or simultaneous processing).

Moreover, in practice, scheduling environment tends to be dynamic, i.e. new jobs arrive at unpredictable intervals, machines breakdown, jobs can be cancelled and due dates and processing times can change frequently.

The main elements of the Extended Job-Shop Scheduling Problem (EJSSP) problem could be modeled as shown in the following subsections.

3.1 Jobs

- A set of multi-operation jobs $J_1,\ldots,J_n$ has to be scheduled. d_j is the due date of job J_j. t_j is the initial processing time of job J_j . r_j is the release time of job J_j.
- The existence of operations on the same job, on different parts and components, processed simultaneously on different machines, followed by components assembly operations (multi-level jobs).
- The existence of different job release dates r_j and due dates d_j.
- The possibility of job priorities definition, reflecting the importance of satisfying their due dates, being similar to the weight assigned to jobs in scheduling theory.
- Precedence constraints among operations of the different jobs.
- The existence of operations on the same job, with different parts and components, processed simultaneously on different machines.
- New jobs can arrive at unpredictable intervals.
- Jobs can be cancelled.
- Changes in task attributes can occur: Processing times, date of deliver and priorities.

3.2 Operations

- Each operation O_{ijkl} is characterized by the index (i, j, k, l), where i defines the machine where the operation k of job j is processed and l the graph precedence operation level (level 1 correspond to initial operations, without precedents).
- Precedence constraints among operations of the different jobs.
- Each job J_j consists of one or more operations O_{ijkl}, where:
  - IO_{ijkl} is the time interval for starting operation O_{ijkl}
  - r_{ijkl} is the release time of operation O_{ijkl}
  - t_{ijkl} is the earliest time at which O_{ijkl} can start
  - T_{ijkl} is the latest time at which O_{ijkl} can start
  - p_{ijkl} is the processing time of the operation O_{ijkl}
  - C_{ijkl} is the k operation completion time from job j, level l on the machine i
- Each operation O_{ijkl} must be processed on one machine of the set M_i, where p_{ijkl} is the processing time of operation O_{ijkl} on machine M_i.
- The existence of operations on the same job, on different parts and components, processed simultaneously on different machines, followed by components assembly operations (multi-level jobs).

3.3 Machines

- The shop consists of a set of machines $M_1,\ldots,M_n$.
- A machine can process more than one operation of the same job (recirculation).
- The existence of alternative machines, identical or not..

In this work, we define a job as a manufacturing order for a final item that could be Simple or Complex). It may be Simple, like a part, requiring a set of operations to be processed. We define it as Simple Product or Simple Final Item. Complex Final Items, requiring processing of several operations on a number of parts followed by assembly operations at several stages, are also dealt with.

We consider the existence of two different types of tasks:

- Jobs with linear structure - where operations are sequentially processed, considering that an operation can be processed when its precedent has already been finished. Job-Shop benchmark tests referred on literature are of this type (Madureira, 2003).
- Jobs with concurrent operations - where operations of same task can be processed simultaneously. An operation can have more than one precedent operation and more than one succeeding operation. This category is common in Complex Final items.

Moreover, in practice, scheduling environment tend to be dynamic, i.e. new jobs arrive a unpredictable intervals, machines breakdown, jobs are cancelled and due dates and processing times change frequently. This non-basic JSSP (Portmann,), focused in our work, which we call Extended Job-Shop Scheduling Problem (EJSSP), has major extensions and differences in relation to the classic or basic JSSP. The existence of operations on the same job, on different parts and components, processed simultaneously on different machines, followed by components assembly operations, which characterizes EJSSP, is not typical of scheduling problems addressed in the literature. However, such is common in practice. This approach to job definition, emphasizing the importance of considering complex jobs, which mimic customer orders of products, is in accordance with real world scheduling in manufacturing.

4. MASDScheGATS system

Distributed environment approaches are important in order to improve scheduling systems flexibility and capacity to react to unpredictable events. It is accepted that new generations of manufacturing facilities, with increasing specialization and integration, add more problematic challenges to scheduling systems. For that reason, issues like robustness, regeneration capacities and efficiency are currently critical elements in the design of manufacturing scheduling system and encouraged the development of new architectures and solutions, leveraging the MAS research results.

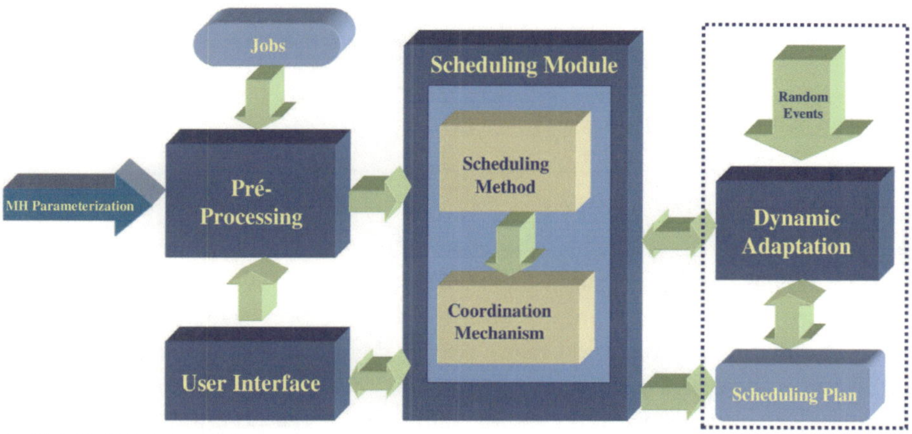

Fig. 1. MASDSCHEGATS System

4.1 MASDScheGATS scheduling system

It starts focusing on the solution of the dynamic deterministic EJSSP problems. For solving these we developed a framework, leading to a dynamic scheduling system (Fig. 1) having as

a fundamental scheduling tool, a hybrid scheduling system, with two main pieces of intelligence.
One such piece is a Hybrid Scheduling Module that could be a combination of Tabu Search and Genetic Algorithm based method and a mechanism for inter-machine activity coordination. The objective of this mechanism is to coordinate the operation of machines, taking into account the technological constraints of jobs, i.e. job operations precedence relationships, towards obtaining good schedules. The other piece is a dynamic adaptation module that includes mechanisms for neighbourhood/population regeneration under dynamic environments, increasing or decreasing it according new job arrivals or cancellations.

4.1.1 Hybrid scheduling module

In this work solutions are encoded by the direct representation, where the schedule is described as a sequence of operations, i.e. each position represents an operation index with initial and final processing times. Each operation is characterized by the index (i, j, k, l), where i defines the machine where the operation k is processed, j the job that belongs, and l the graph precedence operation level (level 1 correspond to initial operations, without precedents).

m – Number of machines
n – Number of jobs
l – Operation level defined on precedence graph
O_{ijkl} – Operation k from job j, to be processed on machine i with level l (defined on precedence graph)
IO_{ijkl} – Time interval for starting operation O_{ijkl}
d_j – Due date of job j
t_j – Initial processing time of job j
r_j – Release time of job j
r_{ijkl} – Release time of operation O_{ijkl}
t_{ijkl} – The earliest time at which O_{ijkl} can start
T_{ijkl} – The latest time at which O_{ijkl} can start
p_{ijkl} – Processing time of the operation O_{ijkl}
C_{ijkl} - Operation completion time from job j, level l on the machine i
L_j – Lateness ($L_j = C_j - d_j$)
T_j – Tardiness ($T_j = \max \{ L_j , 0 \}$)

Table 1. Notation

Initially, we start by decomposing the deterministic EJSSP problem into a series of deterministic Single Machine Scheduling Problems (SMSP). We assume the existence of different and known job release times rj, prior to which no processing of the job can be done and, also, job due dates dj. Based on these, release dates and due dates are determined for each SMSP and, subsequently, each such problem is solved independently by a TS or a GA (considering a self-parameterization issue). Afterwards, the solutions obtained for each SMSP are integrated to obtain a solution to the main EJSSP problem instance. The scheduling method is described in table 2.
The completion due times for each operation of a job are derived from job due dates and processing times by subtracting the processing time from the completion due time of the immediately succeeding job operation.

1st PHASE	**Finding a 1st job shop schedule based on single machine scheduling problems**
Step 1	Define completion time estimates (due dates) for each operation of each job.
Step 2	Define the interval between starting time estimates (release times) for all operations of each job.
Step 3	Define all SMSP $1 \mid r_j \mid C_{max}$ based on information defined on Step1 and Step 2.
Step 4	Solve all SMSP $1 \mid r_j \mid C_{max}$ with those release times and due dates using TS or GA.
Step 5	Integrate all the obtained near-optimal solutions into the main problem.
2nd PHASE	**Check feasibility of the schedule and, if necessary apply the IMACM coordination mechanism**
Step 6	Verify if they constitute a feasible solution and terminate with a local optimum; If not, apply a repairing mechanism.

Table 2. Scheduling method algorithm

$$C_{ijk-1l} = C_{ijkl} - p_{ijkl} \quad (1)$$

This procedure begins with the last job operation and ends with the first. When an operation is precedent to more than one operation, i.e. there exists a multilevel structure, the completion due time is the lower value as defined on equation 2.

$$C_{ijkl-1} = min\{C_{ijkl} - p_{ijkl}\} \, \forall l > l-1 \quad (2)$$

The operations starting due time intervals $[t_{ijkl}, T_{ijkl}]$ are also defined considering the job release times and the operation processing times. The earliest starting time t_{ijkl} corresponds to the time instant from which the operation processing can be started. The latest starting time T_{ijkl} correspond to the time at which the processing of the operation must be started in order to meet its completion due time (due date). This means that no further delay is allowed. When an operation has more than one precedent operation, i.e. there exists a multilevel structure, the interval $[t_{ijkl}, T_{ijkl}]$ is the interval intersection from precedent operations correlated by the respective processing times. At this stage, only technological precedence constraints of operations and job due dates will be considered for defining completion and starting times.

The starting time interval (STI) for operations without precedents is defined as follows:

$$STI_{ijkl} = [r_{ijkl}, C_{ijkl} - p_{ijkl}] \quad (3)$$

The starting time interval of an operation with one precedent operation is defined by equation 4.

$$STI_{ijkl} = [t_{ijk-1l}, T_{ijk-1l}] + p_{ijk-1l} \quad (4)$$

The starting time interval of an operation with more than one precedent operation is the intersection interval of the starting time intervals from all precedent operations correlated by the respective processing times (Equation 5).

$$STI_{ijkl} = [t_{ijK1L}+p_{ijK1L}, T_{ijK1L}+p_{ijK1L}] \cap [t_{ijK2L}+p_{ijK2L}, T_{ijK2L}+p_{ijK2L}] \cap \ldots \cap [t_{ijKnL}+p_{ijKnL}, T_{ijKnL}+p_{ijKnL}] \text{ with } Kn<k \text{ and } L<l \quad (5)$$

Following this procedure it is easy to deal with situations were an operation has more than one precedent operation, i.e. there exists a multilevel task structure involving assembly operations. In this case the previous operations may be processed simultaneously, and therefore a relaxation of an underlining characteristic of the EJSSP problems is assumed. This situation is typical of real world manufacturing requirements. This means that a more generalized and realistic problem is dealt with the scheduling approach adopted in this work.
At this stage, only technological precedence constraints of operations and job due dates will be considered for defining completion and starting times (Fig.2).

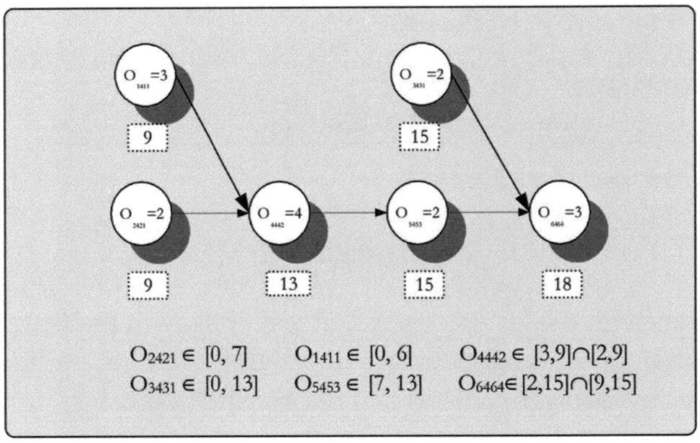

Fig. 2. Processing Precedence Graph with operation completion due times and starting times

The release date r_j correspond to the earliest starting times of each operation. The due date d_j correspond to the operation completion times. The notation r_j and d_j used at this point, considers that we are dealing with single machine problems.

Coordination Mechanism

The integration of the SMSP solutions may give an unfeasible schedule to the EJSSP. This is why schedule repairing may be necessary to obtain a feasible solution. The repairing mechanism named Inter-Machine Activity Coordination Mechanism (IMACM) carries this out. The repairing is carried out through coordination of machines activity, having into account job operation precedence and other problem constraints. This is done keeping job allocation order, in each machine, unchanged. The IMACM mechanism establishes the starting and the completion times for each operation. It ensures that the starting time for each operation is the higher of the two following values (Table 3):

Step 1	Start from initial operations, without precedents, which correspond the level 1 on the sequence for processing on the machine. At this level, the starting and the completion times are the same, i. e., they are equal to those defined by the scheduling algorithm on the previous phase.
Step 2	At level 2, we will have all the operations which immediately precedents (defined on the precedence graph) and on the machine sequence has been already scheduled.
Step 3	The process will be repeated until all the operations have been scheduled.

Table 3. Inter-Machine Activity Coordination Mechanism

- the completion time of the immediately precedent operation in the job, if there is only one, or the highest of all if there are more
- the completion time of the immediately precedent operation on the machine.

Most of the research on JSSP focuses on basic problems as described above. The method developed and just described is in line with reality and away from the approaches that deal solely with static and classic or basic job-shop scheduling problems. Thus, the method is likely to perform worse than the best available algorithms found for such problems. However, it is not our purpose, neither it would be reasonable, to rate our method against such good performing algorithms for academic and basic JSSP. Our aim is to provide an efficient tool, which we think we managed with our method, for obtaining good solutions, for a variety of criteria, for many real world scheduling problems, i.e. complex non-basic JSSP as described above, which we named Extended JSSP. For these problems, the referred best performing algorithms are unable to give solutions. Further, through the survey we made to the literature we were unable to find methods to solve the EJSSP as here described.

4.1.2 Dynamic adaptation module

For non-deterministic problems some or all parameters are uncertain, i.e. are not fixed as we assumed in the deterministic problem. Non-determinism of variables has to be taken into account in real world problems. For generating acceptable solutions in such circumstances our approach starts by generating a predictive schedule, using the available information and then, if perturbations occur in the system during execution, the schedule may have to be modified or revised accordingly, i.e. rescheduling is performed.

In the scheduling system for EJSSP, rescheduling is necessary due to two classes of events (Madureira, 2003):

- Partial events which imply variability in jobs or operations attributes such as processing times, due dates and release times.
- Total events which imply variability in neighbourhood structure, resulting from either new job arrivals or job cancellations.

Considering the processing times involved and the high frequency of perturbations, rescheduling all jobs from the beginning should be avoided. However, if work has not yet started and time is available, then an obvious and simple approach to rescheduling would be to restart the scheduling from scratch with a new modified solution on which takes into account the perturbation, for example a new job arrival. When there is not enough time to reschedule from scratch or job processing has already started, a strategy must be used which adapts the current schedule having in consideration the kind of perturbation occurred.

The occurrence of a partial event requires redefining job attributes and a re-evaluation of the schedule objective function. A change in job due date requires the re-calculation of the operation starting and completion due times of all respective operations. However, changes in the operation processing times only requires re-calculation of the operation starting and completion due times of the succeeding operations. A new job arrival requires definition of the correspondent operation starting and completion times and a regenerating mechanism to integrate all operations on the respective single machine problems. In the presence of a job cancellation, the application of a regenerating mechanism eliminates the job operations from the SMSP where they appear.

After the insertion or deletion of genes, population regeneration is done by updating the size of the population and ensuring a structure identical to the existing one. Then the scheduling module can apply the search process for better solutions with the new modified solution.

a) Job arrival integration mechanism

When a new job arrives to be processed, an integration mechanism is needed. This analyses the job precedence graph that represents the ordered allocation of machines to each job operation, and integrates each operation into the respective single machine problem. Two alternative procedures could be used for each operation: either randomly select one position to insert the new operation into the current solution/chromosome or use some intelligent mechanism to insert this operation in the schedules, based on job priority, for example.

b) Job elimination mechanism

When a job is cancelled, an eliminating mechanism must be implemented so the correspondent position/gene will be deleted from the solutions.

c) Regeneration mechanisms

After integration/elimination of operations is carried out, by inserting/deleting positions/genes in the current solution/chromosome, population regeneration is done by updating its size. The population size for SMSP is proportional to the number of operations. After dynamic adaptation process, the scheduling method could be applied and search for better solutions with the modified solution illustrated in Fig.1.

4.1.3 Meta-heuristics self-configuration properties

Generally, self-organization can be defined as the process by which systems tend to reach a particular objective with no external interference. All the mechanisms dictating its behaviour is internal to the system e.g. are autonomous. This field of research has received much attention trough Autonomic Computing paradigm (EMA, 2006).

In this paper we consider that Meta-Heuristics self-parameterization could permit a better adaptation to the dynamic situation being considered. The idea is that each agent adopts the MH (TS or GA) in accordance with the problem being solved: the method and/or parameters can change in run-time, the agents can use different MH according with problem characteristics (namely problem size, for smaller use GA for problems with more jobs using TS, considering efficiency constraints for example).

Meta-Heuristics can be adapted to deal with dynamic problems, reusing and changing solutions/populations in accordance with the dynamism. We will use the Dynamic Adaptation Mechanisms defined in (Madureira, 2000) for SMSP that includes a method for neighbourhood regeneration under dynamic environments, increasing or decreasing it according to new job arrivals or cancellations.

4.2 Hybrid multi-agent architecture

The work described in this chapter is a system where a community of distributed, autonomous, cooperating and asynchronously communicating machines tries to solve scheduling problems.

The proposed Team-Work based approach is rather different from the ones found in the literature; as we try to implement a system where each agent (Resource Agent) is responsible for optimize the scheduling of operations for one machine through TS or GA. This consider a specific kind of social interaction that is cooperative problem solving (CPS), where the group of agents work together to achieve a good solution for the problem.

Each Resource Agent must be able: to find an optimal or near optimal local solution trough Tabu Search meta-heuristics (or Genetic Algorithms); to deal with system dynamism (new jobs arriving, cancelled jobs, changing jobs attributes, etc); to change/adapt the parameters of the basic algorithm according to the current situation; to switch from one Meta-Heuristic algorithm to another and to cooperate with other agents.

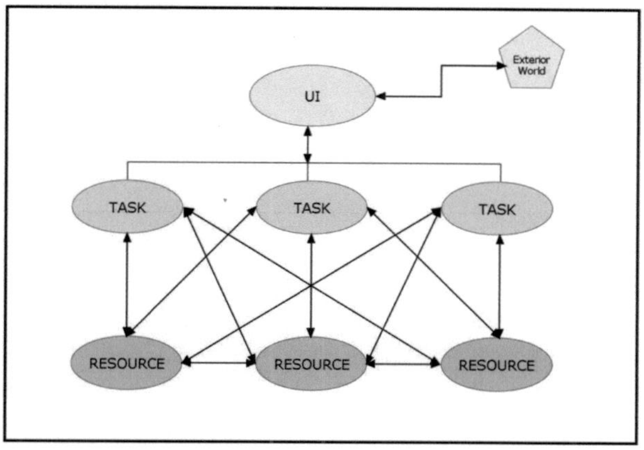

Fig. 3. MASDScheGATS System Architecture

The original Scheduling problem defined in section 3, is decomposed into a series of Single Machine Scheduling Problems (SMSP) (Madureira, 2001). The Resource Agents (which has a Meta-Heuristic associated) obtain local solutions and later cooperate in order to overcome inter-agent constraints and achieve a global schedule.

The proposed Team-Work architecture is based on three different types of agents (Fig. 5). In order to allow a seamless communication with the user, a User Interface (UI) Agent is implemented. This agent, apart from being responsible for the user interface, will generate the necessary Task Agents dynamically according to the number of tasks that comprise the scheduling problem and assign each task to the respective Task Agent(Fig. 3).

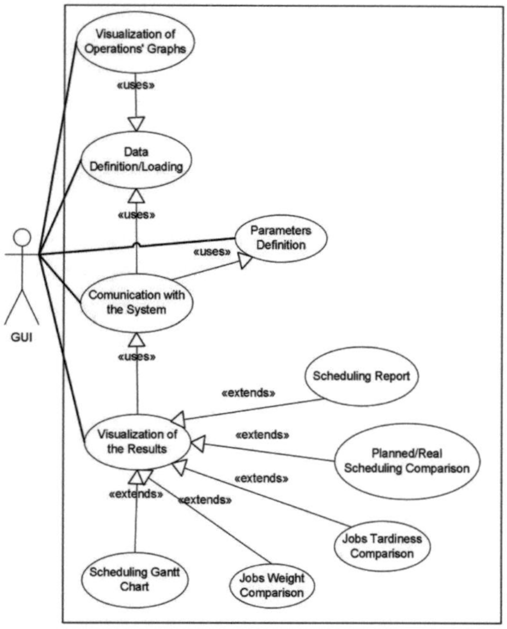

Fig. 4. User Interface Agent Functionalities

The Task Agent will process the necessary information about the job. That is to say that this agent will be responsible for the generation of the earliest and latest processing times, the verification of feasible schedules and identification of constraint conflicts on each job and the decision on which Machine Agent is responsible for solving a specific conflict.

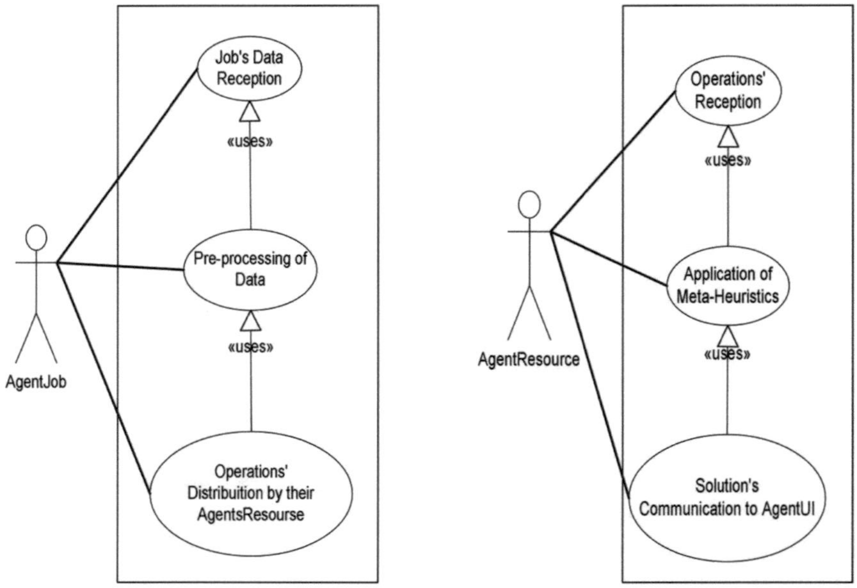

Fig. 5. Agent Job and Agent Resource functionalities

Finally, the Resource Agent is responsible for the scheduling of the operations that require processing in the machine supervised by the agent. This agent will implement metaheuristic and local search procedures in order to find best possible operation schedules and will communicate those solutions to the Task Agent for later feasibility check (Fig. 5).

5. Computational study

The proposed architecture was implemented using the Java Agent Development framework (JADE). Some computational tests were carried out to evaluate the performance of the referred scheduling systems under different manufacturing scenarios.

This section presents the results obtained by MASDScheGATS with TS and GA on the resolution of a set of academic instances of the Job-Shop problem (OR-library), considering the difficulties in finding test problems and computational results for EJSSP. The MASDScheGATS performance will be compared with MAPS - MultiAgent Production Planning System (Wellner and Dilger, 1999).

5.1. Tabu search parameterization

In developing a Tabu Search algorithm we must have in mind that its performance depends largely on the careful design and set-up of the algorithm components, mechanisms and parameters. This includes representation of solutions, initial generation of solutions, and evaluation of the solutions, such as neighbourhood size, tabu list length, tabu list attributes and stop criteria.

Details of the algorithm parameterization are briefly described as follows:

- Solution Representation - The solutions are encoded by the natural representation, where the schedule is described as a sequence of operations, i.e., each position represents an operation index.
- Initial Neighbourhood Generation - An initial solution is generated by a procedure, where the operations are sequenced in order of non-decreasing processing level (defined on precedence graph), giving priority to operations that are processed earlier. Thus, we expect to generate a good initial solution from which an initial neighbourhood will be obtained.
- Tabu list attributes and length - It is used a tabu list that stores the pairs of jobs involved on exchanging of positions (on the neighbourhood generation process), with length 4.
- As stopping criteria in the Tabu Search algorithm, we use a maximum of 100 iterations.

5.2 Genetic algorithms parameterization

In developing a genetic algorithm, we must have in mind that its performance depends largely on the careful design and set-up of the algorithm components, mechanisms and parameters. This includes genetic encoding of solutions, initial population of solutions, evaluation of the fitness of solutions, genetic operators for the generation of new solutions and parameters such as population size, probabilities of crossover and mutation, replacement scheme and number of generations.

Details of the algorithm parameterization are briefly described as follows:

- Solution Encoding - In this work, solutions are encoded by the natural representation (Davis, 1991). In this representation each gene represents a operation index. The geneposition in a chromosome represents the operation position in a sequence, defining, therefore, the operation processing order or priority. The number of genes in the chromosome represents the number of operation in a solution.
- Genetic Operators - Individuals, i.e. solutions, are randomly selected from the population and combined to produce descendants in the next generation. Depending on the problems to solve and their encoding, several crossover operators may be used namely one point, two points, uniform and order crossover(Davis, 1991). Here, we use the single point crossover operator with probability Pc=0.8. The single point crossover operator will be applied to M pairs of chromosomes randomly chosen, with M=N/2, where N is the size of the population. The mutation operator is applied with probability Pm=0.001, to prevent the lost of diversity. Thus, a single point in a chromosome is randomly selected, the current select resource, for the task, is replaced for another in the set of alternatives resources.
- Replacement Scheme - When creating a new population by crossover and mutation we must avoid loosing the best chromosomes or individuals. To achieve this, the replacement of the less fit individuals of the current population by offspring is based on elitism (Davis, 1991) . Thus, the best individuals, i.e. solutions, will survive into the next generation.
- As stopping criteria in the Genetic Algorithm we use a maximum of 100 generations.

5.3 Computational results

For our experiments, we consider some benchmark problems (OR-library). For release dates, we consider zero for all instances. Due dates are considered to be the optimal makespan value. The obtained results with our method based on Tabu Search (TS) and Genetic Algorithms (GA) are compared with those obtained from using the MAPS system (Wellner & Dilger, 1999).

With a simple implementation of the TS and GA and a small parameterization effort it was possible to achieved good performance for most instances of the problem when compared with MAPS system (table 4).

It is important to refer that our scheduling framework, which here uses TS and GA, is flexible in several ways. It is prepared to use other Local Search Meta-Heuristics and to drive schedules based on practically any performance measure. Moreover, the framework is not restricted to a specific type of scheduling problem, as is the case with many methods.

One novel approach, rarely addressed in the literature, but very important in practice, is considered in our scheduling framework, namely that of being able to schedule jobs with complex processing structures, i.e. with both parallel processing of product component parts followed by their assembly at several stages.

Additionally the proposed coordination mechanism is of very simple implementation. We consider that with a more effective cooperation mechanism (that is on ongoing developing) it is possible to improve MASDScheGATS performance.

Instância	*n*	*m*	C_{max} Óptimo	MAPS - TCS			MAPS - LCS			MASDSCheGATS TS				MASDSCheGATS GA		
				Average	Best	Worst	Average	Best	Worst	F. Obj.	Average	Best	Worst	Average	Best	Worst
FT06	6	6	55	69.6	62	82	65.8	57	76	C_{max}	61.4	59	64	78.4	65	97
										WT	63.2	59	68	74	65	89
										L_{max}	99	99	99	74.6	66	96
FT10	10	10	930	1203.4	1164	1242	1277	1172	1373	C_{max}	1519	1408	1612	1476.4	1448	1540
										WT	1368.8	1319	1416	1627.2	1427	1816
										L_{max}	1634.8	1542	1739	1504.6	1399	1611
FT20	20	5	1165	1603.4	1513	1723	1470	1417	1503	C_{max}	1715	1707	1726	1761.4	1692	1952
										WT	1678.8	1664	1714	1696	1662	1755
										L_{max}	1784.6	1686	1889	1740.6	1714	1833
La01	10	5	666	782	725	832	861	822	891	C_{max}	812.2	764	858	919.8	810	1160
										WT	772.6	740	795	865	782	921
										L_{max}	1059	947	1122	1049.2	888	1164
La02	10	5	655	886.6	840	911	821.6	744	873	C_{max}	869.6	839	920	914.4	847	985
										WT	859.4	839	876	940.8	839	1117
										L_{max}	968.4	849	1099	979	871	1152
La03	10	5	597	778.8	726	823	793.6	716	858	C_{max}	834.6	776	916	888	804	997
										WT	794.2	749	830	849	809	894
										L_{max}	947.4	875	990	898.2	823	988
La04	10	5	590	835	801	894	786.2	724	819	C_{max}	865.8	798	924	904.8	746	979
										WT	875.2	767	989	846.6	773	950
										L_{max}	959.2	842	1085	915.4	822	1003

Table 4. Computational Results

6. Conclusions and future work

This chapter presented MASDScheGATS Scheduling System that assumes the combination of different Meta-Heuristics and Multi-Agent Systems potentialities. To solve the scheduling problem, Machine Agents and Task Agents must interact and cooperate with other agents in order to obtain optimal or near-optimal global performances trough Meta-heuristics. The idea is that from local, autonomous and often conflicting agent's objectives, a global solution emerges from a community of machine agents solving locally their schedules while cooperating with other machine agents. Agents have to manage their internal behaviours and their relationships with other agents via cooperative negotiation in accordance with business policies defined by the user manager.

We believe that a new contribution for the resolution of more realistic scheduling problems (Extended Job Shop Problems) was described in this paper. The particularity of our approach is the procedure to schedule operations, as each machine will first find local optimal or near optimal solutions, succeeded by the interaction with other machines trough cooperation mechanism as a way to find an optimal or near-optimal global schedule.

In most practical environments, scheduling is an ongoing reactive process where the presence of real time information continually forces reconsideration and revision of preestablished schedules.

Considering that natural evolution is a process of continuous adaptation, it seemed us appropriate to consider Genetic Algorithms and Tabu Search for tackling Dynamic Scheduling Problems. Thus, the MASDScheGATS based scheduling system developed adapts the resolution of the deterministic problem to the dynamic one in which changes may occur continually. A population/solution regenerating mechanism is put forward, for adapting the population/neighborhood of solutions, according to disturbances, to a new population, which increases or decreases according to new job arrivals or cancellations.

7. Acknowledgments

The authors would like to acknowledge FCT, FEDER, POCTI, POSI, POCI 2010 for their support to R&D Projects and the GECAD Unit.

8. References

Aytug, H., Lawley, M.A., McKay, K.,S. M. and Uzsoy, R. (2005). Executing production schedules in the face of uncertainties: A review and some future directions, European Journal of Operational Research,Volume 16 (1), pp. 86 - 10.

Bartz-Beielstein, Thomas, Blesa, M.J., Blum, C., Naujoks, B., Roli, A., Rudolph, G. &Sampels, M.(2007). Hybrid Metaheuristics. Proceedings of 4th International Workshop H. Dortmund, Germany, Lecture Notes in Computer Science. Vol. 4771. ISBN: 978-3-540-75513-5.

Blazewicz, Jacek., Ecker, Klaus H,.& Trystram, Denis(2005). Recent advances in scheduling in computer and manufacturing systems. European Journal of Operational Research, 164(3), 573 574.(1), pp.86-110.

Boeres, Cristina, Lima, Alexandre, Vinod, E.&Rebello, F.(2003). Hybrid Task Scheduling: Integrating Static and Dynamic Heuristics. 15th Symposium on Computer Architecture and High Performance Computing, 199.

Branke, J. (2000). Efficient Evolutionary Algorithms for Searching Robust Solutions, In Proc: Fourth Intl. Conf. on Adaptive Computing in Design and Manufacture (ACDM 2000), pp. 275-286.

Cowling, P. and Johansson, M. (2002). Real time information for effective dynamic scheduling. European J. of Operat. Research,139 (2), 230-244.
Davis, Lawrence(1991). Handbook of Genetic Algorithms, Van Nostrand Reinhold, New York. EMA (2006). Practical Autonomic Computing: Roadmap to Self Managing Technology - A White Paper Prepared for IBM , Enterprise Management Associates.
Gonzalez, Teofilo F. (2007). Handbook of Approximation Algorithms and Metaheuristics. Chapman & Hall/Crc Computer and Information Science Series
Hasan Kamrul, S.M.; Sarker, R.; Cornforth, D. (2007). Hybrid Genetic Algorithm for Solving Job-Shop Scheduling Problem, In: ICIS 2007 - 6th IEEE/ACIS International Conference pp:519-524.
Horling, Brian, Lesser: Victor. (2005). A Survey of Multi-Agent Organizational Paradigms, University of Massachusets.
Lu, T., Yih, Y. (2001). An Agent-Based Production Control Framework for Multiple-Line Collaborative Manufacturing, International Journal of Production Research, 39/10: pp.2155--2176.
Madureira, A., Ramos, C. and Silva, S. (2004). Toward Dynamic Scheduling Through Evolutionary Computing. In WSEAS Transactions on Systems. Issue 4. Volume 3, pp.1596--1604.
Madureira, A., Santos J., Gomes N. and Ramos C. (2007). Proposal of a Cooperation Mechanism for Team-Work Based Multi-Agent System in Dynamic Scheduling through Meta-Heuristics,In Proc. 2007 IEEE International Symposium on Assembly and Manufacturing (ISAM07), University of Michigan, Ann Arbor (USA), pp. 233--238, ISBN: 1-4244-0563-7.
Madureira, A. (2003). Meta-Heuristics Application to Scheduling in Dynamic Environments of Discrete Manufacturing. Ph.D. Thesis, University of Minho, Braga, Portugal, (in portuguese).
Madureira, Ana M., Ramos, Carlos and Silva, Sílvio. (2000). A Genetic Algorithm for The Dynamic Single Machine Scheduling Problem, In 4th IEEE/IFIP Intl. Conf. on Information Technology for Balanced Automation Systems in Production and Transportation, Berlim (Germany), pp 315—323.
Madureira, Ana M., Ramos, Carlos and Silva, Sílvio. (2001). An Inter-Machine Activity Coordination based Approach for Dynamic Job-Shop Scheduling, International Journal for Manufacturing Science and Production, Freund Publishing House Ltd., vol 4, nº2.
MANUFUTURE High level group. (2004). MANUFUTURE A vision for 2020, Report of High level group, European Commission.
Nwana, H., Lee, L. and Jennings, N. (1996). Coordination in software agent systems, In: BT Technol J, Vol 14 No 4 October. OR-library, http://people.brunel.ac.uk/~mastjjb/jeb/info.html
Pinedo, M. (2005). Planning and Scheduling in Manufacturing and Services, Springer-Verlag, New York, ISBN:0-387-22198-0.
Portmann, M. C. (1997). Scheduling Methodology: optimization and compu-search approaches, in the planning and scheduling of production systems, Chapman & Hall.
Wellner, Jörg and Dilger, Werner (1999). Job Shop Scheduling with Multiagents, In workshop planen und Konfigurieren.
Xhafa, Fatos, Abraham, Ajith.(2008). Metaheuristics for Scheduling in Industrial and Manufacturing Applications Series: Studies in Computational Intelligence , Vol. 128 (Eds.), ISBN: 978-3-540-78984-0.

18

Conversational Characters that Support Interactive Play and Learning for Children

Andrea Corradini[1], Manish Mehta[2] and Klaus Robering[1]
[1]*University of Southern Denmark, IFKI*
[2]*Georgia Institute of Technology, College of Computing*
[1]*Kolding, Denmark*
[2]*Atlanta, GA, USA*

1. Introduction

Over the last decade, digital technology has been increasingly used for educational purposes. The rationale behind this emerging trend is the belief that information technology can be utilized as a powerful means to assist learners with the acquisition of general knowledge, literacy, narrative competence, social skills like teamwork and negotiation capabilities, logical and spatial reasoning, eye-hand coordination and fine motor control, etc. In particular computer games and interactive technology have attracted a great deal of attention and much active research is currently being carried out in an effort to investigate their possible benefits in education (Squire, 2005).

In this paper, we report on the development and evaluation of an educational agent architecture that allows for instructive communication and natural human-computer interaction between humans, in particular children and adolescents, and embodied historical characters. Our e-learning software platform is built around a three-dimensional animated portrayal of the world famous writer Hans Christian Andersen. Users can interact with the graphical character through a combination of speech, (pen and/or mouse) gesture, and keyboard and, in so doing, ask the virtual character questions about Andersen's life, family, historical background, fairy tales and stories. The avatar is endowed with basic affective and emotional capabilities, and uses both synthesized speech and gestures to converse with the pupils. The intent of the system is educational while the interactive nature of the character is designed to help children learn and retain information about the subject matter to a greater extent than would be possible with traditional media. The educational content is pervasive for it is blended within the game-like system interface. In fact, there is no clear cut distinction between the system and the educational content which is always presented in different ways according to the conversational situation thus providing children with new opportunities for effective, immersive and rewarding computer-aided learning experiences.

Conceptually, our system is backed by theories of user-centered learning as well as cognition. The constructivist theory of education (Mantovani, 2001) that recognizes the importance of active experience of students with the learning material supports our approach to education. Findings in the theory of multimedia learning (Mayer, 2001) that show how multimedia presentations are more effective in terms of measured learning outcomes when auditory information is presented alongside of visually complementary images or redundant textual information furnish instead the conceptual justification for the deployment of graphical characters capable of multimodal information generation.

A series of studies that we ran with school pupils show that the implemented agent system is a promising step towards our ambitious long term goal to develop interactive game-like interfaces that enable multimodal communication between users and game characters for edutainment purposes.

The remainder of this paper is structured as follows. First, we present the motivation for this research and discuss a few relevant works that links the game community with educational science and practitioners. We then briefly outline our interactive software system and a few main issues encountered during its development. Further, we focus on a user study that we carried out to gauge our implementation and to assess the system performance. Eventually, we conclude with a discussion of lessons learned and propose a number of possible extensions and future improvements.

2. Convergence of education and game technology

2.1 Our approach: a platform for e-learning

E-learning is a domain that attempts to use information technology to improve people's learning process and skills. A variety of software systems are used within this area in order to organize and present content for didactic purpose according to a variety of design methodologies, target audience and interaction styles. One may distinguish two main forms of e-learning: asynchronous and synchronous e-learning. In asynchronous e-learning the content is created beforehand for learners to access and study the information they need at any time from anywhere. In synchronous e-learning the teacher and the student(s) interact in an actual class, usually over a broadband network. In both situations, the learning material is stored and communicated digitally as text, audio and/or video clips and can be accessed via Internet or from a storage device such as CDROMs, etc.

The development of e-learning systems relies on the assumption that software instruments could enable students to easily assimilate the learning material while simultaneously help decongesting overcrowded classes by allowing students (teachers) to attend (lecture) a class from their own location. Moreover, e-learning inherently supports the idea of life-long education and represents a valuable opportunity for some specific groups of individuals, such as children or disabled people, who can have learning materials tailored and made accessible to them according to their needs.

Real-life training of people and children in particular, is a highly challenging and demanding task. There are no standards or agreed upon guidelines for computer supported learning. Typically, special-purpose multimedia software tools that resort to experimental learning strategies and methods have been deployed in a variety of applications targeted at different audiences (Savidis et al., 2007). These approaches are backed by constructivist theories of education (Mantovani, 2001; Steffe & Gale, 1995) and by the theory of multimedia learning (Mayer, 2001). Constructivist learning theory emphasizes the importance of active experience of students with the learning material. The theory of multimedia learning is relevant in this context because of its "dual-channel" assumption based on the evidence that humans have separate processing systems for visual/pictorial versus auditory/verbal channels of information. Both processing systems have limited processing capacity.

Meaningful learning requires mental processing in both verbal and visual channels, in order to build connections between them (Wickens, 2002). Thus multimedia presentations are more effective in terms of measured learning outcomes when auditory information is presented alongside of visually complementary images or redundant textual information (Mayer & Moreno, 2003; Moreno & Mayer, 2002). The fact that multimodal redundancy serves to focus attention is buttressed by studies on infant language acquisition (Gogate et al., 2001; Bahrick et al., 2004).

The importance of emotions in learning processes is also more and more acknowledged (Anolli et al., 2006; Kort et al., 2001; LeDoux, 1998). Regarding this aspect though, multimedia presentations are only a little more powerful than conventional textbooks in conveying the rich emotional and social information that is exchanged by people when they communicate with each other and that also occur in traditional classes. While teachers can modify their teaching style and methods based on perceived learner's feedback, e-learning platforms are often too rigid in their design and rarely account and accommodate for the emotional and motivational aspects of their users.

Insights in the theory of user-centered learning, constructivist learning theory, multimedia learning along with the need to develop an e-learning software platform endowed with basic affective and emotional capabilities, have been taken into account in the development of a 3D animated conversational character that impersonates the Danish fairy tale writer Hans Christian Andersen (HCA). The target audience of our system is pupils of age 10 to 18. The intended goal is to teach them about the writer's life, historical period, works, family and the characters featured in his writings in a game-like interface. The educational content is presented within a gaming application and depends on the conversational situation. This provides children with new opportunities for a more effective, immersive and rewarding computer-aided learning experience.

2.2 Learning theory desiderata

A growing number of researchers and practitioners in education have recognized the inherent limitations of the traditional large lecture class as pedagogical instrument (Foreman, 2003). The major critic to this way of delivering information is that it cannot deal with the very specific needs of the individual participants. Every student confronted with a new learning situation has a unique knowledge level and a given set of dispositions that cannot be accounted for in a traditional lecture. Moreover, when students encounter problems they must be given immediate feedback in terms of clarification or amplification. This is not always possible in a standard class.

More and more pedagogues and educators advocate for constructive learning environments that allow students to explore learning materials, ideally multi-sensorially, and that encourage comprehension through the active discovery of new knowledge (Mantovani, 2001; Narayanan & Potamianos, 2002; Steffe & Gale, 1995) while also integrating cognitive and emotional factors (Goleman, 1995, Picard et al., 2004). If the learning process is perceived as a rewarding activity, students are motivated to learn regardless of any external imposed requirements and devote more time to the material that is to be learnt. This contributes to the creation of enduring neural structures that ensure that concepts are stored into long-term memory rather than just crammed up for the upcoming test or examination.

2.3 Interactive game technology and game-based learning

Computer games have the power to engage and maintain the attention of players over long periods of time. Most commercial computer games are built around the common conceit of game as a karmic wheel: the user plays, dies, reloads and repeats this operative loop until he gets it right. Digital game-based learning detaches from and goes beyond this common pattern. It aims at exploiting the pedagogical promise of interactive technologies and applies them to the development of games that have educational goals. This kind of learning has its roots in both interactive adventure games and simulation games.

Before successful computer games such as *Zork* and *PacMan* hit the market, there was the world of adventure games. Adventures such as *Hunt the Wumpus* (Ahl, 1979) and *Colossal Caves Adventure* (Hafner & Lyon, 1996) were among the first text interactive fiction games which lured players into immersing themselves in a magical world. They both featured a competent text parser that could understand advanced commands from the player who could control the main character's movements with the arrow keys on the keyboard (Montfort, 2003; Wolf & Perron, 2003). This game concept was later extended to include animated color graphics, a pseudo 3D-perspective of the world game, music playing in the background, and sound feedback and turned into the game *King's Quest I: Quest for the Crown*, a story based on classic fairy-tale elements where a knight has to save a kingdom in distress by recovering a set of lost treasures. A game like this had never been made before and marked the beginning of a new era in interactive graphical games (Levy, 2001).

Real-life training of people is a highly challenging and demanding process that can be effectively improved with the deployment of special-purpose software. New developments in the fields of speech recognition, natural language processing, and computer graphics have given rise to the emergence of more sophisticated game-like computer interfaces and simulations to learning systems (Rieber, 1996). Also called serious games, these recent interfaces have attracted the interest of educators, military and professional practitioners who are interested in the possible benefits of bringing gaming and simulation together by immersing real people into possible critical situations that they should be prepared to deal with. 3D virtual environments of a large-bodied aircraft cargobay and turbine engine blades coupled with interaction modalities based on a head-mounted display and a 6 degrees-of-freedom mouse have been utilized for the training of inspection methods for aviation maintenance technicians (Washburn et al., 2007). The *Mission Rehearsal Exercise* (Gratch & Marsella, 2005) is a system designed to teach leadership skills in high-stress social and emotionally charged situations. *Carmen's Bright IDEAS* is an interactive health intervention system designed to train communication skills and social competence of medical personnel interacting with mothers of pediatric cancer patients (Marsella & Gratch, 2003). In *FearNot* (Aylett et al., 2005) children can watch bullying incidents that take place between scripted agents in a virtual school and are asked to act in support to the victimized characters. The system aims to enable children to develop strategies to cope with bullying situations through empathic interaction with the synthetic characters that inhabit the virtual school. While most research on embodied conversational characters has concentrated on the graphical representation and conversational capabilities of virtual agents, (Oviatt et al., 2004) investigated the question of whether auditory embodiment can provide cues that influence user behaviors and ultimately affects the learning performance of children interacting with a cartoon-like character to learn about marine biology. The *Colorado Literacy Tutor* (Cole et al., 2005) is a set of software tools that aims to improve literacy and student achievement in any subject area by helping pupils learn to read fluently, to acquire new knowledge through understanding of texts, and to appropriately express their ideas in writing. (Massaro et al., 2006) developed a speech and language tutor centered about a talking head as conversational agent for children with language challenges. Synthetic characters have also increasingly been used in storytelling and tutoring applications for children (Ryokay & Cassell, 1999; Robertson & Oberlander, 2002; Vaucelle, 2002).

Both the immediacy of the interaction with interactive characters and the encapsulation of people into a gaming environment add a natural and entertaining experience to the user and can be geared toward a specific learning objective in a way that is consistent with the constructivist theory of education. Users can perform complex activities such as driving a virtual vehicle or navigating through a 3D photorealistic artificial world populated by autonomous characters that can interact and engage in social interaction with human users and/or other in-world avatars according to patterns governed by artificial intelligence programs designed to achieve specific learning objectives.

A series of cognitive processes like e.g. active discovery, analysis, problem-solving, memorization, conversation, visual and emotional stimulation, interpretation and/or physical activity that occurs while using these game-like interfaces deeply contributes in rooting learning in internal brain circuits and ultimately supports the learning process. The high degree of interactivity results in users actively engaged in communication with the virtual world and its inhabitants and is seen as an important factor for effective learning (Stoney & Wild, 1998). Moreover, besides facilitating learning, most of these interfaces are also designed to participate towards the educational goal in a cooperative manner so as to reflect the observation that children collaborate with peers naturally and often rely on each others support during learning processes. Game-based learning has been used quite a lot in adult learning programs too. Business strategy games have been used for many years in the management and financial areas[1] (Prensky, 2000) as well as more recently to introduce computer science programming assignments (Giguette, 2003).

The benefits of using graphical characters, by contrast to plain learning applications, lie in the distinctive use of (sometimes stylized) face and gestures to reflect interpersonal attitudes, deliver communicative content, and provide feedback to which users naturally pay a great deal of attention (Knapp, 1978; Fabri et al., 2002).

Digital learning environments such as computer games, simulations, and embodied conversational characters have all the potential to provide a cognitive bridge between actual experiences and abstractions which is crucial for teaching children to deal with complex problem solving and comprehension issues. The big challenge in educational software for children is to understand how to utilize the available technology in order to engage them directly in collaborative interactions in a way as to benefit their cognitive development.

3. Game-like interface for children edutainment

3.1 System overview

Our current real-time game scenario consists of a player interacting with a full-body single embodied character (Figure 1, left) impersonated by the fairy-tale author Hans Christian Andersen (HCA). Interaction takes place in an entertaining and educational manner within

[1] See for instance www.learningware.com, www.games2train.com, www.socialimpactgames.com, or www.corporatelearningforum.com

a 3D graphical world via spoken dialogue as well as pen gestures. Several other characters can be added to the system. However, since we did not create a large enough knowledge base large enough for all characters, they would currently interact the same way as the HCA virtual character does. Typical input gestures are ink markers like lines, points, circles, etc. entered at will via a mouse-compatible input device or using a touch-sensitive screen.

Fig. 1. (*left*) HCA full-body conversational character in his study; (*right*) Cloddy Hans is one of HCA's fairy tale characters that can be encountered in the fairy world.

Some objects in the author's study have been designed to resemble events experienced by the character and/or works that he created during his real life. For instance, a picture of the Colosseum in Rome hanging over his desk serves as a visual link to his visit to Italy and more specifically the Italian capital city. Similarly, books are stored in shelves while a small set of the writer's personal objects of the writer, such as his umbrella and walkstick, are placed at different locations within the study. These objects had a central role in the writer's life and thus offer a topic of conversation to the user and form the basis for multimodal interaction with the character. Object behaviors are used as visual feedback in deictic utterances as well as for their selection and manipulation. Apart from them, the system offers other domains of discourse including: the writer's fairy tales, his life, his physical presence in the study, and the domain of solving meta-communication problems that occurs during speech/gesture interaction. In order to reinforce the learning experience and make the interaction even more entertaining, in a companion system (Boye & Gustafson, 2005), the user is also granted access to a 3D fairy tale world populated by HCA's fairy tale characters (Figure 1, right). The user can wander about, manipulate objects and collect information useful to solve tasks, which arise while exploring the fairy world, such as e.g. passing a bridge guarded by a witch. For the user to have the impression that she is interacting with distinct, believable agents, each virtual character has its own proper appearance, voice, actions, and personality.

Users perceive the world around them through a first-person perspective. They can explore HCA's study, talk to him, in any order, about any topic within HCA's knowledge domains, using spontaneous speech and mixed-initiative dialogue, change the camera view, refer to and talk about objects in the environment, and also point at or gesture to them. HCA reacts emotionally to the user input by displaying emotions and by employing a meaningful combination of synchronized verbal and non-verbal behaviors. He can get angry or sad because of what the user says, or he gets happy if the user, for instance, likes to talk about his fairy tales.

3.2 Agent architecture

A software system that is supposed to behave in a human-like manner needs to be able to perform a large set of tasks, both externally (talking, gesturing, moving about etc.) and internally (interpreting sensory data, evaluating user's input, monitoring plan execution, etc.). The flexible and responsive nature of multi-agent architectures in which agents communicate, cooperate, coordinate and negotiate to meet particular goals under specified timing constraints naturally lends itself to such an application.

The theory and development of software agents has been an active field of research for a few decades. Several working definitions have been proposed and eventually a consensus was reached in (Jennings at al., 1998) where an agent is deemed as a computer system operating in a certain environment and capable of flexible autonomous actions towards its design objectives. Several models for agent communication have been put forward, the agent broker and agent to agent being the two most representative (Cheyer & Martin, 2001; DiPippo et al., 1999). The agent to agent model is a completely distributed framework where each agent knows the name of any other agents with which it might need to communicate. In the agent broker model instead, a special agent is tasked with finding agents to fulfill services required by other agents requesting that specific services. To that extent, this model relies on a central facilitator, the broker agent that administers communication among agents. Those, in turn need to register with the facilitator in order to advertise the services they offer.

The widely used Open Agent Architecture (Martin et al., 1999) relies on this latter model and is also the inspiring model of the architecture of our choice. We have been using the agent architecture developed by colleagues in our companion project[2]. It is simple to use, easy to implement, and lightweight. For platform independence and to facilitate debugging, agent communication occurs with text only over standard TCP/IP. A central facilitator routes messages among registered agents. It also knows which servers are deployed and how to start them to allow automatic restart in case of unexpected server crash. Agent to agent communication to bypass the broker is also possible and is even enforced whenever the data exchanged is binary given that the facilitator can deal with text only messages.

As a whole, the HCA system is realized as an event driven, modular, asynchronous multi-agent architecture. Several single agents take care of different aspects of the interaction with the user: a speech recognizer senses the user input, a gesture recognition agent interprets ink entered by users, the input fusion agent ensures modality fusion, a response generation module deals with speech synthesis and graphical animations and a dialogue manager (DM) manages the conversation with children as it evolves. Resorting to an agent architecture allows the different developers involved to focus on a specific well-defined functionality. In this way, the architecture makes it possible to create a bigger application from a set of agents that were not necessarily designed to work together. This also facilitates a wider reuse of the expertise embodied by each single agent, their maintenance and debugging.

In our system, the broker coordinates input and output events by time-stamping all module messages and associating them to a certain conversation turn. The behavior of the broker is controlled by message-passing rules, specifying how to react when receiving a message of a certain type from one of the modules. Despite a facilitator-centered configuration, the

---

[2] www.speech.kth.se/broker/

information flow typically occurs in a pipeline-like manner. As depicted in Figure 2, any time an input is sensed, the n-best hypothesis lists from either the speech recognizer or the gesture recognizer or both are sent to the natural language understanding (NLU) module and the gesture interpreter, respectively. The gesture interpreter consults the animation module to figure out which on-screen objects the user has referred to while gesturing. Output from those two agents is then forwarded to the gesture/speech input fusion module which, in turn, provides input for the dialogue manager (DM) which is responsible for the management of the interaction with the user. It has, among others, to plan for the next response to the user, to update the characters' emotional state, and to keep track of the dialogue history. Eventually, the response generator, informed by the DM, coordinates a text-to-speech message to play back synchronized with the rendering of the corresponding character animation.

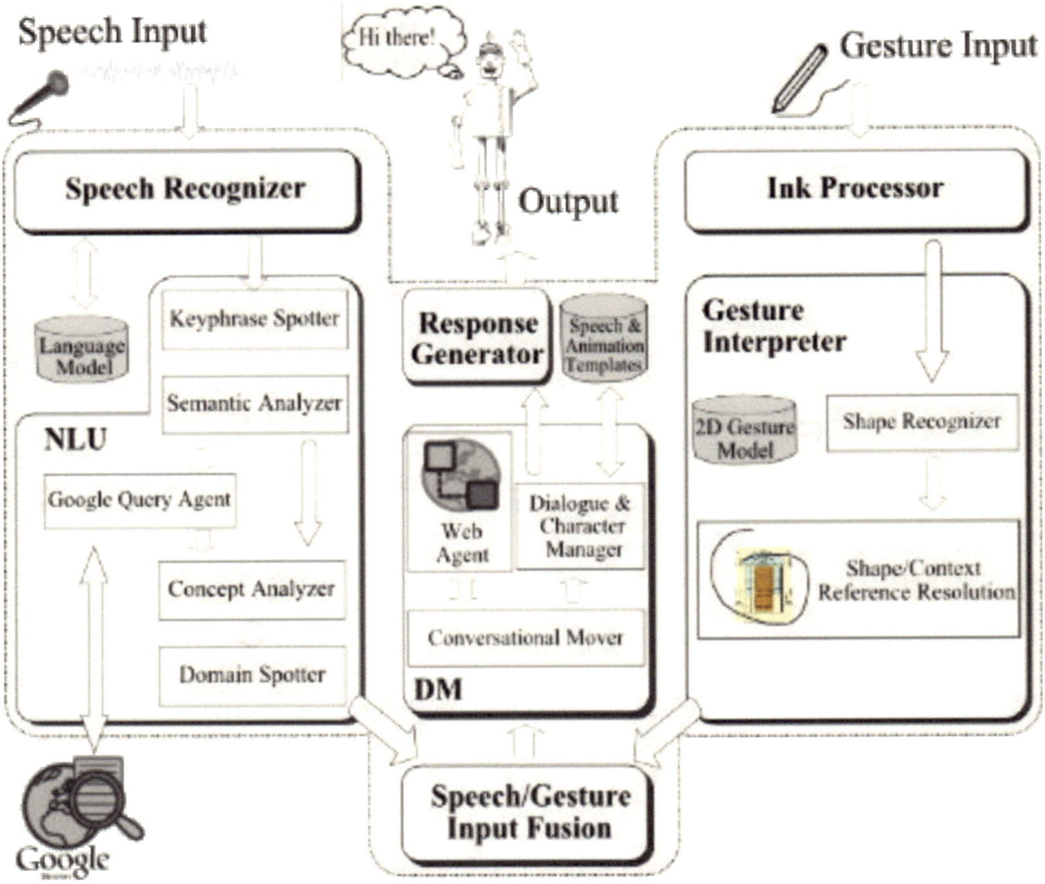

Fig. 2. Detailed view of the whole system architecture and information processing flow.

An ontology is used as common knowledge representation formalism shared among the system modules to create a domain independent architecture. In this way, moving to another character only requires a modification of the ontology-based knowledge representation. We described the input fusion, response generator and dialogue manager modules in details in (Corradini et al., 2003; Corradini et al., 2005a; Corradini et al., 2005b).

The next subsections focus on and address some issues encountered while dealing with the speech modalities of users, and notably children, during interaction with the system.

3.3 Children spoken language recognition: issues

Despite the growing number of kids accessing speech operated applications, spoken dialogue systems developed so far have an inherent problem that directly transfers in the development of our conversational prototype: they have been mainly designed for adult users. While the state of the art in automatic speech recognition and synthesis is still not completely satisfactory for the adult population, the endeavor of enabling speech technologies for children represents even a greater research challenge. In fact, past investigations have shown that children's voices are more variable in terms of acoustic characteristics and prosodic features, are more disfluent when compared to adult speech (Darves & Oviatt, 2002; Oviatt et al., 2004) and change developmentally (Yeni-Komshian et al., 1980; Oviatt & Adams, 2000). Shy and introvert children can be hard to engage in interaction with a conversational character and are reluctant to speak or they speak low in volume if at all (Darves & Oviatt, 2004). A study on a reading tutor for preschool children showed that off-the-shelves speech recognizers perform poorly unless a new acoustic model created from the speech of children in the target age range is employed. By explicitly accounting for common mispronunciations, speech recognition rose to an astounding 95% rate (Nix et al., 1998). Research also indicated that young people tend to employ partly different strategies when interacting with dialogue systems than adults do (Coulston et al., 2002; Oviatt et al., 2004). For instance, younger children use less overt politeness markers and verbalize their frustration more than older children (Bell & Gustafson, 2003). Moreover, children seem to adapt their response latencies and the amplitude of their speech signal to that of their conversational partners. Differently from adults, children do not often modify the lexicon and syntax of an utterance (Bell & Gustafson, 2003). Moreover, in case of communication problems while interacting with conversational agents, research indicates that kids tend to repeat critical original utterances verbatim with just a few modifications of certain phonetic cues, notably by increasing the tone and volume of their voice (Bell & Gustafson, 2003).

Fig. 3. (*left*) A human actor impersonating HCA interacting with school pupils in the writer's native town of Odense; (*middle*) snapshots of an animation; (*right*) face expressing surprise.

These research findings motivated us to collect a corpus of children conversational data. In fact, the few existing corpora of children speech turned out to be not usable in our system for none of them was in Danish and moreover consisted of either prompted speech or monologues of children recounting stories (D'Arcy et al., 2004; Eskenazi, 1996; Gerosa & Giuliani, 2004; Hagen et al., 1996).

We transcribed and analyzed several hours of collected video and audio-taped conversation of young subjects involved in a series of interactive sessions in both *Wizard of Oz* studies and in an after-school class where they played with a real human actor impersonating Hans Christian Andersen (Figure 3, left). The video data was partly used to generate the graphical animations (Figure 3, middle and right). The audio data from these interactive sessions was instead used to create two corpora of children-computer spoken conversation containing spontaneous dialogue data in English and in Danish, respectively. A similar task was also carried out by our project partners for the Swedish language (Bell et al., 2005). The corpora were then used for the creation and training of dedicated acoustic models for the speech recognizer. The deployment of such acoustic models from the speech of children in the target age range of our system immediately boosted the recognition rate of our speech recognizer and confirms the experimental results reported in (Nix et al., 1998).

3.4 Children conversation with the virtual character

Beside differences in the speech signal, there are additional distinctions between adults and children that directly influence and make the development of automatic spoken systems for children difficult. Their behavioral patterns of interaction with a computer are different from those of adults because they are still learning linguistic rules of social communications and conversation. Moreover, there are significant differences in those patterns even among children according to their age range, gender, and the socio-economic and ethnic backgrounds. Children's behavioral patterns are quite different from those of adults in terms of attention and concentration as well. Preschoolers are generally able to perform an assigned task for not longer than about half an hour (Bruckman & Bandlow, 2002). In (Halgren at al., 1995) it was found that children tend to click on visible feature just to see what happens as reaction to their actions. If an action gave rise to some feedback event that they judged interesting (like a nice sound or an animation), many kids kept on clicking to experience the feedback over and over again. In a similar work, (Hanna et al., 1997) discovered that if a funny noise was used as an error message several children repeatedly generated the error just to hear it again.

There are still many additional general issues of technical nature that need to be addressed and solved before computer interfaces can properly become conversational and multimodal. Question-answering systems, command and control dialogues, task-oriented dialogues and frame-based dialogues (Allen et al., 2001; Rudnicky et al., 1999; Zue et al., 2000) are subclasses of practical natural dialogue for which very robust and successful language processing methods have been already proposed. Their main limitation - its fixed context - is simultaneously its greatest strength since it allows building very robust and feasible spoken dialogue systems. However, they are a simplification of real human conversational behavior for they control and restrict the interaction rather than enrich it. By contrast to task-oriented and information spoken dialogue system, we propose a domain-oriented conversation that has no task constraints and can be enriched by either accompanying or complementary pen-gestures. The user is free to address, in any order, any topic within HCA's knowledge domains, using spontaneous speech and mixed-initiative dialogue, and pen markers to provide context to the interaction.

We dedicated a great deal of attention in defining proper design strategies that motivate children, keep them engaged for a certain period of time, and make them produce audible speech that can be reasonably processed by a speech recognizer. To reflect the finding that they tend to use a limited vocabulary and often repeat utterances verbatim, we created a database of possible replies for our back-end that lexically and grammatically mirror the expected input utterance. In other words, we decided that the parser for the user input utterances should also be capable of parsing output sentences i.e. the sentences produced by the conversational agent. Moreover, we never aimed at nor did we need a parser capable of full linguistic analyses of the input sentences. The analysis of data collected in *Wizard of Oz* studies and other interactive adult-children interactive sessions showed that most information could be extracted by fairly simple patterns designed for a specific domain and some artificial intelligence to account for the context at hand.

The key idea underlying our semantic analysis is the principle of compositionality for which we compose the meaning of an input sentence from both the meanings of its small parts and based on the relationships among these parts. The relatively limited grammatical variability in children' language and their attitude of repeating (part of) sentences, made it possible for us to build a very robust language processing systems based on patterns and finite state automata designed for each specific domain. This strategy proved sufficient for the understanding of most practical children spontaneous dialogues with our system and empirically confirms both the practical dialogue hypothesis for which '*..the conversational competence required for practical dialogues, while still complex, is significantly simpler to achieve than general human conversational competence..*' (Allen at al., 2000) as well as the domain-independence hypothesis which postulates that practical dialogues in different domains share the same underlying structures (Allen at al., 2000).

Technically, the NLU module consists of four main components: a key phrase spotter, a semantic analyzer, a concept finder, and a domain spotter. Any user utterance from the speech recognizer is forwarded to the NLU where a key phrase spotter detects multi word expressions from a stored set of words labeled with semantic and syntactic tags. This first stage of processing usually is helpful to adjust minor errors due to misrecognized utterances by the speech recognizer. Key phrases are extracted, and a wider acceptance of utterances is achieved. The processed utterance is sent on to the semantic analyzer. Here, dates, age, and numerals in the user utterance are detected while both the syntactic and semantic categories for single words are retrieved from a lexicon.

In fact, relying upon these semantic and syntactic categories, grammar rules are then applied to the utterance to help in performing word sense disambiguation and to create a sequence of semantic and syntactic categories. This higher-level representation of the input is then fed into a set of finite state automata, each associated to a predefined semantic equivalent according to data used to train the automata. Anytime a sequence is able to traverse a given automaton, its associated semantic equivalent is the semantic representation corresponding to the input sentence. At the same time, the NLU calculates a representation of the user utterance in terms of dialog acts. At the next stage, the concept finder relates the representation of the user input, in terms of semantic categories, to the domain level ontological representation. Once semantic categories are mapped onto domain level concepts and properties, the relevant domain of the user utterance is extracted. The domain helps in providing a categorization of the character's knowledge set. The final output in form of concept(s)/subconcept(s) pairs, property pairs, dialog act and domain is sent on to other system components that deal with the current dialogue modeling. More details about the processing steps of this module along with few explanatory examples can be found in (Mehta & Corradini, 2006).

On the one hand, the proposed NLU is not capable of capturing fine distinctions and subtleties of language since it cannot produce a detailed semantic representation of the input utterance. One the other hand, it is not possible to create a system grammar that covers all possible variations and ambiguities of the natural language used by children in our data set. Altogether, as evinced in the system evaluation (see section 4), our shallow parsing approach which employs the use of semantic restrictions in the grammar (captured by a series of rules) to enforce semantic and syntactic constraints has proved a feasible and robust trade-off approach.

3.5 Out of domain conversation

During a set of usability test sessions, we realized that children frequently ask out-of-domain questions that are usually driven by external events or characters which are popular at the time of the interaction. For instance, in early sessions children frequently asked about the *Lord of the Rings* while this subject was completely ignored in later studies where e.g. *Harry Potter* was a much more common topic of discussion (Bernsen et al., 2004).

We were thus confronted with the difficult and ambitious objective of developing conversational agents capable of addressing everyday general purpose topics. In fact, we cannot expect conversational characters to conduct a simulated conversation with children that exclusively revolves around the agent's domains of expertise. Such a situation, coupled with the decreasing capability of children to focus on a specific subject for prolonged period of times (Bruckman & Bandlow, 2002), would make any interface pretty boring and ultimately conflict with the educational objectives.

The synthetic character should be endowed with the capability of reaching out into topics that could not be covered by the developers during the creation of the system. Previous systems have typically used simplistic approaches of either ignoring or explicitly expressing inability to address out of domain inputs. We could avoid in advance or limit situations where children ask questions related to an unconstrained range of utterances by keeping the conversational flow on a specific, well defined (from the system's perspective) track and leave room for as less opportunities as possible for the human interlocutor to take the initiative (Mori et. al., 2003). However, maintaining full control of the interactive session is a strategy that conflicts with the mixed initiative nature of our system. Another approach is to engage users in small talk when they go out of topics (Bickmore & Cassell, 1999) yet the range of discussion topics is still limited since it is dependent on the amount of templates that can be created off-line. We wanted to reduce the authorial burden of content creation for different general purpose discussion topics. In (Patel et. al., 2006) an approach to handle out of domain input through a set of answers that explicitly state that the character either doesn't know or doesn't want to reveal the answer is presented. This approach is in general better than saying something completely absurd, however this strategy is more suitable for training simulations where the goal of the system is to keep the conversation on track so as to achieve the training goal. For our domain where the goal of our agent is to provide an appropriate educational reply along with a rich social experience to kids, that strategy does not work either. *Façade* (Mateas & Stern, 2004), an interactive drama domain, uses various deflection strategies to bring back the discussion onto the main conversation as well as to limit the depth in which players can drill down on any one topic. These strategies present an interesting solution to avoid out of domains input for a story based domain. An ongoing story provides the user with enough narrative cues to integrate the deflection output used

by characters into the ongoing narrative flow. Differently from this latter work, in our approach, we wanted to address the general purpose topics apart from the domain topics rather than deflecting them to bring the conversation back onto the domain topics.
As we have seen in the previous section, in our implemented system the NLU module has generic rules for detecting dialog acts present in the user utterance. These dialog acts provide a representation of user intent like types of question asked (e.g., asking about a particular place or a particular reason), expression of opinion (like positive, negative or generic comments), greetings (opening, closing) and repairs (clarification, corrections, repeats). These dialog acts are reused across different domains of conversation. Moreover, generic rules are used to detect the domain independent properties (e.g., dislike, like, praise, read, write etc). The NLU categorizes the word(s) that are not processed internally into an unknown category. The longest unknown sequence of words is combined into a single phrase. These words are then sent to a web agent that uses Google's directory structure to find out whether the unknown words refer to a name of a movie, game, or a famous personality and the corresponding category is returned to the NLU. The web agent eventually finds a quick and concise output using three freely available open-domain Question-Answering systems: AnswerBus (Zheng, 2002), Start (Katz, 1997), and AskJeeves[3] or the web page at specific game and movies websites[4]. The web agent employs a set of heuristics, such as removing output with certain stop words, to pick one single reply. Once a sentence is selected, we remove control/graphical characters to get a plain string that can be played by the TTS component. We also make a first attempt at categorizing the retrieved information in order to generate appropriate non-verbal behaviors synced up with spoken utterances (Mehta & Corradini 2008).

4. System evaluation

4.1 Are animated characters effective?

To date there is no clear answer to this question. The evaluation of the effectiveness of including conversational animated characters in user interfaces is a complex and arguable task. In (Dehn & van Mulken, 2000) a review of several interfaces with synthetic agents seems to indicate that there is little or no improvement in user performance. Nonetheless, the authors of that review also suggest to take this conclusion very carefully on the ground that the systems analyzed could not be compared consistently due to the different evaluation methods employed.
Despite ambiguous or inconclusive results and the lack of experimental evidence, we argue that animated agents enhance the user experience first and foremost because they allow for a simulated face-to-face communication that is the most effective mean of communication as well as method of instruction among humans. Moreover, animated agents have the potential of increasing user motivation, stimulating learning activities, enhancing the flow of information, and fulfilling the need for personal relationship in learning (Gulz, 2004).
It is however extremely difficult to assess pedagogical benefits of character enhancement and then to generalize the results. As noted in (Cole at al., 2004) the ideal evaluation of computerized learning environments would consist of repeated interaction with the

[3] www.askjeeves.com
[4] www.game-revolution.com and www.rottentomatoes.com

animated agents over long periods of time to validate the observations on the basis of factors such as e.g. the nature of the task, the personal characteristics of the users, and the believability of the graphical agent.

4.2 Setting the stage

We ran many pilot studies involving children in the attempt to discover the main factors that contribute in creating better computer games with an educational objective in the foreground. How computers are able (or perceived) to play, the degree of challenges, entertainment and interaction they offer, the amount of new knowledge assimilated, and the believability of the game characters, seem to be important factors.

We report here on a study with thirteen young subjects evenly split between males and females (6 and 7 subjects, respectively) recruited in local schools in the city of Odense in Denmark. Each user session had a duration of approximately 50-60 minutes including an exploratory phase with the interface and a post-session informal discussion with each participant. The average age was 13.1 years (12.8 for males and 13.3 for females).

All pupils were Danish native speakers with advanced skills in speaking English. Fifty-three percent of them (100 percent of males and 43 percent of females) declared themselves as being a frequent (i.e. more than 1 hour/week) videogame and/or console player, with a peak of 45 hours/week spent in gaming by a male teenager. 38.5 percent of the participants (28.6 percent of females and 50 percent of males) had been exposed before to computing systems able to process speech and/or gesture; all of them were acquainted with an earlier version of our system. When asked about their favorite games, children said that they like to play with games of any genre, ranging from shoot-'em-up (66.6 percent of males and 0 percent of females), action, platform, to sports and strategy games (40 percent of males and 50 percent of females). With regard to pre-interaction knowledge about the writer, his life, his fairy tales and the historical period he lived in, 53.8 percent of the children (42.8 percent of females and 66.7 percent of males) declared to have a fair to very good knowledge of these historical and literacy facts and events. Despite surprising at first, this high level of knowledge is due to the fact that Odense is Hans Christian Andersen's hometown. In local schools he is often subject of discussion and several cultural events organized by the Odense municipality are often related to its world-renowned citizen.

Fig. 4. (*left*) A child interacting with the system; (*right*) hand gesturing on a touch sensitive screen to operate a virtual object within HCA's study.

To be able to play with the system, each subject had to wear a microphone headset to enter spoken utterances. They could choose among a touch screen, a mouse and a keyboard for entering ink gesture markers. Initially, the participant was given a 15 minutes session to get accustomed with the system. During this time an assistant was present to help out in case of questions about system functioning. At the end of the introductory session, after a short break, each subject was given a set of tasks to carry out during an additional interaction session lasting for approximately 20 minutes without any external human assistant support (Figure 4). We video and audio taped each session while system events were all automatically logged into XML files for further dialogue analysis. Players were allowed to break up the game at any time for any reason. At the end of the interaction each participant was interviewed according to a set of predefined questions. Informal discussions also typically occurred. Eventually each child was handed out (without being told in advance) a theater ticket as a reward for the time spent in the interaction. The questions were used to survey four main aspects, namely user's gaming habits, system interaction capabilities, system's educational and entertainment values, as well as open-ended questions for the subject to provide us with valuable insights and suggestions for creating a better system.

4.3 Results from the interviews

Two persons independently evaluated the questionnaires. User interviews were transcribed and mapped onto numerical values on a Likert scale from 1 to 5. For instance, when looking at the subjective entertainment degree experienced by the user, we mapped sentences such as e.g. '*I had no fun at all*' and '*the interaction was very entertaining, amazing!*' to 1 and 5, respectively. Inter-rater reliability for second scoring of the questionnaire data was 94%. Data analysis over the single categories revealed numerical value distributions of sufficient regular shape.
Thus, despite the limited sample size, the obtained results can be shown in terms of statistical measures like the mean and the standard deviation. These values for a few categories, each characterized by a reasonably symmetric distribution of and no outliers among its numerical values, are:

Interface easy of use (difficult = 1, very easy = 5):	mean = 3.9	stdev = 0.28
Graphics and quality of animations (bad = 1, great = 5):	mean = 3.38	stdev = 0.75
Agent's understanding skills (very poor = 1, great = 5):	mean = 3	stdev = 0.57
Entertaining degree (not at all = 1, very exciting =5):	mean = 3.77	stdev = 0.44
Degree of learning (none = 1, much = 5):	mean = 3.08	stdev = 0.64
Use of gestural input (superfluous = 1, very useful = 5)	mean = 3.98	stdev = 0.22
System's overall rate (very bad = 1, great = 5):	mean = 3.62	stdev = 0.87

In other words, the system was overall rated fairly well. It was perceived as exiting and funny, with a reasonable degree of added educational value. With regard to the educational content, most of the users did not indicate what exactly they have learnt, yet when they did they mostly referred to the writer's life and family while stating that they already knew a great deal about his fairytales and therefore there was nothing new to learn about this topic. In the light of that, more specific questions on what aspects of the writer subjects have learnt about while playing should be considered in future studies.
The interaction with the character is driven primarily by the speech modality however a small set of pen gestures is available to operate on objects in the room as well. Interestingly,

53.8% of the subjects (50% males and 57.1% females) stated that they liked the gesture modality and/or wanted to do more with it. Despite gestures were not used extensively by the subjects, we hypothesize that they ease shy users into the conversation (shy users generally start with clicking on a picture and then just wait for something to happen; rarely they ask about it). Gestures may help breaking the initial hesitance on the part of the user and help to establish a relationship with the interactive character, which forms the basis of a smooth overall conversation.
From a dialogue management point of view we were interested in evaluating aspects like conversation success, domain coverage, robustness, etc. Table 1 depicts the average number of turns over each domain as well as their percentage of domain coverage during interaction sessions analyzed for the usability study.

Domain Name	Average # of Turns	Percentage
Fairy Tales	8.2	9.6
Life	6.9	8.1
Physical Presence	4.8	5.7
Study	13.3	15.6
User	7.7	9.0
Generic	44.2	51.9
All Domains	**14.2**	**100**

Table 1. Domain coverage.

The study domain relates to information about the objects in HCA's study, so every time the user points at something in the study the study domain is triggered. This can be a good indicator of the multi-modality input behavior of the users. The generic domain is the one most addressed by kids confirming empirical evidence regarding their attention and concentration difficulties (Bruckman & Bandlow 2002) and ultimately pointing out the need of a reliable mechanism that makes out-of-domain conversation possible. The generic domain contains also meta-communication turns which were triggered e.g. anytime a low confidence score occurred in the speech or gesture recognizer or the NLU. In a study with 186 input sentences we analyzed our approach in dealing with out-of-domain questions. The results are depicted in Table 2.

Question Type	*Coverage*	*Correct Answer*	*Some Answer*	*Wrong Answer*	*No Answer*
When	8 (4.3%)	2	1	2	3
Who	36 (19.4%)	14	8	3	11
What	65 (34.9%)	51	1	3	10
Keyword(s) list	51 (27.4%)	15	2	2	32
Other	26 (14.0%)	8	2	2	14
Total	**186 (100%)**	**90 (36.4%)**	**14 (7.5%)**	**12 (6.5%)**	**70 (37.6%)**

Table 2. Results of handling out-of-domain questions.

The evaluation study provides also empirical evidence that the interaction with the character is driven primarily by the speech modality despite the availability of 2D pen gestures to operate on objects and entities in the three dimensional virtual room. On average, about 6.3% of the actual turns were gesture only, 80.7% speech only and 13% displayed a multimodal speech-gesture content. Despite this latter figure may seem to be low at a first glance, it should be noted that not all turns necessarily required gestural input (e.g. when the user asked about the age, name, etc.). By comparing the set of potential multimodal situations occurring during the interactions as identified by the human transcribers with the set of the actual multimodal situations (i.e. these covering 13% of the user study interaction), we had an astonishing 96.4% overlap. These correct multimodal turns typically occurred anytime speech was accompanied by deictic words to refer to objects or entities in the virtual world. The 3.6% agreement discordance between the actual multimodal situations and the ideal case, was mostly due to anaphoric expressions used to refer to entities in the game that were talked to in the previous turn(s). In other words, while children considered speech as the main communicative modality, the study provides empirical evidence of a balanced use of modalities and a preference of gesture for manipulable objects and entities.

Interestingly, 53.8% of the subjects (50% males and 57.1% females) stated they liked the gesture modality and/or wanted to do more with it. Despite gestures were not extensively used by the subjects, we hypothesize that they ease shy users into the conversation. Shy users were indeed also those who displayed most interaction patters like scribbling or random on-screen clicking just to see if they get any feedback. In those situations, despite there is no clear cut to define when a user turn starts and a computer turn ends, we recognized some 6.3% of the total turns as being characterized by being gesture only patterns. This behavior pattern is common among users, and thus we believe that gestures may help breaking the initial hesitance on the part of the user and help form a relationship with the interactive character, which forms the basis of a smooth overall conversation.

We haven't performed any data correlation analysis because of the limited number of subjects and thus the lack of a large set of data. A very preliminary examination about the correlation between entertainment and favorite game genre and gameplay expertise, respectively, proved itself inconclusive.

4.4 Comments from the subjects

In this subsection, we report a set of quotes from children subjects together with the results of the user studies that highlight the interface aspects in relation to the pedagogical goals, the way of interaction, the graphical design, as well as desirable improvements of our game-like interface.

<u>*Educational Content*</u>

Children highlighted that their interaction with the agent either extended ".. *information about his life is more fun than about his fairy tales. The user knows his fairy tales but not his life ..*" or brushed up ".. *I haven't really learnt anything than I didn't already know but it helped me recall a number of things ..*" their knowledge about HCA.

We actually did not expect much of an increase in knowledge about HCA because this is also a subject that they learn in great detail and in different courses at school and with after-school activities offered by the Odense municipality. Boys expressed twice time more than girls that they had increased their set of knowledge after the interactive session. Girls were more likely to highlight already existing knowledge on the subject.

Nonetheless, the user study indicates that children believe that they increased their knowledge after playing with our system. This ultimately tells us that we are on the right track to achieve the educational objectives that we envisioned at early stages of development and supports the belief that animated agents in virtual environments provides an interactive experience that helps children learning.

Interaction with the characters

Altogether children enjoyed the interaction with the character which´they thought ".. *it was really cool* .." and was ".. *good enough but he* (HCA) *is not the most polite person around* .." Some reports point out a few cases where the character did not act upon the wish and expectation of the player. They felt that their interaction was ".. *frustrating when he did not answer my questions* .." and HCA ".. *didn't understand everything. One has – by trial and error – to find a formulation which he can understand to bring the system is on the right track* .." We further examined also the goodness of the technical system in term of reliability and accuracy of all its single components with particular emphasis on the speech processing and gesture processing modules. This technical evaluation revealed expected shortcomings on the side of the speech recognizer (Mehta & Corradini 2006) which are however out of our control. The lack of barge-in capabilities in our current prototypes was highlighted in a few comments such as in ".. *it would be good if HCA stopped talking when asked* .."

Graphics and Character Believability

Children appreciated the life-like animations and graphical appearance of the character judging that ".. *The good graphics also makes it* (the system) *entertaining* .." However, the repertoire of HCA's actions was sometimes perceived as rather limited. A few subjects felt that ".. *maybe he should also be able to do more things such as smoke his pipe* .."

Suggestions for Improvements

Children found the overall system interesting and useful, ".. *it is different, more lively, to be told (about HCA life, fairy tale, family etc.) rather than just to read about it all* .. " and ".. *it was entertaining to hear what he told* .." Most children expressed the wish that they would definitely prefer to use the software compared to a classroom session. They thought that ".. *it was more fun than learning the same at school* .." Interestingly, the system has potential also in teaching new words or expressions to children interested in learning a foreign language as stated by ".. *his vocabulary is fine; I learnt some new words in English* .."

Subjects were asked what features of the current prototype needed to be improved. Excerpts from children quotes on this issue highlighted the current limitations of the game in terms e.g. of ".. *missing actions. Maybe there are not so many 12 year old kids who are interested in HCA. It is not really what you would really like to go home and play with. Maybe better suited for smaller children* .." as well as regarding the lack of a clear underlying storyline as highlighted in ".. *HCA's life story should be told up-front. It helps create a context and makes easier to understand the pictures* .."

One child reported that ".. *users should be allowed to visit other parts of his house* .." and brought up the issue of having a small number of places currently available for the user to explore and experiment with. As a consequence not every youngster was keen to play with our system on a daily basis. As a boy participant put it: ".. *I would not spend hours on such game every day. There are not so many challenges* .."

We need to address the wish expressed by a couple of pupils to ".. *add more new things one can point to and get a story about. There could also be stories spanning two pictures where the view angle changes automatically when HCA starts talking about the second picture* .." Comments like ".. *it would be desirable to have more things to point to with creative stories attached to which could even be a bit surprising* .." seem to indicate the wish for more manipulable objects. At the same time, however, other partecipants were pretty happy about the current amount and

behavior of the existing ones as it can be inferred from the comment *".. the use of pictures one can point to is creative, it would have been boring with a book to browse instead .."*
The addition of more sound or music to make the interface more funny and attractive was also suggested through the opinion expressed as *".. it could be funny to have music played in certain situations for instance when you click on a picture or HCA crashes against the wall.."*

5. Discussions and conclusions

Play is more than just entertainment for children. It is a fundamental activity that supports them in developing communication skills, managing feelings and emotions, learning the foundations of social rules, and abstracting concepts. The efforts to exploit the motivation and engagement that computer games naturally offer have recently given rise to a tremendous interest in the use of game-like applications for training and learning. Such kind of applications shifts the player into the participant role and acts as a catalyzer that turns an interactive session into a learning-by-doing experience. Differently from the traditional teacher-based learning paradigm, such a constructivist approach places the learner at the center of the learning process.
It is also indisputable that computers are compelling for children and adolescents. By giving them the control on the pace and kind of actions, they can repeat any activity as often as they like and experiment with variations. Hence, appropriate software can engage children in creative play, problem solving, and conversation with positive effects on their cognitive and social learning and development (Clements 1994; Haugland & Shade 1994).
Technology for children broadly falls into two categories: educational products and digital entertainment. Edutainment is what results in blending these two genres and it is also the framework of the system we have developed. We have created an aesthetically elegant, entertaining and intellectually challenging interactive architecture for young people of age ranging from 10 to 18 years to play and interact with a synthetic conversational agent impersonating the Danish historical luminary Hans Christian Andersen.
The conceptual goal of the project was to allow children and teenagers to collect information representing an organic history and a coherent body of knowledge through conversation and narrative in a funny way. The underlying idea was that a combination of an educational informative system and a gaming environment into a single application offers new opportunities towards more effective and rewarding learning experience. Technically, the task of building game-like interfaces populated by conversational characters represents a tremendous challenge for the research community and involves several large research questions: how to deal with children spoken language, how to deliver the appropriate behavior and information over different modalities in an interesting and engaging manner in every given dialogue situation, how to present a wide spectrum and depth content structure, how to keep up with a dialogue over virtually any topic without interrupting the flow of conversation in case of misunderstanding or out of domain topics, and many more. At the same time, we had to face usuability issues related to the target users of the system. For instance, we had to account for the importance of emotions in a learning process. Depressed or anxious children cannot assimilate new knowledge and learn as effectively. Therefore the assessment and/or display of emotions play an important role and help in improving the effectiveness of computer-based learning environments populated with

virtual agents. We have learnt that anthropomorphism in the interface is not a benefit in itself unless it is coupled with proper expressive, interactive and conversational capabilities; a finding confirmed also by previous research (Cassell at al., 2000). Our research seems to confirm the ability of animated characters to engage and motivate children especially when they can communicate with a system capable of displaying emotions and personality and when they can choose from several input modalities (Narayanan & Potamianos, 2002).

The set of user studies that we ran with school pupils showed a high degree of satisfaction in our system in terms of graphical appearance, ease of use, interaction modalities as well as pedagogical goals. While the world of computer games mirrors the dominance of male programmers and designers in the production lines and is geared for a male audience (Bae et al., 2004, Bryce & Rutter, 2003), our system seems to hint towards interactive game-like interfaces that appeal both girls and boys and therefore has a potential to reduce gender bias towards digital technologies. This partially confirms findings of other studies on gaming and gender (Brunner et al., 1998, Gorriz & Medina, 2000, Lucas & Sherry, 2004) regarding girls' preference for role playing games and narrative. On the long term, we therefore see a significant potential in the use of such kind of interactive systems for the promotion of gender balance enrollment in computer science and information technology courses which are currently characterized by a large gender imbalance (Vegso, 2005).

From the subjects' wish lists, we notice a demand for cunning, challenging and adapting environments. Participants want more fun, interaction, action and competition. They wish for more clickable objects and entities, mobility and actions.

We believe that our system can be useful for developing and designing conversational systems with improved error handling of speech recognition and language processing for children as well as adults. To that extend we plan to examine users' error handling strategies in real human-human dialogues and transfer the findings to human-computer and more specifically to children-computer interaction computer dialogue systems. By responding with a blend of text-to-speech and nonverbal behaviors the animated character can provide an empirical foundation for developing effective adaptive strategies.

Additional benefits of software systems of this kind to pedagogy and education are their availability over the time as a sort of digital tutor on-demand and the possibility to individualize the interaction.

More studies, with more subjects and over longer periods of time should be nonetheless carried out before drawing any strong conclusions of general validity (Cole et al., 2004). We are aware of the fact that usability studies conducted with subjects that already participated in previous field tests should be taken with care for the past experience could have some influence on what the subjects later chose as discussion topics with the character and how they chose to interact with it.

On a conclusive note, we recognize that despite learning being a highly challenging and demanding process it can be improved with the deployment of special-purpose software instruments. We believe that computers supplement childhood activities and materials, such as art, books, exploration with writing materials, and dramatic play but cannot replace them. Educational software can offer highly valuable opportunities for collaborative play, learning, and creation but it can also be misused. Eventually, the final decision about whether and how educational software tools can be used lies exclusively in the hands of the educators and their professional judgments.

Finally, we think that such a complex system could have been implemented only within the framework of a multi-agent architecture. This gave the developers of each single agent a large freedom in the choice of programming language, developing environment, etc. and made the system highly modular thus ultimately easily expandable and easy to debug. Nonetheless, there still are some technical issues to be resolved regarding such kind of software architectures. 3D graphical conversational agents and other emergent technologies demand more research with focus on interactive and autonomous systems. Recent developments in multi-agents research have come closer to the goal of building intelligent systems of general competence. Nonetheless, several areas such as design description, security, reusability, and implementation must be investigated further before agents can be universally accepted as a reliable and robust framework.

6. Acknowledgements

We would like to thank Marcela Charfuelan, Dymtro Kupkin, Holmer Hemsen and Mykola Kolodnytsky for design and programming support and Svend Killerich for data entry.

7. References

Ahl, D. H. (ed.) (1979) *More BASIC Computer Games*. New York: Workman Publishing

Allen, J., Byron, D. K., Dzikovska, M., Ferguson, G., Galescu, L. & Stent,, A. (2000) An Architecture for a Generic Dialogue Shell. *Journal of Natural Language Engineering*, 6(3)

Allen, J. F., Byron, D. K., Dzikovska, M., Ferguson, G., Galescu, L. & Stent, A. (2001) Towards Conversational Human-Computer Interaction, AI Magazine, 22(4):27-37

Anolli, L., Mantovani, F., Balestra, B., Agliati, A., Realdon, O., Zurloni, V., Mortillaro, M., Vescovo, A. & Confalonieri, L. (2006) The Potential of Affective Computing in E-Learning: MYSELF project experience

Aylett, R. S., Paiva, A., Woods, S., Hall, L. & Zoll, C. (2005) Expressive Characters in Anti-Bullying Education. Animating Expressive Characters for Social Interaction, Canamero, L. and Aylett, R. (eds.), John Benjamins Publisher

Bae, Y., Choy, S., Geddes, C. Sable, J. & Snyder, T. (2004) Trends in educational equity of girls and women. *Technical Report 2005016*, National Center for Education Statistics, U.S. Department of Education

Bahrick, L. E., Lickliter, R. & Flom, R. (2004) Intersensory redundancy guides infants' selective attention, perceptual and cognitive development. *Current Directions in Psychological Science*, 13

Bell, L. & Gustafson, J. (2003) Child and Adult Speaker Adaptation during Error Resolution in a Publicly Available Spoken Dialogue System. *Proceedings of Eurospeech*, Geneva, Switzerland

Bell, L., Boye, J., Gustafson, J., Heldner, M., Lindström, A. & Wirén, M. (2005) The Swedish NICE Corpus – Spoken dialogues between children and embodied characters in a computer game scenario. *Proceedings of Interspeech*, Lisabon, Portugal

Bernsen, N. O., Dybkjær, L. & Kiilerich, S. (2004) Evaluating Conversation with Hans Christian Andersen. *Proceedings of the 4th International Conference on Language Resources and Evaluation*, pp. 1011-1014

Bickmore, T. & Cassell, J. (1999) Small talk and conversational storytelling in embodied conversational interface agent. *AAAI fall symposium on narrative intelligence*, pp. 87-92

Boye, J. & Gustafson, J. (2005) How to do dialogue in a fairy-tale world. *Proceedings of the 6th SIGdial Workshop on Discourse and Dialogue*, Lisbon, Portugal, September 2-3

Bruckman, A. & Bandlow, A. (2002) HCI for Kids. *The Human-Computer Interaction Handbook: Fundamentals, Evolving Technologies, and Emerging Applications*, Jacko, J. and Sears, A. (eds.), Lawrence Erlbaum and Associates

Brunner, C., Bennett, D. & Honey, M. (1998) Girl games and technological desire. *From Barbie to Mortal Kombat: Gender and computer games*, Cassell, J. and Jenkins, H. (eds.), MIT Press, Cambridge

Bryce, J. & Rutter, J. (2003) Gender dynamics and the social and spatial organization of computer gaming. *Leisure Studies*, 22:1-15

Cassell, J., Sullivan, J., Prevost, S. & Churchill, E. (eds.) (2000) *Embodied Conversational Agents*. MIT Press, Cambridge, MA, USA

Cheyer, A. & Martin, D. (2001) The Open Agent Architecture. *Journal of Autonomous Agents and Multi-Agent Systems*, 4(1):143-148

Clements, D.H. (1994) The uniqueness of the computer as a learning tool: Insights from research and practice. *Young children: Active learners in a technological age*, Wright, J.L. and Shade, D.D. (eds.), pp. 31–50. Washington, DC: NAEYC

Cole, R., van Vuuren, S., Pellom, B., Hacioglu, K., Ma, J., Movellan, J., Schwartz, S., Wade-Stein, D., Ward, W. & Yan, J. (2004) Perceptive Animated Interfaces: First Steps towards a New Paradigm for HCI. *Proceedings of the IEEE*, 91(9):1391-1405

Coulston, R., Oviatt, S. L. & Darves, C. (2002) Amplitude Convergence in Children's Conversational Speech with Animated Personas. *Proceedings of the 7th International Conference on Spoken Language Processing*, Vol. 4, pp. 2689-2692

Corradini, A., Mehta, M., Bernsen, N.O., Martin, J.-C. & Abrilian, S. (2003) Multimodal Input Fusion in Human-Computer Interaction on the Example of the on-going NICE Project. *Proceedings of the NATO-ASI conference on Data Fusion for Situation Monitoring, Incident Detection, Alert and Response Management*, pp. 223-234

Corradini, A., Mehta, M., Bernsen, N.O. & Charfuelan, M. (2005a) Animating an Interactive Conversational Character for an Educational Game System. *Proceedings of the ACM International Conference on Intelligent User Interfaces*, pp. 183-190

Corradini, A., Mehta, M. & Charfuelan, M. (2005b) Interacting with an Animated Conversational Agent in a 3D Graphical Setting. *Proceedings of the Workshop on Multimodal Interaction for the Visualization and Exploration of scientific data*, pp. 63-70

D'Arcy, S. M., Wong, L. P. & Russell, M. J. (2004) Recognition of read and spontaneous children's speech using two new corpora. *Proceedings of the 9th International Conference on Spoken Language Processing*

Darves, C. & Oviatt, S. L. (2002) Adaptation of Users' Spoken Dialogue Patterns in a Conversational Interface. *Proceedings of the 7th International Conference on Spoken Language Processing*, Vol. 1, pp. 561-564

Darves, C. & Oviatt, S. L. (2004). Talking to digital fish: Designing effective conversational interfaces for educational software. *From brows to trust: Evaluating Embodied Conversational Agents*, Pelachaud, C, and Ruttkay, Z. (eds.), Kluwer Academic

Dehn, D.M. & van Mulken, S. (2000) The impact of animated interface agents: A review of empirical research. *International Journal of Human-Computer Studies*, Vol. 52, pp. 1-22

DiPippo, L. C., Hodys, E. & Thuraisingham, B. (1999) Towards a real-time agent architecture - A Whitepaper. *Proceedings of the 5th International Workshop on Object-Oriented Real-Time Dependable Systems*, pp. 59-64

Eskenazi, M. (1996) KIDS: A database of children's speech. *Journal of the Acoustical Society of America*, Vol. 100

Fabri, M., Moore, D.J. & Hobbs, D.J. (2002) Expressive Agents: Non-verbal Communication in Collaborative Virtual Environments, *Proceedings of International Conference on Autonomous Agents*, Bologna, Italy

Foreman, J. (2003) NEXT-Generation Educational Technology versus the Lecture. *Educause Review*, July/August 2003, pp. 13-22

Gerosa, M. & Giuliani, D. (2004) Investigating automatic recognition of non-native children's speech. *Proceedings of the International Conference on Spoken Language Processing*, pp. 1521-1524

Gratch, J. & Marsella, S. (2005) Lessons from Emotion Psychology for the Design of Lifelike Characters, *Applied Artificial Intelligence*

Gogate, L. J., Walker-Andrews, A. S. & Bahrick, L.E. (2001) The Intersensory Origins of Word Comprehension: an Ecological-Dynamic Systems View. *Development Science*, 4(1):1-37

Gorriz, C. M. & Medina, C. (2000) Engaging girls with computers through software games. *Communications of the ACM*, 43(1):42–49

Giguette, R. (2003) Pre-games: Games Designed to Introduce CS1 and CS2 Programming Assignments. *Proceedings of the ACM SIGCSE*, pp. 288-292

Goleman, D. (1995) *Emotional intelligence*. Bantam Books, New York

Gulz, A. (2004) Benefits of Virtual Characters in Computer Based Learning Environments: Claims and Evidence. *International Journal of Artificial Intelligence in Education*, Vol. 14, pp. 313–334, IOS Press

Hafner, K. & Lyon, M. (1996) *Where Wizards Stay Up Late*. Simon & Schuster Trade, 1996

Hagen, A., Pellom, B. & Cole, R. (2003) Children's speech recognition with application to interactive books and tutors. *Proceedings of the IEEE ASRU Workshop*

Halgren, S., Fernandes, T. & Thomas, D. (1995). Amazing AnimationTM: Movie Making for Kids Design Briefing. *Proceedings of the ACM CHI*, Denver, CO, USA

Hanna, L., Risden, K. & Alexander, K. (1997) Guidelines for Usability Testing with Children. *Interactions*, 4(5):9-14

Haugland, S.W. & Shade, D.D. (1994) Software evaluation for young children. *Young children: Active learners in a technological age*, Wright, J.L. and Shade, D.D. (eds.), pp. 63–76. Washington, DC: NAEYC

Jennings, N.R., Sycara, K. & Wooldbridge. M. (1998) A Roadmap of Agent Research and Development. *Autonomous Agents and Multi-Agent Systems*, Vol. 1, 275-306, Kluwer Academic Publishers

Katz, B. (1997) Annotating the World Wide Web using natural language. Proceedings of RIAO Conference on Computer Assisted Information Searching on the Internet

Knapp, M.L. (1978) *Nonverbal Communication in Human Interaction*. 2nd edition, Holt, Rinehart and Winston Inc., New York

Kort, B., Reilly, R. & Picard, R. W. (2001) An Affective Model of Interplay Between Emotions and Learning: Reengineering Educational Pedagogy-Building a Learning Companion, *Proceedings of International Conference on Advanced Learning Technologies*

LeDoux, J. (1998) The emotional brain: The mysterious underpinnings of emotional life. Weidenfeld & Nicholson, London, UK

Levy, S. (2001) *Hackers: Heroes of the Computer Revolution*. Penguin Putnam, New York

Lucas, K. & Sherry, J. L. (2004) Sex Differences in Video Game Play: A Communication-Based Explanation. *Communication Research* 31(5):499-523

Mantovani, F. (2001). VR learning: Potential and Challenges for the Use of 3D Environments in Education and Training. *Towards Cyber-Psychology: Mind, Cognitions and Society in the Internet Age*, Chapter 12, IOS Press

Marsella, S. & Gratch, J. (2003) Modeling coping behavior in virtual humans: don't worry, be happy. *Proceedings of the AAMAS*, pp. 313–320, ACM Press

Martin, D.L., Cheyer, A. & Moran. D.B. (1999) The Open Agent Architecture: A Framework for Building Distributed Software System. *Applied Artificial Intelligence*, (13):91-128

Massaro, D.W., Liu, Y., Chen, T.H. & Perfetti, C. (2006) A Multilingual Embodied Conversational Agent for Tutoring Speech and Language Learning. *Proceedings of the 9th International Conference on Spoken Language Processing*, pp. 825-828

Mateas, M. & Stern, A. (2004) Natural Language Undertanding in Façade: Surface-text Processing, Lecture notes in computer science, Vol. 3105, Springer Verlag, pp. 3-13

Mayer, R. E. (2001) *Multimedia Learning*. Cambridge University Press, New York, 2001

Mayer, R. E. & Moreno, R. (2003) Nine Ways to Reduce Cognitive Load in Multimedia Learning. Educational Psychologist, 38(1):43-52

Mehta, M. & Corradini, A. (2006) Understanding Spoken Language of Children Interacting with an Embodied Conversational Character. *Proceedings of the Combined Workshop on Language-Enabled Educational Technology and Development and Evaluation of Robust Spoken Dialogue Systems* at the ECAI, Riva del Garda, Italy, pp. 51-58

Mehta, M. & Corradini, A. (2008) Handling Out of Domain Topics by a Conversational Character. *Proceedings of the 3rd ACM International Conference on Digital Interactive Media in Entertainment & Arts*, Athens, Greece

Montfort, N. (2003) *Twisty Little Passages: An Approach To Interactive Fiction*. The MIT Press

Moreno, R. & Mayer, R. E. (2002) Verbal Redundancy in Multimedia Learning: When Reading Helps Listening. *Journal of Educational Psychology*, 94(1):156-163

Mori K., Jatowt A. & Ishizuka M. (2003) Enhancing Conversational Flexibility in Multimodal Interactions with Embodied Lifelike Agents. *Proceedings of the ACM International Conference on Intelligent User Interfaces*, pp. 270-272

Narayanan, S. & A. Potamianos (2002) Creating conversational interfaces for children. *IEEE Transactions on Speech and Audio Processing,* 10(2):65-78

Nix, D., Fairweather, P. & Adams, B. (1998) Speech recognition, children, and reading. *Proceedings of the ACM CHI,* Los Angeles, CA

Oviatt, S. L. & Adams, B. (2000) Designing and evaluating conversational interfaces with animated characters. *Embodied Conversational Agents,* Cassell, J,. Sullivan, J., Prevost, S. and Churchill, E. (eds.), MIT Press, Cambridge, MA, USA, pp. 319-343

Oviatt, S. L, Darves, C. & Coulston, R. (2004) Toward Adaptive Conversational Interfaces: Modeling Speech Convergence with Animated Personas. *ACM Transactions on Computer-Human Interaction (TOCHI),* Vol. 11, Nr. 3, pp. 300-328

Patel, R., Leuski, A. & Traum, D. (2006) Dealing with Out of Domain Questions in Virtual Characters. *Proceedings of the International Conference on Intelligent Virtual Agents*

Picard, R. W., Papert, S., Bender, W., Blumberg, B., Breazeal, C., Cavallo, D., Machover, T., Resnick, M., Roy, D. & Strohecker, C. (2004) Affective Learning - A Manifesto. *BT Technology Journal,* 22(4):253-269

Prensky, M. (2000) Digital Game-Based Learning. McGraw-Hill.

Ryokai, K. & Cassell, J. (1999) StoryMat: A Play Place with Narrative Memory. *Proceedings of the ACM International Conference on Intelligent User Interfaces*

Rieber, L. P. (1996) Seriously considering play: Designing interactive learning environments based on the blending of microworlds, simulations, and games. *Educational Technology Research and Development* 44(2):43-58

Robertson, J. & Oberlander, J. (2002) Ghostwriter: Educational Drama and Presence in a Virtual Environment. *Journal of Computer Mediated Communication,* Vol. 8

Rudnicky, A., Thayer, E., Constantinides, P., Tchou, C., Shern, R., Lenzo, K., Xu W. & Oh, A. (1999) Creating natural dialogs in the Carnegie Mellon Communicator system. *Proceedings of Eurospeech,* Vol. 4, pp. 1531-1534

Savidis, A., Grammenos, D. & Stephanidis, C. (2007) Developing inclusive e-learning and e-entertainment to effectively accommodate learning difficulties. *Journal on Universal Access to the Information Society,* 5:401–419, Springer Verlag

Squire, K. D. (2005) Changing the game: What happens when videogames enter the classroom? *Innovate,* Vol. 1, Nr. 6

Steffe P. L. & Gale J. (eds.) (1995) *Constructivism in Education.* Lawrence Erlbaum Associates

Stoney, S. & Wild, M. (1998) Motivation and interface design: maximising learning opportunities. *Journal of Computer Assisted Learning,* Vol. 14, pp. 40-50

Vaucelle, C. (2002) DollTalk: A computational toy to enhance children's creativity. *Proceedings of the ACM CHI,* pp. 20-25

Vegso J. (2005) Interest in CS as a major drops among incoming freshmen. *Computing Research News,* 17(1):17–18

Washburn, C., Stringfellow, P. & Gramopadhye, A. (2007) Using Multimodal Technologies to Enhance Aviation Maintenance Inspection Training, Proceeding of International Conference on Human Computer Interaction, Beijing, P.R. China, July 24-27

Wickens, C. C. (2002) Multiple Resources and Performance Prediction. *Theoretical Issues in Ergonomics Science, 3* (2)159-177

Wolf, M. J. P. & Perron, B. (2003) *The Video Game Theory Reader,* Routledge

Yeni-Komshian, G., Kavanaugh, J. & Ferguson, C. (eds.) (1980) *Child Phonology*, Volume 1: Production, Academic Press, New York

Zheng, Z. (2002) AnswerBus Question Answering System. *Proceedings of the Human Language Technology Conference*

Zue, V., Seneff, S., Glass, J., Polifroni, J., Pao, C., Hazen, T. & Hetherington, L. (2000) Jupiter: A Telephone-based Conversational Interface for Weather Information. *IEEE Transactions on Speech and Audio Processing*, 8(1):100-112

19

Auctions and Electronic Markets

Donna Griffin and Dirk Pesch
Centre of Adaptive Wireless Systems,
Cork Institute of Technology,
Ireland

1. Introduction

Adam Smiths' *invisible hand* argument presented the concept that opening up a market will result in a globally efficient mechanism where consumers have the ability to choose freely what to buy, sellers or service providers are allowed to choose freely what and how to produce and sell, which in turn leads the market to settle on product and price distributions that are beneficial to all members of the community. Over the past decade, the Internet has facilitated the proliferation of new markets, called electronic Marketplaces (eMarkets) and corresponding opportunities for service providers and consumers alike. According to Feldman adopting an eMarket approach to service provisioning helps to improve economic efficiency, reduce margins between price and cost, and speed up complicated business deals, where the services they provide will expand many companies purchasing and selling abilities and will make processes more dynamic and responsive to economic conditions, thereby helping to realise the goal of Adam Smiths' *invisible hand.*

To enable transactions within eMarkets, electronic Commerce (eCommerce) is employed, allowing entities to conduct their business over the Internet [He, 2003]. According to the nature of such transactions, the following types of eCommerce are distinguished: Business-to-Business (B2B), Consumer-to-Consumer (C2C), Consumer-to-Business (C2B) and Business-to-Consumer (B2C). B2C refers to online retail transactions where the buyers are individual consumers and the sellers represent themselves as business cooperation's, whereas B2B refers to the transactions where both buyers and sellers are business cooperation's. With the rapid growth of the number of transactions conducted via electronic channels such as the Internet, there exists an ever increasing demand to develop advanced computational tools to streamline B2C and B2B eCommerce. Most of the initial Internet based eCommerce was focused on B2C markets. However B2B constitutes a much larger portion of the overall eCommerce landscape and it is widely believed that B2B will continue to grow and will be the predominant means of doing business in the near future [Shaw].

Agents are seen as a key enabler for eCommerce where according to He (2003) "Electronic Commerce is the most important allocation for Agent technologies, because it is reality-based and constitutes a massive market". To support the integration of eMarkets and agents, Collins et al, designed a generalised multi-agent market architecture that can provide explicit and integrated support for complex agent interactions, such as that required in eMarkets. They defined three fundamental elements of the generalised multi-agent market architecture, including an *exchange*, the *market* and the *market session.*

Within eCommerce and eMarkets, negotiations are ubiquitous and are considered an essential business activity for establishing trade relationships and fine-tuning terms and conditions in both B2C and B2B markets [Kim]. Given the ubiquity and importance of negotiations in various contexts, research into negotiation theories and techniques have attracted attention from multiple disciplines such as distributed AI [Kraus], social psychology [Pruitt], game theory [Nash, Rubinstein], operations research [Nash, Neumann], and more recently agent mediated electronic commerce.
It is the purpose of this chapter to examine the main concepts that relate to: Market design, auctions, automated negotiation, agents and eMarkets. The chapter will show how these related technologies work to enable the vision of Adam Smiths *Invisible hand* argument and how the Internet is paving the way towards a globally efficient mechanism for establishing trade agreements.

2. Market design

Ever since the conception of auctions in Roman times, their history has been traditionally fraught with misery. Auctions have been used in the sale of wives in Babylonia in 500 BC [Rawlinson], prisoners of war in ancient Rome, and African slaves in the 16th Century [Jenman]. Rules surviving from the auctions of these eras show that in some cases, at least, bids were called out sequentially with the bidder remaining at the end obtaining the object at the price she/he bid. A variant of this mechanism, in which a time limit is imposed on the bids, is reported by the English diarist and naval administrator Samuel Pepys (1633-1703). The auctioneer lit a short candle, and bids were valid only if made before the flame went out. Pepys reported that a flurry of bidding occurred at the last moment. At an auction on September 3, 1662, a bidder "cunninger than the rest" told him that just as the flame goes out, "the smoke descends", signaling the moment at which one should bid [Pepys]. In fact the word *auction* is derived from the Latin *augere*, which means *to increase.*
Early auctions mostly involved misery, trickery and low prices, used as a business of exploitation and sudden opportunity, and were rarely a serious part of traditional business. More recently however, auctions are used to sell artwork, United States Treasury bills, houses and corporations to name a few. The auction houses of Sotheby's and Christie's were founded in the mid 18th century, and one of the more recent Sotheby's chairmen, A. Alfred Taubman, was once quoted stating "*God help us if we ever take the theatre out of the auction business or anything else. It would be an awfully boring world.*" A. Alfred Taubman, lived up to his own personal *drama* however, with the media frenzy surrounding his conviction in conspiring and colluding with his counterpart at Christie's auction house to fix the commissions paid by sellers of art, antiques and celebrity bric-a-brac [New York Times, 2001].
At the beginning of the twenty first century, auction houses, such as Sotheby's and Christie's are being eclipsed, at least in the value of the goods they sell, by online auction companies. For example eBay, founded in September 1995, sold US$3.27 billion in 2004. Sotheby's and Christie's, on the other hand together sell around US$1 billion of art and antiques each quarter. The mechanism used by eBay shares a feature with the one that Pepys observed: all bids must be received before some fixed time. The way in which the price is determined differs. In an eBay auction, a bidder submits a "*proxy bid*" that is not revealed, the prevailing price is a small increment above the second highest proxy bid. As in the 17th century auctions, Pepys observed, many bidders on eBay act in the last moment - a

practice known as "*sniping*" in the argot of cyberspace. Other online auction houses use different termination rules, for example, Amazon waits ten minutes after a bid before closing an auction. The fact that last minute bidding is less common in Amazon auctions than it is in eBay auctions has attracted the attention of game theorists, who have begun to explore models that explain it in terms of the difference in the auction's termination rules.

Despite the long history of auctions and other exchanges, market design had not gained momentum as a scientific discipline until recently. The momentum has emerged due to the large body of theoretical and empirical market literature that has been published in the field, particularly in the area of auction based protocols. A driving factor for this research has been the growth of eCommerce transactions over the Internet which has presented a large number of challenges in the design of eMarkets that support such eCommerce transactions. eMarket designers now need to deal with geographically distributed traders who have multiple complex factors that they need to consider in their negotiations. In general a market designer's task is to: create a meeting place for buyers and sellers; and a format for transactions that enforces a set of market rules that will lead to a "*desired*" outcome. This outcome of trade will be represented as the final allocation of traded objects and by the exchange of monetary payments between the participants. Market design is still in stages of infancy and comprises of tools and methodologies such as: equilibrium analysis; game theory; mechanism design theory; experimental economics; and computation. Within these methodologies, Game theory and mechanism design has provided some very valuable contributions to the field and as a result are further outlined below.

2.1 Game theory

Game theory is a set of analytical tools designed to help one understand the phenomena that we observe when decision makers interact. The basic assumptions that underlie the theory are that decision makers pursue well-defined exogenous objectives and take into account their knowledge and expectation or other decision makers' behaviour. In other words, decision makers can be said, to be rational and they reason strategically. Gibbons and Osborne & Rubenstein provide useful introductions into the subject.

Game theory assumes that there is a set of agents $\boldsymbol{n} = \{i, i= 1, 2, \ldots, n\}$. The action (strategy) space of agents is represented as A_i , where A_i is the set of all available actions to player i , and an outcome $a = (a_1,...,a_n)$ is thus simply an action profile. The most common and easiest game to solve problems in Game theory is known as a Bayesian game. In a Bayesian game, let agent i's possible payoff function be represented by $u_i(a_1,...,a_n;t_i)$, where t_i is called player i's type and belongs to a set of possible types (or type space) T_i. Each type t_i corresponds to a different payoff functions that player i may have. Given this definition of a player's type, saying that player i knows his or her own payoff function is equivalent to saying that player i knows her type. Likewise, saying that player i, may be uncertain about the payoff functions of the other players is equivalent to saying that player i may be uncertain about the types of the other players, denoted by $t_{-i} = (t_1,...,t_{i-1},t_{i+1},...,t_n)$. We use T_{-i} to denote the set of all possible values of t_{-i}, and we use the probability distribution $p_i(t_{-i} \mid t_i)$ to denote player i's belief about the other players' types, t_{-i}, given player i's knowledge of his own type, t_i.

A key concept in game theory is a strategy which is a complete contingent plan, or decision rule, that defines the action an agent will select in every distinguishable state of the world.

For example, in an auction, the strategy of an agent would dictate what bid the agent should submit, given its type and the actions taken by the other agents. A pure strategy for player i in a Bayesian game is a function which maps player i's type into her strategy set, in that $a_i : T_i \rightarrow A_i$, so that $a_i(t_i)$ is the strategy choice of type t_i of player i. A mixed strategy for player i is $\alpha_i : T_i \rightarrow \Delta(A_i)$ so that $\alpha_i(a_i \mid t_i)$ is the probability assigned by α_i to action a_i by type t_i of player i. Each agent will have a preference over outcomes and will try to choose a strategy so that its preferred outcome occurs. These preferences are expressed in terms of utility functions, where $u_i(a_1,...,a_n;t_i)$ is some real number and if agent i prefers outcome $u_i(a_1,..,a_n;t_i) > u_i(b_1,...,b_n;t_i)$, then we understand that player i likes outcome $a=(a_1,...,a_n)$ strictly better than outcome $b=(b_1,...,b_n)$. The goal of each agent is to maximize it utility.
Game theory is interested in finding equilibria. An equilibrium is a strategy profile which satisfies certain properties. The best known equilibrium concept is the *Nash equilibrium*. A *Nash equilibrium* of a game G in strategic form is defined as any outcome $(a_1^*,...,a_n^*)$ such that $(a_i^*,...,a_{-i}^*) \geq u_i(a_i, a_{-i}^*)$ for all $a_i \,\varepsilon\, A_i$ holds for each player i. The set of all Nash equilibria of G is denoted $N(G)$. In Bayesian Nash equilibrium every agent involved is assumed to share a common prior knowledge about the distribution of agent types, type $F(t)$, such that for any particular game the agent profiles are distributed according to $F(t)$. In equilibrium each player or agent selects a strategy to maximize its expected utility in equilibrium with expected-utility maximizing strategies of other players, in other words each player's strategy must be a best response to the other player's strategies. That is, a Bayesian Nash Equilibrium is simply a Nash equilibrium in a Bayesian game. A stronger equilibrium concept in game theory is the dominant strategy equilibrium.
In the dominant strategy equilibrium, the problem of forming a conjecture about the action choice of other players does not arise, because there is an optimal way of taking an action *independently* of the intended play of others. Games with dominant strategy equilibria are easy for agents to play since it is obvious what their optimal strategy is and they do not need to worry about what the other agents are doing. While many games do not have dominant strategy equilibria, in many practical implementations it is possible to carefully design games in order to guarantee that dominant strategies of the agents are such that agents are best off truthfully telling their true preferences to the auctioneer.

2.2 Mechanism design

In a mechanism design problem one can imagine that each agent holds one of the "inputs" to a well formulated completely specified optimization problem, perhaps a constraint or an objective function coefficient, and that the system wide goal is to solve the specific instantiation of the optimization problem specified by the inputs [Hurwicz].
The system wide goal in mechanisms design is defined with a social choice function, which selects the optimal consequence, given an agent's type, where a social choice function $f : T_1 \times ... \times T_n \rightarrow C$, chooses a consequence $f(t) \,\varepsilon\, C$, given types $t_i = (t_1,...,t_n)$. A Mechanism $M = (S_1,...,S_n; g(.))$ defines the set of strategies S_i available to each agent, and an outcome rule $g : S_1 \times .... \times S_n \rightarrow C$, such that $g(s)$ is the consequence implemented by the mechanism for strategy profile $s = (s_1,...,s_n)$. Game theory is used to analyze the consequences or outcome of a mechanism. Given mechanism M with outcome function $g(.)$, we say that the mechanism implements a social choice function $f(t)$, if the consequence computed with equilibrium

agent strategies is a solution to the social choice function for all possible agent preferences. The equilibrium concept can be either Nash, Bayesian-Nash, dominant - or some other solution concept, so long as the strongest one is used [Varian, Jackson].
The most important properties, according to Bichler, for designing a mechanism include equilibrium, efficiency, stability, incentive compatibility and speed of convergence. A mechanism is efficient, meaning that the allocation resulting from the auction is *Pareto optimal*, where no agent can improve its allocation without making another agent worse off. This means that the auction is efficient if there are no further gains from trade, and that the goods are allocated to the agents who value them most highly. The solution is said to be *stable* if there are no subset of agents who could have done better by coming to an agreement outside the mechanism. If a mechanism is stable then it is Pareto efficient, although the reverse is not true. A direct auction *is incentive compatible* if honest reporting of valuations is a Nash equilibrium. A particularly strong and strategically simple case is a mechanism where truth telling is a dominant strategy. This is a desirable feature because as an agent's decision depends only on its local information, and it gains no advantage by expending effort to model other agents. Mechanisms that require agents to learn or estimate another's private information do not respect privacy. Speed of convergence is another important issue in markets where transactions need to occur at a rapid rate. A good example is the Dutch flower auction. Since these auctions deal with large volumes of perishable goods, each individual transaction needs to be completed quickly.
Mechanism design theory now forms an integral part of modern economics where it's most successful use has been its application to auction theory. These two areas intersect in the area of optimal auction design, where principles from mechanism design are combined with auction theory to design auctions that achieve the desired optimal outcomes [Bichler].

3. Automated negotiation

While market design helps decide the rules of the negotiation, and can also assist in the design of auctions to achieve optimal outcomes, a rationale for using auctions in eMarkets has yet to be discussed. It is the purpose of this section, where the reasons why automated negotiation techniques are important in eMarkets, how and why different auctions are appropriate for different situations, and the main auctions types and their optimal strategies as computed using Game theory are discussed.
According to Bichler, within negotiation, "current human-based procedures are relatively slow, do not always uncover the best solution", and are, furthermore, according to Beam and Segev (1997) constrained by issues of culture, ego and pride. In addition, human participants in the negotiation process often reach suboptimal agreements thereby "leaving money on the table". Human's inability to find better agreements is due to the fact that negotiation is a search process for the optimum agreement. The main difficulty in this optimisation search process is that each party involved in the negotiation has private knowledge and each side does not normally know this private knowledge and their corresponding utility functions. Furthermore both sides often have an incentive to misrepresent their preferences, thereby making the formation of an optimal agreement/solution an extremely challenging task. Essentially, both sides are in competition but must jointly search for possible agreements.
For the past few decades researchers in the field of economics, game theory and behavioural sciences have investigated this negotiation process. However despite the large amount of

research conducted a solid and comprehensive framework is still lacking. A basic principle of microeconomics and negotiation sciences is that there is not a single "*best*" protocol for all possible negotiation situations. Wurman et al, asserts that different negotiation protocols are appropriate in different situations, and, thus, any generic mediation service should support a range of options. To demonstrate this point the abstract, in Table 1 below will analyse key countries (i.e. Britain, Switzerland and Denmark) and the chosen auction protocols used in the sale of the 3G spectrum licences, which cost European telecommunication operator's approx $700 billion US Dollars [Klemperer].

The sale of the European 3G spectrum licences began in Britain in March 2000. Because Britain was the first country to sell such licence agreements it had what is called "first moreover advantage". Britain originally planned to sell just four licenses but faced the problem that there was exactly four incumbent "2G" mobile phone operators who had advantages over the other bidders. In this situation if Britain decided to use an ascending auction protocol it would be susceptible to the problems of: collusion; and could deter the weaker bidder to enter the race since a weaker potential bidder knows that a stronger bidder can always re-bid to top any bid he makes. If Britain used a pure sealed bid auction this could allow a situation where a bidder with lower values could beat opponents with higher values leading to potentially an inefficient outcome compared to an ascending auction. As a result, Britain planned to use a hybrid of the ascending and sealed bid auctions, called "Anglo-Dutch" auction. In this configuration, the ascending auction continued until just five bidders remain, after which the five survivors made sealed bids. In this scenario the sealed bid stage would attract entry and so also raise revenue, while the ascending would mean less loss of efficiency that might result from a pure sealed-bid auction. In this auction nine new entrants' bids strongly against the incumbents, creating intense competition and record-breaking revenues of 39 billion Euros. The Swiss auction experience presented the most embarrassing result, where it decided to use the ascending auction protocol. Although the auction received initially considerable interest from numerous bidders the type of auction protocol turned the weaker bidders off participating where the number of bidders reduced from nine to four. As a result the telecom operators just had to pay the reserve price for the spectrum licence agreements which were one thirtieth per capita of the UK and German prices, and one-fiftieth of what the government had once hoped for. Denmark ran the last of the auctions in September 2001 and was in a particularly tricky position. Valuations were now low and to further complicate matters Denmark planned to sell the same number of licenses as it had incumbent operators. As a result it choose a sealed bid auction to give weaker bidders a chance of winning, in the hope of attracting new entrants and of scaring the incumbent operators into making higher bids. The auction was a resounding success, attracting a serious bid from a new entrant and shocking analysts with a revenue more than double most expectations. What is visible from above is that one generic auction protocol does not fit all. The auction protocol selected must bear in mind a number of factors, such as the number of bidders, possibility of collusion, and market stability. The countries that borne these factors into their design produced an outcome that generated the most revenue for their corresponding governments while countries like the Netherlands that just copied other countries choice suffered the consequences.

Table 1. Abstract - discussing how one size does not fit all when it comes to auction protocol design [Klemperer]

Recent developments in electronic market research offer the promise that new negotiation protocols will not only leave less money on the table but will also enable new types of transactions to be negotiated more cost effectively. There have been many approaches for supporting or automating commercial negotiations, such as bargaining and auctions. Bargaining situations can concern as few as two individuals, who may try to reach an agreement on a range of transactions. Over the past decade, there have been several approaches to supporting or describing one-on-one negotiations, ranging from game theory to negotiation support systems to intelligent agents who bargain the details and finally close the deal without any further user interactions. According to Bichler, however, although much research has been accomplished, automated bargaining using agents is currently restricted to a small number of applications in commercial environments. The reason for this, is that game theory has failed, thus far, to describe human bargaining, where Linhart et at state that *"inadequate theories of bargaining exist only for the degenerate, polar cases of competition and monopoly"*. In addition negotiation support systems require constant human input, both at the initial problem setup and all final decisions are left to the human negotiators, making automated bargaining not so automated.

McAfee [McAfee] defined an auction as "a market institution with an explicit set of rules determining resource allocation and prices based on bids from the market participants". Auctions constitute one type of dynamic pricing, in which the price of the product varies, depending on the demand characteristics of the consumer and the supply situation of the seller and are often used rather than posting a fixed price on an item, in cases where products have no standard value. In addition to price determination, according to Kagel (1997), auction theory is also important for practical, empirical and theoretical reasons. The roots of electronic auction and negotiation mechanisms are in auction and negotiation theory. See for instance, Raiffa, Milgrom, Kagel and Roth (1995), Klemperer, and Rothkopft et al.

Using auctions as a means of automating negotiation in eMarkets has been described by Binmore and Vulkan (1999) as *"an effective way of resolving the one to many bargaining problem"*. According to experiments described in Kagel et al (1995) the outcome of market competition is more likely to conform to game-theoretical rationality than the outcome of a bilateral negotiation. In addition compared to the bargaining process, being a bid taker puts less of a burden on the seller's knowledge and abilities than being a negotiator in a bargaining process, simply because the human or agent does not need to know the range of possible buyer valuations. In general the price set by the eMarket i.e. the winning bid is on average below the item's true but unknown value, but with the introduction of more and more bidders, the price approaches its true value.

In addition, to further advocate the use of auctions in automated negotiation procedures, the technical infrastructure required to support auctions in an online environment is currently available and well accepted. Wurman (2001) outlined how auctions are a very efficient and effective method of allocating goods/service, in dynamic situations to the entities that value them most highly, whereas Bapna et al stated that *"Online auctions, bought about by the synergetic combination of Internet technology and traditional auction mechanisms present a significant new dimension for mercantile processes"*. Intelligent software agents can also represented their owners in an auction, where the agent activities may involve monitoring, analyzing the market conditions and/or deciding when and how much to bid for the desired items.

There are many different forms of auctions, where [Wurman, 1998] defines a taxonomy of auction parameters that allows for approximately 25 million types of auctions. Beam and Segev (1997) also examined 100 online auctions and analyzed their characteristics. However despite this vast range of auction protocols there are only four common types of single sided auctions, which include: English, Dutch, First Price Sealed Bid (FPSB), and Second Price Sealed Bid (SPSB) which are outlined below. Included in the description of each of these auction types is the strategy that the human or agent needs to employ to receive the highest utility in the process. Within these auction types the Dutch auction and First-Price Sealed-Bid are strategically equivalent to each other, while the English auction protocol and the Second-Price Sealed-Bid auction are strategically equivalent to each other. To see how these strategies were computed in more detail, please see [Gibbons].

However, the strategies shown in Table 2 only hold true under the auction model more commonly known as the symmetric Independent Private Value (IPV) model and perceived valuations in the common-value-model. Under the IPV model, Bidder i knows his own valuation, v_i , where this valuation is the true valuation in the independent-private-values models. Each bidder is assumed to know the number of bidders, their risk attitudes, and the probability distributions of valuations, and he knows everyone else knows that he knows this, and so on. At a Bayes-Nash equilibrium, each bidder bids an amount that is some function of his own valuation, such that, given that everyone else chooses his bid in this way, no individual bidder could be better by bidding differently [McAfee].

At the other model extreme, consider the sale of an antique that is being bid for all dealers who intend to resell it, or the sale of mineral rights to a particular tract of land. Now the item being bid for has a single objective value, namely the about the antique is worth on the market, or the amount of oil actually lying beneath the ground. However no-one of course knows its true value and so the bidders, perhaps having access to different information, have different guesses about how much the item is objectively worth. If V is the unobserved true value, then the bidders' perceived values, v_i , $i = 1,2,....,n$, are independent draws from some probability distribution $H(v_i \mid V)$. All agents know the distribution H . This is called the *common-value model.* A frequently observed phenomenon under this auction model is the so called *winner's* curse phenomena. In this situation the winner bids more that the goods true value and suffers a loss. The main lesson learned from the common value model is that bidders should shade their bids, as the auction always selects the bidder as the winner who received the most optimistic estimate of the items value [McAfee].

Another important point to note that under these conditions the revenue equivalence theorem holds, which essentially states that in any auction that has [Klemperer] *"a given number of risk neutral potential buyers of an object has a privately known signal independently drawn from a common, strictly increasing, atomless distribution. Then any auction mechanism in which (i) the object always goes to the buyer with the highest signal, and (ii) any bidder with the lowest-feasible signals expects zero surplus, yields the same expected revenue (and results in each bidder making the same expected payment as a function of their signal)"*. What the above states is that when the object goes to the buyer with the highest valuation, then the outcome of the auction is said to be *Pareto efficient*. The Revenue Equivalence Theorem also proves that for in [Vickrey] *"each of the English auction, the Dutch auction, the first-price sealed bid auction, and the second price-sealed bid auction yields the same price on average"*. Therefore all four types of auctions yield the same expected revenue for the seller in the case of independent private values and risk neutrality.

Auction Protocol	Description	Strategy
Ascending Bid or English auction	The price is successively raised until at least one bidder remains. This can be done by having an auctioneer announce prices, or by having bids submitted electronically with the current best bid posted. The essential feature of the English auction is that, at any point in time, each bidder knows the current best bid. Antiques, art work and houses are sometimes sold using this type of auction.	The agent's dominant strategy (the best thing to do, irrespective of what the others do []) is to bid a small amount more than the current highest bid and stop when the user's valuation is reached. For example, in Yahoo auctions, "*autonomic bidding*" allows users to input their maximum bid and an agent will bid incrementally when it is necessary to win the auction.
Descending Bid or Dutch auction	The agent's dominant strategy (the best thing to do, irrespective of what the others do [Gibbons]) is to bid a small amount more than the current highest bid and stop when the user's valuation is reached. For example, in Yahoo auctions, "*autonomic bidding*" allows users to input their maximum bid and an agent will bid incrementally when it is necessary to win the auction.	Strategically equivalent to First-Price Sealed -Bid
First-Price, Sealed-Bid (FPSB) auction	Each bidder independently submits a single bid, without knowledge of what bids is submitted by other participants. The object is sold to the bidder who makes the highest bid. This type of auction is used in auctioning mineral rights in government-owned land, and is sometimes used is the sales of artwork and real estate. Of greater quantitative significance is the use of sealed bid tendering for government procurement contracts - that is competing contractors submit prices and the lowest bidder wins and receives her price for fulfilling the contract.	The dominant strategy in First-Price Sealed -Bid of complete information is to bid the second highest bidders valuation, while in First-Price Sealed-Bid of incomplete information the dominant strategy, computed using game theory is that he bids a fraction $((n\text{-}1)/n)v$ of his valuation v, when a total of n parties are bidding. Further analysis of this strategy is provided in [Gibbons].
The Vickrey or Second-Price, Sealed-Bid auction	Operates in the same manner as FPSB and while the object is still sold to the bidder who makes the highest bid, the winning bidder pays the second-highest bidders bid, or "second price". While this auction has useful theoretical properties, it is seldom used in practice due to its vulnerability to a lying auctioneer, lower revenue when compared to the English auction and undesirable private information problems [Gibbons].	The (weakly) dominant strategy used in Vickrey auctions is to bid the valuation v_i for player i. Strategically equivalent to the English auction protocol.

Table 2. Main auction types and corresponding strategies

3.1 Terms and extensions to the main auction protocols

In many real world situations, competition and negotiation involve many quality dimensions in addition to price. In Rothkopf and Harstad's critical essay, the authors outlined how it would be useful to expand their limited focus, because isolated, single good auctions are not the most common or interesting auction type from a practical perspective. As a result there have been several extensions to the traditional auction paradigm in recent years, which are further discussed below.

One active field of study has been *multiple unit* and *multi-object* auctions. At multi-unit auctions, the objects for sale are assumed identical, so it matters not which unit a bidder wins but rather the aggregate number of units he wins. At multi-object auctions, the objects for sale are not identical, so it matters to a bidder which specific objects he wins. Thus an example of a multi-object auction would involve the sale of an apple, orange, and a pear, while an example of a multi-unit auction would involve the sale of three identical apples. In the auction's simplest case, the bidders are allowed to buy only one unit of merchandise. In the more realistic case, such restrictions cannot be imposed. The consequence of the additional quantity dimensions is that traditional bidding strategies and auction design mechanisms should be reconsidered and adjusted. As Bapna et al, and Rothkopf and Harstad, among others have pointed out, the strong theoretical results obtained for isolated single good auctions, are not necessarily transferable to the more complicated multiple unit situation.

Another extension is the development of *combinatorial auctions*, in which bidders desire to buy or sell bundles of goods rather than one single good. For example, a seller may want to sell several kinds of related goods where many bidders may have preferences over a combination of items. After the seller receives all the bids, it will decide a non-conflicting allocation among these goods that maximizes its revenue. These sorts of auctions are involved in many situations in the real world especially the computational issues associated with winner determination and final allocation [Kelly]. For example in the sale of the Germans spectrum licences, bidders placed bids on different combinations of spectrum licenses. However, combinatorial auctions are currently rare in practice. The main problems confronted in implementing these auctions are that they have computational uncertainty, in that there is no guarantee that the winning bids for such an auction can be found in a reasonable amount of time when the number of bidders become larger, and that the auction is cognitively complex and can lead participants to pursue perverse bidding strategies [Kelly].

Double-sided auction is a further auction type extension. The most common type of this auction type is the Continuous Double Auction (CDA), which allows buyers and sellers to continuously update their bids at any time in the trading period. This type of auction is easy to operate, efficient and can quickly respond to changing market conditions. A variety of CDA models have being constructed [Easley] and these vary in terms of whether bids/asks are for multiple or single units, whether unaccepted offers are queued or replaced by better offers and so on. Nevertheless all these protocols allow traders to make offers to buy or sell and to accept other trader's offers at any moment during a trading period. The messages exchanged generally consist of bids (offer to buy) and asks (offers to sell) for single units of the commodity, and acceptances of the current best bid or ask. Several bidding strategies have been proposed in the literature. The ZERO Intelligence strategy [Gode], generates a random bid within the allowed price range decided by the agent's budget constraint. The adaptive agent bidding strategy is based on stochastic modelling of the auction process using a Markov chain [Park]. A sequential bidding agent method using dynamic programming is proposed in [Tesauro]. In [He , 2003], heuristic fuzzy rules and fuzzy reasoning mechanisms are used to determine the best bid given the state of the marketplace.

Another extension to the traditional auction paradigm is *multidimensional auctions,* also referred to as multi-attribute auctions. Multi-attribute (reverse) auctions combine the advantages of auctions, such as high efficiency and speed of convergence, and permit negotiation on multiple attributes with multiple suppliers in a procurement situation. A multi-attribute auction is defined *"as an item characterized by several negotiable dimensions"* and first arose in the tenders and procurement area [Dasgupta]. The advances in information technology also allow the use of varied and more complex auction mechanism, where Fieldman [cf. Bichler] stated that ''*We've suddenly made the interaction cost so cheap, there's no pragmatic reason not to have competitive bidding on everything*''. If the multidimensional auction has the variable quantity, it is referred to as *multiple issue* auctions. Laffont and Tirole, describes many of the critical issues in procurement negotiations from an economics point of view and also mention the need for a generalization of auction theory to so called *"multi-dimensional bidding"*. Perhaps since multidimensional/multiple issue auctions hold great promise for the improvement of B2B transactions, their development has largely been practice driven. Generalizations of standard auction theory to the multi-attribute case has been discussed by Thiel, Che, Branco and more recently David et al, and De Smet.

An important distinction to make with regards to auctions is that there exist forward or reverse auctions. In the forward auction the seller offers a product to numerous buyers, where the seller "controls" the market because a product is being offered that is in demand by a number of buyers. The price offered by the buyer continues to increase until a theoretical rational market price is met in the market. Supply and demand sets the price. In a reverse auction, the buyer "controls" the market because the item being offered is available from a number of sellers. The price offered by the sellers continues to decrease until a theoretical rational market price is achieved. The basic premise of a reverse auction is that a sufficient supply exists and seller's profit margins are sufficient to offer reduced prices. The reduced price will be offered because the suppliers can instantaneously observe the prices being offered by other sellers [Smeltzer, Carter].

4. Electronic marketplaces (eMarkets)

The previous sections described how optimal markets are designed using techniques such as Game theory and Mechanism design. They outlined how automated negotiation techniques aim to overcome the problem of "leaving money on the table" in the negotiation process and how auctions have been proposed (with the use of intelligent software agents) to overcome this problem. This section will describe the main elements that constitute real world eMarkets and a classification scheme to help distinguish and provide a comparison of eMarkets currently in existence.

A multi-agent eMarket is highly complex, possessing a large number of attributes connected to its architecture such as security, tools for communication between agents, and distribution of roles played by agents and the marketplace. According to He et al, it is important to classify eMarkets according to some attribute, where He et al, defines the most important classification attribute to be the negotiation attribute. In negotiations the topology can be classified according to:

Nature of interactions between agents - which is important for an eMarket to distinguish whether participants are allowed to negotiate on a multilateral basis i.e. with several other participants or not. On either side - on the buyer or sellers side - one or more participants may be negotiating. Denoting the seller as M ("Merchant") and the buyer as C ("Consumer"), Figure 1 shows the three possible situations given by models A, B and C.

Number of negotiating factors - is an important characteristic in every negotiation as it represents the dimension of the space of negotiation issues. In more complicated "real" cases, a number of issues relating to price, quality, penalties, terms and conditions may be discussed i.e. multidimensional.

Whether the negotiation constraints are fuzzy or crisp - the preferences regarding the negotiation issues may also be represented as either crisp or fuzzy, which makes it possible to evaluate a proposal and generate a counter proposal based on a certain strategy. If the issues are crisp then the preferences for these issues cannot be changed to generate a proposal or counter proposal, where if the issues are fuzzy then the various entities can truly negotiate by proposing values outside of their preferences.

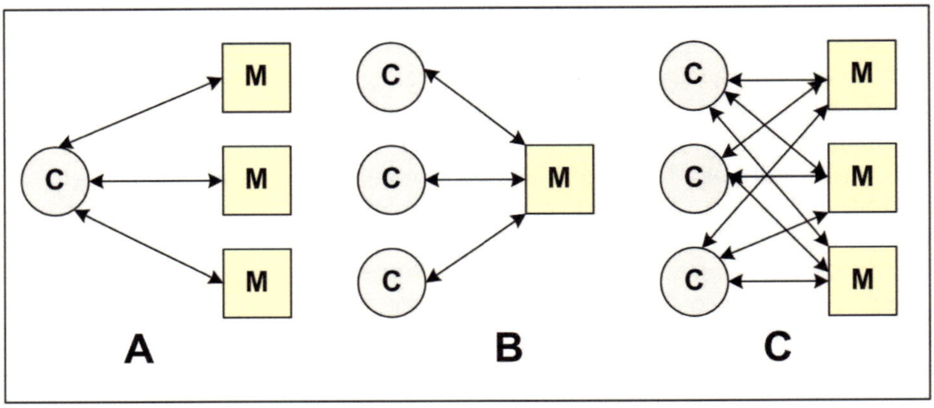

Fig. 1. Three models of competitive negotiation in eMarketplaces

Using the above attributes, Kurbel developed a classification scheme presented by using a technique of morphologic boxes, as shown in Table 3, where the field 'Type of Negotiation' corresponds to nature of interactions between entities i.e. A, B or C denoted in Figure 1. In addition to the classification technique presented by He et al, Guttmann et al, outlined how it is useful to explore the roles of agents as mediators in B2C and B2B eCommerce in the context of a common model, such as the Customer Buying Model (CBB) and the Business Buyer Model (BBT). However this classification scheme is not presented within the scope of this chapter, for further information please see the associated literature. Based on the used and presented classification scheme a survey of well known eMarkets is presented in the section below.

Criterion	Possible Values		
Type of e-marketplace	B2B	B2C	C2C
Type of negotiation model	1:n (A)	m:1 (B)	N:m (C)
Negotiation Issues	One issue (price)	Many Issues	
Type of consumers constraints	Crisp	Fuzzy	
Type of merchants constraints	Crisp	Fuzzy	

Table 3. Classification of controlled multi-agent e-marketplaces

4.1 Survey of electronic marketplaces (eMarkets)

Andersons Consulting's BargainFinder [Krulwich] was the first shopping agent for on-line price comparisons. Given a specific product, the BargainFinder agent requests its price from nine different merchant Web sites using the same request from a Web browser. The retailers play passive roles in this process, they just provide information to the buying agents. Although a limited proof of concept, BargainFinder offered valuable insights into the issues involved in price comparisons in the on-line world. However, value added services that merchants offer in their Web sites are bypassed by BargainFinder as it compares merchants based on price alone. Strictly speaking, eMarkets like BargainFinder are not multi-agent eMarkets because the merchants are statically represented through information about their products and not through software agents. Neither are the consumer's agents sufficiently intelligent as they possess some autonomy and very little features for cooperation. Nevertheless, some of these online shopping markets can be regarded as important steps on the way to multi-agent eMarkets.

Another similar example to BargainFinder is Priceline[1] which carries out the same set of tasks for airline tickets, hotel rooms and cars. However a more important contribution within this domain is Jango [Doorenbos], which can be viewed as an advanced BargainFinder providing a more intelligent solution by having the product requests originate from each of the consumers Web browsers instead of from a central site as in BargainFinder. Jango's modus operandi is simple: once a shopper has identified a specific product, Jango can simultaneously query merchant sites for its price. The results allow a consumer to compare merchant offerings based on price. However in many cases price is not the only important factor to the user. Other relevant issues, for example, might include delivery time, warranty and gift services. Also many merchants prefer their offering not be judged on price alone. Naturally the importance of different attributes will vary between consumers and so there needs to be a way for this information to be easily conveyed to the agent.

This limitation was overcome in the Frictionless[2] scoring platform, "*vendor scorecards*" a form of multi-attribute auction that was used to measure the performance of suppliers. For example, when evaluating the performance of different laptop computer suppliers, the key factors considered include reliability, responsiveness, environmental friendliness and business efficiency. A total score is then calculated for each supplier based on the weighted score of these individual constituent components. Although quick and easy to use, the Frictionless engine neglects one essential aspect of decision making in a vague environment with fuzzy constraints and preferences. A consumer has no means to enter into the system how important the different negotiation issues or product features compared to each other. All are assumed to be equally important. This problem was tackled by the Active Buyer's Guide System developed by Active Research, Inc. [Kurbel] The users are not only asked how desirable are certain product features for them but also how important is each product feature is when compared to others, and even how important are certain combinations of features compared to other combinations.

Two further eMarkets are MAGMA [Tsvetovatyy] (Minnesota AGent Marketplace Architecture) and MAGNET [Collins] (Multi-Agent NEgotiation Testbed) developed by

[1] http://www.priceline.com/

[2] http://www.frictionless.com

University of Minnesota. MAGMA was an attempt to develop a prototype of an agent-based eMarket together with additional infrastructure including a banking system, communication, transport and storage system, plus administrative and policing systems. MAGMA includes trader agents, which are responsible for the buying and selling of goods and negotiating prices, and an advertising server for searching and retrieving adverts by categories. Negotiation is based on the Vickrey auction, where bids are submitted in written form with no knowledge of bids from others where the winner pays the second highest amount. In contrast to the MAGMA system, the MAGNET eMarket was intended to provide support for complex agent interactions such as automated contracting in supply-chain management. Evaluation of the bids received is based not on cost but also on time constraints and risk, providing a very simple multi-issue negotiation technique.
MIAMI Marketplace (MIAMAP) [Esmahi] is an open virtual eMarket where agents process their marketing transactions, providing a generalised mediation model that supports a variety of transactions types, from simple buying and selling to complex multiagent contract negotiations. The negotiation strategy presented from this work takes advantage of the services located within the market to construct beneficial contracts. In its findings Esmahi, states that the introduction of an explicit mediator can help resolve conflicts and add value to multiagent contracting. These eMarkets and the differences between them are compared according to method outlined in [Kurbel] the results of which are shown in Table 4.
Two further notable eMarkets specifically within the domain of telecommunications are the Digital MarketPlace (DMP) [Irvine] and the Telecommunication Service Exchange (TSE) [Griffin]. These eMarkets have been proposed to assist mobile users in being able to exert their bargaining power. This problem has emerged due to the fact that at present, mobile users are typically tied to their service provider via a long term contract lasting usually 12 months or more. Within this time mobile users cannot switch from one service provider to another to avail of special offers and services that the alternative service provider may be capable of offering. This causes an inefficiency of competition in telecommunications from the mobile user's perspective. However, allowing consumers to purchase services on a per request basis, while at the same time maintaining their contract with their chosen service providers however would provide more competition within the sector, and will force service providers to better serve the interests of users.

	Neg. Model	**Type of Neg.**	**Issues**	**Type of consumers constraints**	**Type of merchants constraints**
BargainFinder	A	Search and comparison	Price	Crisp	Crisp
Frictionless	A	Search and comparison	Price, product features, merchants services	Fuzzy	Crisp
Active Buyers Guide System	A	Search and comparison	Price, product features	Fuzzy	Crisp
MAGMA	A	Auction	Price	Fuzzy	Fuzzy
MAGNET	A	Auction	Price, time, constraints, risk	Fuzzy	Fuzzy
MIAMAP	A	Mediator	Cost, price, risk	Fuzzy	Fuzzy

Table 4. Comparison of eMarkets

The DMP presents one such solution to this problem, where mobile users can purchase calls on a per call basis. Internally, the DMP adopts an eMarket where Buyers, service providers and network operators are represented by their respective agents such as: User Agents (UA); Service Provider Agents (SPA); and Network Operator Agents (NOA). The UA are responsible for acquiring the mobile user's preferences over attributes such price and QoS. Upon receipt of this request the UAs initiate an auction with the SPAs using a variant of First-Price Sealed-Bid (FPSB), where the buyer selects the bidder which maximises its objective function, while meeting its valuation. Although the system allows the User Agent (UA) to specify their requirements from a multi-attribute perspective, when the Service Provider Agent (SPA) receives the request it does not formulate a bid based on these attributes. Instead it responds with a single attribute, price when is then used by the UA along with the SPA performance rating (or commitment) to determine the winner of the auction round. This limitation inherently lies in the auction protocol chosen, First Price Sealed Bid, where it prevents the user from correctly evaluating, what it wanted in the original request to what it actually received in the call in terms of these attributes. It also prevents the UA in performing a proper comparison between the various service providers. The DMP is classified according to [Guttman] scheme below in Table 5.

Criterion	**Possible Values**		
Type of e-marketplace	**B2B**	**B2C**	**C2C**
Type of negotiation model	**1:n (A)**	**M:1 (B)**	**n:m (C)**
Negotiation Issues	**One issue (price)**	**Many Issues (partially)**	
Type of consumers constraints	**Crisp**	**Fuzzy**	
Type of merchants constraints	**Crisp**	**Fuzzy**	

Table 5. The Digital Marketplace (DMP) morphologic box classification

The TSE on the other hand supports both B2C and B2B transaction allowing mobile users to purchase services on a per request basis and also allows the dynamic formation of Virtual Organisations in the B2B to create composite services using a Service Oriented Architectural (SOA) approach to service provisioning. While the internal architecture is similar to the DMP with the existence of Buyer User Agents (BUA), SPA and NOA, the TSE also has two notable additional agents, those being the Trusted Intermediary Agent (TIA) and the Better Business Bureau Agent (BBBA). The TIA essentially acts as the auctioneer in the eMarketplace and is responsible for acting on behalf of the buyer in the market. The BBBA is a similar to the Better Bureau Agent employed in Kasbah [Chavez], where post purchase feedback and consumer satisfaction is monitored to provide a rating of the service provider in the eMarketplace. The negotiation model employed in the TSE is similar to that of MAGNET [Collins] using call for proposals, propose and accept/reject message sequence. However, the TSE allows the BUAs to specify their requests in terms of multiple attributes as well as the relative importance of each attribute in terms of each other using the multi-attribute auction protocol. The various SPA bids are then returned to the BUA and the winner is determined using a scoring function. A unique and novel feature of the TSE is that it is an exchange market infrastructure, as advocated by Collins et al, facilitating two separate but co-related markets, the B2B and the B2C. Table 6, further describes the TSE under the classification scheme discussed in [Guttman].

Online auctions are doubtless the largest class of Internet-based eMarketplaces. There are literally thousands of auctions both in the B2B, B2C and C2C areas. Bean and Segev (1998)

examined 100 online auctions and analyzed their characteristics. Examples of these marketplaces include eBay and Amazon, which both use a variant of the English auction to sell its goods over the Internet. To sell something on eBay, one has to provide a description of the item together with some constraints including payment method, where to ship, who will pay for the shipment, minimum bid and reserve price. In fact by providing this information the seller initializes an agent to negotiate about one issue - price. On the bidder side, one can employ a "phantom" bidding service that utilizes the common bidding strategy of 'sniping'. Such examples include eSnipe and Phantom Bidder. The Fishmarket [Napoli] electronic auction house is another example of an eMarketplace that uses the age-old institution of a fish market using the Dutch bidding protocol.

Criterion	Possible Values		
Type of e-marketplace	**B2B**	**B2C**	C2C
Type of negotiation model	**1:n (A)**	**M:1 (B)**	n:m (C)
Negotiation Issues	One issue (price)	**Many Issues**	
Type of consumers constraints	Crisp	**Fuzzy**	
Type of merchants constraints	Crisp	**Fuzzy**	

Table 6. The TSE characteristics for Negotiation Model A

5. Agents and eMarkets

Woolridge et al defined an agent as a "computer system, situated in some environment that is capable of flexible autonomous actions in order to meet its design objectives". Agents over the past number of decades have been applied to a wide range of applications, not least in the area of automated negotiation and auctions. In recent years initiatives such as the Trading Agent Competition (TAC) have attempted to drive research forward to enable scientists to evaluate programmed trading techniques in a market scenario by competing with agents from other design groups [Petric]. The following section will outline where agent technology has made the most impact with a particular emphasis on the topic of this chapter, eMarkets and auctions.

Within the area of Grid computing - the agent and grid communities are both trying to address the problem of "*coordinated problem solving in dynamic, multi-institutional (Virtual) Organizations*". Within this objective the Grid community has historically focused on what Foster et al, refers to as the "*brawn*" i.e. an interoperable infrastructure for secure and reliable resource sharing within dynamic and geographically distributed Virtual Organization (VO), while the agent community has focused on the "*brains*" i.e. on the development of concepts, methodologies, and algorithms for autonomous problem solvers. According to Foster et al, integrating the '*brawns*' of the grid, with the '*brains*' of the agent could result in "*a framework for constructing large scale, agile distributed systems that are qualitatively and quantitatively superior to the best practice today*".

Because of the horizontal nature of agent technology, it is also envisioned according to Luck et al, that the successful adoption of agent technology with Web services will have a profound, long term impact both on the competitiveness and viability of IT industries and also on the way in which future systems will be conceptualized and implemented. With Web services, the World Wide Web Consortium (W3C) has described agents as the "*running programs that drive Web services – both to implement them and to access them as computational resources that act on behalf of a person or organisation"*. In the previously discussed Telecommunication Service Exchange (TSE), the implementation of the B2B market within the exchange focused on dynamic Web service composition, using automated negotiation techniques and multi-attribute auctions to decide which atomic service element best suits a service provider's non-functional Quality of Service (QoS) requirements [Griffin].

A key aspect within eMarkets is the eCommerce and negotiation activities of such markets. Within these, agents are used to fully realise the economic benefits of its existence, where according to He et al *"Electronic Commerce is the most important allocation for Agent technologies, because it is reality-based and constitutes a massive market"*. As a result the adoption of agent technology is a central element to the operations within any eMarket, where these agents negotiate of behalf of their owners. Automating these activities through the use of agents can save time, and in complex settings it has been shown by research by Das et al, that when agents and humans participate simultaneously in a realistic auction, the software agents consistently produce greater gains compared to their human counterparts. The application of agents in B2B eCommerce transactions has been viewed as particularly promising, since manual bidding would obviously not be practical, and negotiations in such eMarkets would have to be preformed by the selling and buying agents with sophisticated agent strategies. In B2C and C2C eMarkets agent technology is not foreseen to make as big an impact. The reason for this is that human customers like the bidding frenzy and they enjoy placing the bids and the entertainment value of an online auction is an important component of the experience [Beam, 1997]. The disadvantage of such frenzied actions is that the participants sometimes can fall victim to a phenomenon known as the "winners curse".

As previously stated these eCommerce transactions take place within an eMarket, where Section 5 provided an in-depth overview of existing implementations. In order for software agents to represent their human owners within the eMarket they need to communicate with each other. Such communication is normally represented through some kind of Agent Communication Language (ACL) and is used to share information and knowledge among agents in distributed computing environments, but also request the performance of a task. The main objective of ACL is to model a suitable framework that allows heterogeneous agents to interact and to communicate with meaningful statements that convey information about their environment or knowledge.

The most recent evolution of ACLs is the draft standard proposed by the Foundation for Intelligent Physical Agents (FIPA). This foundation is a non-profit association whose objective consists of promoting the success of emerging agent-based technology and was officially accepted by the IEEE at its eleventh standards committee meeting in June 2005. It operates through an open international collaboration of companies and universities who are active members in the field. FIPA assigns tasks (ontologies, semantics, architectures, gateways and compliance) to technical committees, each of which has primary responsibility for producing, maintaining and updating the specifications applicable to its tasks. FIPAs Agent Communication Language (FIPA-ACL) is based on speech act theory and messages are considered to be communicative acts, whose objective is to perform some action by virtue of being sent. FIPA-ACL also defines a set of interaction protocols, as detailed in Table 7 which deal with pre-agreed message exchange protocols for ACL messages. What is clear from the Table 7 is the incorporation of existing standard auction protocols into FIPA interaction protocols, demonstrating a clear importance of the use of agent technology with auction protocols.

FIPA Identifier	Title of Interaction Protocol	Function
SC00026	Request	Allows one agent to request another to perform some action
SC00027	Query	Allows one agent to request to perform some kind of action on another agent
SC00028	Request When	Allows an agent to request that the receiver perform some action at the time a given precondition becomes true
SC00029	Contract Net	One agent takes the role of manager and wishes to have some task preformed by one or more other agents and further wishes to optimize a function that characterizes the task. For a given task, any number of the participants may respond with a Proposal message
SC00031	English Auction	Auctioneer calls are expressed in Call for Proposals (cfp) acts, and are multicast to participants in the English auction. Participants propose bids in a propose act, and the auctioneer notifies winner in an accept-proposal act
SC00032	Dutch Auction	Models the Dutch auction by using a series of acts such as inform-start-of-auction, cfp, propose, accept and reject proposal
SC00033	Brokering	Is designed to support brokerage interactions in mediated systems and in multi-agent systems. A broker is an agent that offers a set of communication facilitation services to other agents using some knowledge about the requirements and capabilities of those agents
SC00034	Recruiting	Is designed to support recruiting interactions in mediated and multi-agent systems, where a recruiter is another type of broker agent
SC00035	Subscribe	Allows an agent to request a receiving agent to perform an action on subscription and subsequently when the referenced object changes
SC00036	Propose	Allows an agent to propose to receiving agents that the initiator will do the actions described in the propose communicative act when the receiving agent accepts the proposal

Table 7. FIPA ACL Interaction Protocol

6. Conclusion

In summary, it is important to note that the Internet does not really change much of the fundamental characteristics of the general negotiation process. However the expansion and integration of the Internet into our everyday lives has resulted in work being conducted to support the ever increasing demand of mostly B2B eCommerce transactions, where according to [cf. Bichler] "*Internet based electronic marketplaces leverage information technology to match buyers and sellers with increased effectiveness and lower transactions costs, leading to more efficient "friction-free" markets*. The complexity to support such eMarkets lies in the fact that the parties involved in these transactions are located across geographically distributed locations with complex requirements that will form part of their trade agreements. As a result in the future, market design will play an ever more important role in the automated negotiation process, as sellers and service providers will want to ensure that the outcome is efficient giving them the highest utility possible. Of course, auctions play a crucial element in automated negotiation and while a huge variety of auctions exist, it is important to note that some of the more interesting auction types such as multi-attribute auctions consider multiple considerations in the negotiation. As a result, multi-attribute auctions will play a vital element in B2B eCommerce in the future. To automate such negotiations in B2B eMarkers, it is envisioned that agents will negotiate on behalf of their human owners, with implemented strategies calculated using Game theory to ensure the highest utility from the process.

7. References

R. Bapna, Goes, P., and Gupta, A., Insights and analysis of on-line auctions, Communications of the ACM, Vol. 44 pgs. 43-90

Beam, C., and Segev, A., Automated Negotiations: A Survey of the State of the Art, CMIT Working Paper 97-WP-1022, May 1997

Beam, C., and Segev, A., Auctions on the Internet: A field study, Working Paper 98-WP-1032

Bichler, M., The future of eMarkets, Multidimensional Market Mechanism, Cambridge University Press, 2001

Binmore, K., Vulkan, N., Applying game theory to automated negotiation, Netnomics, Vol (1):1, pgs. 1-9, 1999

K. Binmore, K., Klemperer, P., The Biggest Auction Ever: the Sale of the British 3G Telecom Licenses, Economic Journal, 2002

Branco, F., The design of multidimensional auctions, RAND Journal of Economics, Vol. 28 (1), pg.63-81, 1997

Carter, C., Kaufmann, L., Beall, S., Carter, P., Hendrick, T. and Petersen, K., Reverse Auctions - Grounded Theory from the Buyer and Supplier Perspective, Transportation Research Part E: Logistics and Transportation Review, Vol: 40(3), 2004

Chavez, A. and Maes, P., Kasbah: An Agent Marketplace for buying and selling goods, First International Conference on the Practical Application of Intelligent Agents and Multi-Agent Technology (PAAM'96)

Che, K. Y., Design Competition through multidimensional auctions, RAND Journal of Economics, Vol. 24 (4),1993

Collins, J., Jamison, S., Mobasher, B. and Gini, M., A Market Architecture for Multi-Agent Contracting, Proceedings of the 2nd International Conference on Autonomous Agents, 1998

Collins, J., Tsvetovatyy, M., Gini, M. and Mobasher, B., MAGNET: A Multi-Agent Contracting System for Plan Execution, in Proc. of the Workshop on Artificial Intelligence and Manufacturing, New Mexico, August 1998

Das, R., Hanson, J., Kephart, J.O. and Tesauro, G., Agent-Human Interactions in the Continuous Double Auction, in Proc. International Joint Conference of Artificial Intelligence, Seattle, USA, August 2001

Dasgupta, S., and Spulber, D.F., Managing procurement auctions, Information Economics and Policy, Vol 4, pg.5-29, 1989

David, E., Azoulay-Schwartz, R. and Kraus, S., Protocols and Strategies for Automated Multi-Attribute Auctions, In Proc. First Joint Conference on Autonomous Agents and Multiagent Systems, Bologna, Italy, 2002

Doorenbos, R.B., Etzioni, O. and Weld, D.S., A Scalable Comparison-Shopping Agent for the World-Wide Web in Proc. of the First International Conference on Autonomous Agents, California, USA, Feb5-8, 1997

Easley, D. and Ledyard, J., Theories of price formation and exchange in double oral auctions, In Friedman, D. & Rust, J., eds., The Double Auction Market: Institutions, Theories and Evidence, pgs. 3-25, Addison-Wesley, Reading, MA, 1993

Esmahi, L., Bernard, J-C. and Dini, P., MIAMAP: A Virtual Market Place for Intelligent Agents, in Proc. of the 33rd International Conference on System Sciences, Hawaii, 2000

Feldman, S., Electronic Marketplaces, in IEEE Internet Computing, Vol 4(4), pg. 93-95, Aug 2000

Foster, I., Jennings, N.R. and Kesselman, C., Brain Meets Brawn: Why Grid and Agents Need Each Other, in Proc. 3rd Int. Conf. on Autonomous Agents and Multi-Agent Systems, New York, USA, 2004

Foundation for Intelligent Physical Agents, http://www.fipa.org

FIPA ACL Message Structure Specification, XC00061D, http://www.fipa.org/specs/fipa00061/XC00061D.pdf

Gibbons, R., A Primer in Game Theory, London, Prentice Hall, 1992

Gode, D. and Sunder, S., Lower bounds for efficiency of surplus extraction in double auctions, In Friedman, D. & Rust, J., eds., The Double Auction Market: Institutions, Theories and Evidence, pgs. 199-219, Addison-Wesley, Reading, MA, 1993

Griffin, D. and Pesch, D., Mobile Communications Systems - The Telecommunication Service Exchange, IEEE Transactions on Network and Service Management, Vol:3(2), Second Quarter 2006

Guttman, R.H., Moukas, A.G. and Maes, P., Agent-mediated Electronic Commerce: A Survey, The Knowledge Engineering Review, Vol 13 (2), pg. 147-159, 1998

He, M., Jennings, N.R. and Leung, H-F., On Agent-Mediated Electronic Commerce, IEEE Transactions on Knowledge and Data Engineering, 15(4), pg. 985-1003, 2003

He, M., Leung, H-F., and Jennings, N.R., A fuzzy logic based bidding strategy for autonomous agents in continuous double auctions, IEEE Transactions on Knowledge and Data Engineering, Vol: 15(6), 2003

Hurwicz, L., The Design of Mechanisms for Resource Allocation, the American Economic Review, Vol. 63 (2), Papers and Proceedings of the Eighty-fifth Annual Meeting of the American Economic Association, 1973

Irvine, J., Adam Smith Goes Mobile: Managing Serviced Beyond 3G with the Digital Marketplace, Invited Paper to European Wireless 2002, Florence, Italy, February 2002

Jackson, M.O., Mechanism Theory, In The Encyclopedia of Life Support Systems. EOLSS Publishers, 2000

Jenman, N., Don't sign anything, Auctions-Trickery and Deception on a Massive Scale, Simon & Schuster, Australia, 2002

Kagel, J.H., Auctions: A survey of experimental research, In Kagel, J.H., Roth, A.E., (eds.), The handbook of experimental economics (pp.501-586), New Jersey: Princeton University Press

Kagel, J.H., A. E. Roth, Handbook of Experimental Economics, Princeton University Press, New Jersey, 1995

Kelly, F., and Steinberg, R., A combinatorial auction with multiple winners for universal science, Management Science, Vol: 46(4), 2000

Kim, J.B. and A. Segev, A Web Services-enabled marketplace architecture for negotiation process management, Decision Support Systems, Volume 40, Issue 1, July 2005, Pages 71-87

Klemperer, P., Auction Theory: A Guide to the Literature, Journal of Economic Surveys, Vol 13(3), July 1999

Kraus, S., Negotiation and cooperation in multi-agent environments, Special issue on economic principles of multi-agent systems in Artificial Intelligence, Vol (94):1-2, pgs. 79-97, 1997

Krulwich, B., The BargainFinder agent: Comparison price shopping on the Internet, In. Williams, J., ed., Bots and Other Internet Beasties. SAMS.NET, 1996

Kurbel, K. and Loutchko, L., Towards Multi-Agent Electronic Marketplaces: What is There and What is Missing?, The Knowledge Engineering Review, Vol 18(1), pg. 33-46, 2003

J-J Laffont, and Tirole, J., A Theory of Incentives in Procurement and Regulation, Cambridge:MA, The MIT Press

Linhart, P.B., Radner, R. and Satterthwaite, M.A., (eds.), Bargaining with Incomplete Information, San. Diego, Academic Press, 1992

Luck, M., McBurney, P. and Priest,C., A Manifesto for Agent Technology: Towards Next Generation Computing, Autonomous Agents and Multi-Agent Systems, Vol. 9(3), pg. 203-252, 2004

McAfee, R.P and McMillian, J., Auctions and Bidding, Journal of Economic Literature, Vol. 25 (2), 1987

Milgrom, P.R. and Weber, R.J., A Theory of Auctions and Competitive Bidding, Econometrica, 50, pgs.1089-1122

Di Napoli, C., Sierra, Giordano, M., Norlega, P. and Furnari, M.M., A PVM implementation of the Fishmarket Multiagent System, in Proc. Collaboration in Intelligent Systems Technologies, Mexico,1996

Nash, J.F., The Bargaining Problem, Econometrica 18 (1950), pgs. 155-162

von Neumann, J. and Morgenstern, O., The Theory of Games and Economic Behavior, Princeton University Press, 1994

Osborne, J-J. and Rubinstein, A., A Course in Game Theory, The MIT Press, London, 1994

Park, S., Durfee, E and Birmingham, W., An Adaptive agent bidding strategy based on stochastic modelling, in Proc. of the third international conference on Autonomous Agents, the Netherlands, 1999

Pepys, S., Diary, September 3rd 1662, Retrieved from: http://www.pepys.info/1662/1662sep.html, The High Cost of Collusion, Editorial, New York Times, 12/8/01, p. A22.

Petric, A., Podobnik, V., Grguric A. and Zemljic, M., Designing an effective e-market: an overview of the CAT agent. Proceedings of the International Trading Agent Design and Analysis Workshop (TADA 2008). Chicago, IL, USA, July 2008

Pruitt, D., Negotiation Behaviour, Academic Press, 1981

Raiffa, H., The art and science of negotiation, Harvard University Press, Cambridge, MA

Rawlinson, G. and Translater, G., The History of Herodotus, Retrieved from, http://classics.mit.edu

Rothkopf, M.H. and Harstad, R.M., Modelling competitive bidding: A critical essay, Management Science Vol 40(3), pgs. 364-384

Rubinstein, A., Perfect Equilibrium in a bargaining model, Econometrica 50 (1), pgs. 97-109, 1982

Shaw, A., Electronic commerce: state of art. In Shaw M, Blanning R, Strader T, Whinston A (eds). Handbook on electronic commerce. Springer, Berlin

Smith, A., ed., Campbell, R.H., ed., Skinner, A.S., Wealth of Nations, An inquiry into the nature and causes of the wealth of nations, Clarendon Press, Oxford, 1976

De Smet, Y., Butterfly auctions: clustering the bidding space, In Proc. of 6th International Conference on Electronic Commerce Research, Dallas, USA, 2003

Smeltzer, L.R. and Carr, A.S., Electronic reverse auctions: Promises, risks and conditions for success, Industrial Marketing Management, Vol: 32(6), 2003

Tesauro, G. and Bredin, J., Strategic sequential bidding in auctions using dynamic programming, in Proc. in the first international joint conference on Autonomous Agents and Multi-Agent Systems, Italy, 2002

Thiel, S.E., Multidimensional auctions, Economic Letters, vol. 28, pg. 37-40, 1988

Tsvetovatyy, M., Gini, M., Mobasher, B. and Wieckowski, Z., MAGMA: An Agent-Based Virtual Market for Electronic Commerce, Journal of Applied Artificial Intelligence Vol. 11 (6), pg. 501 - 523, September 1997

Varian, H.R., Economic Mechanism Design for Computerized Agents, in Proc. of the First Usenix Conference on Electronic Commerce, New York, July 1995

Vickrey, W., Counterspeculation, Auctions, and Competitive Sealed Tenders, Journal of Finance, 16(1), pp. 44-61, March 1961

Woolridge, M. and Jennings, N.R., Intelligent Agents: Theory and Practice, Knowledge Engineering Review, 10(2) pg. 115-152, 1995

Wurman, P.R., Dynamic Pricing in the virtual marketplace, IEEE Internet Computing, Vol: 5(2) pgs. 36-42, 2001

Wurman, P., Walsh, W. And Wellman, M., Flexible double auctions for electronic commerce: Theory and implementation, Decision Support Systems, Vol 24(1), pgs 17-27, 1998

Wurman, P.R., Wellman, M. and Walsh, W., The Michigan Internet Actionbot: a configurable auction server for human and server agents, in Proc of the 2nd International conference on Autonomous Agents, pgs. 301-308, Minnepolis, USA, 1998

20

Distributed Optimisation using the Mobile Agent Paradigm through an Adaptable Ontology: Multi-operator Services Research and Composition

Hayfa Zgaya and Slim Hammadi
LAGIS UMR 8146 – Ecole Centrale De Lille
France

1. Introduction

Giving transport customers relevant, interactive and instantaneous information during their travels, represents a real challenge according to the exponential growth of services available on large distributed networks. Unfortunately, distributed applications through wide networks are not easy to realize because of the limited aspect of bandwidth that remains restricted and also because of a high incidence of network errors (bottleneck, failure, crash…). Our goal is to properly access and share distributed data located in an Extended Transport Multimodal Network (ETMN). In this context, mobile technology (Pharm & Karmouch, 1998; Theilmann & Rothermel, 1999) can complement artificial intelligence because it can reduce considerably network traffic (Carzaniga et al., 1997). Giving the mobility character to a software agent will allow him to migrate towards any node on the network that can receive mobile entities. Nodes to be visited by a Mobile Agent (MA) correspond to his route called Workplan. Many researchers have long discussed the benefits of the MA paradigm and conclude that it might be efficient in some cases (Picco & Baldi, 1997; Buse et al., 2003). In a recent work (Zgaya & Hammadi, 2006b), we demonstrated that using the MA paradigm in a Transport Multimodal Information System (TMIS) to collect needed data, is widely beneficial than using classical paradigms such as the Client Server (CS) one, if we use an optimization approach. The verification was successful thanks to a two-level optimization approach (Zgaya et al., 2005a, 2005b) that optimises, using metaheuristic, the total number of mobile entities and their different Workplans through the ETMN. However, some network errors (bottleneck, failure, crash…) can occur during the moving of MAs through the network nodes. In our work, we define a MA negotiation process in order to reassign non-attributed services, to available network nodes. Therefore we designed a flexible transport ontology that allows an easy handling of the terms and messages for negotiating. The remainder of this chapter is organized as follows: the problem complexity and the correspondent general formulation are presented in the next section. The global architecture of the Multi-Agent System (MAS) is proposed in section 3 and the optimisation approach in section 4. The proposed negotiation protocol is specified in section 5, followed by the used flexible transport ontology in section 6. Simulations are given in section 7 and finally the conclusion and prospects are addressed in last section.

2. Problem formulation

The main concern of a TMIS is to satisfy users, respecting the delays of the responses (due dates) and minimizing their costs; this is a two-step optimization problem: firstly the assignment of an effective set of MAs to all existent network nodes. This assignment builds initial Workplans of the MAs in order to explore, in an optimal manner, the ETMN entirely. The second step corresponds to the best assignment of a sub-set of the ETMN nodes to identified tasks, deducing final Workplans. The selected sub-set of nodes corresponds to the possible providers to the identified tasks. A single identified task corresponds to an independent recognized sub-request which belongs to one or several requests formulated simultaneously by one or different customers through different devices (laptop, PDA…). More precisely, a single task can correspond to a transport service (sub-route, well-known geographical zone…) or to a related service (cultural event, weather forecast…). After the decomposition process, information providers (distant nodes), which propose services to the correspondent identified tasks, are recognized (fig. 1). Finally, nodes must be assigned to tasks in order to satisfy all connected users. A user is satisfied if his request was answered

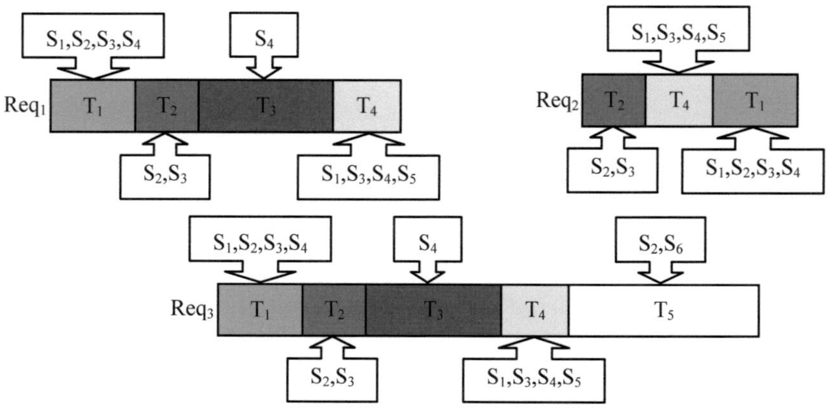

Fig. 1. Nodes identification

rapidly with a reasonable cost. This problem is called the Distributed Tasks Assignment Problem (DisTAP) and defined by:

- R requests, waiting for responses at the same instant *t*. The set of these requests is noted by R_t,
- The set of independent I tasks, representing all available services on the ETMN, is noted by $T=\{T_1,\ldots, T_I\}$,
- Each request $req_w \in R_t$ $(1 \le w \le R)$ is decomposed into a set of independent tasks, noted by $I_{t,w}=\{T_{r_1},\ldots,T_{r_{n_j}}\}$ $(1 \le n_j \le I$ and $I_{t,w} \subseteq T)$,
- The set of independent I′ tasks $(I' \le I)$, composing globally R_t, is noted by I'_t ($I'_t \subseteq T$ and $\bigcup_{w=1}^{R} I_{t,w} = I'_t$),
- Each request req_w has a due date d_w initially known, an ending date D_w and a total cost C_w,
- The realization of each task $T_i \in T$ requires a resource, or node, selected from a set of J registered nodes in the ETMN, noted by $S=\{S_1,\ldots, S_J\}$,
- The set of J′ nodes $(J' \le J)$, selected from S to perform I'_t, is noted by S′ $(S' \subseteq S)$,
- There is a predefined set of processing time; for a given node S_j and a given task T_i, the processing time of T_i using the resources of S_j, is defined and noted by $P_{i,j}$,

- There is a predefined set of information cost; for a given node S_j and a given task T_i, the cost of the information to collect from S_j, corresponding to the service referenced by T_i, is defined and noted by $Co_{i,j}$,
- The size of the collected data to ensure a service is defined; for a given node S_j and a given task T_i, the data size is defined and noted by $Q_{i,j}$,
- We have partial flexibility; the realisation of each task T_i requires a node selected from a set of nodes, which propose the same service performing the task T_i, with different cost, processing time and data size.

The three characteristics described above, namely ($P_{i,j}$;$Co_{i,j}$;$Q_{i,j}$), represent successively the first, second and last term of each element of what we call a service table (table 1).

	S_1	S_2	S_3	...	S_J
T_1	(0;0;0)	(0.2;5;3)	(0.4;3;3)		(0.2;5;3)
T_2	(0.2;4;5)	(0.1;5;2)	(0.4;5;1)		(0.3;8;3)
T_3	(0.1;0;3)	(0;0;0)	(0.2;0;3)		(0.4;2;2)
T_4	(0.3;2;1)	(0.3;1;1)	(0;0;0)		(0,0,0)
...					
T_I	(0.2;3;1)	(0.1;1;3)	(0.4;5;2)		(0.4;5;3)

Table 1. Example of a service table

We notice that if a provider does not offer a response to a task (partial flexibility); the correspondent term in the table above is (0,0,0). Otherwise we have $P_{i,j}\neq0$, $Co_{i,j}\neq0$ and $Q_{i,j}\neq0$. It is also possible to have $P_{i,j}\neq0$, $Q_{i,j}\neq0$ and $Co_{i,j}=0$ for a free information in the case of a promotional operation. In order to situate the complexity of our problem, an analogy was performed (table 2) between the problem described above (DisTAP) and the well-known Flexible Job Shop Problem (FJSP).

FJSP	DisTAP
N jobs	R requests
M machines	J servers
n_j non preemptable ordered operations /job_j	n_j non preemptable ordered tasks /$request_j$
The problem: to organize the execution of N jobs on M machines	The problem: to organize the execution of R requests on S servers
The execution of each operation i of a job j ($O_{i,j}$) requires one resource or machine selected from a set of available machines	The execution of each task i (T_i) of a request j (req_i) requires one resource or server selected from a set of available servers (similarities of requests)
The assignment of the operation $O_{i,j}$ to the machine M_k entails the occupation of this machine during a processing time called $d_{i,j,k}$	The assignment of the task T_i to the server S_k entails the occupation of this server during a processing time called $P_{i,k}$
At a given time, a machine can only execute one operation: it becomes available to other operations one the operation that is currently assigned to is completed (resource constraints).	At a given time, a server can only execute one task: it becomes available to other tasks one the task that is currently assigned to is completed (resource constraints).

Table 2. Analogy between FJSP and our problem

In DisTAP, we manage the similarities of requests in order to avoid the same data research. Besides, we have to assign the servers to tasks as well as to assign MAs to remote nodes (servers), taking into account the network state. Therefore our problem presents more difficulty than the FJSP which has been shown to be NP-hard. In addition, the distributed character of our system and the requirement to cooperate different autonomous static and mobile entities, confirm the choice of a multi-agent architecture for our system.

3. The multi-agent system

To resolve the problem described previously, we propose a system based on the coordination of five kinds of software agents (fig. 2):

- Interface Agent (IA): this agent interacts with the user of the system allowing him to choose an appropriate form of response to his demand, so this agent manages the request and then displays the correspondent result. Therefore, when a user accesses to the TMIS, an agent IA deals with the formulation of his request and then sends it to an available identifier agent. This one relates to the same platform to which several users can be simultaneously connected, thus he can receive several requests formulated at the same time,
- Identifier agent (IdA): this agent manages the decomposition of the requests that were formulated through a same short period of time ε* (ε-simultaneous requests). The decomposition process generates a set of sub-requests corresponding, for example, to sub-routes or to well-known geographical zones. Sub-requests are elementary independent tasks to be performed by the available set of distributed nodes (information providers) through the ETMN. Initially, each node must login to the system registering all proposed services knowing that a service corresponds to the response to a defined task with fixed cost, processing time and data size. Therefore, an agent IdA decomposes the set of existing simultaneous requests into a set of independent tasks, recognizing possible similarities in order to avoid a redundant search. The decomposition process occurs during the identification of the information providers. Finally, the agent IdA transmits cyclically all generated data to available scheduler agents. These ones must optimize the selection of providers, taking into account some system constraints,
- Scheduler Agent (SA): several nodes may propose the same service with different cost, processing time and data size. The agent SA has to assign nodes to tasks, minimizing total cost and total processing time to respect due dates (data constraint). Selected set of nodes corresponds to the sequence of nodes which build the Workplans (routes) of the collector agents. An agent SA has firstly to optimize the number of collector agents before assigning nodes to tasks.
- Intelligent Collector agent (ICA): an agent ICA is a mobile software agent who can move intelligently from a node to another through a network in order to collect needed data and finally returns to his home node, noted by H. This special kind of agent is composed of data, code and a state and has an intelligent behaviour. Collected data should not exceed a capacity threshold in order to avoid the overloading, so the agent SA has to take into account this aspect when assigning nodes to tasks. When they come back to the system, the agents ICA must transmit collected data to the available fusion agents,
- Fusion Agent (FA): the agents FA have to fusion correctly collected data in order to compose responses to the simultaneous requests. The fusion procedure needs information on behalf of IdA and SA agents and progresses according to the collected data availability. Each new answer component must be complementary to the already merged ones.

---

* Fixed by the programmer

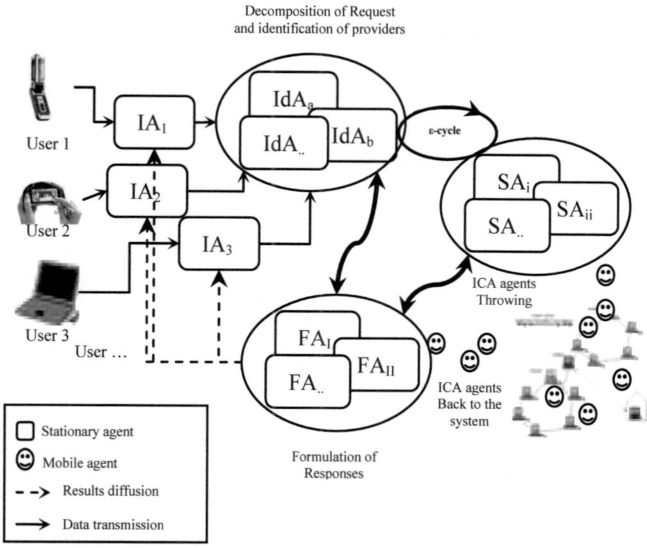

Fig. 2. System architecture

The needed data, required to satisfy the demands of the customers, are distributed through the ETMN and their collect corresponds to the jobs of ICA agents. Consequently, the SA agents have to optimize the assignments of the nodes to the identified tasks, minimizing total cost and response time. To this problem, we propose a two-level optimization solution (Zgaya et al., 2005a, 2005b) corresponding to the complex behaviour of the SA agents.

4. Scheduler Agent behaviour

The SA agent has two different basic behaviours: firstly the generation of an effective number of ICA agents in order to explore the ETMN entirely. This behaviour starts each time the network state varies considerably, in order to prepare the initial Workplans of ICA agents. Thus, we assume the existence of a network module that provides information to the system about the latest variations. The second behaviour is an ε-cyclic one, supervising the reception of the required services and their possible information providers, identified by the agents IdA. This second behaviour optimizes the assignments of nodes to the tasks in order to deduce the final Workplans of ICA agents from initial ones. The SA agents have to interact in order to share information and negotiate the different part of assignment for a global optimisation. For this problem, we just underline that we propose a solution using the formation of coalitions approach but this is not the topic of this chapter. For example, in the case of possible overlapping of the simultaneous requests, concerning SA agents have to gather, forming coalitions, in order to share the assignments about the different identified similarities. Hence, we focus here on the individual behaviour of a SA agent apart from his interaction with the other agents. We describe the two individual behaviours mentioned above in what follows.

4.1 Generation of the initial workplans

The Cost-Effective Mobile Agent Planning (CE-MAP) Algorithms, suggested by (Baek et al., 2001), are the most appropriate to our problematic. In fact, a proposed dynamic algorithm, called BYKY2, optimizes the number of MAs minimizing the total execution time, taking into account the network state. In a previous work (Zgaya, 2005a), we adopted the same approach but we considered the transported data and then the state variation of mobile entities. The MA Workplan problem is described in what follows, assuming some hypothesis:

- Collecting data on a visited node requires a processing time. We suppose that the size of the data to collect from a network node is equal to the average of the total data size on this node,
- Initially, we assume that an ICA agent is not totally empty because it contains an initial quantity of data Q_0,
- We suppose that minimal latency between each pair of nodes in the network is available tanks to an existent network monitoring module,
- Information can have a multimedia aspect, so we assume that the transmission of a quantity of data from a node to another depends on current latency.

4.1.1 Description

The MA Workplan problem can be described as follows: ICA agents are created and initially launched from an originally node (Home node). The other network nodes represent available information providers where an ICA agent can move to collect data corresponding to the claimed services. These ones are expressed in term of independent tasks. A same service can be proposed by different nodes with different cost, processing time and with different formats. We call a response time to a service on a node, the processing time of the correspondent task to this service on this node. So the response time on the Home node is null. Latencies are known and may affect navigation time of ICA agents. Our goal is to minimize the number of ICA agents and their navigation time in order to explore all the ETMN, taking into account network state. Initially, we introduce some definitions using variables described in table 3.

Variable	Description
m	Number of ICA agents
$ICA_1,\ldots,ICA_m$	Identifiers of ICA agents
H	Home node
$Wk_{i,p}$	Nodes sequence representing the Workplan of an ICA_i agent: $(S_{i_1},\ldots,S_{i_p})$ with $1 \le p \le J$
$T(Wk_{i,p})$	Routing time for $Wk_{i,p}$
$Qte_{k,u}$	The size of the transported data by the agent ICA_k until the node S_u included
$Tr(Qte_{k,u},S_u,S_v)$	Transmission time for $Qte_{k,u}$ from node S_u to node S_v
CT_j	Processing time on node S_j for the data quantity Qt_j
Qt_j	Data quantity on node S_j
$d(S_i,S_j)$	Data transfer rate between nodes S_i and S_j

Table 3. Notations

Definition 1: CT_j (Processing time on node S_j) corresponds to needed computing time on the node S_j to extract the data quantity Qt_j.

Definition 2: Qt_j (Data quantity on node S_j) it is the average data size to extract from S_j.

T_i represents a task corresponding to a service proposed by S_j. Therefore:

$$Qt_j = \frac{\sum_{i=1}^{I} a_{i,j} Q_{i,j}}{\sum_{i=1}^{I} a_{i,j}} \quad (1)$$

$$CT_j = \frac{\sum_{i=1}^{I} a_{i,j} P_{i,j}}{\sum_{i=1}^{I} a_{i,j}} \qquad (2)$$

Where $a_{i,j}$ is a Boolean value as follows: $a_{i,j}=1$ if the node S_j proposes a service for the task T_i and $a_{i,j}=0$ otherwise (according to the given service table). Moreover, we remind that $P_{i,j}$ corresponds to the processing time of a given task T_i on the node S_j (section 2).

Definition 3: $Qte_{k,u}$ (Data quantity transported until S_u by ICA_k) corresponds to the size of the collected data by the agent ICA_k during his route, until the node S_u included.

$Qte_{k,u}$ is calculated by:

$$Qte_{k,u} = Q_0 + \sum_{r=1}^{u} Qt_{k_r} \qquad (3)$$

We remind that Q_0 corresponds o the initial quantity of data within an ICA agent (parag.4.1).

Definition 4: $Tr(Qte_{k,u},S_u,S_v)$ (Transmission time) needed time for the agent ICA_k to migrate from S_u to S_v transporting the data quantity $Qte_{k,u}$.

$Tr(Qte_{k,u},S_u,S_v)$ is computed like this:

$$Tr(Qte_{k,u}, S_u, S_v) = \frac{Qte_{k,u}}{d(S_u, S_v)} \qquad (4)$$

Definition 5: $T(Wk_{k,p})$ (Routing time for $Wk_{k,p}$) needed time for the agent ICA_k to visit the sequence of network nodes $(S_{k_1},...,S_{k_p})$ with $1 \le p \le J$.

$T(Wk_{k,p})$ is computed like this:

$$T(Wk_{k,p}) = T_{go}(k, p=1) + T_{travel}(k,p) + T_{return}(k,p) \qquad (5)$$

	$Wk_{k,p}$	T_{go}	T_{return}	T_{travel}
p=1	(S_{k_1})	$Tr(Q_0,H,S_{k_1})$	$Tr(Qte_{k,p},S_{k_p},H)$	CT_{k_1}
$1<p\le J$	$(S_{k_1},..., S_{k_p})$			$X_{k,p}$

Table 4. Routing Time

With:

$$X_{k,p} = \sum_{i=1}^{p} CT_{k_i} + \sum_{i=1}^{p-1} Tr(Qte_{k,i}, S_{k_i}, S_{k_{i+1}}) \qquad (6)$$

4.1.2 Proposed workplan schemes

To propose a cost-effective Workplan MA scheme, we assume that a monitoring module exists in the system providing information about the network status (latency, bandwidth, traffic, bottleneck, failure…). Therefore, we can get data transfer rate values among all pairs of nodes through the ETMN. The goal is to find an effective set of ICA agents minimizing their navigation time, in order to explore all the ETMN nodes, taking into account network state. It is clear that sending an ICA agent to each node gives us the best total computing time because, in this case, agents are launched simultaneously into each network node. Therefore, we keep this best total computation time to build nodes partitions, minimizing the number of ICA agents. Consequently, we just care about the data size and the processing time in the service table (section 2), ignoring the data cost. As described previously, $d(S_i,S_j)$ namely data transfer rate among two network nodes S_i and S_j, is available. We give here a brief description of the algorithm detailed in (Zgaya et al., 2005a):

The initial Workplan algorithm description
- *Step 1*: Sort the nodes in decreasing order according to their correspondent routing time $T(Wk_i{=}S_i)$ $\forall 1 \leq i \leq J$. Set the threshold δ which is the routing time of the first node in the sorted list: $$\delta = \max_{1 \leq i \leq J}(T(Wk_i = S_i)) \qquad (7)$$
- *Step 2*: Partition the given network into several parts by gathering nodes so that the routing time of each part does not exceed the threshold δ.

This proposed dynamic algorithm tries to find the next node to visit from the current position where the agent resides. In other words, this algorithm looks for the next node for a part calculating, each time, the new routing time. A node is selected if the new routing time does not exceed the threshold δ. Otherwise, a Workplan is ready to be assigned to an ICA agent and the algorithm ends if each available node belongs to a Workplan. The algorithm distributes all available nodes to a set of m ICA agents in order to explore the network entirely. Each built route corresponds to the initial Workplan of the correspondent ICA agent. Then, final Workplans will be deduced from initial ones thanks to our evolutionary approach described in next section. This will be done by selecting a subset S′ from S (the total number of available nodes in the ETMN) in order to optimise the management of the data flow through the network. Thus, some nodes will not be selected from S what can decrease the total number m of ICA agents. This will be happen when all the nodes composing the initial Workplan of an agent ICA are not selected. Let m' be the new number of ICA agents. We have also $J'=|S'|$ the new number of nodes so $m' \leq m$, $J' \leq J$ and $S' \subseteq S$. Thanks to the generated final Workplans, required data will be collected in an effective manner, in order to reach as soon as possible and with reasonable costs, the best schedule of the simultaneous requests.

4.2 Composition of services using an evolutionary approach

The Evolutionary Algorithms (EA), inspired from genetic algorithms, added a new aspect to the field of artificial intelligence. These algorithms use various computational models of evolutionary processes to solve problems on a computer. EA are stochastic search methods that mimic the metaphor of natural biological evolution; they operate on a population of potential solutions applying the survival principle of the fittest results, in order to produce successively better approximations to a solution. At each generation, a new set of approximations is created by the process of selecting individuals according to their level of fitness in the population, then breeding them together using genetic operators such as crossover and mutation. Compared to traditional optimization methods such as gradient descent, EA are robust and global search technique. For this reason, the scheduling community has been quick to realize the potential of EA. In this section, we use an evolutionary approach to resolve our assignment problem. Therefore, we use some aspects that must be clarified:

- A specific genetic representation (or encoding) appropriate to the problem, to determine feasible solutions of the scheduling optimization problem,
- Original genetic operators that alter the composition of children during the reproduction. As it was mentioned previously, a task (sub-request) must be managed by only one provider selected from the set of nodes that propose the correspondent service. Therefore, we choose to correct generated solutions in order to respect this constraint. Consequently, each crossover or mutation operation must be followed by a correction process,
- Parents are selected randomly from current population to crossover/mutation with some probability p_c/p_m $(0 < p_c, p_m < 1)$. We believe that this technique gives more chance to weak individuals to survey,
- A non-elitist replacement technique is adopted to generate the new population from the previous one,
- The evaluation functions estimate a possible solution according to two criteria: the cost and the delay.

4.2.1 The representation of an evolutionary solution

The research and the composition of distributed transport services are generated thanks to an evolutionary algorithm, managed by the active SA agents in the system. We notice that the selection of an appropriate representational scheme of a solution is fundamental to the success of EA applications. Therefore, in a previous work (Zgaya et al., 2005b), we designed an efficient coding (possible solution) for the chromosome respecting our problem constraints. Thus, we propose a flexible representation of the chromosome called Flexible Tasks Assignment Representation (FeTAR). The chromosome is represented by a matrix CH(I'×J') where rows represent independent tasks (the services), composing globally simultaneous requests and columns represent identified nodes (the providers). Each element of the matrix specifies the assignment of a node S_{c_j} (1≤j≤J') to the task T_{c_i} (1≤i≤I') as follows:

Value of CH[i,j]	Condition
1	S_{c_j} is assigned to T_{c_i}
*	S_{c_j} may be assigned to T_{c_i}
X	S_{c_j} cannot be assigned to T_{c_i}

We notice that each task must be performed by a single node, selected from the available set of nodes that propose the service corresponding to a response to the concerned task. Indeed, the assignment and the scheduling of all distributed nodes to the required services, represent the optimisation of the services composition that provide transport customers effective responses to their requests.

4.2.2 The genetic operators

(a) The crossover algorithm

Crossover involves combining elements from two parent chromosomes into one or more child chromosomes. The role of the crossover is to generate a better solution by exchanging information contained in the current good one. The following algorithm specifies the crossover operator:

CrossFeTAR Algorithm

The creation of C_1 (resp. C_2) representing the child 1 (resp. child 2) is given by:
- ***Step 1***: Choose randomly two parents and one node; suppose that P_1, P_2 and S_{c_j} ($1 \le j \le J'$) are randomly selected,
- ***Step 2***: Tasks assignment of S_{c_j} in C_1 (resp. C_2) must correspond to the same assignment of S_{c_j} in P_1 (resp. P_2),
- ***Step3***:
k :=1 ;
while (k ≤ J') and (k ≠ j) {
Tasks assignment of S_{c_k} in C_1 (resp. C_2) corresponds to the same assignment of S_{c_k} in P_2 (resp. P_1);
k := k + 1 ;
}
- ***Step 4***: if (C_1 (resp. C_2) is not a feasible solution)
Correct randomly C_1 (resp. C_2);

We notice that sometimes, a generated solution resulting from a crossover process is not feasible. If it is the case, we propose a correction process that changes, in a random way, a non-feasible solution to a feasible one knowing that a feasible solution is a FeTAR instance that assigns each task composing it, only once. The algorithm ***CorrectFeTAR*** illustrates this correction process as follows:

CorrectFeTAR Algorithm

```
The correction of the FeTAR instance CH is given by:
for (i:=1; i ≤I'; i:=i+1){
    initialize to zero the vectors IndexAssigned[] and IndexNotAssigned[] of dimensions J';
    k1:=0; k2:=0;
    for (j:=1; j ≤J'; j:=j+1){
      if( CH[c_i,c_j]=1) {
        k1:=k1+1;
        IndexAssigned[k1]:=j;
      }else if( CH[c_i,c_j]=*) {
        k2:=k2+1;
        IndexNotAssigned[k2]:=j;
      }
    }
    if(k1=0) {
      Draw randomly an index p with 1≤p≤k2 ; s:=IndexNotAssigned[p];
      CH[c_i,c_s]:=1;
    }else if(k1>1) {
          Draw randomly an index p with 1≤p≤k1 ; s:=IndexAssigned[p];
          for (x:=1; x ≤J'; x:=x+1){
          if( CH[c_i,c_x]=1 et x≠s)
             CH[c_i,c_x]:=*;
        }
}
```

For example, we suppose that a Crossover process generated, from two FeTAR instances parents P_1 and P_2, two new FeTAR instances childs C_1 and C_2 like so:

P_1	S_{12}	S_6	S_3	S_{24}
T_1	X	*	*	1
T_5	*	*	1	*
T_3	1	X	*	*
T_9	*	*	1	X
T_2	*	*	1	*

P_2	S_{12}	S_6	S_3	S_{24}
T_1	X	*	1	*
T_5	*	*	1	*
T_3	*	X	*	1
T_9	*	*	1	X
T_2	*	*	1	*

C_1	S_{12}	S_6	S_3	S_{24}
T_1	X	*	*	*
T_5	*	*	1	*
T_3	*	X	*	1
T_9	*	*	1	X
T_2	*	*	1	*

C_2	S_{12}	S_6	S_3	S_{24}
T_1	X	*	1	1
T_5	*	*	1	*
T_3	1	X	*	*
T_9	*	*	1	X
T_2	*	*	1	*

Both C_1 and C_2 are not feasible solutions because C_1 does not assign the task T_1 and C_2 assigns the task T_1 more than one time (T_1 is assigned twice by S_3 and S_{24}). After correction, C_1 will be randomly C_{1x}, C_{1y} or C_{1z} and C_2 will be randomly C_{2x} or C_{2y} like so:

C_{1x}	S_{12}	S_6	S_3	S_{24}
T_1	*X*	*1*	*	*
T_5	*	*	*1*	*
T_3	*	*X*	*	*1*
T_9	*	*	*1*	*X*
T_2	*	*	*1*	*

C_{1y}	S_{12}	S_6	S_3	S_{24}
T_1	*X*	*	*	*1*
T_5	*	*	*1*	*
T_3	*	*X*	*	*1*
T_9	*	*	*1*	*X*
T_2	*	*	*1*	*

C_{1z}	S_{12}	S_6	S_3	S_{24}
T_1	*X*	*	*1*	*
T_5	*	*	*1*	*
T_3	*	*X*	*	*1*
T_9	*	*	*1*	*X*
T_2	*	*	*1*	*

C_{2x}	S_{12}	S_6	S_3	S_{24}
T_1	*X*	*	*	*1*
T_5	*	*	*1*	*
T_3	*1*	*X*	*	*
T_9	*	*	*1*	*X*
T_2	*	*	*1*	*

C_{2y}	S_{12}	S_6	S_3	S_{24}
T_1	*X*	*	*1*	*
T_5	*	*	*1*	*
T_3	*1*	*X*	*	*
T_9	*	*	*1*	*X*
T_2	*	*	*1*	*

(b) **The mutation algorithm**

Mutation represents another important genetic operator. Although mutation is important, it is secondary to crossover. It introduces some extra variability into the population and typically works with a single chromosome to create a new modified one. The mutation algorithm is presented as follows:

MuteFeTAR Algorithm
- ***Step 1***: Choose randomly one chromosome CH, one task T_{c_i} (1≤i≤I') and one node S_{c_j} (1≤j≤J');,
- ***Step 2***:
if(CH[i,j]= *){
Find j_1 with 1≤j_1≤J' and CH[i,j_1]=1 ;
CH[i,j_1] := * ;
CH[i,j] := 1 ;
} else
if(CH[i,j] = 1 and ∃ j_1 / 1 ≤ j_1 ≤ J' and CH[i,j_1]=*){
CH[i,j_1] := 1 ;
CH[i,j] := * ;
}

For example, if the chromosome C_{1x} undergoes a mutation process, muted C_{1x} may be C'_{1x} like so:

C'_{1x}	S_{12}	S_6	S_3	S_{24}
T_1	X	1	*	*
T_5	*	*	1	*
T_3	*	X	*	1
T_9	*	*	1	X
T_2	1	*	*	*

With the mutation point (T_2,S_3).

4.2.3 Evaluation functions

At each iteration, individuals (chromosomes) in the current population are evaluated according to the same measure of fitness. There are a number of characteristics of the evaluation function that enhance or hinder the evaluation of a program performance. In our case, the fitness function intends to maximize the number of satisfied transport travellers, minimizing response delay and total cost. In other words, a chromosome is firstly evaluated according to the number of responses respecting due dates, then according to the average of total costs. Thus, a chromosome has to express ending responses date and the information cost (Zgaya et al., 2005b). The first evaluation function, called Fitness_1, computes the ending dates of all the requests according to the generated FeTAR solution, in order to deduce the number of satisfied users in term of response time. Then the second evaluation function, called Fitness_2, computes the total cost of each request. As we previously mentioned, a request req_w (1≤w≤R) is decomposed into $I_{t,w}$ tasks and the algorithm Fitness_1 computes the total processing time D_w for each req_w. This time does not include only the effective processing time on the nodes because we have to take into account the routing time of ICA agents. For that, we assume that, the ending date D_w (EndReq[w]) corresponding to the total execution time of a request req_w, includes also some value noted by γ which is the average navigation time of ICA agents (Zgaya et al.,2008). Besides, the total cost C_w (EndReq[w]) is computed for each request req_w by the algorithm Fitness_2.

***Fitness_1* Algorithm**

- ***Step 1***: Initialisation (1≤k≤m)
  - Initialize to Ø each set of tasks U_k which should be performed by each ICA_k
  - Initialize to γ the total time EndU[k] to perform each set of tasks U_k.
- ***Step 2***: Compute the set of tasks U_k performed by each ICA_k and the total time to perform them as follows:

```
for (i:=1; i ≤ I'; i:=i+1) {
    Find k and j while ICA_k performs T_{c_i} on S_{c_j};
    U_k = U_k ∪ {T_{c_i}};
    EndU[k] := EndU[k] + P_{c_i,c_j} ;
}
```

- ***Step 3***: Compute ending time for each request i: EndReq[w] with 1≤w≤R, by looking for each task composing this request. An ending time of a request is the maximum necessary time for all the agents ICA responsible for all the tasks composing this request, in order to carry out their Workplan. Ending time for each request is computed as follows:

```
for (w:=1; w≤R; w:=w+1){
 Initialize to false TreatedICA[k] for each ICA_k (1≤k≤m);
    EndReq[w] = 0;
    for (j :=1; j ≤I'; j:=j+1){
      if (T_{c_j} ∈ req_w) {
        k:=1;
        while ((k ≤ m) and (T_{c_j} ∉ U_k)) k:=k+1;
              if (not TreatedICA[k]) {
                EndReq[w]:=max(EndReq[w], EndU[k]);
                TreatedICA[k] = true;
        }
      }
    }
}
```

***Fitness_2* Algorithm**

The total cost for a request is the total cost of all independent tasks composing this request. It is calculated as follows:

Step 1: Initialisation (1≤w≤R)

Initialize to 0 CostRe[w] for each req_w

Step 2:

```
   for (w:=1; w≤R; w:=w+1){
for each T_{c_i} ∈ I_{t,w} {
 Find j/ S_{c_j} assigns T_{c_i} in the FeTAR instance CH;
  CostRe[w]= CostRe[w] + Co_{c_i,c_j} ;
}
   }
```

The evaluation of a chromosome is illustrated by a vector, which express, for each request w (req_w), its required total time for the execution (D_w) and also its total cost (C_w). From the generated vector, we deduce the average total cost C_{av} and the maximum ending date D_{max} of all the requests managed by the chromosome.

4.2.4 Best solution

To determinate the best solutions, we adopted an elitist approach (Zgaya & Hammadi, 2008) using an external storage to memorise the most adapted individuals during the search. The evolutionary adopted approach is shown in fig. 3. During the evaluation process to crossover and mutation, best solutions are saved in external archives. Knowing that $d_{max} = \max(d_w)_{1 \le w \le R}$, we discern two archive sets:

- Main solutions archive (M) representing best solutions which respect all due dates. In other words, a chromosome CH∈M if and only if ∀w (1≤w≤R), $D_w \le d_{max}$. This archive set is decomposed into two sub-archives :
  - dominant solutions archive (d)
  - ε-dominant solutions archive (ε-d)

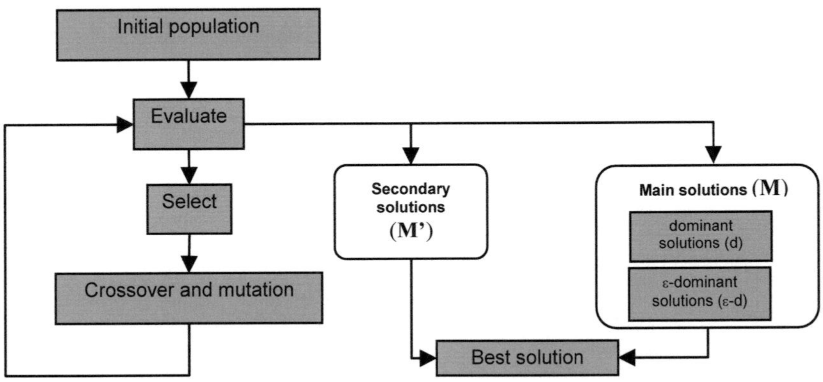

Fig. 3. Evolutionary approach

Secondary solutions archive (M′) representing best solutions which exceed at least one due date. In other words, a chromosome CH∈M′ if and only if ∃w (1≤w≤R) and $d_{max} < D_w$.

We discerned two archive sets according to delay criterion satisfaction because we assume that if a response exceeds its due date, the user is not satisfied. That's why we consider that the first criterion has more priority that the second one. Consequently archive sets are firstly sorted according to delay criterion, then according to cost criterion. We notice by f1 the response delay function evaluated by Fitness_1 algorithm and by f2 the cost function evaluated by Fitness_2 algorithm. Considering two different solutions CH and CH′, if CH∈M and CH′∈M′ then CH dominates CH′. Otherwise, CH dominates CH′ if and only if f1(CH)=f1(CH′) and f2(CH)<f2(CH′) . Each archive set has a maximum number size equals to the population size. If the number of individuals in an archive exceeds this fixed size, a crowding process must occur to decide which solutions must kept in the archive. The non-selected solutions are deleted; and the others contribute to the next selection procedure; archive members can then transmit their characteristics to offspring populations. M and M′ archive sets represent generated solutions having minimum f1 and f2 values, so if a chromosome CH of the offspring dominates any archive member CH′, the archive member

is deleted and the offspring is accepted. Fig. 4 represents the Pareto-optimal fronts with $\varepsilon_1=\varepsilon_2=\varepsilon=0.75$ (Zitzler & Thiele, 1998). We use a population size of N=100 with a crossover probability $p_c=0.8$ and mutation probability $p_m=0.2$.

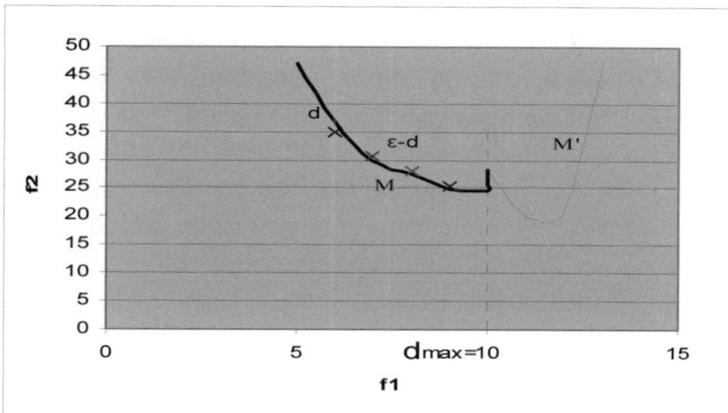

Fig. 4. Optimal fronts

4.2.5 Final workplans generation

According to the generated FeTAR instance CH, the equations (1) and (2) become:

$$Qt_{c_j} = \sum_{i=1}^{I'} (a_{c_i,c_j} \times Q_{c_i,c_j}) \tag{1'}$$

$$CT_{c_j} = \sum_{i=1}^{I'} (a_{c_i,c_j} \times P_{c_i,c_j}) \tag{2'}$$

With a_{c_i,c_j} a Boolean value as follows: if CH[c_i,c_j]=1 ($1 \le i \le I'$ and $1 \le j \le J'$) then $a_{c_i,c_j}=1$ else $a_{c_i,c_j}=0$. Routing time of the final Workplans are deduced using equations (1'), (2'), (3), (4), (5) and (6) according to table 4 (parag. 4.1.1).

Until this stage, the MA paradigm integrates a perfect structure without any incidence. But this is an improbable scenario because, in reality, errors may often occur (crash, bottleneck, failure…), especially in huge systems distributed through large networks. If it is the case, ICA agents have to interact with SA agents in order to negotiate the reassignments of potential cancelled services, keeping the whole robustness of the system. Consequently, we developed a negotiation protocol, described in next section.

5. The negotiation process

Some perturbations can occur through the network when ICA agents are following their correspondent final Workplans, according to the generated FeTAR instance. In this case, the ICA agents have to avoid unavailable nodes in their remained final Workplans. In addition, they have to change their itineraries in order to take into account the cancelled tasks that still need assignments because of the perturbation. Therefore, a new assignment process has to occur to find suitable new available providers. To do this, we have to benefit of active ICA agents who are still travelling through the network and to launch new ones otherwise. So ICA agents have to interact with SA agents in order to find suitable solution to the current situation. Thus, we propose a negotiation process inspired from the well-known contract net protocol (Smith, 1980) between ICA agents representing the participants of the negotiation and SA agents who are the initiators. In our proposed solution, we allow a partial agreement of the proposed contract (a FeTAR instance) from each ICA agent, to be confirmed partially or totally by the initiator of the negotiation (SA agent). A renegotiation process is necessary while there are still tasks that need reassignment. The purpose of this solution is to allow the ICA agents to cooperate and coordinate their actions in order to find globally near-optimal robust schedules according to their priorities, preferences and constraints, which depend on their current positions in their correspondent Workplans. Through the negotiation process tours, SA agents must assure reasonable total cost and time. In what follow, we describe in detail the proposed protocol. Firstly, we present a brief description of the initiators and participants of the negociation process.

5.1 Initiators and participants

An initiator of a negotiation is a SA agent who never knows the exact position of each travelling ICA agent. However, he knows all initial Workplans schemes and the final assignments of the servers (final effective Workplans). SA agent does not need to wait for all answers to take a decision, since he can accept a subset of responses to take pressing sub-decisions; urgent actions must be taken according to the current positions of ICA agents. Consequently, SA agent can take decisions every short period of time. In that case, he must update the set of services that need to be reassigned by providers through the confirmation step. After that, SA agent has to propose a new contract according to the updated services set and to the different capabilities of the participants of the negotiation. We suppose that errors on the network are identified before that an ICA agent leaves one functioning node toward a crashed one. A participant of a negotiation is an autonomous ICA agent who never knows anything about the other participants of the same negotiation process. Obviously, he knows his own initial Workplan scheme and his final assignments of servers (final effective Workplan). In addition, each ICA agent has his own priorities, preferences and constraints that are dynamic, depending on the network state and on his current position in the already defined final Workplan. Constraints of an ICA agent express tasks that he can't perform or servers he can't visit because they might cause problems (overloading, time consuming, high latency…). Priorities express servers where the ICA agent prefers visit because they are already programmed in his remained final Workplan. Finally, preferences express servers that are already programmed in the remained initial Workplan and not in the final one. Each time an ICA agent receives a new contract, he analyzes it to make a decision (refusal or total/partial acceptance).

5.2 The protocol

A protocol defines the language used by agents to exchange information. The proposed negotiation protocol (fig. 5) is characterized by successive messages exchanges between initiators corresponding to the agents who initiate a negotiation (SA agents) and participants of the negotiation (ICA agents). We designed our protocol so that a negotiation process can occur between several initiators and participants; it can be, for example, the case of simultaneous requests overlapping. Presently, we describe a negotiation protocol between a unique initiator and several participants. Negotiation always begins with the creation of a contract by the initiator agent, proposing it to active participants. The first contract corresponds to final Workplans that were already optimized thanks to our two-level optimization approach (Zgaya et al. 2005a, 2005b). A renegotiation means a round of modification request for a contract that "a part" has not been accepted the round before. In what follows, we show the adopted form for a communication before detailing the different exchanged messages between initiators and participants.

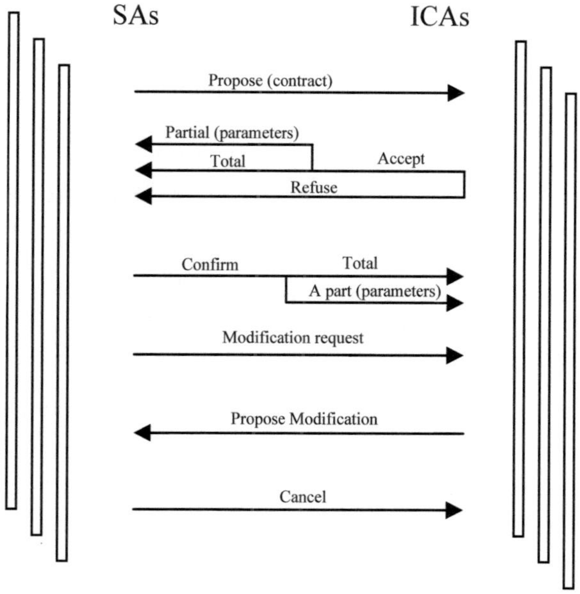

Fig. 5. The protocol

5.2.1 The agent message

We adopt the following structure for an agent message exchange:

<sender, receivers, service, perform, content, content-lang, ontology, f>

With:

- sender: the sender of the message,
- receiver: the list of receivers, they represent the recipients of the message,
- service: the "yellow-pages" service proposed by the receiver of the message,
- perform: the performative, which expresses the communicative intention,
- content: the information included in the message,
- content-lang: the content language, which represents the used syntax to express the content,
- the ontology: the vocabulary of the symbols used in the content and their meaning, used ontologies will be expressed in next section,
- f = <f1, f2, f3, f4, f5> represents some fields used to control several concurrent conversations and also to specify timeouts for receiving a reply. For the present, we don't assign this field but we just explain it for a best comprehension of message exchanges:
  - f1: reply-to *A*: the recipient of the message reply is the agent A,

- f2: conversation-id *ide*: a conversation identifier which may be fixed by the sender of the message in order to identify the ongoing sequence of communicative acts, that together form a conversation,
- f3: reply-with *exp*: identifies the reply to the current message with the expression exp,
- f4: in-reply-to *exp*: to denote that this message is a reply to an earlier action of which the reply was denoted by exp (f3) ,
- f5: reply-by *d*: time and/or date expression which indicates the latest time by which the sending agent would like to receive a reply.

5.2.2 Proposition of the contract

The contract message is a proposition of a new organization (the first contract) or reorganization of final Workplans to achieve tasks. If the execution of some services was cancelled because of some network perturbations, it is indeed the case of reorganization. This will be done by reassigning, ones more, servers to these tasks tht represent the set of the Dynamic Reassigned Tasks (DRT). The initiator sends an individual contract to each active ICA_k agent who proposes the contract-reception service. The correspondent message is:

<SA_i, ICA_k, contract-reception, propose, ∂, fipa-sl, MASOntology, f>

With:

- $\partial = \partial 1$ if it acts of the first contract and $\partial = \partial 2$ otherwise,
- $\partial 1 \equiv$ Workplan (Owner : ICA_k ; Initial : $i_1,...,i_{k_i}$ Final : $f_1,...,f_{k_f}$),
- $\partial 2 \equiv$ FinalWk (Owner : ICA_k ; Final : $f_1,...,f_{k_f}$),
- $i_1,...,i_{k_i}$ represent references of nodes which belong to the initial Workplan of ICA_k,
- $f_1,...,f_{k_f}$ represent references of nodes which belong to the final Workplan of ICA_k,
- $k_i \leq k_f$.

In what follow the third field in an agent message (parag.5.2.1), corresponding to the service, will be null because the conversation will be identified thanks to the last field f to shape a conversation.

5.2.3 Response to the contract

When a participant receives the proposed contract, he studies it and answers by:

- A total acceptance if he agrees to coordinate all tasks chosen by the initiator, included in his remaining trip (remained final Workplan) and according to his current position. The correspondent message is:

  <ICA_k, SA_i, Ø, accept-proposal, Ø, fipa-sl, ICANegotiationOntology, f>

- A partial acceptance if he agrees to coordinate a sub-set of the tasks selected by the initiator, included in his remaining trip (remained final Workplan) and according to his current position, the partial-accept-proposal message content expresses the references of cancelled tasks and those of non available servers (the reason of the non total-acceptance). The correspondent message is:

  <ICA_k, SA_i, Ø, partial-accept-proposal, ∂, fipa-sl, ICANegotiationOntology, f>

  With $\partial \equiv$ (tasks: $c_1,...,c_n$; nodes : $r_1,...,r_m$)

- A refusal if he does not agree with any task in the proposed contract, the refusal message content expresses the references of non available servers (the reason of the refusal). The correspondent message is:

<ICA$_k$, SA$_i$, Ø , refuse, ∂, fipa-sl, ICANegotiationOntology, f> with $\partial \equiv (r_1,\ldots,r_m)$

The initiator does not wait for all answers because he must act rapidly, so he just waits for some answers for a very short period of time to make a decision; this feature is expressed in the last field f of an agent message, through the reply-by facet (5.2.1).

5.2.4 Confirmation

An initiator has to confirm independently the agreed part of each contract proposed to an agent ICA$_k$ who represents an autonomous participant of the negotiation, the confirmation can be:

- Total if the initiator agrees with the total response to the previous proposed contract:

< SA$_i$, ICA$_k$, Ø, confirm, Ø, fipa-sl, Ø ICANegotiationOntology, f>

- Partial if the initiator agrees with a partial response to the previous proposed contract, the partial-confirm-proposal message content expresses the references of agreed tasks:

< SA$_i$, ICA$_k$, Ø, partial-confirm-proposal, ∂, fipa-sl, ICANegotiationOntology, f> with $\partial \equiv (g_1,\ldots,g_p)$.

We notice here that through a confirmation, the set of tasks to reassign (the DRT table) is updated.

5.2.5 Modification request

If the DRT table is not yet empty, the initiator asks participants to propose a new distribution of the assignments of the services which are been cancelled, the request-modification message content expresses the DRT table:

<SA$_i$, ICA$_k$, Ø, request-modification, ∂, fipa-sl, ICANegotiationOntology, f>

With $\partial \equiv$ (DRT).

5.2.6 Proposition of a modification

In a previous work (Zgaya & Hammadi, 2006a), we designed a reassignment procedure strategy of servers to tasks, taking into account not only the dynamic positions of ICAs in their Workplans, but also their constraints, priorities and preferences, according to their respective current positions. Constraints of an ICA agent express tasks that he cannot perform or servers he cannot visit because they might cause problems (overloading, time consuming, high latency…). Priorities express servers where the ICA agent prefers visit because they are already programmed in his final Workplan. Finally, preferences express servers that are already programmed in the initial Workplan and not in the final one. The proposition message content expresses for each participant the new proposition of his remained Workplan according to his current state:

< ICA$_k$, SA$_i$, Ø, propose-modif, ∂, fipa-sl, ICANegotiationOntology, f>

With:

- $\partial \equiv$ FinalWk (Owner : ICA_K ; Final : $f_1,...,f_{k_f}$)
- $f_1,...,f_{k_f}$ represent references of nodes which belong to the final Workplan of the agent ICA_K.

5.2.7 Cancel

To avoid indefinite modifications tours (lack of resources, no available providers…), the initiator agent must cancel the negotiation process following a fixed period of time, illustrated by the last field of an agent message (parag. 5.2.1). Therefore he cancels the current contract creating, if it is yet possible, new ICA agents to execute the convention:

< SA_i, ICA_K, Ø, cancel, Ø, fipa-sl, ICANegotiationOntology, f>

In this section, we used MASOntology and ICANegotiationOntology which express a special vocabulary and semantic modules related to the MAS and the ICA negotiation process respectively. We present in next section the proposed ontology packages corresponding to a flexible Transport Ontology matched with the combinatorial aspect of the negotiation search space of our problem.

6. The proposition of a transport flexible ontology

We aim to define a proper vocabulary to the whole proposed multi-agent system (section 3) in order to automate the different kind of exchanges between agents. Therefore, we propose extensible ontologies packages (Fig. 6) that can adapt to all possible kind of interactions. In this chapter, we derive our different edges of ontologies from a basic one (level 0) that already defines fundamental features. Thus, in order to keep a flexible ontology aspect, we start our derivations with a Generic Ontology (level 1). This one defines the concept Element representing each constituent in any target logistic field: transport, hospital In order to perform a proper semantic checks on a given agent expression, it is necessary to classify all possible elements in the domain of discourse. Thus, we have to distinguish between predicates and terms. This classification is derived from the Agent Communication Language (ACL) defined in FIPA that requires the content of each ACLMessage to have a proper semantics according to the performative of the ACLMessage (Caire & Cabanillas, 2004). Thus, in our system, each element is identified with a distinctive reference that represents it in the global ETMN and an order number for the management. In our work, we focus on the transport field (level 2) represented by the TransportOntology where we define the Task, Server, Request, Service and ServiceTable concepts and also the "Provides" and the "Available provider" predicates. Besides, according to our system architecture, we adopted the multi-agent system methodology (level 3) so we designed the MASOntology where we define the Workplan concept, the "Performs" agent action and the "available agent", the "IsInitialOf", the "IsFinalOf" predicates. Through our proposed multi-agent approach we used a negotiation strategy (level 4) so we designed the ICANegotiationOntology that defines a special vocabulary to the negotiation of agents ICA with agents SA. This ontology is flexible for possible expansions. Initially, it contains "PartialConfirm" and "PartialAccept" agent actions that express respectively a partial confirmation or acceptation of an agent. The ICANegotiationOntology includes also "IsPriorityOf", "IsPreferenceOf" and "IsConstraintOf" predicates which express respectively the membership of a node to the priorities, preferences or constraints of an ICA agent. Predicates and terms mentioned above are represented more in details in what follow.

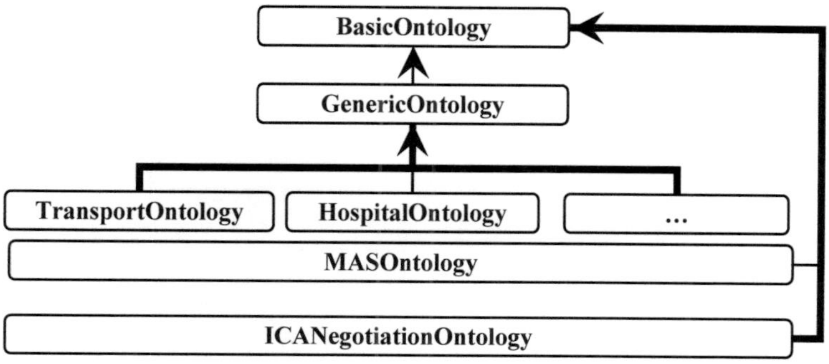

Fig. 6. Ontology Packages

6.1 Predicates

Predicates are expressions that say something about the status of the world and can be true or false. For the negotiation process, we define some useful predicates in the different proposed levels of ontologies (Fig. 7).

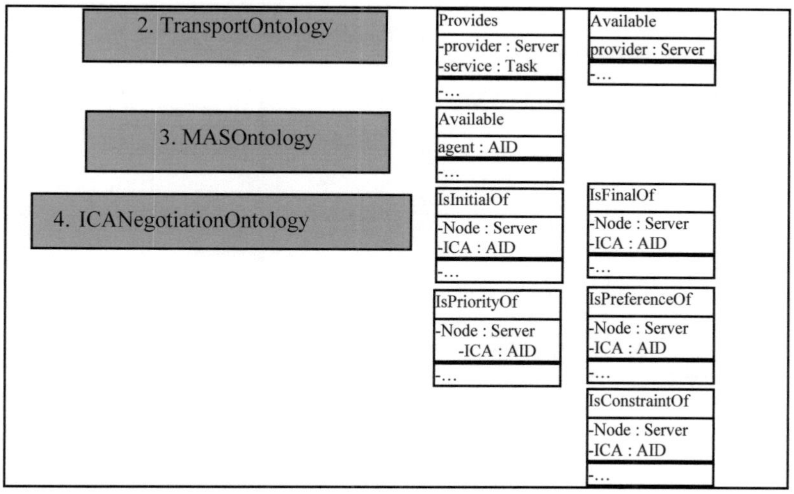

Fig. 7. Predicates

6.2 Terms

Terms are expressions identifying entities (abstract or concrete) that "exist" in the world and that agents talk and reason about. We distinguish in our design: Concepts and Agent actions (Fig. 8):

- Concepts: expressions that indicate entities with a complex structure that can be defined in terms of slots. As we previously mentioned, each element in our system is identified by a distinctive reference which represents it in the global ETMN and an order number for the management, examples:
  - (Element: ref 14 : order 2),
  - (Task: ref 2 : order 15 : providers 2 12 15 : nbProviders: 3),

- AgentActions: special concepts that indicate actions that can be performed by some agents, examples:
    - (Performs (node: ref 2 : order 5: services 2 8 6 : nbServices 3) (Task: ref 5 : order 5 : providers 2 6 : nbProviders 2)),

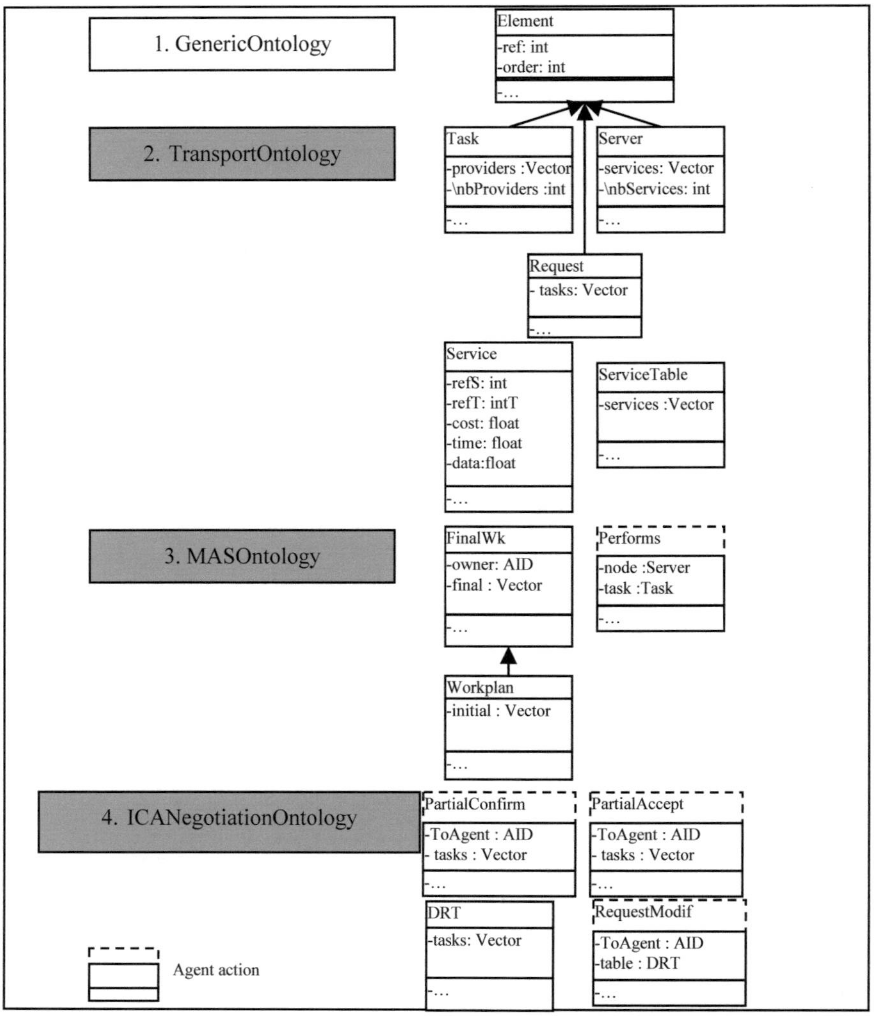

Fig. 8. Terms

7. Simulations

7.1 Global system and communication

For the implementation of our whole system (agent behaviours, communication, interactions…), we use Java Agent DEvelopment framework (JADE). It is a middleware which allows a flexible implementation of multi-agents systems and offers an efficient transport of ACL messages for agent communications complying with FIPA specifications. Jade offers the "yellow pages" service which allows agents to publish one or more services they provide so that other agents dynamically find them and successfully exploit the proposed "yellow pages" services at a given point in time. Besides, this middleware includes a proficient support for content languages and ontologies, that's why we are implementing our semantic hierarchy of ontologies with JADE framework. Also, JADE offers a graphical tool to debug sniffs message exchange between agents. This tool is useful to debug a conversation between agents. On the left side window of the Sniffer graphic tool (fig. 9), we can see available servers containers on the network, where ICA agents can move in order to collect data according to the adopted contract model.

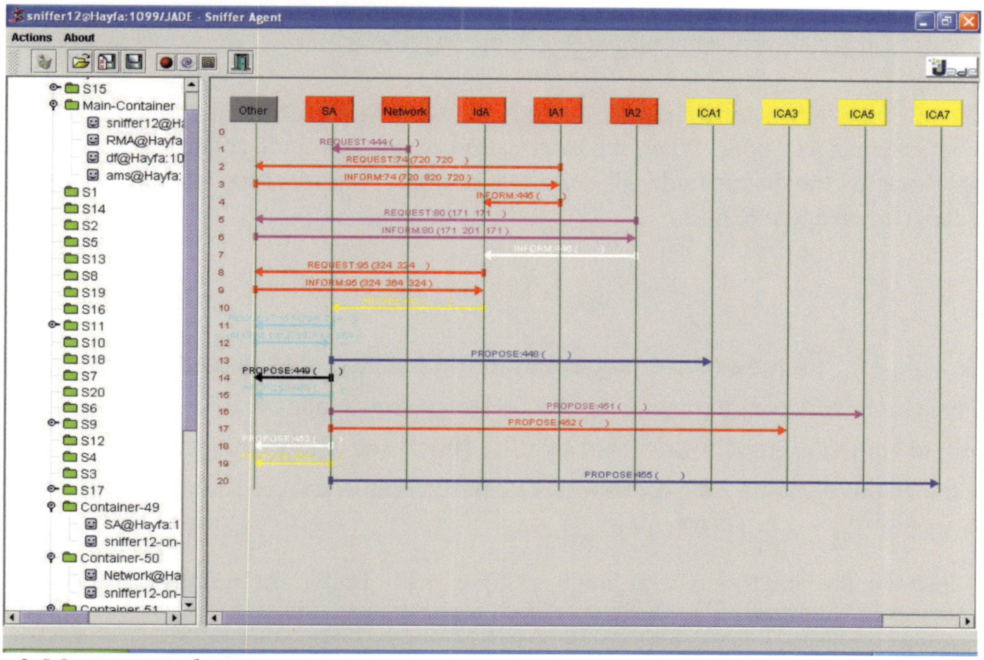

Fig. 9. Messages exchanges

7.2 Comparison of the Mobile Agent paradigm with the classical CS

Many researchers have long discussed the benefits of the MA paradigm and conclude that it might be efficient in some cases (Picco & Baldi, 1997; Buse et al., 2003). Indeed, the MA paradigm illustrates some efficient utility in several system architectures (Lu & Mori 2003; Buse et al., 2003). In a recent work (Zgaya & Hammadi, 2006b), we justified the usage of MA paradigm in our system, proposing an efficient procedure through a multi-agent transport system to optimize the management of services in the transport business domain. In order to evaluate the efficiency of our optimization approach, we propose to compare it to the classical CS paradigm (Picco & Baldi, 1997; Ketel et al., 2005); η_{CS} represents the overhead function used to send message request and $\tilde{\eta}_{CS}$ the one used for replies. Maximum response time in the CS case is:

$$T_{CS} = \sum_{j=1}^{J'} \left(\frac{\sum_{i=1}^{I'} a_{c_i c_j} (\eta_{CS} q_{c_i c_j} + \tilde{\eta}_{CS} Q_{c_i c_j})}{d(H, S_{c_j})} \right)$$

With $q_{c_i c_j}$ and $Q_{c_i c_j}$ correspond respectively to the size of the request message and the response message for the tqask T_{ci} on the server S_{cj}. The data transfer rate between nodes S_i and S_j is denoted by $d(S_i,S_j)$ and H symbolises the common home node. For a generated FeTAR instance solution CH, provided by SA agent, $a_{c_i c_j}$ is a Boolean value as follows: if $CH[c_i,c_j]=1$ ($1 \le i \le I'$ and $1 \le j \le J'$) then $a_{c_i c_j}=1$ else $a_{c_i c_j}=0$. Therefore, the overall transmission overhead for the CS case is:

$$\phi_{CS} = \sum_{j=1}^{J'} \left(\sum_{i=1}^{I'} a_{c_i c_j} (\eta_{CS} + \tilde{\eta}_{CS}) \right)$$

In the MA case, when an ICA agent moves to the node S_{cj}, he carries all the replies collected on the previous j-1 nodes. When the information on the last node collected, the ICA agent sends back to the home node all collected results. Therefore, the overall transmission overhead for an agent ICA_k is:

$$\phi_{MA_k} = \sum_{j=1}^{J'} b_{c_j c_k} \eta_{MA} + \tilde{\eta}_{MA}$$

Where η_{MA} ($\tilde{\eta}_{MA}$) represents the protocol overhead function used to send message requests (replies) in the MA paradigm and $b_{c_j c_k}$ is a Boolean value as follows: if S_{cj} belongs to the final Workplan of the agent ICA_{ck} denoted by Wk_{ck} ($1 \le j \le J'$ and $1 \le k \le m'$) then $b_{c_j c_k}=1$ else $b_{c_j c_k}=0$. The maximum response time corresponds to the maximum total travelling time of all active ICA agents: $T_{MA} = \max_{1 \le k \le m'} (T(Wk_{c_k}) + \phi_{MAc_k})$

Besides, we are interested into huge systems with important number of nodes and important request flow so ϕ_{CS} is likely to be greater than ϕ_{MA}. Therefore we do not take into account the transmission overhead in the experimental results. For example, we generated a FeTAR instance to response to 2s-simultaneous requests, decomposed globally into 8 tasks and requiring data from 19 providers. This solution required 1,4s in the MA paradigm and 14,71s in the CS one (fig. 10). Besides, when we randomly generate several FeTAR instances for the same example, we observe the benefit of the usage of our optimization approach, using MA paradigm instead of the CS one through our system (fig. 11).

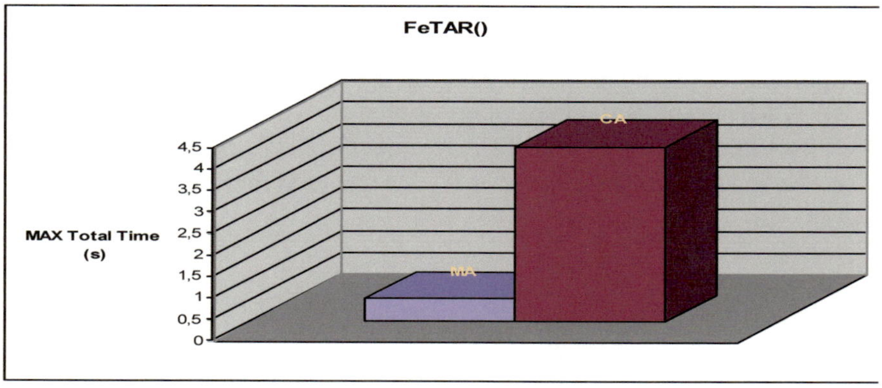

Fig. 10. The result of a FeTAR instance

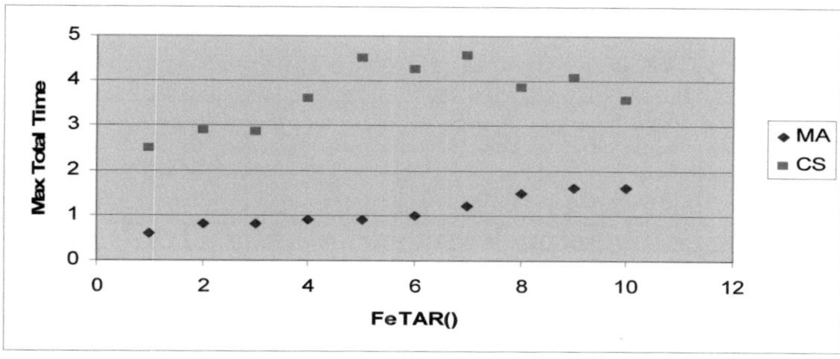

Fig. 11. Variation of FeTAR instances

7.3 Full transport application example

Through 2 seconds (ε=2s), we suppose the existence of a number of users who were connected to our system at t=11 o'clock today using different devices and then formulated a number of requests as follows; req_1: to travel at t o'clock from B to C, req_2: to travel next weekend from A to B with the minimum cost. Ask for the weather forecasting and cultural events for next weekend in B, req_3: to travel at t o'clock from A to C, req_4: to ask for a current transport perturbations from B to C, req_5: look for the best service connecting with the train X, predicted in A at 12:00 today to go to C, req_6: to travel at t o'clock from A to B, req_7: to look for a good price/quality hotel in D during next weekend and to make reservation, looking for the best route and departure time to go from B to D with car taking into account the tailback forecasting, etc. we situate our example in a ETMN composed of I=100 different services, proposed by J=20 different providers. To simplify this example, we suppose that IA agents send the ε-simultaneous requests to a single available IdA agent. This one decomposes the requests into a set of I'=64 independent tasks: $I'_t=\{T_1,T_2,T_3,T_6,T_9,T_{13},T_{16}\ldots\}$. We notice here that, we do not focus on the decomposition process, but we suppose that IdA agent decomposes R_t into independent tasks as follows: T_1= "Transport perturbations from B to C (at t o'clock)", T_2= "Weather forecasting in B (next week-end)", T_3= "To look for a good price/quality hotel in D during next weekend and to make reservation", T_6= "To look for the shortest route to go with car from B to D", T_9= "To look for the best departure time to go from B to D with car taking into account the tailback forecasting for next weekend", T_{13}= "Cultural events in B (next week-end)", T_{16}= "To travel from B to C (today, at t o'clock /today, from 12:00)", T_{19}= "To travel from A to B (today, at t o'clock / next week-end with the minimum cost/ the best service connecting with the train X at 12:00 today)", etc. We just underline the fact that there is not a direct service connecting from A to C. So the decomposition takes into account this aspect. In this paper, we do not detail the decomposition process but we point out that a task can represent several services with different constraints. For example, T_{19} represents 3 services corresponding to the same task "To travel from A to B" with different constraints: "now", "this week-end, with the minimum cost" and "The best service connecting with the train X at 12:00 today". Besides, a service is identified by a key work corresponding, for example, to an "action" and specified according to constraints which are mentioned in brackets. The full response will be composed thanks to FA agent who has to fusion services according to the user constraints, taking into account the pertinence of the information. The generated solution at t+ε is as follows:

- The generated FeTAR instance evaluated by fitness_1 and fitness_2 as follows: C_{av}=3.51 and D_{max} with d_k=6, 7 $\forall k$:

	S_1	S_2	S_3	S_4	S_5	S_6	S_7	S_8	S_9	S_{10}	S_{11}	S_{12}	S_{13}	S_{14}	S_{15}	S_{16}	S_{17}	S_{18}	S_{19}	S_{20}
T_1	0	×	0	0	0	0	1	0	0	0	0	0	×	0	0	×	0	0	×	×
T_2	0	×	0	0	×	×	0	0	0	1	×	0	0	0	0	×	0	0	0	0
T_3	0	×	0	0	0	×	0	0	0	0	0	0	×	0	0	0	×	0	1	0
T_6	0	×	0	1	0	×	0	0	0	0	0	0	×	×	0	0	0	0	0	0
T_9	×	×	×	0	×	×	×	0	1	0	0	0	0	×	0	×	0	×	×	0
T_{13}	0	×	0	0	1	×	×	0	0	0	0	0	×	×	0	0	×	0	0	×
T_{16}	×	×	×	×	1	×	0	×	×	×	×	×	×	×	×	×	×	×	0	×
T_{19}	1	×	×	×	0	×	×	×	×	×	×	×	×	×	×	×	×	×	×	×
T_{20}	×	×	0	×	0	×	×	×	×	1	×	×	×	×	0	×	×	×	×	0
T_{21}	×	×	0	0	×	×	×	×	×	×	×	×	×	×	×	×	×	1	×	×
T_{22}	×	×	×	×	×	×	×	×	×	×	×	×	×	×	×	×	0	×	1	0
T_{25}	×	×	×	0	×	×	×	×	×	×	×	×	×	×	×	0	1	×	×	0
T_{26}	×	0	0	×	×	×	×	×	×	×	0	1	×	×	×	×	×	0	×	×
T_{28}	×	1	0	×	0	×	×	×	×	0	×	0	×	×	0	×	×	×	0	0
T_{29}	0	0	×	×	×	×	×	×	×	×	0	×	1	×	×	×	×	×	×	×
T_{30}	×	×	×	×	×	×	×	×	×	×	×	×	×	×	×	×	0	0	0	1
T_{31}	1	×	0	0	×	0	×	0	×	×	×	0	×	0	×	×	×	0	×	×
T_{32}	0	×	0	0	×	×	0	1	0	×	×	0	×	0	×	×	×	0	×	×
T_{33}	0	×	0	0	×	×	0	×	×	×	×	1	×	×	×	0	×	×	×	×
T_{34}	0	0	0	×	×	×	1	×	×	×	×	×	×	×	×	×	×	×	×	×
T_{35}	0	×	0	×	×	×	×	0	×	×	×	×	×	×	×	×	×	1	×	×
T_{36}	0	×	1	×	×	×	×	×	×	×	×	×	×	×	×	×	×	0	×	×
T_{37}	×	×	0	×	×	×	×	×	×	×	×	×	×	×	×	×	×	0	×	1
T_{38}	0	×	0	×	×	×	×	×	×	0	×	×	×	0	×	×	1	×	×	×
T_{39}	×	×	×	×	×	×	×	×	×	1	×	×	×	×	×	×	0	×	×	0
T_{40}	×	×	×	×	×	×	×	×	×	×	0	×	×	×	×	0	1	×	×	×
T_{41}	×	×	1	×	0	×	×	×	×	×	×	×	×	×	×	×	×	0	×	×
T_{42}	0	×	0	×	×	×	×	×	×	×	1	×	×	×	×	×	×	0	×	×
T_{44}	×	×	×	×	×	×	×	×	×	×	1	×	×	×	×	×	0	×	×	×
T_{52}	×	×	×	×	×	×	×	×	×	×	×	×	×	×	×	×	1	×	0	×
T_{53}	0	×	×	×	×	×	×	×	×	×	×	×	0	×	×	1	×	×	×	×
T_{56}	×	0	0	×	×	×	×	×	×	×	1	×	×	×	×	×	×	0	×	×
T_{57}	×	×	×	×	×	×	×	×	×	×	×	×	×	×	×	×	×	1	0	×
T_{58}	×	1	0	×	×	×	×	×	×	0	×	×	×	×	0	×	×	×	0	×
T_{59}	0	1	×	×	×	×	×	×	×	×	0	×	0	×	×	×	×	×	×	×
T_{60}	×	×	×	×	×	×	×	×	×	×	×	×	×	×	×	×	1	0	0	×
T_{61}	×	×	0	×	×	×	×	×	×	×	×	×	×	×	1	×	0	×	×	×
T_{63}	0	×	0	0	0	×	0	0	0	×	×	×	×	×	×	1	×	0	×	×
T_{64}	0	0	0	0	0	×	×	×	1	×	×	×	×	×	×	×	×	×	×	×
T_{65}	0	×	×	×	×	×	×	×	×	×	×	×	×	0	×	×	×	1	×	×
T_{66}	1	×	0	×	×	×	×	×	×	×	×	×	×	×	0	×	×	×	×	×
T_{67}	×	×	0	×	×	×	×	×	×	×	×	×	1	×	×	×	×	×	0	×
T_{68}	0	×	0	×	×	0	×	1	×	×	×	×	×	×	×	×	0	×	×	×
T_{69}	×	×	×	×	×	×	×	×	0	×	1	×	×	×	×	×	×	×	×	×
T_{71}	×	×	0	×	×	×	1	×	×	×	×	×	×	0	×	×	×	×	×	×
T_{73}	×	×	×	×	×	×	×	×	×	×	×	×	×	×	1	0	×	×	0	×
T_{74}	×	×	×	×	×	×	1	×	×	×	×	×	×	0	×	0	×	×	×	×
T_{75}	0	×	0	×	×	×	×	×	×	1	×	0	×	×	×	×	×	×	×	×
T_{76}	×	0	0	×	×	×	×	×	×	×	×	×	×	×	×	×	×	1	×	×
T_{77}	×	×	×	×	×	×	×	×	×	×	×	×	×	×	×	×	×	1	×	0
T_{78}	×	0	×	×	×	×	×	×	×	×	×	1	×	×	×	×	×	×	×	×
T_{79}	1	0	×	×	×	×	×	×	×	×	×	×	×	×	×	×	×	×	×	×
T_{80}	×	×	×	×	×	×	×	×	×	×	×	×	×	×	×	×	0	×	×	1
T_{81}	0	×	0	0	×	×	×	×	×	×	×	1	×	×	×	×	×	0	×	×
T_{82}	0	×	0	×	×	×	0	0	1	×	×	×	×	0	×	×	×	×	×	×
T_{83}	×	×	×	×	0	×	0	×	×	×	×	1	×	0	×	×	×	×	×	×
T_{84}	0	1	0	×	×	×	×	×	×	×	×	×	×	×	×	×	×	×	×	×
T_{85}	1	×	0	×	×	×	×	×	×	×	×	×	×	×	×	×	×	0	×	×
T_{86}	1	×	0	×	0	×	×	×	×	×	×	×	×	×	×	×	×	0	×	×
T_{88}	0	×	1	×	×	×	×	×	×	×	×	×	×	×	×	×	×	×	×	×
T_{90}	×	×	×	×	×	×	×	×	0	×	×	×	×	1	×	0	0	×	×	×
T_{95}	×	×	×	×	1	×	×	×	0	×	0	×	1	×	×	×	×	×	×	×
T_{96}	×	×	×	×	×	×	×	×	×	×	×	×	×	×	×	×	×	×	1	×
T_{99}	1	×	×	×	0	×	×	×	×	×	×	×	×	×	×	×	×	×	×	×

- $m=5$, initial Workplans are:

$Wk_1=\{S_{20},S_{15},S_1,S_3\}$, $Wk_2=\{S_{18},S_7,S_{10},S_8\}$, $Wk_3=\{S_{16},S_{14},S_5,S_{17}\}$, $Wk_4=\{S_{19}, S_{12}, S_{11},S_6, S_9\}$,$Wk_5=\{S_2, S_{13},S_4\}$;

- $m'=5$, final Workplans are :

$Wk_1=\{S_{20}\{T_{30},T_{37},T_{80}\},S_{15}\{T_{61},T_{73}\},S_1\{T_{19},T_{31},T_{66},T_{79},T_{85},T_{86},T_{99}\},S_3\{T_{36},T_{41},T_{88}\}\}$,$Wk_2=\{S_{18}\{T_{21},T_{35},T_{57},T_{65},T_{76},T_{77}\},S_7\{T_1,T_{34},T_{71},T_{74}\},S_{10}\{T_2,T_{20},T_{39},T_{75}\},S_8\{T_{32},T_{68}\}\}$,$Wk_3=\{S_{16}\{T_{53},T_{63}\},S_{14}\{T_{90}\},S_5\{T_{13},T_{16},T_{95}\},S_{17}\{T_{25},T_{38},T_{40},T_{52},T_{60}\}\}$,$Wk_4=\{S_{19}\{T_3,T_{22},T_{96}\},S_{12}\{T_{26},T_{33},T_{78},T_{81},T_{83}\},S_{11}\{T_{42},T_{44},T_{56},T_{69}\},S_9\{T_9,T_{64},T_{82}\}\}$,$Wk_5=\{S_2\{T_{28},T_{58},T_{59},T_{84}\}, S_{13}\{T_{29},T_{67}\},S_4\{T_6\}\}$;

- We assume that ICA agents are already visiting their first node of their correspondent final Workplans without incidence before the announce of the set of unavailable set of nodes. For the current example, we suppose that the set of unavailable node is :

$S_1,S_3,S_7,S_{10},S_{14},S_5,S_{17},S_{12},S_9,S_{13}$

- We deduce tasks to reassign:

$TDR=\{T_{19},T_{31},T_{66},T_{79},T_{85},T_{86},T_{99},T_{36},T_{41},T_{88},T_1,T_{34},T_{71},T_{74},T_{90},T_{13},T_{16},T_{95},T_{25},T_{38},T_{40},T_{52},T_{60},T_{26},T_{33},T_{78},T_{81},T_{83},T_9,T_{64},T_{82},T_{29},T_{67}\} \rightarrow$ 33 tasks to reassign,

The proposed negotiation process allows the reassignment of the cancelled services. F6, F7 and F9 in fig. 12 below represent three different generated FeTAR instances assignments for the same network error scenario, where the number of agreed assigned tasks was respectively 6, 7 and 9 in the priorities of ICA agents. Thanks to our proposed negotiation process, cancelled services find new available providers through an agreement between static scheduler agents and mobile collector agents of the system so the correspondent transport users are satisfied in spite of some network perturbations.

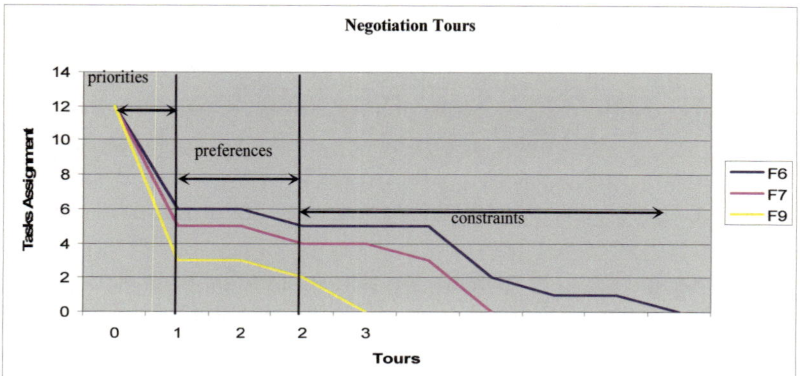

Fig. 12. Negotiation tours

8. Conclusion and prospects

In this paper, we firstly presented the proposed multi-agent architecture for the Transport Multimodal Information System. Then, we described the problem and situated the correspondent complexity. The main goal of our work is to give to transport customers the best responses to their demands, optimising the composition of services in term of cost and total response delay. Therefore, we proposed a two-level optimization solution which optimizes the workplans of mobile entities in order to find the best management of the required information. Besides, we take into account the constraint of the possible network perturbations. In this case, mobile entities have to negotiate with the other entities of the system, in order to optimize the reassignment of the cancelled services. This procedure considers the positions of the mobile entities, their constraints, their preferences, their priorities and also the variable state of the network. However, the complex interaction between the different entities of the system exceeds the limits of the traditional negotiation procedures. That's why, the recourse to the ontologies was essential to design a special vocabulary to perform a proper semantic checks on a given agent expressions. In a future work, we aim to manage the interactions between several initiators and participants in different negotiation processes in case, for example, of simultaneous requests overlapping. Thus, the control of several concurrent conversations is indispensable. Moreover, the extension or the generalization of the proposed protocol is conceivable. Besides, until now, we have used the reference as a service index. In future works, we will offer to providers the possibility to be totally free in terms of services indication. Thus, to market its services through our system, an information provider will not be obliged to change anything locally in its structure. So, a supplier can register each proposed service with the already chosen label. In this context, the usage of a common ontology guarantees the consistency (an expression has the same meaning for all the agents) and the compatibility (a concept is designed, for the same expression, for any agent) of the information present in the system. However, it is not sure that all the agents will use a common ontology. Consequently, we will focus, in future works, on the data heterogeneity problem within our system, when each agent uses different terms with the same meaning or the same term for different meanings.

9. References

Baek, J.W.; Yeo J.H.; Kim, G.T. & Yeom, H.Y. (2001). "Cost Effective Mobile Agent Planning for Distributed Information Retrieval", *Proceedings of the* 21st International Conference on Distributed Computing Systems, pp. 65-72, School of Computer science and Engineering, Seoul national University, USA, 2001.

Buse, D.P.; Feng, J.Q. & Wu, Q.H. (2003). "Mobile Agents for Data Analysis In Industrial Automation Systems", *Proceedings of the IEEE/WIC Int'l Conf. on Intelligent Agent Technology (IAT'03)*, pp. 60-66, Halifax, Canada, October 2003.

Caire, G. & Cabanillas, D. (2004). *Jade Tutorial Applications-defined Content languages And Ontologies*, Tutorial JADE, November 2004.

Carzaniga, A.; Picco, G. P. & Vigna, G. (1997). "Designing distributed applications with mobile code paradigms", *Proceedings of the 19th Int'l Conf. on Software Engineering*, pp. 22-32, July 1997.

Ketel, M.; Dogan N.S. & Homaifar, A. (2005). "Distributed Sensor Networks based on Mobile Agents Paradigms", dept. of Computer Science, North Carolina A&T State

University, NC 27411, System Theory, SSST'2005, Greensboro, USA 2005, pp. 411-414.

Lu, X. & Mori, K. (2003). "Autonomous Information Services Integration and Allocation in Agent-Based Information Service System", *Proceedings of the IEEE/WIC Int'l Conf. on intelligent Agent Technology (IAT'03)*, pp. 290-296, Halifax, Canada, October 2003.

Pharm, V.A. & Karmouch, A. (1998). "Mobile Software Agents: an overview". *IEEE Communication Magazine*, University of Ottawa, Ontario, (July 1998) 26-37.

Picco, G.P. & Baldi, M. (1997). "Evaluating the Tradeoffs of Mobile Code Design Paradigms in Network Management Applications", *Proceedings of the 20th IEEE Int'l Conf. on Software Engineering (ICSE'97)*, pp.146-155, Kyoto, Japan, April 1998, In R. Kemmerer et K. Futatsugi.

Smith, R. G. (1980). "The Contract Net Protocol: highlevel communication and control in a distributed problem solver", *IEEE Transactions on computers*, Vol.29, No.12, (December 1980), 1104–1113.

Theilmann, W. & Rothermel, K. (1999). "Efficient Dissemination of Mobile Agents", *Proceedings of the 19th IEEE Int. Conf. on Distributed Computing Systems Workshop (ICDCSW')*, IEEE Computer Society, pp. 9-14, USA, May 1999.

Zgaya, H. & Hammadi, S. (2006a). "Dynamic Approach to Reassign Tasks when Servers Breakdown in a Multi-Modal Information System", *Proceedings of the 2006 IMACS Multiconference on Computational Engineering in Systems Applications (CESA'2006)*, pp. 985-990, Beijing, China, October 2006, Tsinghua University Press, Beijing, China.

Zgaya, H. & Hammadi, S. (2006b). "Assignment and Integration of Distributed Transport Services in Agent-Based Architecture", *Proceedings of the IEEE/WIC Int'l Conf. on Intelligent Agent Technology (IAT'06)*, HongKong, China, December 2006.

Zgaya, H. & Hammadi, S. (2008). "Combination of mobile agent and evolutionary algorithm to optimize the client transport services". *RAIRO-Operations Research Special Issue on Cooperative methods for Multiobjective Optimization RAIRO Oper. Res.*, Vol.42, No 1, (January 2008) 35-67.

Zgaya, H.; Hammadi, S. & Ghédira K. (2005a). "Workplan Mobile Agent for the Transport Network Application", *Proceedings of the 17th IMACS World Congress Scientific Computation Applied Mathematics and Simulation (IMACS'2005)*, pp. 11-15, Paris, France, July 2005.

Zgaya, H. ; Hammadi, S. & Ghédira K. (2005b). "Evolutionary method to optimize Workplan mobile agent for the transport network application", *Proceedings of the International Conference on Systems, Man and Cybernetics (IEEE SMC'2005)*, pp. 10-12, Hawaii, USA, October 2005.

Zgaya, H. ; Hammadi, S. & Ghédira, K. (2008) . "A migration strategy of mobile agents for the transport network applications". *International Journal, Mathematics and Computers in Simulation (MATCOM)*, Vol.76, No.5-6, (January 2008) 345-362.

Zitzler, E. & Thiele, L. (1998). "Multiobjective Optimization Using Evolutionary Algorithms: A Comparative Case Study". *In Lecture Notes in Computer Science*, Vol. 1498, (1998) 292-301, UK.